American Continental Philosophy

Studies in Continental Thought

John Sallis, general editor

American Continental Philosophy

A Reader

Edited by
Walter Brogan *&* James Risser

INDIANA UNIVERSITY PRESS
Bloomington and Indianapolis

This book is a publication of

Indiana University Press
601 North Morton Street
Bloomington, IN 47404-3797 USA

http://www.indiana.edu/~iupress

Telephone orders   800-842-6796
Fax orders   812-855-7931
Orders by e-mail   iuporder@indiana.edu

Library of Congress Cataloging-in-Publication Data

American continental philosophy : a reader / edited by Walter Brogan and James Risser.
p.   cm. — (Studies in Continental thought)
Includes bibliographcal references and index.
ISBN 0-253-33729-1 (cloth : alk. paper) — ISBN 0-253-21376-2 (pbk. : alk. paper)
1. Philosophy, American—20th century. I. Brogan, Walter, date.   II. Risser, James,
date.   III. Series.

B935 .A44 2000
191—dc21

99-088427

1 2 3 4 5   05 04 03 02 01 00

CONTENTS

ACKNOWLEDGMENTS

The editors thank the following authors and publishers for permission to reprint previously published work in this volume:

Seyla Benhabib, "Feminist Theory and Hannah Arendt's Concept of Public Space," *History of the Human Sciences* 6.2 (1993): 97–114. Reprinted by permission of the publisher, Sage Publications, Ltd.

Robert Bernasconi, "The Invisibility of the Others within the Public Space of Appearance," in *Phenomenology of the Political* (Dordrecht: Kluwer Academic Publishers, 2000). Reprinted by permission of the publisher, Kluwer Academic Publishers.

Judith Butler, "Subjection, Resistance, Resignification: Between Freud and Foucault," in *The Psychic Life of Power: Theories in Subjection* (Stanford: Stanford University Press, 1997). Reprinted by permission of the publisher, Stanford University Press.

John D. Caputo, "Otherwise than Ethics, or Why We Too Are Still Impious," in *Against Ethics* (Bloomington: Indiana University Press, 1993). Reprinted by permission of the publisher, Indiana University Press.

Edward S. Casey, "Keeping the Past in Mind," *Review of Metaphysics* 37 (September 1983): 77–95. Reprinted by permission, *The Review of Metaphysics*.

Drucilla Cornell, "The Ethical Message of Negative Dialectics," in *The Philosophy of the Limit* (New York: Routledge, 1992). Reprinted by permission of the publisher, Routledge, Inc.

Rodolphe Gasché, "Towards an Ethics of Auseinandersetzung," in *Enlightenments: Encounters between Critical Theory and Contemporary French Thought*, edited by H. de Vries and H. Kunneman (Leuven: Peeters Publishers, 1993). Reprinted by permission of the publisher, Peeters Publishers.

David Farrell Krell, "Unhomelike Places: Archetictural Sections of Heidegger and Freud," in *Archeticture: Ecstasies of Space, Time, and the Human Body* (Albany: State University of New York Press, 1997). Reprinted by permission of the publisher, State University of New York Press.

Alphonso Lingis, "The Murmur of the World," in *The Community of Those Who Have Nothing in Common* (Bloomington: Indiana University Press, 1994). Reprinted by permission of the publisher, Indiana University Press.

William J. Richardson, "In-the-Name-of-the Father: The Law?" in *Questioning Ethics: Contemporary Debates in Philosophy*, edited by Richard Kearney and Mark Dooley (London: Routledge, 1998). Reprinted by permission of the publisher, Routledge, Inc.

Richard Rorty, "Private Irony and Liberal Hope," in *Contingency, Irony, and Solidarity* (New York: Cambridge University Press, 1989). Reprinted by permission of the publisher, Cambridge University Press.

John Sallis, "Imagination and Metaphysics," in *Delimitations: Phenomenol-*

ogy and the End of Metaphysics (Bloomington: Indiana University Press, 1986). Reprinted by permission of the publisher, Indiana University Press.

Charles E. Scott, "Institutional Songs and Involuntary Memory: Where Do 'We' Come From?" in *The Time of Memory* (Albany: State University of New York Press, 1999). Reprinted by permission of the publisher, State University of New York Press.

Calvin O. Schrag, "Transversal Rationality," in *The Resources of Rationality: A Response to the Postmodern Challenge* (Bloomington: Indiana University Press, 1992). Reprinted by permission of the publisher, Indiana University Press.

INTRODUCTION

This reader in continental philosophy presents, paradoxically, the work of American philosophers. The paradox, though, is only an apparent one, which can be removed by clarifying the very idea of "American continental philosophy." Naturally, one associates the term "continental philosophy" with a geographical location. The term points to a tradition that began on the European continent, and, in this context, North Americans have been readers and interpreters of European continental philosophy since the 1950s, when phenomenology and existentialism were first broadly introduced here. If, however, we take seriously what occurs in the reception of a tradition, then continental philosophy does not designate primarily, if at all, geographical location. Rather, it would be more proper to identify continental philosophy from its very history and the body of questions that emerge from that history. Today many of the most original voices working in continental philosophy live in North America and write principally in English. By "American philosophers," then, we do not mean what one might naturally assume, namely, those Americans who write in the tradition of pragmatism, a philosophical current that has flourished in our distinctly American culture. The pragmatist tradition in American philosophy —which begins with William James, Charles Sanders Peirce, John Dewey, and others, and continues today in the work of such thinkers as John Lachs, John Smith, and John McDermott—certainly has affinities with continental philosophy. However, this volume does not aim to fuse continental philosophy with the pragmatist tradition. Rather, it recognizes that the work that falls under the rubric "continental philosophy" is no longer something that happens solely on European soil. Accordingly, our specific purpose is to gather a representative selection of some of the most important and original American continental philosophers. We have tried to select texts that have helped to define the field and shape the increasingly influential philosophical movement that goes by the awkward name "continental philosophy."

To introduce the selections in this volume, we first offer a concise historical overview of continental philosophy, especially with regard to its reception in North America. Second, we highlight those features of continental philosophy that reflect a peculiarly American spirit. The final part of the introduction defines the central topics according to which the selection of readings has been organized.

History in Context

The story of continental philosophy is much richer and more complex than we are able to convey here. Continental philosophy is itself a twentieth-century phenomenon and as such has a history that now covers the entire century. For American readers, the first detailed account of continental philosophy was given by Herbert Spiegelberg in 1963 in his monumental two-volume *The Phenomenological Movement.*[1] This book chronicles not only the work of Edmund Husserl, Martin Heidegger, Jean-Paul Sartre, and Maurice Merleau-Ponty but also the "older" phenomenological movement that Spiegelberg locates in the writings of Alexander Pfländer and Max Scheler, among others. The complexity of the story of continental philosophy, suggested by the range of figures that Spiegelberg considered, is even more apparent when one realizes that it presents a story only of phenomenology. At the time, phenomenology was understood to mean, in the most general terms, the return to experience, i.e., the return to the phenomenon as that which gives itself (*Selbstgebung*) either immediately to consciousness (Husserl) or interpretively from itself (Heidegger). There are, of course, profound differences between the work of Husserl and of Heidegger, which one first approximates by comprehending the turn of pure phenomenology in the direction of hermeneutic phenomenology. But phenomenology as a return to experience, although certainly integral to any definition of continental philosophy today, no longer completely accounts for what falls under the rubric continental philosophy. Spiegelberg's book is now itself a work that belongs to the history that it once tried to tell. While he might have crystalized and given clarity to one aspect of this divergent tradition, it still remained to be seen how broader interests and orientations would contribute to continental philosophy.

In France after 1960, the theme of language, which came to prominence most notably through the later work of Heidegger and Merleau-Ponty, was no longer addressed solely through the work of phenomenology but received significant attention from a new movement called structuralism. In its conception, structuralism, like phenomenology, was not understood as a philosophy so much as a method for scientific research. Whereas phenomenology was a method of descriptive analysis, structural analysis turned to the contextual linkage of the parts of a phenomenon. The seeds for the structuralist movement in France in the 1960s had been planted in 1916 by Ferdinand de Saussure in his work *A Course in General Linguistics,* based on lectures at the University of Geneva in the first decade of the twentieth century. Saussure broke free of what was then the traditional view, which considered language primarily with respect to its referential relation to things. He argued for a theory of language as a system of signs displayed by its structural relationships. With this science of signs (semiology) it was now possible to interpret any cultural system of signification. Claude Lévi-Strauss, teaching at the University of Paris and the Collège de France, as well as at the New School for Social Research in New York, brought structural analysis to bear directly on cultural anthropology.

The structuralist project had an immediate influence on the writings of Paul Ricoeur and Jacques Derrida. Ricoeur who, while in a prison camp during World War II, began a translation of Husserl's *Ideen I,* came to develop phenomenology in the direction of hermeneutics. As a result of the influence of structuralism, Ricoeur's hermeneutics took issue with the hermeneutics of both Heidegger and Hans-Georg Gadamer. For Ricoeur, the explanatory function of interpretation, missing from the work of Heidegger and Gadamer, came to be viable with the aid of structuralist analysis. Derrida combined structuralism and phenomenology in a different way in his works *Edmund Husserl's The Origin of Geometry: An Introduction* (1962), *Speech and Phenomena,* and *Of Grammatology* (both in 1967). The first two works deal directly with Husserl's phenomenology. Derrida maintained, with the aid of a radicalized structuralist program, that the belief in the experiential character of language conveyed by phenomenology, the belief in the immediacy of language as a conveyor of experience, must be called into question. However, this critique of the traditional dependency of a metaphysics of presence on a representational theory of language did not lead Derrida away from language back to the epistemological tradition prior to the turn to experience, nor did it cause him to further develop the line of hermeneutics. Rather, it brought him to a new "program" in which the text was given a position of prominence. The reading of texts was a strategy of deconstruction by which the very indeterminacy of meaning was set free.

This shift from phenomenology to poststructuralism in France went far beyond the arena of philosophy, entering into the main currents of psychoanalysis, linguistics, literary theory, feminist studies, and cultural studies. In its generalized formulations, poststructuralism became almost indistinguishable from the ubiquitous term postmodernism.[2] As a distinct term, poststructuralism claims that structuralism is committed to the discovery of over-arching structures and foundational frameworks that govern the meaning of a text. This commitment has a particular metaphysical bias in favor of the notion that there are basic governing principles that make philosophical as well as other work meaningful and capable of giving coherent explanations of reality. Poststructuralism, often drawing from resources in the philosophy of Friedrich Nietzsche, is anti-foundational and committed to the uncovering of a plurality of meanings that arise out of a text or event. Gilles Deleuze and Felix Guattari are among those poststructuralists who have brought a new dimension of interest to these issues of structure and meaning by connecting them to a critique of Freudian psychoanalysis.[3] In similar fashion, Jacques Lacan's post-Freudian analysis of subjectivity and sexuality has influenced greatly the postmodern direction of contemporary continental philosophy and the development of what is sometimes called French feminism, found in the work of such thinkers as Julia Kristeva and Luce Irigaray. Also prominent in this regard is Michel Foucault, whose work during the 1970s on the history of the systems of thought dramatically changed the direction of intellectual life in France.[4]

The shift that was occurring in continental philosophy received yet another impetus when Emmanuel Levinas published his important and influential work *Totality and Infinity* in 1961. Levinas, like Ricoeur, was known initially as a specialist in Husserlian and Heideggerian phenomenology. In *Totality and Infinity,* Levinas engaged in a critique of humanism and subjectivity that went beyond even the radical critique that had already been presented by Heidegger. Levinas argued that beyond phenomenology, beyond what manifests itself in the subject's inhabiting of a world, is the other, who precedes and stands in an asymmetrical relation to the experience of the subject. This relation of one to the other is the basis of all responsibility, which means that before ontology there is ethics, an ethics rooted in alterity.

Meanwhile, in Germany in the 1960s, a second generation of thinkers was already in place. Hans-Georg Gadamer, who was a student of Heidegger in the 1920s, developed a distinctive contribution to hermeneutic theory with the publication of *Truth and Method* in 1960. In *Truth and Method* the issues of language, text, and interpretation were further expanded beyond the confines of a representational view of language and the authority of the subject. At the same time Jürgen Habermas and others, such as Herbert Marcuse, who was also a student of Heidegger, began to carry out their own program directed at a critique of natural scientific knowledge as it applied to issues in social life. For this program of "critical theory," Habermas drew his philosophical commitments not from phenomenology but from a neo-Marxist Enlightenment project that provided a new orientation for the development of social reason. This neo-Marxist concern for issues of social life initially gained recognition with the establishment of the Institute for Social Research in 1923. When in 1930 the Institute came under the directorship of Max Horkheimer, who was himself a student of Husserl and Heidegger in the 1920s, work shifted from an emphasis on Marxist empirical social science to a more theoretical orientation.

By the time Horkheimer, with Theodor Adorno, wrote the *Dialectic of Enlightenment* (1947), the identity of the Institute, also known as the Frankfurt School, was well established. The school marked a clear break with the phenomenological tradition, if only for its "utopian" thinking regarding social life, a point Gadamer continued to insist upon in his own debate with Habermas. This break was compounded by the fact that Adorno and Habermas both strongly attacked the work of Martin Heidegger for its lack of critical perspective on the distinct issue of social life, an omission that became all too obvious with the rise of National Socialism. And yet, critical theory must certainly be understood as a turn within continental philosophy. The critical perspective of the role of natural science in social life had always been a concern of phenomenology.

What is known as "continental philosophy" in America can quite naturally only be understood against the background of these developments on the European continent. These concepts and issues were first introduced to America during the Second World War by expatriate Europeans such as Alfred Schutz and Aron Gurwitsch, and by Dorion Cairns, who taught in New York at the New School for Social Research. The work of both Gurwitsch and Cairns was quite close to that of Husserl, although Gurwitsch himself did not study directly with Husserl. Schutz was initially trained as a sociologist and had a strong interest in the work of Max Weber. In his later work, Schutz drew on the work of William James to explore the meaning of Husserl's *Lebenswelt,* or lifeworld. Other "first generation" American continental philosophers include American-born Marvin Farber, whom Spiegelberg singles out for his role as organizer of the International Phenomenological Society in 1939 and as publisher of the journal *Philosophy and Phenomenological Research;* and John Wild, who, while at Harvard and later at Northwestern, made the work of phenomenology and existentialism academically respectable in North America.

During the 1950s and 1960s American-born philosophers began to assimilate, in addition to the work of Husserl, the full development of the phenomenological movement found in the thought of Heidegger, Merleau-Ponty, Sartre, and other Europeans. This was in part due to the appearance of translations of the texts of these philosophers, most notably the translation of Heidegger's *Being and Time,* which was published in 1962. In the early 1960s existentialism was entering popular culture, and continental philosophy, as phenomenology and existentialism, was making inroads in sociology, psychology, and theology—although phenomenology was then being studied and practiced in only a few universities such as the New School for Social Research, Northwestern University, the Pennsylvania State University, and Duquesne University.

During this same period, continental philosophy in America began to establish its unique voice. In 1962 the first meeting of the Society for Phenomenology and Existential Philosophy (SPEP) was held at Northwestern University. The society was formed to promote the academic exchange of views regarding continental philosophy. Subsequent annual meetings were held at Yale University, the University of Wisconsin, the Pennsylvania State University, and Purdue University. In these early years, it was not uncommon to hear presentations about issues in perception, experience, and language that attempted to establish links with the American pragmatists as well as the American analytic tradition.[5] The society is now the second largest philosophy organization in North America and reflects the broadening of perspectives that has come to constitute continental philosophy in America. A further indication of the growth of continental philosophy was the expansion of professional meetings to include "circles" dedicated to the work of individual European thinkers. In a meeting of Heidegger scholars, first in 1964, then in subsequent years at Duquesne University and De Paul University, a decision was made to form a society for Heidegger scholarship. The first meeting of the society was held at the Pennsylvania State University in 1967. In 1969 the first meeting of the Husserl Circle was held at Washington University, and in 1976 the Merleau-Ponty Society was formed. During the 1970s, other major universities developed programs that specialized in continental philosophy, among them Boston College, Loyola University, De Paul University, and the State University of New York at Stony Brook. In 1976 the first meeting of the Collegium Phaenomenologicum was held in Perugia, Italy. The Collegium was conceived as a unique opportunity to bring Americans and Europeans together to learn from one another through lectures, seminars, and discussions held over the course of several weeks. Over the years it has gained a reputation for its promotion of advanced and original research. In recent years, other groups devoted to the promotion of international dialogue in continental philosophy have also held annual meetings in Italy.

America, it seems, was becoming a place not only where European thinkers found a new home but where many new ideas were given a forum. During the 1970s, Paul Ricoeur taught regularly at the University of Chicago, where he continued to develop his project in conjunction with contemporary analytic philosophy and then in the direction of the question of narrative. Hans-Georg Gadamer made frequent visits to America and eventually accepted a regular appointment at Boston College. Jacques Derrida, who in the early 1970s found himself engaged with the problem of Anglo-American speech act theory, also came to America. He lectured and taught first at the Johns Hopkins University and Yale University, then later at the University of California, Irvine, and New York University. Through these lectures and teaching the work of "deconstruction" took root in a way that was not duplicated in France. Throughout the early years, the New School for Social Research continued to flourish with the contributions of such notable philosophers as Hannah Arendt, whose political philosophy stimulated discussions of the broader issues of human community that resonated with the growing interest in Habermas's work on communicative action.

The Unique Voice of American Continental Philosophy

The preceding historical sketch is drawn from the perspective of the experience of continental philosophy in America. Our purpose, in part, is to address the distinct and original voice of American continental philosophy relative to European continental philosophy. We do not claim that American continental philosophy's distinctiveness is the result of breaking away from its European counterpart and developing on its own. American continental philosophy is not a new movement, a new methodology, or another "ism" but an original appropriation that has grown through its own complex relationship to European perspectives. In the context of its own sense of newness, American continental philosophy has assimilated and reinterpreted this tradition. Building on this history it speaks with a distinctive voice and a unique contemporary perspective.

We have traced these developments in continental philosophy from the 1950s to the 1990s not only to contextualize the mature American continental philosophy that the authors in this volume exemplify but because the American experience figures prominently in this growth and is in part responsible for the directions in which continental philosophy has moved. An interesting connection might well be made between the experience of being American and the practice of American continental philosophy. The central themes and concerns of phenomenology, hermeneutics, post-structuralism, and postmodernism over the last four decades are consonant with an American spirit. To varying degrees, these themes are at the heart of the philosophy of the contributors to this volume. In fact it can be said that these themes have been given special nourishment in North America, though naturally they are by no means unique to America and belong also to European continental philosophy. To be sure, many of the most prominent European philosophers of our times, Gadamer, Ricoeur, Derrida, and others, have done much of their work while in North America.

In the transference of European philosophy to North America, continental philosophy is not merely reproduced in a new milieu. In crossing back and forth over the ocean that separates and connects the European and American experience, continental philosophy undergoes a transformation. But this transformational dimension is not derived simply from the fact that this passage has occurred; it is not solely the result of the fact that American continental philosophers have received this tradition. Rather, continental philosophy, as Deleuze argues,[6] is itself a kind of transformational thinking, that is, a thinking that occurs through its repetition. Thus, American continental philosophers do not merely re-present what has been created in Europe. Rather, they engage in the philosophical practices of such philosophizing and thereby release the fundamentally transformative character of this way of thinking.

Like America itself, continental philosophy is "transitional," at the crossroads of culture, dismantling classical structures and establishing new connections between past and future. What makes the experience of continental philosophy peculiarly at home in North America is precisely this dialogical component, which sustains its unique expression while holding itself open in conversation with its European counterparts. For this reason, America is best described as a particularly appropriate site for continental philosophy, a site which, because of North America's history as a displaced culture, is not a national site in the typical sense. Like continental philosophy itself, the transitional and transformational nature of American culture sustains a thinking that is open to alterity and difference and is responsive to the facticity and fluidity of experience.

This multifaceted quality characterizes the work of American philosophers in the last decade in a way that was not true of the first generation of American continentalists, whose task was to absorb European continental philosophy and bring it back to America. Now this tradition has taken hold, and, as is inevitable whenever absorption is at issue, it has become something new, a continental philosophy that belongs to America and often, as a gift of its own, is returned to Europe to again contribute to the ebb and flow of dialogue and reciprocal thinking. American continental philosophy no longer has the tone of commentary. The voices reflected in the essays contained in this volume are those of independent thinkers, thinkers who above all recognize the importance of translation, not because German and

French texts must be rendered into English but because translation occurs within the very dynamic of philosophizing from a continental perspective. To claim that all philosophizing engages in translation is to say that no language is privileged and that every text is interpretation.

The American experience, because of its immigrant roots, has always been imbued with a sense of the foreign. Philosophizing in the face of the foreign, of what is not one's own, is part and parcel of the American experience. There is a certain sense in which our capacity to remember is infiltrated with a sense of the loss of memory. Our sense of ourselves is one of being cut off from our past, only able to recover ourselves in an experience of fragmented and displaced identity. In a way, America is a siteless site, a place for experience and thinking whose boundaries are not sedimented but open to the recovery of the foreign sites that define us. The experience of belonging and not belonging, of being at home and yet not at home, is very American. The theme of an unrecoverable distance is one of the central themes that continental philosophy has taken up in the last decade, but it resonates especially among contemporary American continental philosophers.

This non-sedimented, open spirit, which shuns a narrowly nationalistic perspective, makes America uniquely receptive to the multiple directions of continental philosophy that emerge from many different countries. The voices of Germany and France merge with those of Italy, Eastern Europe, and Asia; and American philosophers are uniquely positioned to establish a confluence between these voices. Recent continental philosophy has committed itself to such a non-dogmatic perspective, recognizing the legitimacy of the unique and multiple perspectives through which philosophical thinking is achieved.

In America continental philosophy has had a strong impact on fields outside of philosophy, attaining a truly interdisciplinary character. Continental philosophy has radically altered the approaches to literary theory, redefined the field of aesthetics, shifted the issues addressed in many theological circles, and, through the influence of critiques of authority and power structures stemming from the work of Foucault and Habermas, changed the landscape in the social sciences, and, more recently, in psychoanalysis. The interdisciplinary character of American continental philosophy often makes it impossible in many universities to know where philosophy ends and other disciplines begin. The breakdown of discrete disciplines that are rooted in longstanding European tradition is releasing intellectual energy from its narrow academic confines. Yet this American appropriation of continental philosophy is completely in line with the deconstructive and hermeneutic principles that belong to the continental way of philosophizing.

The experience of being American today is of belonging to a culture that no longer aspires to be a melting pot, that no longer blends differences together to create a community of the same. Continental philosophy has provided a way of thinking and speaking that addresses and affirms multiculturalism in America. The emphasis on difference and alterity, often influenced by Levinas and Derrida, that pervades so much of the work of the contributors to this volume is at the heart of continental philosophy; but it can certainly be said that this commitment to pluralism speaks directly out of an American need and an American experience. Several of the authors that appear in this volume have turned from the critique of liberalism and the paradigm of modernity to a new sense of community based on a concept of singularity appropriate to our own factical experience as Americans and as human beings. For example, the attention to the singular voices of those who have not been incorporated into a culture of common identity has created in continental philosophy a space for the feminine voice that has in many ways transformed contemporary thinking. The voices of the other have to some extent become the voices of continental philosophy.

Finally, one cannot fail to take some account of the experience of translation as a uniquely American dimension of continental philosophy. On the surface, this simply means the recognition that Americans speak in many languages. To speak metaphorically, North America is itself a translation. Americans may sense a tension between their own voice and that of the foreigner, but they have had the task of developing a unique voice that does not deny its ear for what is foreign. This fragility with regard to identity creates conditions for expressing the uniqueness of American continental philosophy. It is precisely this sense of ambivalence in the face of the other, this distance from Europe that nevertheless wants to listen to Europeans, that creates American continental philosophy. It allows philosophers to do philosophy in a way that is open to sharing with others, speaking with others, and embracing a dialogical spirit that is open to the voices of the other.

This Volume

The radicality, uniqueness, and originality of contemporary American philosophy is reflected in the sections into which we have grouped the essays in this volume. The essays do not fit into the usual categories of philosophy. It is impossible to group them along the traditional lines of ontology, theory of knowledge, logic and language, and ethics and social and political philosophy. Something new has emerged that makes the usual categories unworkable. Contemporary critiques of language and systems of knowledge that were aimed toward the overcoming of metaphysics or an overarching meaning of being were also meant to revolutionize the sense of the political. Critiques of patriarchy and structures of authority disrupted normative ethics and social organizations rooted in foundationalist metaphysics. Therefore our attempt to suggest headings under which to group these essays is offered as a tentative scheme for gathering issues that in the end intertwine in a way that undermines these designations.

The first grouping, "Intersecting the Tradition," was chosen with the realization that American continental philosophy, and the works of these authors in particular, grows out of and confronts an ongoing project of interpretation. Each of the three authors included in this section relates to tradition in a way that may be appropriately called an intersection. John Sallis's work on imagination, metaphysics, and wonder attempts to release the imagination from bondage to rationality and thus cuts apart (intersects) the unity of tradition. In turn, Richard Rorty's work, often inspired by the attempt to bring various traditions—analytic, pragmatic, and continental—into communication with each other, seems to be inspired by an attempt to think from out of the linkage (intersection) of these various American traditions. Finally, Dennis Schmidt addresses the issue of metaphor, the crossing over (and intersecting) of language, and the tragedy of the impossibility of such an intersection ever finally occurring.

The second group of essays, "Rephrasing Discourse," addresses contemporary continental philosophy's rejection of grand meta-narratives and its insistence that there can be no overarching theory of language. The authors included in this section address the turn from epistemology and the language of the proposition that arises out of certain traditional models of knowledge. The notion of re-phrasing discourse is not meant to stand against logic but to be a positive attempt to think the character of intelligibility and communication that resides in language. Thus Alphonso Lingis's essay, "The Murmur of the World," asks about the communication of those whose voices are excluded. Calvin Schrag talks about the character of rationality in response to the postmodern critique of reason and subjectivity. Who, he asks, is the contemporary communicator and how is communication possible? Drucilla Cornell's essay discusses Adorno's negative dialectics as an example of communication that has become communicative responsibility.

"Places of Identity" is meant to displace the traditional notion that the discussion of human identity simply revolves around questions about who we are. The facticity of human being is discussed in different ways, and each of the authors addresses the problem of identity from a perspective that is no longer rooted in the existentialist question of personal identity (and its lack). Rather, the question of identity is seen to emerge out of the radicalization of experience. Thus, it is in terms of time and history that the human being's sense of self begins to understand its location. The question of identity no longer arises out of the understanding of subjectivity; but it emerges from our sense of dwelling and embodied experience. David Krell's essay, "Unhomelike Places: Archetictural Sections of Heidegger and Freud," sees the creation of sites for thinking in the experience of building. Charles Scott and Edward Casey address the issue from the perspective of memory that is no longer tethered to the *cogito* but is a lived, situated remembrance.

"Locating the Ethical" picks up on the previous theme of place and hints at an issue that has evolved into one of the most original and creative aspects of continental philosophy, the issue of the ethical. At an early stage, under the influence of Heidegger, continental thinkers were wary of discussing ethical issues. They were aware that such issues were almost irretrievably wedded to metaphysical presuppositions. They respected Heidegger's declaration that the question of the ethical was pivotal for the future of thinking, a question that perhaps needed both to be deferred and asked in a new way. The essays in this group reflect the success of continental philosophy in coming to grips with the tradition. Thinking is freed to create a new approach to the ethical, an ethics that no longer thinks under the shadow of a foundational metaphysics and that calls patriarchal and authorial privilege into question. John Caputo offers a discussion of a sense of obligation that is against ethics. William Richardson addresses the important issue of law and patriarchy from a Lacanian perspective. Finally, Rodolphe Gasché develops the basis for an ethics of confrontation.

In "Voices of the Other" we hoped to convey that the thinkers whose work is found in this section have moved beyond logocentrism in their way of speaking and addressing the matter for thinking. The authors speak in fragmented voices that no longer claim the authorial privilege to establish what is proper to truth. In these essays, traditional questions of social and political philosophy have been transformed in light of the issues that emerge in the spirit of pluralism and multiculturalism. Thus, Seyla Benhabib discusses feminist philosophy in the context of a critique of Hannah Arendt's distinction between the public and the private. Judith Butler addresses the issue of power and subjection in an attempt to contrast Foucauldian critiques of institutional power with psychoanalytic interpretations in order to open a space for thinking of the voices of resistance. Robert Bernasconi, who was born and schooled in Britain, contributes an essay on the philosophy of race that distinctly belongs to the politics and history of America.

We have prefaced each selection with a brief introduction that situates the essay in relation to the overall project of the philosopher. In addition, each selection is followed by a bibliography that will serve as a guide for further study. In the end, it is our hope that this reader indicates the diverse and widespread contributions of all American continental philosophers to the important questions that philosophers address.

Camano Island, 1999

Notes

1. Herbert Spiegelberg, *The Phenomenological Movement* (The Hague: Martinus Nijhoff, 1963). The first edition of this text covered the phenomenological movement up to 1958, when Spiegelberg completed the original manuscript.

2. For a clear philosophical account of postmodernism, see Jean-François Lyotard's *The Postmodern Condition: A Report on Knowledge*, trans. Geoff Bennington and Brian Massumi (Minneapolis: Minnesota University Press, 1984). Lyotard develops the notion of postmodernism from classical sources in phenomenology and cultural studies.

3. See Gilles Deleuze and Félix Guattari, *Anti-Oedipus*, trans. Robert Hurley, Mark Seem, and Helen Lane (New York: Viking, 1977).

4. The phrase, "history of the systems of thought," was used by Foucault as the name for his chair at the Collège de France.

5. Selected papers from the first two meetings were published in *An Invitation to Phenomenology*, ed. James Edie (Chicago: Quadrangle Books, 1965). A second volume, *Phenomenology in America*, also edited by James Edie and containing the papers from the next three years, appeared in 1967. A third volume, *New Essays in Phenomenology*, followed in 1969 with papers from the sixth and seventh annual meetings. Both volumes were published by Quadrangle Books.

6. See Gilles Deleuze, *Difference and Repetition* (New York: Columbia University Press, 1994).

Part 1

Intersecting the Tradition

1

Imagination, Metaphysics, Wonder

JOHN SALLIS

John Sallis's importance to the development of continental philosophy in America cannot be exaggerated. His impact as a teacher on generations of students is almost legendary. He is the editor of one of the most important journals in continental philosophy, *Research in Phenomenology*, editor of a prestigious series of books, Studies in Continental Thought, published by Indiana University Press, and one of the guiding forces in the Collegium Phaenomenologicum, an annual, internationally renowned summer program in Umbria, Italy. He is also the author of many groundbreaking philosophical works in American continental philosophy.

Sallis's confrontations with the history of Western philosophy are among the most salient in contemporary philosophy. His work crosses through the usual divisions of theories of knowledge, political philosophy, aesthetics and philosophy of nature. He is an art critic who has brought a contemporary philosophical voice to the interpretation of art. Among the themes that are prevalent in Sallis's work, three deserve special mention. The theme of imagination is never far removed from the center of Sallis's philosophical concern. Sallis attempts to rethink imagination as playing a central role in all dimensions of human experience, action, and poetic production. This can be seen as an attempt to recover the profound sense of imagination found in Kant, the German Idealists, and the Romantics—and to rethink this sense of imagination independently of subjectivity and at the limit of metaphysics. Art is the focus of much of his work, and he attempts not only to bring philosophical reflection (such as that on imagination) to bear on the arts but to let the disclosive and deconstructive capacities of the arts reflect back upon philosophy. The question of nature, especially elemental nature, has influenced Sallis's work. In his discussions about nature, he shows how comportment to nature is profoundly determinative of human beings, especially comportment to and envelopment by the elements.

The trajectory of John Sallis's work is defined by the conclusion of his first book: "The question is whether there can be a philosophy of imagination which is not also a philosophy of the cogito." The question of imagination emerged and took shape through his early research in phenomenology and his studies of Plato and of Kant during the 1970s. This work was followed by a period of intensive engagement with German Idealism, Nietzsche, and Heidegger. During this period, his efforts concentrated especially on determining the limit of both metaphysical questioning and the Heideggerian question of the sense of being. He explored how questions of the sensible, of nature, and of artistic production and disclosure emerge in mutated form at this limit. Sallis's work in the history of philosophy exhibits careful phenomenological and deconstructive strategies that open texts to their own radicality and excess. His more recent work has directly addressed the arts, nature as disclosed in the arts and as thought in advance of metaphysics in Plato's *Timaeus,* and a systematic elaboration of the question of imagination.

The essay that appears in this volume shows how the question of imagination has operated at the limit of metaphysics, how it has exercised an oblique resistance that can come to reorient thinking toward another opening. The essay also shows how wonder, precisely as the beginning of philosophy, operates at the limit and can return in response to a new opening upon nature which discloses its radically sensible and profoundly elemental character.

⤛⫸⬤⫷⤜

In the end of metaphysics—suspending initially all the questions that haunt this phrase—what becomes most decisive are those forces and comportments that have always remained marginal in metaphysics, those that harbor a kind of oblique resistance to the fundamental axes by which metaphysics would measure everything that is. Since such moments will never have been fully appropriated to and by metaphysics, they retain a unique capacity, in the end of metaphysics, to reorient the entire field of thinking in a manner so fundamental as to displace the very schema that determines the sense and value of *fundamental,* that is, of ground. In this essay I attempt to address two such oblique moments, those that in the history of metaphysics have gone by the names of *imagination* and *wonder,* respectively. It will be a matter both of tracing the dynamic relation of each to metaphysics and of offering some indications of the manner in which each comes into play in the end of metaphysics, contributing to an unheard-of reinscription of what is to be thought.

1. Imagination and Metaphysics

As a way of broaching the question of imagination, let me adopt a little flight of fancy that Kant inscribes near the beginning of the *Critique of Pure Reason.*[1] I shall adopt it in a way that may itself appear a bit fanciful. The flight is that of a dove. The dove, cleaving the air in its flight and feeling the resistance, ventures out toward empty space, upward toward the heavens, supposing that there its flight would be still easier and freer. The dove is an image of metaphysics, and its flight represents the ascent that metaphysics would enact, the ascent out beyond the world of the senses, the ascent into the beyond. The question concerns the power of flight: Does the dove ascend on the wings of imagination?

Metaphysics has never given an unqualifiedly affirmative answer to this question, has never been—or at least has never taken itself to be—a flight of fancy. In metaphysical discourse there is nothing comparable to that discourse that Shakespeare, referring to the poet, put into the mouth of Theseus in *A Midsummer Night's Dream*:

> The poet's eye, in a fine frenzy rolling,
> Doth glance from heaven to earth, from earth to heaven;
> And as imagination bodies forth
> The forms of things unknown, the poet's pen
> Turns them to shapes, and gives to airy nothing
> A local habitation and a name.[2]

Metaphysics, on the contrary, would have nothing to do with airy nothing; it wants to know nothing about the nothing. Nor would it have anything to do with such illicit trafficking back and forth between heaven and earth.

Accordingly, metaphysics has always been suspicious of imagination. Recall the case of Descartes, of those strategies by which he would protect properly metaphysical understanding from the corruptive intrusion of imagination, for example, his resolve that in the search for the true self there is to be no reliance whatsoever upon imagination:

> And thus I know manifestly that nothing of all that I can understand by means of the imagination is pertinent to the knowledge which I have of myself, and that I must remember this and prevent my mind from thinking in this fashion, in order that it may clearly perceive its own nature.[3]

Much the same suspicion of imagination is expressed, more imaginatively, by Samuel Johnson:

> Imagination, a licentious and vagrant faculty, unsusceptible of limitations, and impatient of restraint, has always endeavored to baffle the logician, to perplex the confines of distinction, and burst the inclosures of regularity.[4]

Or again, it is expressed by Dryden's warning that

> Imagination . . . is a faculty so Wild and Lawless, that, like an high-ranging Spaniel it must have Cloggs tied to it, least it out-run the Judgment.[5]

Or finally, Shakespeare, again through the mouth of Theseus:

> Such tricks hath strong imagination,
> That, if it would but apprehend some joy,
> It comprehends some bringer of that joy;

> Or in the night, imagining some fear
> How easy is a bush supposed a bear![6]

The operation of this suspicion is not, however, simply an operation at a distance. The suspicion does not operate simply by setting imagination once and for all at a distance, by excluding it from the project of metaphysics as something simply opposed to that project. It will be recalled that even Descartes has, in the end, to summon imagination to the aid of that very understanding that he would protect from it. It is, then, precisely the impossibility of any simple exclusion that renders the suspicion so radical, that makes it necessary for it to be exercised ever anew, that binds it so closely to metaphysics. Imagination can be neither simply excluded from nor simply appropriated by metaphysics.

Here I shall undertake to investigate the dynamics of this relation between imagination and metaphysics. It will be, at least initially, a matter of tracing the double gesture by which metaphysics both appropriates imagination and yet excludes it, sets it at a distance. By investigating this strange dynamics, this gesture bordering on contradiction, I hope to venture a few steps in the direction of a question responsive to our time: What becomes of imagination at the end of metaphysics? Is imagination—that is, the word, the concept, perhaps even the thing itself (if I may use, provisionally, this very classical schema)—entangled in the web of metaphysics in such a way that it too cannot but fall prey to a deconstruction that today would dislodge all metaphysical securities? Is the closure of metaphysics also the closure of imagination and of its field of play? Or, on the contrary, does the closure of metaphysics perhaps serve precisely to free imagination and to open fully its field? Is it perhaps even on the wings of imagination that one can effectively transgress metaphysics and station oneself at the limit, hovering there without security?

But let me be more specific about how, this side of such questions, I shall proceed. I shall focus on certain pivotal texts from the history of metaphysics and shall attempt to show how the dynamics of the relation between imagination and metaphysics is traced in those texts. First of all, I shall consider certain Platonic texts. Here it will be a matter of observing how the relation between imagination and metaphysics takes shape, how its dynamics is constituted, with the very inception of metaphysics. The second text to be examined is Pico della Mirandola's treatise *On the Imagination*. This text, standing at the threshold of modern thought, at the same time gathers up virtually the entire ancient and medieval reflection on imagination. The third text, Kant's *Critique of Pure Reason*, is a pivot on which modern thought turns perhaps most decisively. In it the question of imagination and metaphysics is vigorously renewed.

Before I proceed, some preliminary points need to be mentioned for the sake of clarity. It is especially important to call attention to the way in which metaphysics, the nature of metaphysics, is to be understood here, a way which is rooted in continental philosophy since Hegel and which I cannot adequately develop here. Suffice it to mention two points in this regard.

First, metaphysics is taken to have a history that is not simply extrinsic to it—that is, it is taken as something which was founded, which has run a certain course, and which since Hegel has come to a kind of end, as something which cannot be defined independently of this history. And yet, though I cannot deal with the issue here, clearly one could not indefinitely postpone taking some account of the torsion already installed within such a concept of metaphysics as historical, the torsion resulting from the fact that metaphysics is also constituted as a turning away from history. Second, metaphysics is to be understood here not so much as a particular discipline alongside others within philosophy as a whole but rather as the execution and elaboration of the fundamental movement or gesture which first opens up philosophy as a whole, which founds it—as, to take an example that I shall have to deal with later in some detail, the Socratic turn from sensible to intelligible opens up the very space in which philosophy moves. But here again one must be careful not to construe matters too straightforwardly, for this example is, of course, not really an example at all but, on the contrary, first constitutes the very field of oppositions in which there can be anything like an example.

Finally, it is important to note that, formally considered, the relation between imagination and metaphysics has a certain twofold character. This twofoldness is indicated perhaps most clearly by the grammatically twofold genitive: metaphysics *of* imagination. The phrase refers both to a metaphysical theory about imagination and to a metaphysics in the very accomplishing of which imagination would play a major role, a metaphysics which would be the work—or, perhaps better, the play—of imagination. It will be important to observe how these two sides of the relation are interwoven in the history of metaphysics.

⋅❯❯❂❰❰⋅

It is in the *Phaedo* that Socrates, recounting his own history, tells of that decisive turn by which he was set once and for all on his way. According to his account, that turn came only after he had repeatedly experienced failure in his efforts to investigate things by the method of his predecessors, namely, that direct method of investigation which would proceed to explain certain things by referring them directly to other things. Socrates relates that as a result of this experience he came eventually to have recourse to a kind of indirect way of investigating things, a way which he describes as analogous to the procedure of studying things in an image rather than looking at them directly. He says: "So I thought I must have recourse to λόγοι and examine in them the truth of beings."[7] This recourse he describes as a matter of "placing something under," as one might place a foundation under an infirm structure. What is thus placed under he calls a ὑπόθεσις; he mentions the beautiful itself, the good, the great. In other words—words which are, however, decisive for the entire history of metaphysics—the recourse is a matter of positing explicitly certain εἴδη that are already tacitly posited, expressed, in λόγος. Thus, in the recourse certain εἴδη are posited over against the sensibly present things, posited as "standing under" those things, as their foundation. Hence, the Socratic turn consists in the opening of the difference between immediately, sensibly present things and those εἴδη that would be their foundation—or, more precisely and literally, those εἴδη in which the sheer unobstructed look of things would be had. Note especially the remark that Socrates is careful to add: Though his turn is analogous to the procedure of turning from things (that is, originals) to images (of those things), it is ultimately quite distinct from such a procedure. It is ultimately even an inversion of that procedure, a turn not from original to image but, conversely, from immediately present things (recognized as images) to their originals. The Socratic turn thus differentiates between things in their immediate, sensible presence and those things in their original truth, in their originary presence; and it shifts away from immediately, sensibly present things, away from the fragmented presence of the immediate and sensible—shifts away in order to prepare a reappropriation of those things in their originary presence. By marking this difference between τὸ νοητόν and τὸ αἰσθητόν, the Socratic turn poses the task of mediating this difference and in posing this task founds metaphysics. More precisely, the Socratic turn constitutes the field of metaphysics as a field of presence and metaphysics itself as the drive to presence.

In the Platonic dialogues there are many representations of this difference, this field—for example, that line which is drawn and divided near the center of the *Republic*. The schema of image-original is explicit in Socrates' description of the relation between the two segments which represent the divisions of the sensible as a whole: in the transition it is a matter of εἰκασία, of apprehending images (εἰκών) *as* images in such a way that one sees through them to the originals which they image. It is, for example, a matter of apprehending the shadow of an artifact as a shadow and hence as disclosing the artifact itself, a matter of that kind of apprehending that comes to be exercised by the exceptional one among those cave-dwellers described in that image at the very center of the *Republic*. But it is not only underground, not only within the sensible, that the schema of image-original is in play. For when, emerging from the cave into the open space above, the escaped prisoner prepares to lift his gaze from the earth to the heavens, he makes his preparation by gazing at things as they are *imaged,* as they are, for example, reflected in pools of water. This schema determines the entire course represented by the cave and the line. It constitutes the structure within which the metaphysical reappropriation of presence would be played out. The field of metaphysics, the field of presence, is structured by the dyadic relation between image and original; it is structured by the indeterminate dyad.

In this sense, then, one may say that metaphysics is a matter of imagination, provided, of course, that imagination is distinguished from mere fancy. It is a matter of eikastic imagination, not of phantastic imagination. Granted this limitation, the two sides of the genitive, the two senses of metaphysics *of* imagination, become perfectly complementary: the metaphysical theory regarding imagination would be simply the self-understanding of meta-physics accomplished by imagination.

And yet, the Platonic Socrates incessantly sets imagination, even eikastic imagination, at a distance. The poets, the painters, the sophists, all those who deal in images are ferreted out, distinguished from the philosopher, and banished from the city. One would, of course, need to insist on the subtlety and irony of the Socratic criticisms of the image-makers; and one would need to take account of the massive self-reference of these criticisms, to take account, for example, of the fact that an image stands at the beginning, the middle, and the end of the very dialogue in which image-making is most explicitly condemned, viz., the *Republic*—indeed, not just an image but the image of images, the image of a realm in which all would be mere images, mere shades.[8] Nevertheless, the taking of distance from imagination belongs structurally to the metaphysical project no less than does the appropriation of imagination. For though the schema of image-original structures the field of metaphysics in such a way that the drive to presence can be oriented and carried out, it also, on the other hand, serves to inhibit that drive and to divert it into a play of presence and absence. Insofar as the structure remains in force, every original remains withdrawn, concealed, behind its image, glimpsed only through that image, not in its originary presence. And if indeed one did succeed in traversing the distance from image to original, one would do so only at the cost of opening up another such space behind what would then prove not to have been truly original.

Such is, in briefest outline, the dynamics that governs the relation between imagination and metaphysics in the Platonic texts: imagination both empowers and inhibits the metaphysical drive to presence, and metaphysics must, accordingly, both appropriate and take distance from imagination. The metaphysical theory regarding imagination is not only a matter of metaphysical self-understanding but also one of distinguishing metaphysics from an other from which, as from the sophist, it can never free itself once and for all.

⁎⁌◉⌐⁎

During the period of nearly two millennia that separates the Platonic texts from Pico's treatise of 1500 *On the Imagination,* several shifts occur which affect the relation between imagination and metaphysics and the dynamics of that relation. The most significant shift occurs in the conception of imagination; it is a shift from εἰκασία to φαντασία, from eikastic imagination to phantastic imagination; and it is marked linguistically by the fact that both Latin words, *imaginatio* and *phantasia,* are translations of forms of the Greek φαντασία.[9] Remarkably, εἰκασία goes virtually untranslated. This shift prescribes a whole series of realignments in the relation between imagination and metaphysics, and one of the virtues of Pico's treatise is the transparency with which these realignments are presented.

The shift is announced at the very outset of Pico's text: he identifies his theme as that power of the soul which the Greeks call φαντασία and which in Latin is called *imaginatio*. It is so called in Latin, he notes, because of those images which it forms in itself, images which are linked to those likenesses of things that are conveyed through the exterior senses. Deferring the explanation of that link of imagination to sense, Pico focuses momentarily on those things themselves:

> For whatever the object of sensation, and that means everything corporeal which can be perceived or felt by any sense, the object produces, insofar as it can, a likeness and image of itself, in imitation of incorporeal and spiritual nature. This spiritual nature communicates its powers to the inferior world in imitation of God himself, who in his infinite goodness, spread far and wide, has established and preserves the universe.[10]

The passage is remarkable, for it broaches on both a horizontal and a vertical axis that schema of image-original which according to the Platonic texts structures the field of metaphysics and corresponds to eikastic imagination. Objects, such as the senses can present, produce images of themselves; they are image-makers of themselves, originals necessarily distinct from those images of themselves which they produce in the soul. Furthermore, on the vertical axis, this image-making accomplished by objects is an imitation, an image, of that superior image-making practiced by the soul insofar as it impresses its form on the inferior, corporeal world, for example, in the practice of an art in the classical sense. In turn, and finally, the soul's image-making is an imitation, a moving image, of that absolutely original image-making practiced by the creator. This utterly Platonic beginning is even identified as such: Plato's name is mentioned, and a reference is made to the *Timaeus*. But then, as though it might otherwise displace the discussion of φαντασία that has been promised, Pico abruptly sets the entire eikastic structure aside: "But enough of such reflections, since here is not the place for them." Pico's text has begun by reenacting the shift away from εἰκασία.

A new, more controlled beginning is made, and now the authority of Aristotle is explicitly invoked. Now the constitution of the field of metaphysics, its structuring, hardly comes into question. Instead, the investigation centers on imagination—phantastic imagination—as a power of the soul. As such, imagination proves to be essential to all knowledge, an ally that must come to the aid of all other human powers if they are not to fail in the function bestowed upon them by nature. As Pico writes, actually shifting at this point in his text to the word *phantasia:* "Nor could the soul, fettered as it is to the body, opine, know, or comprehend at all, if phantasy were not constantly to supply it with the images themselves."[11] Imagination is the great mediator: it receives the impressions of objects from the senses, retains them within itself, and renders them purer before passing them on to the higher powers of the soul. As in the Platonic texts, imagination mediates the ascent from the sensible, though now it is a mediation withdrawn into the soul rather than one that draws the soul into a dyadically structured field of presence.

However, Pico's text is by no means written to celebrate the mediating role which imagination plays in the soul's ascent. On the contrary, almost from the beginning—the new, more controlled beginning—Pico stresses that "imagination is for the most part vain and wandering."[12] As he proceeds, the condemnation becomes more and more severe, and an entire chapter—chapter 7, entitled "On the numerous Evils which come from the Imagination"—is devoted to enumerating the charges. Imagination is identified as the mother and nurse of ambition. Cruelty, wrath, and passion are said to be born from and nourished by imagination; likewise with the insatiable thirst for gold and the ardor of lust. Imagination is also charged with bringing about "all monstrous opinions and the defects of all judgment"; it is at the origin of most sins and is the source of those heresies that pervert the Christian faith. However, more significant than any of these charges is the one made in defense of philosophy:

> And if we turn our attention to the functions of the philosophic life, we shall see that no lesser disadvantage has accrued to it from false phantasies. Indeed, when I consider the source of the shifting, the manifold, differences in opinion that have come down even to our time from those great philosophers, Thales, Democritus, Empedocles, Zeno, Pythagoras, and the others, nothing strikes me as more reasonable than that we should pass sentence upon the treacherous imagination.[13]

Philosophy itself, empowered by imagination, is also corrupted by it, by its vanity and its wanderings. Thus, Pico writes his treatise not to celebrate imagination, nor even just to understand it, but to condemn it:

> But imagination is for the most part vain and wandering; for the sake of proving this to be so I have assumed the present task of demonstration.[14]

Above all, Pico writes his treatise in order to condemn the corruption with which imagination threatens philosophy; or, rather, since it cannot be a matter of simply excluding imagination, his task is to set imagination at a distance from philosophy, to render its threat ineffective by developing a theory of imagination in which that threat is exposed. And yet, even this kind of defense is limited; for imagination, empowering knowledge, is always already in play in that very knowledge, that theory of imagination, by which it would be exposed and set at a distance. Indeed, Pico explicitly marks this limit: "Since the imagination itself is midway between incorporeal and corporeal nature and is the medium through which they are joined, it is difficult to grasp its nature through philosophy. . . ."[15] The dynamics of the relation between philosophy, that is, metaphysics, and imagination is such that appropriation and distancing are mutually limiting.

Pico stresses the need for distancing. His metaphysics of imagination, that is, his metaphysical theory regarding the nature of imagination, belongs to metaphysics, to metaphysics as empowered by imagination, belongs to it not so much as positive self-understanding but as a necessarily limited taking of distance from imagination and thus from the threat which it poses to metaphysics. Nevertheless, it is only a matter of stress within a dynamics which, despite the shift from εἰκασία to φαντασία, remains essentially the same as that traced in the Platonic texts.

⋅⭢⊨⊚⊜⊨⭠⋅

In the *Critique of Pure Reason,* written nearly three centuries after Pico's treatise, there remains scarcely a trace of eikastic imagination. On the other hand, the conception of phantastic imagination is greatly enriched and expanded, and its various forms are differentiated. Correspondingly, Kant's conception centers on imagination not just as a power of the soul but rather as the fundamental synthetic power of the subject, the synthetic power necessary for the constitution of an object for the subject.

The sense of this shift in the conception of imagination is closely linked to another, more extensive shift, the shift which makes the *Critique of Pure Reason* such a pivotal text in the history of metaphysics. This text announces a radical shift in metaphysics as such, announces it through the very form assumed by the text, the form of critique, announces it by giving voice to the need to institute a tribunal by which the claims of metaphysics can be decided. What are the claims that require such critical judgment? The claim to purely intellectual knowledge, to knowledge through pure concepts. What is the decision rendered by the tribunal of pure reason? On its negative side, the decision is that metaphysics has no legitimate claim to a knowledge of purely intelligible being, of things as they would be independently of their way of appearing to human sensibility. On its positive side, however, the tribunal upholds the claim that metaphysics makes to purely intellectual knowledge of objects as they appear to human sensibility; it upholds this claim by demonstrating that those purely intellectual determinations, those pure concepts, those categories, are at work in the very constituting of the sensible object, to which they must then subsequently have objective application.

The primary shift is thus a kind of closure, a shift of the intelligible into the sensible. More precisely, insofar as the intelligible is to the slightest degree accessible to human knowledge, it is no longer to be simply contrasted with the sensible but rather is regarded as merely a dimension within the sensible, its categorial determination. The difference originally opened by the Socratic turn, the difference between sensible and intelligible, is now, in Kantian critique, opened within the sensible itself—or, if you will, confined within the sensible. Such is the shift which metaphysics thus undergoes, a shift, a relocation, a confinement, of its very field.[16]

In the constitution of this field, thus shifted, the role played by imagination is no less fundamental than in the classical instance. Now it is a matter of the constitution of the sensible object as such, specifically, of the mediation between the poles of the new field, between the intuitive and the conceptual or categorial. To perform this mediation is the role of imagination, a role which it plays, not (as in the classical instance) by moving eikastically through image to original, but rather by bringing into play its power of synthesis. And yet, even in this decisively modern conception of imagination and of its function, one can still discern a trace of the dynamics that governed the Platonic conception in its relation to metaphysics and to the field of metaphysics. For, in Kant's words, "*imagination* is the faculty of representing in intuition an object that is *not itself present*"[17]—that is, it is the faculty by which one brings to presence something which is not present, or, more precisely, the faculty by which one brings to presence something which remains in another regard absent. To the same degree as eikastic vision through image to original, imagination as redetermined in Kantian critique both empowers and inhibits the metaphysical drive to presence. The difference is, however, that Kantian critique installs imagination within a field which has itself been displaced, a field which is no longer simply governed by the drive to presence, a field which is reconstituted this side of the purely intelligible, this side of the thing-in-itself, this side of that originary presence that provides classical metaphysics with its τέλος. The field of metaphysics as reconstituted in the *Critique of Pure Reason* is a field in which the play of presence and absence, the play of self-revelation and self-withholding, the play of imagination, is released from that repression that would subordinate it in the end to the ideal of sheer revelation, of pure presence.

Thus, imagination and metaphysics, as redetermined in the *Critique of Pure Reason*, are utterly appropriate to one another—so much so that the Kantian theory of the nature of imagination is wholly continuous with critique as such, which provides metaphysics with that self-understanding requisite for delimiting its possibilities and its limits, that is, its field. Such delimitation is sufficient, and there is no need to supplement it with an indictment of imagination such as Pico found it necessary to provide in his treatise. Now, with the *Critique of Pure Reason*, there is no need to set imagination at a distance from metaphysics. This utter appropriation gets expressed most transparently two decades later, when Schelling, in his *System of Transcendental Idealism*, comes to identify theoretical reason as such with imagination.[18] This identity, this appropriation, is echoed by the great English Romantic poets—for example, by Coleridge's account of imagination as that power that "urges us up the ascent of Being,"[19] by Wordsworth's identification of imagination as "reason in her most exalted mood."[20]

And yet, this appropriation of imagination to metaphysics is not unlimited. On the contrary, it is most decisively limited by the most fundamental division within reason itself and, correspondingly, within critique, viz., by the division between theoretical and practical reason, between the *Critique of Pure Reason* and the *Critique of Practical Reason*. However much imagination, extending between sensible and intelligible, can empower theoretical reason and make it possible to delimit a metaphysics of nature, imagination is, on the other hand, that power which, perhaps most of all, must be rigorously excluded from the domain of reason's practical employment. Practical reason must be *pure* practical reason, unmixed with elements of sense such as would otherwise be drawn into it by imagination. It is a matter of a determination, a self-determination, unmediated by imagination.[21] It is a matter of a pure, practical presence to self, unmediated by that play of sense and imagination that contaminates that cognitive presence to self that is based on inner intuition. However much imagination is appropriated to theoretical reason, to the metaphysics of nature, it is with equal rigor excluded, distanced, from practical reason, from the metaphysics of morals. For critical metaphysics as a whole the dynamics of the relation between imagination and metaphysics remains essentially the same as that traced in the texts of Plato and of Pico.

-+=◎c=+-

And yet, there remains another moment of the metaphysical project that I have quite deliberately avoided making explicit up to this point. It is a moment that supervenes upon that dynamic relation between metaphysics and imagination that has now been outlined in texts of Plato, of Pico, and of Kant.

One can perhaps discern this moment most distinctly, most thoroughly separated, in reference to the specific form which the dynamics assumes in critique. In the Kantian conception of practical reason there is operative not only a distancing of metaphysics from imagination but also a rigorous stabilizing of that distance, a setting of practical reason in a domain in which it would be essentially free of imagination. In other words, it is a matter of establishing a certain refuge beyond the play of imagination, a refuge in which, delivered from that play of presence and absence, reason could be self-determining, genuinely one with itself, present to itself in an originary way. The *Critique of Practical Reason* in effect compensates for that shift which the field of metaphysics underwent in the first *Critique*, compensates by positing a new intelligible order: "If freedom is attributed to us, it transfers us into an intelligible order of things."[22]

That moment of the metaphysical project that I want now to make explicit can thus be characterized as a certain stabilizing of the otherwise dynamic relation between imagination and metaphysics. It is a matter of positing a refuge beyond the play of imagination, a refuge in which pure presence would be protected from the threat of imagination. It is a matter of decisively limiting the dynamic relation between imagination and metaphysics by means of a repression of imagination.

This moment is constantly in force in Pico's text and is precisely what allows him to pass so lightly over the positive role which imagination plays in metaphysics. He can pass beyond this role because metaphysics itself is genuinely realized, is genuinely metaphysics itself, only in that domain in which imagination is repressed. Pico outlines this domain in his conception of *intellectus,* that highest power of the soul, the power by which one can contemplate those purely intelligible things that are absolutely removed from the region of sense. Within this domain of intellectual contemplation, one is able, in Pico's telling phrase, to "dominate phantasy." He continues:

"When the soul has withdrawn itself into the intellect, there, as in its own protected palace and enclosed citadel, it reposes and is perfected."[23]

This movement of repression is also in force in the Platonic texts—or, rather, one might say, at *play* in them, since it is rarely traced in those texts without being set within a dialogical play of the utmost subtlety and irony. Within the *Republic* the discussion at the end of Book VI is exemplary, especially if read along with its resumption in Book VII. I am referring to the discussion in which Socrates speaks with Glaucon about that segment of the divided line that represents dialectic, that is, the uppermost of the four segments, if, for convenience, I may assume the usual vertical representation. Socrates describes this final stage of the soul's ascent by contrasting it with the kind of movement in which the soul engages at its penultimate stage, represented by the third, the next-to-highest, segment of the line. At its penultimate stage the soul continues, as at the lower stages, to make use of images, but now, as Socrates explains, "using as images the things that were previously imitated."[24] It proceeds, then, upon hypotheses, that is, originals posited for what now show themselves to be images. Thus, the penultimate stage preserves the dyadic structure—that is, this stage is constituted by shifting to another, more original level, the image-original structure that is most manifestly operative at those stages represented by the lower segments of the line. It is precisely this dyadic structure that would finally be left behind—or, if you will, repressed—at the level of dialectic. Socrates says that in its ultimate ascent the soul, proceeding now without images, would move away from hypotheses toward an ἀρχή, a beginning or ground, that would be aloof from the dispersive play of imagination.

Glaucon is moved by what Socrates says about dialectic; and after Socrates has, in Book VII, gone through the penultimate stage in its full articulation from arithmetic to harmony, Glaucon is eager to move on to dialectic and to go through it in the same way so as to reach that place that would be, in his words, "a haven from the road." Socrates' response is most remarkable:

> You will no longer be able to follow, my dear Glaucon, . . . although there wouldn't be any lack of eagerness on my part. But you would no longer be seeing an image of what we are saying, but rather the truth itself, at least as it looks to me.[25]

It would be a matter of seeing the truth itself instead of an image, a matter of seeing the original truth, the true original—at least, Socrates says, *as it looks to me*, that is, in that appearance that it offers to me, the *image* that it casts in my direction. Need it be said that Socrates reintroduces here the play of subtlety and irony that had almost been lost as the discourse became more and more single-mindedly oriented to what Glaucon calls the end of the journey, the haven from the road?

In the discourse woven by the history of metaphysics, however, such subtlety and irony tend to disappear more irrevocably, to disappear in favor of a massive repression of imagination. It is a matter of stabilizing the otherwise dynamic relation between imagination and metaphysics, of positing a refuge, a haven, aloof from the play of imagination. This moment makes of metaphysics an unqualified drive to presence by subordinating it to a τέλος of pure presence, the end of the journey, the place of the true original whose presence is undivided by any casting of images. This τέλος is equally ἀρχή, the original which grounds. The concept of ground is thus put in force and metaphysics is made a drive to ground.

But let me no longer pretend that this moment is something added to metaphysics, something that would alter an already constituted field and the orientation within that field. On the contrary, this moment belongs to the very constitution of metaphysics as such, that is, as it runs through its great orbit from Aristotle (metaphysics as knowledge of origins and first causes) to Hegel (metaphysics as the arrival at absolute self-presence). Metaphysics as such is drive to presence, drive to ground, and the repression of imagination belongs integrally to it.

And yet, I have deliberately kept this moment detached from a certain field, the field in which obtains the dynamic relation between imagination and metaphysics. I have kept it detached because it is precisely the moment that gets detached at the end of metaphysics, in that closure of metaphysics announced most forcefully by Nietzsche and analyzed most thoroughly in recent continental thought. In this end, this closure, that strategy by which the dynamic relation between imagination and metaphysics was stabilized, that strategy by which imagination was finally repressed, comes to show itself precisely *as a strategy*. The closure of metaphysics is precisely the emptying of every refuge in which pure intelligibility might find protection from the threat of imagination.

The end of metaphysics is, then, the release of imagination into the entire field, the return of the repressed. And yet, the field does not remain the same; it is not, as I pretended earlier, merely the field of metaphysics without its final moment. For that final moment, the τέλος of originary presence, is precisely what orients the field of metaphysics. Once that moment is detached, the field is no longer simply a field of presence, a field oriented to presence.

And yet, as a field of eikastic imagination, it must be an oriented field, a field in which certain lines of directionality mark the difference between image and original, prescribing the movement in the field. But it must be also a field of indeterminate and irreducible duality, a field in which the movement of imagination never comes to rest in an absolute original aloof from the field and the play.

Let me recall some words of that author to whom Nietzsche was referring when in the 1880s he wrote, perhaps exorbitantly, that "the author who has been richest in ideas [*gedankenreichste*] in this century so far has been an American."[26] Nietzsche's reference is to Emerson, and it is from Emerson's essay "Circles" that I cite these words:

> Our life is an apprenticeship to the truth, that around every circle another
> can be drawn; that there is no end in nature, but every end is a beginning;
> that there is always another dawn risen on mid-noon, and under every deep
> a lower deep opens.[27]

It would be a matter of a field that would compound the way up and the
way down, a field upon which two suns might cast shadows and beneath
which the caverns might open endlessly. It would be a matter of joining
end and beginning, of bending the line around into a circle, and of redraw-
ing that circle indefinitely.

More precisely (perhaps), it would be a matter of taking the directional,
oriented character and the reiterably dyadic character of the field as traces
or residues of what metaphysics began by calling λόγος and εἰκασία and
ended by calling reason and imagination. It would be a matter of venturing,
beyond the closure of metaphysics, to reassemble these moments which
metaphysics from its beginning has set apart. Writing under erasure, attending to the subtlety and risk of the move, one might then broach the
demands of a logic of imagination.

Let me recall the flight of fancy, the flight of the dove. The dove of metaphysics soars off into the heavens, ventures out into empty space where
nothing any longer offers support, where flight becomes finally impossible.
The dove may then realight upon the ground in search of security; it may
even seek refuge, a haven, by creeping down into those caverns which
open endlessly, inching along through them, molelike. But just as the emptiness above is an absolute absence which precisely as such is the promise
of full presence grown silent, so the ground below is equally compromised
by those endlessly opening caverns in which, as in Hades, there are only
shades, only images. What the dove must learn is to *hover* between heaven
and earth, drifting a bit with the currents, resisting the lure of the emptiness above and the illusion of fullness below.

2. Wonder and the Determination of Philosophy as Metaphysics

Let me turn now to the word—to what was said in the word—by which the
beginning of philosophy was named in the beginning of philosophy, the
word by which, even if always with a certain reference back to the Greek
beginning, it has never ceased to be named in the historical course that
philosophy, determined as essentially metaphysics, has followed. Both Plato
and Aristotle call the beginning of philosophy θαυμάζειν. Both Hegel and
Heidegger repeat the name, even if in order to mark a certain distance from
the Greek beginning.

Yet here it will be a matter of tracing more openly an exceeding of philosophy that philosophy itself already broached in its beginning: the return
to the beginning, the move back from philosophy to the ἀρχή that precedes
it and first makes it possible, the regression across the limit of philosophy to

the ἀρχή from which it would first be delimited. It will be a matter, then, of an archaic thinking that is at the same time a remembrance. In turning toward the ἀρχή, remembrance will always have been determined also by it. When one comes to pose a question of the beginning, that beginning will already, long since, have been in play, depriving the question of its privilege. One will not have been able to begin without being engaged in the beginning, engaged by it; and when one comes to question it, one only returns differently to it, interrogatively, turning toward what already determines the question.

Remembrance will translate the beginning. Into the stable, well-established English translation of θαυμάζειν it will undertake to translate what is bespoken in the decisive discourses on θαυμάζειν, in those discourses that at the limit of philosophy turn back to name its ἀρχή. The structure of such translation is quite different from that in which a Greek word is merely transliterated or reinscribed in English; it is different, too, from that in which an English cognate of a Latin translation is activated. For *wonder* offers a certain resistance to the translation, that is, it brings its own semantic force into play in a kind of oblique resistance that skews the translation, yet in such a way as to promise a translation in which those ancient discourses may be opened beyond themselves. It is a matter of bringing the semantic force of *wonder* to supplement what is sounded in those discourses, echoing them in another tongue, making them resound in the sounding of *wonder*.

What are some of the things that sound in *wonder*?

There sounds amazement in the face of extraordinary occurrences, the rapture into which one is drawn in beholding mysterious or magical events that appear to bespeak the unknown or to portend what is to come. As in the case of Macbeth, whose letter to his wife tells of his wondrous encounter with the three witches. Hailed by them not only as Thane of Cawdor but also as king to be, he burned with desire to question them further about their more than mortal knowledge. Yet, charged by him to reveal the origin and intent of their prophecy, the witches vanish:

When I burned in desire to question them further,
They made themselves air, into which they vanished.
Whiles I stood rapt in the wonder of it, . . .
(*Macbeth* I, v, 4–6)

Its sound is not very different from that of its Anglo-Saxon ancestor *wundor:* a wondrous thing, a portent, something outside the usual course of nature, like the tracks of the dragon pursued in *Beowulf,* like the dragon itself or the strange creatures (*wundra*) that assaulted Beowulf in the deep (*Beowulf* 840, 1509). Transliterating the Latin, opening *wonder* to its history, one says: monster.

There sounds too the wonder of a vision in which one comes to see the world anew, in which it opens as if for the first time so as to disclose something wondrous. As when Miranda exclaims:

> O, wonder!
> How many goodly creatures are there here!
> How beauteous mankind is! O brave new world
> That has such people in't!
> (*The Tempest* V, i, 181–84)

Wonder, as in the face of a young child suddenly beholding something for the first time.

--=◎=--

The Aristotelian discourse on wonder occurs within a discussion of the knowledge (ἐπιστήμη) that is most archontic (ἀρχικωτάτη), that is, most royal, most suited to rule. Both the knowledge thus determined and the treatise to which the discussion belongs will later be designated by the word *metaphysics*. Such knowledge is said to consist in speculation (θεωρητική) regarding first beginnings and causes (τῶν πρώτων ἀρχῶν καὶ αἰτιῶν). Aristotle's concern is to show that such speculation is not a matter of production (ποιητική), that philosophy is not pursued in order to produce something. This is shown by consideration of the first philosophers, by turning to the beginning of philosophy, to that beginning from which philosophy proceeded in its beginning. In the turn Aristotle thus doubles the beginning: "It is through wonder that men now begin and first began to philosophize" (*Metaphysics* I, 982b12–13).[28] Hence, wonder is identified as the beginning of philosophy both in the beginning and now. All begin from wonder (ἀπὸ τοῦ θαυμάζειν) (*Metaphysics* I, 983a12–13) both in the past and in the present. Only as regards the operation of this beginning in the future does Aristotle remain—initially—silent.

Aristotle outlines a progression through which wonder moves: from perplexities regarding things close at hand to perplexities about the genesis of all that is. Thus, wonder would function as beginning not only in the beginning of speculation but throughout its entire course up to the point at which it would finally open upon the whole of what is.

How does wonder function as a beginning throughout the course of speculation? It functions by bringing about an awareness of ignorance: "Now he who wonders and is perplexed considers himself ignorant" (*Metaphysics* I, 982b12–13). Wonder is like the sting of the gadfly, driving men out of their pretense to know, setting them adrift in their ignorance, as if paralyzed by a stingray. It is in order to escape the ignorance made manifest through wonder that men pursue philosophy, the aim of which is thus simply knowledge and not production. Thus, it is by making ignorance manifest, by bringing about perplexity, that wonder incites the pursuit of knowledge and functions as the beginning of philosophy.

Yet, wonder is only the beginning, inciting men in the beginning and now. Wonder does not belong to the future toward which the pursuit of knowledge moves. Rather, that pursuit, Aristotle insists, must lead to the opposite (εἰς τοὐναντίον) of that with which inquiry began (983a12).

He repeats that all begin by wondering that things are as they are. But now—most remarkably—he presents wonder not only as making ignorance manifest but also as essentially linked to, even constituted by ignorance: the incommensurability of the diagonal of a square seems wonderful (θαυμαστόν . . . δοκεῖ) to everyone who has not beheld the cause thereof. One ends, he says, with the opposite and the better: the opposite not only of ignorance but also of wonder. Thus, in the end knowledge is opposed, as the better, to wonder. Though it is through wonder that one comes to pursue knowledge, that pursuit has the effect finally of dissolving wonder. In the end there would be no place for wonder in knowledge, no place for a knowledge to which wonder would be essential and not merely an incitement. In the end there would be only knowledge, beyond the wonder of perplexity. Philosophy would achieve its end by putting an end to wonder.

Hegel renews the Aristotelian discourse on wonder. One such renewal occurs in the philosophy of subjective spirit, specifically, in that part of the psychology devoted to intuition (*Anschauung*). In displacing wonder from metaphysics to psychology Hegel only carries out the displacement that Aristotle has fully prepared by linking wonder to ignorance and opposing it in the end to the knowledge in which it would finally have been dissolved. Hegel puts an end to wonder still more decisively by assimilating wonder to intuition. Thus, it is in a discussion in which Hegel is concerned to explain how intuition is only the beginning of knowledge (*der Beginn des Erkennens*) that he recalls and confirms the Aristotelian discourse:

> *Aristotle* refers to its [intuition's] place when he says that all knowledge begins from *wonder* [Verwunderung]. Initially, the object is still loaded with the form of the irrational, and it is because it is within this that subjective reason as intuition has the certainty, though only the *indeterminate certainty*, of finding itself again, that its subject matter inspires it with wonder and awe. *Philosophical* thought, however, has to raise itself above the standpoint of wonder.[29]

With Hegel it is a matter of putting an end to wonder as soon as knowledge progresses beyond intuition. That end, that aim, that function, that Aristotle granted to wonder as the beginning of philosophy is now virtually withdrawn from it, even in confirming the Aristotelian statement that all knowledge has its beginning in wonder. For it is no longer wonder but the power of negativity that drives the advance of knowledge. Wonder belongs neither to the future nor to the present of philosophy but only to its past. And even if, like every past, it is retained in the depth of the present and the future, it is not retained *as wonder*.

Beyond the past of philosophy, hardly a trace of wonder is still to be found. And yet, even a trace may make one hesitant to join in putting an end to wonder. Or rather, it may prompt a reversal in which one would submit the end to wonder, bringing wonder to bear upon that very end that would have alleged to bring it to an end. Now, opening wonder to the future.

The Platonic discourse on wonder occurs in the *Theaetetus*. Indeed this entire dialogue can be read as a discourse on wonder, gathered around a single passage in which wonder is identified as the beginning of philosophy. The entire dialogue is framed by occurrences of forms of the word, both in the final speech by Socrates and, at the outset, in the conversation between Euclides and Terpsion that frames the main conversation between Socrates and Theaetetus.

For the question that Socrates asks Theaetetus, "What is knowledge [ἐπιστήμη])?" it suffices neither merely to number (ἀριθμῆσαι) the various forms, to collect them in an enumeration of types, nor to divide, as Theodorus and Theaetetus had divided the numbers into square and oblong. He must, rather, says Socrates, try to address the many knowledges with one discourse (λόγος). Or rather, Theaetetus must try to give birth to such a discourse; for, as Socrates tells him in response to his plea of incapacity, "you're suffering labor pains, on account of your not being empty but pregnant" (148e). Socrates, the midwife ready to assist him, thus launches on his own discourse describing his peculiar art. It is a wonderful art that this son of a midwife practices, also an art over which the Socratic daimon exercises a certain authority. The greatest thing (μέγιστον) in this art is that it can test whether the thought of a young man is giving birth to an image and a lie (εἴδωλον καὶ ψεῦδος) or to something fruitful and true (γόνιμόν τε καὶ ἀληθές).

Theaetetus is quickly delivered: he declares that knowledge is nothing else than perception or sensing (αἴσθησις).

Socrates sets to work determining whether the declaration is fruitful or only a wind-egg. He refers indeed to the wind, applying to it the maxim of Protagoras that man is the measure of all things, observing thus that the same wind may be cold to one person and not cold to another. He continues: sensing is always the sensing of something that is (τοῦ ὄντος), of something existent that appears (φαίνεται) to sensing. Because, according to Theaetetus, sensing is knowledge, it cannot be false. The consequence can be foreseen: such sensing as knowledge, such sense-knowledge, must be knowledge of things that truly are, knowledge of them in their truth. Yet— most remarkably—Socrates foregoes saying that the wind is in truth both cold and not cold, invoking the Graces instead of declaring openly such mixing of opposites, invoking the Graces and then charging Protagoras with having put forth enigmas while reserving the truth for his pupils.

Theaetetus' response is most telling: "How, then, are you saying this, Socrates?" (152d). The response may of course be taken as a request that Socrates explain what his reference to Protagoras' esoteric teaching only suggests. Yet, it may also be taken to refer back to the consequence that Socrates left unsaid; for what Socrates goes on to say in the uncommon discourse that immediately follows is precisely how one says the mixing (κρᾶσις) of opposites. Again it is a matter of birth, of a birth attested to by a great line of philosophers and poets (including Protagoras, Heraclitus, Empedocles, Epicharmus, Homer, and excluding only one philosopher, Parmenides): the birth of all things from flow and motion. Thus it is that nothing is one itself by itself (ἐν . . . αὐτὸ καθ᾽ αὑτό). Socrates continues: "But if you address it as large, it will also appear small, and if heavy, light . . . " (152d). It is not as though the opposites simply appear mixed with one another such that something is then said, for example, to be both large and small. Such is precisely the kind of saying that Socrates has left unsaid. Rather, the mixing of opposites comes to light precisely in and through discourse: if you *address* it as large, it will also appear small. Even its appearing small cannot, given the flow of all things, be independent of discourse and of the determinacy (the being one itself by itself) that discourse puts into effect. It is in discourse that the determinate opposition is constituted, and thus it is only in relation to discourse that the mixing of opposites can become manifest as such.

Extending the discussion, Socrates remarks finally to Theaetetus: "We're being compelled somehow to say recklessly some wondrous and laughable things [θαυμαστά τε καὶ γελοῖα], as Protagoras would say and everyone who tries to say the same as he does" (154b). What is wondrous and laughable is (to say) that one cannot say the same, that there is no same to be said, or rather, that sameness (being one itself by itself) belongs only to saying. And yet, for that reason the mixing-up of opposites in discourse is even more wondrous. As in the paradigm that Socrates offers in response to Theaetetus' query: the six dice that are more than four and less than twelve—that, therefore, not only are both more and less but also can become more without being increased. Theaetutus' response is now itself mixed, both affirming and denying the mixing that Socrates has posed. When Socrates goes on to elaborate the conflict, Theaetetus finally responds by confessing his wonder: "Yes indeed, by the gods, Socrates, I wonder exceedingly [ὑπερφυῶς . . . θαυμάζω] as to what these things are, and sometimes in looking at them I get truly dizzy" (155c). Thus is Theaetetus wonderstruck by what must and yet cannot be said in reference to the mixing-up of opposites. Thus is his wonder provoked by the mixing-up of opposites.

Socrates remarks that Theodorus' guess about Theaetetus' nature—that it is philosophic—is not a bad one, since the pathos of wonder (τὸ πάθος, τὸ θαυμάζειν) is very much that of a philosopher: "for nothing else is the beginning [ἀρχή] of philosophy than this, and, seemingly, whoever said that Iris was the offspring of Thaumas made a not bad genealogy" (155d). One who said this was of course Hesiod: according to his genealogy Thaumas married Electra, and among their offspring was Iris (*Theogony* 265–66). If one takes the names for what they say, then one may say: The rainbow (Iris) is the offspring of wonder (Thaumas) and shining (Electra). Furthermore, both Thaumas and Electra are linked genealogically to Ocean and Tethys;[30] earlier in the conversation, in that uncommon discourse in which Socrates marshalled the great line of philosophers and poets, Homer's saying "Ocean and mother Tethys, the genesis of the gods" is interpreted as saying that everything is the offspring of flowing and motion (152e). Hence, in the beginning there is flowing and motion; and then, born therefrom, if not directly, there is wonder and shining (that is, appearing to sense). There is, as in Theaetetus, the wonder provoked by the appearance of a mixing-up of opposites. The offspring of Thaumas (wonder) is the rainbow and philosophy. Not only this, but also the determination of wonder as the beginning of philosophy is presented as confirmation of the genealogy by which the rainbow is the offspring of wonder.

What does philosophy have to do with the rainbow? Iris is a messenger of the gods to men, and it is this vocation that is evoked in the *Cratylus:* "Iris [Ἶρις] also seems to have received her name from εἴρειν [to speak], because she is a messenger" (*Cratylus* 408b). Both philosophy and the rainbow have to do with discourse; for instance, with the discursive distinction between the different colors that blend into one another in the shining rainbow that joins heaven and earth.

Homer speaks of "rainbows that the son of Chronos has set in the clouds, a portent for man" (*Iliad* 11.27–28). A portent (τέρας) is a sign, a marvel, something wonderful that serves as an omen; it may be even some wondrous creature, a monster (Latin: *monstrum*). As in Theaetetus (and perhaps in every philosophic nature), there is a bit of monstrosity: for it is Theaetetus' nature to wonder exceedingly (ὑπερφυῶς); it is his nature to exceed nature.

Yet, the rainbow is not merely a sign sent from heaven to earth but rather is such that in being sent it spans and thus discloses in its openness the very space across which it is sent, that between earth and sky, between the abode of mortals and that reserved for immortal gods. As philosophy, beginning in the discourse of wonder, opens the space between that which appears to sense and that which is said, that is, set forth in and through discourse.

The difference will be called that between the visible (ὁρατόν) and the intelligible (νοητόν) (see *Republic* 524c).[31] Thus philosophy opens. Thus it begins in the Platonic beginning. Provoked by the mixing-up of opposites, philosophy begins from wonder.

⤚◉═⤙

Not only in the beginning but also now, in the end, in the future perfect, wonder will have remained the beginning.

Thus one returns to wonder in the end, returns again finally to the beginning, putting the end to wonder, or rather, letting the end be provocative, letting it provoke wonder, or rather—one suspects—reawaken wonder from its metaphysical slumber.

For the end is that which has been called the end of metaphysics. No doubt a great deal of caution is required if this phrase is to be used in a rigorous discourse. One must distinguish the relevant sense of end from others that have been posed for—and by—metaphysics: most notably, that by which the end would consist in a gathering of metaphysics into its fulfillment; and, all too symmetrically opposed to this, the sense that would make of the end of metaphysics its mere termination. In every case one must be attentive also to the slippage to which the sense of end is exposed in the end of metaphysics, since it is within metaphysics that the sense(s) of end (to say nothing of the sense(s) of sense) will have been determined. One must also hold in a certain suspension the assumption of homogeneity that would otherwise be put in play by discourse on the end of metaphysics—that is, one will need to leave the name suspended between singular and plural. Nonetheless, whatever the extent of the pluralizing heterogeneity, the Platonic beginning remains decisive. Metaphysics—whether singular, plural, or both—will always have begun with the opening between intelligible and sensible. Even if this beginning remains largely unrecalled, metaphysics circulates within the space thus opened; and insofar as it assumes that space, taking the opening for granted, it is authorized to put an end to wonder. For wonder, provoked by the mixing-up of opposites, is what first draws one into the opening. It is as such that wonder is the beginning of philosophy.

But what is wonder? The question comes too late. For when one comes to ask the philosophical question "What is . . . ?" ("τί ἐστι . . . ?"), one moves already within the opening and wonder has already come into play in prompting that opening. The operation of wonder belongs to the very condition of the question "What is wonder?"; and one will never be able simply to disengage that question from the wonder about which it would ask. One will never be able to interrogate wonder philosophically except by way of a questioning that the operation of wonder will already have determined. To say nothing of all the means that philosophy would bring into play in response to the question, in declaring wonder to be, for instance, a passion of the soul, in assimilating it, for instance, to intuition.

The end of metaphysics inhibits the question even more. For this end brings, in Nietzsche's formula, the final inversion of Platonism, the inversion which constitutes the final possibility of metaphysics, the possibility which announces the exhaustion of all possibilities of circulating within the space of the Platonic opening. Once—in Nietzsche's phrase—the true world finally becomes a fable, once what was called the intelligible drifts away further and further and finally without limit, rendering the space of metaphysics unlimited, or rather, reducing it again to the plane of sense, then the very resources that would enable the question are themselves put into question, set adrift. And yet, one is then drawn back to the place of wonder, to the place where, in a discourse addressed to the mixing-up within what came to be called the sensible, wonder was in the beginning provoked.

Let it, then, be said: the end of metaphysics brings a return to wonder, prompts a return of wonder.

Yet, the provocation of wonder at the end, of a wonder that would be the beginning of a thinking at the limit of metaphysics, would not be quite the same as in the beginning. One would of course be drawn back toward the discursively articulated mixing-up of sensible opposites. And yet, precisely because the discourse in relation to which the mixing-up would appear to sense is nothing other than the discourse fashioned and empowered by the history of metaphysics, that discourse cannot but effect the double separation, that between opposites and that between the mixed-up sensible opposites and the distinct intelligible opposites. It is a discourse that *means* something, a discourse that in its very operation is taken to mean something, to exceed what appears to sense, to open the difference between meaning and sense, between two different senses of sense. Even if in the end of metaphysics meaning is set utterly adrift, language does not cease to mark the difference that two millennia of shaping and theorizing have taught it to mark. Inasmuch as one continues to speak the language of metaphysics—is there any other?—one continues to exceed the plane of sense, opening the difference that is bespoken by the ambiguity in the word *sense,* the gigantic difference within *sense.*

What now cannot but provoke wonder is the γιγαντομαχία into which one is thus drawn. For the end of metaphysics brings a double effacement of that which would be opposed to the sensible (that is, to what has been called the sensible). On the one hand, the intelligible is effaced as original, as independent of its sensible imagings and as governing such imagings. Now there will be no preventing its becoming in turn an image, if not in a simple reversal then at least in a perhaps unlimited chain of pairs, related as image/original without any final anchoring in an original as such that would be itself immune to the play of imaging. On the other hand, the intelligible is effaced as meaning, or, more precisely, as preestablished meaning such as would antedate discourse, as a transcendental signified that would precede and govern from without the play of signifiers.

However much meaningful discourse drives one beyond sense, the intelligible can no longer be released from the play of discourse and sense and posited over against that play, aloof from it. The dyads cannot be submitted to final determination by reference to a term that would no longer be itself determined by dyadic linkage. Thus would wonder be provoked at the end of metaphysics: wonder at the play of the indeterminately dyadic, wonder at the gigantic opening within the word *sense.*

One could also call it poetic wonder, provided *poetic* is either diverted toward what Jacques Derrida calls *invention* or referred back to the ποίησις that Heidegger sought to preserve in advance of its determination as production *(Herstellung).* It is a matter of wonder at the power of the sense image to bring forth its original and of discourse to bring forth meaning, to bring forth in the double (one would have said, at least, almost contradictory) sense of both first giving place to (letting take place) *and yet* uncovering as already there (not simply produced). It is a matter of wonder at a bringing-forth that is both inaugural and memorial—like remembrance. One could call it a wonder of imagination.

--→≡◦⊂≡←--

Can wonder be provoked still more archaically? Can it be provoked by what one might call still—even in the end of metaphysics—the ἀρχή: neither an intelligible nor *the* intelligible nor even the beginning of the intelligible, but rather the opening, the openness, within which sense could be exceeded and dyads brought into play? Such wonder would be in place before one could come to address something *as* something, for instance, to address as large what then would appear small, such that a mixing of opposites would become manifest, provoking the wonder at the beginning of philosophy. Archaic wonder would also be in place before discourse could exceed sense and broach the opening, setting in play the dyads that, even in the end of metaphysics, still would provoke wonder. Such archaic wonder would be, not just the beginning of philosophy (in its beginning or in its end and transmutation), but rather a beginning that would precede philosophy, a turning toward the beginning in which the very space of philosophy would open. The place of such wonder would be the very unfolding of place as such, the spacing of the ἀρχή, archaic spacing.

Heidegger attests to a wonder that, like such archaic wonder, would not simply stand at the beginning of philosophy. Referring to a wonder that, instead, would sustain and in a sense govern philosophy throughout, he writes: "To say that philosophy arises from wonder means [*heisst*]: it *is* essentially something wondrous and becomes more wondrous the more it becomes what it is."[32]

In *What Is Philosophy?* Heidegger refers to the πάθος of wonder *(Erstaunen)* and translates πάθος as *Stimmung* or *dis-position*, proposing thereby to avoid understanding it in the modern psychological sense. Wonder (θαυμάζειν) he then characterizes as a stepping back in the face of beings ("Wir treten gleichsam zurück vor dem Seienden"), a stepping back that becomes attentive to beings, that they *are* and that they are *so* and not otherwise. Thus to step back is at once to be also transported to and bound by that before which one has stepped back. Wonder is, hence, the "dis-position in which and for which the Being of beings opens up."[33]

In the lecture course of 1937–38, *Basic Questions of Philosophy*, Heidegger discusses wonder at much greater length. Again he regards wonder as *Stimmung*, taking the latter as a displacement *(Versetzung)* by which one is brought into a fundamental relation to beings as such. Wonder (θαυμάζειν —now Heidegger writes it: *das Er-staunen*) is the fundamental attunement *(Grundstimmung)* that—at least for the Greeks—was the origin of philosophy. Heidegger carefully distinguishes wonder from a variety of related forms of attunement: surprise *(Sichwundern, Verwundern)*, in which one is struck by something out of the ordinary; admiration *(Bewundern)*, in which one frees oneself, sets oneself over against, the extraordinary thing or event by which one is struck; astonishment *(Staunen, Bestaunen)*, in which one is thrown back by the extraordinary. Wonder, Heidegger insists, is essentially different from these forms; for in all three of them there is a determinate individual thing, something extraordinary, that is set off, contrasted, with the things of ordinary experience. In wonder, on the other hand, "the most ordinary becomes itself the most extraordinary" (GA 45:166). Everything becomes extraordinary (GA 45:174), and one is displaced into the utter unfamiliarity of the familiar, into an inverted world.³⁴ Yet, what is most ordinary is simply that which is, beings; and what is extraordinary about them is that they *are*. Wonder, says Heidegger, brings the most ordinary forth in such a way that it announces its extraordinariness, shines forth as extraordinary. Wonder attends to the outbreak of the extraordinariness of the ordinary. Wonder, says Heidegger, opens to what is "uniquely wondrous, namely: the whole as the whole, the whole as being [*als das Seiende*], beings as a whole [*das Seiende im Ganzen*], *that* they *are what* they *are;* beings *as* beings, *ens qua ens,* τὸ ὂν ἦ ὄν." He adds: "What is named here by the *as,* the *qua,* the ἦ, is the 'between' thrown open in wonder, the open space . . . in which beings as such come into play, namely, as the beings *they* are, into the *play of their Being* [Spiel seines Seins]" (GA 45:168–69).

In a sense, then, Heidegger ventures to say what wonder is: not, however, by submitting it to the philosophical question of *what* it *is,* but rather by situating it, delimiting its place, with respect to the very shining forth of the *is,* by bringing out its attunement to the very opening of the *as* of beings *as* beings. Thus, in spite of all that he says of wonder, Heidegger can also insist that such wondrous displacement withdraws as such from explanation, from analysis of the sort that would resolve it into various components. If one can in a sense say what wonder is, one can do so only through a *Wiederholung,* only by "a reproject [*Rückentwurf*] of the simplicity [*Einfachheit*] and strangeness *of that displacement* of man into beings as such, which takes place [*sich ereignet*] as wonder, which remains just as incomprehensible as the beginning [*Anfang*] to which it is bound" (GA 45:171).

One could think archaic wonder only in the return to it, only in a certain doubling back to its place as that of the opening of beings as such. It is a matter, then, of how the opening is to be thought, or, more precisely, a matter of that *from which* the opening is to be thought, a matter of that from which the spacing of the ἀρχή would take place. No doubt it is to be thought, as Heidegger insists, from beings *as* beings. Then one may, extending the project of fundamental ontology, undertake to think the space in which beings come into the play of their Being—that is, to think what would be called *Temporalität, Lichtung, Ereignis,* to think (the) beyond (of) Being (ἐπέκεινα τῆς οὐσίας), as did also Plato. Or one may insist on pairing such a project with another, with one that would be attentive to the eruption of questioning from out of beings as a whole; a project that in adhering to beings *as* beings would in the end be no project at all but rather a return to thrownness, a *Wiederholung* of the thrownness of the project (as in metontology, to recall the most striking title that Heidegger gave it).

And yet, beings as beings always also—from the beginning, before every beginning—*appear to sense;* the opening is always also an opening within what one can call (twisting it free of the metaphysical opposition) *the sensible.* Is archaic spacing not, then, to be thought from the sensible? Is it not in the opening from and within the sensible that archaic wonder has its place? *From and within* the sensible—a spacing that would trace within the sensible the opening from the sensible, the opening in which the sensible would be exceeded, either in the metaphysical opposition of intelligible to sensible or in the play of indeterminate dyads that commences in the end of metaphysics. From and within the sensible—just as the word *sense*, which comes to be divided from itself (divided into two different senses of sense—an abysmal division, presupposing itself), is nonetheless divided within itself, enclosing the gigantic space in which both imaging and discourse have their place.

One would return, then, to a wonder placed at an opening from and within the sensible, an opening that in a sense—in *sense* itself, if there could be sense *itself*—would precede even the play of beings in their Being, a foreplay, a prelude, as with Wordsworth:

As if awakened, summoned, roused, constrained,
I looked for universal things; perused
The common countenance of earth and sky.
(*The Prelude*, 3:105–107)

One would return, then, to a wonder whose place would be to hover, like a dove, between heaven and earth, open to the wondrous shining of the rainbow that joins earth and sky even while setting them apart. Then one might abandon oneself to the wondrous sights and sounds of earth and sky and, in Emerson's sense, draw a new circle, a circle that would open upon everything that could be said or that could appear to sense:

> The one thing which we seek with insatiable desire, is to forget ourselves, to be surprised out of our propriety, to lose our sempiternal memory, and to do something without knowing how or why; in short, to draw a new circle. Nothing great was ever achieved without enthusiasm. The way of life is wonderful: it is by abandonment.[35]

Notes

1. *Kritik der reinen Vernunft*, ed. Raymund Schmidt (Hamburg: Felix Meiner, 1956), A 5/B 8–9.

2. *A Midsummer Night's Dream* V, i, 12–17.

3. *Meditations on First Philosophy*, trans. Laurence J. Lafleur (Indianapolis: Bobbs-Merrill, 1960), p. 27.

4. Samuel Johnson, *The Rambler* 125 (Tuesday, 28 May 1751) (*The Yale Edition of the Works of Samuel Johnson*, vol. 4, ed. W. J. Bate and Albrecht B. Strauss [New Haven: Yale University Press, 1969], p. 300).

5. John Dryden, Epistle Dedicatory to "The Rival Ladies," in *The Works of John Dryden*, general editor H. T. Swedenberg (Berkeley: University of California Press, 1962), vol. 8, p. 101. Dryden's remark is directed specifically at "Imagination in a Poet" and is put forth in defense of rhyme, which "Bounds and Circumscribes the Fancy."

6. *A Midsummer Night's Dream* V, i, 18–22.

7. *Phaedo* 99e.

8. Cf. *Being and Logos: Reading the Platonic Dialogues*, 3rd ed. (Bloomington: Indiana University Press, 1996), chapter 5.

9. *Imaginatio* translates φαντασία, and *phantasia* renders φάντασμα. Cf. Murray Wright Bundy, *The Theory of Imagination in Classical and Medieval Thought* ([Urbana]: University of Illinois, 1927), pp. 193, 278.

10. Gianfrancesco Pico della Mirandola, *On the Imagination*, Latin text with English translation by Harry Caplan, *Cornell Studies in English*, vol. 16 (New Haven: Yale University Press, 1930), p. 25.

11. Ibid., p. 33.

12. Ibid., p. 29.

13. Ibid., p. 47.

14. Ibid., p. 29.

15. Pico refers this statement to Synesius (*De Insomniis*); ibid., p. 37.

16. Cf. *The Gathering of Reason* (Athens: Ohio University Press, 1980), especially chapter 7, section 2.

17. *Kritik der reinen Vernunft*, B 151.

18. F. W. J. Schelling, *System des transzendentalen Idealismus* (Hamburg: Felix Meiner, 1957), p. 227.

19. "Lecture on the Slave-Trade (June 1795)," in *Imagination in Coleridge*, ed. John Spencer Hill (Totowa, N.J.: Rowman and Littlefield, 1978), p. 27.

20. *The Prelude*, 14:192.

21. See especially the section entitled "Of the Typic of Pure Practical Judgment," in *Kritik der praktischen Vernunft*, vol. 5 of *Kants Werke: Akademie Textausgabe* (Berlin: Walter de Gruyter, 1968), pp. 67–71.

22. Ibid., p. 42.

23. Pico, *On the Imagination*, p. 81.

24. *Republic* 510b.

25. Ibid., 533a.

26. To this sentence, written during the period of *Die fröhliche Wissenschaft*, Nietzsche adds the following parenthetical comment: "(unfortunately made obscure [*verdunkelt*] by German philosophy—frosted glass)" (*Gesammelte Werke. Musarionausgabe* (Munich: Musarion Verlag, 1920–29), vol. 11, p. 284.

27. "Circles," in *The Collected Works of Ralph Waldo Emerson* (Cambridge: Harvard University Press, 1979), vol. 2, p. 179.

28. In *Metaphysics* V 1, Aristotle enumerates the various senses of ἀρχή and concludes: "It is common to all beginnings [κοινὸν τῶν ἀρχῶν] to be the first [thing] from which something either is or comes to be or becomes known" (1013a18–19).

29. *Enzyklopädie der philosophischen Wissenschaften. Dritter Teil: Die Philosophie des Geistes. Werke* (Frankfurt a.M.: Suhrkamp, 1970), vol. 10, p. 255. The passage cited occurs in the Zusatz to §449.

30. See *The Being of the Beautiful: Plato's Theaetetus, Sophist, and Statesman*, translated and with commentary by Seth Benardete (Chicago: University of Chicago Press, 1984), vol. 1, p. 107.

31. I have discussed this passage in detail and in context in *Being and Logos: Reading the Platonic Dialogues*, pp. 428–31.

32. *Grundfragen der Philosophie: Ausgewählte "Probleme" der "Logik,"* volume 45 of the Gesamtausgabe (GA) (Frankfurt a.M.: Vittorio Klostermann, 1984), p. 163.

33. *Was Ist Das—Die Philosophie?* (Pfullingen: Günther Neske, 1956), p. 26.

34. This formulation comes from Eugen Fink: "What breaks out in wonder . . . is an unfamiliarity of the familiar. . . . In wonder the world is inverted [*verkehrt sich die Welt*]" (*Einleitung in die Philosophie*, ed. Franz-A. Schwartz [Würzburg: Königshausen & Neumann, 1985], p. 19). Klaus Held has also taken up these discussions and

described differently the transformation that the world undergoes in wonder: for the wonderer the world comes forth as though emerging for him for the first time, as though it were completely new and utterly surprising. In its reflective moment, Held adds, wonder lets one experience oneself as though one were a newborn child. (See "Fundamental Moods and Heidegger's Critique of Contemporary Culture," in *Reading Heidegger: Commemorations*, ed. John Sallis [Bloomington: Indiana University Press, 1993], esp. pp. 298–300).

35. "Circles," in *Collected Works of Ralph Waldo Emerson*, vol. 2, p. 190.

John Sallis: Selected Bibliography

Books

Force of Imagination: The Sense of the Elemental. Bloomington: Indiana University Press, forthcoming.

Chorology: On Beginning in Plato's "Timaeus." Bloomington: Indiana University Press, 1999.

Shades—Of Painting at the Limit. Bloomington: Indiana University Press, 1998.

Double Truth. Albany: State University of New York Press, 1995.

Stone. Bloomington: Indiana University Press, 1994.

Crossings: Nietzsche and the Space of Tragedy. Chicago: University of Chicago Press, 1991.

Echoes: After Heidegger. Bloomington: Indiana University Press, 1990.

Spacings—Of Reason and Imagination. In Texts of Kant, Fichte, Hegel. Chicago: University of Chicago Press, 1987.

Delimitations: Phenomenology and the End of Metaphysics. Bloomington: Indiana University Press, 1986. 2nd, expanded edition, Bloomington: Indiana University Press, 1995.

The Gathering of Reason. Athens: Ohio University Press, 1980.

Being and Logos: The Way of Platonic Dialogue. Pittsburgh: Duquesne University Press, 1975. 3rd edition, Bloomington: Indiana University Press, 1996.

Phenomenology and the Return to Beginnings. Pittsburgh: Duquesne University Press, 1973.

Chapters in Edited Volumes and Journal Articles

"Interrupting Truth." In *Heidegger Toward the Turn: Essays on the Work of the 1930s*, ed. James Risser. Albany: State University of New York Press, 1999.

"Doubles of Anaximenes." In *The Presocrates after Heidegger*, ed. David Jacobs. Albany: State University of New York Press, 1999.

"Nietzsche's Platonism." In *Between the Last Man and the Overman: The Question of Nietzsche's Politics.* Vol. 4 of *Nietzsche: Critical Assessments*, ed. Daniel W. Conway. London: Routledge 1998.

"Voices of Stone." In *Cathexis*. Catalogue for the exhibition of works by Paul Kipps at Oakville Gallery. Toronto, April 1998.

"Beyond the Political: Reclaiming the Community of the Earth." In *Phenomenology of Interculturality and Life-World*, ed. Ernst Wolfgang Orth and Chan-Fai Cheung. Freiburg/Munich: Verlag Karl Alber, 1998.

"Daydream." *Revue Internationale de Philosophie* (1998).

"A Time of Imagination." In *Interkulturelle Philosophie und Phänomenologie in Japan:*

Beiträge zum Gespräch über Grenzen hinweg, ed. Tadashi Ogawa, Michael Lazarin, and Guido Rappe. Munich: Judicum Verlag, 1998.

"Uranic Time." In *Time and Nothingness,* ed. Michael Lazarin. Kyoto: Institute of Buddhist Cultural Studies, Ryukoku University, 1997.

"Platonism at the Limit of Metaphysics." *Graduate Faculty Philosophy Journal* 20 (1997).

"Double Truths: An Interview with John Sallis." *Man and World* 30 (1997).

"The Politics of the Χώρα." In *Ancients and Moderns,* ed. Reginald Lilly. Bloomington: Indiana University Press, 1996.

"Mixed Arts." In *Proceedings of the Eighth International Kant Congress,* ed. Hoke Robinson. Milwaukee: Marquette University Press, 1995.

". . . a wonder that one could never aspire to surpass." In *The Path of Archaic Thinking: Unfolding the Work of John Sallis,* ed. Kenneth Maly. Albany: State University of New York Press, 1995.

"Mimesis and the End of Art." In *Intersections: Nineteenth-Century Philosophy and Contemporary Theory,* ed. David Clark and Tilottama Rajan. Albany: State University of New York Press, 1994.

"Flight of Spirit." *Diacritics* 19.3–4 (1989).

"Heidegger's Poetics: The Question of Mimesis." In *Kunst und Technik. Zum 100. Geburtstag Martin Heideggers,* ed. Walter Biemel and F.-W. von Hermann. Frankfurt a.M.: Vittorio Klostermann, 1989.

"Time Out . . . " In *The Collegium Phaenomenologicum: The First Ten Years.* The Hague: Martinus Nijhoff, 1988.

"Dionysus—In Excess of Metaphysics." In *Exceedingly Nietzsche: Aspects of Contemporary Nietzsche Interpretation,* ed. David Farrell Krell and David Wood. London: Routledge, 1988.

"Metaphysical Security and the Play of Imagination: An Archaic Reflection." In *Philosophy and Archaic Experience.* Pittsburgh: Duquesne University Press, 1982.

"Fichte and the Problem of System." *Man and World* 9 (1976).

"Toward the Showing of Language." *Southwestern Journal of Philosophy* (1973).

"Schelling's System of Freedom." *Research in Phenomenology* 2 (1972).

"Nietzsche's Underworld of Truth." *Philosophy Today* 16 (1972).

"Time, Subjectivity, and the Phenomenology of Perception." *Modern Schoolman* 48 (1972).

"Nietzsche's Homecoming." *Man and World* 2 (1969).

2

Private Irony and Liberal Hope

RICHARD RORTY

Richard Rorty is perhaps the most versatile and philosophically cosmopolitan philosopher in America. Before turning his energies toward continental philosophy, and the attempt to establish a dialogue between American, Anglo-American, and continental philosophies, he was already a major intellectual force in analytic philosophy circles and a well-known adherent of the American philosopher John Dewey.

Throughout his writings he has sought to identify connections between the work of the classical pragmatists, recent analytic philosophers, and continental philosophers such as Heidegger and Derrida. His work *Philosophy and the Mirror of Nature* establishes a link between Dewey, Heidegger, and Derrida and thus opens up a dialogue across philosophical traditions that had appeared almost impossible because of seemingly unrelated methodologies and styles of language. Richard Rorty brought to all of American philosophy a sense of mutual respect and civility, as well as a sense of renewed interest in the range of projects on the philosophical scene in the United States.

While the breadth of Rorty's interest in continental philosophy is impressive, he has been especially interested in the work of Martin Heidegger. From Heidegger he learned the importance of history to philosophy, an importance often underappreciated by logical positivism. Rorty multiplies the senses in which the current age can be defined in terms of being "post," adding to the often-used notion of "postmodern" such other phrases as "postanalytic" and even "postphilosophical." His work has persistently stood opposed to narrowly defined epistemological argumentation in favor of a quasi-Habermasian concept of philosophy as cultural criticism, a project for philosophy which he outlines in *Consequences of Pragmatism* and in *Contingency, Irony, and Solidarity*. In the latter book, Rorty appeals to the Socratic and Kierkegaardian lineage of philosophy as irony in an attempt to reclaim for philosophy its transgressive intellectual and social value. Rorty's commitment to pragmatism is perhaps the ideal basis for one whose philosophical work is dedicated to opening up avenues for philosophical communication. Just as Rorty has situated his thinking at the crossroads that divide various approaches to philosophy, so too he has attempted to open philosophy to influence and to be influenced by other disciplines. In *Consequences of Pragmatism,* he analyzes the influence of Derrida and de Man on the field of literary theory in America and coins the term "textualism" in contradistinction to "deconstruction." Rorty shares with much of contemporary continental philosophy an approach to the text that attends to its dramatic and literary character. He argues that much of philosophy is and can be accomplished in the form of narrative. In his latest work, Rorty returns to political questions and develops a notion of "liberal utopia" that rethinks the connections between democracy and equality. The primary focus of Rorty's work has been to develop this insight: if it does not make a difference to practice, it should not make a difference to philosophy.

This essay "Private Irony and Liberal Hope" explains the postmodern, postmetaphysical philosophical position in terms of a notion of irony that goes back to Socrates but has both a nominalist and historicist philosophical spirit. Rorty sees Hegel as the first modern ironist who breaks with the metaphysical tradition from Plato to Kant, and the one who begins the tradition of ironist philosophy that is continued by Nietzsche, Heidegger, and Derrida. He draws a comparison of Hegelian dialectic to literary criticism and calls for recognition of the significant contribution ironists make to the redefinition of liberal society.

⇀⇒◑◉⇐↼

All human beings carry about a set of words which they employ to justify their actions, their beliefs, and their lives. These are the words in which we formulate praise of our friends and contempt for our enemies, our long-term projects, our deepest self-doubts, and our highest hopes. They are the words in which we tell, sometimes prospectively and sometimes retrospectively, the story of our lives. I shall call these words a person's "final vocabulary."

It is "final" in the sense that if doubt is cast on the worth of these words, their user has no noncircular argumentative recourse. Those words are as far as he can go with language; beyond them there is only helpless passivity or a resort to force. A small part of a final vocabulary is made up of thin, flexible, and ubiquitous terms such as "true," "good," "right," and "beautiful." The larger part contains thicker, more rigid, and more parochial terms, for example, "Christ," "England," "professional standards," "decency," "kindness," "the Revolution," "the Church," "progressive," "rigorous," "creative." The more parochial terms do most of the work.

I shall define an "ironist" as someone who fulfills three conditions: (1) She has radical and continuing doubts about the final vocabulary she currently uses, because she has been impressed by other vocabularies, vocabularies taken as final by people or books she has encountered; (2) she realizes that argument phrased in her present vocabulary can neither underwrite nor dissolve these doubts; (3) insofar as she philosophizes about her situation, she does not think that her vocabulary is closer to reality than others, that it is in touch with a power not herself. Ironists who are inclined to philosophize see the choice between vocabularies as made neither within a neutral and universal metavocabulary nor by an attempt to fight one's way past appearances to the real, but simply by playing the new off against the old.

I call people of this sort "ironists" because their realization that anything can be made to look good or bad by being redescribed, and their renunciation of the attempt to formulate criteria of choice between final vocabularies, puts them in the position which Sartre called "meta-stable": never quite able to take themselves seriously because always aware that the terms in which they describe themselves are subject to change, always aware of the contingency and fragility of their final vocabularies, and thus of their selves.

The opposite of irony is common sense. For that is the watchword of those who unselfconsciously describe everything important in terms of the final vocabulary to which they and those around them are habituated. To be commonsensical is to take for granted that statements formulated in that final vocabulary suffice to describe and judge the beliefs, actions, and lives of those who employ alternative final vocabularies.

When common sense is challenged, its adherents respond at first by generalizing and making explicit the rules of the language game they are accustomed to play (as some of the Greek Sophists did, and as Aristotle did in his ethical writings). But if no platitude formulated in the old vocabulary suffices to meet an argumentative challenge, the need to reply produces a willingness to go beyond platitudes. At that point, conversation may go Socratic. The question "What is x?" is now asked in such a way that it cannot be answered simply by producing paradigm cases of x-hood. So one may demand a definition, an essence.

To make such Socratic demands is not yet, of course, to become an ironist in the sense in which I am using this term. It is only to become a "metaphysician," in a sense of that term which I am adapting from Heidegger. In this sense, the metaphysician is someone who takes the question "What is the intrinsic nature of (e.g., justice, science, knowledge, Being, faith, morality, philosophy)?" at face value. He assumes that the presence of a term in his own final vocabulary ensures that it refers to something which *has* a real essence. The metaphysician is still attached to common sense in that he does not question the platitudes which encapsulate the use of a given final vocabulary, and in particular the platitude which says there is a single permanent reality to be found behind the many temporary appearances. He does not redescribe but, rather, analyzes old descriptions with the help of other old descriptions.

The ironist, by contrast, is a nominalist and a historicist. She thinks nothing has an intrinsic nature, a real essence. So she thinks that the occurrence of a term like "just" or "scientific" or "rational" in the final vocabulary of the day is no reason to think that Socratic inquiry into the essence of justice or science or rationality will take one much beyond the language games of one's time. The ironist spends her time worrying about the possibility that she has been initiated into the wrong tribe, taught to play the wrong language game. She worries that the process of socialization which turned her into a human being by giving her a language may have given her the wrong language, and so turned her into the wrong kind of human being. But she cannot give a criterion of wrongness. So, the more she is driven to articulate her situation in philosophical terms, the more she reminds herself of her rootlessness by constantly using terms like "Weltanschauung," "perspective," "dialectic," "conceptual framework," "historical epoch," "language game," "redescription," "vocabulary," and "irony."

The metaphysician responds to that sort of talk by calling it "relativistic" and insisting that what matters is not what language is being used but what is *true*. Metaphysicians think that human beings by nature desire to know. They think this because the vocabulary they have inherited, their common sense, provides them with a picture of knowledge as a relation between human beings and "reality," and the idea that we have a need and a duty to enter into this relation. It also tells us that "reality," if properly asked, will help us determine what our final vocabulary should be. So metaphysicians believe that there are, out there in the world, real essences which it is our duty to discover and which are disposed to assist in their own discovery. They do not believe that anything can be made to look good or bad by being redescribed—or, if they do, they deplore this fact and cling to the idea that reality will help us resist such seductions.

By contrast, ironists do not see the search for a final vocabulary as (even in part) a way of getting something distinct from this vocabulary right. They do not take the point of discursive thought to be *knowing*, in any sense that can be explicated by notions like "reality," "real essence," "objective point of view," and "the correspondence of language of reality." They do not think its point is to find a vocabulary which accurately represents something, a transparent medium. For the ironists, "final vocabulary" does not mean "the one which puts all doubts to rest" or "the one which satisfies our criteria of ultimacy, or adequacy, or optimality." They do not think of reflection as being governed by criteria. Criteria, on their view, are never more than the platitudes which contextually define the terms of a final vocabulary currently in use. Ironists agree with Davidson about our inability to step outside our language in order to compare it with something else, and with Heidegger about the contingency and historicity of that language.

This difference leads to a difference in their attitude toward books. Metaphysicians see libraries as divided according to disciplines, corresponding to different objects of knowledge. Ironists see them as divided according to traditions, each member of which partially adopts and partially modifies the vocabulary of the writers whom he has read. Ironists take the writings of all the people with poetic gifts, all the original minds who had a talent for redescription—Pythagoras, Plato, Milton, Newton, Goethe, Kant, Kierkegaard, Baudelaire, Darwin, Freud—as grist to be put through the same dialectical mill. The metaphysicians, by contrast, want to start by getting straight about which of these people were poets, which philosophers, and which scientists. They think it essential to get the genres right—to order texts by reference to a previously determined grid, a grid which, whatever else it does, will at least make a clear distinction between knowledge claims and other claims upon our attention. The ironist, by contrast, would like to avoid cooking the books she reads by using any such grid (although, with ironic resignation, she realizes that she can hardly help doing so).

For a metaphysician, "philosophy," as defined by reference to the canonical Plato-Kant sequence, is an attempt to know about certain things—quite general and important things. For the ironist, "philosophy," so defined, is the attempt to apply and develop a particular antecedently chosen final vocabulary—one which revolves around the appearance-reality distinction. The issue between them is, once again, about the contingency of our language—about whether what the common sense of our own culture shares with Plato and Kant is a tip-off to the way the world is, or whether it is just the characteristic mark of the discourse of people inhabiting a certain chunk of space-time. The metaphysician assumes that our tradition can raise no problems which it cannot solve—that the vocabulary which the ironist fears may be merely "Greek" or "Western" or "bourgeois" is an instrument which will enable us to get at something universal. The metaphysician agrees with the Platonic Theory of Recollection, in the form in which this theory was restated by Kierkegaard, namely, that we have the truth within us, that we have built-in criteria which enable us to recognize the right final vocabulary when we hear it. The cash value of this theory is that our contemporary final vocabularies are close enough to the right one to let us converge upon it—to formulate premises from which the right conclusions will be reached. The metaphysician thinks that although we may not have all the answers, we have already got criteria for the right answers. So he thinks "right" does not merely mean "suitable for those who speak as we do" but has a stronger sense—the sense of "grasping real essence."

For the ironist, searches for a final vocabulary are not destined to converge. For her, sentences like "All men by nature desire to know" or "Truth is independent of the human mind" are simply platitudes used to inculcate the local final vocabulary, the common sense of the West. She is an ironist just insofar as her own final vocabulary does not contain such notions. Her description of what she is doing when she looks for a better final vocabulary than the one she is currently using is dominated by metaphors of making rather than finding, of diversification and novelty rather than convergence to the antecedently present. She thinks of final vocabularies as poetic achievements rather than as fruits of diligent inquiry according to antecedently formulated criteria.

Because metaphysicians believe that we already possess a lot of the "right" final vocabulary and merely need to think through its implications, they think of philosophical inquiry as a matter of spotting the relations between the various platitudes which provide contextual definitions of the terms of this vocabulary. So they think of refining or clarifying the use of terms as a matter of weaving these platitudes (or, as they would prefer to say, these intuitions) into a perspicuous system. This has two consequences. First, they tend to concentrate on the thinner, more flexible, more ubiquitous items in this vocabulary—words like "true," "good," "person," and "object." For the thinner the term, the more platitudes will employ it. Second, they take the paradigm of philosophical inquiry to be logical argument—that is, spotting the inferential relationships between propositions rather than comparing and contrasting vocabularies.

The typical strategy of the metaphysician is to spot an apparent contradiction between two platitudes, two intuitively plausible propositions, and then propose a distinction which will resolve the contradiction. Metaphysicians then go on to embed this distinction within a network of associated distinctions—a philosophical theory—which will take some of the strain off the initial distinction. This sort of theory construction is the same method used by judges to decide hard cases, and by theologians to interpret hard texts. That activity is the metaphysician's paradigm of rationality. He sees philosophical theories as converging—a series of discoveries about the nature of such things as truth and personhood, which get closer and closer to the way they really are and carry the culture as a whole closer to an accurate representation of reality.

The ironist, however, views the sequence of such theories—such interlocked patterns of novel distinctions—as gradual, tacit substitutions of a new vocabulary for an old one. She calls "platitudes" what the metaphysician calls "intuitions." She is inclined to say that when we surrender an old platitude (e.g., "The number of biological species is fixed" or "Human beings differ from animals because they have sparks of the divine with them" or "Blacks have no rights which whites are bound to respect"), we have made a change rather than discovered a fact. The ironist, observing the sequence of "great philosophers" and the interaction between their thought and its social setting, sees a series of changes in the linguistic and other practices of the Europeans. Whereas the metaphysician sees the modern Europeans as particularly good at discovering how things really are, the ironist sees them as particularly rapid in changing their self-image, in re-creating themselves.

The metaphysician thinks that there is an overriding intellectual duty to present arguments for one's controversial views—arguments which will start from relatively uncontroversial premises. The ironist thinks that such arguments—logical arguments—are all very well in their way, and useful as expository devices, but in the end not much more than ways of getting people to change their practices without admitting they have done so. The ironist's preferred form of argument is dialectical in the sense that she takes the unit of persuasion to be a vocabulary rather than a proposition. Her method is redescription rather than inference. Ironists specialize in redescribing ranges of objects or events in partially neologistic jargon, in the hope of inciting people to adopt and extend that jargon. An ironist hopes that by the time she has finished using old words in new senses, not to mention introducing brand-new words, people will no longer ask questions phrased in the old words. So the ironist thinks of logic as ancillary to dialectic, whereas the metaphysician thinks of dialectic as a species of rhetoric, which in turn is a shoddy substitute for logic.

I have defined "dialectic" as the attempt to play off vocabularies against one another, rather than merely to infer propositions from one another, and thus as the partial substitution of redescription for inference. I used Hegel's word because I think of Hegel's phenomenology both as the beginning of the end of the Plato-Kant tradition and as a paradigm of the ironist's ability to exploit the possibilities of massive redescription. In this view, Hegel's so-called dialectical method is not an argumentative procedure or a way of unifying subject and object but simply a literary skill—skill at producing surprising gestalt switches by making smooth, rapid transitions from one terminology to another.

Instead of keeping the old platitudes and making distinctions to help them cohere, Hegel constantly changed the vocabulary in which the old platitudes had been stated; instead of constructing philosophical theories and arguing for them, he avoided argument by constantly shifting vocabularies, thereby changing the subject. In practice, though not in theory, he dropped the idea of getting at the truth in favor of the idea of making things new. His criticism of his predecessors was not that their propositions were false but that their languages were obsolete. By inventing this sort of criticism, the younger Hegel broke away from the Plato-Kant sequence and began a tradition of ironist philosophy which is continued in Nietzsche, Heidegger, and Derrida. These are the philosophers who define their achievement by their relation to their predecessors rather than by their relation to the truth.

A more up-to-date word for what I have been calling "dialectic" would be "literary criticism." In Hegel's time it was still possible to think of plays, poems, and novels as making vivid something already known, of literature as ancillary to cognition, beauty to truth. The older Hegel thought of "philosophy" as a discipline which, because cognitive in a way that art was not, took precedence over art. Indeed, he thought that this discipline, now that it had attained maturity in the form of his own Absolute Idealism, could and would make art as obsolete as it made religion. But, ironically and dialectically enough, what Hegel actually did, by founding an ironist tradition within philosophy, was help decognitivize, de-metaphysize philosophy. He helped turn it into a literary genre.[1] The young Hegel's practice undermined the possibility of the sort of convergence to truth about which the older Hegel theorized. The great commentators on the older Hegel are writers like Heine and Kierkegaard, people who treated Hegel the way we now treat Blake, Freud, D. H. Lawrence, or Orwell.

We ironists treat these people not as anonymous channels for truth but as abbreviations for a certain final vocabulary and for the sorts of beliefs and desires typical of its users. The older Hegel became a name for such a vocabulary, and Kierkegaard and Nietzsche have become names for others. If we are told that the actual lives such men lived had little to do with the books and the terminology which attracted our attention to them, we brush this aside. We treat the names of such people as the names of the heroes of their own books. We do not bother to distinguish Swift from *saeva indignario,* Hegel from Geist, Nietzsche from Zarathustra, Marcel Proust from Marcel the narrator, or Trilling from The Liberal Imagination. We do not care whether these writers managed to live up to their own self-images.[2] What we want to know is whether to adopt those images—to recreate ourselves, in whole or in part, in these people's image. We go about answering this question by experimenting with the vocabularies which these people concocted. We redescribe ourselves, our situation, our past, in those terms and compare the results with alternative redescriptions which use the vocabularies of alternative figures. We ironists hope, by this continual redescription, to make the best selves for ourselves that we can.

Such comparison, such playing off of figures against each other, is the principal activity now covered by the term "literary criticism." Influential critics, the sort of critics who propose new canons—people like Arnold, Pater, Leavis, Eliot, Edmund Wilson, Lionel Trilling, Frank Kermode, Harold Bloom—are not in the business of explaining the real meaning of books, nor of evaluating something called their "literary merit." Rather, they spend their time placing books in the context of other books, figures in the context of other figures. This placing is done in the same way as we place a new friend or enemy in the context of old friends and enemies. In the course of doing so, we revise our opinions of both the old and the new. Simultaneously, we revise our own moral identity by revising our own final vocabulary. Literary criticism does for ironists what the search for universal moral principles is supposed to do for metaphysicians.

For us ironists, nothing can serve as a criticism of a final vocabulary: save another such vocabulary; there is no answer to a redescription save a re-re-redescription. Since there is nothing beyond vocabularies which serves as a criterion of choice between them, criticism is a matter of looking on this picture and on that, not of comparing both pictures with the original. Nothing can serve as a criticism of a person save another person, or of a culture save an alternative culture—for persons and cultures are, for us, incarnated vocabularies. So our doubts about our own characters or our own culture can be resolved or assuaged only by enlarging our acquaintance. The easiest way of doing that is to read books, and so ironists spend more of their time placing books than in placing real live people. Ironists are afraid that they will get stuck in the vocabulary in which they were brought up if they only know the people in their own neighborhood, so they try to get acquainted with strange people (Alcibiades, Julien Sorel), strange families (the Karamazovs, the Casaubons), and strange communities (the Teutonic Knights, the Nuer, the mandarins of the Sung).

Ironists read literary critics, and take them as moral advisers, simply because such critics have an exceptionally large range of acquaintance. They are moral advisers not because they have special access to moral truth but because they have been around. They have read more books and are thus in a better position not to get trapped in the vocabulary of any single book. In particular, ironists hope that critics will help them perform the sort of dialectical feat which Hegel was so good at. That is, they hope critics will help them continue to admire books which are prima facie antithetical by performing some sort of synthesis. We would like to be able to admire both Blake and Arnold, both Nietzsche and Mill, both Marx and Baudelaire, both Trotsky and Eliot, both Nabokov and Orwell. So we hope some critic will show how these men's books can be put together to form a beautiful mosaic. We hope that critics can resdescribe these people in ways which will enlarge the canon and give us a set of classical texts as rich and diverse as possible. This task of enlarging the canon takes the place, for the ironist, of the attempt by moral philosophers to bring commonly accepted moral intuitions about particular cases into equilibrium with commonly accepted general moral principles.[3]

It is a familiar fact that the term "literary criticism" has been stretched further and further in the course of our century. It originally meant comparison and evaluation of plays, poems, and novels—with perhaps an occasional glance at the visual arts. Then it got extended to cover past criticism (for example, Dryden's, Shelley's, Arnold's, and Eliot's prose, as well as their verse). Then, quite quickly, it got extended to the books which had supplied past critics with their critical vocabulary and were supplying present critics with theirs. This meant extending it to theology, philosophy, social theory, reformist political programs, and revolutionary manifestos. In short, it meant extending it to every book likely to provide candidates for a person's final vocabulary.

Once the range of literary criticism is stretched that far there is, of course, less and less point in calling it *literary* criticism. But for accidental historical reasons, having to do with the way in which intellectuals got jobs in universities by pretending to pursue academic specialties, the name has stuck. So instead of changing the term "literary criticism" to something like "culture criticism," we have instead stretched the word "literature" to cover whatever the literary critics criticize. A literary critic in what T. J. Clarke has called the "Trotskyite-Eliotic" culture of New York in the '30s and '40s was expected to have read *The Revolution Betrayed* and *The Interpretation of Dreams*, as well as *The Waste Land, Man's Hope,* and *An American Tragedy.* In the present Orwellian-Bloomian culture she is expected to have read *The*

Gulag Archipelago, Philosophical Investigations, and *The Order of Things* as well as *Lolita* and *The Book of Laughter and Forgetting.* The word "literature" now covers just about every sort of book which might conceivably have moral relevance—might conceivably alter one's sense of what is possible and important. The application of this term has nothing to do with the presence of "literary qualities" in a book. Rather than detecting and expounding such qualities, the critic is now expected to facilitate moral reflection by suggesting revisions in the canon of moral exemplars and advisers and suggesting ways in which the tensions within this canon may be eased—or, where necessary, sharpened.

The rise of literary criticism to preeminence within the high culture of the democracies—its gradual and only semiconscious assumption of the cultural role once claimed (successively) by religion, science, and philosophy—has paralleled the rise in the proportion of ironists to metaphysicians among the intellectuals. This widened the gap between the intellectuals and the public. For metaphysics is woven into the public rhetoric of modern liberal societies. So is the distinction between the moral and the "merely" aesthetic—a distinction which is often used to relegate "literature" to a subordinate position within culture and to suggest that novels and poems are irrelevant to moral reflection. Roughly speaking, the rhetoric of these societies takes for granted most of the oppositions which I think have become impediments to the culture of liberalism.

This situation has led to accusations of "irresponsibility" against ironist intellectuals. Some of these accusations come from know-nothings—people who have not read the books against which they warn others and are just instinctively defending their own traditional roles. The know-nothings include religious fundamentalists, scientists who are offended at the suggestion that being "scientific" is not the highest intellectual virtue, and philosophers for whom it is an article of faith that rationality requires the deployment of general moral principles of the sort put forward by Mill and Kant. But the same accusations are made by writers who know what they are talking about and whose views are entitled to respect. As I have already suggested, the most important of these writers is Habermas, who has mounted a sustained, detailed, carefully argued polemic against critics of the Enlightenment (e.g., Adorno, Foucault) who seem to turn their back on the social hopes of liberal societies. In Habermas's view, Hegel (and Marx) took the wrong tack in sticking to a philosophy of "subjectivity"—of self-reflection—rather than attempting to develop a philosophy of intersubjective communication.

I want to defend ironism, and the habit of taking literary criticism as the presiding intellectual discipline, against polemics such as Habermas's. My defense turns on making a firm distinction between the private and the public. Whereas Habermas sees the line of ironist thinking, which runs from Hegel through Foucault and Derrida, as destructive of social hope, I see this line of thought as largely irrelevant to public life and to political questions.

Ironist theorists like Hegel, Nietzsche, Derrida, and Foucault seem to me invaluable in our attempt to form a private self-image but pretty much useless when it comes to politics. Habermas assumes that the task of philosophy is to supply some social glue which will replace religious belief and he sees Enlightenment talk of "universality" and "rationality" as the best candidate for this glue. So he sees this kind of criticism of the Enlightenment, and of the idea of rationality, as dissolving the bonds between members of liberal societies. He thinks of the contextualism and perspectivalism for which I have praised Nietzsche as irresponsible subjectivism.

Habermas shares with the Marxists, and with many of those whom he criticizes, the assumption that the real meaning of a philosophical view consists in its political implications and that the ultimate frame of reference within which to judge a philosophical, as opposed to a merely "literary," writer is a political one. For the tradition within which Habermas is working, it is as obvious that political philosophy is central to philosophy as, for the analytic tradition, that philosophy of language is central. But it would be better to avoid thinking of philosophy as a "discipline" with "core problems" or with a social function. It would also be better to avoid the idea that philosophical reflection has a natural starting point—that one of its subareas is, in some natural order of justification, prior to the others. For, in the ironist view I have been offering, there is no such thing as a "natural" order of justification for beliefs or desires. Nor is there much occasion to use the distinctions between logic and rhetoric, or between philosophy and literature, or between rational and nonrational methods of changing other people's minds.[4] If there is no center to the self, then there are only different ways of weaving new candidates for belief and desire into antecedently existing webs of belief and desire. The only important political distinction in the area is that between the use of force and the use of persuasion.

Habermas, and other metaphysicians who are suspicious of a merely "literary" conception of philosophy, think that liberal political freedoms require some consensus about what is universally human. We ironists who are also liberals think that such freedoms require no consensus on any topic more basic than their own desirability. From our angle, all that matters for liberal politics is the widely shared conviction that we shall call "true" or "good" whatever is the outcome of free discussion—that if we take care of political freedom, truth and goodness will take care of themselves.

"Free discussion" here does not mean "free from ideology" but simply the sort which goes on when the press, the judiciary, the elections, and the universities are free; social mobility is frequent and rapid; literacy is universal; higher education is common; and peace and wealth have made possible the leisure necessary to listen to lots of different people and think about what they say. I share with Habermas the Peircelike claim that the only general account to be given of our criteria for truth is one which refers to "undistorted communication,"[5] but I do not think there is much to be said about what counts as "undistorted" except "the sort you get when you have democratic political institutions and the conditions for making these institutions function."[6]

The social glue holding together the ideal liberal society consists in little more than a consensus that the point of social organization is to let everybody have a chance at self-creation to the best of his or her abilities, and that this goal requires, besides peace and wealth, the standard "bourgeois freedoms." This conviction would not be based on a view about universally shared human ends, human rights, the nature of rationality, the Good for Man, nor anything else. It would be a conviction based on nothing more profound than the historical facts which suggest that without the protection of something like the institutions of bourgeois liberal society, people will be less able to work out their private salvations, create their private self-images, and reweave their webs of belief and desire in the light of whatever new people and books they happen to encounter. In such an ideal society, discussion of public affairs will revolve around (1) how to balance the needs for peace, wealth, and freedom when conditions require that one of these goals be sacrificed to one of the others, and (2) how to equalize opportunities for self-creation and then leave people alone to use, or neglect, their opportunities.

The suggestion that this is all the social glue liberal societies need is subject to two main objections. The first is that as a practical matter, this glue is just not thick enough—that the (predominantly) metaphysical rhetoric of public life in the democracies is essential to the continuation of free institutions. The second is that it is psychologically impossible to be a liberal ironist—to be someone for whom "cruelty is the worst thing we do" and to have no metaphysical beliefs about what all human beings have in common.

The first objection is a prediction about what would happen if ironism replaced metaphysics in our public rhetoric. The second is a suggestion that the public-private split I am advocating will not work: that no one can divide herself up into a private self-creator and a public liberal, that the same person cannot be, in alternate moments, Nietzsche and J. S. Mill. I want to dismiss the first of these objections fairly quickly in order to concentrate on the second. The former amounts to the prediction that the prevalence of ironist notions among the public at large, the general adoption of antimetaphysical, antiessentialist views about the nature of morality and rationality and human beings, would weaken and dissolve liberal societies. It is possible that this prediction is correct, but there is at least one excellent reason for thinking it false. This is the analogy with the decline of religious faith. That decline, and specifically the decline of people's ability to take the idea of postmortem rewards seriously, has not weakened liberal societies but has indeed strengthened them. Lots of people in the eighteenth and nineteenth centuries predicted the opposite. They thought that hope of heaven was required to supply moral fiber and social glue—that there was little point, for example, in having an atheist swear to tell the truth in a court of law. As it turned out, however, willingness to endure suffering for the sake of future reward was transferable from individual rewards to social ones, from one's hopes for paradise to one's hopes for one's grandchildren.[7]

The reason liberalism has been strengthened by this switch is that whereas belief in an immortal soul kept being buffeted by scientific discoveries and by philosophers' attempts to keep pace with natural science, it is not clear that any shift in scientific or philosophical opinion could hurt the sort of social hope which characterizes modern liberal societies—the hope that life will eventually be freer, less cruel, more leisured, richer in goods and experiences, not just for our descendants but for everybody's descendants. If you tell someone whose life is given meaning by this hope that philosophers are waxing ironic over real essence, the objectivity of truth, and the existence of an ahistorical human nature, you are unlikely to arouse much interest, much less do any damage. The idea that liberal societies are bound together by philosophical beliefs seems to me ludicrous. What binds societies together are common vocabularies and common hopes. The vocabularies are, typically, parasitic on the hopes—in the sense that the principal function of the vocabularies is to tell stories about future outcomes which compensate for present sacrifices.

Modern, literate, secular societies depend on the existence of reasonably concrete, optimistic, and plausible political scenarios, as opposed to scenarios about redemption beyond the grave. To retain social hope, members of such a society need to be able to tell themselves a story about how things might get better, and to see no insuperable obstacles to this story's coming true. If social hope has become harder lately, this is not because the clerks have been committing treason but because, since the end of World War II, the course of events has made it harder to tell a convincing story of this sort. The cynical and impregnable Soviet Empire, the continuing shortsightedness and greed of the surviving democracies, and the exploding, starving populations of the Southern Hemisphere make the problems our parents faced in the 1930s—Fascism and unemployment—look almost manageable. People who try to update and rewrite the standard social democratic scenario about human equality, the scenario which their grandparents wrote around the turn of the century, are not having much success. The problems which metaphysically inclined social thinkers believe to be caused by our failure to find the right sort of theoretical glue—a philosophy which can command wide assent in an individualistic and pluralistic society—are, I think, caused by a set of historical contingencies. These contingencies are making it easy to see the last few hundred years of European and American history—centuries of increasing public hope and private ironism—as an island in time, surrounded by misery, tyranny, and chaos. As Orwell put it, "The democratic vistas seem to end in barbed wire."

I want to disentangle the public question, "Is absence of metaphysics politically dangerous?" from the private question, "Is ironism compatible with a sense of human solidarity?" To do so, it may help to distinguish the way nominalism and historicism look at present, in a liberal culture whose public rhetoric—the rhetoric in which the young are socialized—is still met-aphysical, from the way they might look in a future whose public rhetoric is borrowed from nominalists and historicists. We tend to assume that nom-inalism and historicism are the exclusive property of intellectuals, of high culture, and that the masses cannot be so blasé about their own final vo-cabularies. But remember that once upon a time atheism, too, was the ex-clusive property of intellectuals.

In the ideal liberal society, the intellectuals would still be ironists, al-though the non-intellectuals would not. The latter would, however, be commonsensically nominalist and historicist. So they would see themselves as contingent through and through, without feeling any particular doubts about the contingencies they happened to be. They would not be bookish, nor would they look to literary critics as moral advisers. But they would be commonsensical non-metaphysicians, in the way in which more and more people in the rich democracies have been commonsensical nontheists. They would feel no more need to answer the questions, "*Why* are you a liberal? Why do you *care* about the humiliation of strangers?" than the average sixteenth-century Christian felt to answer the question, "Why are you a Christian?" or than most people nowadays feel to answer the question, "Are you saved?"[8] Such a person would not need a justification for her sense of human solidarity, for she was not raised to play the language game in which one asks and gets justifications for that sort of belief. Her culture is one in which doubts about the public rhetoric of the culture are met not by Socratic requests for definitions and principles but by Deweyan requests for concrete alternatives and programs. Such a culture could, as far as I can see, be every bit as self-critical and every bit as devoted to human equality as our own familiar, and still metaphysical, liberal culture—if not more so.

But even if I am right in thinking that a liberal culture whose public rhetoric is nominalist and historicist is both possible and desirable, I cannot go on to claim that there could or ought to be a culture whose public rheto-ric is ironist. I cannot imagine a culture which socialized its youth in such a way as to make them continually dubious about their own process of so-cialization. Irony seems inherently a private matter. On my definition, an ironist cannot get along without the contrast between the final vocabulary she inherited and the one she is trying to create for herself. Irony is, if not intrinsically resentful, at least reactive. Ironists have to have something to have doubts about, something from which to be alienated.

This brings me to the second of the two objections I listed above, and thus to the idea that there is something about being an ironist which un-suits one for being a liberal and that a simple split between private and pub-lic concerns is not enough to overcome the tension.

One can make this claim plausible by saying that there is at least a pri-ma facie tension between the idea that social organization aims at human equality and the idea that human beings are simply incarnated vocabular-ies. The idea that we all have an overriding obligation to diminish cruelty, to make human beings equal in respect to their liability to suffering, seems to take for granted that there is something within human beings which deserves respect and protection quite independently of the language they speak. It suggests that a nonlinguistic ability, the ability to feel pain, is what is important, and that differences in vocabulary are much less important.

Metaphysics—in the sense of a search for theories which will get at real essence—tries to make sense of the claim that human beings are something more than centerless webs of beliefs and desires. The reason many people think such a claim essential to liberalism is that if men and women were, indeed, nothing more than sentential attitudes—nothing more than the presence or absence of dispositions toward the use of sentences phrased in some historically conditioned vocabulary—then not only human nature, but human *solidarity*, would begin to seem an eccentric and dubious idea. For solidarity with all possible vocabularies seems impossible. Metaphysicians tell us that unless there is some sort of common ur-vocabulary, we have no "reason" not to be cruel to those whose final vocabularies are very unlike ours. A universalistic ethics seems incompatible with ironism, simply because it is hard to imagine stating such an ethic without some doctrine about the nature of man. Such an appeal to real essence is the antithesis of ironism.

So the fact that greater openness, more room for self-creation, is the standard demand made by ironists on their societies is balanced by the fact that this demand seems to be merely for the freedom to speak a kind of ironic theoretical metalanguage which makes no sense to the man on the street. One can easily imagine an ironist badly wanting more freedom, more open space for the Baudelaires and the Nabokovs and not giving a thought to the sort of thing Orwell wanted: for example, getting more fresh air down into the coal mines, or getting the Party off the backs of the proles. This sense that the connection between ironism and liberalism is very loose, and that between metaphysics and liberalism pretty tight, is what makes people distrust ironism in philosophy and aestheticism in literature as "elitist."

This is why writers like Nabokov, who claim to despise "topical trash" and to aim at "aesthetic bliss," look morally dubious and perhaps politically dangerous. Ironist philosophers like Nietzsche and Heidegger often look the same, even if we forget about their use by the Nazis. By contrast, even when we are mindful of the use made of Marxism by gangs of thugs calling themselves "Marxist governments," the use made of Christianity by the Inquisition, and the use Gradgrind made of utilitarianism, we cannot mention Marxism, Christianity, or utilitarianism without respect. For there was a time when each served human liberty. It is not obvious that ironism ever has.

The ironist is the typical modern intellectual, and the only societies which give her the freedom to articulate her alienation are liberal ones. So it is tempting to infer that ironists are naturally antiliberal. Lots of people, from Julien Benda to C. P. Snow, have taken a connection between ironism and anti-liberalism to be almost self-evident. Nowadays many people take for granted that a taste for "deconstruction"—one of the ironists' current catchwords—is a good sign of lack of moral responsibility. They assume that the mark of the morally trustworthy intellectual is a kind of straightforward, unselfconscious, transparent prose—precisely the kind of prose no self-creating ironist wants to write.

Although some of these inferences may be fallacious and some of these assumptions ungrounded, nevertheless there is something right about the suspicion which ironism arouses. Ironism, as I have defined it, results from awareness of the power of redescription. But most people do not want to be redescribed. They want to be taken on their own terms—taken seriously just as they are and just as they talk. The ironist tells them that the language they speak is up for grabs by her and her kind. There is something potentially very cruel about that claim. For the best way to cause people long-lasting pain is to humiliate them by making the things that seemed most important to them look futile, obsolete, and powerless.[9] Consider what happens when a child's precious possessions—the little things around which he weaves fantasies that make him a little different from all other children—are redescribed as "trash" and thrown away. Or consider what happens when these possessions are made to look ridiculous alongside the possessions of another, richer, child. Something like that presumably happens to a primitive culture when it is conquered by a more advanced one. The same sort of thing sometimes happens to non-intellectuals in the presence of intellectuals. All these are milder forms of what happened to Winston Smith when he was arrested: They broke his paperweight and punched Julia in the belly, thus initiating the process of making him describe himself in O'Brien's terms rather than his own. The redescribing ironist, by threatening one's final vocabulary, and thus one's ability to make sense of oneself in one's own terms rather than hers, suggests that one's self and one's world are futile, obsolete, *powerless.* Redescription often humiliates.

But notice that redescription and possible humiliation are no more closely connected with ironism than with metaphysics. The metaphysician also redescribes, even though he does it in the name of reason rather than in the name of the imagination. Redescription is a generic trait of the intellectual, not a specific mark of the ironist. So why do ironists arouse *special* resentment? We get a clue to an answer from the fact that the metaphysician typically backs up his redescription with argument, or—as the ironist redescribes the process—disguises his redescription under the cover of argument. But this in itself does not solve the problem, for argument, like redescription, is neutral between liberalism and anti-liberalism. Presumably the relevant difference is that to offer an argument in support of one's redescription amounts to telling the audience that they are being *educated* rather than simply reprogrammed—that the Truth was already in them and merely needed to be drawn out into the light. Redescription which presents itself as uncovering the interlocutor's true self, or the real nature of a common public world which the speaker and the interlocutor share, suggests that the person being redescribed is being empowered, not having his power diminished. This suggestion is enhanced if it is combined with the suggestion that his previous, false, self-description was imposed upon him by the world, the flesh, the devil, his teachers, or his repressive society. The convert to Christianity or Marxism is made to feel that being redescribed amounts to an uncovering of his true self or his real interests. He comes to believe that his acceptance of that redescription seals an alliance with a power mightier than any of those which have oppressed him in the past.

The metaphysician, in short, thinks that there is a connection between redescription and power and that the right redescription can make us free. The ironist offers no similar assurance. She has to say that our chances of freedom depend on historical contingencies which are only occasionally influenced by our self-redescriptions. She knows of no power of the same size as the one with which the metaphysician claims acquaintance. When she claims that her redescription is better, she cannot give the term "better" the reassuring weight the metaphysician gives it when he explicates it as "in better correspondence with reality."

So I conclude that what the ironist is being blamed for is not an inclination to humiliate but an inability to empower. There is no reason the ironist cannot be a liberal, but she cannot be a "progressive" and "dynamic" liberal in the sense in which liberal metaphysicians sometimes claim to be. For she cannot offer the same sort of social hope as metaphysicians offer. She cannot claim that adopting her redescription of yourself or your situation makes you better able to conquer the forces which are marshaled against you. On her account, that ability is a matter of weapons and luck, not a matter of having truth on your side, or having detected the "movement of history."

There are, then, two differences between the liberal ironist and the liberal metaphysician. The first concerns their sense of what redescription can do for liberalism; the second, their sense of the connection between public hope and private irony. The first difference is that the ironist thinks that the *only* redescriptions which serve liberal purposes are those which answer the question, "What humiliates?" whereas the metaphysician also wants to answer the question, "Why should I avoid humiliating?" The liberal metaphysician wants our *wish to be kind* to be bolstered by an argument, one which entails a self-redescription which will highlight a common human essence, an essence which is something more than our shared ability to suffer humiliation. The liberal ironist just wants our *chances of being kind,* of avoiding the humiliation of others, to be expanded by redescription. She thinks that recognition of a common susceptibility to humiliation is the *only* social bond that is needed. Whereas the metaphysician takes the morally relevant feature of the other human beings to be their relation to a larger shared power—rationality, God, truth, or history, for example—the ironist takes the morally relevant definition of a person, a moral subject, to be "something that can be humiliated." Her sense of human solidarity is based on a sense of a common danger, not on a common possession or a shared power.

What, then, of the point I made earlier: that people want to be described in their own terms? As I have already suggested, the liberal ironist meets this point by saying that we need to distinguish between redescription for private and for public purposes. For my private purposes, I may redescribe you and everybody else in terms which have nothing to do with my attitude toward your actual or possible suffering. My private purposes, and the part of my final vocabulary which is not relevant to my public actions, are none of your business. But as I am a liberal, the part of my final vocabulary which is relevant to such actions requires me to become aware of all the various ways in which other human beings whom I might act upon can be humiliated. So the liberal ironist needs as much imaginative acquaintance with alternative final vocabularies as possible, not just for her own edification, but in order to understand the actual and possible humiliation of the people who use these alternative final vocabularies.

The liberal metaphysician, by contrast, wants a final vocabulary with an internal and organic structure, one which is not split down the middle by a public-private distinction, not just a patchwork. He thinks that acknowledging that everybody wants to be taken on their own terms commits us to finding a least common denominator of those terms, a single description which will suffice for both public and private purposes, for self-definition and for one's relations with others. He prays, with Socrates, that the inner and the outer man will be as one—that irony will no longer be necessary. He is prone to believe, with Plato, that the parts of the soul and of the state correspond, and that distinguishing the essential from the accidental in the soul will help us distinguish justice from injustice in the state. Such metaphors express the liberal metaphysician's belief that the metaphysical public rhetoric of liberalism must remain central to the final vocabulary of the individual liberal, because it is the portion which expresses what she shares with the rest of humanity—the portion that makes solidarity possible.[10]

But that distinction between a central, shared, obligatory portion and a peripheral, idiosyncratic, optional portion of one's final vocabulary is just the distinction which the ironist refuses to draw. She thinks that what unites her with the rest of the species is not a common language but *just* susceptibility to pain and in particular to that special sort of pain which the brutes do not share with the humans—humiliation. On her conception, human solidarity is not a matter of sharing a common truth or a common goal but of sharing a common selfish hope, the hope that one's world—the little things around which one has woven one's final vocabulary—will not be destroyed. For public purposes, it does not matter if everybody's final vocabulary is different as long as there is enough overlap so that everybody has some words with which to express the desirability of entering into other people's fantasies as well as into one's own. But those overlapping words— words like "kindness" or "decency" or "dignity"—do not form a vocabulary which all human beings can reach by reflection on their natures. Such reflection will not produce anything except a heightened awareness of the possibility of suffering. It will not produce *a reason to care* about suffering. What matters for the liberal ironist is not finding such a reason but making sure that she *notices* suffering when it occurs. Her hope is that she will not be limited by her own final vocabulary when faced with the possibility of humiliating someone with a quite different final vocabulary.

For the liberal ironist, skill at imaginative identification does the work which the liberal metaphysician would like to have done by a specifically moral motivation—rationality, or the love of God, or the love of truth. The ironist does not see her ability to envisage, and desire to prevent, the actual and possible humiliation of others—despite differences of sex, race, tribe, and final vocabulary—as more real or central or "essentially human" than any other part of herself. Indeed, she regards it as an ability and a desire which, like the ability to formulate differential equations, arose rather late in the history of humanity and is still a rather local phenomenon. It is associated primarily with Europe and America in the last three hundred years. It is not associated with any power larger than that embodied in a concrete historical situation, for example, the power of the rich European and American democracies to disseminate their customs to other parts of the world, a power which was enlarged by certain past contingencies and has been diminished by certain more recent contingencies.

Whereas the liberal metaphysician thinks that the good liberal knows certain crucial propositions to be true, the liberal ironist thinks the good liberal has a certain kind of know-how. Whereas he thinks of the high culture of liberalism as centering around theory, she thinks of it as centering around literature (in the older and narrower sense of that term—plays, poems, and, especially, novels). He thinks that the task of the intellectual is to preserve and defend liberalism by backing it up with some true propositions about large subjects, but she thinks that this task is to increase our skill at recognizing and describing the different sorts of little things around which individuals or communities center their fantasies and their lives. The ironist takes the words which are fundamental to metaphysics, and in particular to the public rhetoric of the liberal democracies, as just another text, just another set of little human things. Her ability to understand what it is like to make one's life center around these words is not distinct from her ability to grasp what it is like to make one's life center around the love of Christ or of Big Brother. Her liberalism does not consist in her devotion to those particular words but in her ability to grasp the function of many different sets of words.

These distinctions help explain why ironist philosophy has not done, and will not do, much for freedom and equality. But they also explain why "literature" (in the older and narrower sense), as well as ethnography and journalism, is doing a lot. As I said earlier, pain is nonlinguistic: it is what we human beings have that ties us to the non-language-using beasts. So victims of cruelty, people who are suffering, do not have much in the way of a language. That is why there is no such thing as the "voice of the oppressed" or the "language of the victims." The language the victims once used is not working anymore, and they are suffering too much to put new words together. So the job of putting their situation into language is going to have to be done for them by somebody else. The liberal novelist, poet, or journalist is good at that. The liberal theorist usually is not.

The suspicion that ironism in philosophy has not helped liberalism is quite right, but that is not because ironist philosophy is inherently cruel. It is because liberals have come to expect philosophy to do a certain job —namely, answering questions like, "Why not be cruel?" and "Why be kind?"—and they feel that any philosophy which refuses this assignment must be heartless. But that expectation is a result of a metaphysical up-bringing. If we could get rid of the expectation, liberals would not ask iron-ist philosophy to do a job which it cannot do, and which it defines itself as unable to do.

The metaphysician's association of theory with social hope and of liter-ature with private perfection is, in an ironist liberal culture, reversed. With-in a liberal metaphysical culture the disciplines which were charged with penetrating behind the many private appearances to the one general com-mon reality—theology, science, philosophy—were the ones which were ex-pected to bind human beings together and thus to help eliminate cruelty. Within an ironist culture, by contrast, it is the disciplines which specialize in thick description of the private and idiosyncratic which are assigned this job. In particular, novels and ethnographies which sensitize one to the pain of those who do not speak our language must do the job which demonstra-tions of a common human nature were supposed to do. Solidarity has to be constructed out of little pieces rather than found already waiting in the form of an ur-language which all of us recognize when we hear it.

Notes

1. From this point of view, both analytic philosophy and phenomenology were throwbacks to a pre-Hegelian, more or less Kantian, way of thinking—attempts to preserve what I am calling "metaphysics" by making it the study of the "conditions of possibility" of a medium (consciousness, language).

2. See Alexander Nehamas, *Nietzsche: Life as Literature* (Cambridge, Mass.: Har-vard University Press, 1987), p. 234, where Nehamas says that he is not concerned with "the miserable little man who wrote [Nietzsche's books]." Rather he is con-cerned (p. 8) with Nietzsche's "effort to create an artwork of himself, a literary character who is also a philosopher [which is also] his effort to offer a positive view without falling back into the dogmatic tradition." In the view I am suggesting, Nietzsche may have been the first philosopher to do consciously what Hegel had done unconsciously.

3. I am here borrowing John Rawls's notion of "reflective equilibrium." One might say that literary criticism tries to produce such equilibrium between the proper names of writers rather than between propositions. One of the easiest ways to express the difference between "analytic" and "continental" philosophy is to say that the former sort trades in propositions and the latter in proper names. When continental philosophy made its appearance in Anglo-American literature depart-

ments in the guise of "literary theory," this was not the discovery of a new method or approach but simply the addition of further names (the names of philosophers) to the range of those among which equilibrium was sought.

4. Where these webs of belief and desire are pretty much the same for large numbers of people, it does become useful to speak of an "appeal to reason" or to "logic," for this simply means an appeal to a widely shared common ground by reminding people of propositions which form part of this ground. More generally, all the traditional metaphysical distinctions can be given a respectable ironist sense by sociologizing them—treating them as distinctions between contingently existing sets of practices, or strategies employed within such practices, rather than between natural kinds.

5. This is not to say that "true" can be defined as "what will be believed at the end inquiry." For criticism of this Peircian doctrine, see Michael Williams, "Coherence, Justification and Truth," *Review of Metaphysics* 34 (1980): 243–72, and section 2 of my "Pragmatism, Davidson and Truth," in Ernest Lepore, ed., *Truth and Interpretation: Perspectives on the Philosophy of Donald Davidson* (Oxford: Blackwell, 1987), pp. 333–55.

6. In contrast, Habermas and those who agree with him that *Ideologiekritik* is central to philosophy think that there is quite a lot to say. The question turns on whether one thinks that one can give an interesting sense to the word "ideology"—make it mean more than "bad idea."

7. Hans Blumenberg takes this transfer as central to the development of modern thought and society, and he makes a good case.

8. Nietzsche said, with a sneer, "Democracy is Christianity made natural" (*Will to Power*, no. 215). Take away the sneer, and he was quite right.

9. See Judith Shklar's discussion of humiliation on page 37 of her *Ordinary Vices* (Cambridge, Mass.: Harvard University Press, 1984) and Ellen Scarry's discussion of the use of humiliation by torturers in chapter 1 of *The Body in Pain*.

10. Habermas, for example, attempts to save something of Enlightenment rationalism through a "discourse theory of truth," which will show that the "moral point of view" is a "universal" and "does not express merely the moral intuitions of the average, male, middle-class member of a modern Western society" (Peter Dews, ed., *Autonomy and Solidarity: Interviews with Jürgen Habermas* (London: Verso, 1986). For the ironist, the fact that nobody had ever had such intuitions before the rise of modern Western societies is quite irrelevant to the question of whether she should share them.

Richard Rorty: Selected Bibliography

Books

Philosophy and Social Hope. London: Penguin, 1999.

Achieving Our Country: Leftist Thought in Twentieth-Century America. Cambridge, Mass.: Harvard University Press, 1998.

Truth and Progress: Philosophical Papers III. Cambridge: Cambridge University Press, 1998.

Objectivity, Relativism and Truth: Philosophical Papers I. Cambridge: Cambridge University Press, 1991.

Essays on Heidegger and Others: Philosophical Papers II. Cambridge: Cambridge University Press, 1991.

Contingency, Irony, and Solidarity. Cambridge: Cambridge University Press, 1988.
Consequences of Pragmatism. Minneapolis: University of Minnesota Press, 1982.
Philosophy and the Mirror of Nature. Princeton: Princeton University Press, 1979.

Journal Articles

"Nietzsche and the Pragmatists." *New Leader* 80.9 (1997).
"The Ambiguity of Rationality." *Constellations* 3.1 (1996).
"Duties to the Self and to Others." *Salmagundi* 111 (1996).
"Is Truth a Goal of Enquiry? Davidson vs. Wright." *Philosophical Quarterly* 45.180 (1995).
"Richard Rorty Responds." *Dissent* 42.2 (1995).
"Is Derrida a Quasi-Transcendental Philosopher?" *Contemporary Literature* 36.1 (1995).
"Feminism, Ideology, and Deconstruction: A Pragmatist's View." *Hypatia* 8.2 (1993).
"Human Rights, Rationality and Sentimentality." *Yale Review* 81 (1993).
"A Pragmatist View of Rationality and Cultural Difference." *Philosophy East & West* 42 (1992).
"Feminism and Pragmatism." *Michigan Quarterly Review* 30 (1991).
"Intellectuals in Politics." *Dissent* 38.4 (1991).
"An Exchange on Truth, Freedom, and Politics." *Critical Inquiry* 16 (1990).
"The Banality of Pragmatism and the Poetry of Justice." *Southern California Law Review* 63.6 (1990).
"Foucault/Dewey/Nietzsche." *Raritan* 9 (1990).
"A Post-Philosophical Politics?" *Philosophy and Social Criticism* 15.2 (1989).
"Deconstruction and Circumvention." *Critical Inquiry* 11 (1984).

3

Stereoscopic Thinking
and the Law of Resemblances

Aristotle on Tragedy and Metaphor

DENNIS J. SCHMIDT

Dennis Schmidt's philosophical project is directed toward uncovering the ways in which we experience ourselves as finite and as dwelling at a threshold—of language, of intelligibility, of community. In short, his abiding concern is with the sense that the world continually exceeds the individual as it simultaneously defines the individual. This excess is the experience of finitude. His work addresses the forms of finitude and, increasingly, the ways in which these limit experiences are explored outside of the conceptual language of philosophy proper, especially as they are explored in works of art. However, his concern with the achievement of the work of art in experience is not governed by traditionally aesthetic issues. Rather, following the leads of Kant and Hegel, the framework for Schmidt's concern with works of art is defined by a concern with ethical and political life. For Schmidt, the question of community, like the workings of art, has to do with how we solicit and come to respond to the insight that experience opens up a world which is larger than what one can know, define or control, and yet for which one is nonetheless responsible.

There are several trajectories that define the development and direction of Schmidt's thought; and for the most part these paths can be followed back to experiences that turned him to philosophy as a student, namely, the experience of living abroad and his opposition to the Vietnam War. On the one hand, he is concerned with questions of language and cultural practices; on the other hand, he is also concerned with questions of justice, power, resistance, and community. Over time, these two problematics have drawn closer together for Schmidt. As a result, he has become increasingly interested in the question of language as it concerns community—and here the topic of translation takes on a special significance. He is equally interested in the work of art as it opens up experience in new ways—ways that challenge the hegemony of the concept in philosophical reflection, especially in matters concerning political and ethical life.

Schmidt's essay takes up the question of tragedy, which is often regarded as the summit of the possibilities from which art is born. The larger work from which this essay is drawn is guided by the way in which tragedy is taken up—both in antiquity and in post-Kantian German philosophy—as a work that can only be grasped ethically. More precisely: a tragedy is regarded as a work that opens up the question of ethical life in new and productive ways, independently of the law of the concept and of the concept of law. Western philosophy arises in the span between Plato's exile of the tragic poets from the *polis* and the reversal of this gesture (in Nietzsche and Heidegger above all), and so the question of tragedy serves as one of the themes in which the questions posed by the end of philosophy and the limits of Western culture become visible. Dennis Schmidt's philosophical work has been devoted to the task of returning philosophy to questions opened by the topic of tragedy.

-»≡○◎≡«-

Aristotle's *Poetics* presents itself as a specialized text inquiring into the specific character of poetic practice; more precisely, since the word is taken to be the highest form in which such practice is set to work, it presents itself as an inquiry into the nature of literary practices and genres.[1] Despite its self-presentation, in the end, it will be clear that the *Poetics* needs to be read in the context of other Aristotelian texts—most notably the *Physics, Ethics,* and *Politics*—and when it is thus situated it quickly becomes clear that the *Poetics* poses questions that reach far beyond the resources that it uncovers. The connection of the *Poetics* with the *Ethics* and *Politics* is most evident in the concern of each text with the various dimensions of human πρᾶξις. The link to the *Physics,* where φύσις is presented as the perfected form of μιμησις,[2] is less evident but no less significant. Aristotle, like Kant and Heidegger, regards the question of art as inextricably wedded to the enigma of φύσις, and in this he is perhaps most remote from his teacher Plato. When one reads Aristotle it is important then that one take seriously the remarks which suggest that our impulse toward mimetic πρᾶξις is "according to nature [κατὰ φύσιν]" (1448b7) and that the language, the proper diction [λέξεως] of tragedy, namely the iambic meter, is "from nature itself [αὐτὴ ἡ φύσις]" (1449a18). From the outset it is clear: for Aristotle the urge to make poetry needs to be understood as a "natural" impulse: "Speaking generally, poetry seems to owe its origin to two particular causes, both natural" (1448b2). The naturalness of the impulse to make works of art is such that Aristotle suggests that poetry is produced "out of improvisations" (1448b8). The word he uses here, "αὐτοσχεδιασμάτων"—"off-handed" or "impromptu"—carries with it a sense of the casualness and ease, the naturalness with which we make art. Poetry then needs to be understood simply as the most refined and reflected form of that impulse. It is the natural result of human nature. In the end, the riddle of mimetic practices belongs to the even larger enigma of nature itself and to the question of how we ourselves are of nature.

Nonetheless, his introduction into the investigation of our love of making art is much more narrowly focused: art is to be thought initially according to the guidelines opened by μίμησις itself. Aristotle makes it clear that a work is a work of art first of all by virtue of its mimetic element. Criticizing those who would define a work by virtue of its meter alone, Aristotle points out that "Homer and Empedocles have nothing in common except the meter, so it is proper to call one a poet and the other not a poet but a scientist" (1448a11). One is not a poet simply because one plays with the metric possibilities of language. In other words, the musical element of language alone cannot convert an experience into a work of art—some element other than meter provides the passage to the poem. Aristotle is blunt here: the distinctive element of the work of art lies in its mimetic potential, and so it is this potential which forms the axis of Aristotle's interpretation of art in general. If we are to understand the work of art and its fascination for us, then we must understand the secret of μίμησις itself, but to do that we need to know something about our own nature since, as Aristotle introduces it, μίμησις is to be understood with reference to human instincts and pleasures. We need to know that "from childhood human beings have an instinct [σύμφυτον] for representations [μιμεῖσθαι], and in this respect they differ from other animals in ... learning first lessons by representing things" (1448b2).[3] We must also know that μίμησις is something "pleasurable" [τὸ χαίρειν] for us (1448b3). The pleasure and the education imparted by mimetic works collaborate with one another, and understanding their special symbiosis is the first stage in understanding the nature of art.

In order to understand Aristotle's conception of this natural delight that we take in μίμησις, it is helpful to refine its sense by contrasting it with the way in which Plato links the notion of μίμησις with desire. Plato argued that desire characterized the operations of a "lower" region of the soul and consequently that the cultivation of desires which one finds in mimetic works is never able to educate the soul to its full capacity. Furthermore, he argued that such desires leave one vulnerable to the foibles of the world; in our emotions we are invaded by the world and thus we are vulnerable to its variability, we lose our independence, we even lose our reason. This is especially evident in children, in whom the rational powers of the soul are not fully developed, and who are consequently most vulnerable to the force of desire. On the other hand, the rational part of the soul is reliant upon nothing but itself, and this rational power of the soul, which is independent, opens avenues for thinking how it is that we belong together. The economy of the soul is a closed one and so the pleasures of desire are cultivated at the expense of the well-being of reason; consequently, the more desires are cultivated the less we are able to be free. In short, for Plato, the undeniable pleasure that one can find in mimetic works hinders, if not outright damages, the human capacity to answer ethical questions. Aristotle's sense of our delight in mimetic works is quite different. Though the child who plays and toys with imitative life seems to take a natural delight in μίμησις, that is not a signal that such delight is a lower form of the soul. Quite the contrary; such delight in "imitation" is native to human nature, and therefore it needs to be understood as the delight we take in the free expression of our own nature. The play space of imitation is a realm in which possibilities are explored (just as a child might play at being a doctor or a philosopher), and it is a realm in which our instinct to enlarge our world is unfolded. Later (1451a36), Aristotle argues that this kinship of mimetic works to possibility is what distinguishes such works from history (where a story is also told). It also accounts for the bond (and so strains) between art and philosophy: both refer themselves to generalities that escape the confines of the particularities that have happened. Art is thus not simply the expression of feelings, it is rather an exploration of what can be otherwise. Far from disfiguring or weakening the soul, mimetic practices for Aristotle number among the most basic forms in which human nature exercises itself and grows beyond the orbit of the given.

Aristotle is aware that pleasure is elemental and so has no "reason" that can be inspected according to a certain form of analysis. But there is a dynamic in pleasure, and he is especially intent upon unpacking that dynamic in order to better understand just where the delight that we take in imitations might lead us. To that end, Aristotle notes that this delight is so strong that it is capable of transforming the character of our experience: "We enjoy looking at likenesses of things which are themselves painful to see, obscene beasts, for instance, and corpses" (1448b3). Kant too will call attention to this power of art to convert experiences into something that holds and attracts us—even those experiences that might otherwise repel us. But, unlike Aristotle, Kant sets limits on this power of art to illuminate experience anew: art, he says, cannot render beautiful what would otherwise disgust us. When Kant unpacks the pleasure we take in this transformation effected by the work of art, he does so by arguing that it is a pleasure rooted in a sense of the common. It is, he argues, the pleasure we take in being alerted to that to which we belong but do not define alone. It is, for Kant, the pleasure of belonging, a pleasure that we cannot conceive but can only know symbolically. Aristotle has a different account of the roots of this pleasure; but, insofar as it eventually leads to the pleasure we find in metaphor and riddles, it bears significant affinities with Kant's account.

The specific character of this pleasure is described by Aristotle rather abruptly when he says simply that "the reason we enjoy seeing likenesses is that, as we look, we learn and infer what each is, for instance, 'that is so and so'" (1448b5–6). The point is clear but not terribly illuminating: we find pleasure in such works because they instruct us. What is not said here is precisely how we are instructed by such works. The "logic" of this instruction, at least insofar as it happens in words, will not be explained until Aristotle takes up the nature of "resemblances" in words—that is, metaphor and riddle—and seeks to show just how it is that these move the mind beyond the given. There we learn more clearly that the mimetic operation involves an otherwise impossible collaboration of sameness and difference. Aristotle is aware that a perfect imitation is a contradiction that would destroy itself, since it would cease being an imitation by being perfect, and that every "imitation" is a repetition that involves the recognition of samenesses in differences. This means that there is an ambiguity in the law of resemblances operative in μίμησις. Aristotle, like Heraclitus, knows that resemblances are never simple matters and that, as such, genuine μίμησις, the play of resemblances, is by its very nature inventive.

The specific nature of the ambiguity that inhabits the likeness, the resemblance, characterizing mimetic works needs a more precise determination. Aristotle will not help much to fill this need at this stage of the *Poetics*, although later, in the treatment of riddle, pun, and metaphor, we do find some further clues about how the projection of sameness upon difference active in mimetic works is to be thought. But there are other texts in which we find a fascinating and revealing structure parallel to that found in μίμησις, namely, in some of Aristotle's remarks about friends. Aristotle defines the relationship of friends as a sort of resemblance, and one can clearly see that it is, like μίμησις, a sort of re-presentation which is disclosive. One sees this clearly in a passage from the *Magna Moralia*: "Now supposing a person looks upon his friend and marks what he is and what is his character and quality; the friend—if we figure a friend of the most intimate sort—will seem to him to be a kind of second self, as in the common saying, 'This is my second Hercules.' Now to know oneself is a very difficult thing—as even philosophers have told us—and a very pleasant thing. . . . Direct contemplation of ourselves is moreover impossible. . . . And so just as when wishing to behold our own faces we have seen them by looking upon a mirror, whenever we wish to know our own characters and personalities, we can recognize them by looking upon a friend; since the friend is, as we say, our 'second self'" (1213a12–23). Again, we are referred to a resembling, a repetition. This time it is not people acting that is being mirrored; it is the soul that is being reflected for itself. What we are told is that a more revealing likeness of the soul than the likeness of one's image in a mirror is the likeness found in the eyes of the friend. In the repetition, the re-presentation of myself in the eyes of those I love, I find the clearest insight into to the nature of my own soul. We can recognize the structure of representation working in μίμησις in this structure of the event of revelation communicated in the eyes of the friend. Something is exposed that can only be exposed in a representation that is not a simple copy.

Mimetic re-presentation thus escapes the logic of identity governing the operations of reflection. It is more like the self-discovery one finds in the eyes of a friend than it is like the self-identification one achieves by looking in a mirror. In mimetic re-presentation the resemblance, the "imitation," which is produced is simultaneously the communication of differences. As such the knowledge it imparts is what one might call stereoscopic: in it the mind holds together two notions that otherwise could not be brought together. In its best forms, for example, in metaphor, riddle, and witticism—ultimately in tragic poetry—this stereoscopic mimetic operation enables something to be recognized that is otherwise impossible; it enables the mind to combine what is otherwise simply distinct. The logic of the concept prohibits us from holding certain thoughts together such as the position of a thing and its velocity, or, as Hegel will repeatedly remind us, the thought of the beginning. But in metaphor, which Aristotle will argue belongs naturally to mimetic works, we break the bonds of the logic of identities governing ordinary reflection and stereoscopically hold otherwise impossible combinations together as when we say, with Sappho, that eros is "sweetbitter" [γλυκύπικρον].[4] As Empedocles, cited by Aristotle, will say: "From the two comes one seeing [μία γίνεται ἀμφοτέρωνψ]" (1458a19). The most developed forms of μίμησις thus enable the mind to recognize something and to surpass it at the same time: "And the soul seems to say—'how true, but I missed it.'"[5] This liberation, this creative stereoscopy, that belongs to μίμησις is the delight specific to the learning that belongs to the human instinct for mimetic practices. This pleasure cannot give an account of itself as a pleasure, but we can say that it is the pleasure that belongs to synthesis, the pleasure simply of knowing. Furthermore, as will be seen, once this pleasure achieves its fullest formulation in tragic poetry we learn that it is instructive for ethical life and one of the ways we affirm the risks of such a life.

But it needs to be noted that while the mimetic dimension of the artwork is privileged in the explanation of tragic poetry, especially insofar as it accounts for the delight we take in art, μίμησις is not the only human instinct that lies at the roots of poetic practices. Harmony and rhythm—instincts that belong to what Plato analyzed as music (instincts as well that are temporal and mathematizable)—also number among the instincts that gradually develop into poetry. So it is that Aristotle traces the varieties of poetic forms (tragedy, comedy, epic) according to the various permutations by which these instincts work and develop together. Saying that such art forms evolve out of the improvisations of our natures means of course that these forms are, in some manner, exteriorizations of human nature as such. It is to say, with Hölderlin, that "man is born for art"[6] or, with Schelling, that there is a "*Bildungstrieb*," an impulse to art, which belongs to our nature. That does not mean that art is a form of "self-expression" in the rather private and trivial sense of that phrase where it refers to a sort of self-display. Rather, saying that art emerges from our instincts means that it is the presentation, Kant will call it the "free play," of our very nature. By giving an account of poetic practice that grounds such practices in our natures, Aristotle provides an explanation for the power of art in human life. It is not, as with Plato, a power we need to master because it might otherwise disrupt the harmony of the soul with itself; rather, it is a power to be cultivated because it is revelatory in a unique manner.

→✦←

Suggesting that epic poetry and comedy will be dealt with later, Aristotle turns his attentions specifically to tragic poetry. The promised analysis of epic will form the concluding section of the *Poetics;* the section on comedy, like Aristotle's three-book dialogue entitled *On Poets,* is lost among the casualties of history. When the treatment of comedy was lost for posterity, the significance of the analysis of tragedy was shifted since it lost an essential counterpoint, not a mere pendent. One can only wonder what might have been said about comedy in light of what is said of tragedy. More: one wonders what that which must be said of comedy would mean for what might be said of tragedy.[7]

Finally, then, Aristotle wagers a definition of tragedy. As Aristotle himself notes, much of what is said here has been prepared for by the earlier discussion; but there is unquestionably a new key to interpreting tragic poetry introduced here in the form of the notion of κάθαρσις. It is a notion that is introduced after a slight preparation. Aristotle begins by saying that "tragedy is a μίμησις of an action [πρᾶξις] that is heroic and complete and of a certain magnitude—by means of language enriched with all kinds of ornament [ἡδυσμένῳ λόγῳ]" (1449b24–25). Here, even before the new elements to be introduced are mentioned, Aristotle refines, and thereby advances, his earlier discussion of μίμησις. Now it is made clear that tragedy is the μίμησις of a πρᾶξις as such; it is not the μίμησις of the people engaged in actions. The qualification is significant. Since Aristotle holds that all πρᾶξις is purposive, this means that tragedy is a reflection or repetition, a μίμησις, of the aims of human life, not of individual human beings. What is at issue is not the character or the psychological complexes of those who are acting; rather, what is crucial, what makes tragedy ethically instructive and gives us delight to see, is the illumination into the nature and possibilities of πρᾶξις, of purposive action. Aristotle will reinforce this claim later, saying that "while character makes people what they are, it is their actions and experiences that make them happy or the opposite. . . . You could not have a tragedy without action, but you can have one without character-study" (1450a12–15).[8] In tragedy we see into the nature of human πρᾶξις and into the ends of such actions; ultimately, we see into the possibilities of happiness and there we find the insight of the *Nicomachean Ethics* confirmed by tragic poetry: "Happiness is not a thing that we possess all the time, like a piece of property" (1169b33). Tragedy then is the representation of action in such a way that we win a glimpse into the possibilities of action as such. More precisely, it is an insight that is directed by "embellished language" and that is imparted by pity, fear, and the κάθαρσις which these emotions are able to effect. The comments on language here seem to be made as if in passing. The more sustained analysis of the language of tragedy comes later. But the reference to κάθαρσις, which is the only use of the word in the *Poetics,* marks one of the most original contributions of Aristotle's presentation of tragedy.[9]

By and large, Aristotle regards the "embellishments" of language as an extraneous matter. The word he uses here—ἡδυσμένῳ—refers to something added to food to give it a heightened flavor. It is the same word that Plato uses as a sign of his contempt for poetry in the *Republic* (607a).[10] Aristotle seems to be simply saying that the language of tragedy, like a spice, is best when it heightens the effect of the μίμησις of a πρᾶξις—here κάθαρσις—but that embellished language alone not does accomplish that effect. To amplify this point Aristotle remarks that the language of tragedy is not narrative but dialogue, since dialogue is the supreme form of language in action. Narrative will be reserved for epic where the compression of action is not an issue, since epic can be presented over long periods of time. Here, though, the point is that the language of tragedy is in the service of the μίμησις of a πρᾶξις that, by means of an alchemy of pity and fear, solicits a κάθαρσις.

When Aristotle introduces his definition of tragedy here he says that it has been prepared for by the foregoing discussions. But there is one apparent exception to this claim: the notion of κάθαρσις seems to have no antecedents to its appearance here. Κάθαρσις is a medical word and typically is interpreted according to the ideal of a purgation; in other words, it effects a moral purge of the soul; in it the emotions that are toxic for the healthy ethical life of the soul are removed. It is can also be understood in the less specialized but still related sense of a "clarification" of the soul.[11] Much as tears remove toxins from the body when one cries, the experience of the κάθαρσις in tragedy leaves one feeling cleansed. The idea of κάθαρσις here clearly signals a sort of return or restoration of a balance in the soul. It is a clarified state; just as sometimes the air is uncommonly clear after a storm, so too does the soul achieve a sort of clarification after fear and pity have moved through it.

Aristotle will unpack this claim when he says that "two of the most important elements in the emotional effect of tragedy [are] 'reversals' [περιπέτειαι] and 'discoveries' [ἀναγνωρίσεις]" (1450a18). But before the relation of those elements to κάθαρσις is taken up, it is first necessary to be clear about an assumption underpinning Aristotle's conception of fear and pity, namely, that they are indicative of a solidarity, not, as in Plato, of a weakness. We feel such emotions for those whom we resemble, those in whom we see ourselves. There is a healthy fellow feeling, a mimetic identification, that lies at the basis of κάθαρσις. The reason for this is clear: if I do not identify with those who arouse my fear and pity, κάθαρσις is not possible.[12] The effect of the μίμησις of a πρᾶξις itself rests on a μίμησις that operates between the witness and the tragic drama. The identification and difference that operates in the tragedy is also operative between the audience and the performance of the tragedy. In other words, κάθαρσις itself rests upon a sort of mimetic identification that involves those it effects in the πρᾶξις itself. By virtue of this mimetic identification, κάθαρσις belongs to the witness as well as to those who suffer a πρᾶξις. It is a form of πρᾶξις suffered but diluted greatly. Much like the homeopathic conception of medicine, such a diluted form of suffering should, according to Aristotle, have a very significant effect. It is an emotional event in which a knowledge about the aims of life is imparted through a double mimetic act: it is the μίμησις of an action with which the witness mimetically identifies. In it a certain clarity, an insight, is obtained about the aims of life. One learns to see without, like Oedipus, needing to go blind. The supreme cathartic moment comes when one sees oneself in the empty sockets where once Oedipus had eyes. When that void becomes the mirror wherein one sees one's own soul reflected, one experiences what Aristotle calls κάθαρσις.

Such an experience is difficult to bring about, and so from this point forward Aristotle is interested in asking how one can achieve it in the drama. Aristotle, who was an avid theatergoer, thus tries to sort out the components of the successful tragedy before he asks about the specific knowledge of this cathartic experience, namely, the knowledge of our "error" [ἁμαρτία]. The remarks about the six components of a successful tragedy (1450a9) both build and expand upon the definition of tragedy up to this point. Collectively these components reaffirm the centrality of πρᾶξις in tragedy. Aristotle even warns against letting any of these elements overwhelm the representation of πρᾶξις in the drama. So, for instance, he expresses the concern that the visual component of the play, the spectacle [ὄψις] of its staging, not "kidnap the soul" [ψυχαγωγικὸν] by being too dazzling (1450a18). In other words, the playwright should not turn to gimmicks in order to startle the audience: if, for example, the staging of *Oedipus Rex* overly exploits the sight of his appearance on stage with bloody eye sockets, if there the visual effect overwhelms the emotional effect, then the drama has failed.

But the most important of the components of the tragedy is, according to Aristotle, its "plot" [μῦθος] (1450a12), which he describes as "the synthesis of events" (1450a12). The sense of Aristotle's use of this notion needs some clarification. Aristotle, unlike Plato, is not interested in the adaptation of traditional legends for tragic poetry. He knows that tragic poets typically dramatized traditional stories (1451b8), but he also suggests that tragic poetry need not be bound to such stories since poetry, like philosophy, belongs to the realm of the possible, to general truths, and not, like history, to particular events. The work of the tragic poet is not to tell the story of an individual, but to compose the course of events in such a way that we might all recognize ourselves in the way such a plot illuminates human πρᾶξις as such. For Plato, on the other hand, the poet fiddles with a sort of cultural icon or memory in taking up its legend [μῦθοι]; for Aristotle, the appropriation of such legends is merely to lend a sort of added dimension of force to the whole drama. But, for Aristotle, a tragedy can quite well have both plots and characters that are completely invented "as is shown in Agathon's *Antheus*" (1451b8). So the discussion of plot in Aristotle does not refer to content of the stories which might provide a sort of fund from which tragic poets draw; rather, it refers simply to the ordering of the events as the drama unfolds them.

As Aristotle elaborates upon the nature of the successful plot, he remarks that what is most crucial is that it have both "reversals" and "discoveries" (1450a18). In a moment he will add it has a third part, perhaps the most fatal element, the root of what we fear and pity, namely, suffering [πρᾶξις] (1452b9). But in order for the specific character of the suffering that belongs to tragedy to be fully appreciated, the dynamics of the plot that pivot around "reversals" and "discoveries" need to be made more precise. In the reversal and discovery that animate the plot, the sufferings of the tragic figure are compressed and sharpened; by means of them, suffering is not protracted but is compacted and thereby powerfully delineated. What is most important, and yet most difficult, is the need to understand how it is that in these elements of the plot the ambiguity that inhabits the law of resemblances at the heart of mimetic practices, the stereoscopic riddle that drives the tragic drama, finds its manifestation. Just as this ambiguity in the law of resemblance belonging to mimetic practices rendered metaphor the preeminent form of language for the tragic poem, so too does this ambiguity find expression in the reversals and discoveries that propel the plot of the tragic poem.

The definitions of these elements are unproblematic. "A 'reversal' is a change [μεταβολὴ] in what is being practiced [τῶν πραττομένων] into its opposite" (1452a22). Furthermore, it is a change that is probable or even necessary; that is, it belongs naturally to the evolution of events. Part of the surprise that belongs to this reversal is precisely that it is so unsurprising from another point of view. "A 'discovery' . . . is a change [μεταβολὴ] from ignorance to knowledge" (1452a31). The key to the plot, then, is found in these two transformations in the situation of πρᾶξις, both changes being metabolic—sudden. In them the tragic vision of human life is first performed: they disclose a situation that is rent by contradictions and ambiguities that easily—and without warning—convert into their opposite. They thus expose the fragility, the vulnerability, of human affairs. Aristotle indicates that while such changes can operate independently of one another, they are most effective, most potent in their capacity to solicit fear and pity, when they happen simultaneously, as they do in *Oedipus Rex:* the instant in which Oedipus learns the truth he sought is the same instant that his happiness is gone forever. Everything changes in a flash, there is no reversal that subsequently takes time to unfold its meaning. What is most important, though, is to see that a reversal of fortune such as Oedipus's—from savior to pariah—is not merely a trick that the dramatist introduces to win our attentions; rather, it must be understood as reflecting the divided possibilities that human beings confront in acting. Likewise, the recognition of this reversal, the discovery that what one believed to be true has turned out to be otherwise, is not a comment upon the stupidity of those involved but upon the opacity that belongs to human life generally. In reversal and recognition, in these elements of plot, the tragic poem imparts a sense of the conflict and the opacity belonging to human πρᾶξις as such. In this way tragedies illuminate the ultimates, the extreme possibilities, of human life. More precisely, what is illuminated is how hidden such possibilities remain from us for the most part. Not by accident does Oedipus first encounter his fate at a crossroads where he proves that he is blind to the choices that he makes.

What is crucial then is to see that here the poetic work is not about characters but about the possibilities that inhabit the very nature of human πρᾶξις. The cathartic effect is indexed not to the characters and our feelings about them but to the action and the reflection of the possibilities of human life that such action offers us. Thus Aristotle argues that the work of art is, like philosophy, indexed to the realm of possibility: "A poet's object is not to tell what actually happened but what could and would happen. . . . The difference between a historian and a poet is not that one writes in prose and the other in verse—indeed the writings of Herodotus could be put into verse and yet would still be a kind of history. . . . The real difference is that one tells what happened and the other what might happen. For this reason poetry is something more philosophic and of graver import than history, since its statements are of the nature of universals, whereas those of history are singulars" (1451b2–4). The relation of history to πρᾶξις is different than that found in poetry, where the elements of plot illuminate its hidden possibilities as possibilities to which we, the audience, belong as well. What is more problematic, but not addressed by Aristotle at this point, is the question of the respective relations of poetry and philosophy—the relation that is of suffered knowledge presented mimetically to reasoned knowledge presented conceptually.

At this point Aristotle's concern is rather to complete his analysis of plot by introducing its third, and final, constituent—suffering [πάθος]. But before he does that we find a passing, and puzzling, reference to beauty [τὸ καλὸν]—a word that, for Aristotle, refers to something that is good to look at. Speaking of the well-constructed plot, he remarks that "in everything that is beautiful . . . [its] parts must not only exhibit a certain order in its arrangement of parts, but also be of a definite magnitude" (1450b36).[13] The reference to beauty is surprising: one might expect that a text on poetics, on the achievement of art in human life, would have made the beauty of art a central concern. But here we find a remark made almost en passant and not in order to introduce the topic of beauty but in order to clarify the orderliness of the plot. The marginal role that beauty plays in the question put to us by art only serves to reinforce the point that Aristotle made at the outset of the *Poetics:* mimetic practices are, at bottom, an exploration of the possibilities of πρᾶξις; and the pleasure that accompanies the experience of such works is best explained as an example of the delight we take in all learning and self-disclosure.

When Aristotle finally introduces the third element of tragic art—namely, suffering, misery, calamity—he does so abruptly, without clear preparation and without much subsequent discussion. All that is said—but of course this says a great deal here—is that "suffering is a πρᾶξις of a destructive or painful nature, such as the presentation of death, torture, woundings and the like" (1452b12). After noting that the other two elements of plot have been explained, he drops the topic of plot and the question of how to conceive this suffering. Or so it seems.

The question posed by the operations of πάθος is one of the central questions of the *Poetics*. It is not immediately clear, however, how we are to think this third element of the plot in light of the brief remarks Aristotle makes about it. In the end, the full sense of the πάθος of tragic art, and of the knowledge that it communicates, becomes clear only after we have understood why it is that death is preeminent among the ways in which πάθος is experienced. Here the discussion refers both backward—to the sudden change that characterized the other two elements of plot—and forward—to the "error" belonging to the human condition.

From the reversals and discoveries in the plot of the tragic poem we learn something about the mutability of human πρᾶξις. We learn that things may well, without warning, convert into their opposite. We learn that what was once divine can, in a flash, become monstrous. We learn, as Oedipus does, that at any moment we might approach a crossroads and meet another who could become for us either a god or a monster (or, as in the case of Oedipus, both: his father, who in belonging to his own creation is a god, becomes, unwittingly, a monster). In these elements of plot, then, one learns that one is ultimately "enigmatic, without consistency . . . with no defined essence, [one realizes that one] oscillates between being the equal of the gods and the equal of nothing at all."[14] What becomes visible here is the expanse of the human condition—the possibilities belonging to πρᾶξις—an expanse so great that it is capable, at any given moment, of converting its situation into its other. In the end, all life belongs to the possibility of this conversion insofar as life, at any given moment, is convertible into death. This inevitable conversion of the whole of life that every life suffers is the reason that death plays a preeminent role in the conception of tragedy. What is opened up in the exposure of this change is a space of strangeness, a space that is abyssal. It is enough, as Plato repeatedly reminds us, to drive one mad. Μανία is one of the real possibilities of how reversals and discoveries are experienced: "Quem deus vult perdere, demantant prius."[15] When Aristotle refers to the πάθος, the suffered experience, of tragic art he calls attention to a knowledge that we cannot resolve but can only endure. It is the knowledge that πρᾶξις is riddled with ambiguities and contradictions that are opaque and yet motile and thus powerfully disruptive. It is also the knowledge that one cannot lift oneself out of this torn condition. Tragic πάθος is the signal of the "gap between our goodness and our good living, between what we are . . . and how humanly well we manage to live."[16] It is a reminder that being of good character is not sufficient for human happiness, which depends in part upon good fortune.

When Aristotle discusses the possible trajectories of such disruptions, when he examines the representation of such upheavals in tragic art, he asks which sort of change of fortune best arouses our pity and fear. Is it the change from good to bad fortune, from bad to good? Is it the change in the situation of a cruel person or a good person? In response to his own question he introduces the notion of ἁμαρτία: we feel "pity for undeserved misfortune [and] fear for the person like ourselves" (1453a4). This is made more precise when he says, "this is the sort of person who is not preeminently virtuous and just, and yet it is through no badness or villainy of his own that he falls into misfortune, but rather through some error of judgment [ἁμαρτία]" (1453a9). The reversal of fortune that is most pitiable and fearful, and which we do well to understand as the greatest form of suffering, is one that is owing to ἁμαρτία, to some sort of mistake in πρᾶξις that is intelligible—that is not, in other words, simply sheer "bad luck"—and yet that is not simply a matter of bad character.[17] Aristotle makes this explicit: "It must not be due to villainy but to some great error [ἁμαρτίαν μεγάλην] in such a person as we have described" (1453a15). Fear and pity are not the response summoned for the villain who suffers; they are rather reserved for those who call suffering upon themselves through an act of ignorance, an act of bad judgment, that is not to be explained by reference to the malice or ill-will traceable to a bad character.

Something unwelcome, dangerous, and disruptive makes its appearance in the possibility described by the notion of ἁμαρτία. In the literature of suffering, in tragic poetry, ἁμαρτία functions as the word that best explains why people suffer. The κάθαρσις we experience when a light is shined upon the operations of ἁμαρτία teaches us something about how we need to understand beings capable of such profound suffering. A chronic possibility of human life and an "error" that even a person of good ἕξις, of good ἔθος, can suffer ἁμαρτία names the axis along which tragic reversals are formed. Since we live and act in a world that is larger than our knowledge of the world, we are persistently confronted with questions that are matters of judgment rather than clear knowledge. As finite beings we are, as Socrates never ceases to remind us, defined by our relation to our ignorance. Acting in the dark we are thus exposed to reversals of fate since the orders in which we live and act are clearly far larger and more powerful than the human capacity to know them. Plato is clearly trying to harness such orders and to steel the soul against desires that might admit powers into soul which the soul can neither know nor master (powers such as ἔρος). Aristotle, on the other hand, is willing to grant that human life is risky and that the elements of the plot of tragic poetry—reversal, discovery, and suffering —cooperate to call attention to this risk insofar as it is a matter of ἁμαρτία, of errancy. The differing assessments that Plato and Aristotle accord to tragedy for human understanding are thus traceable to the differences in their respective conceptions of human life. In both the *Politics* and *Ethics* Aristotle affirms the importance of the risk that belongs to human life, the risk that is a matter of judgment but never control: the risk of loving another or of having a friend. There he argues that, besides being a futile gesture—one can never, in the end, close off the world that possesses the power of invading a life, no matter how well armored, at any moment—the desire to eradicate such risks would be the desire to erase what enriches life. It would be the desire for a life closed to human goods that are greater than those that one defines alone. It would be the desire for an arid life. But it is also the desire for a life without the possibility of suffering.

But insofar as we, like Aristotle, affirm the risks of finite human πρᾶξις, insofar as we acknowledge that the reach of human knowledge and the realm of human affairs are not commensurate, then we open ourselves to the sort of suffering disclosed by tragic art. The incommensurability between the spheres of knowing and acting that tragic art illuminates is the space in which ἁμαρτία, errancy, is possible. It is this abyssal space, this impossible gap we must continually traverse, that we see mirrored, for example, in the vacant eyes of Oedipus. According to Aristotle, the healthy response to it is to know how deeply it must be suffered to be understood and to have the twin feelings of fear—for ourselves—and pity—for others—as we experience its mimetic contagion. The high esteem in which Aristotle holds tragic art emerges out of his fundamental agreement with the view of human life it presents. It is a view of life that cultivates a deep sensibility to the enigma of finite life and to the proximity of monstrosity and divinity, of suffering and happiness, in such a life. Such a sensibility is profoundly ethical in nature: it is a sense of life, of its strangeness and largeness, born out of the solidarity belonging to fear and pity. But more so: it is a view of life and of oneself that emerges out of the law of resemblances in which we see ourselves mirrored in the eyes of the other.

-->=◉⊂⊷-

With the presentation of the notion of the errancy exposed by the μίμησις of πρᾶξις, the analysis of the plot, the composition, of the work of art is completed. But, according to Aristotle, there are five additional elements that belong to such works and so the *Poetics* continues with an analysis of these as they function in the tragedy before turning to the concluding remarks about epic art. Of those five other elements, two (spectacle and song) have been dismissed as largely marginal, possibly even distracting, matters that are more about the theatrical production of the work than about the insights proper to tragedy. A third element (character) has been limited in its importance for our understanding of tragedy; it is simply that "most important is that the character [ἤθη] be good" (1454a22). The remaining two elements (diction and thought) dominate the second half of the *Poetics*. The reason for this dominance is clear, even though Aristotle himself never makes it explicit: both of these elements concern language, and the effort here is to demonstrate how it is that language itself, the medium of human πρᾶξις, is destined to the presentation of action as tragic. In other words, the attempt here is to illuminate the tragic possibilities borne by language itself. This demonstration of the kinship between language and tragedy runs even into the capillaries of language, even into the alphabet.[18] Here the stereoscopy of the law of resemblances governing mimetic practices is made clearer.

Aristotle's concern here is chiefly with the question of diction or style [λέξις], since thought [διάνοια], which he defines as "all the effects produced by words" (1456a34), is more proper to the inquiry of the *Rhetoric*. One notices immediately that Aristotle's approach to the question of style is conspicuously different from that found in the *Republic*, where Plato both mimetically performs the question in his own distinctive philosophical style and translates the question into the topic of music and harmony. Here, in Aristotle, the discussion is mostly concerned with metaphor, riddle, and pun as well as with the analytic of the components of language in general. But what is most notable, given the discussion, is that here one can no longer avoid the question of Aristotle's own relation to style in the *Poetics*.

Of course, there are several reasons that such a question, though important to pose, cannot be properly addressed. The status of the text of the *Poetics* is simply too unclear for any judgment to be made about its own style. It is, it seems, a compilation of notes, for lectures perhaps, likely never intended for publication; and so it is simply illegitimate to assume that anything could be gleaned from the nature of the writing here. Nonetheless, a general question, one that reaches beyond Aristotle, needs to be posed about the language of criticism, the language of theory, the language in which art—with its deliberative and reflected relation to style—is most properly addressed. It is also a question that recoils upon these very words. The issue is simple: If style is so significant to what is communicated in the work of art, can that which comes to be known thanks to the experience of such a work be said again but in a different style? Is the knowledge that emerges out of a sensitivity to matters of style betrayed once it is taken up again in a language that is governed by the logic of the concept? More generally: Can philosophy appropriate the insights of art without distorting, or even simply missing, those insights insofar as they are indebted to elements of language absent from the language of philosophy? Can a knowledge that is performed simply be said? Such questions can be taken up as referring to the problematic of translation, but that might already be a theorization of a question and so a privileging of the language of theory. In antiquity Plato is clearly most alert to this problematic (though it is said that Aristotle's own dialogues were delightful, flowing and like a "golden river"),[19] but otherwise it is not often taken up as a question. However, when the reappropriation of the question of art from antiquity sets to work in German philosophy, this question of the propriety of philosophic style to its insights becomes one of the most pressing of all questions. That is why we find such stylistic acrobatics and innovations in writers such as Hegel, Kierkegaard, Nietzsche, and Heidegger. With them we are confronted forcefully with the question of philosophic writing. Aristotle, however, is mute on such matters. What we do find is an extended analysis of language that illustrates how it is able to represent the ambiguity at work in the law of resemblances governing μίμησις. We learn, in short, how it is that language can lend itself to the special insights of tragic art.

That analysis begins with a microscopic look at the radical elements of language; namely, the vowel, consonant, and syllable. In an attempt to clarify the distinctive features of human language, Aristotle notes that "animals utter indivisible sounds but none I should call a letter" (1456b20). He continues by saying that for an intelligible sound to be made, a vowel or semi-vowel is requisite. Pure consonants, which Plato said had "no voice"[20] (such as, d, j, s) are unpronounceable without the addition of the breath provided by a vowel. The innovation of the Greek alphabet, to which both Plato and Aristotle were very alert, was the representation of a system of writing in which the separate elements of the act of speech are noted (the Phoenician sign, by contrast, represented the consonant plus any vowel determined by the context).[21] Aristotle begins his discussion of poetic language by drawing upon the possibilities of abstraction provided by the alphabet and so by stripping language in general down to its most radical element. He then reassembles language, as it were, discussing the possibility of words, phrases, and parts of speech, always emphasizing the complex character of language involved in the unique process of symbolization that belongs to words that can be written according to such an alphabet.[22] Suddenly Aristotle introduces the notion of metaphor, saying that "metaphor consists in giving the thing a name that belongs to something else" (1457b9). Later, while commenting upon the various possibilities of language that have been enumerated in this discussion, he will underscore the fundamentality of metaphor for the task of tragic poetry: "It is a great thing, indeed, to make a proper use of these poetical forms, as also of compounds and strange words. But the greatest thing by far is to be a master of metaphor. It is the one thing that cannot be learned from others; and it is a sign of genius, since the right use of metaphor implies an eye for resemblances" (1459a4–5). Metaphor, then, is the most fitting possibility of language for the μίμησις of πρᾶξις.

In metaphor we give a name to otherwise nameless things: "For instance, to scatter seed is to sow, but there is no word for the action of the sun in scattering its fire. Yet this has to the sunshine the same relation as sowing has to the seed, and so you have the phrase 'sowing the god-created fire'" (1457b25). The specific dynamic of such naming is, according to Aristotle, helpful in illuminating something of the nature of tragic poetry. Metaphor is "an intuitive perception of the similarity in dissimilars" (1459a5), and in this one can easily see how it is that the delight we take in metaphors is like the delight we find in the eyes of the friend: it is the experience of the mind moving beyond the dichotomous taxonomy of either/or. In some regard there is a fundamental metaphoricity of all thinking insofar as to think is more than to merely calculate and is instead the creative movement of the mind beyond the terms that it is given. We project sameness upon difference and by means of this act of impertinence we are able to stereoscopically expand the horizon of what we know and can understand. A Chinese proverb has it that "no brush can write two words at the same time";[23] yet in metaphor language is able to do just that. A name unknown is brought forward by virtue of its intuited resemblance with a name known. Two things are known at once, both the same, both different. The gap that defines their differences becomes the space in which language and knowing play. It is a sort of stereoscopic knowing that violates the law of identity governing conceptual reason.[24] The line that Aristotle cites from Empedocles at this point—it is cited simply as an example of how a word can be compressed—is perfectly revealing: "From the two comes one seeing [μία γίνεται ἀμφοτέρωνψ]" (1458a4).

But here one must ask what metaphor has to do specifically with the inquiry into tragic art in the *Poetics*. What does language accomplish in metaphor that advances, or at least augments, the insights proper to tragic art? Why is metaphor a privileged mode of "diction" in mimetic practices? By overcoming, or by not being contained by, the dichotomies of either/or metaphor becomes the manner in which language compresses contradictories in itself and is thereby the way in which unresolved differences are able to be expressed in their belonging together. Metaphor thus has a dual advantage for tragedy: first, it is able to speak what is otherwise unspeakable; second, it is able to present a double truth without thereby extinguishing the ambiguity proper to it. Both of these features need to be unpacked with reference to the general nature of tragic art.

To say that metaphor is able to name the otherwise nameless is to affirm that it is a way in which language gropes into the realm of our ignorance. Language then becomes a sort of compensation for our blindness. What is important here is to understand that it is when metaphor is necessary, and not simply as a poetic device to spice the poem, that it first reveals its imaginative reach and the significance of that reach for knowing. Metaphor is necessary when what must be said presents itself simply as unknown, as lacking a word, as even unnamable and yet still summoning speech. The truth of the metaphor belongs thus to the finitude of our knowing. Metaphor is the imaginative countermovement of language before the limitations of my knowledge; by means of it I can struggle to say something about what I do not fully grasp. With respect to the task of tragic poetry it is clear that metaphor is more than what Aristotle earlier characterized as an "embellishment" of language; rather, it is an essential manner in which language in the tragic poem contributes to naming what we know most of all through πάθος, through suffering. I cannot, for instance, know my death— that necessary ultimate that perfects human πρᾶξις—but in metaphor I can, in a paradoxical manner, know something of it. Likewise with the error of judgments to which I am blind (which is why the image of blindness belongs so natively to Greek tragedy). Likewise with the ability to know myself. Insofar as tragic art is dedicated to marking the ἁμαρτία, the ineluctable errancy of πρᾶξις which we cannot, in the end, fully know, it needs to rely upon this gift of metaphor to speak, without betraying, what cannot be named.

By means of the metaphor we accede to the importance of what we cannot fully know. In metaphor, then, we elliptically disclose what is hidden and otherwise inscrutable. Metaphor accomplishes this stereoscopic disclosure thanks to the ambiguity that belongs to the law of resemblance: as in a translation, there is a double disclosure, a doubled naming, that belongs to metaphor. Like paternal twins, the operations of metaphor are twinned—the same but not identical. This means, though, that there is also a natural kinship of the metaphor with the riddle as well as to the expression of an ἀγών, a conflict. The ambiguity, the difference, belonging to the two things named gives rise to a semantic friction that jars us. One example that Aristotle provides moves rather clearly in this direction: "For instance a cup is to Dionysus what a shield is to Ares; so one can speak of the . . . shield as 'Ares's cup'. . . . Having given the thing a strange name, one may by a negative addition deny it some attribute of that new name [as when] one calls the shield not 'Ares's cup' but a 'wineless cup'" (1457b33). By violating our expectations, language in the metaphor arrests us and fixes our attention upon the friction, the disparities, between what is hidden (Dionysus's shield), its name (wineless cup), and the indirect manner in which it is named (metaphor). In the semantic friction of the metaphor, language in the tragic poem repeats the logics of both the reversal and the discovery belonging to the plot. It thereby adds to the liveliness and the force of the new idea: "Because the hearer expected something different, his acquisition of the new idea impresses him all the more. His mind seems to say 'Yes, to be sure, but I never thought of that'. . . . the thought is startling because, as Theodorus puts it, it does not fit in with the ideas you already have."[25] In this way, the experience of naming in the metaphor mimes the experience of the plot; both are mimetic of an ἀγών that is characteristic of πρᾶξις and of our capacity to speak about our experience. Speaking as it does in a double register, metaphor operates on the axis of a paradox; so does the plot of the tragedy: "The dramatist plays on this to transmit his tragic vision of a world divided against itself and rent with contradictions."[26] In both cases the mind of those who hear and witness the tragic poem is brought into a conversation with itself because of the contradiction.

But Aristotle finds more still to be said about the propriety of metaphor for the tragic poem; namely, that its relation to riddle, and to jokes as well, renders it especially well suited to impart the insights of tragic art.[27] "The essence of the riddle consists in describing a fact by an impossible combination of words. By merely combining the ordinary names of things this cannot be done, but it is made possible by combining metaphors" (1458a28). By bringing together impossible combinations of words, by the play of ambiguities animating it, the metaphor opens the enigmatic space of the riddle in which the nature of the impossible is presented as such. Delineating a special form of unknowability, the riddle belongs natively to the logics of reversal and discovery, and, by extension, to the dynamic of human πρᾶξις itself. That is why the riddle plays such an important role in tragedy. The force of the riddle is nowhere more evident than in the tragedy that serves as the model tragedy for Aristotle, that is, *Oedipus Rex*. "*Oedipus Rex* is not only centered on the theme of the riddle but . . . in its presentation, development, and resolution the play is itself constructed as a riddle. The ambiguity, recognition, and περιπέτειαι all parallel one another and are all equally integral to the enigmatic structure of the work."[28] In thinking about the nature of the riddle we learn just how much the tragic art is about what is irreconcilable and impossible, about what is indispensable for us to know yet impossible at the same time. We learn that human πρᾶξις cannot, in the end, be substantivized, it cannot be defined or essentialized, it cannot even be described; it is rather a riddle, full of double meanings and ambiguities that exceed our abilities to answer in a simple or final fashion. Tragedy turns to the riddle precisely because it presents such an enigma: "The Greeks were drawn to enigmas. But what is an enigma? A mysterious formulation you could say. Yet that would not be enough to define an enigma. The other thing you have to say is that the answer to an enigma is likewise mysterious."[29] Therein lies the difference between the enigma and the problem: the problem admits of a solution, the enigma does not, but rather demands that we shift our perspective in order to grasp what is disclosed by the riddle. Such a shift is, in part, aided by the metaphor. Like Oedipus without eyes, we learn to see differently once we learn to grasp the nature of the riddle.

Of course it is precisely Oedipus who is an enigma to himself, the paradigmatic enigma perhaps. At the outset of his story he appears as the solver of a riddle and so comes to be greeted as the savior of the city of Thebes. In the course of governing the city he is confronted with a new riddle, namely, who killed Laius? As that question moves toward its resolution, Oedipus becomes a riddle to himself. He no longer knows who he is, and he who was once a king and savior becomes an outcast. The solver of the riddle about everyone becomes the very embodiment of the riddle of human identity. At the moment he discovers this, the chorus speaks of Oedipus as "strange, monstrous and mad" with one of the most compact expressions of the enigma of human πρᾶξις found in tragedy: ᾧ δεινὸν ἰδεῖν πάθος ἀνθρώποις, ὦ δεινόταον ὅσ'ἐγὼ προσέκυρσ' ἤδη."[30] The reversal that belongs to πρᾶξις, the errancy of our knowing, is not always benign. In these possibilities of human πρᾶξις, which are illuminated in tragic art, we are exposed to what can leave us strange to ourselves and those we love, to discovering that one who was once a god can become, in a flash, a monster, to, finally, madness. We learn that such are the possibilities belonging to every life, and that even the well-conducted life cannot immunize itself against such risks that belong to the "flaw" to which we expose ourselves and by which we are able to call disaster down upon ourselves and those we love. The greatness of the work of art is precisely its capacity to present this impossible truth without infecting us with such madness. Nonetheless it presents us with the cathartic event that lets us understand something of what makes such madness possible. Risk belongs to the realm of πρᾶξις. Ἁμαρτία, calling the damage of such risk down upon oneself, does not come about through some irresponsibility—the notion of responsibility does not belong to what art teaches us of ethics—but through a simple defect of the mind, a lapse in judgment. Art, the μίμησις of πρᾶξις, gives us the peculiar pleasure of knowing something of that risk and of being able to see into our own defect. Aristotle is of the conviction that such a truth, which complements the insights of ethical inquiry, should make a difference in how one lives.

That, and simple good fortune, can make all the difference in the question of one's happiness.

⊷═◉═⊷

But Aristotle does not end the *Poetics* on such a note. Rather, he continues by reminding us that tragedy—with its dialogue form and specific elements—is not the sole mimetic practice that illuminates something of the possibilities of human πρᾶξις. Epic, which has a somewhat different structure than tragedy, also qualifies for treatment in a text such as the *Poetics*, which is devoted to investigating the nature of art's capacity to educate us about ethical life. Comedy, too, according to Aristotle's promises at the outset of the *Poetics*, belongs to such an investigation; but that section of the text—whether never written or lost—does not exist.[31] So it is that the analysis of epic brings the *Poetics* to a close. It does not, however, bring it to full closure with respect to the question the text lays out for itself.

What is striking from the outset is the disproportion between the quantities of the text devoted to tragedy and to epic: tragedy occupies Aristotle for the bulk of twenty-two chapters; epic, on the other hand, is dealt with in three chapters (two of which seem rather out of touch with the remainder of the *Poetics*). The chapters on tragedy contain few references to epic; those on epic are primarily concerned with comparing it to tragedy. But this disproportion in the respective sizes of the analyses is not alone in making clear that Aristotle regards tragedy as the highest and more far-reaching form in which art is able to shed light upon human affairs. Aristotle is unhesitating about passing judgment here: "Since it attains the poetic effect better than epic, tragedy is clearly the higher form of art" (1462b13). Tragedy sets the standard for literature, and the formal differences between epic and tragedy (they differ chiefly in length and meter) do not challenge that standard but confirm it with only one significant exception. The exception is that epic is better at portraying the marvelous [θαυμαστόν] since the illogical [ἄλογον] is more readily achieved in the epic where we do not actually see the persons in the story (1460a12–14). It is an exception about which Aristotle makes no further comment. What one finds instead is a catalogue of the ways in which tragedy achieves the form of art with greater force than epic does. Thus, for example, Aristotle points out that tragedy is a more concentrated form than epic: "Suppose Sophocles's *Oedipus* were to be turned into as many lines as there are in the *Iliad*. . . . it would seem thin and diluted" (1462b15). But then one must ask why, if everything epic does tragedy does better, Aristotle devotes any time to epic at all? Why discuss a diluted form of art after the more concentrated form has already been presented? The answer to this question comes in the form of a proper name: Homer. Homer, who is the only poet Aristotle ever calls "divinely inspired" (1459a29), is not regarded as a typical epic poet, even though Aristotle formulates the definition of epic largely with reference to him. What makes Homer such an exemplary poet is precisely that, as Aristotle reads him, he is basically a dramatist and not a narrator. In the final analysis, Homer's literary gifts, while best exemplifying the genre of epic, are themselves not contained by the form of that genre. Nonetheless, one must say that, despite his gifts and innovativeness, Homer does not represent the final form of poetic art: *Amicus Homer magis amica veritas.*

But to follow Aristotle as he tries to sort out the lines between epic and tragedy, and tries as well to find the place of Homer in those lines, risks leaving one entangled in subtleties that might obscure an important point about the definition of tragedy already achieved up to this point. In that definition Aristotle not only created a new genre of literary criticism, he also set in motion a shift in Greek thought about art. That shift is twofold. On the one hand, it is simply the solidification of the claim already tacit in Plato; namely, that tragic art marks the summit of the possibilities of art in general. On the other hand, it signals the recentering of the accomplishment of tragic art from Homer to Sophocles. Despite all of the praise for Homer found in the *Poetics* and the unqualified admiration expressed for his achievements, it is evident that the most perfected form of the possibilities of tragedy are found in Sophocles. This shift—from the heroic Achilles to the pathetic Oedipus—is fundamental. It marks a displacement of the Homeric vision of πρᾶξις by a Sophoclean one; a move from one temperament to another. It is a decisive shift and one that will remain in force, and largely unquestioned, for centuries to come. Plato sought to replace Achilles with Socrates as the image of the hero, but it was Aristotle who removed Achilles from the premiere place in tragic art and in that place inserted Oedipus. Both Socrates and Oedipus are figures defined by their incessant questioning. Both "suffered" in order to persist in that need to interrogate the world. But they remain indisputably distinct as models for how we might best probe the regions of our ignorance as illustrating the ethical significance of that ignorance which so profoundly defines human being. In the figure of Socrates, Plato sets up a new model for a life with questions, a bios theoretikos, one that is not, like the bios politikos that he finds presented in tragedy, attached to πρᾶξις and to the ambiguities that belong to it.[32] By being dispassionate and disengaged, Socratic questioning armors itself against the divisions and reversals that are the ever present possibilities of human πρᾶξις. Socrates recognized the necessity of removing himself from mimetic practices precisely because such practices are, by their very nature, wedded to the tragic possibilities of πρᾶξις. Aristotle's reply, his acknowledgment of the worth of the work of art for the understanding of human life, is to call attention to a very different kind of questioning as it unfolds in the figure of Oedipus.

-→=◉⊂=←-

Both Plato and Aristotle argue that mimetic works, representations or imitations of πρᾶξις, expose the soul to ambiguities, conflicts, enigmas, and other destabilizing forces that can present themselves in a human life. Although the differences in their respective presentations of tragedy are significant—differences that crystallize in the differences between epic and tragic drama, Homer and Sophocles—they are in accord in suggesting that the experience of tragic art cultivates an openness to the multiple forces which can divide the soul against itself and its world. Both suggest that in tragedy one is alerted to the gap between the respective horizons of our knowledge and our actions, as well as to the conflicts and risks inherent in our desires. Both grant that the experience of the work of art as it presents such gaps touches us profoundly and so both take this experience to be a serious matter worthy of sustained reflection. But whereas Aristotle finds that art sheds a light on human affairs that adds a certain texture to what is disclosed in the theoretical analysis of πρᾶξις, Plato argues that when it is properly understood art issues a warning about the danger that art itself poses to the soul. In other words, for Plato, the dangers that art illumi-nates—all of which can be explained as the danger of a soul not one with itself—are precisely what the experience of art cultivates. That is why art, for Plato, poses a threat that needs to be controlled. For Aristotle the matter is different: such a danger is native to human πρᾶξις, and to wish to elimi-nate it would be to drain πρᾶξις of its nature. Art poses not a threat but a delight, since in it we come to learn something of that danger, something of ourselves, that we cannot control but we can respect. We witness a danger-ous truth about ourselves that—reflected in a language, re-presented in the structure of the drama, and mediated by the distance of the theater—we stereoscopically come to understand without ourselves being destroyed. The hero of the work of art, the one to whom we are beholden for its plea-sure and its knowledge, is (for example) Sophocles, thanks to whom the sufferings of Oedipus can be instructive. The merit of the work of art is that it introduces an element of what is dangerous, without itself being danger-ous; as such, it homeopathically serves the health of the just soul.

This disagreement between Plato and Aristotle about the significance of art reflects their obviously differing view on the nature of human πρᾶξις, as well as the nature of the vantage point from which the truth of πρᾶξις is best made visible. The theater of the truth of ideas and the theater of the tragedian offer competing insights about human affairs. But what is per-haps less obvious, but no less significant, are the different conceptions of language at work here. Plato dialogues are like palimpsests—full of puns and rhetorical transitions—expressing a concern about language that is not self-consciously enlisted in the task of moving the soul beyond the reach of time. For Plato, it is the eidetic possibility of language that needs to be sum-moned by our speaking. When we participate fully in the dialogue, we are drawn forward by the draft of that possibility: everything that begins in a now exposes itself as belonging to an always.[33] We are, as it were, translated into the idea by the dialogue. By contrast, Aristotle, whose own texts have a spare and even skeletal quality, celebrates the ability of language to ex-pose the ambiguities and conflict of those who live and die in time. The agonistic possibilities of language as they are expressed in metaphor and riddles amplify and drive home the deep conflicts and enigmas that belong to all human πρᾶξις. Governed by different languages (the eidetic and the mimetic), different relations to πρᾶξις (detached and displayed), these different theaters (of the truth of ideas and of the tragedy of life in time) are, in the end, different ways of thinking the lives of those who die in time.

Notes

1. This philosophic prejudice that judges artworks that appear in the word as somehow "higher" forms is made explicit by Hegel, who traces the migration of art from mute stone (sculpture) up to the arrival of the word in the poem. However, neither Aristotle nor Hegel problematizes this assumption as such. Nietzsche, for whom wordless music outstrips the poetic power of the word, will be among the first to raise this question as such and in so doing challenge even the power of the language of philosophy to grasp the work of art at all. Others will make this challenge in other ways. Merleau-Ponty's analysis of images likewise challenges the tacit pan-linguisticality dominant in philosophic treatments of art.

2. See *Physics* B, ii. See also my "Economies of Production," in *Crises in Continental Philosophy,* ed. Arleen Dallery and Charles Scott (Albany: State University of New York Press, 1990), pp. 145–57, 265–68.

3. Saying that we learn our first lessons "mimetically" helps to clarify the sense of the word "μίμησις"—one only need think of how one learns a language, that is by means of repetition. More precisely, Aristotle's remark specifies the nature of the "imitation" at work in μίμησις: it is not a matter of producing a copy, a duplicate; rather, in the imitation that is μίμησις we find a curious sort of repetition or re-enactment. It is of utmost importance for understanding Aristotle that one not take μίμησις to refer to a sort of "copy" or "reproduction." To say that the work of art is mimetic is not to say that it produces copies. When one has a proper sense of the Greek conception of μίμησις one is not puzzled by the fact that, for the Greeks, music is counted among the most clearly mimetic arts. Contemporary conceptions of "imitation" tend to be shaped by technological conceptions of "reproduction" (this, for instance, is what Andy Warhol made such a theme for art).

4. See Anne Carson, *Eros: The Bittersweet* (Princeton: Princeton University Press, 1986), pp. 3–9, 116 (henceforth cited as *EB*). Carson's book is among the best presentations of this paradox of the impossible knowing that belongs to poetic language proper. What she does not mention, though, is the way in which translation bears a kinship to metaphor in this regard. By moving between two languages one holds together resemblances that are not full identities. From this point of view, translation is a stereoscopic experience and a model for thinking μίμησις in general.

5. *Rhetoric* 1412a25. See Anne Carson, "Just for the Thrill," *Arion* (Winter 1990): 153; see also, *EB*, p. 116.

6. Friedrich Hölderlin, "Der Gesichtspunct aus dem wir das Altertum anzusehen haben," in *Sämtliche Werke und Briefe* (Munich: Hanser Verlag, 1992), vol. 2, p. 63.

7. From what evidence we have it is likely that Aristotle disapproved of the comedy of his day, finding its attacks upon individuals and its foul language not to his liking. Curiously it seems that Plato had a deeper appreciation of comedy (see the *Philebos,* 48a–50a). Certainly many of the dialogues are comic masterpieces in their own right and exhibit a genius for lampooning those who make excessive claims to wisdom. On this question, see Gerald Else, *Aristotle's Poetics* (Cambridge, Mass.: Harvard University Press, 1967), pp. 185–95.

8. Although Freud chose to name psychological complexes after figures in ancient tragedies, it is clear that those figures themselves did not, as Aristotle notes, display their interior lives.

9. In two lengthier discussions of κάθαρσις, *Politics* 1341a21 and 1341b32ff., he suggests that κάθαρσις is discussed in greater detail in the *Poetics*.

10. See D. W. Lucas's commentary on his Greek edition of the *Poetics* (Oxford: Clarendon Press, 1968), p. 97.

11. See Martha Nussbaum, *The Fragility of Goodness* (Cambridge: Cambridge University Press, 1986), pp. 388–90, for Nussbaum's compelling arguments to this effect (henceforth cited as *FG*). See also Else, *Aristotle's Poetics*, pp.158–60, for an interesting retranslation and rethinking of the entire passage in Aristotle.

12. In the *Rhetoric* (1390a23) Aristotle distinguishes the impulse to pity in the young and the old by saying that the young feel it because they identify with others while the elderly pity because they believe that suffering is always nearby. The first form of pity is the only one capable of effecting a κάθαρσις.

13. This seems to be a tacit reply to Plato's comment in the *Phaedrus* (264c) that any discourse, like a living thing, has a body that is best composed of proportionate parts. There seems little doubt that in the *Poetics* Aristotle is responding to the presentation of tragedy in the *Phaedrus*.

14. Jean-Pierre Vernant and Pierre Vidal-Naquet, *Myth and Tragedy in Ancient Greece* (New York: Zone Books, 1990), p. 139 (henceforth cited as *MT*).

15. "Whom God wishes to destroy, He first makes mad." The source of this remark is unknown; see Ruth Padel, *Whom Gods Destroy* (Princeton: Princeton University Press, 1995), pp. 3–8 (henceforth cited as *WGD*).

16. *FG*, p. 382.

17. On the word "ἁμαρτία," see *WGD*, pp. 197–99, and *MT*, p. 62. See especially the *Nicomachean Ethics* (1135b11–25), where Aristotle distinguishes the various forms of involvement we might have in a wrongful deed. There ἁμαρτία is located between simple misfortune and an outright crime. It should also be noted that Socrates uses the word when he makes the celebrated claim that "No one willingly does wrong [ἁμαρτανεῖ]." It would be interesting to think through this word in relation to the opening words of Dante's *Divine Comedy*: "In the middle of the course of life I found myself astray in a dark woods." There is a sense in which ἁμαρτία refers to a going astray, to a deviation from the proper path of action.

18. A full discussion of this point would need to draw upon the *Rhetoric* and would do well to counterpose the analysis of the elements of language in Aristotle to that found in Plato's *Cratylus*. On this, see my "Putting Oneself in Words . . . ," in *Library of Living Philosophers: Hans-Georg Gadamer*, ed. Lewis Hahn (Chicago: Open Court Press, 1995), pp. 483–95.

19. See both *FG*, p. 392, and Else, *Aristotle's Poetics*, pp. 67–73.

20. *Theaetetus*, 203b.

21. See Eric A. Havelock and Jackson P. Hershbell, *Communication Arts in the Ancient World* (New York: Hastings House, 1978), p. 31. See also *EB*, pp. 53–55.

22. An interesting parallel is found in the symbolic nature of the Arabic system of numbering that we use today. It is a system of counting that involves an intellectual operation quite different, and far more complex, than that required of the Roman numeric system.

23. Cited in Carson, "Just for the Thrill," p. 153.

24. Here it would be interesting to bring into the discussion Kant's claim that there are two different forms of "logical" hypotyposis: the schematic (which he

treats in the *Critique of Pure Reason*) and the symbolic (which he treats in the *Critique of Judgment*). The latter form is, from the perspective of the former, somewhat impertinent. See *Critique of Judgment*, paragraph 59.

25. *Rhetoric,* 1412a17.

26. *MT,* p. 113.

27. See *Rhetoric,* 1412a22.

28. *MT,* p. 120.

29. Roberto Calasso, *The Marriage of Cadmus and Harmony* (New York: Knopf, 1993), p. 334.

30. *Oedipus Rex,* line 1298. It is a line that echoes the opening of the celebrated choral ode in *Antigone:* πολλὰ τὰ δεινὰ κοὐδὲν ανθρώπου δεινότερον πέλει (line 338).

31. There is an anonymous Byzantine work on comedy that bears some relationship to the *Poetics,* but just what that relationship is remains unclear. See Else, *Aristotle's Poetics,* pp. 185–95.

32. See Jacques Taminiaux, *Le théâtre des philosophes* (Grenoble: Millon, 1995), pp. 33–47.

33. Such is also the description of the funeral oration given by Nicole Loraux in *The Invention of Athens* (Cambridge, Mass.: Harvard University Press, 1986), pp. 13–14.

Dennis J. Schmidt: Selected Bibliography

Books

Lyrical and Ethical Subjects. Albany: State University of New York Press, forthcoming.
On Germans and Other Greeks. Bloomington: Indiana University Press, forthcoming.
Edited, with Günter Figal, *Die Zukunft der Hermeneutik.* Tübingen: J.C.B. Mohr (Paul Siebeck), 2000.
The Ubiquity of the Finite: Hegel, Heidegger and the Entitlements of Philosophy. Cambridge, Mass.: MIT Press, 1988.

Chapters in Edited Volumes and Journal Articles

"Socrates mit Gehstock." In *Begegnungen mit Gadamer,* ed. Günter Figal. Reclam Verlag, 2000.
"Heidegger and the Greeks: History, Catastrophe and Community." In *Heidegger toward the Turn: Essays on Work of the 1930's,* ed. James Risser. Albany: State University of New York Press, 1999.
"Was wir nicht sagen können." In *Die Zukunft der Hermeneutik,* ed. Günter Figal and Dennis J. Schmidt. Tübingen: J. C. B. Mohr (Paul Siebeck), 2000.
"On Blank Pages, Storms and Other Images of History." *Research in Phenomenology* 29 (1999).
"Gadamer." In *Companion to Continental Philosophy,* ed. Simon Critchley. Oxford: Blackwell, 1997.
"Solve et Coagula: Something Other than an Exercise in Dialectic." *Research in Phenomenology* 26 (1998).
"What We Owe the Dead." *Research in Phenomenology* 28 (1997).
"The Ordeal of the Foreign." *Philosophy Today,* ed. John D. Caputo and Debra Berghofen, 40.1 (1996).
"What We Didn't See." In *Phenomenology: Past and Future.* Duquesne: Simon Silverman Phenomenology Center of Duquesne University, 1995.

"Putting Oneself in Words . . . " In *Library of Living Philosophers,* ed. Lewis Hahn. Chicago: Open Court Press, 1995.

"Lyrical and Ethical Subjects." *Internationale Zeitschrift für Philosophie* 1 (1995).

"Can Law Survive?" *Toledo Law Review* 26.1 (1994).

"Why I Am So Happy." *Research in Phenomenology* 24 (1994).

"Toward 'Another Time.'" *Southern Journal of Philosophy* 32 (1993).

"On the Memory of Last Things." *Research in Phenomenology* (1993).

"Fission and Fusion: Gadamer, Hegel and Heidegger on History and Language." *skepteon* 1.2 (1993).

"Acoustics: Nietzsche on Words and Music." In *Dialectic and Narrative,* ed. Thomas R. Flynn and Dalia Judovitz. Albany: State University of New York Press, 1993.

"Black Milk and Blue/Bodies: Heidegger and Celan on the Politics of Language." In *Word Traces,* ed Aris Fiorettos. Baltimore: Johns Hopkins University Press, 1993.

"Changing the Subject: Heidegger, 'the' National and 'the' Epochal." *Graduate Faculty Philosophy Journal* 14.2–15.1 (1991).

"Economies of Production." In *Crises in Continental Philosophy,* ed. Arleen Dallery and Charles Scott. Albany: State University of New York Press, 1990.

"Poetry and the Political." In *Festivals of Interpretation,* ed. Kathleen Wright. Albany: State University of New York Press, 1990.

"Strangers in the Dark: On the limits of *praxis* in Heidegger." *Southern Journal of Philosophy* 28 (1989).

"Hermeneutics and the Poetic Motion." *Hermeneutics and the Poetic Motion: Translation Perspectives* 5 (1989).

"In Heidegger's Wake: Belonging to the Discourse of the Turn." *Heidegger Studies* 5 (1989).

"Circles—Hermeneutic and Otherwise." In *Writing the Future,* ed. David Wood. London: Routledge & Kegan Paul, 1988.

"The Hermeneutic Dimension of Translation." In *Translation Perspectives IV,* ed. Marilyn G. Rose. Binghamton: State University of New York, 1988.

"Kunst, Kritik und die Sprache der Philosophie." *Philosophische Rundschau* 34 (1987).

"In the Spirit of Bloch." Introduction to the translation of Ernst Bloch's *Natural Law and Human Dignity.* Cambridge, Mass.: MIT Press, 1986.

Part 2

⊹⇌◎⇋⊹

Re-Phrasing Discourse

4

The Murmur of the World

ALPHONSO LINGIS

Alphonso Lingis is, by some accounts, the quintessential phenomenologist. This is not only because of his early work on Husserl, Merleau-Ponty, and Levinas—Lingis provided beautiful translations of the latter two authors—but especially because of his realization that the call of phenomenology to return to the matter as such must be taken to mean the call *from* what is. No one has gone to further lengths to listen with pure attentiveness to this remote call and listen to the expressions of its voice that have not been coopted by the dominant philosophical and cultural paradigms of the West. In his recent work, Lingis has sought to free himself from the methods and presuppositions around which he had organized his earlier work in order to find the lucidity to address new issues and formulate concepts and methods directly out of his effort to see what had not been seen before.

Lingis is one of the few Western philosophers who has done for philosophy what Gauguin did for art. He has allowed the foreign and native to gain their own unique, untranslated expression and recognition in our language. In *Foreign Bodies,* he sought to discover the sentient and mobile body in different cultural experiences. In *Deathbound Subjectivity,* he addressed the relationship between subjectivity and mortality, traversing the philosophical landscape from Kant and Nietzsche through Husserl, Heidegger, and Levinas, while drawing from them an understanding of the rupture in the armor of the sovereign self that exposes it to alterity. His widely admired explorations of intense personal experiences in foreign places are "chronicled" in such works as *Excesses* and *Abuses.* One of his most recent works, *The Community of Those Who Have Nothing in Common,* focuses on a basis for community even after the collapse of the modern paradigm—a community in laughter and tears, eroticism, sacrifice, and heroism. His latest work, *The Imperative,* indicates a turn in Lingis's thought toward the ethical and political, though the imperatives he uncovers are not subjectivistic.

This essay by Alphonso Lingis establishes a relationship between human discursive language and the non-discursive elements in that language as well as with the sounds of the animate and inanimate world. This topic is the basis for his forthcoming book, *Dangerous Emotions,* where he criticizes the Enlightenment model of communication, reciprocal recognition, and respect.

-->==O==<--

Information and Noise

We communicate information with spoken utterances, by telephone, with tape recordings, in writing, and with printing. With these methods we communicate in the linguistic code. We also communicate information with body kinesics—with gestures, postures, facial expressions, ways of breathing, sighing, and touching one another. The communication here too uses abbreviations, signs, and conventions.

To make drawn lines into writing, we have to conform to the convention that dictates that certain strokes correspond to a certain word and notion. Even those among us with excellent manual dexterity, good training, good health, and alertness make slips in our penmanship and our typing. There are always typos in the many-times copyedited critical editions of classic authors. There is no speaking without stammerings, mispronunciations, regional accents, or dysphonias. Typing and printing are designed to eliminate the cacography, yet in every book we have seen some letters and words that are so faintly impressed that they are inferred rather than seen. Recording, and radio and television transmission, are designed to eliminate the cacophony, but there can be static, cut-offs, and jamming; there is always hyteresis, the lagging of transmission due to shifting in the electromagnetic field; and there is always background noise.

Entering into communication means extracting the message from its background noise and from the noise that is internal to the message. Communication is a struggle against interference and confusion. It is a struggle against the irrelevant and ambiguous signals which must be pushed back into the background and against the cacophony in the signals the interlocutors address to one another—the regional accents, mispronunciations, inaudible pronunciations, stammerings, coughs, ejaculations, words started and then canceled, and ungrammatical formulations—and the cacography in the graphics.

Communication and Contention

It is striking that the development of knowledge is conceived in military terms, such as *hunt, raid, strategy, battle,* and *conquest.* Yet is not knowledge developed in and for communication? When individuals shielded and armed encounter one another and make a move to communicate—extending bared hands and speaking—their violence comes to a stop. Discourse interrupts violence and words silence the clash of arms. Communication finds and establishes something in common beneath all contention.

But communication itself has been classically conceived as an agon, a contention between interlocutors. Communication takes place in discourse, that is, a dialectics of demand and response, statement and contestation, in which interlocutors oppose one another.

One sees communication as a continuation of violence but with other means. One sees in the dialectical cadence of communication, proceeding by affirmation and contestation, an interval in which each makes himself other than the other, when one sees each one speaking in order to establish the rightness of what he says. To speak in order to establish one's own rightness is to speak in order to silence the other. Yet Socrates from the beginning excluded the possibility of establishing one's own rightness. Communication is an effort to silence not the other, the interlocutor, but the outsider: the barbarian, the prosopopoeia of noise.

Michel Serres argues that there is indeed force being exercised to resist and silence another in all communication[1]—but it is not in the dialectic of demand and response, statement and contestation, in which interlocutors position themselves and differ the one from the other. What the one says may oppose—question, deny, or contradict—what the other says; but in formulating opposing statements that respond to one another, interlocutors do not entrench themselves in reciprocal exclusion. For speaker and auditor exchange their roles in dialogue with a certain rhythm; the source becomes reception, and the reception, the source; the other becomes but a variant of the same.[2] Discussion is not strife; it turns confrontation into interchange.

However, when two individuals renounce violence and set out to communicate, they enter into a relation of non-communication and violence with outsiders. There could well be, and in fact always is, an outsider or outsiders who have an interest in preventing communication. Every conversation between individuals is subversive—subversive of some established order, some established set of values, or some vested interests. There is always an enemy, a big brother, listening in on all our conversations, and that is why we talk quietly behind closed doors. There is nothing you or I say to one another in conversation that we would say if the television cameras were focused on us for direct broadcast.

There are outsiders who have an interest in preventing *this* rather than *that* from being communicated; they do so by arguing for that, by presenting it in seductive and captivating ways, or by filling the time and the space with it. There are outsiders who have an interest in preventing us from communicating at all. They do so by filling the time and the space with irrelevant and conflicting messages, with noise.

Formerly the street walls of buildings were blind, without windows; anyone who came to speak had to ring a bell and tell his name. Today the street walls of buildings are screens upon which messages written in neon flashes—irrelevant and conflicting messages which are not received and responded to but which agitate and merge into images that dazzle, inveigle, and excite the consumer frenzy of contemporary life. The roads and the paths to the furthest retreats in the country are lined with wires tense with stock exchange pandemonium; beams bounced off satellites in outer space penetrate all the walls.

The walls we have to erect about ourselves are immaterial walls, the walls of an idiolect whose terms and turns of phrase are not in the dictionary and the manuals of rhetoric. Not only the talk of lovers, but every conversation that is resumed again and again becomes, over time, incomprehensible to outsiders. There is secrecy in every conversation. In the measure that this wall of secrecy gets thinner, we more and more utter but current opinions, conventional formulas, and inconsequential judgments. Heidegger quite missed that; it is the big and little Hitlers lurking in every hallway, every classroom, and every bar where we went to relax and get our minds off things that produce *das Gerede*—"talk."

There are also allies—outsiders who have an interest in promoting the communication between us. The company wants the section members to communicate with one another; in disputes the police want us to try to communicate with our neighbors before calling them. Even authoritarian governments want their citizens to communicate at least their fears and resignation to one another.

When we cannot communicate, we appeal to outsiders to help. We enroll in classes to learn from professors mastery of the established forms of discourse and the state of the current debate so as to be able to communicate our insights effectively. We appeal to the scientific community, its established vocabulary and rhetorical forms, in trying to communicate with fellow scientists from Japan or agricultural workers in Africa. Descartes, having established the existence of his own mind and his own thoughts, then appeals to the great outsider, God, before he moves on to consider the existence of other minds and the possibility of communicating with them.

In making philosophy not the imparting of a doctrine but the clarification of terms, Socrates, like analytic philosophers, like recent pragmatic philosophers, makes philosophy a facilitator of communication. Socrates, who evolved from soldier to philosopher in the service of the community, struggled against the babble and the barbarian who is the real enemy of truth. But Michel Serres interprets the Socratic effort in such a way as to make the elimination of noise, in the rational community, a struggle against the rumble of the world and to make the struggle against the outsider a struggle against the empiricist.

The Signified, the Signifier, the Referent

To communicate is to take an emitted signal to mean the same to the speaker and to the auditor. And it is to take an emitted signal to mean the same as a signal emitted before. The meaning designated by conventional signifiers at different times and in different places is recognized to be the same; Husserl characterizes the meaning of expressions as ideal. Meanings exist, not intemporally and aspatially, but by the indefinite possibility of recurring and by the indefinite possibility of being designated by signifiers issued anywhere, anytime.

There is, in language, no first or last occurrence of a word. A word can have meaning only if it can be repeated. The words that have suffered obsolescence can still be referred to, by linguists and students of literature, and can be returned to the language; their demise is never definitive. The first time a word is constructed, if it is to be able to enter into the usages of language, it must appear as already latent in the structures and paradigms and rules of formulation of the language.

It is not only the signification but the signifier, too, that is ideal. What signals in a sound is not its particular sonorous quality as really heard but the formed sound that is taken to be ideally the same as that of other sounds uttered before and yet to be uttered. To hear sounds as words, to hear signals in the noise, is to abstract from the soprano or bass, thinness or resonance, softness or loudness, or tempo of their particular realizations and to attend only to the distinctive feature that conventionally makes the sounds distinct phonemes in the phonetic system of a particular language. The word as a signifier is already an abstraction and the product of an idealization.

Recognizing what is written involves epigraphy, a skill in separating out the ill-written features of the letters and words. The geometry class abstracts from the fact that the drawing the teacher has put on the board is only approximately a right triangle or a circle. When she draws a circle with a compass, one ignores the fact that the pencil angle shifts as she draws and the line is thicker on one side than on another. The reader systematically neglects not only the erroneous lines but also the particularities with which the letters have to be materialized. He disregards the fact that they are written in blue or black ink, or set in a Courier 10 or Courier 12 typeface. Reading is a peculiar kind of seeing that vaporizes the substrate, the hue and grain of the paper or of the computer screen, and sees the writing as will-o'-the-wisp patterns in a space disconnected from the material layout of things.

To communicate is to have practiced that dematerializing seeing that is seeing patterns as writing and that dematerializing hearing that is hearing streams of sounds as words and phrases. It is to push into the background, as noise, the particular timbre, pitch, volume, and tonal length of the words being uttered and to push into the background, as white noise, the particular color, penmanship, and typeface of the visible patterns. Communication—by words and also by conventionalized kinesic signals—depends on the common development of these skills in eliminating the inner noise in signals and in dematerializing vision and audition.

To communicate with another, one first has to have terms with which one communicates with the successive moments of one's own experience. Already to have a term which, when one pronounces it now, one takes to be the same as when one pronounced it a moment ago, is to have dematerialized the sound pattern, dematerialized a vocalization into a signifier, a word. Memory works this dematerialization. When one conveys something in words to another, how does one know that the communication is successful? Because one hears the other speaking about that experience, responding to it, and relating it to other experiences, in terms one would have used. To recognize the words of another as the words one used or would use, one departicularizes those words of their empirical particularities: their pitch, timbre, rhythm, density, and volume—their resonance. One disengages the word from its background noise and from the inner noise of its utterance. The maximal elimination of noise would produce successful communication among interlocutors themselves maximally interchangeable.

The meanings we communicate—the ways we refer to objects and situations—are abstract entities: recurrent forms. The signifiers with which we communicate are abstract, universal: ideal. But the referents, too, are abstract and idealized entities.

If we speak to another of a mountain vista, it is because that mountain landscape spoke to us; if we speak of a red, not brown, door, it is because that door emitted signals in the vibrations that made contact with our eyes. If our words, signals addressed to one another, have referents, it is because things address signals to us—or at least broadcast signals at large.

The medium teems with signals continually being broadcast from all the configurations and all the surfaces of things. To see that color of red, to pick up the signals from that door or that vista, is to constitute an enormous quantity of irrelevant and conflicting signals as background noise.

But to refer to that color of red with a word that one has used to refer to red things before and that will be used by one's interlocutor who does not see it or who sees it from his own angle of vision is to filter out a multiplicity of signals given out by this particular door in the sun and shadows of this late afternoon and received by one who happens to be standing just here. What we communicate, with the word and concept "red," is what, in this red door, can recur in other things designated by this word. The reception of signals from referents in view of communicating them is not a palpation that discerns the grain and pulp and tension with which each thing fills out the spot it so stubbornly and so exclusively occupies. It is seeing the red of the door and the gloom of the forest and the shapes of the leaves as modular patterns stamped on the unpenetrated density of things. Only this kind of leveling and undiscerning perception, Serres argues, could be communicated. "The object perceived," he complains, "is indefinitely discernible: there would have to be a different word for every circle, for every symbol, for every tree, and for every pigeon; a different word for yesterday, today, and tomorrow; and a different word according to whether he who perceives it is you or I, according to whether one of the two of us is angry, is jaundiced, and so on *ad infinitum*."[3] To communicate is to consign to noise the teeming flood of signals emitted by what is particular, perspectival, and distinctive in each thing.

To abstract from the noise of the world is to be a rationalist. The first effort at communication already begins the dematerialization that thought will pursue. The effort to render a form independent of its empirical realizations issues in the constitution of the universal, the scientific, the mathematical.

The City Maximally Purged of Noise

We face one another to emit signals that can be received, recognized, and reiterated, while about us extends the humming, buzzing, murmuring, crackling, and roaring world. Our interlocutor receives the information by not harkening to the pitch, volume, accent, and buzz of our sounds, and attending only to the recognizable, repeatable form, consigning the singular sonority of our voice and sentence to noise internal to the message. And he turns to the thing, situation, or event referred to by our message as a recurrent and abstract entity, not as the singular vibrant density sunk in the morass of the world and emitting its particular signals, static, and noise. The practice of abstraction from the empirical implantation of things is what brings about communication. To eliminate the noise is to have successfully received the message. To communicate it is to reissue the abstract form. The abstract is maintained and subsists in the medium of communication.

The community that forms in communicating is an alliance of interlocutors who are on the same side, who are not each Other for each other but all variants of the Same, tied together by the mutual interest of forcing back the tide of noise pollution.

The Socratic effort to communicate with strangers is, in reality, the effort not to rationally certify the existing Athenian republic but to found an ideal republic of universal communication—a city maximally purged of noise.[4] It is an effort to found a scientific and mathematical discourse and to silence the rumble of the world. In constructing an objective representation of nature out of abstract mathematical entities, one produces a community in quasi-perfect communication, a transparent Rousseauian community where what is formulated in the mind of each is what is also formulated in the minds of the others. That community would be imminent today, as all information becomes digitally coded and transmitted by satellite in the silences of outer space.

But is it really true that universal, abstract, objective, scientific discourse is departicularized and is the discourse of anyone? It can't be just accidental that to do philosophy is to compose one's own philosophy, a philosophy that will decompose with one. "If philosophy is autobiographical, in a sense that science is not . . . ," I was saying, when a philosopher of science interrupted me to refuse the distinction. "It is fatuous to say that if Einstein did not invent the special theory of relativity, someone else would have," she objected. "Everybody now understands that the data he was working with and the theories he was trying to integrate could be formulated and integrated in any number of different, imaginable and so far unimaginable, ways. If Einstein had not slipped out in time from Nazi Germany, there is every reason to think we would never have the special theory of relativity." The term "electricity" has a different sense for a television repairman than for an electrical engineer working on urban power generators or on cat-scan equipment, but also for a meteorologist, a solid-state physicist, or an astronomer. Its meaning is different in each laboratory; the different models and paradigms with which any scientist works spread a different array of paths about the movement of his terms. It is not only the new hypotheses posited and new experiments devised that generate new conceptions; when a scientist reads the work of another scientist, the terms may generate a different movement in the paths of the conceptual operations of the reader than they had in those of the writer.

Is not, then, the ideal of the kind of maximally unequivocal transmission of messages in the industry of a social space maximally purged of noise that Serres invokes another idol of the marketplace—idol of the communication theory (devised for the service of our military-industrial complex)?

Serres's argument leads him to identify, as noise, the whole of the empirical as such. "To isolate an ideal form is to render it independent of the empirical domain and of noise. Noise is the empirical portion of the message just as the empirical domain is the noise of form."[5] "The 'third man' to exclude," Serres now concludes, "is the empiricist, along with his empirical domain. . . . [I]n order for dialogue to be possible, one must close one's eyes and cover one's ears to the song and the beauty of the sirens. In a single blow, we eliminate hearing and noise, vision and failed drawing; in a single blow, we conceive the form and we understand each other."[6]

Rationalists—mathematicians, scientists, and the miraculous Greeks—eliminate the signals emitted by the particularities of empirical particulars and transmit only the abstract idealities; empiricists pick up all the static being emitted by the particularities of empirical realities and use different words for every circle and every pigeon, for the circles and pigeons others see from their perspectival points of view, and for circles and pigeons perceived with jaundiced eyes or the feline eyes of carnivorous interlocutors. They are Evil Geniuses of interference butting into every effort at communicating an unequivocal information-bit from one to the other. "The more [empiricists] are right, the less we can hear them; they end up only making noise."[7]

Empiricists are the demons that rule the world. But one cannot progressively assimilate more and more of these ephemeral proper names for the signals of the world; one has to struggle against them. The only solution is to say, with Leibniz against Locke, that "empiricism would always be correct if mathematics did not exist."[8] The community that establishes communication has to take its existence as proof of its validity. The only solution is to "not *want* to listen to Protagoras and Callicles—because they are right." This, Serres writes, "is not an *ad hominem* argument; it is the only logical defense possible."[9] The community we must want must not want to hear the glossolalia of nonhuman things—the humming, buzzing, murmuring, crackling, and roaring of the world, must not want to hear the stammerings, quaverings, dronings of one another's voices, and must want its hearing perfectly adjusted to hear the mathematics relayed by satellites in outer space.

What an extraordinary outcome of the ancient Socratic philosophy of dialogue completed now in a contemporary theory of communication! The struggle for the establishment of transparent intersubjectivity is a battle against the relayers of the signals of the world. Communication depends on, is the other side of, non-communication—a *wanting* to not communicate and an active battle to silence the empiricist demons. The only logical defense of rationality and logic is the active and combative will to not listen to Protagoras and Callicles—because they are right!

The Encounter with the Other

Serres conceives of communication as an exchange of expressions that have the same informative value for the receiver as for the emitter, expressions whose value reduces to exchange-value. Expressions that would discern what differentiates one circle from another; one symbol, tree, or pigeon from another; one yesterday, today, or tomorrow from another; or your angry or jaundiced perception from mine, have no communicative value. Serres then conceives of interlocutors as emitters and receptors which interchange their functions. In the measure that what was received was what was emitted and that what was communicated was the abstract, departicularized message, each partner in conversation becomes the same for the other: the auditor becoming speaker of what he heard and the receptor source of what he received.

Serres argues that in a dialogue, the two interlocutors are "in no way opposed"[10] but are variants of each other, are variants of the Same, because the questioner and the respondent exchange their reciprocal roles, with the source becoming reception and the reception source, "according to a given rhythm." But does not this rhythm oppose them? Is it not the time-gap between emission of the signal and its reception that opens up the space of hyteresis where the interferences and the misconstructions enter? In the ideal republic that Serres invokes—the city of communication maximally purged of noise—would not the emission and reception have to be simultaneous? The less time involved in the communication means the less thermodynamic energy involved and the less entropy. Two modems, transmitting and receiving information-bits simultaneously, would be the model.

But to affirm something is not simply to make oneself the momentary source of a formulation whose abstractness makes it equivalent of what any interlocutor does or can issue and receive; it is to present something to someone for his judgment, his confirmation or contestation. To set oneself forth as a subject of discourse is to expose oneself to being contested and discredited. To make oneself a subject in discourse is to subject oneself to another. Already, to greet someone is to recognize his or her right over one.

To question someone is not simply to make oneself a receptor for information which one will soon reissue; it is to appeal to another for what is not available to oneself. To address a query or even a greeting to another is to expose one's ignorance, one's lacks, and one's destitution and is to appeal for assistance to one non-symmetrical with oneself.

To address someone is not simply to address a source of information; it is to address one who will answer and answer for his or her answer. The time delay, between statement and response, is the time in which the other, while fully present there before one, withdraws into the fourth dimension—reaffirming his or her otherness, rising up behind whatever he presents of himself, and rising up ever beyond whatever I represent of her and present to her—to contest it or to confirm it.

To enter into conversation with another is to lay down one's arms and one's defenses; to throw open the gates of one's own positions; to expose oneself to the other, the outsider; and to lay oneself open to surprises, contestation, and inculpation. It is to risk what one found or produced in common. To enter into conversation is to struggle against the noise, the interference, and the vested interests, the big brothers and the little Hitlers always listening in—in order to expose oneself to the alien, the Balinese and the Aztec, the victims and the excluded, the Palestinians and the Quechuas and the Crow Indians, the dreamers, the mystics, the mad, the tortured, and the birds and the frogs. One enters into conversation in order to become an other for the other.

The Noise in the Message

We are necessary as efficient causes of new sentences, producers of new information formulated with old words. But in our particularities, our perspectival points of view, and our distinctive capacities to issue and to receive meanings, we are part of the noise. The time it takes to formulate those sentences is a time filled with the opacity of our own voices. How transparent communication might be if there were not resistance in the channels that conduct it: no lilting, bombastic, stammering voice pronouncing it!

Yet is there not also a communication in the hearing of the noise in one another's voices—the noise of one another's life that accompanies the harkening to the message? What kind of communication would that be?

The particular, the material, the empirical, Serres says, is indefinitely discernible. It is a succession of signals, each with its own name, in a static that cannot be recorded or reproduced. Yet surely every day we do succeed in communicating to one another, not only the abstract formula of an insight, but the unique spell of the encounter with an early-winter afternoon, the charm of something someone said that was never before said, or the weirdness of a feeling never before felt. Language is the amazing power to say, with a limited number of words and grammatical structures, sentences never before said that formulate events that have never before occurred.

Every new sentence that succeeds in saying something does so, Merleau-Ponty said, by a coherent deformation of the sentence paradigms already in the language. Every new sentence also continues the bending, extending, and deforming of the code. "Let us agree," Serres writes, "that . . . communication is only possible between two persons used to the same . . . forms, trained to code and decode a meaning by using the same key."[11] But when an American, brought up on Indian legends, says to an Englishman, brought up on legends of imperial conquerors, "He's brave . . . ," they do not have the same key to this word. If, nonetheless, the one understands the other, it is by improvising the key as one goes along.

Is it not also false to suppose that only the meaning attached to words by a code, fixed or evolving, communicates? The rhythm, the tone, the periodicity, the stammerings, and the silences communicate. In the rush of the breathless voice, the tumult of events is conveyed; in the heavy silence that weighs on the voice, the oppressive tedium of a place is communicated. "'Prove it,' demands the logocentric system that the art historian worships. 'Prove that you still love me. . . .'" Joanna Frueh, performance art critic, is saying it in different intonations, volumes, and crescendos—sparring with the voice of the academic demand and circling around the male: "Prove it. . . . *Prove* that you still love me. . . ." "Prove that you still *love* me. . . ."

The noise of our throats that fills the time it takes to convey the message communicates the noise of the things or makes the things discernible in their empirical plurality. By the utterance of every insight we have into an empirical particular—a particular circle, tree, or pigeon we contemplated yesterday when we were angry or jaundiced—breaking into the universal circulation of passwords, watchwords, and orders; by singling out a particular interlocutor; and by interrupting the narrative or the explanation with an intonation, an attack and cadence, or with the redundancies that blur and interjections that wail, bray, or strike speechless; we do succeed in communicating the differentiation, the plurality of facets and of perspectives and the indefinite discernibility of empirical particulars. Anyone who thinks we are only emitting noise is one who does not *want* to listen.

The one who understands is not extracting the abstract form out of the tone, the rhythm, and the cadences—the noise internal to the utterance, the cacophony internal to the emission of the message. He or she is also listening to that internal noise—the rasping or smoldering breath, the hyperventilating or somnolent lungs, the rumblings and internal echoes—in which the message is particularized and materialized and in which the empirical reality of something indefinitely discernible, encountered in the path of one's own life, is referred to and communicated.

With this internal noise it is the other, in his or her materiality, that stands forth and stands apart making appeals and demands. The other is not simply the recurrent function of appealing to and contesting me; he or she is an empirically discernible vulnerability and intrusion. In *Visage* Luciano Berio composed not with words but with the sonorous elements with which words are formed—the sighs, gasps, waverings, dronings, hissings, sobs, giggles, whimperings, snivelings, screams, snortings, purrings, mutterings, and moanings—out of which, sometimes, words are shaped. He plunged them into a vast space in which electronic sounds hum, pound, sing, scatter, dissipate and where, finally, the roar of machines drowns out the human voice. In them, Cathy Berberian exposes herself more than her intentions and judgments could have revealed—exposes her sensibility, her susceptibility, her mortality, and the flux and scope of her carnal existence.

As efficient causes of expressions that convey information, we are interchangeable. Our singularity and our indefinite discernibility are found in, and are heard in, our outcries and our murmurs, our laughter and our tears: the noise of life.

The Background Noise

If the neo-Socratic communication theory of Michel Serres has not understood—has not *wanted* to understand—the noise internal to communication: the pulse and the wobble, the opacity of the timber and density of the voice, the noise of life, the noise each of us is in his or her particularity; it has also not understood—has not *wanted* to understand—the background noise in the midst of which we speak.

Advances in soundproofing technologies and digital recording promise the complete elimination of background noise. Sensory-deprivation tanks were first invented in the '60s, by Johy Lilly, who was working with dolphins and, like every diver, loved the silence and the bliss of deep-sea diving and thought to duplicate it on land. But the technology that eliminates the noise also eliminates the communication. In the absence of auditory, visual, and tactual background signals, one no longer senses the boundaries between outside and inside, past and present, perception and images, and one soon hallucinates. If the reception of a determinate signal is impossible beyond a certain level of background noise, the intention to emit a determinate signal becomes unrealizable without a certain level of ambient drone to escalate, punctuate, and redirect. Recorded white noise—forest murmurs, the rumble of the city—was added to space capsules; the recordings are sold to terrestrials living in soundproofed apartments.

We understand that background noise is essential to communication when we understand that reception in the communication system of our bodies is not the passive exposing of a preprogrammed surface of sensibility to outside stimuli but picking a signal out of the multiplicity of irrelevant and conflicting signals. Where the receptor organ can receive a wide variety of signals, perception is the active power to focus in on, isolate, segregate, shape a figure, and reduce the rest to indifferentiation. If, each time we look, we see a figure standing out against the adjacent objects, this is not due to the physical stimulation that is being spread across our retinas; it must be due to an active power in our gaze. Since communication is, for the receiver, actively separating a figure from the background, then in the absence of the background there can be no figure either. If one looks into a closed, elliptically shaped box painted black and uniformly illuminated with white light, one cannot see the black and cannot see the surfaces at all; all one sees is a luminous gray density. But if one then sticks a white strip of paper on the wall of that box, suddenly the light becomes transparent and the hue of the medium recedes and condenses into black on the walls of the box. When the psychologist seats a subject in a room such that he sees only the homogeneous surface of a broad wall uniformly illuminated, the subject cannot see how far it is from him, cannot see any surface at all, sees only a medium in depth about him, and cannot say what color it is. John Cage once emerged from a soundproof room to declare that there was no such state as silence. In that room he heard the rustling, throbbing, whooshing, buzzings, ringings, and squeakings with which the movements of his muscles and glands resounded with the ripples and rumbles of the never-ending movements of the atmosphere.

If the reception of a determinate signal is the segregation of a sonorous field into figure and background drone, the emission of a determinate signal forms in the hum of the field. Communication theory identifies the background hum as a multitude of irrelevant or conflicting signals. To designate it, thus, as noise is to conceive it from the point of view of the individual teleologically destined to citizenship in an ideal republic maximally purged of the noise of life and of the empirical domain—the miraculous Greece or the totally transparent Rousseauist society. We shall conceive a different understanding of the background noise if we put vocalization among us in the perspective of evolutionary biology.

One day, while trying to drive in the chaotic traffic of Teheran, with each move I tried to make provoking taps on the horns of cars beside, behind, and advancing toward me, I remarked to a hitchhiker I had picked up that after five blocks of this I felt like a road lizard on bad amphetamines. Oh, they are not, like we Westerners, using the horn as a warning or a threat, he said. They are like quail clucking as they feed on a ripe wheat field. They are, he meant, creating a sound environment with which they symbiotically merge with one another. I understood at once, because my mind flashed back to the long nights I had driven across Turkey and Iran when the next town proved to take, not the hour I had calculated, but six hours due to the devastated condition of the road and the flooded rivers, and how I had thought that night driving in a car is the absolute form of hermitage that civilization had finally invented. When you are alone in the middle of the night in a hotel room in an alien country, you cannot moan out your loneliness and misery without someone hearing you on the other side of the wall; but if you are driving nights on the highway you can scream and none of the cars crossing you in the opposite lane will hear anything. When I drive distances at night, I, like Simeon Stylites on his pillar in the Syrian deserts, invariably fall into the same extremist spiritual exercises revolving around the theme *Memento mori,* reviewing the meaning or meaningless of my life in the cosmic voids ahead. With the tappings of the horns, the yearnings or outcries of solitude penetrate the hull of roar with which one's car encases its motion, and merge and become common.

When one lives with birds one sees how the noise level of the birds keeps up with the noise level of the house, with the wind that begins to whisper and whistle across the sidings, with each notch up you turn the volume dial on your record player. It is the rumble and rasping of the inert things that provokes the vocalization of the animals; fish hum with the streams and birds chatter in the crackling of the windy forest. To live is to echo the vibrancy of things. To be, for material things, is to resonate. There is sound in things like there is warmth and cold in things, and things resonate like they irradiate their warmth or their cold. The quail and the albatross, the crows and the hummingbirds, the coyotes and the seals, the schooling fish and the great whales, the crocodiles infrasonically and the praying mantises ultrasonically continue and reverberate the creaking of the branches, the fluttering of the leaves, the bubbling of the creeks, the hissing of the marsh gasses, the whirring of the winds, the shifting of the rocks, the grinding of the earth's continental plates.

This noise is not analytically decomposable, as communication theory would have it, into a multiplicity of signals, information-bits, that are irrelevant or that conflict: that become, in Serres's word, *equivocal*. The noise figures as resonance and vocalization that, like the scraping wings of crickets we hear, contains no message.[12] Olivier Messiaen, in his *Chronochromie*, did not compose into music, into rhythm and harmony and melody, the enormous quantity of signals being emitted by the birds of the jungle that he had in his vast collection of tapes of bird cries; we hear in *Chronochromie* the sounds of metals—cymbals, bells, blocks, pipes, and rasps; woods—mahoganies, oaks, and bamboos; hides—cords and drums; fibers—whisks; and strings, gums, and fluids transforming into the wild exultant racket of multitudes of feathered and flying things. And as we listen, it transforms again into our own sounds.

For we too communicate what we communicate with the background noise, and we communicate the background noise. The communication takes place when the vibrancy of the land, the oceans, and the skies is taken up, condensed, and unfurled in the hollows of one's own body, then released, and when one hears its echo returning with the wind and the sea.

In the highlands of Irian Jaya it seemed that no matter how late it was at night, there was always someone who could not sleep and who spent his insomnia singing and drumming. "Are they preparing a ceremony or feast?" I asked a missionary with whom I had taken shelter and who was keeping me up for Christmas midnight mass. "No," he answered. "It goes on every night. In fact they are afraid of the night. They are like children," he said, with the weariness of his years. But their vocalizations did not sound to me to be issuing out of breasts where fear trembled. It seemed to me that their chants and yodelings picked up and reverberated sounds their own throats made, sounds other throats made, sounds the marshes and the birds of the night and the winds were making. J. M. G. Le Clézio lived long among the Indians in the Chiapas in Mexico and in Panama; to live among them is to live in the days and nights of their music: music made with bamboo tubes, perforated pipes, drums, shells, rattles, and also with a taut falsetto use of the voice, the throat having become a flute or whistle. Le Clézio heard it in the midst of the din of the rain forest: in the barking of dogs, the cries of the spider monkeys, the agoutis, the hawks, the jaguars, and in the vocalization of the frogs which fills the whole length of every night in the rain forest. It seemed to him that any musicologist who just studied the tapes of Indian music in the laboratories filled with synthesizers in Paris or Frankfurt would inevitably connect the specific scales, pitches, rhythms, and phrasings of Indian music with cultural values and conventions, and would try to connect it with their myths and tragic cultural history. But theirs is a music made of cries and chants without melody or harmony, a music not made for dancing or pleasing; it is a music with which they see, hear, and feel in the anesthesia of the night. "Melodious music is first the conviction that time is fluid, that events recur, and that there is what we call 'meaning.'" But "for the Indian, music has no meaning. It has no duration. It has no beginning, no end, no climax."[13] Words are prisons in which the breath of life is imprisoned in human form; in a music without melody and without meaning, the Indian hears the animal, vegetable, mineral, and demonic realms. One had to listen to it there, in the nights of the Lacandon rain forest, to understand that this "music" is not an aesthetic production, that is, a creation of human subjectivities attempting to communicate immanent states like moods, feelings, values, or messages to other human subjectivities. It is a prolongation of the forest murmurs, the whispering sands, and the hum of the heavenly bodies.

Separated from the vocalizations, rumblings, creakings, and whirrings of animate and inanimate nature, music becomes a means of communicating between humans only. Words can be added to it, speaking of the loneliness of individuals overcome through human love. But this communication in a city maximally purged of noise is a recent creation. A friend recently played for me, on his state-of-the-art equipment, a CD of the only complete recording of the Balinese Kechak. Listening to it, I was at once astonished and mesmerized by the purity, transparency, and beauty of the digitally recorded and cleansed sounds. But after a few moments, I began to think of how abstract it was; one was hearing only a tonal mapping of the Kechak, like reading the score of a concerto for harp without hearing the tinkling crescendos or seeing the elegant and aristocratic figure of the harpist seated there in the baroque concert hall of old Prague. I had never succeeded in doing anything but irritate anyone who was riding in my car while I had Balinese or Javanese music on the tape player in the car, and I would apologetically explain that, in fact, I had myself come to be so captivated by this music because of the whole setting: drifting through the dark and wet jungle after the day's work is done; idling for an hour or two among the gossiping Balinese quite unconcerned that the players have not yet arrived two hours after they said they would; settling into the throbbing of the frogs and night insects; seating myself on the ground as the circle of seated men expanded and the priest lit the torches that awaken the monstrous figures of the demons that guard the temple compound while the incense stirs the spirits that slumber in the flowering trees and vines, and the glistening bare bodies of the men massed on the ground began to sway as the trance spreads among them, the trance ancient as the sea, then abruptly their animal outcries greeting the apparition of the gods weaving among them: dancing gods, bound in exquisite silks and batiks, their heads crowned with delicate-stemmed flowers and smoldering sticks of incense and their jewels throwing off ruby and sapphire flash-fires. The digital recording, cleansed not only of the noise of the reproductive equipment but of the background noise of the performance, does not, I thought, reproduce perfectly the sounds of the Kechak dance; it creates music. Western civilization, which created, in the eighteenth century, the market economy and, indeed, economic activity; which created the abstract universal essence of libido; which created people as female and as male; which created the value-free objective representation of nature and history and culture; which created sculpture out of African fetishes and created paintings out of tang'kas, those cosmic diagrams and instruments for centering in meditation found in Tibetan gompas; which created art, art for art's sake, out of ritual and civic ceremonies; has now created music out of the Balinese Kechak. The Balinese, for their part, have no word in their language for art and do not listen to the music; at night in the temple compound, they rock their squalling children, nurse them, chat with neighbors, go out to get something to eat, admire and severely criticize the performance of the fellow-villager who is dancing the Rama or the Sita, fall into trance, come out of it, are transubstantiated into gods, demons, rivers, storms, and night. But, in fact, when Bach composed, rehearsed, and directed a cantata, he was not simply creating music; he was praising God, earning merit and salvation, paying for the upkeep of his twelve children, competing with Telemann and Purcell, enhancing the status of his prince-patron and his own station, and contributing to a successful Christmas feast for all the town.

The creation, in our time, of music, like every cultural creation, is an inestimable contribution to the wealth of our heritage and makes, Nietzsche would say, this old earth a sweeter place to live on. The music was produced by the electronic elimination of all the marginal, subliminal signals coming from the nonmusical sonorous medium: the chatter of the village, the people, and the history; the remote murmurs and rumblings of the gods and demons; the barking dogs and the crowing roosters prematurely awakened from their somnolence by the dawn they see flickering from the torches; the night insects and the frogs; the rustling of leaves; the clatter of the rain; the restlessness of the air currents in the night skies; and the creaking of the rock strata—the background noise.

We, too, do not vocalize and mark surfaces only because we have some message to transmit. Significant speech, utterances where one can, like

Serres, distinguish the calliphony from the cacophony, the message from the noise, is only an abstract part of speech. When grammarians and linguists analyze any text, they are astonished at how much redundancy there is in all speaking; how much of what we say to one another is repetition, chorus, murmur, and drawn-out resonance. We are no different from the celestial birds, who chime in with one another but know that it is only occasionally, in all this effervescent racket, that some information about a delectable kind of seed that got put in the dish today or some danger is being addressed to them.

You were dozing in your room and you woke, wondering what time it was. You thought, like that disheveled figure on a bed in the French cartoon that you had glued at eye view of your pillow, "Si je continue comme ça, je ne serai jamais maître du monde!" (If I keep on like this, I never will be the master of the world!). You tried to get the blood stirring and some movement started, you shuffled to the kitchen, shaking up some things on the way, making the door creak by opening it with a thrust, so as to get some movement in the dead silence of the house. You came upon your housemate sprawled torpidly on the couch, like a cold-blooded frog in mid-afternoon: "Hey, man, like, whatcha doing, huh?" Where is the information-bit? You said that to get some night sounds going, some rhythm going, some hopping about started.

It is out of and in the midst of the reverberation of ambient materiality that the utterances we make get shaped, and they get sent forth to return to it. The resonance of things animate and inanimate is in the redundancies, the drawn-out vowels and consonants, the hisses and groans and ejaculations, and the babble and mumbling and murmur that is the basso continuo of all our message-laden utterances.

Computer technology, driven by the pilot-industries of the military-industrial complex, places top priority on transmitting the message as effectively, efficiently, and effortlessly as possible. It is computer technology that shaped and forms contemporary communication theory.[14] But so little of what we say to one another makes any sense! So little of it makes any pretense to be taken seriously, so much of it is simple malarkey, in which we indulge ourselves with the same warm visceral pleasure as we indulge in belching and passing air. It really is, Nietzsche long ago pointed out, bad taste to make serious pronouncements and work out syllogistically valid arguments in civilized company. So much of language added to industry and enterprises that are programmed by the laws of nature or rational science and that operate all by themselves, so much of language added to fumblings and breakdowns and even disasters has no other function than to provoke laughter. Laughter mixing moans, howls, screams into the racket of the world. As much of what we say when we embrace we say to release our sighs and our sobs into the rains and the seas.

All these stammerings, exclamations, slurrings, murmurs, rumblings, cooings, and laughter, all this noise we make when we are together makes it possible to view us as struggling, together, to jam the unequivocal voice of the outsider: the facilitator of communication, the prosopopoeia of maximal elimination of noise, so as to hear the distant rumble of the world and its demons in the midst of the ideal city of human communication.

Notes

1. Michel Serres, "Platonic Dialogue," trans. Marilyn Sides, in *Hermes,* ed. Josué V. Harari and David F. Bell (Baltimore: Johns Hopkins University Press, 1983).
   2. Ibid., p. 67.
   3. Ibid., p. 70.
   4. Ibid., p. 68.
   5. Ibid., p. 70.
   6. Ibid.
   7. Ibid., p. 70, n. 11.
   8. Ibid., p. 70, n. 12.
   9. Ibid.
   10. Ibid., p. 67.
   11. Ibid., p. 65.
   12. Crickets communicate in the ultrasonic range, too high for human ears to hear. See Diane Ackerman, *A Natural History of the Senses* (New York: Random House, 1990), p. 195.
   13. J. M. G. Le Clézio, *Haï* (Geneva: Skira, 1971), pp. 51–52.
   14. The late works of Michel Serres are so many contributions toward a reinstated empiricism. See, among others, *Les cinq sens* (Paris: Grasset, 1985).

Alphonso Lingis: Selected Bibliography

Books

Dangerous Emotions. Berkeley: University of California Press, 2000.
The Imperative. Bloomington: Indiana University Press, 1998.
Sensation. Atlantic Highlands, N.J.: Humanities Press, 1995.
Foreign Bodies. New York: Routledge, 1994.
Abuses. Berkeley: University of California Press, 1994.
The Community of Those Who Have Nothing in Common. Bloomington: Indiana University Press, 1994.
Deathbound Subjectivity. Bloomington: Indiana University Press, 1989.
Phenomenological Explanations. Dordrecht: Martinus Nijhoff, 1986.
Libido: The French Existential Theories. Bloomington: Indiana University Press, 1985.
Excesses: Eros and Culture. Albany: State University of New York Press, 1984.

Chapters in Edited Volumes and Journal Articles

"Love Song." In *Engendering French Literature and Culture,* ed. Lawrence Schehr and Dominique Fisher. Stanford: Stanford University Press, 1996.
"Society of Dismembered Body Parts." In *Deleuze and the Theater of Philosophy,* ed. Constantin Boundas and Dorothea Olkowski. New York: Routledge, 1994.
"Bodies That Touch Us." *Thesis* 11 (1994).
"Phantom Equator." In *Merleau-Ponty, Hermeneutics and Post-Modernism,* ed. Thomas

W. Busch and Shaun Gallagher. Albany: State University of New York Press, 1992.

"The Destination." In *Eros and Iris. Contributions to a Hermeneutical Phenomenology. Liber Amicorum for Adriaan Peperzak.* Dordrecht: Kluwer Academic Publishers, 1992.

"The Incomparable." *International Studies in Philosophy* 23.2 (1991).

"Imperatives." In *Merleau-Ponty Vivant,* ed. M. C. Dillon. Albany: State University of New York Press, 1991.

"Painted Faces." *Art and Text* 27 (1989).

"The Elemental Imperative." *Journal of Research and Phenomenology* 18 (1988).

"Substitution." In *Postmodernism and Continental Philosophy,* ed. Hugh J. Silverman and Donn Welton. Albany: State University of New York Press, 1988.

"The Din of the Celestial Birds, or, Why I Crave to Become a Woman." In *Psychosis and Sexual Identity,* ed. David Allison et al. Albany: State University of New York Press, 1988.

"Mastery in Eternal Recurrence." In *Analecta Husserliana,* vol. 21, ed. A. T. Tymieniecka. Dordrecht: Reidel, 1986.

"The Visible and the Vision." *Journal of the British Society for Phenomenology* 196.2 (1984).

"Oedipus Rex: The Oedipus Rule and Its Subversion." *Human Studies* 7 (1984).

"Theory and Idealization in Nietzsche." In *The Great Year of Zarathustra (1881–1981),* ed. David Goicoechea. Lanham, Md.: University Press of America, 1983.

"The Fatality of Consciousness." *Philosophy Today* 27.3–4 (1983).

"Intuition of Freedom, Intuition of Law." *Journal of Philosophy* 73.10 (1982).

"Sensations." *Philosophy and Phenomenological Research* 42.2 (1981).

"The Imperative to Be Master." *Southwestern Journal of Philosophy* 11.2 (1980).

"The Perception of Others." *Philosophical Forum* 5.3 (1974).

"Intentionality and Corporeity." In *Analecta Husserliana,* vol. 2, ed. A. T. Tymieniecka. Dordrecht: Reidel, 1970.

5

Transversal Rationality

CALVIN O. SCHRAG

Calvin Schrag has had a continuing interest in issues surrounding the topic of the being and behavior of the human subject—issues that are routinely discussed in the areas of philosophical anthropology and philosophy of mind—from the time of his first publication, *Existence and Freedom*, to his most recent work, *The Self after Postmodernity*. For him these issues have always been entwined with related issues in cognate disciplines. These have to do with matters concerning historical understanding, social structures and dynamics, and the contribution of the human sciences to the achievement of self-knowledge. His publications *Radical Reflection and the Origin of the Human Sciences* and *Communicative Praxis and the Space of Subjectivity* addressed certain dimensions of these larger issues. Throughout all of his works, the issues of the resources of reason in the odyssey of self and social understanding are a recurring concern. He gave this issue concentrated and critical attention in one of his later works, *The Resources of Rationality: A Response to the Postmodern Challenge*.

It can be said that, in general, the trajectory of Schrag's work has been toward establishing a continuing and critical dialogue with the main philosophical trends and movements that define twentieth-century continental philosophy. He has given studied attention to some of the stalwarts in continental philosophy, beginning with his 1957 study of Heidegger and Kierkegaard in his doctoral dissertation at Harvard and continuing through the subsequent decades with critical examinations of the contributions of Husserl, Sartre, Merleau-Ponty, Gadamer, Habermas, Ricoeur, and more recently members of the deconstruction-postmodernist field, including Foucault, Lyotard, Deleuze, Derrida, and Levinas. He has had intermittent dialogues with philosophers in the Anglo-American tradition, particularly with those associated with the Ordinary Language School. His book *The Self after Postmodernity* was initially presented as the 1995 Gilbert Ryle Lectures at Trent University in Ontario, Canada.

His discussion of "Transversal Rationality" from *The Resources of Rationality* is eminently appropriate for this volume. It provides a sum-mary of his entire work: the interrelated issues of understanding, explanation, reflection, and rationality were issues that for him simply did not go away. Here he offers a comprehensive and sustained analysis of the range and limitations of human reason. This is accomplished against the backdrop of the often volatile debate on modernism versus postmodernism. His argument shows how to split the difference between the modernists' indefensible claims for a reasoning that is able to deliver universal criteria and principles and the postmodernists' rejection of reason because of the fractitious particularity and plurality of concepts and social practices. Transversal reason is able to effect a passage between claims for unchanging and over-arching universals and an anti-reason that courts out and out relativism. Schrag argues that a transversal *logos* keeps our diverse discourses and social practices from succumbing to a chaos of unmanageable particularities.

⫸═◉═⫷

Transversality across the Disciplines

Transversality has appeared on the scene as a recurring figuration of thought across the disciplines for some time. The notion has achieved a rather wide currency among the various disciplinary matrices that make up the academy of the arts and sciences. Mathematicians define transversality as a generalization of orthogonality, enabling a line to intersect two or more lines or surfaces without achieving coincidence. Physiology employs the grammar of transversality in describing the networking of bands of fibers. In anatomy the term is used to define the lateral movements of vertebrae. Physicists make use of the concept of transverse mass in working out the ratio of accelerating forces. In philosophy the concept of transversality has been used to describe the dynamics of consciousness and the interplay of social practices.

Surveying the polysemic figuration of transversality across the disciplines, one is confronted with a plethora of senses that seem to shift as one moves from one discipline to the next. Proceeding in awareness that the meaning of a term resides in its use, one is nonetheless tempted to search for family resemblances that might become visible in its multi-disciplinary usages. Any such search, however, needs to proceed with a high degree of caution. The particularities of the disciplinary practices that guide the sense of transversality should not be glossed over. Yet, it is surely of some consequence that we are here dealing with a grammatical figure and concept that enables us to approach a variety of subject matters, including the topology of lines and surfaces, forces of acceleration, the interweaving of fibers, movements of vertebrae, the dynamics of consciousness, and the interplay of social practices. The use of the concept/metaphor of transversality in all of these approaches exhibits interrelated senses of lying across, extending over, intersecting, meeting and converging without achieving coincidence. By way of complex maneuvers of borrowing and conjugation, metaphorical play and refiguration, the various disciplines make use of these interrelated senses ensconced within transversality to understand and explain geometrical space, events of nature, anatomical structures, physiological processes, human behavior, and cultural and historical configurations. It is thus that transversality, most generally construed, provides a window to the wider world of thought and action.

However, as is the case with all such windows, one is afforded only perspectives on a changing scene. It is thus that certain tendencies in the employment of the vocabulary of transversality need to be resisted. Chief among these tendencies is the rationalistic impulse to sublate the several usages in the various disciplines into a higher concept that totalizes the different faculties of knowledge into a seamless unity viewed from above, as well as the positivistic impulse to determine a usage that is somehow paradigmatic and normative for all the rest, inviting a hegemonic "unity of the sciences" seen from below. A vigilance over the imperialism of a concept or a metaphor, be it that of transversality or some other, needs to be strictly maintained. The task is to discern how the use of each concept or metaphor plays in its own court, without sublation and without reduction. Only then will genuine communication across the disciplines become possible.

Our principal concern is with the use of transversality in the discipline of philosophy, and particularly with regard to its utility for advancing an understanding of the dynamics of reason. In probing its philosophical capital, we of course do not stand at the beginning. Transversality as a figure of philosophical discourse has already made its debut. So we pick up on a story that has already been told; however, we propose to retell this story in such a manner that its pivotal character, its leading figure, undergoes a refiguration.

The story of transversality as a philosophical concept in modernism is an account that links transversality with a subject-centered philosophy of consciousness. The plot of this story has been prominently illustrated in Sartre's appropriation of transversality in his effort to solve the problem of the unity of consciousness. The problem is one that he inherits from Husserl. He proposes to solve it, however, without Husserl's appeal to a transcendental ego wherewith to ground the unity of consciousness. Sartre's position contra Husserl on this issue is well known. The unity of consciousness, according to Sartre, is secured not by way of anchoring it in a transcendental and identical pole of consciousness, residing in the depths of the cogito, but is seen rather as the result of a constituting act of consciousness. A result rather than a given, a product of consciousness rather than a necessary condition within consciousness, unity is an achievement of a performative intentionality. Consciousness, which for Sartre is from bottom up intentional, unifies itself through its own resources by dint of transversal relays that bind present consciousness with its past. Thus, Sartre is able to speak of a "consciousness which unifies itself, concretely, by a play of 'transversal' intentionalities which are concrete and real retentions of past consciousness."[1] Through a species of self-reflexivity, consciousness achieves a bonding with itself by reclaiming the consciousness that it has been through a remembrance of things past. Consciousness comes to a stand, as it were, through an interweaving of the lines of psychic forces that lie across its retentional span.

The philosophical use of the grammar of transversality by Sartre to account for the unification of consciousness may indeed have its own rewards within the limitations of his project, namely, that of providing an internal critique of Husserl's theory of consciousness. But it is precisely the limitations of Sartre's project that require attention, for it is these limitations that have certain consequences for an employment of the concept of transversality. Sartre engineers an internal critique of Husserl's egological concept of consciousness, demonstrating, in a rather imaginative manner to be sure, that the transcendental ego has no clothes. But he stays with the Husserlian project of designing a philosophy of subjectivity that moves out from the primacy of consciousness. In this regard both Sartre and Husserl remain with the programmatics of modernism. They proceed from the postulate of an originating consciousness and seek to render an account of its dealings and contents. In the case of Husserl, this account follows the route of a transcendental and egological turn. Sartre maneuvers his way about sans the services either of transcendental reductions or egological postulates. He sketches instead an "existentialist theory of consciousness." Nonetheless, both Sartre and Husserl proceed from the primacy of consciousness as center and origin. This defines their shared phenomenological prejudice.

Although we stand ready to acknowledge the contribution of postmodernism in its critique of the foundationalist philosophies of subjectivity and consciousness that have been so much a part of the mind-set of modernism, and although we have jettisoned a subject-centered approach to the claims of reason, we are not lobbying for a deletion of the vocabulary of subject and consciousness. A displacement of the sovereignty of the subject, and its consciousness-centered rationality, does not entail a dissolution of the subject and consciousness in every manner conceivable. It may well be problematic to begin with the subject, either as an epistemological and self-reflecting subject or as an existentially isolated self. Yet one still has to end with the subject, duly decentered and refigured. Our topography of communicative praxis enables us to effect such a decentering without loss of either the speaking or the acting subject. The subject finds a new space as an emergent within the dynamics of discursive and institutional practices. Although we are sympathetic with the postmodern problematization of subject-centered philosophy, we are concerned about the failure of nerve in postmodernism to acknowledge the weight of tradition and the background of communicative practices against which the subject assumes a new posture.[2]

There is a further limitation in Sartre's use of transversality, a limitation that travels with his commitments to the sovereignty of the existential subject. This limitation arises from his peculiar stance on temporality, in which a primacy is conferred upon the present at the expense of devaluing the efficacy of the future. Sartre's appeal to transversal intentionality is motivated by a desire to account for the retention of past consciousness within the interstices of present consciousness. It is clear enough that the dynamics of transversal intentionality moves backwards; what is not clear from Sartre's account is how it moves forward. The protentional vector of transversality remains marginalized. Consciousness extends across its past occasions, perpetually defining the present as retentionally qualified. But there is no explicit acknowledgment of the protentional efficacy in intentionality—as there is, for example, in the thought of Heidegger and Merleau-Ponty.

Given these limitations pertaining to the figuration of transversality within a subject-centered philosophy of presence, a refiguration is required. This refiguration is governed by a shift away from a phenomenological description of consciousness as a given datum to an interpretation of the configurations of discourse and action as communicative achievements. Consequent to this shift, the principal focus is no longer on a present event of consciousness, and much less upon a belief structure that accompanies such an event, but rather upon the assemblages and patterns of discourse and action as progeny of communicative praxis. We are no longer dealing with a serial succession of moments of consciousness but rather with societal assemblages and gestalts of praxis.

The transversality of these gestalts of praxis, lying across varying forms of discourse, modes of thought, and institutional configurations, exhibits conjunctions and disjunctions, accommodations and alterations, solidifications and ruptures. Some constellations of thought and action slide into one another, occasioning mutual acknowledgment and consensus; others follow the lines of deviation and difference, occasioning agonistics and dissensus. The transverse mass of our social practices indeed comprises a multiplex phenomenon of converging and diverging gestalts. To be sure, the subject and moments of consciousness are at play in this transversal dynamics. The point, however, is that these emerge as implicates of communicative praxis and never enjoy the metaphysical and epistemological security of originating principles. The sense of transversality that is at issue for our concerns is that of a transversality socially and historically contextualized.

The social contextualization of transversality has received particular attention in Félix Guattari's explication of the workings of "transversality in the group."[3] Guattari, a practicing psychiatrist, details the performance of transversality in the institutional setting of a psychiatric hospital, providing us with a concrete illustration of the effect of the figuration of transversality across the disciplines. He employs the term to help explain the networking of the different constellations of power and seats of decision making that are involved in the psychiatric practice. The institutional setting is structured by a peculiar network of groups and subgroups, types of expertise, lines of authority, and concerned parties. There are the administrators, the doctors, the nurses, the assistants to the doctors and nurses, the patients, and the families of the patients. All of these groups play some role in the program and process of psychiatric healing. The exercise of decision making, with its multiple rationales, is transversal to the different groups and various social roles that make up the institutional complex.

The degree of transversality in operation depends upon the effectiveness of a dialogue across the various groups and sectors of concern, fostering a recognition of the otherness of each of the groups involved and leading to a "dialectical enrichment."[4] Transversality thus at once heightens the self-understanding in each of the involved groups through a mutual acknowledgment and sets the requirement for adjustments and accommodations in recognition of the contributions by the several groups. In developing self-understanding among the several groups and encouraging shared responsibility, transversality avoids both the hegemony of a decision-making process that proceeds vertically from top down and the impasse of horizontally dispersed groups warring with each other.

Guattari summarizes this transversal networking of groups as follows: "Transversality is a dimension that tries to overcome both the impasse of pure verticality and that of mere horizontality; it tends to be achieved when there is a maximum communication among the different levels and, above all, in different meanings."[5] Guattari's location of the dynamics of transversality within the heart of a praxis that informs the management of a psychiatric hospital provides us with a concrete and local exemplification of its workings. What interests us in particular about this appropriation of the figure of transversality is its alignment with the intentionality of social practices as this intentionality operates without appeals to the protocols and postulates of pure theory. Transversality falls out as a praxial accomplishment in which understanding, mutual acknowledgment, dialogic interaction, decision making, and various vectors of concern remain in play. These ingredients of communicative praxis display an indigenous intentionality of an economy of discernment, understanding, articulation, and assessment on the hither side of a priori principles, antecedently specified criteria, and predetermined methodologies. In short, it is an intentionality that operates in advance of any purchases on the holdings of the modern theoretico-epistemological paradigm and its subject-centered concept of rationality.

It is this aggressive move to transversality as an achievement of communicative praxis that places in sharp relief the limitations in Sartre's construal of transversal intentionality as a determinant of a sovereign and subject-centered consciousness. Sartre's "existentialist theory of consciousness," in spite of its warranted assault on the transcendental postulates of modern rationalism, remains at best a late-modern reaction that is unable to dispel the ghosts of a centripetal, originating consciousness.

The grammar of transversality has made its way into the various texts of postmodernism, but only sporadically and quite obliquely. For the most part, it has been called upon in the making of local and isolated observations. No consolidation of its usage has been offered, and much less has a systematic account of it been given. Lyotard invokes the term in discussing the quandaries of translation. "Translation," he submits, "requires pertinences that are 'transversal' to languages."[6] In translating from one language into another one needs to land upon phrase regimens and genres of discourse in the one language that have their analogue in the other. This requires the discernment of pertinences that lie across the two languages, which are somehow analogous, exhibiting a sameness-within-difference. Although Lyotard is markedly pessimistic about the possibility of translations, given the recalcitrance of the *différend* that determines the life of phrase regimens, he does recognize the role that transversality would need to play in a translation project.

Foucault has generalized transversal praxis to encompass the play of power relations that congeal into a variety of social forms, such as the "opposition to the power of men over women, of parents over children, of psychiatry over the mentally ill, of medicine over the population, of administration over the ways people live."[7] The specific forms of these power relations vary from political situation to political situation, but the struggles through which the forms are defined display common concerns and motivations. Foucault speaks of them as "transversal struggles":

> They are "transversal" struggles; that is, they are not limited to one country. Of course, they develop more easily and to a greater extent in certain countries, but they are not confined to a particular political or economic form of government.[8]

A more explicit and somewhat more concentrated use of the figure of transversality occurs in Deleuze's interpretation of Proust. Indeed, according to Deleuze, transversality supplies the "formal structure" on which Proust's entire *Remembrance of Things Past* rests:

> It is transversality which permits us, in the train, not to unify the viewpoints of a landscape, but to bring them into communication according to the landscape's own dimension, in its own dimension, whereas they remain non-communicating according to their own dimension. It is transversality which constitutes the singular unity and totality of the Méséglise Way and of the Guermantes Way, without suppressing their difference or distance. . . . It is transversality which assures the transmission of a ray, from one universe to another as different as astronomical worlds. The new linguistic convention, the formal structure of the work, is therefore transversality, which passes through the entire sentence, which proceeds from one sentence to another in the entire book.[9]

Deleuze's use of transversality to disentangle the formal structure of Proust's masterpiece supplies another example of the utility of the concept across the disciplines, highlighting its relevance for the agenda of literary studies. The principal lesson to be learned from Deleuze's application of transversality within the literary domain is that it affords a thinking about the unity and structure of a work that is not superimposed, is not intro-jected from the outside, but is rather seen to develop within the work itself. Transversality effects a unification and integration, a communication across differences, that does not congeal into a seamless solidarity or locus of coin-cidence. It brings the various viewpoints lying across the landscape of the remembered past into a communicative situation that recognizes the integ-rity of particularity and the play of diversity.

It is the postmodern use of transversality, particularly by Deleuze in the arena of literary studies and by Guattari in the field of psychiatry, that raises the intensity level of the postmodern challenge. They have brought the concept to the forefront and have made us aware of its utility for proble-matizing the traditional and modern appeals to predetermined unities and fixed universals. It is this that comprises for Deleuze the "anti-logos" of the "literary machine," a reactive stance against traditional and modern uses of reason. But it is precisely at this dramatic juncture that the postmodern challenge becomes attenuated and requires supplementation, if not a more radical reformulation.

The limitations of the postmodern use of transversality reside princi-pally in the tendency to define its workings from the perspective of an "anti-logos" reactive stance. This enables postmodernism to undermine the pretentious claims that traveled with the logos doctrine in classical and modern thought, but postmodernism comes up short in addressing the less pretentious claims of reason that continue to be operative in transversal communication. The philosophical stance of postmodernism is principally that of a reaction, an assault on the vagaries of logocentrism, a preoccupa-tion with the motif of "the despised logos," all of which tends to congeal into a battle against the claims of reason itself. Its contribution toward dis-pelling the ghosts of a subject-centered and theory-grounded universaliz-ing rationality needs to be recognized, and herein may well reside its most durable legacy. But its troublesome presupposition that a subject-centered and theory-based rationality is the only candidate for the office of reason has eluded careful scrutiny. The fact of the matter is that postmodernism has been unable to come to terms with the issue of rationality from a more positive perspective. It has landed on the figure of transversality as a prom-ising resource, but it has failed to capitalize on its potential for a trans-formed portrait of reason.

Reason as a transversal dynamics can be seen to be operative, and in a predominant manner, in what we have come to call "praxial rationality." This praxial rationality does not entail a jettisoning of the logos but rather a refiguration of it within an economy of communicative praxis in which the claims of reason become effective by dint of praxis-oriented critique, ar-ticulation, and disclosure. We have followed the descent of the logos into the interstices of communicative praxis and have tracked its inscriptions as they play in the configurations of our discourse and action. An effort has been made to meet the challenge of postmodernism by providing a portrait of the life of reason after the demise of logocentric principles. The logos is refigured and reformed, pruned of its pretentious claims for pure theory, and reinstalled in the life of our praxial engagements.

Our explorations have led us to an acknowledgment of the role of transversality in the economy of reason as it operates within the polis of our practical affairs. This enables us to speak of a transversal rationality after the holdings of the universal logos of traditional metaphysics and epistemology have gone into foreclosure. What is now demanded of us is an explication of this transversal rationality relative to its temporal and spatial determinations, its liberation from the strictures of universalization, and its transhistorical relevance.

The Chronotopal Field of Transversality

The figure of transversality, inscribed across the disciplines as an extending over and intersecting of lines, forces, velocities, fibers, moments of consciousness, and social practices, displays both temporal and spatial determinations. One might be disposed to speak of transversality as "pre-supposing" a spatiotemporal field, whether one is dealing with the transverse mass of subatomic particles in motion or whether one attends to the transverse configurations of social practices and their peculiar constellations of power. Caution, however, should be exercised in the appropriation of the vocabulary of "presuppositions" so as not to abstract time and space from the moving particles and the living practices. Caution also should be used in visiting the various disciplines with a univocal sense of time and space. The time and space of material particles is not that of the time and space of consciousness. The time of historical narratives is not that of fictive inventions. Admittedly, an inevitable borrowing and accommodation of senses occurs in the passage from region to region and discourse to discourse; but one will need to be aware of certain aporias that emerge in the course of this passage.

Paul Ricoeur has given concentrated attention to the aporetic of temporality in his *Time and Narrative,* in which he details the paradoxes and quandaries that follow the separation of objectively measured cosmic time from subjectively lived existential time. He approaches this aporia, resulting from the clash of cosmic and lived time, by consulting the resources of narrativity, suggesting that we first look for the "connectors" between cosmic and lived time in the strategies of emplotment within historical narration. Historical narration bridges the chasm separating these two regions of time by joining measured time with historical events. This involves harmonizing seasons and years with festivals, biological processes with the sequence of generations, and delivered documents with a participatory understanding of the past. Now there is, according to Ricoeur, a complementing response to the disproportion of cosmic and lived time on the part of fictive narration, which in turn occasions an aporia on another level, that of a split between historical fact and fictive invention. This requires a refiguration of the time of narrativity, leading to an acknowledgment of a "third time" that borrows figures from both history and fiction and that articulates through the resources of a productive imagination an intersection of the actual world of lived experience and fictive invention.

The boldness of Ricoeur's project is unparalleled in the philosophical literature dealing with the problematic of temporality. The problematic, most generally stated, is one that results from an inability to forge an immediate access to time, whether one is dealing with cosmic or with lived time, with historical time or with the time of fiction. One thus seems to be left with an unmanageable polysemy of temporality, with a multiplicity of senses, that appears forever to preclude any consolidation of the meaning of time as a unified phenomenon. In the face of this, Ricoeur's bold venture in marking out a "third time" that intersects the complexes of cosmic and lived time, historical and fictive time, is at once provocative and challenging. Indeed, Ricoeur's venture helps to inspire our own, as we experiment with the figure of transversality in addressing the economy of reason. The transversal play in the understanding and communication of our praxial engagements is a play that is peculiarly temporalized in its lying across a spectrum of intertextured senses of time.

We thus project a *Weiterdenken* with Ricoeur on the aporetic of temporality, exploring its relevance for the dynamics of a transversal rationality. As we shall see, this will require an interpretive understanding and reflection that simultaneously moves through the aporetic of spatiality. The dynamics of reason not only envelops configurations of temporality, it also traverses various regions of spatiality. Our social practices are informed by boundaries as well as durations, places as well as moments, passages across space as well as movements through time.

At this juncture it would be helpful to recall Mikhail Bakhtin's merger of the spatial and the temporal in his thought-provoking concept of the chronotope. The claims of reason move about in a chronotopal field of value-imbued times and places. Praxial rationality, as a composite of strategies of critique, interpretive articulations, and incursive disclosures, suffers the qualifications of both time and space. Bakhtin's understanding and use of the chronotope can be of some help in marking out certain directions for our own explorations. However, his interest resided principally in showing how the chronotope, as an intertextured assimilation of time and space, is illustrated by the dialogic imagination in its fictive inventiveness—and, more specifically, within the discourse of the novel. Ricoeur's contribution resides primarily in his isolation of a "third time" that folds over the narratives of historical events and those of fictive invention, providing a new way for dealing with the aporia of the clash of cosmic with lived time. We suggest that what is required in a *Weiterdenken* with both Bakhtin and Ricoeur on the issues at hand is the grafting of a supplementary exploration of "space and narrative" onto Ricoeur's "time and narrative," and an extension of Bakhtin's chronotope beyond the realm of fictive discourse, broadening the assimilative space-time matrix to include the play of intentionality across the life-world of human emotions and human action.

To the extent that one would be successful in such collaborative reflection on the issues with Bakhtin and Ricoeur, one would open up a spatiotemporal field that spans the regions of discourse, perception, human emotions and actions, and institutional involvements. The spatial and temporal determinants within each of these regions retain their praxial orientations. They announce valences of value-imbued and socially defined times and places instead of abstracted instants and points. The chronotope of discourse marks out times and places for assent and disavowal, negotiation and intervention, in response to the claims and activities of the encountered other. The chronotope of perception opens up a perceptual field that assimilates the oriented space of the embodied perceiver with experiences of before and after.[10] The human emotions are qualified by durations of joy and elation, pain and suffering, that are coordinated with places and regions to be visited or avoided. Human action proceeds from places invested with value, enacting projects at the right or opportune moment. The institution of festivals and social events involves a commemoration and anticipation of both times and places. It is thus that temporality and spatiality, in their multiple valences and expressions, invade the expansive terrain of human endeavor and qualify our comprehension of the world.

This comprehension follows the route of an intertextured critique, articulation, and disclosure, which comprise the three moments or phases of the rationality of praxis. The task at hand is that of explicating the transversal dynamics of this rationality, exploring how reason is transversal to the multiple configurations of discourse, perception, human emotions and actions, and institutional complexes. As transversal, reason neither simply transcends the panoply of human experience nor is it simply immanent within it. The metaphysical/epistemological matrix of transcendence versus immanence is more of a conceptual liability than a hermeneutical resource for an understanding of the spatiality and temporality of human reason.

Reason remains transversal to the various forms of our personal and social forms of life. It lies across them diagonally; it is neither vertically transcendent to them nor horizontally immanent within them. It operates "between" them in such a manner that it is able to critique, articulate, and disclose them without achieving a coincidence with any particular form of discourse, thought, or action. The integrity of otherness—other forms of thought and other social practices—is maintained, accomplishing at once a better understanding of that which is one's own and a recognition of the need to make accommodations and adjustments in the response to the presence of that which is other. Within such a scheme of things, the dynamics of transversal rationality falls out as a convergence without coincidence, an interplay without synthesis, an appropriation without totalization, and a unification that allows for difference. Such is the transversal dynamics that motivates rationality as a concernful struggle within communicative praxis.

The effect of time and space on the potentialities of human reason has already received considerable attention in the history of modern philosophy, and particularly in the philosophy of Kant and later in the philosophy of Husserl. Insofar as one is condemned to think with the tradition, even when one thinks against it, a critical dialogue with Kant and Husserl on the role of time and space within the economy of human reason may well be unavoidable.

Kant's doctrine of the unity of apperception, framed as a synthesis of perception, imagination, and conception, places considerations of time and space very much in the foreground. Time and space, defined by Kant as a priori "forms of intuition" *(Anschauungsformen)*, provide the elemental structures of the world as experienced. All experience, from which knowledge begins but does not arise, occurs within a manifold of appearances that are temporalized by virtue of being either simultaneous or successive and spatialized by dint of their separateness from each other. Although time and space are themselves not experienced—there is no direct experiential access to either time or space—they are necessary conditions for experience to occur. On the level of perceptual phenomena, space (as the outer sense) is given equal billing with time (as the inner sense). However, as one moves from perception to conception, via the mediating work of the imagination, the role of temporality is increasingly accentuated. The schematizing operation of the imagination, Kant informs us, finds its grounding in the "transcendental determinations of time."[11] It is thus that the whole range of presentative acts of consciousness (sensation, perception, imagination, conception, and judgment) have some dealings with time.

The accentuation of the role of temporality in the knowledge-bearing odyssey of consciousness reaches a further stage of intensification in Edmund Husserl's *Phenomenology of Internal Time-Consciousness*.[12] In this work Husserl undertakes the task of demonstrating how temporality supplies the immanental unity of consciousness as it moves from a primal present to a past that is perpetually reclaimed as a horizon of retentional modifications of the streaming present. The passing present continues to "sink off" below the surface of the flux of consciousness, becomes sedimented, and requires for its accessibility a performance of retrieval, via both a passive and an active synthesis. The passive synthesis of retentional unification courts an active synthesis of a constituting, recollective act of consciousness. The unity of consciousness is thus the achievement of the workings of a passive synthesis of retentional moments and the active synthesis of an explicit, objectifying recollective act. Through these syntheses the lost primal present is, as it were, perpetually restored. In the more fully elaborated phenomenological program of his subsequent reflections, and particularly during the phase of the transcendental phenomenological idealism of the *Cartesian Meditations*, Husserl secured a theoretico-epistemological guarantee for the

unity of the temporal flux of consciousness by installing a timeless transcendental ego.[13]

Husserl's discussion of temporality in his *Phenomenology of Internal Time-
Consciousness* can be particularly instructive, as Sartre had already clearly
seen. This early work of Husserl offers a veritable object lesson in the performance of detailed and painstaking phenomenological analysis and description. His project is that of articulating the "immanent unities" of internal time-consciousness as they "are constituted in the flux of multiplicities
of temporal shading." The diverse and multiple contents of this temporal
shading are suspended over the past and take their place as "retentional
modifications of the primal content in the now-character."[14] This primal
content is a vehicle or carrier of first-order apprehensions that constitute a
temporal unity as consciousness moves back into its past. The phenomenological importance of the primal content of the now-character resides
principally in providing an "identical materiality" in the "exhibition of the
same" within the "continuing succession" of consciousness.[15]

There is thus a unification that is built into the primal, streaming present itself, as it is surrounded by a horizon of retentional modifications. Admittedly, the primal present sinks off below the surface, but in so doing it is
not dispersed into a random succession of multiplicities on the longitudinal
axis but instead becomes sedimented into a vertical coincidence, a "coincidence of identity."[16] This coincidence of identity ensures a continuity and
sameness, enabling one to remain conscious of that which endures as being
identical with itself. Herein resides the phenomenological constitution of
time, exhibiting at once a passive and an active constitution. It is the latter,
the active constitution, that makes possible the objectification of time and
through a move of generalization is seen to be operative in the constitution
of other objectivities. This early analysis and description of internal time-
consciousness was developed later, against the backdrop of Husserl's mature phenomenological and transcendental idealism, in conjunction with
an explicit egology. This egology enabled Husserl to explain the achievement of a constitution that yields at once coincidence and identity as the
effects of the immanental agency of a transcendental ego, the originating
source and condition for all identification, objectification, and constitution.

We have undertaken this brief excursus into Kant's and Husserl's understanding and use of temporality because there are certain lesson to be
learned from a critical engagement with their reflections on the issues at
stake. One of these lessons instructs us on the limits of a subject-centered
and consciousness-based approach to temporality. The success of Kant and
Husserl in explicating the structure and dynamics of the faculties and presentative acts of consciousness needs to be noted. Indeed, within the requirements of the modern epistemological paradigm, their contributions
may well stand as unparalleled. They have shown, with both clarity and
detail, how the knowing subject with its epistemic consciousness needs to
come to terms with temporality. One might even be inclined to say that

modem epistemology comes to its fulfillment in Husserl's phenomenology as a rigorous science.

We have for some time now argued for a delimitation of the resources of an epistemological, subject-centered approach.[17] In our move beyond epistemology, from philosophy as a subject-centered system of beliefs to philosophy as an elucidation of human discourse and action, the historically conditioned background practices of our world engagements have moved into prominence. Knowledge itself is viewed as being inseparable from its social sources. The determinations of praxis extend even to the epistemic domain. Within such a scheme of things the contributions of Kant and Husserl suffer a consequential delimitation.

In Kant's perspective on temporality, both vis-à-vis its role as a form of intuition in the life of perception and its workings in the schema of the imagination as a transcendental determination of time, as well as in Husserl's doctrine of internal time-consciousness, the socio-historical and politico-institutional constitution of temporality remains abridged. The temporalizing that occurs between the subjective time of consciousness and objectively measured cosmic time is occluded. It is precisely this "third time" (as Ricoeur has suggestively named it), moving between subjective and objective time without becoming coincident with either, that our praxially imbued temporality of transversality exemplifies. The delimitation of the subjective time of consciousness and cognition becomes explicit in this appeal to the transversality of our social practices and their historical inherence.

A second lesson to be learned from a critical engagement with Kant and Husserl on temporality involves an awareness of the pitfalls of overestimating the continuity of memory. Husserl's theory of retentional consciousness, as well as Sartre's existentialized version of it, gives insufficient attention to the fragility of memory. In defining their projects within the conceptual parameters of modernism, as an explanation of the unity of consciousness, they suppress the discontinuities of remembering and the ruptures of recollection. In the case of Husserl, this suppression is principally the result of his purchases on the concept of representation to solidify the retentional continuum. The past is perpetually reclaimed through a process of re-presenting *(Vergegenwärtigung)*, presenting again the past nows of consciousness as they sink off below the surface and achieve an identity with the primal, streaming present. This heavy investment in the resources of representation to deliver the translucency of the past ensconced within the present occludes both the fugitive nows that escape presence and those that undergo transformation in the process of being recalled.

Husserl and Sartre recognize clearly enough that some species of repetition is operative in all forms of remembering. But in their penchant for the founding of sameness they fail to recognize that repetition generates difference. The memory span, both that of personal consciousness and social history, suffers ruptures and refigurations. The past as remembered is never a representation of it as it once occurred. Gary Madison supplies the needed corrective to the epistemological concept of representation when he adduces: "To understand an experience, to reconstruct the past is not to 'represent' it to ourselves; it is to *transform* it."[18]

The third lesson to be learned from our problematizing of the epistemological paradigm of temporality (specifically as employed in the transcendental tradition of Kant and Husserl) involves the requirement to give more attention to the relevance of spatiality. The more that temporality becomes recessed in the depths of subjectivity, the less attention is paid to the spatial determinants. This ascendancy of time over space disturbs the effects of the chronotopal assimilation of forms of discourse and action and tends to restrict memory to a reckoning with time. The subordination of space to time became an increasingly distinctive feature of modernism from Kant to Hegel and from Hegel to Husserl. Even in the philosophy of Heidegger, which is commonly documented as a chief formative influence in the development of postmodernism, temporalization is given preeminent emphasis. Spatiality somehow follows in its wake, a kind supplement to the temporalization of human existence.[19]

This peculiar mind-set of modernism, which grants more importance to time than to space, is a not unexpected consequence of the modern bifurcation of mind and matter, spirit and nature. From Descartes on, the rules of the game have called for an assignment of the category of space to the domain of matter and nature and the category of time to the domain of mind and spirit. This division of categorial labor was made particularly explicit in the philosophy of Hegel. As is well known, the net result in Hegel's metanarrative of the odyssey of Spirit is the sublation of time and space into the Absolute Idea. But what is equally clear is that in Hegel's narrative the temporal and historical determinations of the Spirit keep the advantage. The travail of the Absolute Idea is a story of the victory of time over space. The ensuing "historical consciousness," for which Hegel was so profoundly responsible, quickly spread its mantle over subsequent philosophical developments in the nineteenth century and became a veritable defining feature of modernism.

The chronotopal abode or dwelling, wherein our figure of transversality is situated, emerges on the hither side of the epistemological and subject-centered construal of time-consciousness and its consequent devaluation of spatiality. It displays the time-space nexus within the heart of communicative praxis and its social and institutional practices. Socio-historical configurations antedate the episodical now-points of consciousness, and institutional constitution takes precedence over the phenomenological/ transcendental constitution of the ego. In this chronotopal dwelling there is neither a "vertical coincidence" within the depths of an ever-present now nor a mere sequencing of a longitudinal progression of nows. Instead we find diagonals that cut across the variegated forms of life that make up the chronotopal communicative practices. The transverse mass of our praxial engagements consists of forms of life that lie across each other without coincidence; yet these forms of life do not dissolve into an indeterminate heterogeneity and "pure" incommensurability. Socio-historical practices display an interdependence and a "gathering" by dint of a transversal play of praxial critique, articulation, and disclosure. These moments of rationality, exhibiting a logos-effect of gathering, circumvent both the synchronic verticality of totalitarian hegemony and the diachronic horizontality of anarchic multiplicity. This enables us to speak of the transversal logos.

The Transveral Logos

Our explorations of the dynamics of transversal thought and action within a moving chronotope of assimilated times and places has led us to a reformulation of the classical concept of the logos. This classical concept, so despised in the literature of postmodernism because of its complicity in the misdeeds of logocentrism, is retrieved and refigured in our concept of transversal rationality. An assault on logocentrism does not entail a scuttling of the logos. Throughout we have attempted to show how the claims of reason remain in force, even though they no longer enjoy the metaphysical and epistemological guarantees that have been offered to them in the past. The universal logos of logocentrism is dead. The transversal logos of communicative rationality is alive and well.

The peculiar mark of the Occidental doctrine of the logos as it was taken over in the constructionist designs of metaphysics and epistemology was its putative claim for universality and necessity. Classical metaphysics called upon a doctrine of essence to ensure such a claim. Essences were taken to be permanent, atemporal, and unifying determinations of both the human soul and its proper objects of cognition. The odyssey of reason thus came to be defined as an effort to recall the essential structures of mind and reality alike. The modern epistemological paradigm problematized the auspicious metaphysical architectonics that traveled with the classical concept of the logos and sought to locate the claims for universality and necessity within the structure of the human mind and within a criteriological concept of reason that found its legitimation in the quest for apodicticity.

In both these paradigms, classical metaphysical and modern epistemological, the presentation/representation of that which is universal and necessary finds its proper figure in that of a vertical grounding. There is either a grounding of such claims from above (from the vantage point of transcendent and ahistorical essences) or from below (the vantage point of transcendental, logically a priori, and equally ahistorical conditions). But whether grounded vertically from above or from below, we are proffered a perspective from the other side of history, a view from the perspective of an ahistorical subject that is nowhere and in no time.

The ahistorical subject, whether in the dress of classical metaphysics or modern epistemology, gravitates into the predicament of being unable to render an account of its own genealogy without undergoing reinsertion into the density of history from which it has sought to escape. Both the subject of social practices and the reason that it employs cannot escape their historical inherence. Subjectivity and reason alike arise from a complex networking of contingencies in communication-oriented existence.

Given the requirement for a communicative turn, we find Jürgen Habermas's project of devising "an alternative way out of the philosophy of the subject" by replacing "subject-centered reason" with "communicative reason" to be singularly suggestive.[20] Yet, at that very point where Habermas appears to have surmounted the perplexities in the traditional account of reason, he reverts to an epistemologically oriented doctrine of validity claims and continues to scrounge around in modernism's leftover holdings in theory construction and universalizability. His "theory of communicative action" continues an appeal to criticizable validity claims that have a universal grounding, designed to offer a "theory of rationality with which to ascertain its own universality."[21] Such ascertaining is purportedly accomplished through the exercise of validity claims that are built into the very structure of consensus formation, which "*as claims* . . . transcend all limitations of space and time, all the provincial limitations of the given context."[22] When all is said and done, validity claims are context-free, independent of the context of our socio-historical practices. We need, according to Habermas, something more—something more theoretical, more universal, and more validatable than the everyday know-how that enables us to make do in our quotidian practices. "The horizontal knowledge that communicative everyday practice *tacitly* carries . . . does not satisfy the criterion of knowledge that stands in internal relation to validity claims."[23]

Although Habermas's endorsement of communicative reason as a substitute for the subject-centered reason of modernism is to be commended, the fact remains that he has not taken his own project seriously enough. His notion of communicative reason remains lame and spineless, in need of the backing of validity claims that have the sanction of universality, claims that "transcend limitations of time and space." Habermas grasps clearly enough the importance of communication, but he needs to recognize a more robust, a more vibrant, and a more *full-bodied* notion of communicative rationality. What is required is a notion of communicative rationality that offers its own resources of critique, articulation, and disclosure, no longer requiring the epistemological guarantees of universality and necessity issuing from a vertical grounding.

That which we have found to be particularly instructive in the postmodern challenge is the problematization of such appeals to vertical grounding and claims for universality. Postmodernism has called our attention to the horizontal discontinuities in the flux of our changing and heterogeneous forms of discourse and social practices. Through this subversion of the metaphor of verticality by a persistent accentuation of horizontality, the search for a universal logos is indeed called into question. The unification and totalization promised by classical doctrines of essence, both of the idealist and realist varieties, come up short, and the a priori (universal and necessary) rules that governed the quest for certainty in the epistemological ventures of modernism are reduced to contingent strategies. Whereas the vertical grounding of metaphysically and epistemologically oriented modes of thought sought a view from the other side of history, the horizontal multiplicity celebrated in postmodernism offers only a fragmented vision from this side of history. This privileging of horizontality in postmodernism has its own disturbing consequences. It leaves us with a heterogeneity of socio-historical assemblages of discourse and action in which paralogy and incommensurability, rupture and overturn, have the final word. In such a scheme of things the relativization of all forms of thought and all contents of culture is difficult to avoid.

The problematization of the classical and modern claims for universality has sufficient reactive force to awaken us from our dogmatic metaphysical and epistemological slumbers, but this problematization does not require that we simply tune out the voices of classical and modern thought. After the overlay of philosophical constructionism has been pruned away, certain existential concerns about an understanding of self and world in the tradition of Occidental thought continue to solicit our interest. Indeed, as we have time and again emphasized, we cannot think and act except through an engagement with the tradition. The task is to stand in a critical relation to the tradition. It is thus that our project, simplified possibly to the extreme, comprises an effort to split the difference between the vertically grounded conceptions of reason and the horizontality of the postmodern anti-logos of becoming. We split the difference by calling upon the transversal logos.

The transversal logos requires a critical revision of the postulates of universality, both as essentialist prescription and criteriological a priorism. This critical revision, however, does not scrap the performance of the logos as rational comprehension. The logos is reconstituted, but it is not left behind. It continues to register its effects (and it is discernible only through its effects) in a transversal binding or gathering of the multiplicity and flux of our socio-historical practices. The region in which this binding or gathering is operative is neither that of untrammeled essences nor a priori rules. Its proper region or arena is that of communicative praxis—a praxis that at once acknowledges the multiplicity of forms of discourse and action and discerns that the sense of the multiple does not reside in its historical specificities alone. The meanings that attach to our particular perceptions, speech acts, and local narratives are the result of a gathering and configuring of perceptual and discursive specifics against a background of the intrusion of alterities. As there is no perception at an instant, within an enclosed specificity, so there is no comprehension of a specific form of discourse or action without a background of other discourses and other actions that mutually define the figuration of each.

The overdetermination of the metaphors of verticality and horizontality leads in both cases to a blocking of the performances of critique, articulation, and disclosure, given that these phases of rationality are temporalized and spatialized "between" and "across" the orthodoxy of proclaimed unities and the heterodoxy of difference. Orthodoxy appeals to a vertical grounding to secure the universality and stability of "correct" and "right" opinion *(doxa)*. Heterodoxy valorizes the play of difference within the horizontal dimension of changing forms of thought and action. Framing the issue of rationality in terms of predilections toward orthodoxy and heterodoxy helps to make more explicit the role of doxa in the transversal performance of reason. The verticality of orthodoxy and the horizontality of heterodoxy comprise antipodal approaches to the delivered doxa of our communicative practices—be they scientific, ethical, aesthetical, or political. The challenge of the transversal logos is that of effecting a passage between orthodoxy and heterodoxy.

The privileging of verticality guides the effort to find within the extant doxa that which is "correct," "right," and "true," by virtue of it being grounded in some unimpeachable epistemic guarantee. The formalization and quantification of these epistemic guarantees leads to what Edmund Husserl had already suggestively described as "the despised doxa" of Western rationalism, in which the indigenous intentionality of everyday praxis is progressively occluded. Rationalism's obsession with correctness, grounded in atemporal conditions for universality and necessity, led to a disparagement of the contributions of doxa on the level of concrete life-world experiences. Husserl's celebrated "return to the life-world" was an effort to recover the concrete, functioning intentionality of life-world engagements and activities. Postmodernism radicalizes the Husserlian project of reclaiming the domain of doxa and finds in this domain *nothing but doxa*—nothing but a heterogeneous succession of forms of life and modes of thought. We thus pass from the epoch of the despised doxa to that of the despised epistēmē and the despised logos.

This rite of passage, from verticality to horizontality, from orthodoxy to heterodoxy, from a "politics of reason" to a "politics of opinion,"[24] would seem to justify an identification of the entourage of postmodernists as the *new Sophists*. The prominence of Protagoras and Gorgias in Lyotard's definition of the *différend* as a conflict between two parties that remains insoluble because of the want of a rule of judgment is quite plainly visible.[25] As did the Sophists of old, so do the new postmodernists privilege the way of opinion and disparage the claims of reason. The epistēmē/doxa dichotomy remains normative for both, and the right side of the virgule subverts the left. With the subversion of a logos-grounded epistēmē, all that remains is a succession of hetero-doxa in which each prevailing opinion is countered by a new opinion within a conflictual rhapsody of "rhetorical agonistics" that has neither goal nor purpose.[26]

We find in this dispute between the vertical universalists, the friends of reason, and the horizontal pluralists, the friends of opinion, a double mistake that is shared by both parties. The one mistake is that of analyzing epistēmē into a universal logos, generating the theoretical construct of "epistemology," designed to provide a foundational support for every instance of knowledge. The second mistake, closely tied to the first, is that of bifurcating the realms of epistēmē and doxa and considering this matrix of bifurcation as a given. So long as one stays within a framework of inquiry that exhibits this double mistake, the oppositions of verticality versus horizontality, reason versus opinion, orthodoxy versus heterodoxy, universalism versus historicism, will remain in force and will be taken as normative. The battle lines will continue to be drawn between a logocentric epistemology and a doxastic flux of historical becoming, congealing into a *différend* that neither party can surmount.

That a philosophical resolution of this dispute has not yet been forthcoming is not all that puzzling. What is puzzling is that resolutions continue to be sought and that the problematic premises of the longstanding debate continue to go unrecognized. The dispute, in the end, remains a fight about the grammar of universals. Our response to this state of affairs is that of shifting the grammar and the questioning to see if one might get a better perspective on the issues at hand. The shift of questioning moves from an interrogation of metaphysical and epistemological postulates to the question about what goes on in the play of our quotidian speech and action, our discursive and institutional practices. The shift of grammar is that from the universal to the transversal. The notion of transversality, with its metaphorical resources to move across the disciplines and the differentiated culture-spheres, proves to be more productive in rendering an account of our multiple and interdependent social practices than is the metaphysically sedimented grammar of universality, which fixes the format of discussion in terms of an undecidable option between vertical grounding or horizontal dispersal. Seyla Benhabib points us in a fruitful direction for pursuing these matters when she remarks: "The oppositions within the confines of which much recent discussion has run—universalism versus historicity, an ethics of principle versus judgment in context, or ethical cognition versus moral motivation—are no longer compelling."[27]

The binding rationality of critique, articulation, and disclosure is transversal rather than universal in character. None of the moments of rationality, either singularly or in concert, yield universal validity. They do, however, enable the achievement of shared understanding and solidarity, which is to be distinguished from a consensus grounded in universalizable validity claims. This shared understanding and solidarity is the achievement of the hard struggle for communication across the spectrum of varying forms of life, attentive to the play of similarity within difference and the play of difference within similarity. In this struggle for communication, the myths of universalization and totalization (illustrated, for example, in Habermas's notion of the "ideal speech situation") may indeed continue to play a role, testifying to the inseparability of *mythos* and *logos* in our philosophical narratives. These myths, however, need to be recognized as *broken* myths, discharging their functions in the service of an open-ended process of unifying that does not congeal into a fixity of formal determinations and a closure of historical possibilities. Although the universal logos is problematized, this does not consign us to a *Walpurgisnacht* of irrationality in which all signifiers are black and in which every interpretation and every moral claim is as good as every other interpretation and every other moral claim. Both intracultural and transcultural judgments and assessments retain their efficacy. Indeed, such judgments and assessments are unavoidable given the transversal play of our beliefs and practices in responding to that which is said and done. It is precisely through this *response-dynamics* of communicative praxis, whereby we respond to the discourse and action that is thrust upon us, that the deployment of critique, articulation, and disclosure proceeds.

A requirement that ensues from giving such dominance to transversal rationality is that of squaring it with the hermeneutical demand. Interpretation enjoys a certain ubiquity, operative both in precognitive and cognitive world-comprehension, at work within the projects of understanding and explanation alike. The hermeneutical demand is inescapable; interpretation goes all the way down and all the way back. We now have the task of aligning in some manner the workings of interpretation with the dynamics of transversal rationality.

The alignment of the two, the grafting of the one onto the other, results in a mutual delimitation and reinforcement. Transversal thinking cannot outstrip the bounds of interpretation. The critique, articulation, and disclosure that extend over and move across the orthodoxy of congealed principles and rules and the heterodoxy of conflicting particularities of practice continue to ride the crest of the "hermeneutical as," geared to an understanding that is always that of understanding differently. In such understanding there is an evident circularity, a movement from one portion of discourse and event of action to another, against the backdrop of a whole that envelops them. This part/whole matrix that guides understanding privileges the circle as the root metaphor of rational comprehension. The transversal paradigm of rationality continues to call upon the services of interpretive understanding, but it also delimits the metaphor of circularity with that of diagonality. There is here a shift from the circle of understanding to a diagonal of thinking that intersects the surfaces of hermeneutical circles. Transversality delimits hermeneutics and resituates it within a wider space of rational circumspection. Not only does the diagonal of transversal thinking remain orthogonal to the various interpreted forms of discourse and action, it transversally extends beyond them to an infinity of "other" holistic complexes—an infinity that never congeals into a totality.[28]

The decisive feature in this transversal delimitation of hermeneutics is the intrusion of that which is other, the weight of alterity, the incursivity of disclosure. The directive of the transversal logos is to acknowledge the reality of the other. The effects of such are discernible across the spectrum of our variegated scientific and cultural communicative practices, in contending with an alien and incommensurable paradigm of scientific explanation as well as in negotiating disputes across political and religious lines of force. Disputes between Arab and Jew, Indian and Pakistani, Irish Republican Army and British Crown, all of which exhibit a strong undertow of political and religious differences, become negotiable only to the degree that there is an acknowledgment of the reality and integrity of the other as other. The rationality of such negotiations resides in an understanding of the particular traditions in which each of the parties are situated and in a recognition of the need to make accommodations and adjustments through a transversal movement of responding to that which is at once other and alien.

Hermeneutical and transversal thinking, the circle and the diagonal, delimit each other. But in this mutual delimitation there is also a mutual enrichment and an expansion of resources, providing a wider perspective on the dynamics of rationality. It is within this wider perspective that the refiguration of universality is seen to occur as "the universal" is transmuted into "the transversal."

Merleau-Ponty's suggestions for a refiguration of the classical and modern concepts of universality still await the full recognition that they deserve. Unfortunately, Merleau-Ponty's contribution toward a thinking beyond the stalemate that so often ensues from the confrontation of postmodernism with modernism tends to be lost in the philosophical shuffling of that which is deemed to be the most current and the most revolutionary.[29] We are particularly interested in Merleau-Ponty's thought experiments in refiguring the grammar of universals, in the process of which he designs what one might refer to as a "halfway house" in the journey from the universal to the transversal. He experiments with the vocabulary of "lateral universals," which he distinguishes from "overarching universals," universals that are grounded in a vertical and totalizing objectivity:

> This provides a second way to the universal: no longer the overarching universal of a strictly objective method, but a sort of lateral universal which we acquire through ethnological experience and its incessant testing of the self through the other person and the other person through the self. It is a question of constructing a general system of reference in which the point of view of the native, the point of view of the civilized man, and the mistaken views each has of the other can find a place—that is, of constituting a more comprehensive experience which becomes in principle accessible to men of a different time and country.[30]

That which solicits our particular interest in Merleau-Ponty's figure of lateral universals is his concrete contextualization of the achievement of such universals within the ethnological practice of coming to grips with differing points of view across the spectrum of cultural and historical diversity. Merleau-Ponty recognizes clearly enough the multiplicity and heterogeneity of discourses, actions, and institutions that define the region of ethnological study. This marks out the plane of horizontality with its cultural diversity and historical diachrony. But the projects of cross-cultural understanding and communication deliver the multiplex forms of life on the plane of horizontal diversity from an incommensurable otherness. The drive for understanding and communication works with "lateral universals," which perform the function of gathering the manifold social practices under study into "a more comprehensive experience which becomes in principle accessible to men of a different time and country." This gathering, however, proceeds not by way of appeals to overarching, synchronic, and vertically grounded universals but is rather the effect of a transversal rationality that is able to visit different times and places.

An additional feature to be noted in Merleau-Ponty's revisionary tactics in dealing with traditional claims of universality has to do with the implied requirement for a phenomenology of experience through which the "comprehensive experience" of ethnological understanding is constituted. We too have argued for a phenomenological reclamation of experience, a return to the life-world of functioning intentionality and tacit knowledge, to enable us to deal with the vagaries of linguistic, textualist, and narratological closure. The experienced life-world resists sublation into semiotic systems, textual graphics, and narrational constructs. It retains its integrity and impinges on our discourse and action as the displayed referent of our communicative praxis. The task of transversal rationality is that of scanning the terrain of our life-world involvements, enabling a critique, articulation, and disclosure of the manifold forms of life that these involvements produce.

The Transversal and the Transhistorical

Our refiguration of the universal logos as transversal provides us with a new perspective on addressing the issues spawned by the reactive stance of nineteenth-century historicism, the effects of which are still quite visible today. With its objectivistic attitude toward the past, relativistic attitude toward the present, and progressivistic attitude toward the future, historicism set in motion a plethora of oppositions that guided reflections on the topic of history well into the twentieth century. Chief among these were the oppositions of transcendentalism versus historicism, essentialism versus individualism, and absolutism versus relativism. The debates that moved within the play of these dichotomies were defined principally in terms of the use of the grammar of universals in our understanding of socio-historical reality. The garden varieties of transcendentalism, essentialism, and absolutism sought to find a haven of universally binding conditions of knowledge and regulative principles of action that transcend historical particularity. It was thus that the ahistorical, in the guise of a priori epistemic conditions, invariant essences, and universal principles, was pitted against the particularities and multiplicities of historical change.

The "new" historicism of postmodernism—if indeed the language of history and the historical still remains appropriate here—follows certain directions opened up by Nietzsche's "untimely" anti-historicist reflections, which problematized historicism's objectification of the past and its postulate of progressivism. In these Nietzsche-inspired postmodern developments some of the presuppositions and postulates of classical historicism are indeed undermined. Yet, for all that, the crux of the matter that occasioned the furor in the initial disputes between the historicists and the anti-historicists remains unprobed. This crux of the matter has to do with construing the difference between the historical and the ahistorical by collapsing the *a*-historical into the *trans*-historical. The new historicism of postmodernism continues to buy into a conceptual scaffolding in which the ahistorical and the transhistorical are conflated. It is thus that postmodern reflections on history have resulted in a peculiar paradox. On the one hand, the postmodern problematization of the tenets of the old historicism is suggestive and seems to offer a liberation from the dichotomous thinking in which it was caught up; but on the other hand postmodern reflection buys back into the original dichotomy by setting the universal, the meta-narrational, and the consensual against the multiple, the local, and the dissensual. In such a scheme of things the ahistorical and the transhistorical are again fused, considered as partners in the crime against particularity, plurality, multiplicity, and the evanescence of a "present-becoming."[31]

The peculiar advantage of the grammar of transversality is that it facilitates a thinking beyond the dichotomies of transcendentalism versus historicism, the essential versus the contingent, the absolute versus the relative, and is thus able to avoid confusing the transhistorical with the ahistorical. The dynamics of the transversal logos, in its extending over and lying across the multiplicity of social practices and conventions, makes it possible for us to visit different times and places without either requiring a panoptic standpoint outside of history or having recourse to an incommensurability of local narratives. Understanding and communication across the variegated forms of life is achieved not via an appeal to an overarching or undergirding universal (whatever shape such a universal might assume) but rather through the hard struggle of a transversal communicative praxis that stays with the beckonings of the historical without being bound to the particularities of localized conventions. Transversal communication possesses the resources for transhistorical assessment, evaluation, and critique without the problematic appeals to atemporal essences or transcendental conditions. The performances of praxial rationality—critical discernment, articulation, and disclosure—achieve their efficacy in a transversal communication that is able to move from context to context, from one form of life to that of another. Socio-historical critique may indeed remain *context-dependent,* but this does not preclude an assessment, refiguration, or indeed overturn of different localized contexts as one discerns the play between and among them. Every context-dependency is situated within a wider context-interdependency.

A recognition of the enabling of transhistorical communication and critique within the economy of the transversal logos requires a double shift —a shift away from the domination of verticality in modernism and the domination of horizontality in postmodernism. This peculiar splitting of the difference between modernism and postmodernism gives rise to a transfigured performance of reason "between" them. The subject-centered and criteriological conception of rationality of modernism had its sights set on a vertical grounding of reason in ahistorical epistemic conditions for universality and necessity. Given the paucity of resources for a determination of universality and totality within the horizontality of historical becoming, principles of epistemic justification were located on the other side of history. The reactive stance of postmodernism turned the tables, privileged horizontality, abandoned the quest for universalization and totalization, and valorized the flux and multiplicity of "present-becoming." Within such a perspective, we are proffered only a fragmented and fractured vision from this side of history. The history at issue for postmodernism, shorn of any recollection of the past and any reality of the future, is too thin and fragile to comport a logos that can transcend its specificities and particularities through transhistorical discernment, assessment, and critique.

Both the privileging of verticality in the interests of securing an untrammeled universality and the privileging of horizontality bent toward a random, diachronic pluralization occlude the distinction between the ahistorical and the transhistorical. Indeed, the one is seen to collapse into the other. The integrity of transhistorical comprehension can be secured only through the installment of a praxial rationality transversally defined. In this transversal historical understanding and comprehension neither the metaphorical weight of verticality nor that of horizontality become dominant. It effects a passage between the orthodoxy of sedimented belief-systems and institutional forms and the heterodoxy of changing beliefs and practices, between normativized rules and procedures and revolutionary thought and action.

The transversal extending over and diagonally lying across the interplay of conjunctions and disjunctions of thought and action in their localized differentiations and constituted idealizations, between the standpoints of heterodoxy and orthodoxy, provides the motivation for transhistorical communication. Neither dissensus nor consensus, neither agonistics nor an unbroken communitarianism, provide the proper ends of human discourse and action. The transversal time-space of our communicative practices yields an interplay of dissent and consent, occasioning shared understanding and cooperative endeavors, but only against the background of a recognition of the integrity of the thought and action of the other. From this there emerges a dialectics of achievement and breakdown of communicative projects in which there is a struggle to communicate in spite of misunderstanding and irremediable differences.

Lyotard may indeed have a point in questioning Habermas's assumption that "the goal of dialogue is consensus." But simply to replace this assumption with the counter-assumption that the "end" of dialogue and discussion "on the contrary, is paralogy" does not advance matters all that much.[32] The limitations of dialogue, some of which are admittedly disconcerting, need to be made known; however, the installation of dissensus and paralogy as the proper end of human discourse suffers its own limitations. What is required is a continuing effort to articulate the communicative event as one that illustrates a dialectics operating between the solidarity of consensus and the heterogeneity of dissensus.

Our delineation of the workings of transversal communicative rationality, in what amounts to an end run, either to the right or to the left, around the transcendentalism/historicism aporia and its mistaking of the transhistorical for the ahistorical, provides us with some new perspectives on the rationality of socio-historical criticism and its implied ethical-normative content.

The concrete concerns that motivate any social critique of delivered forms of life and institutions issue from an uneasiness in accepting the stock of taken-for-granted beliefs and practices, even when these congeal into a unanimity of convention. There is no guarantee that the unanimity of convention coincides with ethical requirements for justice, defensible claims concerning rights and duties, and the good life as both a personal and corporate achievement. Justice is not to be identified with the unanimity of convention; rights and duties are not simply historically specific; and the good life exceeds the parameters of any particular tradition. Because of these concrete concerns that motivate ethical behavior, various appeals to rationality, the rationality of both thought and action, have been made. Our own appeal has taken shape as an appeal to a praxial rationality, communicatively situated and transversely postured, displaying interdependent moments of discernment, articulation, and disclosure. Against this background the ethical requirement falls out as the performance of a "fitting response."

In a previous work, *Communicative Praxis and the Space of Subjectivity*, I sketched the outline of an ethics of the fitting response, contextualized against the backdrop of what I called "the rhetorical turn," involving revisionary perspectives on the ancient Greek notions of *kathakonta, ethos,* and *polis.* We saw an ethics of the fitting response as providing an alternative to the traditional theory construction of teleological, deontological, and utilitarian ethical systems.[33] In this previous work our specific interest was that of locating the ethical requirement within the responsivity of an engaged and decentered moral self as it responds to the prior thought and action already inscribed within a historicized polis. An ethical way of life is not an interior construct of a centered and sovereign subject. It is achieved in and through a responsiveness to alterity, to the reality of the encountered other, who intrudes upon one's subjectivity and solicits responses that are proper for discourse and action.

What was implied throughout my previous work, but was never made sufficiently explicit, was the role of rationality in the fitting response of the ethical. The principal aim of the current work has been that of elucidating and describing the role and dynamics of rationality as it operates transversally across the practices in the cultural spheres of science, morality, and art by dint of praxial critique, articulation, and disclosure. It is by calling upon the resources of this praxial rationality that the conventions of our thought and action are tested and contested and become subject to assessment and evaluation.

It is thus again that a possible rejoinder to the postmodern challenge can be offered, and more specifically to the point of Lyotard's willingness to sacrifice a "politics of reason" for a "politics of opinion." In sketching his politics of opinion, Lyotard distinguishes his understanding of opinion (doxa) "from the overly empirical context that many Sophists (and even Aristotle) have given to it.[34] This we consider to be a notable advance. In his own way, Lyotard has rescued what Husserl had already referred to as the "despised doxa" of Western rationalism from certain accumulated distortions. What remains problematic, however, is Lyotard's hurried scrapping of the resources of rationality, whereby the despised doxa of modernism is simply replaced with the despised logos of postmodernism. Indeed, our general continuing argument has been that a reclamation of the concrete intentionality of our doxastic life-world engagements does not entail a scuttling of the claims of a praxis-oriented logos. In the sphere of ethico-political involvement, a revitalized "politics of opinion" works hand in glove with a revitalized "politics of reason." As the doxa of the tradition needs to be pruned of its empiricistic distortions, so also the *logos* of the tradition (both ancient and modern) needs to be shorn of its pretensions to universalization and totalization and refigured within the texture of transversal communicative praxis.

In the expanding current literature on the uses of reason in social and political criticism, the explorations by Kai Nielsen merit particular attention. He has formulated an approach and strategy that he names "wide reflective equilibrium." We are particularly interested in Nielsen's broadened perspective on reflection because it displays remarkable similarities to our own understanding and use of transversal rationality and offers similar potential for transhistorical critique. Nielsen's proposed wide reflective equilibrium borrows features from Rorty's anti-foundationalist neo-pragmatism as well as from Habermas's accentuation of emancipatory interests in his critical theory of society.[35] Indeed, Nielsen's approach effects an imaginative synthesis of these two dominant current strands of thought on the issue, which on first reading are not all that similar. Habermas is intent on continuing the conversation with modernism; Rorty shifts the terrain of discourse and speaks the language of postmodernism. It is thus that Nielsen's project of synthesizing certain features of the thought of Rorty and Habermas offers its own response to the postmodern challenge, marking out possible moves toward socio-political critique within a space between the modernist proclivity to despise doxa and the postmodernist tendency to despise the logos.

Nielsen's notion of reflection as it plays in wide reflective equilibrium, it soon becomes evident, has little commerce with the use of reflection in the subject-centered paradigm of modern epistemology. Reflection is no longer construed as an interior mental event, issuing from a sovereign cogito intent upon forging an access to an exterior world. Reflection, according to Nielsen, is from bottom up social, always situated within the density of world-engagements. Reflection takes on a socio-pragmatic orientation, bent toward a discernment of the intercalation of knowing and doing, thought and action, within the panoply of social practices.

In articulating the dynamics of reflection, Nielsen makes much of the need for a "shuttling back and forth" as we engage in efforts toward "rebuilding the ship at sea." These well-placed metaphors enable him to articulate what we would be disposed to call the transversal play of rationality as it moves across the multiple configurations of thought and action:

> We shuttle back and forth between considered convictions, moral principles, ethical theories, social theories, and other background empirical theories and those considered judgments (at least some of which must be distinct from the initial cluster of considered judgments) that are associated with or are constitutive of or partially constitutive of the moral principles, social theories or other background theories.[36]

This shuttling back and forth between convictions and judgments, moral principles and empirical theories, ethical perspectives and institutional forms, illustrates at once the dynamics and wide scope of the workings of reflection that Nielsen advances. This wide scope encompasses the separated culture-spheres of modernism (science, morality, and art), and the dynamics of wide reflection enables one to move across these spheres, effecting a binding of sorts, whereby each functions as a background for the other. The canvassing of these spheres, moving back and forth between them, occasions adjustments and modifications of theories and practices in each of the spheres and sometimes leads to a disavowal and abandonment of them in the forging of new and untried perspectives:

> In such shuttling we sometimes modify or even abandon a social theory or other background or even come to construct a new one. We move back and forth—rebuilding the ship at sea—modifying and adjusting here and there until we get a coherent and consistent set of beliefs. When we have done that, then we have for a time attained wide reflective equilibrium.[37]

We find Nielsen's strategy of wide reflective equilibrium helpful for fleshing out our portrait of the transversal rationality of praxis. The reflection at work in wide reflective equilibrium possesses features that we highlighted in our explication of the performance of reason as a dynamics of discernment, articulation, and disclosure.

Yet, in continuing the conversation with Nielsen on the matter at hand we are disposed to offer a friendly critique of his construal of reflection. This critique may indeed have something to do with the epistemological sedimentations in the very concept of reflection—sedimentations that are difficult to dislodge. These sedimentations reappear in Nielsen's overdetermination of a "belief-system" orientation in defining the accomplishments of reflective equilibrium. We attain the sought-after equilibrium, says Nielsen, when "we get a coherent and consistent set of beliefs"; and we achieve this coherence and consistency of beliefs by shuttling back and forth between clusters of "theory" (empirical, social, ethical, and aesthetic). It is this heavy accent on the role of beliefs and theories that occasions for us certain concerns.

To be sure, beliefs, connected with theory either explicitly or implicitly, play a role in the forms of life that make up our communicative praxis. They comprise, however, only a part of the web of life-world engagements, which fall out more globally as a networking of social practices, habits, and skills in which beliefs and theories are later arrivals. The life-world, as we have seen, is properly portrayed as an amalgam of configurations of discourse and action, configurations of praxis including speech acts, gestures, habits, skills, and social competencies that comport their own insight and understanding, irreducible to a belief structure and a theory-grounded definition of rationality. One might formulate the requirement for dealing with the issue at hand as one that calls for an even "wider" wide reflective equilibrium than that proposed by Nielsen. This would refigure and expand the range of reason, making its alignment with the social sources of thought and the practices of everyday life more explicit, and provide a corrective to recurring tendencies of privileging a belief-centered approach to rationality.

Notes

1. Jean-Paul Sartre, *The Transcendence of the Ego: An Existentialist Theory of Consciousness*, trans. Forrest Williams and Robert Kirkpatrick (New York: Noonday Press, 1937), p. 39. Sartre mounts two specific arguments against Husserl's doctrine of the transcendental ego. It is superfluous; it remains an abstraction that performs no utility in accounting for the unity and individuality of consciousness. And it is a hindrance; it severs consciousness from itself, functioning as an "opaque blade" that separates present consciousness from its retentional qualification (pp. 39–40).

2. For a sustained discussion of the recovery of the subject in the aftermath of its deconstruction as a metaphysical substrate and an epistemological residuum, see Calvin O. Schrag, *Communicative Praxis and the Space of Subjectivity* (Bloomington: Indiana University Press, 1986).

3. Félix Guattari, *Molecular Revolution: Psychiatry and Politics*, trans. Rosemary Sheed (New York: Penguin Books, 1984), p. 22.

4. Ibid., p. 22.

5. Ibid., p. 18.

6. Jean-François Lyotard, *The Differend: Phrases in Dispute*, trans. Georges Van Den Abbeele (Minneapolis: University of Minnesota Press, 1988), p. 49.

7. Michel Foucault, "The Subject and Power," in Hubert L. Dreyfus and Paul Rabinow, *Michel Foucault: Beyond Structuralism and Hermeneutics* (Chicago: University of Chicago Press, 1982), p. 211.

8. Ibid., p. 211.

9. Gilles Deleuze, *Proust and Signs*, trans. Richard Howard (New York: George Braziller, 1972), pp. 149–50.

10. Merleau-Ponty has given particular attention to the role of time and space in the phenomenon of perception. He speaks of the "phenomenal field" of perception as a figure-background configuration in which perceiving is an event of embodied consciousness that integrates the determinations of a lived time and lived space. See particularly *Phenomenology of Perception,* trans. Colin Smith (New York: Humanities Press, 1962).

11. "Thus an application of the category to appearances becomes possible by means of the transcendental determination of time, which, as the schema of the concepts of understanding, mediates the subsumption of the appearances under the category" (*Critique of Pure Reason,* trans. Norman Kemp Smith [London: Macmillan, 1953], p. 181).

12. Edmund Husserl, *The Phenomenology of Internal Time-Consciousness,* trans. James S. Churchill (Bloomington: Indiana University Press, 1964).

13. Edmund Husserl, *Cartesian Meditations: An Introduction to Phenomenology,* trans. Dorion Cairns (The Hague: Martinus Nijhoff, 1960). See particularly "Fourth Meditation: Development of the Constitutional Problems Pertaining to the Transcendental Ego Himself," pp. 65–88.

14. *Phenomenology of Internal Time-Consciousness,* p. 119.

15. Ibid., p. 120.

16. Ibid., p. 121.

17. *Communicative Praxis and the Space of Subjectivity.* See particularly chapter five, "The Illusion of Foundationalism," pp. 94–111.

18. Gary B. Madison, *The Hermeneutics of Postmodernity: Figures and Themes* (Bloomington: Indiana University Press, 1988), pp. 166–67.

19. In an earlier work I attempted to rectify the subordination of spatiality by showing how time and space are co-primordially constitutive of human experience. Deformalizing time and space as abstracted and lifeless frames for conceptualization, I sketched an "existential coordinate of time and space" in which time and space are understood as living horizon-forms that mark out the concrete deployment of perception and embodiment. See Calvin O. Schrag, *Experience and Being: Prolegomena to a Future Ontology* (Evanston: Northwestern University Press, 1969), chap. 2, "The Temporality and Spatiality of Experience." Edward S. Casey has also responded to the devaluation of space, particularly in discourses on memory. In his book *Remembering: A Phenomenological Study* (Bloomington: Indiana University Press, 1987), he carries through a detailed phenomenological analysis of the intertexturing of temporality and spatiality in what he names the phenomenon of "remembered space." In a highly suggestive passage of this work, he frames the issue as follows: "In actual experiences of remembering, the spatiality and the temporality of the mnemonic presentation are often correlated to the point of becoming indissociable. The 'when' and 'where' are inextricably linked—so that for example, to remember a scene from my grandparents' home is *ipso facto* to remember a scene that took place at a certain period of my childhood" (p. 70).

20. Jürgen Habermas, *The Philosophical Discourse of Modernity,* trans. Frederick Lawrence (Cambridge, Mass.: MIT Press, 1987), chap. 11, "An Alternative Way Out of the Philosophy of the Subject: Communicative versus Subject-Centered Reason," pp. 294–326.

21. Jürgen Habermas, *The Theory of Communicative Action,* vol. 2, *Lifeworld and System: A Critique of Functionalist Reason,* trans. Thomas McCarthy (Boston: Beacon Press, 1987), p. 400.

22. Ibid., p. 399.

23. Ibid., p. 400.

24. "There is no politics of reason, neither in the sense of a totalizing reason nor in that of the concept. And so we must do with a politics of opinion" (Jean-François Lyotard, *Just Gaming*, trans. Wlad Godzich [Minneapolis: University of Minnesota Press, 1985], p. 82).

25. *The Differend*, pp. 6–16.

26. Ibid., p. 26.

27. Seyla Benhabib, "In the Shadow of Aristotle and Hegel: Communicative Ethics and Current Controversies in Practical Philosophy," *Philosophical Forum* 21.1–2 (1989–90): 4.

28. On this topic, see particularly Emmanuel Levinas, *Totality and Infinity*, trans. Alphonso Lingis (Pittsburgh: Duquesne University Press, 1969).

29. A notable exception to this neglect of Merleau-Ponty's thought as it pertains to issues relating to the current modernism/postmodernism controversy is Martin C. Dillon's work, *Merleau-Ponty's Ontology* (Bloomington: Indiana University Press, 1988). See particularly the highly provocative (in the sense of thought-provoking) concluding section "Abyss and Logos," pp. 224–44.

30. Merleau-Ponty, "From Mauss to Claude Lévi-Strauss," in *Signs*, trans. R. C. McCleary (Evanston: Northwestern University Press, 1964), p. 120.

31. The locution "present-becoming" is that of Claire Parnet, used in her dialogue with Gilles Deleuze. "Future and past don't have much meaning, what counts is the present-becoming; geography and not history, the middle and not the beginning or the end" (*Dialogues*, trans. Hugh Tomilson and Barbara Habberjam [New York: Columbia University Press, 1987], p. 23). See also Gilles Deleuze and Félix Guattari, *A Thousand Plateaus: Capitalism and Schizophrenia*, trans. Brian Massumi (Minneapolis: University of Minnesota Press, 1987), chap. 10, "1730: Becoming-Intense, Becoming-Animal, Becoming-Imperceptible," pp. 232–309. The effort to hang everything on a "present-becoming" results in a somewhat bizarre twist or wrinkle in the new historicism. History is shorn of its past and future, any sense of beginning and end, and is subordinated to geography. Time is read back into space, into a topography of rhizomatic multiples, pulverized into an evanescent present-becoming. It is indeed questionable whether such a thin sense of the historical can support a "historicism"—either old or new. Clearly, such a pulverization of the present, devoid of past and future, nullifies any project of historical understanding that would proceed transversally, reclaiming the past whilst anticipating the future. It is precisely the sense of historical presence as the chronotopal intersection of a continuing tradition and a yet-to-be-shaped future that is threatened by the new historicism of postmodernism. Although Deleuze and Guattari have found a place for the dynamics of transversality in the institutional life of humankind, their weak sense of the historical, their preference for geography over history, and their spatialized view of time keeps them from acknowledging the chronotopal texture of the play of transversal forces.

32. See Jean-François Lyotard, *The Postmodern Condition*, trans. Geoff Bennington and Brian Massumi (Minneapolis: University of Minnesota Press, 1984), pp. 65–66.

33. *Communicative Praxis and the Space of Subjectivity*. See particularly chapter ten, "Ethos, Ethics, and a New Humanism," pp. 197–214.

34. *Just Gaming*, p. 82.

35. See particularly Nielsen's "Searching for an Emancipatory Perspective: Wide Reflective Equilibrium and the Hermeneutical Circle," in Evan Simpson, ed., *Anti-Foundationalism and Practical Reasoning* (Edmonton, Alberta: Academic Press, 1987).

36. Ibid., p. 148.
37. Ibid., pp. 148–49.

Calvin O. Schrag: Selected Bibliography

Books

The Self after Postmodernity. New Haven: Yale University Press, 1997.

Philosophical Papers: Betwixt and Between. Albany: State University of New York Press, 1994.

The Resources of Rationality: A Response to the Postmodern Challenge. Bloomington: Indiana University Press, 1992.

Communicative Praxis and the Space of Subjectivity. Bloomington: Indiana University Press, 1986.

Radical Reflection and the Origin of the Human Sciences. West Lafayette: Purdue University Press, 1980.

Experience and Being: Prolegomena to a Future Ontology. Evanston: Northwestern University Press, 1969.

Existence and Freedom: Towards an Ontology of Human Finitude. Evanston: Northwestern University Press, 1961.

Chapters in Edited Volumes and Journal Articles

"Hermeneutical Circles, Rhetorical Triangles, and Transversal Diagonals." In *Rhetoric and Hermeneutics in Our Time*, ed. Walter Jost and Michael J. Hyde. New Haven: Yale University Press, 1997.

"At the Crossroads of Hermeneutics, Rhetoric, and Ethics." *Journal of the Yeungam Center for Research in Eastern and Western Philosophy* 10 (1997).

"From Experience to Judgment in the Aftermath of Postmodern Critique." *Analecta Husserliana* 53 (1997).

"The Story of the Human Subject in the Aftermath of Postmodern Critique." *Revue roumaine de philosophie* 1–2 (1996).

"The Kierkegaard-Effect in the Shaping of the Contours of Modernity." In *Kierkegaard in Post/Modernity*, ed. Martin J. Matustik and Merold Westphal. Bloomington: Indiana University Press, 1995.

"Ultimacy and the Alterity of the Sublime." In *Being Human and the Ultimate*, ed. Nenos Georgopolous and Michael Heim. Atlanta: Rodopi Press, 1995.

"Transversal Rationality." In *The Question of Hermeneutics*, ed. T. J. Stapleton. Dordrecht: Kluwer Academic Publishers, 1994.

"Phenomenology and the Consequences of Postmodernity." In *Reason, Life and Culture*, ed. A.-T. Tymieniecka. Dordrecht: Kluwer Academic Publishers, 1993.

"Communication Studies and Philosophy: Convergence without Coincidence," with David D. Miller. In *The Critical Turn: Rhetoric and Philosophy in Postmodern Discourse*, ed. Ian Angus and Lenore Langsdorf. Carbondale: Southern Illinois University Press, 1992.

"Traces of Meaning and Reference: Phenomenological and Hermeneutical Explorations." In *Current Advances in Semantic Theory*, ed. Maxim Stamenov. Amsterdam and Philadelphia: John Benjamins, 1991.

"Reconstructing Reason in the Aftermath of Deconstruction." *Critical Review* 5.2 (1991).

"On the Hermeneutics of Gadamer and Habermas," with Professor Chong-Mun Kim. *Korean Journal of Philosophy* 1.12–13 (1986).

"Subjectivity and Praxis at the End of Philosophy." In *Hermeneutics and Deconstruction,* ed. Don Ihde and Hugh Silverman. Albany: State University of New York Press, 1985.

"The Question of the Unity of the Human Sciences Revisited." In *The Phenomenology of Man and of the Human Condition,* ed. A.-T. Tymieniecka. Dordrecht: D. Reidel, 1983.

"The Idea of the University and the Communication of Knowledge in a Technological Age." In *Communication Philosophy and the Technological Age,* ed. Michael J. Hyde. Tuscaloosa: University of Alabama Press, 1982.

"Praxis and Structure: Conflicting Models in the Science of Man." *Journal of the British Society for Phenomenology* 6.1 (1975).

"The Crisis of the Human Sciences." *Man and World* 8.2 (1975).

"The Phenomenon of Embodied Speech." *Philosophy Forum* 7.4 (1969).

"The Meaning of History." *Review of Metaphysics* 7 (1963).

6

The Ethical Message of Negative Dialectics

DRUCILLA CORNELL

Drucilla Cornell has brought the work of Hegel, Levinas, Lacan, Derrida and other continental thinkers into discourse with the legal profession. Her efforts to develop an ethical reading of deconstruction have resulted in an original philosophy of alterity that draws from the resources of deconstruction and the philosophy of Emmanuel Levinas. Following the work of Theodor Adorno, her deconstructive readings of critical theory have helped to lay the basis for a positive and affirmative configuration of justice and its significance for legal interpretation. Cornell's work has helped to bring the contributions of continental philosophy in the area of ethics and political philosophy into dialogue with such political philosophers as John Rawls and Thomas Nagel, and, in doing so, has made an important contribution to American liberal analytic jurisprudence.

Cornell has been one of those responsible for the development of deconstruction and Derridean philosophy in America. She has developed, in her work *Philosophy of the Limit*, a positive sense of deconstruction as identifying the limits of philosophical understanding and the quasi-transcendental conditions of any system. Cornell takes this positive sense of limit into her discussion of alterity and friendship in order to offer an account of relationship and community that acknowledges the excess of the Other.

In addition to her special interest in bringing the discussion of alterity to bear on questions of justice and legal interpretation, Cornell has been a unique and important voice in developing feminist perspectives for contemporary continental philosophy. In her work *Transformations,* she offers an interpretation of "ethical feminism" and proposes a feminist theory of the state based on equivalent rights and egalitarian democracy that provides an alternative view of the feminine to both the traditional essentialist and universalist standpoints of liberalism and the social construction theory of femininity offered by Catherine MacKinnon and others. Through her notion of transformation, Cornell attempts to rethink the connection between radical social change and open-ended individuality.

In this essay, by using the work of Adorno, Cornell shows that with-

out the recovery of a playful innocence achieved through the reconnection with the Other in oneself, one cannot become a human being
capable of nonviolent relations to the Other. She develops a notion of
reconciliation to interpret Adorno's notion of communicative freedom
and demonstrates the possibility of thinking of Adorno's metaphor of
the constellation as a method for deciphering what one is studying
without imposing structures on it from the outside. Finally, she draws
the resources for a critique of totality and the "totalizing infinite." From
Adorno's negative dialectics Cornell opens up the possibility for thinking diversity in unity and considers Adorno a crucial voice for those
who aspire to non-appropriative ethical relationships.

→≡◎◎≡←

The need to let suffering speak is the condition of truth.
—*Theodor Adorno*, Negative Dialectics

Introduction

In *Negative Dialectics*, Adorno critiques Hegel for betraying the most radical
implications of his own dialectic in the name of a comprehensive, encircling totality. This critique, the ethical dimension of which I hope to reveal,
gestures toward a deconstruction, which is nevertheless an appropriation,
of Schopenhauer's ethic of pity. In referring to Adorno's project, I use the
word "ethical" deliberately. Adorno's suspicion of the normalizing effect
inherent in the generalization of one behavioral system of "rules" led him
away from the attempt to *determine* a morality and toward a more properly
ethical conception of the relationship with the Other. For my purposes,
"morality" designates any attempt to spell out how one *determines* a "right
way to behave," behavioral norms which, once determined, can be translated into a system of rules. The ethical relation, a term that I contrast with
morality, focuses instead on the kind of person one must become in order
to develop a nonviolent relationship to the Other. The concern of the
ethical relation, in other words, is a way of being in the world that spans
divergent value systems and allows us to criticize the repressive aspects of
competing moral systems.

In his critique of Kant, for example, Adorno addresses the mode of subjection he associates with the Kantian subject of morality. He critiques the
kind of person we are called upon to become if we are to do our moral duty
under his own *interpretation* of Kant's categorical imperative. Like the early
Hegel, Adorno is concerned with the ethical relationship in general. Adorno
seeks to uncover just how one engages with the other in a nonviolent
manner so that the Hegelian aspiration to reciprocal symmetry and mutual codetermination can be achieved. He argues that a truly nonviolent
relationship to the other is foiled by what he calls the dialectic of Enlight-

enment which, for him, subsumes the Kantian theory of the subject of morality.

In the story that Adorno tells in *Negative Dialectics*,[1] the Kantian subject, as a being of the flesh, falls prey to the endless striving to subjugate his own impulses and thus to secure the possibility of moral action. Reason is geared solely to the preservation of the subject, equated here with consciousness; because of Kant's separation of consciousness from the flesh, the subject is pitted against the object, which includes that aspect of the subject conceived empirically. Conceived in this way, the subject-object relationship necessarily gives rise to the master-slave dialectic. The master-slave dialectic is played out in our relations to nature, taken here to mean both against the external world of things and against our internal "nature" as physical, sexual beings. Ultimately, the master-slave dialectic takes its toll. The thinking subject's striving for mastery turns against itself. The part of our humanness that is "natural"—sexual desire, our longing for warmth and comfort—succumbs to a rationality whose mission is to drive into submission an essential part of what we are. The subject itself becomes objectified, an object among other objects. Relations between human beings degenerate into manipulative interaction, the goal of which is to master the other. Relations of reciprocal symmetry and mutual co-determination, in Hegel's sense, are thwarted, if not completely destroyed.

As I hope to show, Adorno makes the point that without the recovery of a playful innocence achieved through the reconnection with the Other in oneself, one cannot become a human being capable of nonviolent relations to the Other. In this sense, his dialectic of "natural" history is "directive"; it calls on us to "be" differently in our relationship to the Other. The emphasis on the "natural," desiring subject, the importance in Adorno's theory of the dissolution of rigid ego dictates, the suspicion of the normalizing impulse in the call to duty, are anti-Kantian, at least on the traditional reading of Kant; but these emphases do not make Adorno's message anti-ethical. Adorno denies that the ethical must be based on the will to limitation and control rather than on the desire for fulfillment. He holds, rather, that the will to limitation, in the call to do one's duty, itself replicates the master-slave dialectic and eventually undermines the possibility of a nonrepressive basis for Kant's own understanding of the importance of goodwill in relations to others.[2]

The young Hegel was also specifically concerned with the "repressive" aspects of Kantian morality and, more generally, with the havoc unleashed by the Enlightenment's radical divide between subject and object, mind and nature, and body and soul. Hegel's system aims to reveal the state of reconciliation underlying a social fabric violently torn asunder. Adorno challenges Hegel on the grounds that Hegel's system turns against the very dialectical reciprocity and mutual codetermination he sought to reveal as the truth of reality. According to Adorno, Hegel's system replicates the self-same violent relationship to the Other that it purports to overcome. Hegelianism becomes a form of imperialism over the object. Adorno rebels against Hegel's ontological identification of meaning and being as an imposed unity. Nonidentity denies that a concept is ever fully adequate to its object. Yet Adorno remains an immanent critic of Hegelianism.

By taking Adorno's Hegelianism seriously we can win back a degree of freedom within Adorno's own categories. Without keeping his Hegelianism in mind, it is all too easy to misinterpret Adorno's "philosophy of redemption" and his dialectic of reconciliation in such a way as to miss its ethical aspiration. If we consider Adorno's statement that "the idea of reconcilement forbids the positive positing of reconcilement as a concept"[3] within the context of his attempt to put Hegel's categories in motion from the inside, we can decipher what Adorno means and does not mean by that statement. As I have already suggested, Adorno argues that the Hegelian reconciliation of the dichotomies in a totalizing system turns against the mutual codetermination Hegel purports to show as the truth of all reality. In Hegel's *Logic,* transcendental categories such as Being and Essence are unfolded in their reciprocal determinations against what they are not—to be something determinate is to be something in distinction to what it is not. The determinations of the categories ultimately are uncovered as reciprocally codetermined in the unfolding of the Absolute Idea. The deconstruction of the philosophy of substance and of constituted essences in the *Logic* shows us how the boundaries which give us the appearance of the existence of atomic entities yield to the reality of mutual codetermination, the dialectical permeation of purportedly opposite categories. The philosophy of substance which asserts that an entity can be understood on its own is exposed as a fallacy. Instead, the relata are shown to be internally interrelated, first negatively, in their contrastive relationship with that which yields their self-definition, and then "positively," as the "belonging together" in and through which the relata become what they are.

The gathering together of the multifold in the logos culminates in the self-recognition of Reason in Being. The awareness that the self-conscious subject comes home in and through the relationship to otherness is what Michael Theneuissen has called "communicative freedom." Communicative freedom is the truth of the belonging together of the relata. Communicative freedom, in other words, is the *coincidence* of love and freedom in which "one part experiences the other not as boundary but as the condition for its own realization."[4] Under the circumstances of communicative freedom, "reality would have found its substantive 'truth' and thus become fully real . . . everything would be related to such an extent that the relata would not retain their separateness."[5] Under Theneuissen's interpretation, which is also the one I adopt, the full integration of the relata is what Hegel means by Absolute Knowledge or "self-recognition in absolute otherness."

For Adorno, communicative freedom cannot be thought of as the unification of the relata into a comprehensive totality without violating the coincidence of love and freedom. The "belonging together" of the relata in conditions of freedom can only be realized if the difference from the Other is maintained in a dialectical interaction that does not yield to the ontologi-

cal unity of meaning and being. Hegel's tendency to turn *Geist* into a deified subjectivity undermines the freedom to be in a relation of reciprocity
to otherness because the status of the Other as Other is ultimately denied.
Yet "communicative freedom" is not simply rejected; it is redefined within
Adorno's deconstruction of the truth of interrelatedness as the *Geist* that
encompasses both self and other. For Adorno, Hegel's *Logic* exhibits a tension between his brilliantly executed deconstruction of the metaphysics
of substances (a perspective marked by the indifference and unrelatedness
of elements) and the metaphysics of constituted essences (a perspective
marked by the subordination of elements to dominant categories), on the
one hand, and his tendency to reintroduce substance in the form of a reified
Spirit, the imposed unity of subject and object, on the other. As Adorno
remarks, "The reconciled state would not be the philosophical imperialism
of annexing the alien, if the proximity it is granted remains what is distant
and beyond the heterogeneous and beyond that which is one's own."[6]

"Reconciliation," as I will use the term in this essay, is Adorno's redefinition of communicative freedom as the state beyond the heterogeneous as
absolute otherness and beyond that which is captured by the Hegelian Concept. Reconciliation is the art of disunion that allows things to exist in their
difference and in their affinity. Adorno, then, is a philosopher of reconciliation in a very specific sense. His defense of a reconciled state is presented
in the name of the plural and of the different. Relations of reciprocal symmetry can only come into existence if the Other remains unassimilated.
Once the unification of the relata into a comprehensive totality can no
longer be conceptualized as the Concept returning to itself in an eternal
present, the ideal of reconciliation can be shown or disclosed but not conceptualized.

The "philosophy of redemption" is the counterpole to Adorno's assertion
that "the whole is false."[7] The "normative standard" of communicative freedom cannot be conceptualized as the truth of an already-achieved reality.
The ideal's critical power lies precisely in its capacity to reveal the world as
distorted and indigent in comparison with the reconciled state. It should be
emphasized, however, that Adorno, in *Negative Dialectics,* denies that we
can conceive of reconciliation; but this denial is not the same as Schopenhauer's insistence on the transcendental disjuncture between reality and
utopia. That disjuncture renders the dream of reconciliation an illusion of
the desiring individual, an illusion that those who pierce the veil of Maya
leave behind. Schopenhauer's message is clear: we can only find peace by
forsaking the futile striving of those who seek to be at home in the world.
Adorno's aspiration is the opposite. In his view it is only by developing
perspectives which illuminate our state of homelessness that we can begin
to glimpse through the cracks and the crevices what it would be to be at
home in the world. These redemptive perspectives displace and estrange
the world so that we are made aware that we are in exile. This exercise,
however, is not intended simply to teach us to forsake the world. Through
the development of redemptive perspectives we can resist "consummate

negativity" without, on the other hand, perpetuating the myth of the ever-the-same, or, put in popular language, the myth that there is "nothing new under the sun." Determinate negation, in Adorno, becomes the form in which every claim to identity conceals its non-identity: the illusion of identity is destroyed and with it the so-called realist perspective,[8] which assumes that social life cannot be radically transformed. According to Adorno, in a corrupt world one can only teach the good life through immanent critique of the form of moralistic self-righteous subjectivity itself. Yet in his dedication to *Minima Moralia*, Adorno nevertheless justifies his reliance on aphorisms against Hegel's own dismissive gesture toward them precisely because aphorisms allow for the expression of subjectivity, even if that subjectivity takes on the voice of the isolated individual:

> In his relation to the subject Hegel does not respect the demand that he otherwise passionately upholds: to be in the matter and not always beyond it, or to penetrate into the innermost content of the matter. As today the subject is vanishing, aphorisms take upon themselves the duty to consider the evanescent itself as essential. They insist in opposition to Hegel's practice and yet in accordance with his thought on negativity: "the life of the mind only attains its truth when discovering itself in absolute desolation."[9]

The unalleviated consciousness of negativity holds fast to the possibility of a different future. As Adorno remarks, "What would happiness be that was not measured by the immeasurable grief at what is."[10] He is in earnest when he argues that his melancholy science should be placed in the region of philosophy devoted to the teaching of the good life.

I have already indicated that there are several ethical dimensions in Adorno's work. Each can be understood as an aspect of the critique of totality on which negative dialectics is premised. The first is the revelation of the "more-than-this" in nonidentity. The presentation of the "more-than-this" serves as a corrective to realist and conventionalist ethics with their shared impulse to enclose us in our form of life or language game. Adorno appeals to nonidentity to undermine what I call the ideology of lesser expectations. The second dimension lies in the redefinition of communicative freedom as the content of the utopian vision of reconciliation. The third is expressed in the critique of the Kantian subject of morality. For Adorno, a moral subject that does not know itself as a desiring, natural being will not recover the compassion for others that can serve as a non-repressive basis for moral intuition and, more specifically, of the goodwill. The critique of the Kantian subject of ethics emerges from the dialectic of natural history. To separate the dimensions of Adorno's message in the way I have just done is admittedly artificial, but it is necessary to decode his own ethical message.

The redefinition of communicative freedom, the dialectic of natural history, and the unleashing of difference in identity are ways of approaching Adorno's immanent critique of Hegel's *Logic*. They are, if you like, different emphases in the unfolding of the immanent critique, different ways of elaborating negative dialectics. My justification for artificially separating the dimensions is strategic; the separation helps us to distinguish Adorno's ethical message. Once we remark the ethical message of Adorno's negative dialectics, we can read his commentaries on the subject and on instrumental rationality, as well as his critique of common sense as tendering a powerful warning. This warning does not, however, degenerate into a harbinger of inevitable disaster; in other words, Adorno does not disparage the very idea of ethical mediation as simply more of the same. It should not be forgotten that for Adorno "he who dies in despair has lived his life in vain."[11]

The Reconstellation of Hegelian Categories

Nonidentity: The Critique of Totality

Adorno brushes aside the accusation that his negative dialectics is just one more replay of a tired and outdated left-Hegelianism with the following remark:

> The fact that history has rolled over certain positions will be respected as a verdict on their truth content only by those who agree with Schiller that "world history is the world tribunal." What has been cast aside but not absorbed theoretically will often yield its truth content only later.[12]

The unleashing of the "truth" of Hegelianism allows Adorno to show that the Hegelian "system was the source of Hegel's dialectics, not its measure."[13] Indeed, according to Adorno, the system turns against itself, choking off the freedom of dialectical movement by the self-containment of the Concept. Once freed from the circle of identification—the closed circle of the infinite—dialectics implies nonidentity between concept and thing. Nonidentity, in other words, is dialectics taken all the way down. For Adorno, Hegel's central error lies in his attempt to recuperate negativity in the Concept self-consciously returned to itself. This attempt leads Hegel to envelop otherness in an all-encompassing subjectivity in spite of himself. All his statements to the contrary notwithstanding, Hegel left the subject's primacy over the object unchallenged. It is disguised merely by the semi-theological "spirit" within its indelible memories of individual subjectivity.[14]

By reifying *Geist* into a deified subjectivity, Hegel's idealism involves an "imperialism" of the subject over the object, an imperialism which negates the very possibility of reconcilement that it purports to reveal.

> In Hegel there was a coincidence of identity and positivity; the inclusion of all-identical and objective things in a subjectivity expanded and exalted into an absolute spirit was to effect reconcilement. On the other hand, the force of the entirety that works in every definition is not simply its negation: that force is itself the negative, the untrue. The philosophy of the absolute and total subject is a particular one. The inherent reversibility of the identity thesis counteracts the principle of its spirit. If entity can be totally derived from that spirit, the spirit is doomed to resemble the mere entity it means to contradict; otherwise spirit and entity would not go together. It is precisely the insatiable identity principle that perpetuates antagonism by suppressing con-

tradiction. What tolerates nothing that is not itself thwarts the reconcilement for which it mistakes itself.[15]

The attempt to achieve pure self-recognition in absolute otherness, in other words, violates the Other by denying its otherness to the Concept. Without the closure of the circle, the Concept can no longer fully incorporate objectivity as its own expression. The object, in other words, escapes ownership in its nonidentity with the Concept. This failure to achieve reconcilement becomes "the motor of disenchantment"—what Hegel called the "highway of despair"—which unleashes the dialectic previously rigidified in the frozen dance of the Concept returning to itself in an eternal present. Thought, confronted with its inability to achieve supremacy, turns against itself. The Hegelian system, according to Adorno, carries within it the seeds of its own destruction as system:

> By negating the concept of the limit and theoretically assuring itself that there always remains something outside, dynamics also tends to disarm its own product, the system.[16]

The "truth" is in the confrontation, in the nonidentity between concept and object. The "truth," in other words, is not to be found in the object, nor in the form of thought of the object, nor in the unity of subject and object in the Concept. The object can neither be grasped in its entirety by the Concept nor can it be known in its immediacy. Adorno took to heart the Hegelian insight into the inevitable conceptual mediation of immediacy. Yet, because of his refusal to complete experience in an infinite which totalizes its contents, he interjects a constitutive outside that is foreign to the Spirit of Hegel's absolute idealism. "The circle of identification—which in the end always identifies itself alone—was drawn by a thinking that tolerates nothing outside of it."[17]

The Hegelian system, as a result, is undermined by the very insight into the unfolding of negativity which is its hallmark. The nonidentity inherent in absolute identification turns against itself. Negativity is the escaped otherness, uncovered by the "logic of disintegration." The "truth" of negativity is the "negative reaction on the part of the knowledge that penetrates the object—in other words, extinguished the appearance of the object being directly as it is."[18] Adorno's materialism, with its recognition of the constitutive outside, reinstates the Hegelian category of essence not as "background world" but as the non-identity inherent in the limits of thought and the deconstruction of totality.

> [E]ssence passes into that which lies concealed beneath the façade of immediacy, of supposed facts, and which makes them as they are. It comes to be the law of doom. Thus far obeyed by history . . . it can be recognized only by the contradiction between what things are and what they claim to be.[19]

To deny essence altogether would be to side with appearance as if things were really what they are claimed to be within any current conventional system of definition. Siding with appearance would reinscribe identity thinking. The reality of the thing would be found to be fully expressed in its concept. For Adorno, essence is expressed as the concept of negativity that makes the world the way it is, but negativity expressed as "essence" can only be known indirectly through the nonidentity of subject and object; negativity is not to be hypostatized as absolute Other.

We can now summarize the difference between Adorno's and Hegel's understanding of negativity. For Hegel, negativity as a determining relation to the other ultimately is explained as the inevitable incompleteness of brute entities. Negativity, in other words, is the expression of an infinite, in contradiction with the finite contents in and through which it is embodied. For Adorno, however, the dialectic proceeds by way of the critique of a totalizing infinite. Adorno takes seriously Hegel's insight that finite reality is not adequate to its concept. Indeed, it is precisely the inadequacy of finitude to its concept that releases Adorno's negative dialectics. Whereas Hegel's dialectic in the *Logic* unfolds through the incompleteness of categories such as Being and Essence until the progression culminates in the self-reflection of the Absolute Idea, Adorno's immanent critique cancels the privilege of "thinking" by its uncovering of difference in identity.

Nevertheless, negative dialectics is not true for all time. It is not another first principle. To make negative dialectics another first principle would be to hypostatize negativity in the exact way Adorno warns against. For Adorno, then, negative dialectics is not a method; nor is it simply material reality, as if material reality in its contradictoriness could be presented to us without mediation through concepts. Negative dialectics is instead the "truth" of an unreconciled reality, or antagonistic entirety, to be found in "the cogitative confrontation of concept and thing."

> To proceed dialectically means to think in contradictions, for the sake of the contradiction once experienced in the thing, and against that contradiction. A contradiction in reality is a contradiction against reality.[20]

The conditions in which negativity can be overcome are those of a reconciled world—a world that can be brought into being only if the antagonistic entirety is itself negated. Negative dialectics awaits its decline in a redeemed world.

> Regarding the concrete utopian possibility, dialectics is the ontology of the wrong state of things. The right state of things would be free of it.[21]

There is an ambivalence in Adorno's use of the expression "antagonistic entirety." Adorno seems to reintroduce the concept of totality as understood within a negative dialectic of history. Such a view of totality, however, takes a different shape from the absolute infinite that totalizes its contents. Robert Neville has succinctly summarized the form of totality in Hegel's negative dialectic of history:

> If *Geist* can be modeled on the negative dialectic of history, then we have a new opportunity to address the question of the determinateness of the totality. We may say that the transcending state is determinate with respect to the

stage it transcends precisely in those respects in which it negates the possibility of the transcended stage and carrying its bit along transformed by the determinate actuality of the later stage. The actuality of the moment then is determinate either with respect to a possibility that it excluded but with respect to a past actuality that it negates and subsumes. There may well be many elements in the moment which are not determinate either with respect to what is rational in the moment itself. But they might become determinate when the moment itself is totalized and negated by its own executioner.[22]

Totality, in the Hegelian dialectic of history, "has reason as a selective principle. Reason which proceeds with necessity distinguishes within a situation between the truly actual and the adventitious."[23] In Adorno's musings on Walter Benjamin's statement that "hope is only for the hopeless," however, it becomes clear that Adorno also rejects totality as a selection principle to distinguish what is crucial to the unfolding of Reason. Reason as a selection principle denies certain groups, peoples, and nations "actuality" on the grounds that they are incidental to the narrative of reason in history. By so doing it violates them, demonstrating once again that Hegel's unifying spirit is a coercive force. In its worst form, Hegel's unifying spirit becomes a "justification" for the imperialism of the West. The dialectic—so the story goes—proceeded in the way it did because it is only in the history of the West that Reason finds its adequate expression.[24] Adorno uses his deconstruction of the totality inherent in Hegel's dialectic of history to introduce *categorical* novelty and to expose the ethnocentricity of Hegel's own unfolding of the history of Reason. In the standard interpretation of Hegel, there is no categorical novelty, only categorical "improvement," of what has already been achieved. Adorno insists on the possibility of a future, a future in which the return of the negated would modulate the established categories allowing for the creation of what is truly new. The ephemeral nature of thought allows for the rising of the *new*, of that which was excluded from the grasp of the Concept or pushed out by the pressure of the Concept's progression. The eternal present is shattered on the bodies of those who were tossed aside in the Concept's development.

Why does Adorno proceed through negative dialectics to introduce the "truly" new and the possibility of categorical novelty from within the deconstruction of Hegel's own system? Adorno and Hegel both consider the philosophy of reflection philosophically false and ethically a distortion of relations of reciprocal symmetry. Adorno, in other words, forthrightly argues that he accepts the most lasting contribution of Hegel's *Logic*—the insight that identity is constituted in and through otherness. Otherness can no longer be understood as an external relation in which a self-identified subject stands over and against the object only to find itself reflected there:

> The individual existence does not coincide with its cover concept of existence at large but neither is it impenetrable, another last thing against which cognition knocks its head in vain. The most enduring result of Hegelian logic is that the individual is not flatly for himself. In himself he is the otherness and linked with others.[25]

In the philosophy of reflection, on the other hand, the "I" sees itself reflected in the other but does not see the other looking back. The other is reduced to a mirror for oneself. Hegel's absolute knowledge, self-recognition in absolute otherness, is the overcoming of the mirror stage, the recognition of the reciprocity of self-consciousness. But for Adorno, the *experience* of interrelatedness in an antagonistic entirety is one of domination and not of communicative freedom. The "normative standard" of a reconciled condition awaits us; it has not been realized in the horizon of absolute knowledge. But, as already suggested, in Adorno the dialectic no longer defeats the philosophy of reflection through the identity of identity and nonidentity as it does in Hegel, but rather the dialectic proceeds through the "nonidentity" in identity. The shift denies that "the negation of the negation"—the "positive" reconstitution of an identity inclusive of otherness—is a possible occurrence within thought, even if it is accomplished in the name of Spirit, which is purportedly the revelation of the truth of the things themselves. It is precisely this identification of things and the Concept that Adorno denies as an accomplished "fact."

The positive, which Adorno understands in Hegel to ultimately overcome negation, has more than its name in common with the positivity Hegel fought in his youth. To equate the negation of the negation with positivity is the quintessence of the politics of identity for Adorno.[26] According to Adorno, Hegel's recuperation of the negative lends legitimacy to the current state of the world which it does not deserve. In this sense, the negation of the negation in Hegel serves as ideology.

> Against this, this seriousness of unswerving negation lies precisely in its refusal to level itself to sanctioning things as they are. To negate a negation does not bring about its reversal; it proves rather that the negation was not negative enough. . . . What is negated is negative until it has passed.[27]

Determinate negation, in other words, can no longer be thought of as a "positive" result of the negation of the negation but only as the self-canceling of the illusion of self-identity. Yet it would be a mistake to read Adorno's rejection of the "negation of the negation" as a retreat into "the predialectical stage: the serene demonstration of the fact that there are two sides to everything."[28] Instead, it leads beyond the circle of identification, to a different approach to the object.

The Metaphor of the Constellation

To quote Adorno:

> The unifying moment survives without a negation of negation, but also without delivering itself to abstraction as a supreme principle. It survives because there is no step-by-step progression from the concepts to a more general cover concept. Instead the concepts enter into a constellation. The constellation illuminates the specific side of the object, the side which to a classifying procedure is either a matter of indifference or a burden.[29]

Because, according to Adorno, the thing's own "identity against its identi-fications" can never be grasped in its immediacy nor in its unity with the Concept, we can only approach the object through a constellation of con-cepts which attempts to bring into the light the specific aspects of the object left out by the classifying process. The constellation does not pretend to totality in the sense of fully expressing the sedimented potential of the ob-ject. What it does is unleash the fullest possible perspective on what the object has come to be in its particular context. Since an object only yields itself to us through the mediation of concept, the goal is not and cannot be the pure illumination of the object beneath the Concept, even through the disclosure of its rightful name.[30] The sedimented history of the object re-vealed through its constellation cannot be separated from its entanglement with concepts. As a result, an object cannot be known except in its context. "Context" here is understood not merely as external relation but also as the internalized characteristics which make an object what is. The "substance" of the object is relational at the core.

> Becoming aware of the constellation in which a thing stands is tantamount to deciphering the constellation which having come to be, it bears within it.[31]

A constellation, then, cannot merely be grasped as a conceptual appara-tus imposed upon the object. Constellation should be understood as a meta-phor for a process of decoding that can never once and for all come to an end in a philosophical system. To the degree that a constellation "succeeds" with the object it does so through a process of decipherment. One deciphers rather than "figures out" the object. The deciphering of the object involves mimetic capacity, a capacity "for those modes of behavior which are recep-tive, expressive and communicative in a sensuous fashion."[32] Mimesis, in other words, is the capacity to identify *with*, in sympathy and in apprecia-tion, rather than the ability to identify *as*, as is characteristic of instrumental logic. In this sense, knowledge through constellation does not privilege the subject's purpose over the object's "right" to be what it has become. In Adorno, mimesis is connected with the attitude toward the other he associ-ates with utopia. Mimesis lets the object be. By so doing, mimetic capacity foreshadows the nonviolative relationship to the other, beyond the hetero-geneous and beyond what is one's own, that can only be fulfilled in a re-deemed world.

Adorno's notion of "identifying with" is not a return to intuition or im-mediacy. The "emphatic idea" of reason can only be recovered by way of immanent critique of the Concept's own claim to identity. We can only form constellations if we have grasped the misrecognition inherent in iden-tity-logical thinking. We cannot immediately see into the object; we can only approach it from different angles of contextual perspectives, know-ing all the while that it is never truly recognized by our conceptual appara-tus. The object ultimately remains outside, unassimilated in its entirety by thought. For Adorno, the re-experiencing of the object as nonidentical is the experience of misrecognition, in which the subject literally runs up against the limits of conceptualization and is opened to the Other as other, the unassimilated. Because Adorno rejects Hegel's move to totality, there is no context of all contexts. We can only know the object as it is in its different contexts, never immediately or as it is in its true reality. As Adorno explains:

> Cognition of the object in its constellation is cognition of the process stored in the object. As a constellation theoretical thought circles the concept it would like to unseal, hoping that it may fly open like the lock of a well-guarded safe deposit box; in response not to a single number but to a combination of numbers.[33]

Yet for Adorno, the relativity of the object to context, and the rejection of the context of all contexts, does not lead to skepticism. The "more-than-this" in the nonidentity of the real is in the object itself. As a result, such thinking does not turn the "object's indissolubility into a taboo for the subject."[34]

The Deconstruction of the Philosophy of Consciousness

Adorno holds that skepticism and relativism inhere in "the philosophy of consciousness." These philosophical positions not only "favor" the subject over the object but also understand the object as a mere derivative of the subject. As already suggested, Adorno reads Hegel as undermining the specular, monological view of the subject in which the subject sees itself mirrored in the other but does not see the other "looking" back. In Hegel, self-consciousness is constituted in and through otherness. Subjectivity is not substantial in and of itself; instead, the subject is correlative and codependent. The awakening of self-consciousness arises in and through entanglement with the other. The priority of interrelationship subverts the exclusive logic of identity; the other cannot be excluded from the internal processes of self-consciousness. The "I" comes to be only in the tissue of relations, in the interplay of "internality" and "externality." The "I" cannot achieve perfect self-containment, that is, the fullness of presence to itself. In other words, the "I" can no longer be grasped as a self-bounded substance prior to its predicates. Only within a metaphysics of constituted essence does Adorno believe it makes sense to privilege the subject's knowledge of itself over its knowledge of its others and to let such knowledge stand as the foundation for "certainty." Thus, for Adorno, the "antithesis" of the lie of the supposed unity of subject and object in the Concept is not to be understood as an essential structure of being. Such a misunderstanding would overlook the insight into the interrelatedness of all things that Adorno's critical reading of Hegel discloses. Adorno therefore warns us very carefully against hypostatizing the subject-object polarity. To do so would be once again to locate truth in the positive, this time in an undialectical structure in which all dialectics take place.

If the dualism of subject and object were laid down as a basic principle it would, like the identity principle to which it refuses to conform, be another total monism. Absolute duality would be unit.[35]

Hegel opens us to the insight that the "substance" of all things is to be found in their interrelatedness and, as we have seen, Adorno accepts this insight as the lasting contribution of Hegel's *Logic*. For Adorno, this interrelatedness is experienced as antagonism and not as "communicative freedom" because of the state of reality in an antagonistic society. Thus the "philosophy of consciousness" is both true and false: true, as the experience of the isolated subject blocked from coming to terms with the intersubjective constitution of the self in such a way as to yield a knowledge of the self as *other,* a knowledge that could assuage fear; false, as the firm foundation for an epistemology.

> The consciousness assumes a monadological shape, that the individual feels knowledge of himself (*Von Sich Selber*) is more immediate and certain than the same knowledge of all others—this is the correct appearance of a false world in which men are alien and uncertain to each other and every individual immediately related only to his particular interests but in which nevertheless universal essential laws are indeed realized.[36]

Cogitative self-reflection yields a knowledge of oneself as other, nonidentical, which in turn opens the self to the nearly suppressed mimetic capacity, the ability to identify with others through access to the other in oneself. Dallmayr explains the process of cognitive self-reflection as understood by Adorno as follows:

> Only insofar as it is non-ego, can the ego relate to the non-ego or alter ego, and can it perform an action, including an act of thought. By means of double reflection thought terminates its supremacy over non-thought, since it is itself shot through from the beginning with otherness.[37]

The Suffering Physical

Nonidentity, an idea Adorno derives from Hegel's own understanding of the constitution of self-consciousness in and through otherness, gives the lie to Hegel's subsequent, absolute identification of object and Concept; at the same time, it opens a breathing space for things which prevents them from being completely stifled by an imposed social totality. The disruption of totality gives us a glimpse of what things in their interrelatedness might become if they were allowed to rest in their affinity, rather than forever being stuffed into a new system of identification. The ethical significance of the disjuncture between meaning and being reminds us that reconciliation cannot be imposed. The oppressed thing—the object itself, the suffering, physical individual—bears witness to the failure of history to realize itself in the unity of subject and object. The disruption of the circle of immanence does not allow history the pretense that it is "second nature." According to Adorno, Hegel's "natural history" bolsters this pretense:

In the midst of history, Hegel sides with its immutable element, with the ever-same identity of the process whose totality is said to be salvation. Quite unmetaphorically he can be charged with mythologizing history. The words "spirit" and "reconcilement" are used to disguise the myth.[38]

Adorno's dialectic of natural history reminds us that neither history nor nature can be turned into a first principle.

If the question of the relation of nature and history is to be seriously posed, then it only offers a solution, if it is possible to comprehend historic being in its most extreme historical determinacy, where it is most historical, as natural being, or if it were possible to comprehend nature as historical being where it seems to rest most deeply in itself as nature.[39]

The intertwinement, and yet disjuncture, between history and nature exposes Hegel's philosophy of history as a myth. Suffering is not merely recognized by Adorno as historical or natural necessity. Rather, suffering, from the standpoint of the particular which endures it, is senseless. The only answer adequate to the suffering physical is the end to suffering, not a new version of the "meaning" of what it has undergone. Again, Adorno's disjoining of meaning and being takes on an ethical dimension. The anti-spiritual side of spirit is the promise of happiness that the desiring individual has been denied. In this sense, Adorno's shift to materialism carried within it a refusal of the continued denial of happiness.

The smallest trace of senseless suffering in the empirical world belies all the identitarian philosophy that would talk us out of that suffering: "While there is a beggar, there is a myth," as Benjamin put it. This is why the philosophy of identity is the mythological form of thought. The physical moment tells our knowledge that the suffering is not to be, that things should be different. Woe speaks, "go." Hence the convergence of specific materialism with criticism, with social change in practice.[40]

The society "demanded" by the suffering physical is one in which a solidarity has been achieved "that is transparent to itself and all the living."[41] "The *telos* of such an organization of society would be to negate the physical suffering of even the least of its members, and to negate the internal unreflexive forms of that suffering."[42]

Adorno and Schopenhauer: The Reinterpretation of the Ethics of Pity

When put in the context of his dialectic of natural history, the "materialism," or indeed the sensualism, of Adorno's philosophy of redemption becomes evident. By getting in touch with the "historicized nature" sedimented in the history of human suffering, we can potentially recapture the "mimetic" identification with otherness which has been pushed under in the subject's drive for self-preservation. The dialectic of natural history not only serves to expose the hardening of social formations into a "second nature"; the dialectic also potentially returns us to what has been "forgotten" within ourselves—our own physicality. The reminder that we, too, are the "suffering physical" marks the feeling of vulnerability that pushes further the knowledge necessary for controlling the Other; this effort to know the Other, and thus to control him, is done in the name of self-preservation. The awareness of our physical vulnerability is expressed in the quest for certainty and control over the Other, but the destructive "moment" inherent in the striving for self-preservation at the expense of otherness is made evident in Adorno's exposure of the basis of the identity logic.

The species "survives" through the domination of the "natural" by instrumental rationality, but it survives in this manner only by sacrificing "the sensual happiness" for which the suffering physical yearns. The subject's striving for self-preservation turns against itself by blocking the very reconciliation with otherness that would make happiness possible. For Adorno, to consciously *experience* our "unhappiness" is to remember the physical moment within ourselves and, with it, the "goal" of our longing, sensual ease.

> Conscious unhappiness is not a delusion of the mind's vanity, but something inherent in the end—the one authentic dignity it has received in its separation from the body. This dignity is the mind's negative reminder of its physical aspect, its capability of that aspect is the only source of whatever hope the mind can have.[43]

Put somewhat differently, the suffering physical "demands" its own redemption in a reconciled world, a world in which sensual ease is not blocked by the subject's striving for sovereignty. It is precisely this insistence that the experience of the suffering physical puts us in touch with the promise of happiness that separates Adorno from Schopenhauer. In other words, Schopenhauer's philosophy of despair is an expression of his identification of the truth of the real with the objectifications of the Will. Adorno contends that materialism controverts Schopenhauer's truth: according to the materialist, the world which includes the suffering physical cannot be reduced to or identified as the objectifications of the Will represented in the mind. The philosophy of redemption can be understood as Schopenhauer's philosophy of denial turned on its head. For Schopenhauer, a redeemed world is an illusion of the desiring Will. For Adorno, it is the promise that clings to the physicality of the particular. Thus, the Schopenhauerian elements in *Negative Dialectics* come to rest in a constellation which negates Schopenhauer's own philosophical conclusions.

In Schopenhauer, "the spell of subjectification" inheres in the *principium individuationis*. The endless spewing out of the expressions of the Will in the form of particular manifestations is utterly beyond our control. Reason cannot chain the Will because it is beyond the reach of its principles. The Will, in other words, is unfathomable, groundless, and free from the dictates of the principle of sufficient reason. The principle of sufficient reason is the universal form of every phenomenon of the Will, not of the Will itself. The expression of the Will in human willing is also subject to the dictates of the principle of sufficient reason but not the Will itself. The individual as a phenomenon of the Will is not free, in spite of the illusion of freedom that is created by the human ability to know the Will in oneself.

> The principle of sufficient reason is the universal form of every phenomenon, and man in his action, like every other phenomenon, must be subordinated to it. But because in self-consciousness the Will is known directly and in itself, there also lies in this consciousness the consciousness of freedom. But the fact is overlooked that the individual, the person, is not Will as thing-in-itself, but is the phenomenon of the Will, as such determined and has entered the form of the phenomenon, the principle of sufficient reason.[44]

Human freedom, then, is not to be found in the human capacity to act according to the dictates of reason nor in the effort to control the Will. Human beings cannot escape the necessity that is expressed in willing, but they can deny the will to live that inheres in the individual phenomenon. Denial, for Schopenhauer, is the only freedom. This denial, of course, changes nothing; one still goes on as one must. To try to change one's fate is to live it out more completely. Our humanity, our unique capacity for reason, is evidenced in stoic denial. In this sense, the striving "self is what is inhuman."[45] By seeing individualism as form only, we can deny the egoism which is expressed in our mulish efforts at self-preservation. Reason lifts the veil of Maya and opens our eyes to the "truth" of individualism. Our individuality is epiphenomenon, the mere expression of the Will. In Schopenhauer, to grasp this truth is to be "humiliated." But the wound to our narcissism opens us to the only true "foundation" of morality—compassion for the suffering of others. Once the veil of Maya is lifted, the individual comes to understand that the sharp distinction between ego and other is an illusion. By penetrating the *principium individuationis,* we learn to identify with the other. We come to see the "true significance" of our own petty striving, its ultimate insignificance. What lingers after the denial of the Will is both the composure of one who knows and the pity of one who experiences the suffering of others as a shared human fate.

> If that veil of Maya, the *principium individuationis,* is lifted from the eyes of man to such an extent that he no longer makes the egotistical distinction between himself and the person of others, but takes as much interest in the sufferings of other individuals as his own, and thus is not only benevolent and charitable in the highest degree, but even ready to sacrifice his own individuality whenever several others can be saved thereby, then it follows automatically, that such a recognition in all beings, his true and innermost self, must also regard the endless sufferings of all these lives as his own and take upon himself the pain of the whole world. No suffering is any longer strange or foreign to him. All the miseries of others, which he sees and is so seldom able to alleviate, all the miseries of which he has indirect knowledge, and even those he recognizes merely as possible, affect his mind just as do his own. It is no longer the changing weal and woe of his person, that he has in view, as is the case with the man still involved in egoism, but as he sees

through the *principium individuationis,* everything lies equally near to him. He knows the whole, comprehends its inner nature and finds it involved in a constant passing away, a vain striving, an inward conflict, and a continual suffering.[46]

Schopenhauer offers us an ethic of pity based on the identification of the "truth" of the human condition. His is the wisdom of disillusionment. The loss of innocence is the price we pay for the knowledge that can open us to the only true human freedom—denial of the Will. To know the world as Will and representation is to live beyond hope. The yearning for utopia is false consciousness, and one pays heavily for the mistake of hope. Hope enchains the utopian individual to the world he would deny. As Adorno explains: "For Schopenhauer any hope for the establishment of humanity was the fond delusion of a man who had nothing but misfortune to hope for."[47]

Adorno, on the other hand, considers the renunciation of hope to be an error of identity-logical thinking. In this sense, "despair is the last ideology."

> The mistake in Schopenhauer's thinking is that the law which keeps immanence under its own spell is directly said to be that essence which immanence blocks, the essence that would not be conceivable as other than transcendent. But the world is better than hell because the absolute conclusiveness which Schopenhauer attributes to the world's course is borrowed in turn from the idealistic system. It is a pure identity principle and as deceptive as any identity principle. The world's course is not absolute conclusive nor is absolute despair; rather despair is its conclusiveness. However void every trace of otherness in it, however much all happiness is marred by revocability: in the breaks that belie identity, entity is still pervaded by the ever-broken pledges of that otherness.[48]

The materialist honors the pledge to otherness which idealism renounces. Adorno prefers "to read transcendence longingly rather than strike out."[49] The longing of the suffering physical is to be protected as a sign of what might be, what I would call the utopia of sensual ease. The confusion of the utopia of sensual ease, in which things are allowed to rest in affinity with death is itself due to the spell of subjectification in which otherness can only appear as the subject's mirror opposite—in this case obliteration. This confusion, for Adorno, was the central error in Wagner's sensualist recasting of Schopenhauer's insight. Schopenhauer even denies the status of otherness to obliteration, whereas Wagner thinks that obliteration is otherness. The hell of our mortal life lingers on in our death. This Schopenhauerian denial of the physical is echoed in Wagner in spite of himself. For Adorno, the spell of subjectification creates a false *either/or: either* the subject's endless, impotent striving *or* its longing for complete annihilation so as to be beyond this striving.

> As long as the world is as it is, all pictures of reconciliation, peace and quiet resemble the picture of death. The slightest difference between nothingness and coming to rest would be the haven of hope, the no man's land

between the border posts of being and nothingness. Rather than overcome that zone, consciousness would have to extricate from it what is not in the power of the alternative.[50]

In a world in which the subject "survives" only through a frantic appropriation of otherness, sensual ease is recast as a death wish, as in Wagner's rendition of Schopenhauer.

The power of the alternatives between death and utopia lies in the individuality "signaled" in the noncaptured physical. Thus for Schopenhauer, the humiliated subject who relinquishes individualism must also relinquish desire for the end of suffering; whereas, for Adorno, the very suffering of the noncaptured physical gestures toward the coming into being of a multidimensional, desiring being. The subject, in its physicality, is something more than its categorization as subject over the object. To be in touch with this something more, one must reach out to the other in oneself that has been denied. To grasp the subject as constituted under the weight of a subjectivity that preserves itself at the expense of the suffering, longing, physical human being is to grasp the "truth" of Schopenhauer's vision of freedom through humiliation. In this sense, "the subject's dissolution presents at the same time the ephemeral and condemned picture of a possible subject."[51] To understand oneself as a "natural" subject is to retrieve in oneself a kind of innocence; denial is denied. The wisdom of disillusionment is exposed as the self-destructive impulse of idealism. The melancholy science is not one of defeat; to be melancholy is to experience deprivation as loss. This is itself a form of resistance in a world in which deprivation is justified as necessary. According to Adorno, to deny the desire of the natural Will is to subject oneself to the rule of the superego—a subjugation that is in league with the Kantian definition of freedom. The association of freedom in Kant with the postulation of a radically autonomous and completely unified ego contaminates freedom through its incorporation of aggression against the hapless, desiring self.

The Critique of the Kantian Subject of Morality

Adorno maintains that freedom cannot be obtained from the heteronomous but only through it. The superego represents, in reified form, the subject's constitution in and through others. To be free from the superego is to render this intersubjectivity transparent to itself as a dialectical relation:

> Instead of sanctioning the internalized and hardened authority of the superego, theory should carry out the dialectics of individual and species. The rigorism of the superego is nothing but the reflex response to the prevention of that dialectics by the antagonistic condition. The subject would be liberated only as an I reconciled with the non-I and thus it would also be above the freedom which is leagued with its counterpart repression.[52]

For Adorno, the paradox in Kant's definition of freedom as the constitution of causality by pure reason is that one is only free if one acts as one *must* as a rational being. One is free only if one obeys the law dictated by one's status as a rational noumenal Will. Adorno finds it no coincidence that "all the concepts whereby the Critique of Practical Reason proposes in honor of freedom, to fill the chasm between the Imperative and Mankind are repressive. A causality produced by freedom corrupts freedom into obedience."[53]

The repressive aspect of Kantian morality stems, in part, from the radical separation of reason and nature and can be overcome only through the dialectic of natural history in which the natural moment of reason itself is not denied.

> The prehistory of reason, that it is a moment of nature and yet something else, has become the immanent definition of reason. It is natural as the psychological force split off for purposes of self-preservation; once split off and contrasted with nature it also becomes nature's otherness. But if that dialectic irrepressibly turns reason into the absolute antithesis of nature, if the nature in reason itself is forgotten, reason will be self-preservation running wild and will regress to nature. It is only as reflection upon that self-preservation that reason would be above nature.[54]

The impulses of physical desire are part of the rational Will itself. The Will must be understood dialectically in its relation to the very desires it unifies and expresses.

> A Will without physical impulses, impulses that survive, weakened in imagination, would not be a Will. At the same time, however, the Will settles down as the centralizing unit of impulses as the authority that tames them and potentially negates them. This necessitates a dialectical definition of the Will. It is the force that enables consciousness to leave its domain and so change what merely exists; as recoil is resistance.[55]

Under a dialectical conception of the Will, there can be no absolute divide between the noumenal and the empirical subject, any more than there can be a transcendental gap between reason and desire. A person is never a completed unity as rational Will. Yet the independence of Will understood as the striving for the unity of the ego is also not denied. Here one hears the echo of Nietzsche. A self is not a given, it is a goal, an aesthetic achievement. "To become what one is" is an accomplishment, and one that is never completed as long as the desiring self continues to live.

As a result, the Will cannot be thoroughly objectified without losing itself as Will. For the Will to be the Will it must retain the subjective moment that makes it irreducible to any categorical expression. As Adorno remarks: "We can as well talk of a Will that is independent and to that extent objective as we can talk of a strong ego or in the latter days of old character."[56] Kant's mistake was to make the noumenal subject into a totality. Only by so doing could he achieve the radical independence of the noumenal self. Adorno understands this move on Kant's part to be progressive as well as regressive:

> According to Kantian ethics the subject's totality predominates over the moments it lives by—moments which alone give life to the totality, although

outside such a totality they would not make up a Will. The discovery was progressive . . . the subject becomes moral for itself; it cannot be weighed by standards that are inwardly and outwardly particular and alien to the subject. Once the rational unity of the Will is established as the sole moral authority, the subject is protected from the violence done to it by a hierarchical society—a society which (as still in Dante's sense) would judge a man's deeds without any previous acceptance of its law by his consciousness.[57]

There is a truth in "free Will" that Adorno does not want to deny. But once the transcendental divide between nature and reason is deconstructed, the notion of free Will takes on a new meaning. What Adorno rejects is the inescapable alternative inherent in the Kantian project: either the Will is free or it's unfree. According to Adorno, it is both:

> Each drastic thesis is false. In their innermost core, the theses of freedom and determinism coincide. Both proclaim identity. The reduction to pure spontaneity applies to the empirical subject the very same law which as an expanded casual category becomes determinism. Perhaps free men would be freed from the Will also; surely it is only in a free society that individuals would be free.[58]

Adorno sees as Hegel's great insight the understanding that concrete freedom is objective, not simply a state of the Will. Marx adds to this view the insistence that "objective" freedom always rests on the satisfaction of material needs. Freedom for the empirical subject cannot be had without the gratification of need. The very materiality of human existence demands a socially realized freedom in which want, in its extreme forms, has been eliminated. As already suggested, such a freedom can only be achieved intersubjectively because the "independent" self can only defeat its longing by alienating itself from the world rather than by making the world a home. Satisfaction demands mutuality and adjustment. The atomic individual cannot lay hold of a world that yields to the need to negate suffering. However, freedom, in the form of the postulation of the radical autonomy of the rational Will, even if philosophically false, expresses a truth of social experience. We feel isolated from one another; our interdependence occurs behind our backs. Reified as social order and internalized as the superego, intersubjectivity is frozen into a context which determines us and appears beyond our control. Individualism, as an imposed social form, turns against the aspiration to be free in the full, material sense precisely because realized freedom demands a "transparent solidarity" which individualism blocks. This view, of course, should not be taken to mean that Adorno rejects the association of freedom with individuality altogether. The relationship, however, is complex.

> The individual feels free insofar as he has opposed himself to society and can do something—though incomparably less than he believes—against society and other individuals. His freedom is primarily that of a man pursuing his own ends, ends that are not totally exhausted by social ends. In this sense freedom coincides with the principles of individuation. A freedom of this type has broken loose from punitive society; within an increasingly rational one,

it has achieved a measure of reality. At the same time in the midst of bourgeois society freedom remains no less delusive than individuality itself.[59]

The delusion inherent in this kind of freedom is that it masks the necessity it imposes.

> The real necessity involved in the kind of freedom praised by radical individualism ideology—in a freedom which the free had to maintain and to enforce with their elbows—this necessity was an image designed to cover up the social necessity that compels an individual to be rugged if he wants to survive.[60]

Adorno ultimately endorses the view of individual freedom put forward in Hegel's *Phenomenology of Mind*. The individual as rational Will is not free of the heteronomous; (s)he comes to the concept of freedom only *against* it and in struggle with it. As material beings, we are beholden to one another and to the outside world more generally. The idea of freedom is entwined with the experience of unfreedom. In this sense, *individual* freedom is a moment, a historical mode, which resists what would deny it.

Freedom Rethought

> As perceived in Hegel's *Phenomenology*, it is only from that which has been divided from it, from that which is against it, that the subject acquires the concepts of freedom and unfreedom which it will then relate to its own structure.[61]

Freedom cannot be "positive" because, in the Hegelian sense, it is freedom against. The material moment of freedom can only be realized socially. But the inevitable social aspect of the conditions of freedom does not mean that freedom can be simply identified with what the collectivity defines freedom to be. Adorno's critique of Marx is that he, too, posited a positive notion of freedom in which the tension between the "individual" and the "community" would collapse. Reconciliation demands that this tension be maintained but not reified. A self-transparent solidarity would allow for much greater fluidity in relations between subjects, but it would not totally end the experience of the divide between the internal and external.

> In a state of freedom the individual would not be frantically guarding the old particularity—individuality is the produce of pressure as well as the energy center for resistance to this pressure—but neither would that state of freedom agree with the present concept of collectivity. The fact that collectivism is directly commanded in the countries which today monopolize the name of socialism, commanded as the individual's subordination to society, this fact belies the socialism of those countries, and solidifies antagonism.[62]

The recovery of "the natural" in reason itself rejects the idea of freedom as the notion of radical autonomy or sovereignty. There is no freedom except in and through otherness, and there is no freedom without an end to material deprivation. Adorno rejects completely the Schopenhauerian view of "freedom" as denial. Where Adorno agrees with Schopenhauer, however, is in his stress on sympathy for the other as the basis for moral intuition. Yet Adorno holds that it is compassion rather than pity which is the basis for sympathy for others. Pity reflects the helplessness inherent in Schopenhauer's idealism. The fate of the desiring individual is indeed pitiful in Schopenhauer. Compassion, for Adorno, is not rooted in the wisdom of disillusionment but in the recognition of the shared human plight that comes from the subject's reflection on his "natural side." The "mindfulness of nature," our grasp of our existence as the suffering physical allows us to be *soft*. Goodness, for Adorno, is a form of tenderness. To the degree that the Kantian "kingdom of ends" imagines something like a reconciled condition between human beings, it retains a utopian content. But the Adornian emphasis on the recovery of compassion, through the subject's reflection on her or his own otherness, breaks with the framework of de-ontological ethics.

In other words, Adorno wishes to preserve goodwill without repression or, more radically, to suggest that repression blocks goodwill. Adorno's moral subject that does not know itself as a "natural" desiring being will not recover the sympathy for others that can serve as a nonrepressive "basis" for moral intuition. Adorno's point, put starkly, is that an ethics separated categorically from what has been called the "natural" will be repressive.

"The mindfulness of nature" opens subjects to otherness in the recognition of their own nonidentity and, by so doing, allows us to appreciate ourselves and others as multidimensional beings. This openness to otherness is demonstrated in Adorno as a non-violative relation to the concrete which does not seek to appropriate or to remain indifferent. The "love" for otherness is blocked by a subject which can only see the Other as its own image or as its mirror opposite. Adorno's deconstruction, and yet incorporation, of Schopenhauer's ethic of pity in the dialectic of natural history helps us to think again about Herbert Marcuse's belief that the only foundation for our moral beliefs is the compassion for the suffering of others. The call to love things "both earnest and ironic" is not a call to focus merely on nature as an abstraction or on things in their concrete individuality at the expense of relations between human beings. Such a shift in perspective is, if you like, the underpinning of a different unrepressed interrelatedness. To argue that there is something "there" that has been repressed, we need not rely on Freud's theory of the drives or on some other notion of an essential human nature. We must simply see the untruth of idealism, the identification of the real with its concept.

Negative Dialectics in Its Relation to Contemporary Trends in Philosophy

Following through Adorno's own insight into nonidentity allows us to reject Adorno's tendency to make negativity absolute. His emphasis, however, continues to provide us with an important reminder. For Adorno, what appears sensible is often that which has been imposed on us. Common sense too easily degenerates into the wisdom of rationalization. The significance of Adorno's warning against the complacent acceptance of common sense can best be brought out through a comparison with both Hans George Gadamer's appeal to tradition[63] and Richard Rorty's appeal to solidarity[64] as means by which we come to make sense of our ethical and political environment. Although they come to Hegel from very different beginnings, I understand both Gadamer and Rorty to be pragmatic Hegelians. While it would be unfair to Gadamer to suggest that his appeal to tradition does not allow for critique—the adherence to a tradition is a self-conscious appropriation of tradition, and such a self-conscious appropriation implies critique—there is nonetheless a quietism in his philosophy. Rarely does Gadamer reflect on *who* are the "we" who *share* a tradition. Rorty, likewise, appeals to "social practice" and "our shared conversation"; in a similar manner, he fails to come fully to terms with the ethical critique of "the conversation of mankind." In Hegelian terms, both Rorty and Gadamer fail to recognize the difference in identity. Adorno's negative dialectics reminds us again and again of the relations of domination and exclusion which are implicated in an abstract appeal to the "we" who *share*. The emphasis on the continuation of "the conversation of mankind" in the present is similarly undermined. An ethic which fails to incorporate the role not only of critique but also of the full disruptive power of the imagination[65] "condemns us to an unending commerce with the familiar objects of thought."[66] Adorno's negative dialectics disrupts this unending commerce at every turn. For Adorno, to gain insight into what is we must know it as other. To know it as other is to know it in the light of a redeemed world.

> Perspectives must be fashioned that displace and estrange the world, reveal it to be with its rights and crevices, as indigent and distorted as it will appear one day in the messianic light. To gain such perspectives without vulgarity or violence entirely from fleeting contact with its objects—this is the task of thought.[67]

Adorno's emphasis on the *unheimlich* need not be read as the denial of ethical mediation. Instead, Adorno should be understood as reminding us that we will not really find "our dwelling" in the world until we stop trying desperately to make a home out of our world by means of identity-logical thinking.

> In fear, bondage to nature is perpetuated by a thinking that identifies, that equalizes everything unequal. Thoughtless rationality is blinded to the point of madness by the sight of whatsoever will elude its rule. . . . Even the theory of alienation, the ferment of dialectics, confuses the need to approach the heteronomous and thus irrational world to be "at home everywhere" as Novalis put it—with the archaic barbarism that the loving subject cannot love what is alien and different, with the craving for incorporation and persecution. If the alien were no longer ostracized there hardly would be any more alienation.[68]

Adorno's melancholy science reminds us of the violence of intersubjectivity. He forces us to confront the content of the solidarity to which we appeal.

And, of course, Adorno continually questions whether or not there can be a truly "self-transparent" solidarity within the frame of mass society. Adorno's suspicion, and indeed fear, of intersubjectivity when taken to its extremes can be understood as an expression of the very hostility to the alien he warns us against. Yet his suspicion does not result because he has no view of intersubjectivity but rather because he adopts the strong Hegelian vision of self-consciousness as a social, interactive achievement. It is precisely his understanding of the intersubjective constitution of self-consciousness which leads him to question whether the conditions of mass society do not completely undermine the social conditions in which critical subjectivity can survive. Thus, Adorno emphasizes the vantage point of the exile for its value in preserving the remnants of critique. Who are the "we" who hear Adorno and why now? How does he speak to us? Why engage in the task of recovering "some freedom for history" within Adorno's own categories? What does it mean to take responsibility for Adorno's signature?

Conclusion

I will begin my conclusion with an answer to my last question. In "taking responsibility for the signature of the other," we are tested in our own ability to exercise our openness to and tenderness toward otherness. To take responsibility for the signature of the other without violation demands that one seek to internalize the attitude toward otherness which shines through the cracks and the crevices of *Negative Dialectics*. It demands that we reflect on the ethical relation in general, the very relation to which Adorno directs our attention. What is at stake in such a project is less the following of rules than the open-minded spirit in which it is accomplished. In part, Adorno speaks to us now because his implicit ethical vision rests on expansiveness rather than on constriction. His is a gentle, directive message which does not demand the universalization of one particular behavioral mode of morality. The focus is less on doing what is right in accordance with one's duty than on the development of an attitude of tenderness toward otherness and gentleness toward oneself as a sensual creature. The dialectical richness of Adorno's deconstructive Hegelianism allows us to overcome the rigid divide between the serious business of ethics and the playfulness of the aesthetic realm. Adorno refuses the Kantian categorical divide between the ethical and the aesthetic. Yet if Adorno is to be rightly accused of "aestheticizing" the ethical, it is only in Charles Peirce's unique sense of aesthetics. For Peirce, the ethical is subordinate to the aesthetic. For Peirce, "esthetics is the science of ends, and the business of the esthetician is to say what is the state of things which is most admirable in itself regardless of any ulterior reason."[69] Adorno's pessimism about the effect of a "fallen world" on positive visions of the ultimate good led him to proceed by indication rather than by direct philosophical elaboration. In Adorno, the ultimate Good can only be *known* negatively. But without redemptive perspectives which, at the very least, indicate the ultimate good of communicative freedom, we would be unable to even glimpse the different way of belonging together which inheres in Adorno's critique of totality. The ultimate good, then, is present in Adorno in its negative force and as the force of the negative. The ultimate question whether Adorno's own formulation of his project degenerates into endless negativity depends, in part, on how seriously we take his attempt to develop constellations as a counter to determinate negation and, ultimately, on what we make of his critique of Hegel's move to totality. As I have suggested, Adorno took seriously the redefinition of "communicative freedom" as an essential aspect of a redemptive perspective. But the following question remains: is the rendering of communicative freedom in terms of a redemptive perspective appropriate enough, or must we, like Heidegger, attempt to think of "belonging together" differently or, like Peirce, develop a vision of "evolutionary love"? In other words, the question to Adorno remains as follows: Can we approach "diversity in unity" without thinking belonging together differently, or must we always fall back on an appeal to the whole, whether we call it Creativity or the Will? In spite of the perplexities which persist even after the most sympathetic reading of *Negative Dialectics*, Adorno remains a crucial voice for those of us who seek to aspire to the ethical relationship.

Notes

1. Theodor W. Adorno, *Negative Dialectics*, trans. E. B. Ashton (New York: Continuum, 1973), p. 139.

2. Immanuel Kant, *Foundations of the Metaphysics of Morals*, trans. Louis White Beck (Indianapolis: Bobbs-Merrill, 1959), pp. 30–31.

3. Adorno, *Negative Dialectics*, p. 145.

4. Michael Theneuissen, *Sein und Schein, der Kritische Funktion Hegelschen Logik* (Frankfurt a.M.: Suhrkamp, 1978), pp. 148–49.

5. Ibid.

6. Adorno, *Negative Dialectics*, p. 191.

7. Theodor W. Adorno, *Minima Moralia: Reflections from Damaged Life*, trans. E. F. N. Jephcott (London: New Left Books, 1974), p. 50.

8. I am using realism in the popular sense rather than in the strict philosophical sense, but there is a relationship between the two that cannot be entirely ignored, particularly as certain forms of moral realism deny the possibility of radical transformation, and also particularly as this realism has been used in moral theory. As the counterexample of a unique understanding of this realism, which could be reinterpreted in moral theory so as not to foreclose radical transformation, see Sabina Lovibond, *Realism and Imagination in Ethics* (Minneapolis: University of Minnesota Press, 1983).

9. Adorno, *Minima Moralia*, p. 16.

10. Ibid., p. 200.

11. Ibid., p. 167.

12. Adorno, *Negative Dialectics*, p. 144.

13. Ibid., p. 161.

14. Ibid., p. 38.

15. Ibid., p. 143.

16. Ibid., p. 27.

17. Ibid., p. 172.

18. Ibid., p. 160.

19. Ibid., p. 167.

20. Ibid., p. 145.

21. Ibid., p. 11.

22. Robert Neville, *Hegel and Whitehead: Contemporary Perspectives on Systematic Philosophy,* ed. George R. Lucas Jr. (Albany: State University of New York Press, 1986), p. 91.

23. Ibid., p. 92.

24. Richard Rorty continues to make this mistake. See "Philosophy in America Today," in *Consequences of Pragmatism* (Minneapolis: University of Minnesota Press, 1982), pp. 211–30.

25. Adorno, *Negative Dialectics,* p. 161.

26. Ibid., p. 158.

27. Ibid., p. 159.

28. Adorno, *Minima Moralia,* p. 247.

29. Adorno, *Negative Dialectics,* p. 163.

30. On one reading this understanding differs from Benjamin's. Cf. "The Language of Man," in *Reflections: Essays, Aphorisms, Autobiographical Writings,* ed. Peter Demetz, trans. Edmund Jephcott (New York: Harcourt Brace Jovanovich, 1978).

31. Adorno, *Negative Dialectics,* p. 163.

32. Ibid.

33. Ibid.

34. Ibid., p. 161.

35. Ibid., p. 174.

36. Theodor W. Adorno, *Against Epistemology; A Metacritique: Studies in Husserl and the Phenomenological Antinomies,* trans. Willis Domingo (Oxford: Basil Black-well,1982), p. 162.

37. Fred R. Dallmayr, *Twilight of Subjectivity: Contributions to a Post-Individualist Theory of Politics* (Amherst: University of Massachusetts Press, 1981), p. 137.

38. Adorno, *Negative Dialectics,* p. 357.

39. Theodor W. Adorno, "The Idea of Natural History," trans. Bob Hullot, *Telos* 60 (Summer 1984): 111–24.

40. Adorno, *Negative Dialectics,* p. 203.

41. Ibid., p. 204.

42. Ibid., pp. 203–204.

43. Ibid., p. 203.

44. Arthur Schopenhauer, *The World as Will and Representation,* vol. 1, trans. E. F. I. Payne (New York: Dover, 1969), p. 104.

45. Adorno, *Negative Dialectics,* p. 299.

46. Schopenhauer, *World as Will and Representation,* p. 104.

47. Theodor W. Adorno and Max Horkheimer, *Dialectic of Enlightenment,* trans. John Cumming (New York: Herder and Herder, 1972), p. 103.

48. Adorno, *Negative Dialectics,* p. 404.

49. Ibid., p. 400.

50. Ibid., p. 38.

51. Ibid., p. 281.

52. Ibid., p. 283

53. Ibid., p. 232.

54. Ibid., p. 289.

55. Ibid., p. 241.

56. Ibid., p. 238.

57. Ibid.

58. Ibid., p. 264.

59. Ibid., p. 262.

60. Ibid.

61. Ibid., p. 220.

62. Ibid., pp. 283–84.

63. Hans-Georg Gadamer, *Truth and Method* (New York: Crossroads, 1975).

64. Rorty, "Philosophy in America Today."

65. Lovibond, *Realism and Imagination in Ethics.*

66. Ibid., p. 195.

67. Adorno, *Minima Moralia*, p. 274.

68. Adorno, *Negative Dialectics*, p. 172.

69. Charles S. Peirce, *The Collected Papers of Charles Sanders Peirce, 1931–1934*, ed. Charles Hartshorne and Paul Weiss (Cambridge, Mass.: Belknap Press of the Harvard University Press, 1960), p. 130. Cf. his "Evolutionary Love," in *Philosophical Writings*, ed. Justus Buchler (New York: Dover, 1955), pp. 361–74.

Drucilla Cornell: Selected Bibliography

Books

At the Heart of Freedom: Feminism, Sex, and Equality. Princeton: Princeton University Press, 1998.

The Imaginary Domain: Abortion, Pornography and Sexual Harassment. New York: Routledge, 1995.

Transformations: Recollective Imagination and Sexual Difference. New York: Routledge, 1993.

The Philosophy of Limit. New York: Routledge, 1992.

Hegel and Legal Theory. New York: Routledge, 1991

Beyond Accommodation: Ethical Feminism, Deconstruction, and the Law. New York: Routledge, 1991.

Feminism as Critique: Essays on the Politics of Gender in Late-Capitalist Societies. Minneapolis: University of Minnesota Press, 1987.

Journal Articles

"Exploring the Imaginary Domain." *Philosophy and Social Criticism* 24.2–3 (1998).

"The Future of Sexual Difference: An Interview with Judith Butler and Drucilla Cornell." *Diacritics* 28.1 (1998).

"Exploring the Imaginary Domain." *Philosophy and Social Criticism* 24.2–3 (1998).

"Re-thinking Consciousness Raising: Citizenship and the Law and Politics of Adoption." *Southern Journal of Philosophy* 35, Supp. (1997).

"Enabling Paradoxes: Gender Difference and Systems Theory." *New Literary History* 27.2 (1996).

"Feminism, Deconstruction and the Law." *Radical Philosophy* 73 (1995).

"Loyalty and the Limits of Kantian Impartiality." *Harvard Law Review* 107.8 (1994).

"Beyond Accommodation: Ethical Feminism, Deconstruction, and the Law." *Harvard Civil Rights–Civil Liberties Law Review* 27.1 (1992).

"Gender Hierarchy, Equality, and the Possibility of Democracy." *American Imago* 48.2 (1991).

"Sex-Discrimination Law and Equivalent Rights." *Dissent* 38.3 (1991).

"The Doubly-Prized World: Myth, Allegory and the Feminine." *Cornell Law Review* 75.3 (1990).

"The Problem of Normative Authority in Legal Interpretation." *Law and Semiotics* 1 (1987).

"Time, Deconstruction, and the Challenge to Legal Positivism: The Call for Judicial Responsibility." *Yale Journal of Law and the Humanities* 2.2 (1990).

Part 3

Places of Identity

7

Unhomelike Places

Archetictural Sections of Heidegger and Freud

DAVID FARRELL KRELL

David Farrell Krell is one of the most influential and original contributors to American continental philosophy. Yet, in many ways, he is as European as he is American. He lived in Germany and taught at German universities for years. While he came to know Martin Heidegger well and became the foremost translator of Heidegger's works into English, he also compiled, in consultation with Heidegger, the first English collection of Heidegger's essays, *Basic Writings.* Before returning to the United States, Krell was Chair of the Philosophy Department at Essex University in England and helped to establish a strong and respected presence for continental philosophy there.

Krell's work began as a confrontation with Heidegger's *Nietzsche.* Marx, Merleau-Ponty, and Freud were important for his work in Nietzschean genealogy and Heideggerian ontology. Issues of metaphysics and ontology—especially in Heidegger's project of a fundamental ontology of Dasein—but also of philosophical anthropology and existential psychology, were at the forefront of Krell's philosophical interest. Krell's work on Heidegger is pervasive but finds specific expression in his books *Intimations of Mortality* and *Daimon Life.* In many ways, Krell's own development as a thinker and writer can be traced through his work on Nietzsche, which has been a continuous yet radically transformed thread throughout his life. Krell's work *Postponements* attempts to show how Nietzsche's postponements—woman, sensuality, and death—pervade his ideas and his styles. *Infectious Nietzsche, Nietzsche: A Novel,* and *The Good European,* from a decade later, show how Nietzsche continues to be one of Krell's philosophical and literary interlocutors. The work that brings together the breadth and uniqueness of Krell's philosophy, as it is focused around the theme of memory, is his *Of Memory, Reminiscence, and Writing.* Over the years, Krell has become more and more preoccupied with questions of literature and art. Derrida's work became crucially important to him once he became convinced by Derrida's response to Heidegger's *Nietzsche.* The writings of

Maurice Blanchot have also been important to him, and in recent years, in works such as *Lunar Voices* and *Contagion*, he has focused on the German Idealists and Romantics, especially Hölderlin, Novalis, Schelling, and Hegel. He has written on topics in eighteenth- and nineteenth-century science and history of medicine, but also on the philosophy of history and art as interpreted by the German Romantics.

As this essay shows, Krell remains concerned with questions developed by Freud and Heidegger. His interest in architecture was sparked by Daniel Libeskind's recently inaugurated Jewish Museum project in Berlin and by his own work over many years with Don Bates, Peter Davidson, and Ben Nicholson. The extended references to Hoffmann and Rilke give some suggestion of Krell's involvement in literature, while references to Irigaray point to questions concerning erotic life.

⟶⊨◉⟜⟞

. . . to be looking with closed eyes at midnight, to dream with open ones at noon.
—Daniel Libeskind

. . . the question of the fragment in architecture is very important since it may be that only ruins express a fact completely. Photographs of cities during the war, sections of apartments, broken toys. Delphi and Olympia.
—Aldo Rossi

Why *archetictural* sections—spelling the word new? Because the ancient Greek word τίκτειν, meaning to engender by lovemaking, may well be older than every notion of τέχνη, more archaic than every architectonic or form of technology. The first two chapters of the book from which this essay is taken, *Archeticture: Ecstasies of Space, Time, and the Human Body,* deal with (1) Plato's account of choric space and materiality/elementality in *Timaeus,* and (2) the "ecstatic" spatiality that begins to unfold in modernity with Kant, Hegel, and Heidegger.[1] It will not be possible for me to summarize these chapters in a few lines in order that the reader might venture with some confidence or at least some sense of familiarity into the present undertaking. Moreover, the essay reprinted here tries to develop a sense of the *uncanny* and *unhomelike* nature—the *Unheimlichkeit*—of both the Platonic discourse on χώρα and the Heideggerian "ecstatic" analysis of space and time. With apologies to the reader for this abrupt beginning *in medias res,* I proceed to the topic of the *unfamiliar* as such.

Neither a choric space, that is, a space for cosmic lovemaking, nor a liberated ecstatic spatiality can be familiar to us. Neither has to do with the usual; neither can be reduced to the technical. Everything about what I am calling *archeticture* is therefore strange and even uncanny. In the present essay I shall call upon Heidegger once again, this time aided and abetted (or

Fig. 7.1. Gisela Baurmann, *Scissors' Skin*. Latex, 1990–91.
"Quetsch: Investigation into Architectural Representation."
LoPSiA Paris/Briey.

Fig. 7.2. Gisela Baurmann, *Scissors' Skin*. Latex, 1990–91.
"Quetsch: Investigation into Architectural Representation."
LoPSiA Paris/Briey.

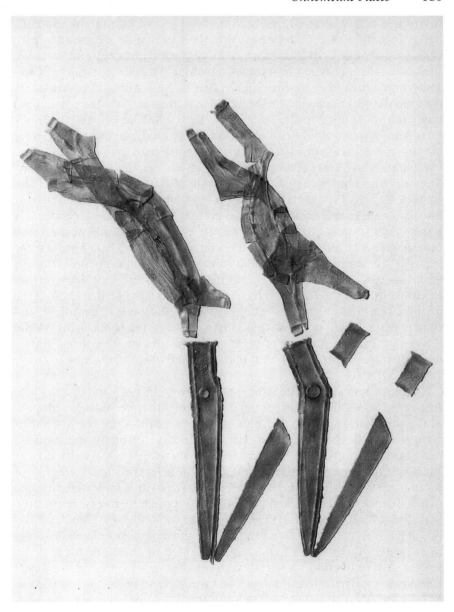

Fig. 7.3. Gisela Baurmann, *Scissors' Skin*. Latex, 1990–91.
"Quetsch: Investigation into Architectural Representation."
LoPSiA Paris/Briey.

interrupted and frustrated) by Freud, seeking insight into the unhomelike quality of archeticture. To be sure, I will not dream of an architectural *plan* or *elevation* composed of equal parts of Heideggerian ontology and Freudian psychoanalysis. For who knows what a plan or elevation of Heidegger and Freud would look like? No one knows. One no longer dreams of structures of thought and knowledge in the way Kant dreamed of them, searching madly for (and failing to find) the bedrock on which to construct a Tribunal of Pure Reason. No, not an elevation of any kind, nor any plan. Here it can only be an attempt to devise and design several *archetictural sections,* odd glimpses and cross sections, snippets of curious alignments and complex configurations in the bodies of thought of Heidegger and Freud.[2] The thought of each of the two, taken singly, is of course demanding enough to foil any amateur archeticton. Such as myself. I shall therefore restrict this inquiry for the most part to Freud's 1919 essay, "Das Unheimliche," and Heidegger's 1925 lecture course at Marburg University, *Prolegomena to the History of the Concept of Time.*[3] Freud's essay is contemporaneous with his work on *Beyond the Pleasure Principle,* his most dazzling speculative work, published in 1920; Heidegger's lecture course is a kind of first draft of his magnum opus, *Being and Time,* published in 1927. However, restricting the number of texts will not really guarantee focus: there is enough material here for an infinite number of juxtapositions—challenging, thought-provoking juxtapositions. I shall restrain myself, and offer thirty-three sections.

•

Heidegger is talking to the editors of *Der Spiegel* in 1966 and looking into the mirror. Ironically, while looking into the mirror, contemplating his own tarnished political image in the faces of these journalists, the old man shortchanges himself, cheats his own thought. He loudly laments the rootlessness and homelessness *(die Heimatlosigkeit)* of contemporary existence, as though the extirpation of rootlessness and homelessness had always been the concern of his thought. The contemporary plight is indicated, he says, by the absence of great art and poetry. It is as though he had never noticed Paul Klee, whose work, however, he cites at the outset of "Time and Being," a piece written only five years before the *Spiegel* interview. (Two decades earlier, Klee's works had been confiscated by the Nazis for the "degenerate art" exhibition.) It is as though he, Heidegger, were the usual type of neoconservative or reactionary, who turns right in politics when there is nothing left of art. However, for the younger man, for Heidegger the phenomenologist and ontologist, and sometimes even for the mature thinker of mortality, homelessness is nothing to be lamented. It is rather the ontological distinction of humankind, the pristine character of *Dasein* or "existence" as such. Homelessness is what every work of art and archeticture bestows on us: neither roots nor domesticity nor the fireside chat but a sense of our being never at home in the face of the uncanny.

•

In *Being and Time* and in the Marburg lecture courses that led up to it, Heidegger defined human existence itself in terms of being *not-at-home.*

Indeed, in the first draft of his analysis of care and concern as the fundamental modes of human comportment, Heidegger gathered these existential, ecstatic structures under the larger notion of the unhomelike or uncanny. Section 30 of his 1925 *Prolegomena to the History of the Concept of Time* declares that human existence *(Dasein)* has essentially nothing to do with homey homes, that its very being is *Unheimlichkeit*, "uncanniness," "unhomelikeness." Our being in the world, the world that serves as our only home, is marked by the uncanny discovery that we are *not* at home in it. *Dasein*, or being-there, when it is truly there, is an absentee; it is stamped and typed by the *Unzuhause*, the not-at-home, the nobody-home. Heidegger's thought, early and late, at least until his belated mirror phase, revolves about this paradox or terrible irony: human being is being in the world and dwelling on the earth—and yet we are never at home in the world, never rooted in the earth. When we finally arrive at the "there" of there-being *(Da-sein)*, as Gertrude Stein knew, there isn't any there there. There there is ash—what Freud knew as traces of "the unconscious," and Heidegger as "being toward the end."

•

Is this feeling of being ill at ease, this uncanny, unhomey sensation—whatever fine distinctions or sweeping claims Heidegger may try to make—merely our fear of death? Or is it more like a pervasive, indeterminate anxiety, a fundamental or founding mood that Heidegger at other times reads variously as joy, melancholy, and, most strikingly, profound boredom? In the face of *what* are we anxious, joyous, melancholy, or deeply bored? Everything and nothing. Everything: beings as a whole. Nothing: no thing at all. An impersonal yet thoroughgoing alienation or expropriation marks our efforts to learn who we are. In his inaugural lecture of 1929, "What Is Metaphysics?" Heidegger finds an appropriately impersonal phrase for it: *Es wird einem unheimlich*, literally, it becomes uncanny for one; more loosely, one begins to feel uncannily not at home, one looks at no one in particular and for no particular reason says, "It's getting strange." Heidegger would insist that this is not an expression of nostalgia, not the predictable homesickness of philosophers, which both Novalis and Nietzsche descried, described, and decried, not anomie, not sentimentality, not the religious longing for a world beyond. Also not a mere prologue to the politics of reaction or capitulation to the allures of "leadership?"

> Indeed, Nathanael's poems were quite boring *[sehr langweilig]*. His revulsion in the face of Clara's cold and prosaic heart grew more intense; for her part, Clara could not overcome her revulsion in the face of Nathanael's obscure, gloomy, and tedious *[langweilige]* mysticism. . . . (Hoffmann, *S*)

•

When and where do human beings begin to feel the uncanniness of human being? Heidegger became increasingly convinced that the *poet's* experience discloses most relentlessly the paradox or terrible irony of human homelessness and disquiet. In the summer of 1927, while discussing Kant—not the most sentimental of thinkers, one must say, except perhaps where bedrock is concerned—Heidegger turned to Rainer Maria Rilke's *The Note-books of Malte Laurids Brigge* in order to get a bit closer to the "fundamental problem" of the manifold meaning of being. Suddenly, instead of an ontology of beings or epistemology of subjects and objects, and instead of Augustine and Aristotle, he invoked the exemplary worlds of the "primitive" and the "child"—Freud's two favorite worlds, the world of totem and taboo and the world of trauma. In order to rejoin these privileged yet remote worlds, as it were, Heidegger injected into his lecture course a piece of poetry, *prose* poetry. About what? About architecture—or perhaps archeticture—in the city. And about ruins. Ruins of home, ruins at home.

•

The passage from *Malte Laurids Brigge* elaborates a kind of archetictural section, a transversal slice through the middle of a dilapidated apartment building. The slice is produced not on the architect's drawing table, however, but by a wrecker working at the behest of a city planner. Rilke writes:

> Will anyone believe that there are such houses? No, they will say, I'm counterfeiting. This time it is the truth, nothing omitted, and, of course, nothing added. Where would I get it from? You know I'm poor. You know that. Houses? However, to be precise, they were houses that were no longer there. Houses that had been demolished from top to bottom. What was there were the other houses, the houses that had stood next to them, high neighboring houses. Obviously, these were in danger of collapsing, now that everything next to them had been removed; for a huge framework of long, tarred poles had been rammed in at an angle between the mud of the vacant lot and the stripped walls. I do not know whether I've already said that it is these walls I am referring to. Yet it was not, as it were, the outside wall of the remaining houses (which is what one would have had to suppose) but the inside wall of the houses that once stood there. One could see the inner surfaces of these walls. On the various stories one could see the walls of rooms where the wallpaper still clung, with here and there the hint of a floor or a ceiling. In addition to the walls of the rooms, a dirty white space ran the entire length of the brick wall, and through that space crept the open, rust-speckled conduits of the toilet pipes, undulating softly in an inexpressibly disgusting wormlike peristaltic movement. Gray, dusty traces marked the paths that gas for the lamps had followed along the edges of the ceilings; they twisted all the way around, here and there, quite unexpectedly, and entered into a hole in the colored walls, a black gap torn carelessly out of the wall. Most unforgettable, however, were the walls themselves. The resilient life of these rooms had not let itself be quashed. It was still there; it clung to the remaining nails; it stood on the hand's breadth of floorboard; it had crept under the hints of corners, where a tiny bit of interior space still remained. One could see it in the colors that had been transformed ever so slowly over the years: blue into moldy green, green into gray, and yellow into an ancient and stagnant white that was rotting away. Yet it was also in the fresher places that had been preserved behind mirrors, pictures, and closets; for it had traced and retraced their contours, and was present in these hidden places too, with their spiders and dust, places now denuded. It was in every scrap that had been stripped away, it was in the moist bulges on the lower edges of the wallpaper, it hovered in the

tattered remnants; the repulsive stains that had come into existence long ago exuded it. And out of these walls at one time blue, green, and yellow, framed by the fissured paths of the now destroyed connecting walls, the atmosphere of this life stood out—the resilient, phlegmatic, halting breath that no wind had yet dispersed. There stood the noondays and the illnesses, the exhalations and the smoke of years, and the sweat that pours from armpits and makes our clothes heavy, the fetid breath of mouths, and the musty smell of fermenting feet. There stood the pungency of urine, the ardor of soot, the gray steam from boiled potatoes, and the heavy, slippery stench of fat gone rancid. The sweet and lingering smell of neglected suckling babes was there, the smell of anxiety in children who go to school, and the moist heat rising from the beds of growing boys. And much had joined this company from down below, from the abyss of alleyways, everything that had gone up in smoke; and other things had trickled down from above with the rain, which, above cities, is not pure. And much had been blown in by the weak and domesticated housewinds that always stay in the same street, and much was there from who knows where. I've already said that all the walls had been demolished, all the way back to the rear wall—? Now, this is the wall I've been talking about all this while. You will say that I stood before this wall a long time; but I swear I began to run the moment I recognized it. For that is the terrifying thing—the fact that I did recognize it. Everything I've mentioned here I recognize, and that is why, without the slightest exertion, it runs me through: it is at home in me.[4]

It is at home in me. . . . How strange, how exceedingly strange, to hear Heidegger invoking prose that is not so much purple as moldy green and off-white; uncanny to hear him citing a fiction that extols the resilient life of fetid breath and fermenting feet. There is not another quotation like it in the Heideggerian corpus. Edifying hymns to gods and portentous worries about the destiny of the planet—that is the usual fare with Heidegger. Columns on the march, not cheesy feet; fateful sendings and fatalities of being, not city planning. However, razed walls too are a fatality, the ruins that one recognizes and that run one through. Ruins of home, ruins at home, ruination. Ruinance. I repeat, I do not know another passage in Heidegger as uncanny as this one. And it comes from *Rilke*—the poet he will accuse (in 1942–43) of Schopenhauerianism, botched Christianity, and a kind of sentimental bestiality.[5]

While conceptualizing buildings as machines eventually led to the demise of meaning in the city of my memory, rational devaluation is violently transcended by this exploded identification. The instruments of torture are also manifestations of architecture as a verb, once and for all replacing the obsolete noun and positing poetic destruction in place of technological building. (Alberto Pérez-Gómez, *Polyphilo*, 1992)

•

It is at home in me—Rilke. *It* is unhomelike for one—Heidegger. Freud of course has much to say about this *It, Id, Ça,* or *Es.* The event that grants time and being, says the later Heidegger; the impersonal life of the drives, the pulsional life that threatens to swallow the diminutive ego, says the later

It seemed to me that human faces appeared all around me, but without eyes—instead, there were profound, horrifying caverns of darkness. "Give me your eyes! Give me your eyes!" cried Coppelius in muffled, moaning tones. (Hoffman, *S*)

Freud. Both *Es*'s could be read in terms of Maurice Blanchot's neuter/neutral *il*, the narrative voice.

•

Heidegger never acknowledges the *Es* in Freud. He recognizes it in Rimbaud and Trakl, in the *It gives/There is* of poetry, especially in the "De Profundis" and "Psalm" of Trakl. Yet there is no *Id* in his confrontation with Freudian psychoanalysis: he finds Freud facile and flaccid, a minor character in the history of metaphysical subjectivity. In fact, I know of no serious references in Heidegger (beyond scathing allusions and animadversions) to Freud's oeuvre, not a single positive reference to the *other* great thinker of the uncanny and unhomelike nature of human existence. For his part, Freud, rescued by the time of his *floruit* and by his aversion to philosophy, had less reason to repress *Being and Time* than he did all of Nietzsche, who, as Freud feared, threatened his originality. Freud's allergy to philosophy—philosophy being his first love, that earlier state to which psychoanalysis wends its way via all its detours—and Heidegger's lack of fame (as the *hidden* king) are enough to explain the absence of references in Freud to Heidegger. As for Heidegger's contempt for Freud, "Das Unheimliche" may well merit it: it is one of Freud's most tentative, tangential, and inconsequential essays; it is poorly organized, even "lumpy"; it is ostensibly about *aesthetics*, which Heidegger scorns. And yet this essay, uncannily, contains most of Freud's final ideas about psychic life. "Das Unheimliche" is about thirty-five pages long and is divided into three parts. The first part introduces the uncanny or unhomelike as a truant theme of aesthetics or literary criticism; the second provides a quasi-phenomenology and a nascent psychoanalysis of the uncanny; the third offers a very odd discussion of the difference between experiencing and reading, *Erleben* and *Lesen*.

•

The aesthetics of literature, which one usually calls criticism, deals with subdued or sublimated affects, dampened or diluted emotions and feelings,

And with that he seized me so violently that my joints cracked. He unscrewed my hands and feet, reattaching them, first at one place, then another. "They don't fit anywhere else! Better the way they were! The Old Man knew what he was doing!" (Hoffmann, *S*)

says Freud. One might well wonder why the analyst refers to aesthetics or literary criticism at all, when any patient on the couch reproduces those affects, emotions, and feelings *without* dilution. Perhaps the analyst reads literature for mere diversion. Or perhaps his is a contribution to criticism out of the goodness of his heart and the depth of his experience, an altruism the aesthete could hardly be expected to withstand. Or do literature and its narrative voice here too play a different sort of role? Do they provide access to the not-at-home that no life experience can provide? We will have to return to this question at the end of the essay—the question of

Fig. 7.4. Gisela Baurmann, *Scissors' Skin*. Etching, 1990–91.
"Quetsch: Investigation into Architectural Representation."
LoPSiA Paris/Briey.

the difference between lived experience and literary gleaning. For the moment, Freud is satisfied to indicate a curious omission in the critical literature: the experience of the uncanny or unhomelike has been neglected, as though it were the (neglected) Heideggerian question of being. What sort of experience is it? One that resists depiction, and one that is hardly uplifting. It is an experience to which Freud himself is scarcely susceptible: he confesses or flaunts his obtuseness *(Stumpfheit)* or lack of receptivity with regard to this subdued emotion. His sober analysis follows two paths: (1) a quasi-phenomenological description of the uncanny in life and literature, wherever and however it seems to arise; and (2) a lexical description of the word as it appears in a battery of dictionaries. It is worth noting that in his presentation of the uncanny Freud reverses the order of the two paths in his itinerary, presenting the dictionary entries first and only then venturing the description. Both paths, he says, lead to the identical conclusion: the uncanny is related to terror, anxiety, and horror, and yet perdures at a safe remove from these affects; the uncanny is thus a species of the terrifying that points back, not to intellectual insecurity in the face of some novelty, as E. Jentsch supposed, but to something long familiar, something experienced and known of old in a nonintellectual way, something both lost and destined to be found again in the mists of time. Freud adopts Friedrich W. J. Schelling's definition: *"Un-heimlich* is what we call everything that should have remained secret, in concealment, but that came to the fore." Uncannily, concealment does not wholly conceal; concealment ultimately gives way to unconcealment; concealment *shows itself* as such. Of all Freud's essays, this is the one that Heidegger—the thinker of concealing and self-showing—ought to have read most closely. In secret. Closely closeted.

•

By the time Heidegger was teaching his *Prolegomena to the History of the Concept of Time* in 1925 he would have had four opportunities to read Freud's "Das Unheimliche," which had been published in four different places. We may be certain that he did not avail himself of these opportunities. Yet it is worth remembering in some detail the role that *Unheimlichkeit* plays in Heidegger's budding ontological analysis of human existence. Uncanniness, or being-not-at-home, is for Heidegger a fundamental structure of existence. Paradoxically, being-not-at-home is to be understood precisely "in terms of being-at-home—familiarity" (20: 348). Familiarity is the normal condition or usual state, at least for an existence that is always "falling," always "ruinous," and even "ruinant." If the ruins of home are always at home, always in some sense "familiar," it is because, as we have already heard, human existence is *Ruinanz*.[6] Familiarity itself is a mark of ruinous falling, an expression of evasion. For what is uncanny is the need of existence to *flee from itself.* What is unhomelike is the need of *Dasein* to escape from itself, to be forever fugitive—to be in φυγή, *fuga, Flucht,* "flight." To be sure, *die Fuge,* "joining," "jointure," "juncture," appears in Heidegger's texts of the 1930s as an elevating architectonic theme. Nowadays, after the publication of the 1936–38 *Contributions to Philosophy (Of Propriation),* Heideggerians are waxing lyrical about the "fugal structure" of the maestro's thought. Yet the fugue that is appropriate to Heidegger's thought is on the run somewhere between fear and anxiety. Φυγή is close to πλήγη, a word we shall soon hear in another context; *Flucht,* "flight," is more *Fluch,* "curse" or "plague," than airy fancy. If anxiety is the *ground* of fear, the uncanny is the *abyss* of anxiety. Anxiety *reveals itself* as the fugal structure or flight pattern of an existence ever on the wing: ruinous, ruinant, falling, and—in its very familiarity—fleeing.

•

Heidegger takes Book 2 of Aristotle's *Rhetoric* to be the original text of Western philosophy and psychology on the πάθη or affects. There the principal πάθος is fear. How to instill fear in the people—perhaps, as Freud reminds us, through the noble lie, which tells of punishments to be meted out in an afterlife, the ruse of Plato's *Republic*—or in those who govern. According to Heidegger, Aristotle's analysis, passed on via the Stoa to Augustine, Thomas Aquinas, and the Renaissance and Reformation, remains at the basis of all modern analyses of affectivity. To be sure, Heidegger does not mention Freud. Yet Freud's analyses of anxiety as the affective outcome of *every* repressed emotion, and of the uncanny as the very mark of repression, analyses that bring the uncanny into closest proximity to anxiety, could certainly be integrated into Heidegger's account of Aristotle's *Rhetoric.* Heidegger's phenomenology of fear and anxiety in 1925 mirrors in an uncanny way Freud's catalog of "lived experiences" in part 2 of "Das Unheimliche." This is not the place to rehearse Heidegger's treatment of the *Wovor* and the *Worum,* "that in the face of which" and "that about which" *Dasein* is afraid or anxious. Yet many details of the analysis would fascinate Freud: the "fright" that arises from an immediate, recognized threat, such as a grenade that lands nearby, with only a few seconds before the tremor of detonation; the "horror" of some unidentifiable threat; the "terror" of sudden horror; the general "anxiousness" of timidity, awe, worry, and so on. Also relevant is Heidegger's insistence on the importance of fear *for* or *about* someone else, the other, whom Freud tends to reduce to the mirror image of a secondary narcissistic projection. However, the purpose of Heidegger's phenomenology of fear is to arrive at that *indeterminate* fear which is generalized anxiety, the anxiety that Heidegger as well as Freud associates with uncanniness. Not only that. Heidegger affirms two of Freud's three principal sites of the uncanny: both thinkers name "darkness" and "solitude" *(Dunkelheit, Alleinsein)* as abodes of the unhomelike, while Freud also writes of "stillness" *(die Stille),* which has a more positive yet also ultimately uncanny resonance for Heidegger. However, not even these two or three sites are essential to what Heidegger calls the unhomelike. Rather, *"that in the face of which we are anxious is the nothing"* (20: 401). The no-thing, that is to say, the very differential structure of our being in the world, which is never a being of "things," not even when *Dasein* dies, is what threatens. Accordingly, that *about* which we are anxious is our being in the world *as such,* what in *Being and Time* Heidegger calls our *being able to be* in the world. Our being (able to be) in the world as such is what is disclosed to us when the *Unzuhause,* our being *not* at home, comes out of the closet. Heigh-ho, nobody home, as the child's ditty says: that is what it means to dwell in the world as *possibility-being.* In his 1925 lectures Heidegger calls it our "naked" being in the world, and he associates the stark nakedness of our being able to be (not at home) in the world with the abyss and with mortal anxiety *(der Abgrund, die Todesangst).* The only possible home for us is the *Unzuhause, Un-heimlichkeit.* The negative prefix does not simply negate or annul, neither for Heidegger nor for Freud. Perhaps in memory of Hegel—or of *one* of the Hegels, namely, the one who thinks the radical exteriority of space and time—both Freud and Heidegger pursue the monstrously uncanny power, the positive power, of the negative. Their pursuit should remind us that however heroic the project of *archeticture* may sound, there is nothing sentimental or comforting about that project. Archeticture is as uncanny as human existence. Surprise.

•

According to Freud, the prefix *Un-* is both the mark of repression—of what criticism has neglected—and a pure supplement to the word *heimlich,* both necessary and utterly superfluous. For *heimlich* means not only what is *heim(e)lig, heimisch, vertraut,* which Grimm calls *vernaculus,* the familiar, homelike, homey, but also what is *geheim,* secret, covert, furtive, and hidden, which Grimm calls *occultus,* a word perhaps best rendered by the pseudonegation *(un)heimlich.* It seems clear that *unheimlich* is a species of *heimlich,* not its negation but a positive scion or subset of it. Freud will interpret the word's uncanny form as the result of the process of ambivalence: the uncanny will in fact be the most familiar; it will be the skeleton or the flesh in the closet of every home, in the most closely closeted closet of the homiest home there ever was.

> She seemed not to notice me, and in general her eyes seemed somehow petrified. I might almost say they were without vision; she appeared to me to be sleeping with open eyes. An altogether uncanny feeling crept over me. . . . (Hoffmann, *S*)

•

Heimlich is—as we have seen—a homonym of a special sort. It means both "familiar, domestic, candid" and "unfamiliar, alien, secret." It thus appears to be a primal word, an *Urwort,* of the Abelian sort.[7] Oddly, the contrary and even contradictory meanings of the word induce a kind of reflexivity in Freud's use of it. He twice (StA, 4:248, 250) says that the word *heimlich* "uncannily collapses into its opposite *[mit seinem Gegensatz unheimlich zusammenfällt]."* (The *Standard Edition* sets off the word *unheimlich* in quotation marks on these two occasions, feigning certainty that Freud is merely making *mention* rather than uncanny *use* of the word.) Freud employs the adverb to express, lexically and syntactically, the uncanny conflation of canny and uncanny, homelike and unhomelike, in the same word, as though both existence and psychoanalysis were at home on the wing. His text on the uncanny both constates and performs its subject. Further,

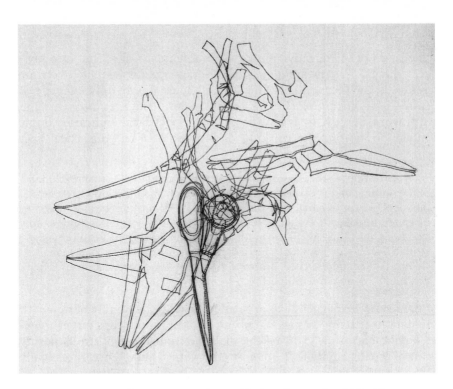

Fig. 7.5. Gisela Baurmann, *Scissors' Skin*. Drawing overlay, 1990–91.
"Quetsch: Investigation into Architectural Representation."
LoPSiA Paris/Briey.

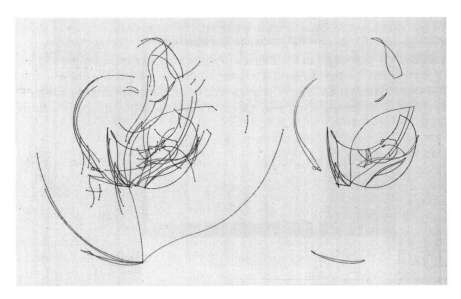

Fig. 7.6. Gisela Baurmann, *Scissors' Skin*. Drawing abstraction, 1990–91.
"Quetsch: Investigation into Architectural Representation."
LoPSiA Paris/Briey.

the negation of the negative prefix works asymmetrically. That is to say, it affects only the first meaning: *un-heimlich* never means candid, overt, un-secretive. In the second field of meanings, the prefix can only intensify the negative, as though *heimlich* were a Greek word. Heidegger too is intrigued by this word, because he is always on the lookout for the uncanny origins of nihilation, beyond the workings of propositional and dialectical negation:

> What testifies to the constant and widespread though distorted revelation of the nothing in our existence more compellingly than negation? Yet negation does not conjure the "not" out of itself. . . . For negation cannot claim to be either the sole or the leading nihilative behavior in which Dasein remains shaken by the nihilation of the nothing. Unyielding antagonism and stinging rebuke have a more abysmal source than the measured negation of thought. Galling failure and merciless prohibition require some deeper answer. Bitter privation is more burdensome.[8]

For Freud and Heidegger alike, nihilation negates the homily of home, the homily of hearth and haven. No negation of negation leaps out of Hegel's speculative hat in order to rescue dialectic from the monstrous positive power of the negativity that drives it. And yet, in some sense, the negative prefix *does* operate on the unfamiliar, alien, and secret. That is to say, the experience of the uncanny toward which Freud and Heidegger are groping implies the *revelation* of the unfamiliar, alien, and secret. That is the sense of Schelling's insight, which Freud embraces. For it is Schelling's definition of *das Unheimliche*, which Freud sets in spaced type, that successfully relates the two contrary or contradictory senses of the word: if *un-heimlich* designates everything that *ought* to have been kept secret but now has come to the fore and been revealed, then the word *unheimlich* does in some sense negate the absolutely secretive, the utterly alien, and the wholly unfamiliar. It is as though in the experience of the uncanny and unhomelike, against which the stolid Freud is all but immured, something like *the nothing*—the Heideggerian *Nichts*—announces itself. However subdued the affect, there is in the uncanny a *showing* and a *revealing.* Of what? Of no thing at all.

•

There is something uncanny about Freud's copying out like Bartleby (or like Flaubert's Bouvard and Pécuchet) those two long dictionary entries on *heimlich,* first from Daniel Sanders, then from the Brothers Grimm, even if it was Theodor Reik who passed the entries along to him. Grimm supplements Sanders (not the Sandman, not just yet) in an odd way. I shall take up the Grimm supplement in a moment. For now, the following uncanny coincidence: as I was working on these dictionary entries in Freud's text, these entries so painstakingly reproduced, so obsessively copied out, as though every lexical detail were of the utmost importance, I received a letter from the German architect Gisela Baurmann.[9] In her letter, written from Corbusier's *Unité* in Lorraine, Baurmann used words related to *heim-*

lich four times. I shall present them back to front here, following Freud's example, in order to approach the supplement of the uncanny.

1. "When I returned from Berlin and Karlsruhe—Berlin was lovely, so familiar *[vertraut]*, the streets, the squares, the faces!—I was at first shocked by the bareness and austerity [of Corbusier's *Unité*]. . . . And yet seldom have I felt as unquestionably at home *[ungefragt heimisch]* as I do here." *Heimisch,* not yet unhomelike, not yet uncanny, although introduced by an "And yet." As though one could be at home in the bareness and austerity of Corbusier's abandoned housing for the syndicalist coal miners, in a dwelling that is uncannily betwixt a monument and a ruin.

2. "For me, all this rigidity (the concrete, glass, corridors, balconies, etc.) has something uncannily *[unheimlich]* calming about it. Here one feels untouchable. . . . The hardness of all the materials—the concrete, the dark wood, the unfurnished apartments—radiates such honesty!" *Unheimlich* is here used adverbially, to modify the calming effect of the rigid and cold, the tranquilizing effect of glass and concrete and dark wood, producing the uncanny honesty that radiates from Corbusier's *Cité Radieuse.*

3. "Each of us is housed in his or her cell of a cement honeycomb. The edifice itself is a giant, a colossus, planted mercilessly in the forest. A tiny, slovenly French village lies ten minutes away by foot. . . . Yet as soon as you pass through the door [of the *Unité*], you are taken up and received; as soon as the door closes behind you, you become part of a tiny secret kingdom, a *heimeligen* realm." The Swiss, Austrian, and South German *e* now sidles up to and into the word, in order to suggest an ardor or warmth radiated by a hearth or a tile oven, the Allemannic *Kunsht,* of which Heidegger was so fond.

4. Finally, Baurmann describes a mechanical iron-ore mine she inspected somewhere near Briey-en-Forêt, a totally automated work site, altogether unmanned. She writes: "The building was in disrepair, everything covered by a rust-red dust, and not a soul in sight. Everything there is automated. It was truly *unheimlich.*" Which is where Freud too begins, without a psyche in sight, and where he will end, with automata.

•

In his 1984 introduction to John Hejduk's *The Mask of Medusa,* Daniel Libeskind refers to "an active trace of homelessness that remains visible in a cultural atmosphere," adding: "The non-dwellable establishes itself as a first principle of architecture: a fault out of which constructive hope emerges, and the destination into which it collapses when the human promise is broken."[10]

•

Why does Freud supplement the long quotation from Daniel Sanders, which gives him the Schellingian definition he will need for his own idea of repression, with the shorter version from Grimm? The rather more obscure treatment there, gathered about the axis *vernaculus/occultus,* gives Freud very little beyond what Sanders has already provided, except perhaps for one odd reference. Grimm cites 1 Sam. 5:12, which recounts Yahweh's striking the Philistines "in their homelike or secret places *[an heimlichen örten]*, so that the city cried to heaven." Freud takes the biblical passage to mean that Yahweh strikes the people—the women as well as the men, presumably—in their private parts, their pudenda. That is what this second lexical entry, the Grimm entry, seems to give Freud. For nowhere in Sanders is there an explicit reference to the genitalia. However, when one becomes as obsessive as Freud and examines the passage in Samuel, at least in Luther's translation, something disconcerting happens. Because of the reference to territory there (*"und alle jre grentze an heimlichen örten"* [1 Sam. 5:6]), and because of the reference to the outcry and tumult in the city of the Philistines after some punitive action by God (*"durch die Hand des HERRN in der Stad ein seer gros Rumor"* [1 Sam. 5:9]), the *heimlichen örten* at first seem to imply no more than the local habitations of the Philistines, and certainly not their private parts. The sense would be that Yahweh strikes the Philistines in their homes or in their homeland—in those primary architectural *Umschließungen* discussed by Hegel in his *Lectures on Aesthetics*. However, a more uncanny sense of *heimlichen örte* awaits. A student and friend, Lyat Friedman, informs me that the Hebrew text says that the hand of Yahweh struck the Philistines in a *dark place,* cursing them with *hemorrhoids.* Thus when the enemies of Israel are blasted by a divine curse, they suffer from a "homelike plague in homelike places *[und kriegten heimliche Plage an heimlichen örten]*" (ibid.). From the editors of the Luther Bible we learn that while *heim sein* means to be at home, the *heimlich gemach* is the latrine, and a *heimlicher ort* is either a place of ambush (the Greek λόχος), a secret location, or "a veiled expression for the anus or buttocks."[11] *Heimligkeit* means "a secret" in Luther's vocabulary; *heimsuchen* means either to visit or to have intercourse with someone. When God does it, "home-seeking" means either to bless *(segnen)* or to punish *(strafen),* an ambivalence Freud's Schreber understood better than most contemporary theologians. An uncanny question for the biblical scholar: Is it Yahweh's custom to treat people in the way scapegoats were treated in Greek antiquity—to beat them about their genitals, driving out the demons from the parts that must be made fertile—or to socratize them with blessing and punishment until a painful swelling ensues? Or is Freud's substitution of the private parts for the anal region one of his oddest anal-genito-hermeneutical fantasies? Who here is Oedipus φαρηακός, and who Sphincter?

•

There is a curious word in Plato's *Phaedrus* (237b 4) describing the crafty lover of youths, the canny lover who cunningly convinces boys that he is in fact *not* a lover, so that they ingenuously place all their trust in him. The word is αἱμύλος. Ficino translates it as *vir sane versutus,* a man well versed in the ways of the world (*versutus,* from *verto,* I turn). One thinks of Odysseus πολύτροπος. Aeschylus has Prometheus tell of his "counsels of craft" on behalf of the Olympian gods, after the Titans had scorned his "clever machinations," αἱμύλας μηχανὰς (*Prometheus Bound,* line 208). Αἱμύλος sounds very much like *heimlich,* uncannily so, especially in its homeliest of down-

home forms, the South German *heimelig.* To be sure, no self-respecting phi-
lologist would venture an etymology beyond the Nordic *Heim* for the whole
sequence of German words; there is certainly no need to hearken back to
some Greek etymon, one that would displace the "home" from the German
heimlich, as though *heimlich* were a Greek word, intensified as *un-heimlich.*
Yet it is tempting to think that the wheedling and wily lover, the seducer
whose speeches are also often described as δεῖνον, clever, sly, cunning, canny, uncannily foxy, is himself the creature that is normally kept in the
closet. Or beaten about the genitals.

•

According to the second part of Freud's "Das Unheimliche," there are
two main sources of the unhomelike and uncanny in life and in letters: (1)
the return of materials and complexes repressed during infancy, and (2) the
reemergence of atavistic beliefs and superstitions that humanity has (if only
in intellectual terms) already overcome. These two sources follow the familiar ontogeny-phylogeny parallel in Freud, homologous with the psy-
chophysical parallelism, with each human infant serving as a microcosm
that in some way mirrors the macrocosm of humankind's infancy. In both
cases (for Freud's examples seem to cross all the parallels), both infantile
humanity and human infancy come into question. Both sites involve the
no-man's-land that divides the living and the dead, a realm peopled by
puppets and automata. Freud's famous reading (or misreading) of E. T. A.
Hoffmann's *Der Sandmann* occurs here, although I will say little about it. (To
insist on Freud's *misreading* seems jejune to me: while Freud distorts certain
details of Hoffmann's story, his reading remains an astonishing and even
uncanny achievement.) One might try to trace the same obsessions—the
automaton that both thrills and kills, the beautiful puppet that both se-
duces to life and induces death—in Melville's "The Bell-Tower," Mérimée's
"La Vénus d'Ille," Poe's "Ligeia" and "William Wilson," and Mary Shelley's
Frankenstein. What fascinates Freud in Hoffmann's tale are two duplex and
duplicitous figures: the sandman, here called Coppelius and Coppola, who
burns and plucks out the eyes of children,
and Olimpia, the enucleated puppet who
tears out the hearts of young men. For Freud,
the character called Nathanael—the boy who
is terrified by the sandman (embodied in the
threats of his governess) and the youth who
is so enamored of Olimpia that he scorns the
love of his faithful Clara—is reminiscent of

> Clara can by no means be said
> to have been beautiful; that is
> what everyone agreed whose
> office it was to know about
> beauty. Yet the architects
> praised the flawless proportions
> of her figure. . . . (Hoffmann, *S*)

the Wolfman, who adopts a feminine position vis-à-vis the father. Again,
both cases, both sources of the unhomelike in life and letters, apply to the
second of the two motifs in the sandman story—the doppelgänger, the doubling and redoubling marked, to repeat, by the names Coppelius-Coppola
(from the Italian *coppo,* "eye socket") in Hoffmann's tale. Freud sees in the
doppelgänger the original *Di Manes,* the guardian spirits or tutelary genii,
the good daimons that now, under the new religion, under the aegis of new

paternal powers, become demons. Among the more familiar doppelgänger are the feet, the left and the right, of an erect humanity. The feet, whose odor offends the obsessively visual human being, the creature that can no longer stand to see its feet, much less suffer their fermentation. What is least homelike and most uncanny is that which is always at home: the human body in all its anonymity and imperious power, with all its gravity and in all its levity, in and out of all the holes and empty ciphers of its desires—the original double, which the wind blew in from who knows where, Descartes certainly cannot figure it out, while Heidegger can only say that it—the body—is "the most difficult problem."[12] For the double, left and right, female and male, has no origin and marks the end of all originary thinking. Freud's lumpy essay limps along from here to Nietzsche's thought of eternal recurrence of the same, and from thence to repetition compulsion, the economy of lifedeath, and primary masochism—all the atavisms that psychoanalysis would have preferred to let lie but that make psychoanalysis psychoanalysis. Which, Freud says, many take to be *unheimlich*.[13]

•

Repression is the very mechanism of anxiety, according to Freud; any affect or emotion that is repressed returns as anxiety. Further, its return is uncanny—the emergence of something both long familiar and long hidden that ought to have remained in concealment. Heidegger speaks of the concealment and even distortion of beings that are always a part of their epiphany. Yet it may be that Heidegger's thought of self-concealing being as enigma, mystery, and secret *needs* the thought of repression. For when repression is primal, when it is *Ur-Verdrängung*, it is utterly beyond every ontic thought of beings. Repression, for its part, has to be thought in terms of the ontological difference. The uncanny, unhomelike return of the repressed is a thought *of being*, subjective genitive, precisely because in it there is no subject.

•

Rudolf Arnheim cites several examples of architectonic thought after Kant.[14] After he mentions Marcel Proust's own depiction of *À la recherche du temps perdu* as a medieval cathedral, with each part of the work designed as a porch or a stained-glass window in the apse, he cites Freud's *New Series of Lectures toward an Introduction to Psychoanalysis* (1932–33). He reproduces Freud's "modest drawing" of the second topological system, reminiscent of, but different from, his more famous drawing in *The Ego and the Id* (1923).

Arnheim comments as follows:

> Freud undertakes to describe the complex interrelation between two sets of fundamental psychoanalytic concepts, namely unconscious, preconscious, and conscious [the *first* topical or topological system, usually called the *dynamic* system, understandably of enormous importance to the author of *The Dynamics of Architectural Form*], and id, ego, and superego [the *second* topical or topological system]. The principal dimension to be represented is that of the distance from the station point of consciousness, i.e., the dimension of depth. Hence an elevation is more appropriate than a horizontal plan. (DAF, 273–74)

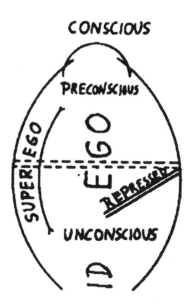

"Can you not see me?
Coppelius deceived you:
those were not my eyes
that burned their way into
your breast; they were
ardent drops of your own
heart's blood—I still have
my eyes, look at me!"
(Hoffmann, *S*)

For Arnheim, consciousness is "the station point." The unconscious, which is deep, lies at a remote distance from the station. Arnheim neglects to mention that in all editions of Freud's works prior to the *Standard Edition*, Freud's "modest sketch," ostensibly appropriate only in elevation, was shown *on the horizontal*—probably in order to save space, say the editors of the *Standard Edition* and the *Studienausgabe* (StA, 1:515 n. 1). No doubt, such a horizon(t)al positioning of Freud's sketch further enhances its appearance as an eye—a bit squashed, to be sure, and therefore reminiscent of the eye of J. D. Salinger's "Almond Man." What lends credence to its *being* an eye is the fact that—in the German, at least—consciousness is always defined as the system W-Bw, *Wahrnehmung-Bewußtsein*, roughly, perceptual consciousness, or perception-plus-consciousness.

Never in his life had he
come across an optical
instrument that brought
objects right up to the eye
so purely, so sharply, in
such clear outlines.
(Hoffmann, *S*)

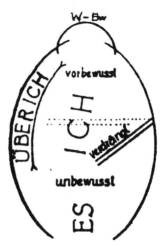

Arnheim notes Freud's own complaint that his drawing is not true to scale: the region of the id or unconscious would have to be significantly larger than those of the ego or the preconscious and perceptual-conscious. "This flaw, however-er," Arnheim adds, "is of minor importance, because the drawing is topological rather than metric" (DAF, 274). Moreover, the use of curved lines indicates that these are only approximate—suggested and suggestive—spaces. Arnheim stresses that Freud's drawing is "entirely visual," and goes on to suggest that "if it were to be executed as a building, the working-out of the actual shapes and dimensions could continue from here without a break" (ibid.). The oddity, the truly uncanny nature of the drawing—the fact that Freud represents essentially unrepresentable psychic forces to a *perceptual consciousness* that is itself represented in (or immediately above) the drawing, indeed, represented as a relatively insignificant supplement to the system, a mere superficies, a kind of lens or cornea or cap—Arnheim does not mention. He takes the fact that Freud *has* to draw drawings for a perceptual consciousness to be the visualist's victory. What Arnheim neglects to ask is: How much of the building would be built by the id, presuming that the powerful id can read drawings? And if only the ego can read and build, what will it make of the inscrutable id at its foundations? Finally, if we compare this drawing to Freud's earlier sketch of the second topological system in *The Ego and the Id,* one uncanny addition strikes us:

"Do me a favor, brother," said Siegmund to him one day. "Do me a favor and tell me how a clever fellow like you could go ogling that wax doll over there, that wooden puppet?" (Hoffmann, *S*)

The figure of Olimpia hovered before him in the gentle winds, emerged from the bushes, and gazed at him from the radiant brook with magnificent, beaming eyes. (Hoffmann, *S*)

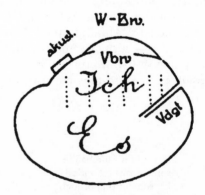

The eye is now oddly squashed or sunken, no longer almond in shape, but sacklike, collapsing under its own weight—or under the weight of the new addition. Above the protuberance of the id or *Es* on the left is an "acoustical cap," *Hörkappe,* presumably the "Wernicke speech center" in the brain, which plays a role in the hearing/understanding of language. Freud compares the entire W-Bw system, the perceptual conscious, to the fertilization spot *(Keimscheibe)* that sits on top of an egg. (Luckily, the superego has not yet arrived on the scene at this stage of Freud's account, so that such a simile remains possible.) From the very beginning of his career, Freud placed great importance on speech and hearing in his accounts of the preconscious and the functioning ego. Clearly, were one to *build* Freud's psychic system, one would need more than a visualist architect. When Arnheim speaks of Freud's drawing as "actually the translation of a system of forces into a perceptually tangible medium," with the metaphor or kinesthesia of "tangibility" left undefined, and when he cites the superego as the "opening" or "bridge" from the id to the ego or "liberating realm of consciousness," deftly surmounting the "horizontal barrier that blocks this upward motion," one wonders how much Freud our architect has understood. Presumably, all that Freud ever wanted to understand and build was the solid double line of *repression,* on a tangent to the dotted double line between id and ego, or, on the right side of the

sack system, the double line that *seems* more like a canal to the outside world than a barrier. What *is* the double line of *Verdrängung?* That is Freud's question to the psychoanalytic architect who has done this drawing. Is

> An angry Nathanael sprang to his feet, repulsing Clara from him: "Damn you, you lifeless thing, you robot!" (Hoffmann, *S*)

it a trapdoor? an open door? diving board? pendulum? And what *is* the repressed itself, which, in spite of all its drawn appearances, itself never appears—except perhaps to return *as* repressed in the phenomenon of the uncanny? No architect, but only an archetict, could pursue these questions.

•

The automaton or puppet—Descartes's man in the street or Kleist's boxing bear and ballet dancer in *Das Marionettentheater*—is the uncanny other, the doppelgänger. It is never far from home. Even when she or he is of the opposite gender, as in the case of Nathanael and the enucleated Olimpia, it is "the voice of the friend that every *Dasein* carries with itself."[15] The mute automaton arrogates to itself the daimonic voice of desire and the demonic voice of conscience and guilt. The origin of the doppelgänger, both in the narcissism of the individual psyche and in the tutelary genius or daimon of the species, would contain the secret of primal repression. It would be the ultimate source of anxiety and of anxiety's shade, the uncanny.

> "Only in Olimpia's love will I find my Self again." (Hoffmann, *S*)

It would be the origin of auto-affection, of hearing and understanding oneself while speaking; hence, the origin of all reflexivity and consciousness, the origin of all oneiric presence in metaphysics. Such "origins" can only be *nonorigins:* the doppelgänger always comes first.

•

Olimpia, the alluring but dangerous puppet—a kind of Edwina Scissorhands—built by Schelling's and Hegel's favorite scientist, Spalanzani, and given Nathanael's eyes by Coppola-Coppelius, is a technitron. Nathanael first sees her through Coppola's pixelated *Perspektiv* or technological looking glass. Indeed, he *always* sees her through the doppelgänger's looking-glass, so that Nathanael seems to be the technitron of his own envisaging, the architect or Demiurge of his own disaster. Hoffmann teases his readers from the very start of the tale, where we are told that the sandman desires "to observe quite closely the mechanism of [Nathanael's] hands and feet," that Coppelius in fact proceeds to "unscrew" the boy's appendages, reattaching them here and there, until he is forced to admit defeat.[16] As a young suitor, Nathanael inveighs against his fiancée, Clara, for failing to respond ardently enough to his gloomy poetry. He accuses her of being an automaton (S, 25), thus betraying the fact that *every* woman he looks at appears to him (in his perspective, which is the doppelgänger's *Perspektiv*) to be the mannequin that *he* is. In a word, if Olimpia's seductive gaze *(Anblick)* communicates love to Nathanael, that gaze is Nathanael's own look *(An-blick)* directed at her gaze. Hers are the "magnificent, beaming eyes" that look back at him "from the radiant brook" *(aus dem hellen Bach)* of his own narcissism (S, 30). Freud's worst nightmare: the ultimate victory of a narcissism so primary that there is no escaping its deadly doubling effects. "Well may Olimpia seem *unheimlich* to you cold, prosaic human beings," cries Nathanael. "Her loving gaze rose like the sun *for me alone*, permeating my senses and my thoughts . . ." (S, 35). Everywhere he looks, Nathanael sees Olimpia's limpid gaze, or Clara's Olimpian gaze, upon him; it is the gaze that will incite him to plunge to his own death. Heidegger's worst nightmare: the essence of technology is a mode of disclosure so overwhelmingly powerful that it blinds us to all other modes, cutting them off as possibilities for us. Heidegger's dearest hope: the disclosure enacted in and by the work of art, especially the work of poetry, the work of language, will resuscitate the disclosure of disclosure as such. Yet what about a poetry or fiction (such as E. T. A. Hoffmann's) whose technique (in the Greek sense of poietic art) confounds nature and artifice, producing a truly ticno-techno-phantasm? What about a work of art that puts to work the art of the technical artificer and the tictonic lover-deceiver? This would be betrayal from below, from the South. For they are all Italians, these Futurist ticnotechnowizards: Spalanzani, Coppola, Rappaccini, Bannadonna (the last two from Hawthorne's "Rappaccini's Daughter" and Melville's "The Bell-Tower," respectively), joined by Casanova and his doll. One recalls Freud wandering anxiously through the red-light district of a small Italian town, uncannily unable to flee, returning again and again to the street where he first recognized the significance of the neighborhood, confronting again and again a fate worse than death. Luckily, Heidegger brought Frau Heidegger along to help him find his way unscathed through Rome.

•

The sandman burns and extracts the eyes of naughty children who disobey their mothers and will not go to bed. Such is Derrida's anxiety in *Mémoires d'aveugle*.[17] Such is the academicians' anxiety in the face of Derrida. Which is why they try to scratch out his eyes.

•

Hoffmann calls Coppola the "accursed *Doppeltgänger* [sic] *und Revenant*." Derrida begins *Of Spirit: Heidegger and the Question* by invoking the *revenant*,

Fig. 7.7. Gisela Baurmann, *Scissors' Skin*. Lead relief, 1990–91.
"Quetsch: Investigation into Architectural Representation."
LoPSiA Paris/Briey.

the ghost, as the return of the repressed.[18] Spiriting Heidegger in the direction of *Geist,* Derrida discloses the uncanniness of Heidegger's corpus, the uncanniness—and the ignoble lie—of Heidegger's politics. Which is why Heideggerians in particular try to scratch out Derrida's eyes.

•

Heidegger's most stubborn doppelgänger in *Being and Time* is none other than the concept of the "self." He continues to appeal to it (as Narcissus to the stream) even after the ecstatic analysis of temporality has left it in tatters. He fails to recognize that all appeals to the self *(das Selbst)* and to propriety *(Eigentlichkeit)* are haunted by the Augustinian-Cartesian ghost—the *cogito.* Freud cites the thought of eternal recurrence of the same in the context of the endless splitting or fission of the father-imago *and* of the ego. That would imply eternal return as Pierre Klossowski thinks it in *Le cercle vicieux,* the self enucleated and catapulted from itself, our multiple selves on the endless cycle of anamnesis and amnesia.[19]

> And how could we fail to refer back to the sexual act, and especially to the feminine sex as place? In its likely confusion with the first "house" of man, but also its confusion with his *skin?* In some way, the feminine sex ought to serve as a skin for the man's sex, for the man himself, who is without access to this other dimension: the mucous. Dimension of the sexual act? Of its accessibility, its economy, its communion beyond skins. (Irigaray, *E,* 50)

•

Recall Heidegger's and Augustine's anxiety in the face of *concupiscentia oculorum* and Augustine's desire to be castrated for the sake of the kingdom of heaven—his need to adopt a feminine position before the divine father. That would be the anxiety, not of losing one's eyes, but of keeping them: an overwhelming horror in the face of the temptations of visibility, Olimpia's seductive *Anblick,* her gaze, her vision, her sight, which is the very sight of her—for, again, her eyes are Nathanael's own eyes—in the *Perspektiv* of the doppelgänger. Bannadonna, says Melville. Narcissus, says Freud; *abscisus,* says Augustine—Oh, to be spayed (the Latin *spado*) for the sake of the father. Desire for the Great Dark of the solar anus. Olimpia's bloody eyes, enucleated by Coppola, are Nathanael's *seeing* eyes—glued to the *Perspektiv.* Heidegger's love of clearing is surpassed by his love of concealing, the mystery, *das Geheimnis,* where the *Heim* of *Ge-heim* is always *un-heimlich.* This puts him too close to Freud for comfort: the style of Heidegger's thinking would be, not Olympian, but Olimpian.

> She gives form to the man's sex, and sculpts it from the inside. She becomes the containing one, and the active *place* of the sexual act. . . . Is she not imagined to be passive only because the man fears the loss of mastery in the act? Whence his violence from to time? (Irigaray, *E,* 49)

•

The mother's body too is a site of the uncanny unhomelike. It is the occasion of fantasies of life-in-the-womb, to be sure: the fascination exercised by intrauterine existence —as Descartes, for example, discusses it in his 1648 correspondence with Arnauld. Descartes says that the infant, who will retain no recollection of its life in the mother's womb, must nonetheless *constantly* be cogitating, gathering and thinking *itself* as existing, even as

Fig. 7.8. Gisela Baurmann, *Scissors' Skin*. Rayogram, 1990–91.
"Quetsch: Investigation into Architectural Representation."
LoPSiA Paris/Briey.

the animal spirits of *her* blood course through *its* arteries and nerve tubes. No wonder weaning is such a thought-provoking experience. At the same time, according to Freud, the female genitalia represent the uncanny un-homelike—at least for "neurotic males"—so that the sight of the site of love, being both Dido's cave and the head of Medusa, inspires both home-sickness and horror.

•

In love, it would be fitting for the parts of the whole—the union of man and woman—to envelop one another *mutually,* rather than for each to destroy the envelope of the other. (Irigaray, *E,* 58)

Would it be possible to think together the enucleated eye or weeping mucous mouth of the male member and the lips of woman? Not for the sake of the witch's brew and war-lock's stew of phallic mother or vaginal fa-ther, but for the sake of difference without war? Without war or even litigation, which is the contemporary way to make love? Would it be possible to think the mouth and lips together as enveloping envelopes?

•

What Freud calls the *Kinderangst* of losing one's eyes is actually the pro-jection of a parental, paternal/maternal anxiety, the terror of every adult who watches the infant child wielding its first pair of scissors, fumbling about the face and eyes. *Kastrationsangst* is shared by mother *and* father, both in terror of the child's losing its eyes. Testimony to the love that Freud sees disturbed by Coppelius, the child's love for its slain father. The child's anxiety is twofold: first, that the violent father will throw sand in its eyes, will continue to say *no* in the name of the father; second, that the gentle father will die, never knowing of the child's *yes* to him. The child's embrace of the father, the sometimes violent, sometimes gentle father, is perhaps both a concession to the unquenchable hatred and a plea for recognition of the ardent love. Hegel and Aristotle say that it is perfectly obvious that parents love their children more than their children love them. Not so. Not more. Perhaps not even differently. Children fear for their fumbling parents as well. Three-year-olds have been known to say, "It's okay, Papi, it's just your nerves." Nietzsche says in a letter to Malwida von Meysenbug (dated May 13, 1877) that fathers are always a bit awkward. He might have added that this does not change even after they have become ghosts.

•

The eye dislodged from the socket *(coppo)* in the head and in the male member: more than a century before Bataille, with his phantasm of the pineal eye, Novalis saw the doppelgänger in this unseeing eye and spewing mouth. If Heidegger, the thinker of the clearing and of ocular concupis-cence, ever saw it, he never said so. Because the thought of being and propriation soars beyond the whole of beings, it misses, as Sartre averred, the holes in beings. Yet nothing, the no-thing of the granting, is all Hei-degger ever desired. Hence the scathing polemics against psychoanalysis. Hence the naïveté of an Olympian Heidegger dispensing wisdom to the analysts at Zollikon.[20]

Fig. 7.9. Gisela Baurmann, *Scissors' Skin*. Rayogram, 1990–91.
"Quetsch: Investigation into Architectural Representation."
LoPSiA Paris/Briey.

•

If the doppelgänger is originally the daimon, tutelary genius, or soul—as guarantor of immortality—she or he or it soon becomes the herald of death, as in Kenneth Branagh's *Dead Again*. This is the historical unhomelikeness of anxiety, which Freud finds in Heine's late work, *Die Götter im Exil*. Heidegger needs this thought, and this poet, for his encounter with Hölderlin, the thinker of the mortality of all gods; he needs Heine as well as Nietzsche for his thought of "the last God," who for the very last time passes by "the futural ones."[21]

•

There is something particularly uncanny about the third and final part of Freud's "Das Unheimliche." Freud would very much like to distinguish between "lived experience" and "reading," life and letters. Heidegger triumphant: without really knowing the Freudian text, he predicted all along that Freud was mired in *Erlebnis*, the mush of "lived experience" that life-philosophy dishes out in order to prove to itself that it is not moribund. According to Heidegger, "lived experience" is the very death of thought, the funeral mask of metaphysics. What is uncanny about Freud's effort is that *all* his sources for the uncanny are literary; even what he claims to be autobiographical, "lived" experiences are in fact marvelously narrated and beautifully crafted pieces of writing—no matter how lumpy the essay as a whole. Freud triumphant: without ever knowing the Heideggerian text, Freud sensed the inevitable turn to poetry—and even to literature—demanded of all thinking.

•

In the fairy tale, writes Freud, virtually everything *is* uncanny, so that nothing is experienced *as* uncanny. It is as though the willing suspension of disbelief both conjures and quiets the uncanny, both spurs and neutralizes the unhomelike at once. Freud has to settle for the paradox "that in literature *[Dichtung]* much is not *unheimlich* that would be if it occurred in real life, and that likewise in literature possibilities abound for attaining *unheimlich* effects that do not occur in real life" (StA, 4:271–72). Life and letters engage in a kind of ring dance of canny/uncanny indeterminacy. However, the amulet of literature serves less well against the ghosts of repressed materials from infancy—materials long familiar to us yet heretofore locked away in the unconscious, *altvertrautes Verdrängtes*—than it does against the collective atavisms of early humanity. The uncanny unhomelike thus returns to each life, even to the most stolidly unphilosophical and immured of existences, in the life of letters.

It is unhomelike with one; it is at home in me.

Freud refers to three anxieties of childhood, anxieties that never fail to produce uncanny and unhomelike effects and affects in both life and letters:

Stillness
"The resilient, phlegmatic, halting breath that no wind had yet
dispersed . . ."
". . . seldom have I felt so unquestionably at home."

Solitude
"The smell of anxiety in children who go to school . . ."
". . . here one feels untouchable."

Darkness
"A black gap torn carelessly out of the wall . . ."
". . . radiates such honesty!"

Notes

1. See David Farrell Krell, *Archeticture: Ecstasies of Space, Time, and the Human Body* (Albany: State University of New York Press, 1997). My thanks to Dana Foote, who designed the book, and to Gisela Baurmann, who provided the extraordinary—the uncanny—graphics. The marginal insertions in the text are principally from Luce Irigaray, *L'éthique de la différence sexuelle* (Paris: Minuit, 1984), cited as *E*, with page number, and from E. T. A. Hoffmann's tale, *Der Sandmann*, cited as *S*, with or without page number.

2. These archetictural sections of Heidegger and Freud took their departure from an event sponsored by DePaul University's College of Liberal Arts and Sciences and the Graham Foundation: the conference, "*Das Unheimliche*: Philosophy • Architecture • The City," took place on April 26–27, 1991, at DePaul. My thanks to all the participants, among them Jacques Derrida, Daniel Libeskind, Don Bates, Stanley Tigerman, Ben Nicholson, Jeffrey Kipnis, Mark Rakatansky, Catherine Ingraham, and Peter Eisenman. These sections of mine could be regarded as responses to Anthony Vidler's wonderful book, *The Architectural Uncanny: Essays in the Modern Unhomely* (Cambridge, Mass.: MIT Press, 1992), which I came to know, however, only after they were written. Vidler's argument runs as follows: "Architecture has been intimately linked to the notion of the uncanny since the end of the eighteenth century. At one level, the house has provided a site for endless representations of haunting, doubling, dismembering, and other terrors in literature and art. . . . But beyond this largely theatrical role, architecture reveals the deep structure of the uncanny in a more than analogical way, demonstrating a disquieting slippage between what seems homely and what is definitively unhomely. As articulated theoretically by Freud, the uncanny or *unheimlich* is rooted by etymology and usage in the environment of the domestic, or the *heimlich*, thereby opening up problems of identity around the self, the other, the body and its absence: thence its force in interpreting the relations between the psyche and the dwelling, the body and the house, the individual and the metropolis" (Vidler, pp. ix–x).

3. I shall quote the *Studienausgabe* of Freud's works (Frankfurt a.M.: S. Fischer, 1969–79 [paperback edition, 1982] throughout, citing it as StA by volume and page. "Das Unheimliche" appears at 4:241–74. For Heidegger's 1925 text, see *Prolegomena zur Geschichte des Zeitbegriffs*, vol. 20 of the Martin Heidegger Gesamtaus-

gabe (Frankfurt a.M.: Vittorio Klostermann, 1979; translated by Theodore Kisiel as *The History of the Concept of Time: Prolegomena* (Bloomington: Indiana University Press, 1985). The Gesamtausgabe volumes too I shall cite by volume and page.

4. Rainer Maria Rilke, *Werke in drei Bänden* (Leipzig: Insel, 1953), 2:39–41; quoted in Martin Heidegger, *Die Grundprobleme der Phänomenologie,* vol. 24 of the Martin Heidegger Gesamtausgabe (Frankfurt a.M.: Vittorio Klostermann, 1975), pp. 244–46. My thanks to Will McNeill for the reference to Rilke.

5. For a discussion of Heidegger and Rilke, see the introduction and chapter 9 of my *Daimon Life: Heidegger and Life-Philosophy* (Bloomington: Indiana University Press, 1992).

6. Martin Heidegger, *Phänomenologische Interpretationen zu Aristoteles: Einführung in die phänomenologische Forschung,* Martin Heidegger Gesamtausgabe, vol. 61 (Frankfurt a.M.: Vittorio Klostermann, 1985), pp. 131–55.

7. See Freud, *Über den Gegensinn der Urworte* (1910), StA 4:227–34.

8. Martin Heidegger, *Basic Writings,* ed. David Farrell Krell, revised and expanded edition (San Francisco: HarperCollins, 1993), p. 105.

9. Baurmann was at that time a member of the Laboratory of Primary Studies in Architecture (LoPSiA), directed by Don Bates, at Corbusier's *Cité Radieuse* in Briey-en-Forêt, France.

10. Daniel Libeskind, in John Hejduk, *The Mask of Medusa* (New York: Rizzoli, 1985), p. 11.

11. See Martin Luther, *Die gantze Heilige* [N.B.: not *Heimliche*] *Schrift,* 3 vols., ed. Hans Volz, Heinz Blanke, and Friedrich Kur (Munich: Deutscher Taschenbuch Verlag, 1974), vol. 3, *Anhang,* p. 339.

12. Martin Heidegger and Eugen Fink, *Heraklit* (Frankfurt a.M.: Klostermann, 1970), p. 234.

13. StA, 4:266. See the thought-provoking reading of *repetition* in Freud's Sandman interpretation in Neil Hertz, *The End of the Line: Essays on Psychoanalysis and the Sublime* (New York: Columbia University Press, 1985), pp. 97–121. I have not even ventured to take into account here the vast amount of literature on Freud's reading (see Hertz, pp. 246–48, who cites Cixous, Deleuze, Derrida, Gasché, Kofman, and Samuel Weber, among others). I am grateful to Cynthia Chase for recommending Hertz to me, and for our discussion.

14. Rudolf Arnheim, *The Dynamics of Architectural Form* (Berkeley: University of California Press, 1977), cited hereinafter as DAF, with page number.

15. Heidegger, *Sein und Zeit,* §34, p. 163; see Derrida's *fourth* Geschlecht, in *Reading Heidegger: Commemorations,* ed. John Sallis (Bloomington: Indiana University Press, 1992).

16. Hoffmann, *S,* 10.

17. Jacques Derrida, *Mémoirs d'aveugle: L'autoportrait et autres ruines* (Paris: Réunion des Musées Nationaux, 1990). On Hoffmann's *Der Sandmann,* see pp. 65–66 n. 59. Translated by Michael Naas and Pascale-Anne Brault as *Memoirs of the Blind* (Chicago: University of Chicago Press, 1993), pp. 62–63 n. 59.

18. Jacques Derrida, *De l'esprit: Heidegger et la question* (Paris: Galilée, 1987), p. 11; translated by Geoffrey Bennington and Rachel Bowlby as *Of Spirit: Heidegger and the Question* (Chicago: University of Chicago Press, 1989), p. 1.

19. See Pierre Klossowski, *Nietzsche et le cercle vicieux* (Paris: Mercure de France, 1969). I have discussed Klossowski in my *Of Memory, Reminiscence, and Writing: On the Verge* (Bloomington: Indiana University Press, 1990), chapter 7, and in my *Infectious Nietzsche* (Bloomington: Indiana University Press, 1996), chapter 11.

20. Martin Heidegger, *Zollikoner Seminare: Protokolle—Gespräche—Briefe,* ed. Medard Boss (Frankfurt a.M.: Vittorio Klostermann, 1987).

21. Martin Heidegger, *Beiträge zur Philosophie (Vom Ereignis),* Martin Heidegger Gesamtausgabe, vol. 65 (Frankfurt a.M.: Vittorio Klostermann, 1989). For the text by Heinrich Heine, see Heine's *Sämtliche Werke,* ed. Jost Perfahl (Munich: Winkler Verlag, n.d.), 2:707–28; see also "Die Göttin Diana," 2:729–39.

David Farrell Krell: Selected Bibliography

Books

Contagion: Sexuality, Disease, and Death in German Idealism and Romanticism. Bloomington: Indiana University Press, 1998.

Archeticture: Ecstasies of Space, Time, and the Human Body. Albany: State University of New York Press, 1997.

With Donald L. Bates, *The Good European: Nietzsche's Work Sites in Word and Image.* Chicago: University of Chicago Press, 1997, and Munich: Knesebeck Verlag, 2000.

Infectious Nietzsche. Bloomington: Indiana University Press, 1996.

Lunar Voices: Of Tragedy, Poetry, Fiction, and Thought. Chicago: University of Chicago Press, 1995.

Of Memory, Reminiscence, and Writing: On the Verge. Bloomington: Indiana University Press, 1990.

Postponements: Woman, Sensuality, and Death in Nietzsche. Bloomington: Indiana University Press, 1986.

Fiction

The Recalcitrant Art: Diotima's Letters to Hölderlin and Other Missives. Albany: State University of New York Press, 2000.

Son of Spirit: A Novel. Albany: State University of New York Press, 1997.

Nietzsche: A Novel. Albany: State University of New York Press, 1996.

Chapters in Edited Volumes and Journal Articles

"A Malady of Chains: Husserl and Derrida on the Origins of Geometry and a Note to the 'Archeticts' of the Future," in *A.D. Architectural Design.* London, 1997.

"Of Spirit and the Daimon: Jacques Derrida's *De l'esprit.*" In *Ethics and Danger: Currents in Continental Thought,* ed. Charles E. Scott and Arleen B. Dallery. Albany: State University of New York Press, 1992.

"Everything Great Stands in the Storm That Blows from Paradise." *Cardozo Law Review* 13.4 (1991).

"Lucinde's Shame: Hegel, Sensuous Woman, and the Law." In *Hegel and Legal Theory,* ed. Drucilla Cornell, Michel Rosenfeld, and David Gray Carlson. New York: Routledge, 1991.

"'I made it on the verge' . . . : A Letter to Daniél Libeskind on the Jewish Museum in Berlin." *Assemblage: A Critical Journal of Architecture and Design* 12 (1990).

"The Crisis of Reason in the Nineteenth Century: Schelling's Treatise on Human Freedom (1809)." In *The Collegium Phaenomenologicum: The First Ten Years,* ed. John Sallis, Giuseppina Moneta, and Jacques Taminiaux. The Hague: Martinus Nijhoff, 1989.

"Ashes, ashes, we all fall . . . " In *Dialogue and Deconstruction: The Gadamer-Derrida Encounter,* ed. Diane P. Michelfelder and Richard E. Palmer. Albany: State University of New York Press, 1989.

"Knowledge Is Remembrance: Diotima's Instruction at Symposium 207c–208b." In *Poststructuralist Classics,* ed. Andrew Benjamin. London: Routledge, 1988.

"Paradoxes of the Pineal: From Descartes to Georges Bataille." In *Contemporary French Philosophy: Proceedings of the Royal Institute of Philosophy,* ed. A. Phillips Griffiths. Cambridge: Cambridge University Press, 1988.

"The Oldest Program toward a System in German Idealism." *Owl of Minerva* 17.1 (1985).

"Phenomenology of Memory from Husserl to Merleau-Ponty." *Philosophy and Phenomenological Research* 42.4 (1982).

"Work Sessions with Martin Heidegger." *Philosophy Today* 26.2 (1982).

"Results." *Monist* 44.4 (1981).

"A Smile and a Sense of Tragedy: Letters from J. Glenn Gray." *Philosophy Today* 25.2 (1981).

"Memory as Malady and Therapy in Freud and Hegel." *Journal of Phenomenological Psychology* 22.1 (1981).

"Hegel Heidegger Heraclitus." In *Heraclitean Fragments,* ed. John Sallis and Kenneth Maly. Tuscaloosa: University of Alabama Press, 1980.

"Phenomenology of Memory: Some Implications for Education." In *Phenomenology and Education,* ed. Bernard Curtis and Wolfe Mays. London: Methuen, 1978.

"Female Parts in *Timaeus.*" *Arion: A Journal of Humanities and the Classics* 2.3 (1975).

"Merleau-Ponty on Eros and Logos." *Man and World* 7.1 (1974).

"Socrates' Body." *Southern Journal of Philosophy* 10. 4 (1972).

"Toward an Ontology of Play: Eugen Fink's Notion of Spiel." *Research in Phenomenology* 2 (1972).

8

Institutional Songs and Involuntary Memory

Where Do "We" Come From?

CHARLES E. SCOTT

Charles Scott's work composes thought that is formed by experiences that arise without indication of transcendental foundations or identities. For him, philosophizing is a matter of thinking in and with options that are provoked by the breakup of traditional metaphysical ways of thinking and knowing. In his work, there are experiments with styles and processes of thought that move through and away from functioning absolutes. He experiments with thinking that operates with a prioritization of questions that do not lead to definitive or substantive answers and gives attention to nonsubjective syntheses and values that are embodied in institutions, practices, and processes of substitution and signification in language.

Scott has found in some of our highest and most cherished values and meanings multiple and often conflicting structures of power, of inheritance and disinheritance, of centralization and marginalization. In his work, he has emphasized the importance of the processes of departure that develop in these dynamic structures and that seem to be embedded in Western culture. In American culture these are also the departures from many different cultures that were "left behind," and yet they are at once the same cultures that provided the initial identities for an immigrant people. His work operates out of an American intellectual culture that is constituted by the translations and processes of transfiguration that characterize these departures, a culture formed in part by the openings and liberty provided by exile, splintered traditions, multiple centers for truths, and valorizations of differences that produce a union far different from the one provided by a definitive, overarching authority.

In the context of the possibilities that come with departures and translations, Scott has written about Plato, Kant, Schelling, Fichte, Hegel, Kierkegaard, Nietzsche, Heidegger, Gadamer, Foucault, Deleuze, and Derrida, and has engaged philosophically with many continental philosophers from America whose works are included in this volume. Scott has been especially interested in the ways by which we can reconsider traditional texts, relearn them, and develop, in a contemporary setting, ways of knowing them that are different from the kinds of knowledge and thought that they traditionally embodied.

There are several trajectories that define Scott's concerns. He began his professional work by giving accounts of experiences of religious meaning that do not have as part of their content disclosure of a divinity. This early interest led to work on experiences of transition and transformation in which identities are found to be formed of multiple boundaries and trajectories of meaning and force. In that work, he found helpful accounts of therapeutic experiences in which something that is recognized as healing occurs, although in those occurrences people find no defining subjectivity. His work became increasingly devoted to thought that is not organized primarily by the force of identity or subjectivity, and a considerable portion of Scott's work has been motivated by the ethical and political implications in processes that either valorize or do not valorize subjectivity and identity. This led Scott to his most recent work on memory, especially on memories that are not voluntary and not within the possession of the person who experiences them. The selection of Scott's work included in this essay is taken from his 1999 book, *The Time of Memory*. The book traces the dimension of loss that is constitutive of memorial occurrences and prepares the way for a reconsideration of physicality and problems that arise in thought about bodies.

-→=●=←-

But all of us have, unconsciously, involuntarily in our bodies values, words, formulas, moralities of opposite descent. . . . A diagnosis of the modern soul—where would it begin? By resolute incision into their instinctive contradiction, by the isolation of opposite values. . . .

—*Nietzsche*, The Case of Wagner

There is an important difference between individuals' sacrificing their selves for the sake of something else and their finding emptiness in themselves. In self-sacrifice people give up priority for their own needs, desires, and interests for the sake of something other than themselves. When they find emptiness in themselves, however—no self at all accompanying their selves—they do not necessarily sacrifice anything. They might rather attend to emptiness and allow by that attentiveness a sense of emptiness to infuse and inform their other experiences, including their self-oriented desires and interests. When that kind of attentiveness happens, their attitudes and feelings and their relations to themselves may well change; but the change happens in association with "nothing" that they find in themselves, and not in association with something outside of themselves in the affirmation of which they sacrifice their own interests and needs. Such sacrificial acts might also happen, but not necessarily because of a sense of emptiness. People might rather experience a dimension that is something like a dispossession that accompanies all that they are and have, a dimension that is not to be grasped or kept, and one that composes a release of determined experiences and things, release in one's involvement with them and care of them. A sense of emptiness can happen like an experience of loss that comes with present, passing events, except this sense of loss is not one of having lost something or given up something. Rather it is like the awareness of being definitely here along with no presence, like being porous in one's singularity, or occurring simultaneously with emptiness and senses of identity and acts of recognition.

"Emptiness" is a difficult word since it speaks metaphorically of no thing. A report that emptiness "happens" in an individual's life—not the empty feeling of melancholy in an experience of weak (or no) motivation to live, but the emptiness of nothing accompanying other specific experiences—such a report describes what appears to be an extremely private experience and indicates that the individual's life in its event is characterized by radical difference from all of the determinations in his/her life. The issue that I wish to note now is not an epistemological one concerning validation or confirmation. The issue is rather the way in which a person might communicate such a "realization" of emptiness. How can one communicate such a nonobjective and nonsubjective dimension of the particular events that he or she undergoes? Probably only by indirection, and in this case indirection that exposes another person to "the" emptiness that one finds. Exposure to no-thing? To indetermination to which one may attend but which does not become an object of attention? To no-thing "that" "is" neither active nor passive, neither subject nor object, neither eternal or finite, not a "this" at all, but happens obliquely like an absence of the signified in a *signifier* or like Lethe that cancels its own image and "communicates" by its passage "beyond" reference and sense? Or like Dionysus who means loss of *all* determination including his own determination? Or Apollo whose power of determination fades into "darkness" without order or determination, or Mnemosyne who names the coming to presence of "things" in their loss of presence? The difficulty of this aspect is complicated by its imperviousness to the manners of knowing and direct speech by which we usually speak about things, define them, clarify them, and understand them. Although it appears to me that speaking of emptiness should be no more awkward than speaking of bodies, which are also impervious to our direct thought and speech, many people are less accustomed to meeting this kind of difference (from intelligibility) than they are to encountering the resistance of bodies to intelligibility. And we are accustomed to speechless gestures that carry intelligibility, are usually not noticed reflectively, and by which people communicate a good deal of meaning and significance—one's arm moving unconsciously in the air, extending a space of silent communication, expressing any one of hundreds of things that an arm's gesture can "say"—such events are themselves remarkable for the palpability and impalpability that accompany them.

If my observations are accurate, the feelings, issues, and questions that accompany memory's loss (events comprising emptiness as well as determination) are a significant, if seldom noticed, part in our culture's lineage of tacit recognition. And if we are to speak out of these experiences and of them, we face the desirability of speaking and thinking with an indirection that can bring them to the explicit awareness of other people. Direct speech about them can contribute to the processes by which we lose touch with their way of happening and thus mislead us by means of our explicit understanding of them: the greater our abstract clarity regarding them, the more decisive can be our departure and distance from them. In indirect communication, our objectivity and rational good sense can become a conduit to occurrences that do not happen the way objectivity, rationality, and good sense happen, and a conduit that happens as a passing means to occurrences that often are not recognized in our ordinary and well-functioning sensibility.[1]

I would like to show how some kinds of thinking can be comprised of an indirect communication in which "something" like lethic "space" that is unfixed, devoid of mass, impersonal, and capable of endless transformation is brought indirectly to awareness by means of direct descriptions of some aspects in our culture's lineages. In this case, the process of *indirection* includes a language by which the priority of subjectivity for experience and thought is replaced by the priority of *lineage* and its transmission. And while I am persuaded of the importance and descriptive accuracy of this move, I will place emphasis on the performative aspect of such thinking (rather than on the issue of accuracy) in order to show a way of descriptive thinking that valorizes memory and attempts to carry out its work in an indirect communication of memory's loss in memory's enactments. In this way I will show that loss and nondetermination can be given expression indirectly in a genealogical manner of placing and specifying determined, bygone occurrences. Such indirect "presentation" happens as involuntary remembering *in* memory's losses, although my direct approach to this indirection will raise problems that I will need to address.

Locating the Present-Past

Memories embedded in our musculature, dreams, sicknesses, feelings, and relations; memories expressed as preferences, attractions, aversions, anxieties; memories that give unconscious depth, range, and force to our "immediacies": involuntary memories form our everyday lives and unexpected interruptions in them, although we seldom think about involuntary memories or recognize them when they happen. But they do happen. We find a significant measure of the present-pasts' manifestation and presentation in involuntary memories which add to the singularity, determination, and affection in our bodies and in the body of our imaginations and systems of self-regulations and recognitions. Pathologizing memories, healing memories, controlling and fateful memories: they are among the patterns of our lives and define our human occurrences. We deny them at the cost of self-deception.

As important as these memories are in their determinations of the ways we come to presence and compose our subjectivity, they constitute only one of several domains of involuntary memory. I would like to look at one of these domains—an institutional one—with an emphasis on the question of ways whereby we might think appropriately as we account for this domain and speak about it. How can we give increased alertness to these memories which do not begin or continue in their courses because of volitional actions on our part? Can we speak of the present-past as it takes place in institutions in a manner that allows the present-pastness of which we speak to appear in its involuntary happening? Can we understand institutions as instances of indirect communication of involuntary memories?

I have indicated that the occurrences of the past-present include losses in "what" comes to presence in memory. Such losses are not more characteristic of voluntary memory than involuntary memory. I have been addressing memorial occurrences in the transpiration of "forces" that are memorialized in such figurations as Mnemosyne, Lethe, Apollo, and Dionysus. I shall turn to the nonmythological figurations in institutions that are memorial, involuntary, forceful, nonsubjective, and strangely, embody nonetheless a kind of awareness as humans live in them and by means of them. As I make this transition from mythology to institutions, consider one of Mnemosyne's figurations. She is the goddess of poetry and poets, and poets in ancient Greece were those who could see immediately into the past, to the origins of things or to the past great ages of their people. People found these past "things" to be invisible to mortal sight and to require for their presenting by sight and song the help of this goddess. Inspired memory is the poet's power to give perceptive presence to what is not perceptively present. J. P. Vernant points to another function of the poet that accompanies his inspiration: poems may include long catalogues of the names of gods, warriors, ships, and horses. These seemingly unpoetic lists "enable a social group to piece its 'past' together. . . . They constitute, as it were, the archives of a society that has no writing."[2] This is a society that exists in lineages of gods as well as people, and the poets provide the genealogies of originary gods and people. They rank and classify them along with their ships and horses, identify their families and their origins, and in this way they tell the stories of their society's time by means of codified, detailed legends and myths. Poems in this era spoke of "what" is originary for the present and of the processes by which the present came to be. They speak, however, of origins and processes that have much less to do with linear time than with divinely established destinies and the mysterious linkages of divine and human lives. The poets *relate* the past and its figures, but in this seemingly unpragmatic activity they establish both a definitive past and a meaningful present in which deathless beings live. They tell a people who they are and where they came from by reference both to bygone days and to an eternal present that is not linear in its disclosure.

Vernant says that the genesis of the world, as related to the poets by Mnemosyne and her daughters and then sung to others by the poets, unfolds by means of genealogies: "the rhythm of this past depends not upon a single chronology but upon genealogies. Time is, as it were, understood in the account of the relations between generations."[3] The primal beings of the past, such as Gaia or the Titans (including Mnemosyne), remain in present effect in the "night of the underworld."[4] And those who gave identity to bygone times "are still present to those who see them. They dwell on the earth, shade-like, or under the earth or in the ocean, or on the island of the blessed. They are available to the poets' eyes as they live timelessly on the edge of time. The poet sees the "things" of the past in their remarkable, obscure, ageless present. . . ." "Never for a moment does the journey back through time make us leave contemporary realities."[5] Rather, poetic sight into the past constitutes a region of discovery of what is contemporary, although invisible and hidden—a discovery of the depths and heights of being that determine present lives without the notice of people in their ordinary awareness and knowledge.

Poets' memory thus eliminated "the barrier that separates the present from the past." "It provides a bridge between the world of the living and that beyond to which everything that leaves the light of day must return."[6] In this movement the lethic element is *like* the darkness through which the poet, by Mnemosyne's power, sees clearly. But the power of Lethe as well as the good sense of everyday understanding are lost in the immediacy of divine sight. Linear time and its lethic envelopment are largely ignored. Time is not reconstituted by the poet. Re-membering is not a part of the process. Rather, past things are seen contemporaneously just as they are in their incorruptibility.

Forgetting ordinary present time, however, for the poet of present, bygone time, is a moment of liberation from the misery and nearsightedness of the present age: knowledge of who lived then and how they lived in a time vastly more privileged than the poet's own time "enables [the poet] to escape from the time of the fifth race which is so fraught with fatigue, wretchedness, and anxiety": we find the balm, Mnemosyne's gift, in its association with Lethe, the god of forgetfulness.[7] Discernment of the past in the oblivion of the present time composes at once discernment of an eternal present that gives freedom from a profound ignorance and the deathlessness that accompanies it. Immortality and salvation are found through this memorial, poetic knowledge.

Note that in this context oblivion is connected with a turn to the present-past. Lethe is the "power" of forgetfulness that is mirrored in human superficiality, ignorance, and consequent misery, the power that is the element through which and beyond which the poet sees what truly is. Without inspired poetic knowledge and memory—Mnemosyne—humankind is lost on earth, surrounded and suffused by a darkness that people cannot perceive, much less see through. I shall connect this ancient sense of memory and knowledge to contemporary genealogy. But first I note a turn of emphasis in the name of Mnemosyne's and Lethe's imagery in order to highlight a moment that is different from the *return* to origins that I have been considering, a moment that will also provide a helpful distinction when I consider twentieth-century thought.

A second orientation for Mnemosyne and Lethe is found in the role that they play in some forms of Greek eschatology that are valorized by belief and reincarnation.[8] In this role they are oriented toward the soul prior to its incarnation and toward the future of souls after physical death rather than toward sight in the present-past. Instead of bringing to mortals the secrets of origins, Mnemosyne now brings the means by which souls can reach the end of time and, in the context of some religious practices that were oriented around reincarnation, put an end to the cycles of generations. Mnemosyne's role in providing liberation from "the world of oblivion" remains, but now that oblivion appears before the souls' earthy life and must be overcome by a recollection discipline. Lethe is that through which the soul passes in coming back into physical life; Lethe is the element by which the soul forgets all that it has learned and suffered in earlier lives, and consequently Lethe is associated even more strongly than earlier with condemnation and misery. And Mnemosyne is the power of remembering that carries the soul back through its many lives and to the many sources of its own life as her devotee engages in the act of the soul's recovery. Mnemosyne provides the knowledge by which the soul can free itself from the body's deathly forgetfulness. The waters of Lethe are crossed as the soul comes to earth: "The water of oblivion is no longer the symbol of death, but of a return to life and to existence within time."[9] By virtue of this water the soul forgets the lessons of its past earthly life and simply lives out again and blindly the travails of mortal existence. By such forgetfulness the soul is condemned to infinite *repetition* of forgetfulness, mortal experience, partial knowledge; it is "chained" to the wheel of birth and death. It becomes merely a leaky sieve, as the Platonic image has it. Instead of on origins, the emphasis falls on each soul's prenatal loss of a sense of itself as well as on the prenatal significance of Lethe.

Now the poet is not the primary perceiving mediator of Mnemosyne's blessings. The individual, rather, learns the discipline of memory and by memory's movements is transported back in time and beyond "this" time to other times and other lives. In this way people gather the knowledge and lessons by which their souls find themselves—beyond the power of temporality and now beyond the power of its earthly blindness and mistakes. And when its body dies and is prepared for rebirth, it can make "informed" choices. If it can avoid Lethe's water (on the left) and come by the road on the right to Mnemosyne's spring-fed lake, it can receive the lake's sacred water and become a deathless god with its complete knowledge of what is and is not. Memory, purification, salvation, past lives, and eternity are joined in this imagery, with which forgetfulness is allied in a hopeless recycling of the soul who in its impurity cannot recall life beyond its present life. "The very effort involved in remembering is in itself a 'purification,' an ascetic discipline. It constitutes a truly spiritual exercise. . . ."[10] This ascetic exercise of memory—this discipline—that the Pythagoreans and others carried out was focused on a person's past lives and will be reflected obliquely in our contemporary disciplines of philosophical genealogy. While the soul's past lives will not focus this contemporary memorial work, the living past in our culture and its institutions, the cultural force of the living past in our affections and recognitions—in our minds' involvement in institutions—will provide a centripetal center for our thought. We are not looking for eternity but we might look for liberation or understanding or new possibilities which, though far distant from "salvation," nonetheless arise through a transforming discipline of memory.

Earlier in this essay I referred to embedded memories and to experiences of emptiness, to something like a space (or nonspace) left as a breath passes. I connected that kind of happening to an "aspect" of nondetermination embedded in present-past events and gave a promissory note that I would return to this connection. Within the context of the promissory note, and not yet in its fulfillment, I note that the ancient Greek interpretations that we are now considering of the soul's collection of itself by means of remembering its past lives is an interpretation that is connected to "concentration on the soul's breath."[11] The exercise of this concentration was directly linked to recollection, to the soul's "eternal nature," and to memory of the soul's deathless difference from body. Memory of specific events of the past was not indicative of anything significant for itself but was simply a technique used in order to "get in touch" with one's soul in a movement toward the fullness of pure being. The benefit of the soul's difference from body was sometimes found by means of trances in which a soul would travel to the "beyond" of its other lives as well as the beyond of the "element" (Mnemosyne) through which the journey took place. In this journey it discovers all of the errors that it has committed and by which it has been contaminated. And in this case, the defilement of Lethe's forgetfulness is overcome, whether the journey be retrospective or a "vertical" and ecstatic ascension to present and complete, timeless being. In these instances, the soul finds its measure in Mnemosyne's enactment and in the purity that she is now understood to require, a requirement which means elimination of Lethe's power of forgetfulness. The soul finds itself not by means of empty indetermination but by fullness of being—immortal being—to which it turns. Lethe is defeated. Without loss, memory now is considered in the context of completion and perfection, and the enlightened soul, free of temporality, exists in timeless being. Lethe, on the other hand, as a force that gives temporality to the soul in the form of self-forgetfulness, self-alienation, and infinite repetition, is absent from the soul's timeless self-enactment. Now the soul never forgets itself. It suffers no forgetfulness at all. *Anamnesis* (memory) brings completion. The soul is free of nondetermination in the sense that it is without forgetfulness, intrinsic need to change, intrinsic uncertainty, and anarchic disorder. It cannot die, and it now knows what is and is not, what has been, and what will be. Memory is imagined to be without loss, and Lethe figures a region "before birth from the powers of which the pure soul departs. Lethe does not name the soul's destiny when the soul comes to the end of time by means of memory's transcendence."[12] Inspired memory, rather, begins timelessly and leads to the end of time in timeless being without Lethe's forgetfulness. Mnemosyne thus figures a separation from temporality that promises salvation and divinity, that is, deathlessness and freedom from the force of human suffering. Time is experienced primarily as "a power of destruction which irremediably ruins everything that . . . makes life worth living."[13]

In this particular complex of images, beliefs, and thoughts, the highest human aspirations thus include transcendence of (escape from?) time. The Pythagoreans, for example, returned to bygone events only for the purpose of reaching the soul's timeless and true dwelling places. Ages, periods, sequences, genealogies, significant moments, and deeds—all that constitute a memorable past—are no more than passing steps toward a catharsis of the soul which is imprisoned by its sojourn in time. The recalling of past things is grounded by Mnemosyne's clear and unfettered power to transmit the soul to true memoria—to the truths of her eternity before unbroken presences of being. Mnemosyne's "flow" has become a timeless transmission that carries the soul to its destiny of no forgetfulness and hence of no change, affection, suffering, or death. It seems that Mnemosyne's gift is not one of freedom from transformation and loss. She no longer gives temporal perspective. Rather, she gives the soul to find itself in eternity. Mnemosyne is here a sign solely of completeness, not one that includes fragmentation or fissure or loss of life in the coming of life. Lesmosyne seems to be forgotten in this figuration. (Does Lethe smile obscurely in this accomplishment?)

We have found Mnemosyne and Lethe functioning differently in two of their figurations, but there are also similarities. Mnemosyne is a power of saving knowledge, and power by which time is transcended—a power in which an inspired person can be in perceptive and transformative touch with Truth and Eternal Presence. In both mythical structures the fragmentation of earthly time, its turbulence, instability, and mortal existence indicate inferiority in ontological status and a kind of existing that is aligned with ignorance, suffering, and death, all of which are inimical to Mnemosyne's and the soul's true nature. And yet, in spite of these unpersuasive beliefs and the dominant conception of time, the power of Mnemosyne continues to transmit the past and human awareness through time in such a way that what happened no longer repeats itself in finite lives. She also continues to be a power of liberation from the otherwise overwhelming finite present with its destiny of blind oblivion. She is a power that relieves mortal suffering and ignorance. And her linkage to Lethe also continues although in the negative and externalized way of overcoming Lethe's power. Lethe has been expelled from Mnemosyne's own event and territory, and that means that forgetfulness is experienced as external to memory, that memory's event is in unblemished touch with radiant eternity. Finally, Mnemosyne continues to be an impersonal "agency" of memory, that is, devoid of mass; but her transmission is to a perceptive psyche to which she brings enlightenment and not, in Lethe's absence, endless transformation.

Aristotle's conception of memory, on the other hand, is radically different from that embodied by Mnemosyne's myths. Memory (*mnemes*) is a secondary faculty, is subject to mistake, and "belongs to the past."[14] It is "a state of affection" of either sensation or judgment; it takes place as "the lasting part of an affection" in the form of something like a picture (449b–450a). It depends on a lapse of time and a distance in the mind from an impressive occurrence, a distance that is spanned by the mental continuation of the picture. By memory we have one kind of temporal perception that is oriented by what caused the affective picture and by that image's "likeness to that of which it is an image" (451a). Memory is most particularly not an aspect of the present, perceptive presentation of things. Rather it constitutes simply an awareness of pastness and past impressions.

Recollection (*anamnesis*) is no less than memory a strictly human and individual occurrence. But it differs, in Aristotle's usage, from "memory." It names a process of influence and recovery by which one deliberately moves from impression to impression until the forgotten one is discovered (451b), "for when a man is recollecting he infers that he has seen or heard or experienced something of the sort before, and the process is a kind of search" (453a). One's deliberations are not "at distance, as some think that visions operates. . . . but one thinks of them by proportionate mental impulse (*análogon kinései*); for there are similar figures and movements in the mind" (*kinései*) (452b). In speaking of recollecting Aristotle understands himself to be speaking of the movements toward a retained state of mind, "a mental picture in the physical sphere," a movement that is affected by other physical states such as weight that bears on the organs of perception or the rates of growth and decline (435b). In thinking this way a person recovers a rational, pictorial affection in the lapse of time, or perhaps better said, a human mind recovers it. There is, on Aristotle's account, an emphasis not only on the deliberative function of *anamnesis* but also on a non-voluntary aspect of memories' return, for retained affections can present themselves persistently in an unregulated and unintended way: ". . . outbursts of temper or fear, when they have once produced an impulse, do not cease even when the subjects of them set up counter movements, but continue this original activity in spite them. This affection is like that which occurs in the case of names, tunes, and sayings, when any of them has been very much on our lips; even though we give up the habit and do not mean to yield to it, we find ourselves continually singing or saying the familiar sound" (453a).

Temporalization of the past, retention of affections, and deliberate recovery of memories are all fallible and conditioned events within human minds for Aristotle; and the transmission of memories retains for him a nonvoluntary power that can be for a time beyond the individual's control. The ideas of memory's independence of directional consciousness and of something approximate to the self-enactment of memory remain in Aristotle's thought despite the thoroughness of his move to temporal, human agency in his explanation and description of memory.

Lethic forgetfulness in memory's enactment is also dimly recognized in Aristotle's essay. I say "dimly" because it receives no careful attention. But the lapse of time that is definitive of memory decisively separates the past, impressive occurrence from its present enactment, and the function of memories as affective, pictorial states of mind divides memories by a representational distance from "what" they hold. Loss of the "things" that memories record as affective states is intrinsic to memorial events; and lapses by which memories are hidden constitute conditions for the exercise of recollection. Memory, according to Aristotle, is characterized by loss, distance in time, forgetfulness, hiddenness, and fallibility. These characteristics happen as an individual's states of mind and do not have any status external to the experiences of a particular mind. Mnemosyne, with her gifts and divine grace, has fallen from view in Aristotle's commonsense account; but aspects of the myths, especially in the name of Mnemosyne's early connection with Lethe, are vaguely reflected in it.

All of the myths of Mnemosyne also share with Aristotle a nonhistorical sensibility. But in contrast to Aristotle, Mnemosyne's and Lethe's mythic affiliations or lack of affiliation interconnect and depart from each other without a sense of mortal time's rule over their origins and transmissions. Mnemosyne's later myths especially carry one away from temporal fragmentation and the contingent existence of orders, including the orders of her own figurations. Mnemosyne's and Lethe's mythic externality before human emotion and mentation directs people toward superhuman insight, ritualized catharsis, and unchanging truths, not to living, finite past-present linkages in human mentation, much less in human cultural experience. Perhaps Mnemosyne's balm is found in her power to divert people away from their despair and affliction. But it also gives authority and power to special people whom she guides to rarified, sublime mystery and whom she graces with the power to return to humans with speech inspired by the mystery and her transmission of it. In many ways she is a goddess who bears humans or, later, their undying souls beyond the limits of time. The songs that she inspires sing out of a timeless presence that gives the possibility of wholeness to people who are lacerated in the brokenness of mortal time.

All that is lyrical nonsense in the context of Aristotle's account, except that he too has a view in which time produces nothing and always takes life away. Such temporality infects memory and prevents it from having the noetic power to reach truth. Memory and recollection constitute a temporal agency which contributes to a human sense of time but not to knowledge of higher, more excellent truth. And although memory does not contribute to the soul's full maturation in which (the soul) is fully and timelessly in attention to itself, memory and recollection do have the virtue of making a fallible if inward capacity to transmit past experiences into present awareness, a glimmer, perhaps, of fallible, historically constituted human beings struggling to recollect the courses and trajectories by which they have come to live the ways in which they find themselves. Even though I find that memory does not happen exclusively in individual minds, it does happen, as Aristotle saw, in loss—obliteration, really—of transcendence beyond time. The temporality of memory produces—now in spite of Aristotle's description of time—possibilities for understanding in temporal terms even the enlightenment provided by memory in lineages in which transtemporal attachments are assumed.

The loss of Lethe and Mnemosyne's figuration—a lethic loss of Lethe's "memory"—radicalized her ritualized religious functions and her association with being without time. On the other hand, Lethe continued to figure radical loss of memory and of the benefits of timeless presence. Such losses, when combined with an understanding of meaning within the constraints of finitude, constitute involuntary memory of memory's own fragmentation. This thought is, of course, beyond the circumference of Aristotle's philosophy. But there is in his interpretation nonetheless the lethic element of forgetfulness and loss within memory's process and this element gives to memory its fragmentation. Memory for Aristotle, in sharp contrast to Orphic and Phythagorean views, cannot provide wholeness or unity or extraction from time. Lesmosyne again? Hardly, but still an oblique appreciation of radical forgetfulness within memory's event.

Against this mythic and Aristotelian background (inclusive of their differences), I shall turn to ways in which institutions not only transmit and embody memories but also actively form people by the power of their memories. We are at a great distance from the mythic consciousness in which Mnemosyne and Lethe moved and in which Mnemosyne and Lethe also moved people by the drawing, transforming power of their figurations. But we remain close to the events of transmission that characterize memory as they and we experience them. In archaic and classical times in Greece, we saw that poets were the bearers of meaning whose reach was completely outside of the capacity of other people; and "Mnemosyne" was the name for the power of transmission and linkage to "what" people either never knew, or forgot in a primordial and original event of forgetfulness. Their songs were constituted by both the spirit and the content that Mnemosyne disclosed to them. And with these songs individuals were carried beyond themselves to hear—perhaps to see—what was not now immediate and perceptible in time, to hear or see what was necessarily forgotten in temporal presence. In the radical change of awareness that marks our differences from those Hellenic devotees, we lack the grace of Mnemosyne's powerful and poetic presence. But we have memorial transmissions nonetheless that have remarkable transformative power and that give all manner of possibilities and figurations of life to arise and blossom. The prosaic, transmissional, and generative powers of institutions in their memorial aspects, though they are fragmented and mortal and certainly are not mythological gods, constitute nonetheless remarkable forces as they make present past events. Without a transcendental reach, they still have a transcending dimension in their cultural events as occurrences of transmission, formation, and carriage of people far outside the reach of their private experiences. Institutions happen as bodies of memorial life, whether for good or ill. And no matter how much we might hate them or fear them or cling to them, they pound out dithyrambic rhythms by which we are borne by strange and largely silent lineages, by things and to things we do not name but in the force of which we live. In these complex figurations of transmission, formation, and transformation, institutions carry out functions analogous to those of the archaic muses, now secularized and largely without beauty, analogous to figures who moved with powers that could convey people to what is hidden and essential for their lives. And those people who attend to institutions in their transmissional aspects? Not poets, usually, but like the archaic seers who found access to "things" that defined destinies and past, forming events, and who would say what they saw for the benefit of people. Everything now, in comparison to the times of mythological expression, is scaled down, without radiance or divinity, perhaps not totally lacking mystery but without uniting, unquestioned beliefs. "We" are without the need for blindness in order to see by memory. But now we see that to which those poets and seers were blind—temporal, unstable, transforming, and decomposing things—re-membered things. Such things now help to compose the element of sight and meaning; and the region of gifted sight includes past-presence, given in part through institutionalized monuments like texts, artifacts, and ancient manuscripts. And, in the absence of gods and seers, perhaps the memory of memory also lives in guises that only Lethe could appreciate were she here and given to admiration.

Consider perhaps the least divine and poetic of established institutions: money. The object as well as bearer of suspicion, greed, and love, money is one of the most powerful means of transmission in the world; and its insubstantial products are among the most prominent universalizing powers among diverse cultures that are otherwise bound to parochial customs and beliefs. It has massively transformed many economic practices as well as entire economies and has led to the formation of many other powerful institutions. It has played a major role in defining social standing and in the process overturned other longstanding social structures. Above all money carries experiences and constitutes experiences of the imaginal, consensual formation of a primary medium in and for our lives and one on which our lives depend. It can properly function as a constant reminder of radical contingency. In its power of transmission it is an opposite of Mnemosyne's early poets. It transmits and transfers with no hint of substantive, transcendent mystery. It occasions power with no requirement of purity. It mirrors a vast indifference to individual survival and can put in suspended relief the traditions by which a people have come to know who they are. It spawned a large vocabulary and transformed work in its development: currency, loan, investment, banking, income, capital, profit, securities, funds, account, debit, credit, fiscal, balance, and change, to name only a few words in English that had nonmonetary meanings that were charged by the functions of money. And all of this without a "natural" origin, a natural law, or any other noncontingent foundation; with no more than human sanction, practice, and agreement for its "laws" of exchange; and nonetheless with a staggering virtuality when one considers the significance and force of its reality. Generative, awesome in its power, originary for customs, roles, social standing, and vast, interlinking networks of exchange and identity, money establishes an organism that carries us back to mutational beginnings—it has only evolved origins without an originary "word" or act or single, unified cause. Money attracts us in its ecstasy of promise and death, in its necessity and ephemeral indifference, in its receptacle-like quality of creation without subjectivity. It draws us like a fate that is spent in our lives, like a movement secreted in our lives, like an elusive memory of illusion, medium, reality, generation, disappearance, and appearance—all at once. Without our consent or preference, we belong to money rather more then it belongs to us.

In that belonging we inherit not only money's memorialized lack of substance, we also inherit histories of exchange and transmission. Consider the origin of nonconvertible paper money during the Revolutionary War. Bills that were not based on conversion into anything else—not gold or silver or tobacco or shells—probably saved the American revolution.[15] After the colonies declared their independence, faced with the necessity of financing a war, unable effectively to levy and collect taxes in large amounts, and without credible standing as a borrower, the new government did what it had to do: it printed money with nothing precious to back it other than enthusiastic trust in the value of independence.[16] Although my use of this example of predispositions and our money's lineage does not depend on any particular interpretation of the wisdom of those policies, my account agrees with those who find the disastrous fiscal policies during the revolution to be justifiable given the conditions of the time. Acceptance of the paper bills constituted an act of loyalty to the revolution, and those who did not accept them were "enemies of liberty." In other words, during this time it was considered treason to insist on convertible money or on gold or silver in financial transactions.[17] The bills that the government printed could be exchanged and used in payment for other things, but one could not go to a bank or to the government and exchange them for a standard weight of anything. At that time, the government did not even use land on a security (as several European governments had in order to increase the availability of money). The major trading nations, on the other hand, enjoyed stable currencies with reliable, convertible values. In the interest of stability and British wealth, King George II in 1751 had restrained the American "Colonies or Plantations" from printing paper bills in order to retain control of trade on this continent and to prevent the inflationary and uncontrollable consequences of large quantities of "bad money." But in 1775, in the interest of liberty and heedless of certain inflation, the colonial government began to print large sums of money. Benjamin Franklin wrote: "This currency, as we manage it, is a wonderful machine. It performs its Office when we issue it: it pays and clothes Troops, and provides Victuals, and Ammunition; and when we are obliged to issue a Quantity excessive, it pays off by Depreciation."[18] An extravagant fiscal policy became a "machine" in the service of the revolution and belief in the value of liberty. Further, printing money during the war occurred in lieu of taxation and embodied a certain freedom from *the* indication of oppression by the state. Money without substantial backing was essential for the birth of liberty on this continent.

I note two elements in the proliferation of government bills in this country's early history: belief in liberty and inevitable hyperinflation. The continental government's paper money was soon almost worthless—not worth "a continental," as the expression goes—and the more money people were paid, the poorer they became. By the end of the war the continental currency had lost ninety-nine percent of its face value and was effectively in default. This situation meant that many debtors paid their creditors with worthless bills and that many well-to-do patriots lost most of their monied wealth. By virtue of its bills' lack of convertibility and intrinsic value, the government was able to supply its army at will, pay its bills, and, as Franklin observed, end up scot-free by virtue of depreciation. In effect, the government had to pay for nothing. And further, paper money violated the scarcity principle as well as the security principle relative to metals that, by general consensus, were precious: as long as the supply of what is accepted as precious is limited, its value will be reasonably steady and its exchange value will be secure. But with unsecured paper bills and no central bank to establish reserves and regulations, the virtuality of a controlled medium of exchange became radical, and ruinous inflation swept the colonies.

In spite of anxiety and financial loss, most people stayed with the revolution: belief in the value of liberty functioned like security, not for the money itself but for the policy of exchange in spite of the worthlessness signified by the bills. If the revolution could be carried out without wealth and if liberty from oppression could be achieved by bills empty of value, so be it. The value of valueless money resided in purposes born of the lure of liberation and faith in this revolution. It was as though the bills were borrowed in debts to this faith and lure. Hope, trust, belief, ideas—the *value*—of liberty were the sources from which the currency was borrowed. And it—the currency—repaid its creditors with the enormous interest of a newly founded republic, democratic at least in rhetoric, and free of England's tyranny. In this case paper money made, instead of wealth, a revolution from tyranny, and it substituted not only for an absence of wealth but also for republican-democratic ideals. This is a strange and compound substitution, . one in which an absence (in this case of wealth) finds its figuration in bills without intrinsic value, bills whose exchange value also signifies, and in that sense figures, hope in a revolution.

This associative dimension of continental paper bills, to which I am call-

ing attention, combines failure and success, catastrophe and victory, liberty
and groundlessness, and highlights a factor common to all paper bills and
banknotes: possibility for growth and disaster on the verge of insubstanti-
ality. I cannot say with certainty whether these aspects of the continental
bills played a positive role in the formation of government and society in
the United States. The formations of central banking systems and the strife
concerning banking in this country in addition to the formation of other
monetary policies make the associative lineage of liberty and paper money
extremely complex. But a suggestion does take shape: the combination of
successful liberation from tyranny, the power and insecurity of bills that are
not (really) convertible into precious metal or land, and passion for the
freedom of self-representation present elements that are familiar in the experience of United States democracy. One might well consider the legacy of
the money from 1775 to 1781 for the association in United States culture of
value without permanent substance, freedom from tyranny, and for a time,
an astonishing degree of optimism based on expansion and depletion of
resources. Perhaps memories of their money and successful revolution took
many transformations in the development of North American ideals, policies, and attitudes.

Memory and money are so strange! Happening as it does in money's
"eventing" and not solely or even primarily in images of money or money
as image of other things—although memories occur "there" too—money's
memorial aspect occurs in transmissions and networkings. This most ma-
terialistic of things from the point of view of "spiritual" perception brings
to presence and transforms in its activities many past events that marked
money's development, brings them to transformative presence in events
of transferal that are quite excessive to any image or representation that
money might also have. This kind of institutional memory has an imageless
dimension in this sense: the memorial aspects of money in its usage occur
in exchanging, in situations of exchange that generate new beginnings and
endings in events. They take place in transmissional processes rather than
only in or through images or pictures that are retained, almost like monuments, with availability for further reference. This memory in transmissional happenings is ephemeral. It does not occur in a clearly marked space
for memory or in a relatively static form. This kind of memory happens,
rather, in buying and selling, saving and spending, in desiring to save or
spend, in empowering moments, and it happens in the interlinking of the
things it enables. Memory in this case happens when we spend money,
accumulate it, gain or lose social leverage by its means, expand our experiences by its networks, or recognize things on its terms. These things *might*
be put into the forms of images, just as I am giving them a particular accessibility by these words and thought. But images and words are secondary
presentations that refer and give appearance not only to signifying images
but to various other happenings. As presentative and immediate in our
lives, however, these other nonimagistic happenings are not simply signs.
They happen as occurrences that transmit memories—give past occurrences

currency—as they occur in other transmissional processes. Events without sign or image are neither more nor less visible than Mnemosyne's presence, yet they are as forceful as people once found her to be. Money, like many other events, composes an environment in which events of the past are transformed into influential, impacting presences, into transformations, we have seen, that also enact forgetfulness of the past as it comes as memory to presence.

Consider further involuntary memory without images. I do not want to say that such memories are without form, but rather that they are not identical with the images that carry them. The eventful forms, such as forms of exchange, are moved in part, I have said, by past events that are born (and born again) in dynamic, current determinations and circumstances—something like a fusion of horizons that I have discussed elsewhere. The renewed happenings of past events occur as obscure forces of influence, that is, as indirect, intangible, effective and affective powers, something like the sounding that moves forms of music. They indwell occurrences as limits, ways of doing things, as attitudes and affections that are engendered by the processes, recognitions, trajectories, and hierarchies of value. Such influences and their lineages can be studied and described by attention to the intangible forces and elements that constitute an event. Such study is not poetic divination like that of archaic Greek seers, but it is nonetheless a study which puts us in touch with forces that elude most of our everyday awareness. Images do carry influences, but inquiring into those influences requires the inquirer to find also what is not an image in the lineage's memorial enactment as well as to find transmissions of influences that exceed images.

Foucault's study of the history of insanity in the Age of Reason is one instance of this kind of inquiry and also a study of a kind of memory that is excessive to the images that carry it. Included in the several agendas in *Madness and Civilization* is the silencing of madness in the seventeenth and eighteenth centuries and a silencing that continues to be manifest in the twentieth-century medical knowledge of insanity and in the modern mental asylum.

Foucault traces and brings to awareness a division between madness and nonmadness that has its origins toward the end of the middle ages. This division itself obscurely carried memory of the exclusion figured by lazar houses and by "the value and images attached to the figure of the leper" in his or her removal from the "normal" world.[19] The leper was recognized as a sign of God's anger and grace, as a revelation of God's will and care in relation to humans. *In the lepers' exclusion,* people saw the hope of God's salvation. Foucault's point is that *abandonment* of the leper in the lazar houses—something distinguishable from the lazar house as a *sign* of abandonment—was itself a constitutive element in a lineage of exclusions that bore on the formation of madness in modern times.[20]

A perception had increased in the middle ages of the ambiguity, power, and danger of madness, that appeared to separate these afflicted ones from the sense of divine grace and revelation that had previously bound them to the communities that banished them. The mad were increasingly associated with folly and with an element of cosmic anomie and deception, with what Foucault calls "unreason"; in the midst of order and lawfulness something "strange" and not lawful came to figure the recognition of the madman. Or, if "natural" is the lawful, something unnatural figured the mad. They appeared to be living epiphanies, not of something past or pending, not even of God's judgment and will, but of "something" in the world "now" that is menacing and chaotic, something divided from normalcy, nature, law, and God's will.

Foucault shows that in the modern period exclusion by means of institutionalization combined with an unconscious terror before the chaos of non-rationality, a consequent desire to contain, "correct" and "normalize" the mad by way of "rational" conduct and by an exercise of socially sanctioned power over their bodies—these combined elements gave a new form of abandonment: the voices of the mad were silenced. They were silenced in the sense that they could not present themselves to society in their own ways of being. They were not allowed their own self-manifestations, and the movements of their minds and bodies were submitted to the informed and rational subjectivity of those who knew themselves to be civilized. They were interpreted and presented by the syntax and practices of those who recognized themselves as reasonable and atoned as appropriate in their rationality to the nature of life and the will of God. The activity of this syntax and practice and the activity of containment and institutionalization memorialized the exclusion of lepers; the memorialized connection of this exclusion to the judgmental and salvific nature of Reality as well as an anxiety before what appeared unordered and a sense of disease connected with exclusion. Containment of the mad also bore a trace of the chaos that their exile was intended to eradicate, and madness in its strange and ostracized differences became increasingly an object of fascination and preoccupation on the part of "normal" people. In their fascination people remained in touch with the "power" from which containment of the mad was supposed to free them. The silence of the chaotic mad was also carried by the institutionalized flow of official knowledge and rhetoric that placed and defined them.

This complex figuration of epiphany, confinement, exclusion, correction, and silencing was memorialized in the formation of mental institutions and psychiatric/psychological knowledge. Or, in other terms, the division between mad and rational people carried, *as division,* a body of many, multiply dimensional memories. These memories, in their elusive quality, are expressed through the functions of institutions. These memories are found not only as divisions by which the mad and the normal are connected, but also as occurrences of exclusion by which the excluded, *as excluded,* continues to occur within the body that forced the exclusion, as confinements by which the confined continued to circulate in the society, as correction by which the errancy is preserved, and as silence by which "something" inarticulate is given a power of indirect communication. These memories have a double quality. On the one hand they constitute retentions of what is lost by exclusion; and on the other, these very processes of division, exclusion, confinement, and silencing carry past events and practices and give them presence in other events and practices. These memories of past occurrences are also presented in such popular associations as those of madness, murder, immorality, and secret folly. They are presented in the establishment of "hospitals" for the mad; the freeing of the mad from prisons and houses for the poor for the purpose of correction in another kind of institution; the transformation of madness into the medical category of insanity; a broadly disseminated sense of the dark mysteriousness of madness; and the modern formation of psychiatry within a framework of diagnosis, cure, and institutionalization.

Foucault shows that in these occurrences and associations the silence of the mad is sheltered and intensified and that the modern asylum is a monument to this silence. In its context of modernity, madness appears as "this ambiguity of chaos and apocalypse."[21] In the appearances of madness, the ordered and rational grounds for life dissolve into an anarchy of emotions, sounds, and images; and madness also marks the end of rational time, the edge of ordered sequence, meaning, and truth. It is a deviant wildness that is kept in a "safe" house of futile containment.

The silence of the mad is measured and figured out only by the asylum. It is also measured and figured by expressions of madness that emerged out of the division of reason and unreason. In the lineage of unreason, Foucault mentions Goya, Nietzsche, Sade, van Gogh, Hölderlin, and Artaud. Their art "*opens* a void, a moment of silence, a question without answer, *provokes* a breach without reconciliation where the world is forced to question itself."[22] In their works these artists and writers indicate a departure from the reign of reason and rational order in the world and allow opening to "what" is without reason. The opening and provocation are not explicit in the work's subject matter or coherence but come to expression as the artwork reaches limits of order, expression, sense, and meaning; incorporates the limits in its presentation; and becomes itself an expression of the ambiguity of chaos without order. It carries one to the edge of expressibility, an edge where "something" without art or device or word gives darkness to the work's shining presence. In such works, lethic oblivion qualifies everything else that is remembered and presented. Foucault finds in this qualification a refiguration of madness, not one that has learned to speak sanely but one that shows madness in the fading of reason, a fading with fragmented shape and form—something like memory of no memory at all, like vague lights blinking in the darkness and intensifying the darkness as they fade out without promise of return.

The one who traces lineages and their transformations, a person we can call an archeologist or genealogist, may also be a participant in the artistic marking of madness's silence and Reason's limits in this sense: he, in this case, finds language and concepts by which to describe and present transformations and figurations in the seventeenth and eighteenth centuries in their own patterns of disclosure and formation. Inclusion of their silence recasts representation. One finds that the transmissions of influence, procedures, meanings, and figurations of recognition do not follow the principles and rules that govern traditional western logics or experiences of reason and meaning. The emergence of "unreason", for example, in the context of seventeenth-century culture showed no rational grounding or fundamental meaning. It showed the different accidental connections in a discourse in which "Reason" was dominant, and a complete lineage of religious practice, disease, and exclusion. Those aspects can fit into a reasonable manner of explanation. But Foucault's account also shows an emptiness—an absence of meaning—that would not fit into an explanatory scheme. There are shifts that are made by a world without images, he says of the experience of madness. This experience "remains silent in the composure of the knowledge which forgets it."[23] He holds in tension, without resolving their ambivalence, chaos and apocalypse in the context of Reason and unreason. Unreason at this time reveals itself aporetically as the limit of Reason—aporetically because in the discourse of its occurrence only Reason can reveal and delimit itself. As Foucault phrases the thought in *The Order of Things,* the space of seventeenth- and eighteenth-century rationality was constituted by the totality of Reason representing itself; and madness, we find in *Madness and Civilization,* occurs in a complete lack of the very representational space that would reveal it and confine it. The paradox of madness's disclosure is found in its lack of representational order and its silence in the context of its appearance as apocalyptic, like a flash of blinding light that shows a density of hidden darkness *in* Reason and Reason's manifestations. And Foucault provides a discourse in which Reason's authority is multiply broken by the ambivalence and ambiguity that compose without resistance his grammatical writing *and* by silence at a brink of experience and expressibility to which his writing and expression repeatedly brings us.

For Foucault the disclosure of madness in the context of Reason gave rise to an identifiable lineage that includes Nietzsche, Hölderlin, Goya, Sade, van Gogh, and Artaud. "Emptiness as such" or "chaos in itself" are not shown. Rather, his work shows emptiness with determinant experiences, no meaning *with* meanings, absence of order *with* order, silence *with* orders of articulation. In this dimension of the lineage that Foucault describes, an inclination falls away to turn either meaning or emptiness into entities that organize or underlie or infinitely transcend the world. And yet such nondetermination composes a memory in its conceptual event in the sense that "it" happens like a recall of making reasonable, meaningful, or sensible, a dimension like utter forgetfulness that happens without lucidity or explanation in the midst of illuminating knowledge, recognition, and truth. In both seventeenth-century madness and in Foucault's account of it nothing comes to nonpresence with present and determined occurrences.

The "art" of this kind of presentation, in contrast to the archaic bard's songs and to the Socratic art of *elenchoes* and recollection, is found as study brings one to the edge of expressibility and meaning, to a boundary that links presentation to nothing presentable, to the passage of order into no order. If the style of presentation in its indirectness and nuance shows the boundaries of showing as well as of indication, connection, and causation, something like the experience of eighteenth-century madness is recalled in the midst of the work's sane rationality; and we can add Foucault's name to the list of those in the lineage stemming from madness's silence in the *formation of modern insanity*. This is a lineage in which the silence of madness in an age of Reason and the silence of insanity in an age of medical authority are given space for their own eruptions at the borders of crafted, disciplined presentations. These are works which not only allow space, as it were, for attentiveness to this silence. They are also works in which connections, communications, and orders, far from being governed by a sense of Reason, are found in the lineage of the eighteenth century's unreason, a lineage in which "unorder" and "no presence" are remembered by the contextual events of absence, emptiness, or unreason.

Transitions and transformations of established orders compose "regions" of unorder's epiphanies. I have said that in the manifestation of unorder, involuntary memory of no presence also happens, that the silence of madness, as Foucault describes it, occasions memory of limits to images, order and meaning, as well as memory of divisions which contribute to the formation of the power or presence of some institutions. These institutions are the present carriers of shifts and differentiations that the genealogist brings to interruptive, indirect expression. He gives another expression to an ephemeral, nonobjective dimension in the institutions' occurrences—a dimension without images. The art of expression is found, for example, in disclosures of uncapturable "silence" in the midst of what appears to be its interpretive master and articulate retainer. The gaps of exposure can be found in transformations or mutations in which one forceful figuration translates into another forceful figuration, the second of which is silently determined in part by loss of the first figuration. This kind of translation seems to "hold" the exclusion of what it was to carry, the events of differentiation that accompanied its arising limits and identity. Such translation appears to carry not only many of the determining factors *in that out of which* it changed but also the contingency of the happening that gave it to be limited and mutated.

Nietzsche, for example, shows that mercy overcomes the cruelty out of which it arises and which is formative of the Western experiences of justice. This overturning happens because of the vital temporality that is part of the composure of justice. The life-force of justice leads by means of its affirmation beyond the life-endangering forms that transmit it. Cruelty expresses a fundamental and unconscious fear of the nonhuman way in which life-force happens, an effort to contain and to control life, and a body of hostile and resentful affections consequent to the futile and unsafe project. Individuals in this fundamental and negative attitude toward the force of life easily enjoy causing pain and justifying cruelty by appeal to principles and "higher" values. But Nietzsche shows as he traces cruelty in the form of some kinds of justice that mercy arises through a transformation of cruel justice as an individual becomes strong enough to affirm others in spite of the "wrongs" committed by them.[24] He also found in the "law of self-overcoming" a movement in Western culture that gave over the values and stabilities of Western morality to change from within because of their own conflicted vitality.[25] This "law" is like a silent, intrinsic inclination toward change and differentiation in practices of self-sacrifice, an inclination toward change and differentiation *by means of* self-sacrifice, an inclination by which western formations move in their internal differences and oppositions toward their own overcoming. They give themselves up, as it were, and transform themselves by the power of their own force of life, which has been formed by contradictions and, in Nietzsche's lineage, by the value of sacrificing oneself for "something higher." But Nietzsche's transitions seem to be full of life-force, not of emptiness, and even though the idea of life-force is itself subject to self-overcoming on Nietzsche's terms, the idea nonetheless posits a continuing presence that provides instigation toward the most radical transformations. These transformations arise from the power of life that in Nietzsche's thought eludes the finality of any identity and "space" absent force, life, and will.

Foucault, on the other hand, finds no life-force that functions as a vital connective tissue joining transitory elements. Even the disordering presence of will to power is lacking in his accounts of transformations.[26] In his study of orders of knowing in *Orders of Things*—orders by which things are gathered and recognized—Foucault emphasizes the mutable structures of established orders of knowledge.[27] Each of the orders he describes is characterized by a "network of analogies" which links different disciplines and provides an unconscious continuity among them. We can see a network of analogies or an "episteme" as a nonvoluntary and nonconscious field of continuity in which, for example, knowledge of language, knowledge of life, and knowledge of numbers operate by the same ordering rules and principles. This continuity is provided by the rules and principles and not by anything that transcends them or is in excess to them. But *this* knowledge on Foucault's part is also informed by the recognition that the exclusive ordering power of the rules and principles that are found in the orders of knowledge shows at once "a space of knowledge," chora-like, that imposes no order on the orders that occur "in it." It is like "emptiness" that has no content to offer. And this knowledge of "the" space of knowledge is itself metaphorical and makes no claim to describe something literally or with calculable exactness. In its metaphorical quality, the descriptive knowledge knows that it reposes with nothing that can be directly described. "It" is like mere difference or simple indetermination, as distinct from something that is active and present and governed by laws. In this lethic space there is nothing to speak of and nothing to say, but "it" marks the limit of determination and order by a boundary of anomic absence. Or, from another perspective, one could say that determined, specific orders stand out, offering their gathering principles without further justification, stark in their singularities, forceful by means of recognitions; and yet, they occur in the muteness of a "dimension" that borders them, making them available for transformation and eradication—strange witnesses to unordered "space" in their established organizations. This metaphor of space means that the orders of knowledge by which we recognize things in their regularities and continuities are governed by describable and finite processes. Foucault's archeological/genealogical work includes a regular recall of the mutable limits of regularities. But this recall, although stateable in declarative sentences, is carried primarily in a manner of knowing that originates in the appearance (*with* determinant appearances) of what I have inadequately named emptiness, nondetermination, or unreason. Foucault's knowing begins with the "madness" that appeared in recognitions and "corrections" in seventeenth- and eighteenth-century rationality. Foucault's way of knowing and recognizing orders of knowing composes an enacted memory of "madness" and its institutional lineage (including disciplined language and established customs). One can say much about this memory and its beginning, but declaration means little in comparison to knowledge that takes its shape in encounters with ends and deaths of orders, with delimiting "space" that seems to deviate completely from orders and yet to allow their distribution through time. In this familiarity and indirection, Foucault's work constitutes an encounter with no order amidst the orders of things.

Transformations of fundamental ordering principles—and the continuity of transformations—take place as problems arise for a given order that the order cannot address adequately on its own terms. Orders change by virtue of problems that they create for themselves. For example, the episteme of Similitude that preceded the dominance of representation for knowledge could not account for the differences among identities as they were recognized within the episteme, or the processes of recognizing, or historical transformations; and as it confronted this cluster of problems, this complex structure of recognitions mutated into an episteme that was focused by the rules of presentation. That is quite a different "network of analogies" in comparison with the network that constituted Similitude and the differences that developed under the power of Similitude by such means as discoveries in linguistics concerning the functions of signifiers, the divisions within disciplines, a growing attention to deception and imagination, discovery of new methods of measurement, and the growth of analysis and discrimination as means for connecting differences and similarities.[28] Foucault finds that basic transformations of orders and ordering principles happened as ways of knowing changed, that these changes were not the consequences of anything like subjectivity. Rather, a different kind of subjectivity formed, slowly, as ways of knowing changed. He thus studies lineages of transformation, not volitional subjects, in order to understand the emergence of a time when knowledge revolved around the axis of subjectivity and representational activity.

Before I turn to an account of the detail of Foucault's description of transformations, I would like to note that we have turned from the rich experience of memory as founded in eternal truth—and from the poets who gave life meaning through songs and sight that originated in the Truth—to memories that are embodied in institutions and that carry with themselves traces of a lack of determination (emptiness) that accompanies their multiple determinations; and we have turned from the artists of truth to those who give articulation to these institutional memories. Cultural establishments transmit past events into present circumstances in the accompaniment of losses of determinations and events. These establishments in their transmissional aspect are themselves memorial events that present in highly mutated ways other times and beginnings that happened in their formation. Beginnings are measured in part by originary, institutional impotence as well as by trajectories of force and by sedimentations that are active in producing contexts and strange appendages for contemporary practice. Institutions (cultural establishments) carry fragmented memories—pieces, as it were, of other events; and they happened in a loss of the past that they also present in their contemporary formations.

Perhaps there is a balm that accompanies the prosaic descriptions of institutions' transmissional and memorial aspects, a balm that comes with recognitions, increased options, and above all, with language and thought that present things in the "element" that I have metaphorized as nondetermination or as emptiness: language and thought that embody recall of these lethic divisions of memory, its kinship with unorder and nondetermination, its undisturbed quiet before the losses and boundaries that permeate things as they come to presence. In that language and thought memory's retention appears with unrecoverable losses whose traces are found in the slippage of past events into something else that we can call presence, or in trajectories that we can control as little as we can grasp them in their flowing, undertowing, or elevating immediacy. We are bathed in memories that we do not choose or create as we live our day-to-day lives. And occasionally we can explicitly present them, like waking dreams, as we weave our futures and give ourselves occasion to add to or reduce, if only slightly, their force and form.

Notes

1. Indirect communication happens in so many ways! As a mood or disposition that "shades" what we say directly and gives it rhythm, expression, tone, inflection, and gesture; as posture or movement; as context; as glance or blink or a small wrinkle by one's eyes; as rate of breathing, relaxation of a muscle group, by even the subjunctive mood in our language. But indirection happens also *as* one attends to something—to hope or fear or something loved. The attention and the attended can affect how one relates to something else or speaks of it or of something else. Some people develop the skill of giving "something" that is not directly expressed intensity and appearance through something else that is said or painted

or sung or written. The thing sung or said is not simply a sign of this other. It belongs to the other in the communication, accords with the other's expression as the other appears in its own, quite distinct expression. The communication that I want to notice in this essay arises from attention to nondetermination or emptiness, a kind of attention that is like overhearing something without objectivity, something both elusive and palpable, like something fading at the edge of a glance or on the brink of meaning, or like the moment I have described elsewhere, when a sound ceases. I remember seeing a border of snow and no snow where heavy snowing stopped. . . .

2. Jean Pierre Vernant, "The Mythical Aspects of Memory and Time," *Myth and Thought in the Greeks* (London and Boston: Routledge and Kegan Paul, 1983), p. 78.

3. Ibid., p. 79.

4. Ibid.

5. Ibid., p. 80.

6. Ibid. The poet is considered to be blind to "day-things" and perceptive of what lies beyond the day's light.

7. In the oracle of Lebadeia, for example, "where a descent into Hades was enacted in the cavern of Trophomius we find Lethe, forgetfulness associated with Mnemosyne, forming with her a pair of complementary religious powers. Before venturing into the mouth of hell, the questor, who has already undergone rites of purification, was taken to two springs named respectively Lethe and Mnemosyne. He drank from the first and immediately forgot everything to do with his human life and, like a dead man, he entered into the realm of Night. The water of the second spring was to enable him to remember all that he has seen and heard in the other world. When he returned he was no longer restricted to the knowledge of the present moment: contact with the beyond had revealed both past and future to him." Through this rite one transcends the opposition of death and life, "and he can move freely from one world to the other." "Memory appears as a source of immortality." Ibid.

8. These remarks are based primarily on ibid., pp. 82ff.

9. Ibid., p. 83.

10. These observations refer to texts by Empedocles. In reference to the Pythagorean discipline of remembering, Vernant says, "the obligation laid on the members of the (Pythagorean) fraternity to recall all of the events of the day gone by, each evening, had more than the moral value of an exercise in soul-searching. The effort involved in remembering, if undertaken following the example of the sect's founder so as to encompass the story of the soul throughout ten or even twenty different lives, would make it impossible for us to learn who we are and to know our own psyche—that daemon which had become incarnate in us" (ibid.).

11. Ibid.

12. "Once it has atoned for everything, the soul, being centered in its original purity, can at last escape from the cycle of births, leaving generation and death behind it, and can gain access to the form of unchanging and permanent existence which is the prerogative of the gods." "Memory is exalted because it is the power that makes it possible for men to escape time and return to the divine state." Ibid., p. 88.

13. Ibid., p. 89. Consider in this context the following statement by Aristotle in *Physics* 221 a–b: ". . . for things to exist in time they must be embraced by time just as with other cases of being "in" something; for instance, things that are in place are embraced by place. And it will follow that they are in some respect affected by

time; just as we are wont to say that time crumbles things and that everything grows old under the power of time and is forgotten through the lapse of time. But we do not say that we have learnt, and that anything is made new or beautiful by mere lapses of time; for we regard time itself as destroying rather than producing, for what is counted in time is movement, and movement dislodges whatever it affects from its present state. From all this it is clear that things which exist eternally, as such, are not in time; for they are not embraced by time, nor is their direction measured by time." This thought that time destroys and does not produce anything new or beautiful is close to the mythological "idea" that by Mnemosyne's eternal power of transmission humans come to what time cannot give: new birth into eternal truth and the beauty of a timelessly pure soul in truth's light.

14. The Greek is *hā dè mnéme toû genoménon* and is translated by W. S. Hett as "memory is of the past." "On memory and recollection," 449b, *Aristotle*, Loeb Classical Library, vol. 8, pp. 288ff. Further citations will be from this volume.

15. See John Chown, *A History of Money: From AD 800* (London and New York: Routledge, 1994), chap. 24; and John Kenneth Galbraith *Money, Whence It Came, Where It Went* (Boston: Houghton Mifflin, 1975), chap. 6.

16. The trust, however, was supported by other means of persuasion. A Resolution passed on January 11, 1776 stated: "Any person who shall hereafter be so lost to all virtue and regard for his country as to refuse the Bills or obstruct and discourage their currency shall be deemed published and treated as an enemy of the country and precluded from all trade and intercourse with its inhabitants." For discussions of opinions by those who condemn the fiscal policies of the revolutionary government see ibid.

17. Chown, *History of Money*, p. 219. Quoted from an act of Congress in 1775.

18. Quoted in Galbraith, *Money*, p. 59.

19. Michel Foucault, *Madness and Civilization: A History of Insanity in the Age of Reason*, trans. Richard Howard (New York: Vintage Books, 1973 [1965]), p. 6.

20. Foucault uses "structures" in referring to the "remainder" of abandonment in combination with theological beliefs and religious experiences that carries a transition from lepers to the mad. This is a word that he soon gave up and one that I shall also drop with the notation that I am placing abandonment and exclusion outside of the language of structures at the same time that I recognize that structures "carry" such intangibles. The past occurrences of abandonment and exclusion in the formation of the asylum, like other nonvoluntary memories, are not identical with the bearing structures and institutions: not separate from them in their lineage but also not identical with them.

21. Ibid, p. 281.

22. Ibid., p. 288, my emphasis.

23. Ibid., xii.

24. *On the Genealogy of Morals* (New York: Vintage Books, 1967), Walter Kaufman, second essay, sections 8–11.

25. Ibid., third essay, sections 27–28.

26. In my opinion, Nietzsche's idea of will to power should be read as strategic and temporary, as an idea whose functions are to show the temporal instability of all "stabilization" and to show human communality in "something" that lacks identity. In that reading, will to power lacks the possibility of providing unifying meaning and, in combination "the law of self overcoming," moves to unsettle its own grounding aspect. Foucault's account of transition and transformation is appropriate to this reading and its turn from the thought of grounding. But one can show

that Nietzsche *also* organizes his thought in the force of the idea of will to power and thereby goes considerably beyond its merely strategic employment as he makes claims for the existence of will to power.

27. The remainder of this paragraph is a gloss on his "Foreword to the English Edition" (Vintage Books, 1970), pp. ix–xxiv.

28. Ibid., chap. 3, pp. iiff.

Charles E. Scott: Selected Bibliography

Books

The Time of Memory. Albany: State University of New York Press, 1999.

On the Advantages and Disadvantages of Ethics and Politics. Bloomington: Indiana University Press, 1996.

The Question of Ethics: Nietzsche, Foucault, Heidegger. Bloomington: Indiana University Press, 1990.

The Language of Difference. Atlantic Highlands, N.Y.: Humanities Press, 1987.

Edited, *Dreaming: An Encounter with Medard Boss.* Atlanta: Scholars Press, 1983.

Boundaries in Mind: A Study of Immediate Awareness Based in Psychotherapy. New York: Crossroads, and Atlanta: Scholars Press, 1982.

Chapters in Edited Volumes and Journal Articles

"Nietzsche: Feeling, Transmission, *Phusis.*" *New Nietzsche Studies* 4 (1999).

"The Work of the History of Philosophy." *Research in Phenomenology* 29 (1999).

"Appearances." *Graduate Faculty Philosophy Journal* 20.2–21.1 (1998).

"*Zuspiel* and *Entscheidung:* A Reading of sections 81–82 in *Die Beiträge zur Philosophie.*" *Philosophy Today* 41, supplement (1997).

"A People's Witness beyond Politics." In *Ethics as First Philosophy,* ed. Adriaan Peperzak. New York: Routledge, 1995.

"The Pleasure of Therapy." In *Speculations after Freud: Psychoanalysis, Philosophy, and Culture,* ed. Michael Munchow and Sonu Shamdasani. New York: Routledge, 1994.

"Thinking Non-Interpretively: Heidegger on Technology and Heraclitus." *Epoché. A Journal for the History of Philosophy* (1993).

"Foucault, Ethics, and the Fragmented Subject." *Research in Phenomenology* 22 (1992).

"The Pleasure of Therapy." *ellipsis* 2 (1992).

"The Question of Ethics in Foucault's Thought." *Journal of the British Society for Phenomenology* (1992).

"Responsibility and Danger." In *Ethics and Responsibility in the Phenomenological Tradition.* Duquesne: Simon Silverman Phenomenology Center, Duquesne University, 1992.

"Authenticity/Nonbelonging." In *Reading Heidegger,* ed. John Sallis. Bloomington: Indiana University Press, 1991.

"Genealogy and Difference." *Research in Phenomenology* 20 (1990).

"Foucault and the Question of Psychotherapeutic Liberation." *Journal for Existential Psychology and Psychiatry* 1 (1990).

"The Middle Voice of Metaphysics." *Review of Metaphysics* 42 (June 1989).

"Heidegger and the Question of Ethics." *Research in Phenomenology* 18 (1988).

"The Destruction of *Being and Time* in *Being and Time*." *Man and World* 21 (1988).

"The Middle Voice in *Being and Time*." In *The Collegium Phaenomenologicum: The First Ten Years*, ed. John Sallis, Giuseppina Moneta, and Jacques Taminiaux. Dordrecht: Kluwer Academic Publishers, 1988.

"On the Unity of Heidegger's Thought." *Research in Phenomenology* 17 (1987).

"Heidegger, Madness, and Well-Being." In *Thinking about Being*, ed. Robert W. Shahan and J. N. Mohanty. Norman: University of Oklahoma Press, 1984.

"Foucault's Practice of Thinking." *Research in Phenomenology* 14 (1984).

"Speech and the Unspeakable in the Place of the Unconscious." *Human Studies: A Journal for Philosophy and the Human Sciences* (1984).

"Psychotherapy: Being One and Being Many." *Journal for Existential Psychiatry and Psychology* 16 (1979).

"Archetypes and Consciousness." *Idealistic Studies* (1977).

"Consciousness and the Conditions of Consciousness." *Review of Metaphysics* (1972).

9

Keeping the Past in Mind

EDWARD S. CASEY

Edward S. Casey has sought to provide intensive and extensive descriptions of phenomena that, though neglected or repressed in mainstream philosophy, are nonetheless of quite basic importance in human experience. Four topics are central to his work: imagining, remembering, place, and the distinctive character of the glance in perception. Imagining and remembering have too often been treated in philosophy as marginal with respect to perception, and place has most often been regarded as a mere subdivision of space. The glance is seen as fickle and trivial in contrast with the seriousness of the gaze and other modes of visual scrutiny. Casey's effort has been to show that what is taken to be marginal is in fact indispensable to the very phenomena being investigated.

Casey's approach to all four topics has been phenomenological. In his earlier works, this was more explicitly so. *Imagining* offers both an intentional and eidetic analysis of the phenomenon, uncovering various distinct art forms and kinds of content as well as eidetic features such as "pure possibility" and "indeterminacy." *Remembering* begins with the same sort of formal analysis, but Casey expands his descriptive methodology in order to capture the richly ramified character of human memory. He explores certain intermediary kinds of remembering such as reminiscing and recognizing as well as such comprehensive sorts of memory as body memory, place memory, and commemoration. These latter entailed the broadening of his descriptive base from an account of individual acts of remembering to collective and communal aspects. The opening of the horizon of description to include history and culture is evident in all Casey's subsequent work. He has also sought to avoid Eurocentrism in his work by referring to other cultures and has especially pursued the experience of place as it figures into these other cultures.

If there is a single general trajectory that would describe the development of Casey's work, it is that from a preoccupation with acts of mind—from their nuanced and detailed descriptions—to a concern with the encompassing universal conditions that make such mental acts as imagining and remembering possible in the first place. In his work, two primary such conditions are identified and traced—body and place. Body is the pivot of concrete memory just as it is the natural subject of the place-world. Just as memory led Casey to discuss place, so too the animating role of the lived body links these central topics of his work. It is not surprising, then, that descriptions of the lived body are central to *Remembering* and *Getting Back into Place. The Fate of Place* is something of a departure from his earlier work in that it is primarily an essay in intellectual history. Yet another departure is anticipated in his forthcoming work, *Representing Landscape,* a book that will trace out the role of place in landscape painting and maps and that will discover the glance which sweeps over the entire landscape, taking them in comprehensively yet instantaneously.

This essay was a true turning point in Casey's work. It marked the moment in which he realized that a supposedly mental act such as remembering could not be confined to the closed domain of mind, a theater of representations. Already in this essay it was clear that just as remembering must be expanded to make room for place, so place itself must be distinguished from space when this latter is understood as homogeneous, infinite, and isometric. Casey shows that place is not a mere medium. It is historical, and it is composed of a series of surfaces at which we glance intermittently yet fatefully.

❖

It was lost to sight but kept in memory.

—*Augustine,* Confessions

Memory, therefore, is certainly not the mental process which, at first sight, one would imagine. . . .

—*Wittgenstein,* Philosophical Grammar

"Keeping the past in mind": where *else* is it going to be kept? We could perhaps try to keep it in the past itself; but then we'd have the past containing itself, swallowing its own tail. An event would die out the moment it was born: it would have no continuing potential halo—fulfilled or unfulfilled—nor would it be rememberable. Yet an event shorn of all these attributes would no longer be an event at all. To keep a past event entirely past, with no possible repercussion in the present, would be to deprive it of its very eventfulness. "Remembrance is now," says George Steiner in *After Babel;* but this is so only because the past itself is now: is now being re-enacted, re-lived.

I

What is bound to mislead us is the dichotomist assumption that keeping in mind must be either an entirely active or an utterly passive affair. This assumption has plagued theories of memory as of other mental activities. On the activist model, keeping in mind would be a creating or recreating in mind of what is either a mere mirage to begin with or a set of stultified sensations. Much as God in the seventeenth century was sometimes thought to operate by continual creation, so the mind was given the same lofty powers in the Romantic thought that represented a reaction to much of what the seventeenth century stood for. But the activist model is by no means limited to the Romantic idealists or *Naturphilosophen*. It reappears in more than one phase of phenomenology, and it informs the sober theorizing of Bartlett and Piaget on the nature of remembering.[1] On the passivist model, on the other hand, the mind is mute and unconfigurating. It takes in but does not give back other than what it takes in. It is a recording mechanism only. Something like this view is at work in empiricist theories of memory, considered as restricted to the contents of Human "impressions" and arranged according to their order and position in time; it continues in Kant's notion of "reproductive imagination" as operating by association alone; and it is found flourishing today in psychological accounts of what is revealingly called "human associative memory."[2]

It is all too evident, I think, that where the activist model gives too little credit to the incomings of experience, the passivist model gives too much. To begin with, there is too much *there* in experience, too much density in it, to claim that we are continually creating or constructing it.[3] And yet it is equally mistaken to believe that it is *all* there, graven in pre-established tablets of truth. Mere "registration," as Sokolowski has recently shown, is only one epistemic stage among others. It is not an adequate analogue for such diverse activities as evocation or reporting.[4] And if it is not all there to begin with, then we have much to do with what we end with, including what we remember of what was there.

II

The extremes of activism and passivism rejoin curiously in their exaggerated monisms, leading us to look elsewhere for a suitable model of keeping the past in mind. Let us begin by asking ourselves what *keeping in mind* amounts to and how it bears on remembering the past. "Keeping" is, to begin with, more than retaining—where "retaining" may mean such diverse things as the mere retention of facts and formulas, the fringe-like retentions that cling to each successive now-point in Husserl's version of James's idea of primary memory, or that "retaining-in-grasp" in Husserl's later conception of a memorial capacity that lies between primary and secondary memory and is considered essential to the method of free variation in imagination. In fact, keeping in mind is more even than secondary memory, "recollection" in the ordinary sense of a depictive representation of past events. The tendency to reduce keeping in mind to recollection is a powerful one, despite early warnings from Bergson (who found "habit memory" an at least equally significant form of keeping) and more recent ones from Heidegger, who inveighs against confining memory to the recovery of the past in the form of "remembrance" *(Wiedergedächtnis)*.[5] The "wieder" of *Wiedergedächtnis* or *Wiedererinnerung* (both of which signify secondary memory) is especially telling, as is the semantically equivalent "re-" of "recollection." Secondary memory is secondary precisely because it is somehow a re-enactment of the past, its return in representational guise. No wonder so many theories of recollection have emphasized its reproductive aspect—without paying sufficient attention to the fact that reproduction normally includes a simulacrum of the scene recaptured. But the past can be recaptured in non-isomorphic modes of representation, just as it can be kept in mind in a more fundamental way than that of explicit recollection or secondary memory.

Memor, the root of *memoria* or memory, means "mindful." Being mindful of something differs from retaining it in any of the senses just discussed as well as from recollecting it or even being reminded of it.[6] Being-mindful-of is being full *of mind* about something: being or becoming *in mind* of it, heeding it in a way that exceeds the simple apprehension that lies at the core of retention, recollection, and being-reminded. It exceeds all of these precisely by virtue of keeping something in mind. What then is such keeping? Its main action is one of *remaining* or *staying with* what we come to be mindful of. Instead of just grasping, or noting, or pigeonholing, or stockpiling, we remain with what we have become mindful of. Remaining-with is a form of abiding by, and it is compatible with *not* representing the minded item or thinking of it in any express form. It is staying alongside the item, letting it linger longer than if one were to classify it, shunt it into a convenient position in secondary memory, or act upon it in some immediately effective way. Such staying has staying power; it stays on beside what is minded.

If remaining or staying with is the essential action of keeping in mind, conservation or preservation is the essential result: hence the "keep," "the innermost and strongest structure . . . of a medieval castle, serving as a last defense" (OED) as well as the "keepsake," which I give to you so that you will keep me in mind. But conserving often involves concealing, *keeping hidden,* keeping out of the daylight of open perception by remaining within the dank cellars of the mind's keep. Far from this being a cause for regret —something to be overcome with an efficient mnemotechnique—it tells us something important about remembering, namely, that it is as much a withholding of the past as a holding of it in mind. We preserve the past as truly in *not* exhibiting it to ourselves or others in so many words or images as in re-presenting it in these ways. Consider only the way the body keeps the past in a veiled and yet entirely efficacious form in its continuing ability to perform certain skilled actions: I may not remember just how, or even when, I first learned the breaststroke, but I can keep on doing it success-fully—remembering how to do it—without any representational activity on my part whatsoever. In such a case, the non-exhibition of a particular past is clearly an advantage, since its sudden recollection might impede my spontaneous bodily movements. Many instances of habitual or skilled re-membering how to do (or say, or think) things are exemplary of a keeping that, withholding its own historical origin, nevertheless re-enacts it in our conduct in the present.

When we play the game of memory we play it for *keeps*. Remember-ing consists in a keeping action that combines elements of remaining and preserving, holding and withholding—all held within the keepful reach of mind. Even the breaststroke is kept in mind as it is displayed bodily; for "mind" is itself a vast keep that guards the past in more forms of re-appear-ance than the apprehension-based notions of retention, recollection, or re-minding can sustain.

III

Here we must ask: how do things stand now with regard to the vexing issue of whether remembering is an active or passive affair?

Let us go back to the language of "keep" for a moment. It is a striking fact that both as a noun and as a verb this word has both active and passive meanings. As a noun, "keep" can mean either "the act of keeping or main-taining" or "the fact of being kept." As a verb, it means either "take in, re-ceive, contain, hold" (and more specifically, to "take in with the eyes, ears, or mind") or to "guard, defend, protect, preserve, save." These bivalent meanings, differing as they do, are not at all incompatible. Indeed, precisely by means of the component actions of keeping traced out just above, they are complementary to each other and (more crucially) *simultaneously realiz-able*. Thus "the act of keeping," by virtue of its remaining with what is kept, helps to constitute "the fact of being kept." And the taking in or holding is a guarding or saving thanks to the element of withholding that conceals the keeping and thus the kept itself.

Consider how this occurs in a concrete case of remembering: I remember my attending a philosophy conference in New York at the New School for Social Research and having to change lecture halls at the last moment to accommodate Hannah Arendt's talk, for which a large crowd had showed up. Since I had helped to plan the conference, I felt responsible for things going smoothly. After the new hall had been arranged, I walked over with Arendt, who had been quite upset over the change. But she cooled down in the course of the walk and went on to deliver a marvelous lecture on the Socratic conception of virtue. As with so many memories, this is very sche-matic in character: I remember little more of the occasion than I have here reported. Yet I would certainly want to say that I have kept it in mind all these years, and in precisely the bivalent senses just discussed. The mem-ory has been actively maintained by being revived from time to time (e.g., whenever I think of Hannah Arendt for whatever reason), and by this very revival it has attained a state of "being kept" in mind throughout. At the same time, it was received, taken in, at a most impressionable point (both in my life and during the meeting itself) and preserved or saved thanks to this very receptive sensitivity.

What we can observe in any such example is a delicate dialectic of the active and the passive, the receptive and the spontaneous. There is, at the very least, a constant going back and forth between these dimensions. Heidegger was attuned to much the same thing when he wrote that "what keeps us in our essential nature holds us only so long, however, as we for our part keep holding on to what holds us."[7] "The hold is held"[8] in remembering, and this is accomplished by its keeping. The hold, what holds me, is constituted by the particulars of a memory (Arendt's ire, her piercing dark eyes, the mollifying walk) as they are assembled by the setting in which they inhere (here the New School meeting itself). These are givens of the past of which I can be no more than a more or less receptive witness; they bear down upon me and may even burden me if I become obsessed by them. But I bear up on them in turn by holding, keeping hold on the memory itself. I bear it in mind actively, keeping it on the agenda there. It is not that I simply store this experience and regain access to it as if it had been packaged or pickled on some psychical or neuroanatomical shelf. Having taken in the experience, being kept by *it* initially ("impressed," "struck," we say inadequately), *I* keep it subsequently by bringing it back to mind again, thereby restoring it. And *myself* as well: for not only Hannah Arendt but my-being-in-her-presence is kept on, re-collected (from the shards of the scene so imperfectly recalled in terms of detail). No matter: the experience has been kept in mind. It has been remembered, and in a way that is at once active and passive—so much so that we are no longer constrained to choose between these traditional alternatives.

IV

Now that we know something about how the past is kept in mind, its basic holding action, we must pursue a quite different line of thought by asking: Is the past kept within the mind alone? Can we confine it to this tenure, critical as it is—and important as it is to stress in the face of efforts to locate remembering elsewhere? Such efforts currently tend to seek the essence, or at least the formal structure, of memory, either in the functioning of the brain or in information-processing mechanisms. Neither is adequate to the task of providing a truly comprehensive account of remembering. Neurophysiologists are still bitterly divided over determining the minimal unit of memory—whether it be cellular, molecular, synaptic, or holographic—and cannot begin to explain its higher-order operations (except to say that these somehow involve the rhinencephalon, the mamillary bodies, and various parts of the cerebral cortex). In fact, the most significant work to emerge from this perspective concerns the *pathology* of memory as this is occasioned by the brain's malfunctioning; and, in this respect, the contribution of neuroanatomy to the understanding of human memory curiously rejoins the findings of psychoanalysis, also adept at telling us about the misfortunes of remembering but inept at explaining how memory functions in the normal case. As for information-processing models, they are elegant but only pseudo-explanatory. Their stage-wise approach to memory breaks it down into such plausible units as iconic, short-term, and long-term stores; but they fail to explain how coherent experiences of remembering emerge from the concatenation of these phases and must resort to such stop-gap notions as "encoding," "rehearsal," and "transfer" to fill in the gaps. Concerning these two dominant modes of construing memory, we can say that each possesses what the other lacks: brain physiology is persuasive as to flow and transmission of memories (given a view of the brain as a dynamic field of electrochemical forces) but disappointing as to ultimate units, while information-processing is lucid on the modular level but opaque when it comes to circulation and development.

It has been characteristic of phenomenologists to underline how much mind matters in a fundamental experience like remembering. This is imperative when confronting expressions of the "natural attitude" such as are found in neurophysiology and information-processing: for them, only matter matters in memory (whether the matter be that of the brain or bits of information mechanically conveyed). Husserl's 1905 lectures on inner time consciousness, which did much to inaugurate phenomenology as we now know it, can be read as an extended plea to consider remembering from an exclusively mental perspective. The "exclusion of objective time" with which the lectures begin is tantamount to a suspension of a naturalistic model of memory, and it is telling that this first use of the phenomenological reduction bears directly on remembering—rather than on, say, perceiving or imagining. For indeed the urgency surrounds memory, which is unusually tempting to grasp in naturalistic terms. The temptation is due to the fact that recollection rescues experiences from "death's dateless night," the oblivion to which every human experience is subject and against which mechanical and physiological models seem to promise hope of fixity, of stable storage of the past.

Against this against, phenomenology offers the counter-defensive of an understanding of memory in strictly physical terms. Thus Husserl denies that we recover the past in any pristine format, a format that continues to be a working assumption in trace and storage theories of memory: "I can re-live the present, but it (the present) can never be given again."[9] One thing Husserl does not provide, oddly enough, is an explicit intentional analysis of memory in terms of its various noetic and noematic phases. In work in progress I have tried to make up for this lacuna by discerning not just two main act-forms, including remembering-to (do X or Y), remembering-on-the-occasion-of, and several species of remembering-that and remembering-how. On the noematic side, I have found meaningful distinctions to be made between the mnemonic presentation, the specific content remembered, the world frame of remembered space and time, and an encircling "aura" (as I call the fading fringe of what we remember).

Yet an intentional approach to memory is still not sufficient to capture the full phenomenon of keeping the past in mind. We can no longer assume, in polemical opposition to naturalistic models, that memory is played out on the surface of the psyche—that mind qua "consciousness of X" is the only, or even the main, arena in which the past abides and is recovered. Where then are we to turn? We already have on hand one instance of extra-mental memory, habitual memory, wherein the past is sedimented into the *body,* becoming amassed there. Not only in the case of skilled actions of the breaststroke sort but in many other ways as well memory moves massively into the body, as we can see in the case of certain ritualistic actions, in dancing (which can be densely memorious without being highly skilled), and even in plain walking (where our body "knows the way" along a familiar route without requiring any recollection).

Habitual remembering of various sorts thus leads us out of mind. Into what? Into the WORLD, which is where the body takes us in any case. *And this is just where we must now take memory itself.* Remembering has been ensconced too long in the cells of the brain, the vaults of computerized memory-banks, and the machinations of mentation. Let us try putting it back in the lived world, where it has always been in any event, though barely recognized as such at the level of either description or theory.

Think of it: *the past kept in things,* those very "things themselves" that phenomenological method was designed to bring us to. It doesn't matter that it didn't always do so in its haste to reabsorb the world into the sphere of immanence known as "pure consciousness." For the things will bring themselves forward *to us,* and in fact are never *not* doing so in some fashion. They come to us bearing the past manifestly in monuments, relics, and mementoes, less obviously but just as forcefully in the dwellings we inhabit (buildings bear memories as much as our bodies do), and still less obviously but crucially in the collective memories we share with each other as co-experiences of certain situations. This is not even to mention such evident keepers of the past as archival documents, the casually and yet tellingly left-over marks of human and non-human activities, or, for that matter, the automobiles in which so much of our lives can come to be encapsulated.

V

I shall, however, restrict consideration here to one basic dimension of the world in which the past is kept. This is *place.* Despite its primordiality in human experience, place has been conspicuously neglected by philosophers. As for memory of place, this is hardly considered a topic worth pausing over, even though an ancient (and still quite effective) method of memorizing used an ordered grid of places as its main device: the "place method" about which Frances Yates has written so eloquently in *The Art of Memory.* Moreover, many memories are, if not expressly *about* places, richly rooted in them and inseparable from them. Even the idea of "keeping the past *in* mind" carries with it distinct echoes of location in place, albeit a non-worldly mental "place."

Notice, to begin with, that it is the body itself that establishes the felt directionality, the sense of level, and the experienced distance and depth that together constitute the main structural features of any given place in which we find ourselves and which we remember. But granting that it is by our mobile bodies that we become oriented in place, what is place itself? Aristotle's definition is the vessel, whose inner boundary coincides exactly with the outer boundary of what it contains (*Physics* 212a20–21). The operative notion here is that of the snug fit of the container, and Aristotle's own favorite analogy to place is the vessel, whose inner boundary coincides exactly with the outer boundary of what it contains: "just as the vessel is transportable place, so place is a non-portable vessel" (212a13–15).

Although Aristotle does not discuss memory of place as such, his basic conception of place is highly suggestive in this regard: a given place may derive its haunting power (a "haunt" is certainly a memorable place) from its "distinct potencies" as a container which exerts an "active influence" on us, whether by way of attraction or repulsion (cf. *Physics* 208b10–25). A place is not a setting of indifferent space, homogeneous and isotropic (I prefer to call this characteristically seventeenth-century view of space a "site"). Place works on us, and on our memories, by its very peculiarities and tropisms, its inhomogeneity.

If we begin pressing in this direction, we very soon reach the notion of *landscape,* which is where the Aristotelian idea of place with its irregular protuberances and non-metrically determinable inclosure to a simultaneously given collocation of places as these form part of our ongoing experience. What holds the collocation there is the landscape's horizon within which I am situated by means of a distinguishable here vs. there that forms the epicenter of the place where I am at. Moreover, within a given landscape, I am always moving from place to place. I am never *not* in place, not placed, even if I do not know precisely where I am in geographic space, the space of sites.[10]

Place as it effloresces in landscape is, therefore, one of the main ways in which my being-in-the-world manifests itself. If landscape can be said to constitute the world's felt texture, place is the congealing of this texture into discrete here/there arenas of possible action. In and through places, what Husserl called the "rays of the world" illuminate the landscape as their horizoned setting. And, through the movements of my "customary body," I come to find something abidingly familiar in the landscape I inhabit, now or formerly.[11] I feel attuned to its sympathetic space—or out of tune when I have been away too long or when painful memories disorient me.

I do not want to suggest that place only draws us outward into the landscape. There is a counter-movement as well. Not only do I inhabit a given landscape but it can be said to inhabit me. The "in" of "inhabitation" is bidirectional. And thanks to this doubly pervasive action, we can begin to grasp one basis of the power of place as remembered. For when I recall myself in a particular place set within a landscape, I am not only recollecting how it was *for me* but how it, the whole visible spectacle, came *to me* and took up dwelling *in me,* as henceforth part of me. It is no longer a matter, as in the experience of site, of parts merely alongside other parts. Place in its landscape being imparts itself to me, permeates me. And, as the "spirit of place," the *genius loci,* enters me, the visible becomes increasingly invisible. As Rilke has it in the ninth *Duino Elegy:*

Earth, isn't this what you want: an invisible re-arising in us? Is not
your dream to be one day invisible? Earth? Invisible?

Indeed, this can occur to such an extent that I may need geography (a map), a painting or photograph, just a fresh look at my surroundings, or (most pertinently) a remembering to make visible again what has become so thoroughly embedded within. By speaking of "embedded within" or "incorporation," I do not mean to suggest that the landscape has been internalized by a voracious *res cogitans.* The invisibility in question can just as well be described as my getting lost in the landscape: as my becoming one with it.[12]

If this is beginning to sound increasingly implausible (have we not merely moved from one kind of invisible, that inherent in mind, to another, that found in the empathic experience of landscape?), consider a concrete case, your own circumstance as you read these lines. You, too, are in a particular place, wherever this may be: and you are also situated within a landscape, whether this be part of unfettered nature, a university campus, or a set of city blocks. Unless you are deeply alienated from them, such a place and landscape offer a snug fit indeed—so much so that it would be difficult to establish the exact boundaries of either. As you inhabit your place so it inhabits you, while landscape provides an abiding setting for habitations of many kinds (cognitive and social as well as corporeal). If and when you come to remember this present experience, place and landscape will together hold and preserve its explicitly recalled content. This latter need not concern place *per se.* Indeed, place and landscape may be more effectively operative in memories when they are *not* the focus of what we remember but are merely adumbrated: their most forceful position is often a marginal one. Yet however indistinctly a given place-*cum*-landscape may have been experienced at first and will be subsequently remembered, it offers enclosure for whatever we do recall in detail. It is the circumambience of our ongoing remembering, that which gives place to the focally remembered. It is the scene for the proscenium brought back to mind.

VI

Back to *what?* Haven't we just been trying to transcend mind by resolutely moving out into place? Is any mediation possible between anything so diaphanous and lambent as mind and something so dense and obdurate as place? If mind is still to matter to us in an account of memory—if we are still to be able to speak of keeping the past genuinely *in mentis*—it becomes evident that mind itself must be reconceived. And it is precisely mind as an internal theater of representations that is at once too confining and incompatible with something as blatantly worldly as place. Before we can get out of mind, however, we must get mind out of itself, out of its own self-encapsulation, its epistemological primary narcissism. It is, in short, a matter of mind-expansion, and one key to it is to be found precisely in memory of place. If we are not to keep the past in a mind from which there are no meaningful exits, we must come to appreciate how it is kept in place.

How then is this possible? Primarily by place's "active power" of holding memories for us. The hold is held in place. This is not mysterious; it does not require invoking a World Soul. It is a given particular place that holds significant memories of ours, acting as a veritable gathering place for them. When I remember certain experiences that took place there, my mind and my past coalesce in, and around, such a place. Each is drawn out of the isolation, the undifferentiation, of forgetful non-remembering and drawn *into* the re-differentiation which remembering realizes.[13] Place furnishes a matrix for mergings of many kinds—most obviously of past with present, a process which could be called "presentment" and which itself has many forms. (Indeed, the remembered past does not merely terminate in the present of remembering but can be said to *begin* there, and to do so every time we recall it. Keeping in memory is a continual re-keeping: hence the many variant versions of the "same" past with which we regale ourselves in remembering and which lead us naturally to assimilate remembering to story-telling.)

Yet a remembered place can also present us not just with a fusion of past and present but with a merging of itself and the remembering mind that wanders freely into its midst—much as happens with the body in its moving insertion into the perceived world. Such a place, a genuine memory-place, gathers in to keep; it not only keeps my past and my memories alive by furnishing them with a "local habitation and a name," it moves my mind there for the duration of the remembrance: *out there,* outside of its own self-imposed strictures.

Notice that I am saying more than that mind is itself some kind of place —which it also is, whether we conceive it (with Aristotle) as "the place of forms" or merely as a passing place for imaginations, recollections, and thoughts. Being mindful, as I remarked earlier, is allowing the mind to fill, to distend, with memories. It is only when we take mind-as-place too literally, getting carried away with its own containing capacities, that the slippery slope to idealisms and representationalisms of many sorts starts in earnest. In fact, the mind is only a "quasi-locality." Merleau-Ponty, who employs this last term, also says that "the mind is neither here, nor here nor here [which it would have to be if it were a genuine place]. . . . And yet it is 'attached', 'bound', it is *not without bonds*."[14] The bonds are not just to body, itself a "place of passage" as Bergson called it, but to place.[15] And mind is attached, and continually re-attached, to place precisely through memory, which is the main means by which we keep the past in mind.

And *mind in place:* which is to say, out beyond its own internally generated indices and icons of a world outside. If the self is mainly what we remember it to be, and if its remembering is inexorably place-bound, bound to be implaced in *some* locale (for not to be so located is not only to be profoundly disoriented; it is not to be at all), then the mind will always already be out there in place, clinging to it as to its own self-definition.[16] Narcissus, after all, gazed at himself not in a mental image but in a reflection given back by a pool, that is, in a place that exceeded his own self-infatuation even as it supported it. Mind and place lose their antithetical relation to one another once they are brought together in remembering, which binds itself to place even as it constitutes the self who remembers. One might say therefore that mind and place are both modulations of our being-in-the-world, along with body, language, and history. Or perhaps even that place is "the body of the mind," its extra-organic organ.[17] More than a simple *Spielraum* for mind's effusions, more than a mere scene for its actings-out, it is that "other scene" (in Freud's descriptive phrase for dreams) in whose very alterity mind comes to know itself as it is and to keep itself as it has been: two activities not separable from each other in the end—or even in the beginning.

Memory recalls mind to place—takes it decisively there and not to its mere representation. We revisit places in remembering (just as we do in dreams), and in so doing our minds reach out to touch the things themselves, which are to be found in the very places they inhabit. *Mind coadunates with world in memory of place.*[18]

VII

Place, then, plain old place, proves to be a liberating factor in matters of memory and mind. An appreciation of the place of place in our experience helps to free us from the naturalistic and mentalistic straitjackets within which both mind and memory have for too long been confined. Memory of place offers a way out of this confinement and back into the lived world, while encouraging us to rethink the mind itself as continuous with this world, coterminous with it, and actively passive (or passively active) there. This is not to say that when we begin to reconceive memory and mind in terms of place we are without problem or paradox. For instance, why is it that place, itself best understood on a container model, aids us in overcoming the persistent temptation to regard mind and memory as themselves forms of strict containment? Meditation on place leads paradoxically to the opening out from within of that which it encloses from without.

Nonetheless, I have persevered in underscoring the primordiality of place, and I have done so not just because it is a generally neglected topic in philosophy (Norman Malcolm's recently published *Memory and Mind* does not deign to mention it), but because most discussions of memory in Western thought (including Aristotle's own seminal discussion in his short treatise on the subject) have emphasized the primacy of *time*, particularly *past* time, in remembering. Almost all such consideration, from Plato to Husserl, Heidegger, and Minkowski, has subsumed memory under a temporal problematic: as if remembering were just one more way of being in time. It matters little in this regard whether we place memory (as *anamnesis)* under the sign of eternity or reduce it to the reproduction of expired durations. Either way, it is assumed that remembering, since it has to do with the past, is exclusively a temporal affair. But is it? Doesn't place, which is at least equiprimordial with time, require us to reconsider this assumption? Thus, when Heidegger claims that "what is past, present, [or] to come appears in the oneness of its own *present* being," we cannot help but notice that "present being" (*An-wesen:* literally, "being *at*") always occurs in place, the arena wherein both temporal and spatial determinations are at once rooted and specified.[19]

The poet puts it best:

I can only say, *there* we have been: but I cannot say just where.
And I cannot say, how long, for that is to place it in time.[20]

I would suggest that "where have we been?" is often a more appropriate heuristic device in matters of memory than "when have we been?"—providing that we do not restrict interpretation of the "where" to the shrunken sense of site. Site is leveled-down place and is functionally and metrically defined (as in a "building site"). To reduce place to site is comparable to reducing lived time to date. The *"just where"* is homologous to the *"just how long."* The where that counts in remembering is, as Eliot indicates, a *there* and thus a matter of place, which we have seen to be structured by a here/there opposition played out within the horizoning spread of landscape. To remember is, in effect, and often in fact, to claim that *"there I was doing X or Y in the presence of A and B."* Place is the operator of memory, that which puts it to work in presenting past experience to us in an inclusive and environing format.

VIII

The most insistent direction, the main drift, of this essay has been from the inside out—from the innards of memory to its exoskeletal outreaches. Most accounts of memory try to keep all the significant action contained within, within the inner acrobatics of representation or within the microstructures of neuroanatomy or of information flow. In this internalization of mem-ory, phenomenology has played its part by conceiving of remembering as a "positing presentification" of the past, its re-presentation to mind by mind.[21] And mind, being thought of almost entirely in terms of consciousness and intentionality, has served as a psychical container for the remembered. In questioning this deeply interiorizing tendency I have had recourse primarily to place, still another form of containment but one considerably more diffuse, elastic, and porous. Mind and memory exfoliate in place, even though place's own activity is that of closing in or down (not pinning down: that is site's task). Time's basic action is one of breaking out (out of the fixed boundaries of calendar and clock) and breaking up (of all that wastes away in time). Time "disperses subsistence," and it is not at all surprising that our distressful thoughts concerning the oblivion to which the past is prone are tied to time, to its dispersing movement.[22] The same movement is evident in the more hopeful, but still threatening, thought (implicit in Nietzsche as in Freud) that "the past begins now and is always becoming."[23]

Place, then, not only offers protection against this very dispersal, against time's diasporadic or "ecstatic" proclivity, which Heidegger made so much of in Being and Time. By its encircling embrace, place shields, holds within (and withholds) rather than scattering subsistence in dissemination.[24]

In contrast with time, therefore, place is eminently suited for the keeping operation which we found earlier to lie at the core of remembering: as remaining-with and conserving, holding and concealing, taking-in and protecting. In fact, it becomes clear that the past itself can be kept in place, right in place, especially when place is taken in its full landscape being. This happens saliently in the simultaneously given, vertically arranged strata of geological formations, which compress their own amassed past within them. Places, even ordinary places, often do much the same, presenting to us their unreduced verticality over against the already reduced horizontality of temporal dissolution.

Place, then, not only offers aegis before time's ravages but may take time into itself, encasing its disarray in its own structure. Something like this happens in all remembering, even when it is not explicitly of place. In keeping the past in mind, it is safekeeping it from an inherent temporal dispersiveness. But we keep the past most effectively in mind when we also keep it expressly in place—when mind embraces place and not just its own representations. This is one more reason why memory of place is liberating, since it frees us from time's dissevering action, its disbanding of human experience into the antagonistic segments of "past" and "future," the "no longer" and the "not yet."

That leaves us, as remembering always does leave us, in the present, a present massively enriched through the coeval actions presentment and implacement (as we may call the "placing" action of memories). Remembrance is indeed now. It is also here reminding us that remembering begins and ends in place even as it traverses the most distantly located personal past, a past it brings incisively into present place, into the now-and-here of remembrance.

Notes

1. For Bartlett, the "schema" is a strictly constructivist notion; for Piaget, the "scheme" serves to "assimilate" experience in keeping with the exact stage of one's

cognitive development: both views are decidedly Kantian in their stress on the mind's actively shaping role. See F. C. Bartlett, *Remembering: A Study in Experimental and Social Psychology* (Cambridge: Cambridge University Press, 1932), pp. 199ff., 300ff.; and Jean Piaget and Barbel Inhelder, *Memory and Intelligence*, trans. A. J. Pomerans (New York: Basic Books, 1973).

2. Cf. John R. Anderson and Gordon Bower, *Human Associative Memory* (Washington, D.C.: Winston, 1973).

3. A phenomenon like nostalgia, with its almost irresistible pull to the past, testifies to the already informed ingression of events we undergo rather than bring forth.

4. Robert Sokolowski, *Presence and Absence: A Philosophical Investigation of Language and Being* (Bloomington: Indiana University Press, 1978), pp. 7–9, 100–102.

5. "Retention is mostly occupied with what is past, because the past has got away and in a way no longer affords a lasting hold. Therefore, the meaning of retention is subsequently limited to what is past, what memory draws up, recovers again and again. But since this limited reference originally does not constitute the sole nature of memory, the need to give a name to the specific retention and recovery of what is past gives rise to the coinage: re-calling memory-remembrance *(Wiedergedächtnis)*" (Martin Heidegger, *What Is Called Thinking?* trans. J. Glenn Gray (New York: Harper, 1968), pp. 140–41; Heidegger's italics.)

6. Plato's use of *anaminmeskesthai* is normally in the passive form of "to be reminded of," as when particular equal things remind me of Equality. Reminding is a matter of being put in mind of X or Y (not themselves necessarily belonging to the past) by a presently perceived particular; and it can be so associative or automatic as not to include being-mindful-of at all. On reminding in Plato, see Richard Sorabjii, *Aristotle on Memory* (London: Duckworth, 1972), pp. 35ff.

7. Heidegger, *What Is Called Thinking?* p. 3; my italics.

8. Merleau-Ponty, *The Visible and the Invisible*, trans. Alphonso Lingis (Evanston: Northwestern University Press, 1968), p. 266.

9. Edmund Husserl, *The Phenomenology of Internal Time-Consciousness*, trans. James S. Churchill (Bloomington: Indiana University Press, 1964), p. 66.

10. "In a landscape we always get to one place from another place, each location is determined only by its relation to the neighboring place within the circle of visibility" (Erwin Straus, *The Primary World of Senses*, trans. J. Needleman [Glencoe, Ill.: Free Press, 1963], p. 319).

11. Maurice Merleau-Ponty, *Phenomenology of Perception*, trans. C. Smith (New York: Humanities Press, 1962), p. 82.

12. On this point, see Straus, *Primary World of Senses*, p. 322.

13. For more on this conception of forgetting, see Merleau-Ponty, *The Visible and the Invisible*, pp. 196–97.

14. Ibid., p. 222; his italics.

15. The body is "a place of passage (for) movements, received and thrown back" (Henri Bergson, *Matter and Memory*, trans. N. M. Paul and W. S. Palmer [New York: Doubleday, 1959], p. 145).

16. "The self can only be remembered" (Louis Dupré, *Transcendent Selfhood* [New York: Seabury, 1976], p. 72). "The non-existent is nowhere" (Aristotle *Physics* 208a30).

17. Merleau-Ponty, *The Visible and the Invisible*, p. 253.

18. It ensues that in this situation mind's modes of operation do not merely correspond to the structures of the world: they are the latter, or at least become profoundly akin to them in remembering. Plato, precisely when discussing rec-

ollection, remarks that "all of nature is akin" (Meno 81d). Merleau-Ponty, who speaks of "the 'Memory of the World,'" says that "Being is the 'place' where the 'modes of consciousness' are inscribed as structurations of Being . . ." (*The Visible and the Invisible*, p. 253; preceding phrase from ibid., p. 194).

19. *What Is Called Thinking?* p. 140; his italics.

20. T. S. Eliot, "Burnt Norton" (*Four Quartets*); his italics.

21. See Husserl, *Ideas*, trans. Boyce Gibson (New York: Macmillan, 1931), sections 99, 111.

22. Aristotle *Physics* 221b2. I owe this felicitous translation to Peter Manchester.

23. Stanley A. Leavy, *The Psychoanalytic Dialogue* (New Haven: Yale University Press, 1980), p. 94. Cf. also pp. 97, 110–11.

24. I take this last word in Derrida's sense and would like to remark that place as I have described it does not fall prey to his critique of the metaphysics of presence. The outgoing "there" of place prevents its collapse into that proximity of the "there" which is of the essence of presence as Derrida interprets this latter term.

Edward S. Casey: Selected Bibliography

Books

The Fate of Place: A Philosophical History. Berkeley: University of California Press, 1997.

Getting Back into Place: Toward a Renewed Understanding of the Place-World. Bloomington: Indiana University Press, 1993.

Spirit and Soul: Essays in Philosophical Psychology. Dallas: Spring, 1991.

Remembering: A Phenomenological Study. Bloomington: Indiana University Press, 1987.

Imagining: A Phenomenological Study. Bloomington: Indiana University Press, 1976.

Chapters in Edited Volumes and Journal Articles

"Smooth Spaces and Rough-Edged Places: The Hidden History of Place." *Review of Metaphysics* 51 (1997).

"How to Get from Space to Place in a Fairly Short Stretch of Time: Phenomenological Prolegomena." In *Sense of Time*, ed. S. Feldman and K. Basso. Santa Fe: SAR Press, 1997.

"The Place of the Sublime." In *Analecta Husserliana*, ed. A. T. Tymieniecka. Dordrecht: Kluwer Academic Publishers, 1997.

"Forgetting Remembered." *Man and World* 25 (1992).

"The Element of Voluminousness: Depth and Place Re-Examined." In *Merleau-Ponty Vivant*, ed. M. Dillon. Albany: State University of New York Press, 1991.

"Heidegger In and Out of Place." In *Heidegger: A Centenary Appraisal.* Pittsburgh: Duquesne University, Silverman Phenomenology Center, 1990.

"Place, Form and Identity in Postmodern Architecture and Philosophy." In *After the Future*, ed. Gary Shapiro. Albany: State University of New York Press, 1990.

"Levinas on Memory and the Trace." In *The Collegium Phaenomenologicum: The First Ten Years*, ed. John Sallis, Giuseppina Moneta, and Jacques Taminiaux. Dordrecht: Kluwer Academic Publishers, 1988.

"Derrida's Deconstruction of Heidegger's Views on Temporality: The Language of Space and Time." In *Phenomenology of Temporality: Time and Language.* Pittsburgh: Duquesne University, Silverman Phenomenology Center, 1987.

"The World of Nostalgia." *Man and World* 20 (1987).

"Origin(s) in (of) Heidegger/Derrida." *Journal of Philosophy* 81 (1984).

"Habitual Body and Memory in Merleau-Ponty." *Man and World* 17 (1984).

"Keeping the Past in Mind." *Review of Metaphysics* 37 (1983).

"Sartre on Imagination." In *The Philosophy of Jean-Paul Sartre, Library of Living Philosophers*, ed. P. A. Schilpp. LaSalle: Open Court, 1981.

"Time Out of Mind." In *Dimensions of Thought: Current Explorations in Time, Space and Knowledge*, ed. R. H. Moon and R. Randall. Berkeley: Dharma, 1980.

"Perceiving and Remembering." *Review of Metaphysics* 32 (1979).

"Imagination and Phenomenological Method." In *Husserl: Expositions and Appraisals*, ed. F. Elliston and P. McCormick. Notre Dame: Notre Dame University Press, 1977.

"Comparative Phenomenology of Mental Activity: Memory, Hallucination, and Fantasy Contrasted with Imagination." *Research in Phenomenology* (1976).

"Toward a Phenomenology of Imagination." *Journal of the British Society for Phenomenology* 5 (January 1974).

"Art, Imagination, and the *A Priori*." In *Analecta Husserliana*, ed. A. T. Tymieniecka. Dordrecht: Kluwer Academic Publishers, 1974.

"Imagination: Imagining and the Image." *Philosophy and Phenomenological Research* 31 (1971).

"Man, Self, and Truth." *The Monist* 55 (1971).

"Truth in Art." *Man and World* 3 (1970).

"Meaning in Art." In *New Essays in Phenomenology: Studies in the Philosophy of Experience*, ed. J. M. Edie. Chicago: Quadrangle, 1969.

Part 4

Locating the Ethical

10

Otherwise than Ethics, or
Why We Too Are Still Impious

JOHN D. CAPUTO

John D. Caputo has tried to settle in the distance that separates philosophy from religious and theological questions in the way that many
continentalists interest themselves in the interaction between philosophy and literature. Caputo has consistently tried to develop a style of
thinking that is driven in two different directions at once: to a more
heartless rendering of things that faces up to the facelessness of what
Nietzsche called the great cosmic stupidity, and to an ethics of the heart
first adumbrated in the biblical ethics of the neighbor. Caputo characterizes these two tendencies in many ways in his work, sometimes calling the former the "Dionysian" and the latter the rabbinic, the religious, or the messianic.

Caputo's first book, *The Mystical Element in Heidegger's Thought,*
worked out the relations between Heideggerian and Eckhartian *Gelassenheit.* In *Heidegger and Aquinas,* Caputo shows that the question of a
mystical element in Heidegger opened up a different way of dealing
with the relationship between Heidegger and Thomas Aquinas, one
that got past arguing whether *esse* was what Heidegger meant by *Sein.*
A philosophical turning point for Caputo occurred in the early 1980s
when he seriously encountered Derrida. Derrida's liberating influence
on his thought can be detected in *Radical Hermeneutics,* where Caputo
shifts to a more impudent style, which also allowed Caputo's more
Kierkegaardian voice to gain expression. In this work, Caputo argues
for a hermeneutics that takes full account of the factical limits of our
situation, of what Kierkegaard called the "difficulty" of life. Caputo's
subsequent work became increasingly wary of Heidegger's *Seinsgesch-
ichte* and its privileging of a special language and epoch for Being's
homecoming. When the wave of revelations about Heidegger's national socialism broke, Caputo wrote *Demythologizing Heidegger* to state his
reservations about the "myth" of Being in Heidegger and his sense of
the deeply elitist and essentializing tendencies of Heidegger's thought.

Against Ethics stated the case for an ethics without foundations, a kind of poststructuralist or postfoundationalist ethics, which had lost its taste for the history of Being and had become more interested in the history of suffering.

In his most recent works, *The Prayers and Tears of Jacques Derrida* and *Deconstruction in a Nutshell,* Caputo shows the possibilities that deconstruction opens for ethical, political, and religious reflection; focus on attaining justice in all situations; and a more radical conception of human existence and social relationships, which turn on an appreciation of the singularity of the situation in which justice must obtain. He reflects on the way deconstruction opens up religious reflection or the way that religious motifs, deconstructively pursued, can open up philosophy to its other, without breaking the "undecidability" or the tension between the Dionysian and the religious, which pull in opposite directions.

Caputo's essay in this volume, first published in *Against Ethics,* is one of his most personal reflections. It is written from the heart, not as a speculative piece of argumentation. In it, he formulates his understanding of an ethics without foundations, of an obligation that overtakes us and that we are not at liberty to decline but one we cannot, for all that, take to be the voice of God, the Categorical Imperative, or the Good, except by a leap beyond the factical limits of our situation.

⋯⊷⊜⊶⋯

I turn now to say what—in sum—I have learned from Abraham and Johannes de Silentio, from the strange painting signed by Abraham of Paris, and from the lyrical-philosophical discourses of Johanna de Silentio, Magdalena de la Cruz et al., by which I was so mysteriously visited. It has not been my task to write a *tractatus de obligatione,* to make obligation safe and to shelter it from attack, to provide it with the protection afforded by *episteme* or *Wissenschaft.* I have instead undertaken to make certain supplementary contributions to a poetics of obligation as an event that happens in the midst of a cosmic night, that regularly disturbs my sleep. In taking a stand against ethics, in never pretending to get as far as ethics, I have produced something that is otherwise than ethics, something a little too impious for ethics, while yet being very attached to its obligations. I move about in the difference between piety and impiousness, between ethics and the innocence of becoming, keeping up a correspondence with Dionysus while staying in constant touch with my rabbi.

On Minimalism

My concern has been to keep metaphysics to a minimum. The last thing I want is to set off another round of German metaphysics. So when I speak of an "event" as "what happens"[1] I am not putting on great metaphysical airs. I am writing from below and saying, in the most unrestricted, least imposing sense possible, that anything at all that happens is an event. I am also saying that I am not sure what is happening, even though things are happening all around me. I am like a man caught up in a swirl of activity who keeps asking "what's happening?"[2] Something is happening, but he cannot say just what, because so many things are happening. The point of talking like this is to find an idiom that carries a minimum of metaphysical baggage, that commits itself at most to a minimalist metaphysics. I am practicing a certain Ockhamism, which puts the razor to whatever I do not need.

We cannot just avoid or simply step outside metaphysics, which would mean to step outside the logic and the ontologic of our grammar and our intellectual habits. That would be a hypermetaphysical undertaking for which I lack the grammar, the logic, and the head. To speak at all is to have recourse to a way of framing and phrasing, to fall back upon a way of dividing up and parceling out, to mark the world up *(archi-écriture)* and to stake it out in one ontocategorial way or another. That is unavoidable. The idea is not to deny our presuppositions but to unfold them with greater penetration, staying on the alert as best we can to the ontocategories that shape our thought, troubling ourselves about them and worrying them a lot.[3] To speak at all is always already to be caught up in a certain amount of violence, of hermeneutic violence, of *archi*-violence and *archi*-incisions.

If you tried absolutely to neutralize metaphysics, to put it out of action *simpliciter,* you would get caught up in a metaphysics of neutralizing consciousness, in the metaphysical idea of a consciousness able transcendentally to neutralize real being. That is what Heidegger caught Husserl doing.[4] It is better to recognize the inevitability of metaphysics, to be vigilant about its omnipresence, and then to try to keep it to a minimum, to treat events as nonviolently as possible, with a maximum of *Gelassenheit.*

The time has come to overcome the "overcoming of metaphysics," or to make it plain that the point of overcoming metaphysics is to "not-be-overcome-by-metaphysics," by too much metaphysics, not to suffocate or to perish from the extravagant, totalizing tendencies of a maximizing metaphysics. A maximizing metaphysics is always too violent for events, which are very delicate and tender little growths; it is more violent than necessary, more violent than archi-violence, which is unavoidable. One cannot avoid some sort of metaphysics or another, but that does not mean that one needs to rush headlong into the most extravagant, totalizing, maximalist, metanarratival, in short, the most meta-physical forms of metaphysics, which are always organized around some Meta-event or other.

My minimalism is what is behind my affection for "anarchy," for the *arche* is always a stroke of violence, a violent incision, a cutting up and ordering about of events, of the singularity of events, by a sweeping principial power, by a *principium*/prince, by a Meta-event that orders everything around. The key to my idea of anarchy is to see that it is always on the side of keeping violence to a minimum. We need just laws and *archai* of

various sorts, tentative, revisable *principia* (put forward in fear and trembling), for the point of the law is to protect the weak against the strong, that
is, to minimize violence. My anarchism is no street-corner antinomianism,
but the cultivation of an eye for the singularity of events. Its aim is not to
level the law but to keep the law honest, to keep the eye of the law on the
withered hand, as Magdalena put it. I do not commit myself to pure anarchy or pure nonviolence. I avoid the metaphysics of purity and willingly
embrace the mutual contamination of anarchy by the law and of the law by
anarchy.

To affirm the anarchy of events is to embrace a polyarchy that con-
cedes that events are indefinitely redescribable, indefinitely reconfigurable,
that we lack the perspective from which to pronounce the meaning or
pass the final judgment on the sense of events. Events belong to multiple,
incommensurable, heteromorphic quasi systems in a kind of flat infinity
that stretches out indefinitely in every direction. In virtue of such flatness,
events never contain or attain an upright, order-giving, vertical infinity,
the infinity of some absolute being—*l'infini:* the Infinite One—some Meta-
event that dominates and organizes other events and serves as their *arche.*
That would amount to vertical violence, the hierarchical violence of an
overarching *arche* that takes itself to have full authority and to speak with
authoritative power, which it is the point of minimalism to keep to a minimum.

Minimalism is a metaphysics without a Meta-event, a kind of decapi-
tated metaphysics. Metaphysics in the traditional sense wants to keep its
head. But I have no head for metaphysics and a metaphysics with no head.

Minimalism thus does not mean absolute simplicity but rather bewilderment before a tangled complex of events, a kind of amazement before the
mazing grace of events, before the dense entanglement of what's happening. Minimalism is a philosophy that begins in a maze *(thaumazein).* The
violence would be to erase the complexity, to simplify the quasi system, to
dominate the textuality of the event with the simplicity of a single system,
of an overarching principle or interpretation. The violence would be to stop
the slippage, to erase the ambiguity, to take the play out of events, to put
events out of play and into order, to hierarchize them, to erect principial
authorities who would give authorized interpretations and definitive solu-
tions and judgments.

Minimalism lets events happen, lets them be, lets them go, without imposing grand and overarching schemata upon them, without simplifying
them. It has decided to come to terms with intractable plurivocity and heteromorphic proliferation, in the spirit of Abraham of Paris.

You cannot avoid linking one event to another and that to another, *ad
infinitum*—again and again, and in different ways, over and over. But in this
minimalist metaphysics or quasi philosophy of events you will never come
up with some Meta-event that organizes all other events, that puts them to
rest, that arrests their play, that sweeps over them all and gathers them to
itself in a final "because" and gives them all a rest. I do not care if you call

such a Meta-event *ousia* or *eidos,* *Bewußtsein* or *Wille zur Macht,* God or the gods, *abba* or *Jahweh,* the *logos* of the Dialectic or the all-gathering *logos* of the primordial Greek Beginning (*pace* father Abraham and the prophets, *pace* Hegel and Heidegger and Greco-German philosophy). Every time somebody tries such a thing, we can show that this schema is always already troubled and disturbed from within. Every time an event is a treated as a Meta-event, there is a power play afoot and the police are not far behind.

The most violent violence arises from thinking one can dispense with archi-violence and lay hold of some nonviolent thing-in-itself, some absolute, unmediated *arche.* It is just when people think they have gained access to the unmediated, Derrida says, that the rest of us are visited by the most massive, most violent mediations.[5] The point of a minimalist metaphysics of events is to avoid putting on the royal airs of the *arche,* to keep events in play, to lift the load the *arche* places on the back of what is happening, even while one recognizes the place of provisional rules. In minimalism, events are taken as tender shoots and delicate growths that need to be protected from such violence.

Es Gibt

"There is" *(es gibt)* is the minimalist way I have chosen to speak. It tries not to say too much, not to be too imposing a saying, not to impose itself on events. It tries to let events be.

There are *(es gibt)* events. They happen "because" *(weil)* they happen. They happen "for the while" *(dieweil)* that they happen. The "because" sinks into events, sinks off in what happens, fades away like an echo in space, leaving only the events.

Events happen without "why." There is no "why" outside what happens, no Meta-event that dominates other events, that serves as the point and purpose of what happens. Whatever is outside what happens is what does not happen. Events link on to other events, forming chains of events of various kinds, too many kinds to count or record. The "why" sinks into the "because" and is submerged in what happens; the Meta-event is submerged in the flow of other events.

What happens is what there is *(es gibt)* That is all. "There is" *(es gibt, il y a)* is the simplest, least encumbered way to speak of what happens. I have nothing up my sleeve; I am not trying to slip something past you. *Es gibt, weil es gibt:* There is because there is. That is a way of speaking that does not weigh events down with heavy ontological burdens or lift them up and carry them off with eagle wings to great mountain heights. "There is" *(es gibt)* is part of a minimalist metaphysics that is trying to travel light.

This very tautological way to speak in fact produces highly heterological effects. This minimalism is part of a corresponding maximalism in the sense that it allows for a maximum of pluralistic possibilities. That is because its very simple way of speaking is not very imposing, not too incisive.

Minimalism gives events some play, lets them play, allows for a maximum of heteromorphic multiplicity. *Es gibt* means *es spielt:* It plays. It plays because it plays. It plays for the while that it plays. It is all like a child playing who plays because she plays. The play is without why; the why sinks into the play.

Es gibt. It gives. What gives *(was gibt)? Es spielt.* It plays. What plays? What is the "it" that gives or plays?

Nietzsche has already warned us about this mistake, about the illusion, induced by grammar, of looking for some subject or agency or author when we use impersonal expressions like "it's lightning," or "it's raining"— or "it happens." Nietzsche is warning us to keep metaphysics to a minimum, to keep William's razor sharp. *"Es gibt"* means "there is" in the sense of "it is given that," "it happens that," "I am saying that." But there is no *"es"* that gives. The "It" is not a Meta-event. To say that what happens is like a child playing is actually a way of saying that there is no child, that nothing watches over what happens, that nothing anchors it down or lifts it up—not even a child. "It is raining" means "the rain falls." The "it" that "rains" sinks into the rain that falls. There is no "it," no agency implied. When we say "there is," "it is," we are conceding that nothing (we know of) is there, that no *thing* is there, that no one is there, behind or beneath or hovering over what is happening, no surpassing *arche* watching over everything. What happens is what happens. "There is" is a way of getting beyond the notion of a deep agency at the heart of what happens that is driving it somewhere, or of a deep *telos* at the end of what happens that draws it to itself. It is a way of speaking very simply, of saying that it happens, and that that is all. It is a way of declining to separate the "it" and the "happens."

Minimalism "declines" to say more. It does not deny that there is more, for how after all would it do that? *"Es gibt"* is a way of saying something happens, who knows what? It is a form of modesty. If that is so, then I do not know whether there is or there is not "any more." That is the region to which maximalist metaphysics proudly stakes its claim, the waters upon which religious faith ventures, full of fear and trembling. All I am saying is that minimalism is the horizon within which more robust assertions must be made, and that more robust assertions are on their own.[6] Minimalism is not a new overarching metaphysics. It is just one more perspective, a very modest perspective that arises when one asks, in genuine bewilderment, "what's happening?" When we say "there is" or "it is," that is a way of saying that nothing Overarching we know of is there, that it's just happening.

This is not a tautology but a heterology, because it does not indulge itself in the thought of a *to autos,* of something Self-same undergirding or overseeing what is happening. It does not try to gather what is happening into a unity and claim that "all is one," or claim that everything that is happening is really "nothing more than" such-and-such a Meta-event, or the history of such-and-such, or the giving and withdrawing of such-and-such, or caused by such-and-such. For any such undertaking I have confessed, again and again, I have no such prodigious head. *Es gibt* is not a way of sustaining or underwriting identity but of making space for difference, of making space for everything. To the extent that it does not indulge itself or impose itself, to the extent that it adopts a very simple, minimalist way to speak, very timid, its hat in its hand, the expression "there is" is very unimposing.

It does, however, impose upon itself a very severe, austere regime, self-effacing and without pretense.

"*Es gibt*/there is" is an impersonal, anonymous expression. If *es gibt* is a game playing, it is a game without a player, without an Overarching Someone or Something throwing the dice and trying to win. It is only a game. Or it is not even a game, if by a game we mean something over and above the play of its elements, the play of events. Events happen. Phrases happen. The forces discharge themselves, or are discharged, in the middle voice—in between agency and passivity, in between causal agents and passive patients, without distinguishing the force and its discharge, the event and its happening. Events, phrases, forces happen *(arrivent)*, one after the other, linking and unlinking and relinking, incessantly; that is what they are.

"*Es gibt*" is an austere way of speaking—it is our ascetic ideal—which confesses that we do not know what is happening. It is even a way of saying that nothing is happening, that is, no *thing* is happening or making-happen, over and above what is happening, no one Great Meta-event. It is a kind of plea that implores us to stick to what is happening; or a kind of confession that we are stuck in what is happening, and that it is impossible to get any further. It is a confession that we do not have such a prodigious head as is required for answering the question what is happening, that we cannot get on top of what is happening, that we are stuck in the middle of *it, in medias res, inter-esse,* amazed and bewildered. We cannot soar over what is happening with philosophy's eagle-wings. What's happening has clipped our wings.

No one we know of is there. No one we know of knows we are here, on the little star. We are like orphans—and widows and strangers. The stars do not care, do not take care of us. We are disasters, all.

"*Es gibt*" is a way of saying that we can lay claim to no star to guide us, no ground to found us, no deep core of *eidos* or *ousia, Sein* or *Geist,* to see us through the flux of events. It is a way of speaking of the "abyss," of the *Abgrund.* "*Es gibt*" exposes all to an abyss, lands us in a void, leaves us without support, with a minimum of foundations.

I have been speaking all along about obligation in minimalist terms. There is—*es gibt*—obligation. Obligation happens with and in terms of proper names, of the singularity of the individual. Obligation is a matter of being attached to a singularity, to something bearing a proper name. The lyrical-philosophical discourses were signed by curious proper names, strange names that provided a minimum of identification. That allows their readers a maximum of substitution; it allows these wondrous proper names to substitute for the names of us all, and in that way to speak to and of the obligations of us all, of each and every one of us.

But *es gibt* is neither a proper name nor a pseudonym but the very name of anonymity, of no-name, of no thing, of no one. It is a name for no one and for nothing, for the emptiness of the space between the stars, for a starless interstellar void. *Es gibt* is the name of the nameless, anonymous anarchy of what is happening. That is why it disturbs my sleep.

So to say *es gibt*/there is obligation, to say "it gives obligation," comes down to saying that when obligation happens it happens in a void, in an abyss.

Unlike Levinas, whom I love very much but whom I am obliged to betray, I do not think that anything can "deaden the heartrending bustling of *il y a.*" I am more inclined to believe Levinas when he says that obligation comes "from I know not where" *(je ne sais d'où).* I am more inclined to believe that we cannot separate the *il* which is Him, God, which is God's own utter illeity, from the *il* of *il y a,* from the rumble of *il y a.* "God" is not the "apex of my vocabulary," something that would organize and stabilize my vocabulary, but another word that puzzles and disturbs my sleep. I am pursued by a more radical anarchy than Levinas's, one without an apex or a deep, founding, preoriginary ethics from which science and law and politics and institutional life can be derived and secured and can draw breath. I am haunted by a more disturbing diachrony, one with which I can never catch up. To say that this diachrony leaves its trace in obligation, and then to say that this trace is the trace of God, is that not to track this trace down, to catch up with it, to catch one's breath? That is too much for me, I who am permanently behind and out of breath and a terrible insomniac. If he— *il,* E.L.—"does not know from where" obligation comes, then why does he say a thing? Why does he say that it *(il)* is the trace of God? Why does he say that what he does not know can put an end to the haunting rumble of *il y a* instead of making it worse? For what else is *il y a* than being caught in the grips of I know not what, than being always already seized by what can never be present? My meditations on *il y a* leave me in a permanently anarchic state, tormented by the truth of scepticism. *Me voici,* here I am, called upon by I know not what, all my nouns and pronouns inwardly disturbed by anonymity.[7]

Il y a. Es Gibt. It happens.

When a proper name is used, when a proper name happens, it is like a voice crying in the void, like a prophet crying in a cosmic wilderness. Standing on the surface of the little star, our hands cupped to our mouth, we shout our proper names into the abyss. *Es gibt:* there are proper names. Proper names happen against the horizon of the impersonal, the improper, defying the anonymity of *es gibt,* rising up and sinking away.

If you press proper names, if you push hard enough against their surface, or probe with your stylus into their core, you will find a core of impropriety, of *différance,* for if they were truly proper they would not happen. So there is something slightly pseudonymous about proper names as well, and we are all slightly pseudonymous characters. The *différance* by which proper names are inhabited is the indifference, the anonymity, of what is happening that infiltrates their idiolect. The pseudonymous is the mask of the anonymous.

Proper names happen in the abyss. They happen for a while. They happen for the while that they happen. Then they die out like a lost language belonging to a lost time. In the long run, that is what they are and that is what our language is or will amount to. Eventually, as the little star grows cold, the noises of our language will disappear into the stellar night.

Eventually, we will all have spoken forgotten, dead languages.

Eventually, the memory of all these people and all these languages and all these proper names and the dates and places by which they are marked will be entrusted to faint and indecipherable traces on listing stones. Not even that.

Il y a là cendre. Not even that.

It gives—proper names. It—that is, nothing—gives them. They are given, but they are not given by anyone or anything. If they are gifts, they are gifts without a giver. If you insist that gifts must have givers, then you abandon minimalism and become pious. Proper names happen; that is all. The rigidity of their designation eventually withers, or it goes up in smoke, like Shulamith.

Es gibt/il y a/there is/it happens: that means there is nothing there that anyone can lay hold of. There is no Overarching agency or doer, no super-causal agent, no transcendent something or other, no *arche* we can grasp. Not as far as we know. It happens. There is no one there to thank or blame, no one archi-thing or archi-person doing it all, behind it all, responsible for it all, none we can grasp. It happens and it is innocent. It happens, for better or for worse. That is all.

Obligations do not derive from some central source of power. Obligations are strictly local events, sublunary affairs, between us. They are matters of flesh and blood, without cosmic import or support.

They happen.

Against Heidegger, or, in the Name of Another Heidegger

All along I have been settling accounts with Heidegger. The minimalism of the *es gibt* is my way of repeating Heidegger—carefully, selectively, warily, differently.[8] I have been repeating Heidegger while all along clipping Heidegger's eagle wings, reading Heidegger against Heidegger. It is a part of my love/hate relationship with father Heidegger (it is not safe to love Heidegger unless you also hate him), of following Heidegger while being against Heidegger. There is a certain Heideggerian tone to what I am saying here, but I am trying to keep Heidegger to a minimum. I am a minimalizing Heideggerian.

I have been egged on by the lyrical-philosophical discourses, which were very irreverent toward Heidegger—who is the father of all of us who are deconstructing this or that, or talking about its delimitation. Like the discourses, I have been throughout as impious as possible toward Heidegger, because Heidegger is far too pious, dangerously pious, about the *es gibt*, about his *Sprache*, his *Volk*, his poets, and his Greeks. But my impiety has been, in part at least, minimally, in the name of another Heidegger. I will not say a higher Heidegger, because I have had enough of Heideggerian heights and the soaring of Greco-German eagles. But I will say of another, simpler and more austere Heidegger, the Heidegger of the *es gibt* and of the groundless play of Being's comings and goings, which is, I think, the austere setting within which obligations are given.[9]

I have been reading with you, vaguely and from afar, and contaminated with other texts, my favorite passage from Heidegger, from *Der Satz vom Grund*, a text that I have been reading for many years[10] and that keeps taking new turns on me, that keeps happening to me anew, again and again. But I have been simultaneously editing it all along, and with a heavy hand. I hold the text and read it with one hand, while in the other I hold my scissors. (That is how I read everything these days; my study is a mess.) That is because Heidegger, as I now think, could never maintain himself in the simplicity of the thought of the *es gibt*. Much as he loved the splendor of the simple, he could not contain himself, he could not hold back from the most extravagant adornments of *es gibt*. Whatever he may have said about *die Strenge des Denkens*, he could never discipline himself to a rigorous minimalism. He always said too much about what's happening, even though he protested against the Gigantic in the *Beiträge*.[11] However provocative his meditations on *es gibt*, he always reduced *es gibt* to silence under his great Greco-German metanarratival outbursts, buried under the massive *Sprechen* of his *Sprache*—with disastrous effects on obligation. My view has been to take a minimal view of *es gibt* in order to maximize obligation. I have found it necessary to deny the History of Being in order to make room for obligation.

I have been reading Heidegger reading Heraclitus, as every Heidegger afficionado will have already noticed. Here is Heidegger "translating" a fragment of Heraclitus about a mysterious child-king:

> The mission of Being *(aion)*, that is a child, at play, playing a board game; the kingdom is a child's. (Frag. 52)[12]

The "kingdom" *(basilein)*, Heidegger comments, means the *arche*—the *principium* or, let us say, the "principality"—which gives the rule for the way Being holds sway in that time, in that epoch. The Being of beings *(the arche)* happens again and again, each time differently in each and every epoch of Being—as *eidos, ousia, esse, Geist, Wille*, etc.[13] But what is the *arche* of the *archai*, the truth of truth, the unity of the manifold senses of Being, the rule that rules over the happenings of Being? That is the child. The *Seinsgeschick*, the giving or sending—the *Es gibt*—of Being, of the Being of beings, is a child at play. This great royal child, Heidegger says, is the "mystery of that play in which humans and their life time are caught up, upon which their essential being is staked." Heidegger asks, why is this great child described by Heraclitus playing his world-game?

> He plays because he plays.
>
> The "because" sinks into the play. The play is without "why." It plays for the while that it plays. There remains only play: the highest and the deepest.

Here is where my editorial work begins, where I brandish my scissors, where I cut the text off (like a rabbi): just at the point where Heidegger abandons the disaster and finds a lucky star to steer him through the groundless play:

> But this "only" is everything, the One, the Unique.

Here is where Heidegger starts heading for his star, where he gets very mono-astro-nomical. As he says elsewhere:[14]

To head toward a star—this only.
To think is to confine yourself to a
    single thought that one day stands
    still like a star in the world's sky.

You can see Heidegger starting to gather everything together, to collect what he has been letting be, letting go, letting happen. He cannot hold himself back; it is among his most fundamental gestures. Now a gigantic *logos* moves in, a single star that gathers the world-play together into the unity and simplicity and singleness of the *Seinsgeschick*, of the all-gathering One, of the Self-same. Like a great invading army, a massive metanarrative moves over the *es gibt* and assumes control of the play so that the play is no longer fully in play but rather gathers itself together under a Single Guiding Star. Something first flashed (like the morning star), for a moment, in the First Beginning, something great and aboriginal, for which we latecomers are too late. But this Something is not over but coming to us in the Other Beginning, for which we today wait and await, for which we are too early. In the meantime, the time of need, everything hangs in the balance. We latecomers, we *Abendländers*, we must wait to see if the evening star will transmute back into the morning star, if the gentle law of the *Es Gibt* (now in capital letters), the hidden law of benefaction in this giving and sending, is coming to save us. Still, we must do our part. The text concludes:

> The question remains whether and how we, hearing the movements of this play, can play along with and join in *(fügen)* the playing.

The question is whether we can join in the fugue *(Fuge)* by hearing the resounding of the First Beginning in the Other Beginning. The question is whether we have the ears to hear the Great Greek Beginning, to resonate with the Great Greek harmony, the Harmony of these Greek Spheres.

That is the end of minimalism and the beginning of another tall tale, an astronomically tall tale. The austere play of the *es gibt* gets its star. The "It" acquires a proper name and a proper language and a proper home, a Beginning and a Future Destiny. The play is watched over by the mildness of a royal child who holds gentle sway over a Great Event. The goalless, anarchic anonymity of what happens gets filled in and filled out with the propriety of Being's own proper name and Greek tongue. That is why I have to edit this text rigorously, to edit out the Greco-German patronyms and astronyms, to take *es gibt* more austerely, more ascetically, more minimally.

That is also why I read *es spielt* in terms of *es gibt*, but not *es ereignet*. For *Ereignis* sets off an uncontrollable chain reaction of Heideggerian events. *Es ereignet* invites an irresistible Heideggerian gesture, promotes the most massive outburst of Heideggerian piety. At the sound of *Es ereignet* Heideggerian knees everywhere bend, their eyes cloud over, their heads laid against the breast of the Event of Appropriation. Then we are inundated by wave after wave of *eigen, eignen, Er-eignis, zu-eignen,* and *ver-eignen,* by a whole avalanche of *Eigentlichkeit*. That spells the end of minimalism and the *es gibt,* of its unadorned, impersonal impropriety, of the anonymity, the anarchy, the abyss.

Even *es gibt* itself is vulnerable to this Heideggerian chain reaction. For even if you avoid hypostasizing the *es,* as Heidegger does, you may not avoid pietizing the *gibt,* just as Heidegger does not. *Es gibt* can ignite another Heideggerian chain of *Geben* and *Entnehmen,* of *Denken* and *Danken,* of thinking as thanking for the gift that Being gives us to think. This massive piety brings *es gibt* under the rule of law, albeit of a higher, more elusive, more essential law, a gentler, eschatological, astronymical law than metaphysical teleology would enforce.

The modesty of my minimalism is not to know what is happening. For my part, the thrust of the *es gibt* or *es spielt* is to divest us of the Gathering *(logos)* of the One and the Unique and the Single Star and to expose us to the wiles of plurivocity and polyvalent multiplicity, of a heteromorphic, anarchic abyss, of stellar oblivion and exploding stars. I am less inclined to bend my knee before the "mystery of the play" than to head for cover. That is why I stick to (or find myself stuck with) "it's happening," the mere happening of Ereignis, if you will. On a minimalist scale, the *Ereignis* is just "event" (maybe even an impropitious event), and that is all, without the propriety and the appropriation, which you are more likely to hear in *"es geschieht"* or *"il arrive"* or *"il y a."* I am trying to stick to something a little more minimalistic, Ockhamistic, and occasionalistic, something a little more fortuitous and chance-like in *Ereignis*—without the flapping wings of the *Seinsgeschick.* Whenever I hear Greco-German eagles soaring overhead I head for shelter. I do not want to be saved by a Greco-German eagle. Far from waiting for such a bird to save me, I hope he never has a clue as to where I am hiding.

Heidegger has a way of seizing upon the sheer facticity of what is happening—that is what I love—and then of annulling or superseding it—that is what is dangerous. He has a way of "deflecting" what his favorite poets kept trying to tell him, Veronique Foti says,[15] even as he kept telling us to listen to the poets and to let them disrupt the complacency of our lives. I would say that Heidegger's entire path of thought is a kind of "deflection" of what he himself was continually reflecting upon, that Heidegger could never catch up with or come to terms with Heidegger, that Heidegger always lagged behind Heidegger. He takes to task the attempt of onto-theo-logic to dominate and totalize what is happening, only to find a higher, more essential way to dominate and totalize it all his own. He has a way of exposing the radical contingency of what is happening and then of covering it up.

Already in *Being and Time*, in the discussion of "truth," Heidegger said "there is" *(es gibt)* truth so long as "there is" *(es gibt)* Dasein. Truth happens, and it happens just because and just so long as and just for the while that Dasein happens. But why does it happen? Why must there be truth? Why does Dasein happen as the place where truth breaks out? To that Heidegger makes a minimalist response: "it is quite incomprehensible why entities are to be *uncovered,* why the *truth* and *Dasein* must be."[16] The question "why?" already belongs to the horizon opened up by truth. The happening of truth, of uncovering, is the condition under which it is possible to ask "why?" so that the "why?" will never be able to circle back behind truth and find the condition under which truth is possible. Truth is the condition of the why; the why cannot find the condition of truth. Truth happens, without why, before why. But in the all-important chapter on historicity Heidegger found a way to take this minimalism back and to transmute the facticity of Dasein's being into a deeper necessity:

> The more authentically Dasein resolves . . . the more unequivocally does it choose and find the possibility of its existence, and the less does it do so by accident *(unzufälliger)*. Only by the anticipation of death is every accidental *(zufällige)* and 'provisional' possibility driven out. . . . Once one has grasped the finitude of one's existence, it snatches one back from the endless multiplicity of possibilities that offer themselves as closest to one—those of comfortableness, shirking, and taking things lightly *(Leichtnehmen)*—and brings Dasein into the simplicity of fate *(Schicksal)*.[17]

Here is where the need to get beyond the *es gibt* breaks loose, the need to "drive out" *(austreiben)* everything fortuitous and accidental, to drive what happens into the resoluteness of destiny, to force the *es gibt* into the destiny of resolving. That is to overload what happens and turn it into the stuff of a *telos* or a *Schicksal*. It says that what happens is not just what happens, that it has all along been ripe and rife with the future, that it groans and wails until it can bring forth the future.

This is exactly what got Heidegger into an enormous amount of trouble in the 1930s, when he thought that the "moment" had come, that it was time to seize the moment, which turned out to be a way of seizing power. This was all tied in with his love of difficulty and distrust of bourgeois ease ("taking things lightly," *Leichtnehmen*). If you make things difficult and laborious enough, you will drive the contingency out of things and force a destiny to the surface. After 1936, this love of destiny grew even worse, even though it assumed a new form. It was no longer a matter of willing and striving and resolving and forcing the contingency out of things, but of poeticizing and thinking and waiting for the gentle law of the One and the Unique to play itself out and send us back to the future, to send us the Future as the coming-back of the early Dawn. But it was still the same idea of submitting what happens to higher or deeper laws, of finding some kind of deeper unity or destiny to gather together the heteromorphic and heterologic plurality of what happens. He was still astronymical, still overloading what happens with destinies, with evening stars and morning stars, and with what is graciously giving and sending itself to us in what happens. He was still organizing what happens into a higher or deeper whole, an eschatological or astronymical whole.

Heidegger would not listen to the poets he was reading, who kept trying to break the bad news to him that what happens is what happens, that it has a mean accidentality about it, and that it is not *unterwegs* to the Other Beginning. His poets kept trying to warn him about soaring off with eagle wings over what happens; they kept trying to tell him to stick to *es gibt*.

The *es gibt* means it's happening without why, which also means without the eschatological turning of Being's errant destinings into the Truth of Being. The *es gibt* means you can't drive the contingency out of events and force them into a destiny or a necessity, that you can't relieve the cold chill of the *es spielt* with the thought that there is some why, some meta-why, which is configuring everything and gathering it into an eschatological climax. That would be to force events, to overload them with a gigantic metanarrative, to steer them toward a guiding star, to say more than we know, to abandon the simplicity of thinking and minimalist austerity. That kind of violence, which goes beyond the archi-violence advocated by a minimalism, inevitably leads into onticoconcrete violence to enforce its *arche*.

The *es gibt* means there is no way to lift yourself up above what happens, to soar over it with eagle wings—be they Hegelian or Heideggerian eagles—and force it into a destiny, a *telos* or a *Seinsgeschick*. The *es gibt* means it's happening without a deep destiny that overrides and mutes obligation in the pieties of *Andenken*. I have found it necessary to deny these temple pieties in order to make room for obligation.

Exultations and Obligations:
Between Nietzsche and Ethics

This talk of being against ethics has put me in a delicate position. I am trying to occupy a spot midway between Ethics, which (like Levinas) I too love more than God, and Nietzsche, who (like Deleuze) I love more than the death of God. I love Nietzsche and Ethics, to excess, really, but I lack the piety demanded by Ethics for its Good and its Infinity and its Categorical Imperatives, even as I cannot muster the lionhearted, macho courage required by Nietzsche's cold cosmic truthfulness. I am neither a Knight of the

Infinite Abyss, ready to hurl myself into the Void, nor a Knight of *l'Infini*, the Infinite One who hovers over all. I am not a knight at all. I distrust favors from the Crown.

My Dionysian rabbi seems not to want to settle down in either Athens or Jerusalem but, if anything, to operate a shuttle between the two, a kind of jewgreek monorail that will allow him to move back and forth as the seasons and his moods dictate. He is not a man to stay where the climate is always the same. It is very embarrassing to lack identity like this, but I will try my best to make a case for such undecidability, to assume at least the appearance of respectability.

Minimalism means having been cut off from a guiding star and a Meta-event, a point outside of what happens that explains, legitimates, or gives meaning to what happens. What is outside of what happens is what is not happening. What happens is like a quilt: it has a pattern but it is not going anywhere. When you get to the edge of a quilt you have not found its *telos*, you have just reached the point at which the quilt ends. If you got to the end of what happens, to where it is going, you would have reached the point at which nothing is happening anymore.

What happens can only be taken for itself, for what it is. One can savor what is happening or not, or something in between. What is at issue is not the purpose of what happens but whether one rejoices in what is happening, whether what is happening is a joy or a disaster, or something in between; whether one is a hapless victim of what is happening or whether one is flourishing.

Events knit themselves together in a kind of middle voice action that is neither purely active nor purely passive. Events form patterns, configurations, or structures that may either lift us up or cast us down, or both; that may prove to be a source of joy or a curse, or something in between. Life is an accumulation of such patterns of innumerable microlinks and microconnections, little linkages that weave our days and works together, that strengthen the fabric of life, that support life against the stress of events—or fail to.

Events give joy or they do not (or something in between). But they do not as a whole have a meaning (*sens*, direction). That gives my minimalism a melancholy look, but I beg the reader to be patient with me just a bit longer; I promise an (almost) happy ending. The point lies in the joy or the disaster, in the flourishing or the loss, not in the meaning. The point is not where events are "going," or where we are going with them, because the only place we seem to be going is stellar oblivion. We are, from that point of view, all disasters, lost stars, lost in space.

Astronomy is the most philosophical of all sciences.

Events do not admit of a *Resultat* that explains or legitimates them, but of an *exsultat*, which allows us to rejoice in them.

The point is not the "meaning" of events but rather the *joie de vivre*, the joy of ordinary life, of our days and works, of the finite, immanent, intermediary goals of daily life, the surpassing joy of the day-to-day, of work and companionship, the exultation in the ordinary, which is, after all, what there is. Great Events and surpassing *Übermenschen* are relatively rare—and certainly beyond me.

The Kingdom of God is here, now. Not in the First Beginning or the Other one; not in History or the Spirit; not in the surpassing discharge of some Greco-German *Übermensch* who prides himself on his feeling of distance from ordinary life. The Kingdom of God is found in daily pleasures, in ordinary joys.

Events happen. They happen for better or for worse. There is nothing outside of events that you could accept in exchange for what happens, that would be better than what happens.

Exultation is the joy one takes in what happens, in the patterns that events forge of themselves, the pleasure of events that one savors with fondness, that give deep, quiet, lasting joys—or loud and oft-repeated ones. *Chacun à son goût.* We do not need Greco-Germans to rank-order the order of joys. Let many joys happen. Let them happen with heteromorphic delirium, delight, and multiplicity. Exultation is the particular course of pleasures and pains, joys and sorrows, that flow our way, that arise in the course of events, whatever form they may happen to take.

When events are torn asunder, when the loss is beyond repair, when events leave us in shreds, in "tears," then you suffer a disaster and you lose your lucky star. That is what activates the lines of obligation, what gives obligation a sense of urgency.

It does not take much for the tenuous gossamer web of life to come apart. A stray bullet, a stray chromosome, a stray virus, a wanton cellular division—and the flesh is hopelessly ruined. Events strike a very delicate balance; they form frail, fragile, vulnerable configurations and microconnections. They are easy prey to chance and misfortune, to mis-hap. Joy is sustained on a tissue-thin surface, a tissue of flesh.

To speak of what happens is to give up thinking that events make sense all the way down, that there is some kind of *eidos* behind appearances, some kind of *Geist* or rule or principle with a deep if elusive grip on things, some *logos* or *nous* keeping what happens in order and holding events mightily in its sway. To speak of what happens is to be willing to take events for themselves, to hope for the best, to make the best of them.

To speak of what happens is to give up looking for the Meaning of events, because while events give joy or sorrow they do not, as a whole, have Meaning. While there are numerous meanings *in* events, there is no meaning *to* events overall, no overarching Meaning that is their point, their *logos* or *telos*, their sum and their substance. The sum and substance of events is nothing other than the events themselves.

There is no deep structure that sustains what we believe or cherish, what we savor in life, none at least that we know of. That is my *docta ignorantia*, the product of my research and numerous sabbatical leaves.

You see how minimal are the resources I marshal against Ethics.

Beneath the surface of ordinary life—the surface of productive, functioning, busy lives—there lurks an abyss. Beneath the surface of healthy agent bodies the abyss of flesh stirs, an abyss of vulnerability that can swallow up every joy. The abyss is forced to the surface—by the desperate circumstances in which one lives, by a personal crisis, by a moment that drives us to the rail of life, that forces us to ask what is going on, what is happening. Sometimes a physiological event, a microscopically slight chemical imbalance, hurls someone into an abyss of depression and melancholy, of torment and pain. The bottom can fall out from the world in a thousand ways. That is the disaster, the danger of irreparable loss, the trigger that sets off the networks of obligation.

My concern in these pages is almost exactly the opposite of Heidegger's in *Being and Time*. Heidegger's concern is with people who are so immersed in daily life that they need an exposure to the abyss in order to break the thoughtlessness of their lives and get their active agent life in gear. My concern is with people whose lives are torn to shreds, or nearly so: who have been consumed by the abyss, or nearly so. My interest lies with people so exposed to the abyss by which events are inhabited that they cannot get as far as ordinary life and its ordinary joys and sorrows.[18]

My concern in these pages is almost exactly the opposite of Nietzsche's. Nietzsche looked with distance and disdain upon the small joys and little sorrows of ordinary people. He made everything turn on the massive discharge of force of a great tragic artist, the overwhelming energy of what is great and overflowing. I regard massive discharges of energy with some suspicion, even with fear and trembling, and I am considerably more interested in the fate of ordinary people. I am inclined to let tragic artists fend for themselves. I do not think that life as a whole, including great quantities of suffering, is justified by an Ionian column or a Greek tragedy. Nothing justifies great quantities of suffering; that is what I mean by a disaster.

My concern in these pages is almost exactly the opposite of Hegel's. I do not think it is worth sacrificing a hair on the head of the least of us to advance the cause of the History of Spirit. The History of Spirit—like the History of Being or the *Überfluß* of the *Übermensch*—is a dangerous invention of Greco-Germans who do not blush to let innocent flowers perish for the advancement of their phallosophical phantasies. I take my stand with Johannes Climacus and the lyrical-philosophical treatises against the System, against the History of Being and the History of Spirit, against Ethics and Metaphysics (although I wish all of them well).

Beware of philosophers: they are too much occupied with strong or healthy people, with autonomous agents and aggressive freedoms. They miss the disasters. They pass right over those who are laid low by the cruelty of events. They take no stock of those who cannot get as far as freedom and autonomy or the origin of the work of art. They pay no mind to people who are crushed by what happens, whose lives are not knit together but in shreds, people who are hap-less, who fall victim to what happens. It is these unhappy, hapless, joyless people who call out when obligation happens. Joylessness is a loss, a disaster. There is nothing one can be offered in return for joylessness. The only response that is appropriate, the only response that is called for, is to offer to repair the loss, to lend a hand when the damage threatens to run beyond control, to help restore the possibility of joy, the rhythms of ordinary things. That is what obligation amounts to.

Obligation proceeds on the assumption that what happens is all there is, that there is nothing to legitimate the destruction of what happens, so that the role of obligation is to help restore the joy to what happens, to make exultation possible, or possible again.

Ethics is intended to answer the scandal of deep and utter joylessness, of utter misery, of unspeakable, unwarranted suffering. The idea behind Ethics is to subject the disaster that befalls the child or the deportees to infinite valorization, to treat their fate as absolutely Evil, as Evil incarnate, Evil in itself. Ethics seeks a deep backup for our condemnation of Auschwitz, one that would make it impossible to redescribe it. But it is always possible—to the chagrin and scandal of Ethics—to adopt a Nietzschean idiom in which the Nazis are taken to be wolves or eagles, parts of a cruel but "innocent" economy, in which the cry of the child dies out like an echo in empty space, in which the smoke of Shulamith dissipates in the air, in which events move on and everything is forgotten. Ethics is intended to counter the abysmal thought that everything is innocent, that there is a dumb anonymity at the heart of things, that the fate of the deportees is absorbed without remainder into what Nietzsche calls "this mighty realm of the great cosmic stupidity."[19] Ethics wants to find the infinity of the personal at the core of events —that is Levinas, that is Ethics—but instead finds itself up against the anonymity of the *es gibt*. Ethics requires infinity of some kind, if not the infinity of the Law, which is instantiated in the person (Kant), then the infinity of the person (Other), which is the Law (Levinas).

Ethics is piety. It cannot abide the impious thought that events happen, the simplicity, the scandal, the asceticism of the thought that events happen, and that the sources of joylessness and misery go unpunished. The sworn enemy of Ethics is the anonymity and innocence by which things are inhabited.

But we who have had the impiousness to take our stand against Ethics, which means to take a stand between Nietzsche and Ethics, between Evil and the Innocence of Becoming, we must confess to having no cosmic backups for our condemnation of Auschwitz. That is our embarrassment and scandal. We have to live with the anonymity that insinuates itself into obligations. But if it is not possible to expel anonymity with infinity, it is at least possible to *defy* the anonymity of the *es gibt* and its cosmic dice game and to attach oneself, almost blindly, with a hypervalorization, with a hyperbolic valorization, to proper names. My stand against Ethics—but for obligation —comes down to taking a finite but hyperbolic stand—without Infinity and its assurances—on behalf of restoring joy and the possibility of exultation. I embrace justice, the jewgreek myth of justice, the hyperbolic emphasis, the conscious exaggeration, the stress and hyperstress on justice—for the least among us, for the widow and the man with the withered hand—the salutary jewgreek savoring of the singularity of the *me onta*. I try to be prepared to face the worst, to deal with the abysmal thought that if you probe deeply enough you will find, at the heart of obligation, the mute anonymity of *das 'es,'* the raw givenness of obligation, the fact, as it were. *Es gibt*, there is, obligation. That is all. Obligation happens in the face, in the facelessness, of Anaximander's anonymous cosmic justice, the *dike* of Nietzsche's cosmic dice game. Obligation rises up as an anarchic, hyperbolic resistance to this *dike*, taking sides with the singularities that come-to-be and pass away in this Greek agonistics.

Justitia fiat, coelum ruat.

The eagles of philosophy soar over disasters, lifting them up and putting them in larger relief, while the jewgreek heroes of obligation, who never leave the ground, hasten instead to their relief *(relève)*. Either way, the stars play heedlessly overhead.

Obligations happen for the while that they happen and then fade away. That is all there is to them. But that is enough. They do not need to last forever. Obligations require proper names, not, *pace* Lacoue-Labarthe, sacred, everlasting names,[20] nor, *pace* Levinas, infinite ones. If Ethics needs Sacred or Infinite names, obligation is willing to get along with simple, proper names. Obligations happen with or without sacred names, with or without the Infinite. To follow the way of obligation means to be stirred by the appeals, to answer the calls of lowly proper names, of what is laid low. The right response to what is laid low is not the invocation of a sacred name but offering relief, lending a hand. Without why. Because. Because flesh is flesh, because flesh calls to flesh, because to promote flourishing and joy, in particular that of the least among us, of the *me onta*, is its own form of life— *pace* Nietzsche.

Flesh flourishes—or it does not—under starless skies, and then it goes under, leaving its memory behind in faded traces on weather-worn stones.

But for the while that it flourishes, for the while that flesh is flesh, flesh calls and makes its needs felt, and the needs of flesh are all you need for obligation.

To say *"es gibt/il y a/*it gives" obligation is to situate obligation within an impersonal "it." The "it" is not an entity but the pregiven, encompassing, impersonal horizon of the "it is," "it happens." The "impersonal" is not the opposite of the personal, its opposing genus or antagonistic type, but rather the encompassing matrix and ever-present horizon of the personal, like the night on either side of the day. It is that from which the personal arises and to which the personal returns. Dusk to dusk. Dust to dust. *Cendres des morts: il y a là les cendres. Lethe* to *lethe*, to cite another Heidegger.

By the personal I do not have in mind any grand metaphysical gesture, anything transcendent or transcendental, infinite or sacred or supersensible, either Being or Otherwise than Being. I am trying to keep the metaphysics to a minimum. I am happy enough to grant that it is mostly a matter of grammar; I do not feel the need for a grand metaphysical backup. I mean, very minimalistically, something that is mostly a matter of phrasing. "You" say; "we" or "I" hear; "he," "she," or "they" are spoken about. Personal phrases happen. There are happenings of a personal kind.

By a person I do not mean an autonomous metaphysical subject but a subject of obligation, something that makes demands on me, that asks for a hand, for the flesh of my hand. A person is a place where obligations happen, where "someone" says "I" to "me," where "you" call upon "me," where "they" call upon "me" or "us." A person is a place where the eyes of the other come over me, overtake me, pulling me up short. From obligations a whole network of interpersonal relations springs up; in persons a whole network of obligations takes root.

Obligations spring up in a void, like grass in the cracks of sidewalks. The personal is a web woven over the impersonal, a filmy, gossamer surface across a dense mass. A name in the midst of namelessness. A bit of light and warmth in the midst of a surrounding darkness and cold, like the window of the house in Trakl's *Winterabend,* lit up within and come upon by the wary traveler or stranger. The person is always the wayfarer, the stranger, like Abraham or Ishmael.

Personal events happen. *Es gibt/il y a/*it gives persons—they, you, we, I —for the while that it gives them, because it gives them, without why. The why sinks into the because, into the bonds that spring up among persons, into the internal connections and inner constellations that they weave among themselves. Obligation is an operation introduced by life to mend its wounds, to let the links of life form their own spontaneous combinations.

For a while, for the while that they last. Cut off from the stars above, obligations form their own earthly microconstellations, knitting themselves together across the surface of our little star.

Flesh flickering under a starless sky; the exultations of flourishing flesh; the cries of joy; the calm cadences of quiet conversations among friends; the quiet repose of solitary thought; the laughter of lovers fading into dark, starless nights. Those are all the stars we have, all the stellar direction we are likely to come upon.

An Unscientific Postscript on a Disaster

I conclude, but without the benefit of conclusion, of a closure, lacking the support of a mighty Meta-event to set everything aright. I run the risk of looking like an experienced speaker who, having reached the end of his lecture, is unable to find a way to inform his audience that he has nothing more to say. He shifts from one foot to the other and begins awkwardly to back off the stage, all the while mumbling something inaudible and smiling foolishly, until at last the audience realizes that, as he has now disappeared from view, the lecture must be over.

I have at my disposal only fragments and singularities, which are what Ethics calls "cases." So it is fitting that I bring these remarks to a close not with a grand conclusion but with a fragment, an example, with a bit of a problem—which is big enough, a disaster really—if you are caught up in it, viz., the problem of suicide or self-destruction. This is a problem that interests me for itself, but also because a good deal of what I think about obligations and events, about exultation and damaged lives, converges here and takes a palpable form.

From time to time the abyss shows through, the anonymous void by which we are inhabited breaks out and we are swallowed up, or very nearly. The tenuous links that events form among themselves give way. We are driven to the edge, or over the edge. The abyss bleeds through the cracks and crevices of ordinary existence; the void peers out from behind the minimalia of everyday life.

The disaster breaks out and we are gone.

Once again, by the abyss I do not mean anything profound or romantic, any dark and mysterious realm upon which only *Denkers* or *Dichters* may venture, a space reserved for heroes of the void. I say again, I am no Knight of the Infinite Void, no knight at all. Far be it from me, minimalist that I am, to venture out on bottomless, uncharted seas. I have no heart for the Abyss. I leave that to the warriors of Being, the Knights and Admirals of Greco-German phallosophy. As for me, I may be seen rowing timidly some distance behind, looking about for the remnants that may have floated to the surface from disasters in the deep.

The abyss is just another name for what happens for the happening of events, for the fact that events happen because they happen, cut off from the comforts of a deep and reassuring ground. The abyss is the decapitation of events, the loss of the Meta-event. But that can be disturbing.

After all, life is through and through questionable, and to be "disturbed" or to lack "balance" at such moments is not, or is not merely, "psychological." It is life's imbalance, the world's disturbance. We suffer not only from mental imbalance—from the inability to ride out the misfortunes and setbacks of life, to laugh off the limits life sets—but from a certain cosmic disturbance, the world's imbalance.

From the disaster. We are a little mad because the world is a little mad.

I do not think that people who are driven to the edge are getting things all wrong so much as that they are unreasonably right, right to an excess. That is their imbalance. (And mine or ours—for their *déraison* is nothing "other.") They pay too close attention to life. They are scrupulously, infinitely attentive to life and—to their misfortune—they see through its masks, the very structures that have been put in place for our own protection. They do not know how to ignore, forget, forgive, repress, move on. They are too demanding of life and life just cannot deliver on their demands. Life is not whole, not reasonable all the way through; it is no match for their expectations.

After all, things do tremble in insecurity. They happen because they happen. They are not propped up, down deep. If you press events tightly enough, you will not seize hold of some necessity in them; events will instead squeeze right through your fingers.

What happens *is* a little mad—a little violent, a little cruel, a little meaningless, a little hopeless, a little unfair.

A little. But enough. Sometimes too much.

There are people who see that, or who are pushed into seeing that, who are not protected from seeing that, and they will not give themselves or the world a break. They will not let it pass. They will not let up until they force the abyss out of hiding and then the abyss gets the better of them.

Those who dare set foot in the space of self-destruction are not always mired in falsity so much as they have overexposed themselves to the truth, to the cold truth, "harmful and dangerous in the highest degree,"[21] to the sort of knowledge that destroys, to the disaster, that the universe is a comfortless place, that we do not know who we are, not if we are honest, and that we huddle together for warmth in this cold night. Self-destruction seems to me often a function of overexposing oneself to something from which most of us have the prudence to take shelter. It is like staying out too long in sub-zero temperatures, like not having the good sense to come in out of the cold.

One gets pushed to a brink, to the edge of the "why?" which sinks into the because, pushed into the discovery that there is nothing deep to sustain what we most cherish, no guardrails around existence, no net to catch us. The web comes undone, the links are broken, the tissue is torn asunder, the immanent system of meanings collapses. There is no sustaining ground beneath what happens, no transcendent aim beyond what happens to explain it. Events are not going somewhere; they are just happening.

The rhythm of everyday life goes limp and loses its purely immanent sense and interwovenness. The individual is cut loose from the world of her involvements and is set adrift, in a dangerous detachment from work, loved ones, friends and companions, drifting on the edge of the world, flirting with world-lessness. In such a state, events undergo a monstrous magnification. People become inordinately afraid of ordinary perils. They experience as sheer terror the world that most of us take in stride. They become compulsively, obsessively preoccupied with matters that hardly matter to others. They translate ordinary defeats and losses into occasions of massive self-contempt and self-hatred. Adolescents take the ordinary setbacks of teenage life to heart, and what to one young person is just a bad day or a bad date or a bad break, which they greet by a shrug or a laugh, takes on truly tragic dimensions. They are filled with fear, anxiety, insecurity, hopelessness, terror, distrust, disgust, or despair by events that most people brush off or just ignore or at least know how to cope with.

They lose the ability to say "that happens," "such things happen," and instead they succumb to what happens, are destroyed by it. "That happens" is not a magic incantation but a formula for keeping one's balance in the midst of what is happening. The medium-sized bumps and chinks in ordinary life become enormous hurdles, gigantic obstacles that throw them into confusion. What happens in ordinary life undergoes a process of magnification and exaggeration that makes it literally larger than life.

Events become monstrous, de-monstrations of the abyss.

Everyday happenings become occasions of utter terror, of insuperable depression, irredeemable self-hatred. People lose their resiliency, their capacity to rebound, to forget, to move on, to put things behind them, to erase the past, to link up in new ways, to re-create themselves, to laugh at themselves and the follies of being human, to take the course of life in stride. Such people have among other things lost the power of genuine (not hysterical) laughter, which was the wise remedy that Zarathustra recommended in the face of the abyss. The order of rank (the best and the toughest), Nietzsche said, is "almost" determined by the ability to suffer. What truly determines the order of rank is the capacity for laughter, which means for him an ability to affirm the endless cycle of joy and suffering: "I would go so far as to venture an order of rank among philosophers according to the rank of their laughter—rising to those capable of *golden* laughter."[22]

Events have their own particular, limited, internal linkages inside the chain, but they do not have ultimate or transcendent purposes. Events are not on the whole going anywhere. They happen. The little planet will eventually grow cold. The will to power will eventually reconfigure and we will all be quite wiped away. For that is what we are, you and I and all things. *Und nichts außerdem!*

The joys that life has to offer are entirely internal. Life is like a game we enjoy playing. One desires life for the sake of life. "If someone asked life for a thousand years, 'why do you live?'" Meister Eckhart said, "then if it could answer, it would say nothing other than 'I live because I live.'"[23] One is not trying to *get* somewhere with life, and it would make no more sense to offer someone help in getting where life is going—death—than it would to offer a jogger a lift in one's car. In fact there are laws against offering such help.[24] There is nothing that one could trade life *for*, nothing that would make a good exchange for life. It is the very joy one feels in one's work, one's companionships, one's surroundings, one's activities that gives life its savor, or in which the taste of life turns sour. Events are self-justifying, self-legitimizing, and self-sustaining. If we take no joy from events, we take no joy from life, for events make up all the life there is; they are what we mean by life.

But the fabric of events is a delicate knit. It does not take a lot for the momentum of ordinary life to wither, for its fabric to unravel. It can unravel in a moment of tragedy from which one never recovers, even as it can deteriorate slowly over time as love or friendship or the ability to work wane. Ill health, a sudden and irrevocable reverse of fortune, or even ordinary misfortunes that other people deal with handily, can send one spinning into the abyss. There are disasters that drive one to the limit, *in extremis*, beyond the bonds and boundaries of ordinary life. The abyss peers out from behind the cracks of daily life, the way a great ravine becomes visible between the tracks of a railroad if we let ourselves look down. There is nothing deep and firm to sustain us, not if we look down, not if we ask *why?* and demand an ultimate response, a final answer. What sustains the elements of life is only their internal connectedness and inherent worth. When that is shattered—whether by misfortune, terminal illness, or simply by a serotonin imbalance[25]—life is shattered and it is extremely hard and often impossible to knit it back together again. Indeed, too often it is not even knit together to begin with; people never even really get the fabric of ordinary life started, and their lives seem shattered right from the start; they are simply born into desperation and neglect and never escape it.

Despite my recommendation to take up reading tombstones, I am not resurrecting the familiar existentialist line on death or suicide. I have no interest in macho confrontations with the abyss, in heroically hurling myself into a void, in "glamorized masculine anxiety." These heroic, *übermenschlich* ruminations on my impending death are always focused on the meaning of "my" life, "my" death, or taking "my" life. My concern has been all along the alarm sent out by others. My standpoint is that of obligation, of the demands made on us by the fortunes and misfortunes of the other. From the standpoint of obligation, the I is always, structurally, the sane, healthy, well-constituted agent body, while the other is flesh laid low. It is always the "other" who is drawn to or "succumbs" to self-destruction. This is not an aggressive phallic operation, a problem for the "lone phallus," out there all alone, without maternal protection.[26] It is a question of activating the feminine operation, of listening to the alarms that are sounded by other flesh.

Once again, we must beware of the philosophers. Philosophers like Hume too often entertain the illusion that the question of self-destruction concerns rational, autonomous agents deliberating the pros and cons of a course of action, rather the way one deliberates about an investment. That is the suicide of the I, the suicide of an *Aufklärer.*[27] While political suicides may be something like that, or the reasoned suicides of honor in Greece and Rome may have been something like that, the fact of the matter is that acts of self-destruction are usually not acts of reason and phallogocentric lucidity. When they are, so be it. But philosophers are too inclined to think that suicide is simply or even primarily a matter of freedom and reason, whereas a good many acts of self-destruction are hardly exercises in philosophical thinking or existential resoluteness. A good many, perhaps most suicidal people are in a state of ambiguity and undecidability about death, not lucidity. They fear death as much as they fear life; they want life as much as they desire death. Their actions are ambiguous, often inconclusive, steeped in undecidability, usually not meant to be conclusive or unconditional, so that many "successful" (= completed) attempts at suicide are really accidents, and the attempts were a call for help that went too far. Suicidal people are in pain and they are calling upon us to respond.

The gestures of self-destructiveness of the Other are a call for help, alarms sounding, the *glas* of obligation ringing in our ears. What has gone wrong with such lives is that the thousand little links, the microconnections of ordinary life have come unstrung. The complex, sustaining networks of life, the minimalia and the microlinks that make up ordinary life, have collapsed.

But what are we called upon to do? What can one do? What is our responsibility?

There is no "answer," no cognitive solution, to the questions that self-destructive people put. They are, I think, putting questions before which philosophers no less than their analysts (if they can afford one) are struck dumb, the difference being that the philosophers' ignorance comes cheaper. Moreover, self-destructive people do not require an answer so much as companionship. We are all children of the same dark night, inhabited by the same demons, haunted by the same spectres. We are all equally beset by the inscrutability of what happens, and none of us, philosophers or analysts, have a hotline that feeds us special information about the *eidos* or *ousia* or *Geist* or *Wille* that is behind what is happening. No one can lay claim to having the *logos* of the abyss. There are no "professionals" in the field of what happens, just laity in various states of being de-laicized.

Professional "therapists" are not to be construed as people who have the *episteme* that governs these matters. That illusion, which does more harm than good, has been mercilessly exposed by Foucault's histories of madness. Therapists are or should be, on my accounting, people who have professed an allegiance to those who suffer lives of enormous and sometimes unbearable pain. (The "unconscious" is an important notion because it is a source of inestimable pain, not because it offers the occasion for provocative literary theories or because it has the structure of a language—if it does.) Therapists and clinical psychologists and counselors of every stripe belong, on this view, to an ancient but very unscientific jewgreek paradigm, the paradigm of the "healer," people who "drive out devils," usually by "laying on hands." I imagine what is behind such old jewgreek stories is the power of a man or woman of compassion to calm a troubled heart, to take the hand of the troubled one in their hands, literally to lend them a hand, to be on hand. They did not have anything special to say to them or the miraculous power to suspend the laws of nature. They did not know anything special. Who does? But they talked with their troubled friends through long nights or lonely days, hand in hand, flesh in flesh. It is not what they said *(le dit)* that matters but the saying *(le dire)*—and the flesh of their hand. That was the miracle of what they did.

What healing they could do, they did in virtue of the power of companionship and friendship, which awakens the power of the flesh to knit itself back together. The healer tries to reactivate the spontaneous bonds of everyday life, to set in motion once again the process by which life heals itself, to reactivate the growth and formation of the protective tissue of life, the web of flesh, the microconnections that everyday life knits around itself. The healer is a healing presence, a "help," someone who is "there," a voice in a world of silence, compassion in a world that has become merciless, support in a world without grounds. In the matter of obligation, "being-there" means being there for the other, for someone who calls out for help.

We are all fellow travelers on the little star, fellow participants in the same cosmic play. What we have to offer one another is our voice, our healing hand, our laughter, ourselves. The hand heals of itself, because it is a hand, because it is flesh. We all have the hands of healers and we can all heal by laying on hands. Our golden laughter is wiser than any words. That is the feminine operation. It is not a question of finding an answer to the night of truth but of sitting up with one another through the night, of dividing the abyss in half in a companionship that is its own meaning. I follow the excellent advice to put in the place of "the fear and trembling of a paternal Abraham or a solitary Nietzschean subject . . . that of a trembling people, a trembling community."[28]

It is not a question of introducing a solution from without, or from above. Life is healed only by life. There is nothing outside life that one can introduce as a remedy or solution to its sorrows, even as there is nothing outside life that grounds it or founds it or gives it a transcendent sense. The wounds of life can be administered to only by more life, life pressed against life; life in life, hand in hand, siblings of the same dark night.

Even a religious belief in a purpose transcendent *to* life can function only if it takes root *in* life. Faith must be a living faith, a significant form *of* life, a living spirituality, a spiritual life. Faith must knit itself into a rich and immanently rewarding pattern of life. Far be it from me to make trouble for religious faith, I who am a devoted admirer of father Abraham, a devout reader of Magdalena's stories of Yeshua, a lover of jewgreek narratives devoted to flesh and healings, a lover of saints and mystics. I am only trying to draw the parameters within which faith happens. A man or woman of faith is not one who knows nothing of the abyss but rather one who has looked down this abyss and construed it in terms of the traces and stirrings of a loving hand, who finds in the abyss of suffering an infinity, who sees the Other as the trace of the Infinite.[29] Faith is a matter of a radical hermeneutic, an art of construing shadows, in the midst of what is happening. Faith is neither magic nor an infused knowledge that lifts one above the flux or above the limits of our mortality. Faith, on my view, is above all the *hermeneia* that Someone looks back at us from the abyss, that the spell of anonymity is broken by a Someone who stands with those who suffer, which is whey the Exodus and the Crucifixion are central religious symbols. Faith does not, however, extinguish the abyss but constitutes a certain reading of the abyss, a hermeneutics of the abyss. Faith is not a way of escaping what happens, but a way of interpreting it and coming to grips with it.

The Anonymous

What haunts my days and disturbs my sleep is the thought of the anonymous, of cold lunar surfaces or an uninhabited deep, of frozen polar regions inhospitable to life. I lie awake imagining a world that consists of nothing other than a certain cosmic rumble, an incessant, dull, inarticulate roar.

My peace is disturbed by the mercilessness of a certain Nietzscheanism according to which there is no one there, nothing within or beyond the stars, no Aristotelian gods inhabiting them and steering them safely about the heavenly vault, nothing but the charging and the discharging of forces, firing and misfiring. *Und nichts außerdem!* Nietzsche and his delegate Felix Sineculpa have cost me considerable sleep.

Imagine a world in which no one is there. Or in which we are alone. A world without proper names, without names at all.

The discourse on obligation is a treatise on proper names, on the affirmation of "someone," something more or less proper, personal, over and beyond or within the cosmic hum. By "someone" I do not mean anything deep or profound, some permanent presence beneath the flux of time, some transcendental *ich* organizing a complex assembly of faculties, habits, and acts, something Infinite or Sacred or Supersensible. On the contrary, I mean the most fleeting and transient of things, the most tender growth, a flickering light, very delicate and fragile, vulnerable to the elements. I mean the several possibilities of joy or sorrow, of pleasure or pain, of exultation or humiliation, attached to proper names, the memories attached to proper names. By "someone" I mean persons long ago, barely remembered now, their names barely legible on weather-beaten stones. The stuff of memory and stories. I also mean the ones who tell the old stories, who understand that they are themselves the stuff of future stories, who anticipate what they themselves will have become.

Were I able to find the time I would write a book on old cemeteries, and I would cultivate the art of making rubbings to save the names that have been effaced by time. Remember my theory of *Seinsvergessenheit:* people who do such rubbings do more to recall the meaning of Being than all German philosophers combined.

Obligations shatter the silence of anonymity with proper names, if only temporarily, shooting proper names into the night-dark sky like darts of light, like shooting stars, fleeting moments of illumination. We send up small, tiny, limited little infinities into the night, as if there were something Infinite that contracts the vastness of the sky, as if there were an Infinity that shrinks the seas and dwarfs the mountaintops, that makes all of nature bow down.

As if these proper names really were infinite and not themselves moments in the life of the seas and the stars and the mountains, as if they were not woven of the same flesh, the same mortal stuff and fragile flesh as the earth.

As if. As it were. Facts as it were. There are no facts, only interpretations.

Obligations are fleeting, finite victories over the anonymity which is older than us, which is stronger and higher and deeper than us, which is before we are. Obligations are our hyperbolic act of affirming infinite worth, of attaching hyperbolic significance to the least among us, of answering infinite demands, within the frail, finite, fragile bounds of our mortality.

Proper names are our temporary triumphs, and passing protests against the anonymity of *il y a*, against the transciency of *es gibt*, against the namelessness that surrounds us.

Obligations forge the links of "you" and "I" and "we" and "he" and "she," forming little links that spread tenuously across the surface of the little star, weaving a thin tissue of tender, fragile bonds and multiple microcommunities. Obligations form a delicate gossamer surface across the face of the little star, like a thin snowfall in early spring covering the thawing ground, providing just the slightest cover of white, and vulnerable to the first rays of the warming sun.

The anonymous is the incessant rumble of events, while obligation is the event of someone, of something personal in the midst of this inarticulate hum. Events happen anonymously, like the roar of the surf, while obligation is like the cry of a small child who has lost his way on the beach calling for help.

The anonymous is the roar of wind and rain on a dark night, while the personal is the voice of a fair and delicate young boy, shivering in the rain, who would rather die than live without his love.

In the Trakl poem "A Winter Evening,"[30] a traveler comes upon a warmly lit house, an inviting table within, set with bread and wine, visible through the window. The anonymous is the winter night, the stellar cold of the winter sky, the frozen earth, the lifeless, lightless night without, while the house within affirms the realm of the I and you and we and they. The house within a small corner of light, warmth, and companionship in the midst of winter's harshness, a brief respite of relief from pain and of shelter from cold and hunger. The house offers a tenuous, temporary hold against the fierceness of the night.

The snow falls on the house, on the fields around the house, on the churchyard over the hill, on the whole region, covering the whole country.[31] At length the whole earth is covered by the snow, through which, here and there, little houses are barely visible, warmly lit, with tables set with bread and wine, inviting weary travelers to their hospitality, offering welcome to wayfarers of every kind. The traveler comes within and shares the bread, and afterwards tells a story of a delicate young boy she once loved, now dead. Travelers weeping over their joys, laughing over their misery and mortality. The next morning they are on their way again.

We are all becoming shades, shadowy spectres of bygone life, vanishing almost without a trace, except for the memory inscribed in barely legible names on listing tombstones.

Flesh clings to flesh in the anonymity of the night. The day is a temporary respite from unrelenting night. Night is the mother of us all: an almost perfect anti-Platonism.

The snow falls on the house, on the churchyard beyond the house, on the sea beyond the churchyard, covering the whole earth, covering the proper names on gravestones and houseplates, covering the whole island, the whole world. Tombstones barely visible through the snow, listing and crooked, the name of young Michael Furey, of all the dead, hardly legible through the drifting snow:

> Yes the newspapers were right: snow was general all over Ireland. It was falling on every part of the dark central plain, on the treeless hills, falling softly upon the Bog of Allen and, farther westward, softly falling into the dark mutinous Shannon waves. It was falling, too, upon every part of the lonely churchyard on the hill where Michael Furey lay buried. It lay thickly drifted on the crooked crosses and headstones, on the spear of the little gate, on the barren thorns. His soul swooned slowly as he heard the snow falling faintly through the universe and faintly falling, like the descent of their last end, upon all the living and the dead.[32]

Obligations happen, bonds are formed, tables are set, while the earth is covered in cold white snow, while the surf roars, while the stars dance their nightly dance, while worms inch their way toward forgotten graves.

(In the Place of a) Conclusion

Obligations happen, like faint flickers of flesh against a black expanse, lights against a great night.

Obligations happen; they happen because they happen; they happen for the while that they happen. Then the cosmos draws a few more breaths, the little star grows cold, and the animals made of flesh have to die.

The snow falls faintly through the universe on all the living and the dead.

Life is justified not as an aesthetic phenomenon but as a quasi-ethical one.

Notes

1. See also chapter 5, "Judging Events," in my *Against Ethics: Contributions to a Poetics of Obligation with Constant Reference to Deconstruction* (Bloomington: Indiana University Press, 1993).

2. You can hear the "minimalism" of "events" in the English expression "What's happening?" or the German *"Was geschieht?"*—particularly if you take it as an actual question and not simply a turn of phrase. Of itself, the question produces a stall, a momentary paralysis or freeze, which is a function of its vacuous (minimalist) open-endedness; and it invites an equally open-ended, vacuous, sometimes even slightly embarrassed response: "Not much." *"Nichts neues."* The question needs a schema, a horizon or a framing, in order to get going.

3. Martin Heidegger, *Being and Time*, trans. E. Robinson and J. MacQuarrie (New York: Harper & Row, 1962), §62, p. 358.

4. I argue this in "Husserl, Heidegger and the Question of a Hermeneutic Phenomenology," *Husserl Studies* 1 (1984): 157–78.

5. Jacques Derrida, *The Truth in Painting*, trans. Geoffrey Bennington and Ian McLeod (Chicago: University of Chicago Press, 1987), pp. 326–27.

6. Before knights of faith everywhere launch their assaults, let me hasten to assure such readers that I am not out to undermine faith but to set forth the parameters and uncircumventable limits within which practices like faith take root. As with everything else, *différance* is the condition of im/possibility of faith. I hope on another occasion to take up the question of faith in a postmodern setting. My impiety is hardly meant to exclude faith, I who am a heteromorphic lover of many possibilities, especially jewgreek ones, but to point to the possibility of an impious form of faith, one which is sensitive to the rights of those without faith, the others of faith.

7. See Emmanuel Levinas, *Otherwise Than Being, or, Beyond Essence*, trans. Alphonso Lingis (Pittsburgh: Duquesne University Press, 1998), pp. 148–49, 150 ("I know not from where"); p. 156 ("apex"); p. 183 ("heartrending bustling"); p. 185 (he, *il*).

8. I have all along been running together Heideggerian "events" and Lyotardian "events" and the resources of the English word "events" in the hope of demystifying and demythologizing the *Ereignis*, of keeping both metaphysics and meta-metaphysics to a minimum.

9. See my *Radical Hermeneutics: Repetition, Deconstruction, and the Hermeneutic Project* (Bloomington: Indiana University Press, 1987), chapters 6–7, for a more careful deconstruction of Heidegger's History of Being.

10. See my study *The Mystical Element in Heidegger's Thought* (New York: Fordham University Press, 1986), chapter 2.

11. GA 65, *Beiträge*, p. 8 *et passim*.

12. This and the next three passages from Heidegger are taken from *Der Satz vom Grund*, p. 188 (my translation). See English trans., *The Principle of Reason*, trans. Reginald Lilly (Bloomington: Indiana University Press, 1991), p. 113.

13. The idea of an "epoch" of Being is itself a violent simplification, too forceful a gathering together of what happens into the unity of a well-ordered *legein* or *epochein*. It is impossible to believe that the complexity of what happens in an "epoch" can be so simplified. Such a notion is unadorned metanarratival mythologizing.

14. Martin Heidegger, *Poetry, Language, Thought*, trans. Albert Hofstadter, 1st ed. (New York: Harper & Row, 1971), p. 4.

15. Véronique Marion Foti, *Heidegger and the Poets: Poiesis/Sophia/Techne* (New Jersey: Humanities Press International, 1992), p. xix.

16. *Being and Time*, p. 271.

17. *Being and Time*, p. 435.

18. My thanks to Michael Thompson for bringing this feature of *Being and Time* home to me.

19. *Daybreak*, No. 130, pp. 129–31.

20. "For what are lacking, now and for the foreseeable future, are names, and most immediately 'sacred names,' which in their various ways governed, and alone governed, the space (public or other) in which ethical life unfolded" (Philippe Lacoue-Labarthe, *Heidegger, Art and Politics*, trans. Chris Turner [Oxford: Blackwell, 1990], p. 33).

21. See Friedrich Nietzsche, *Beyond Good and Evil*, trans. R. J. Hollingdale (Baltimore: Penguin Books, 1972), No. 39, p. 50.

22. *Beyond Good and Evil*, No. 294, p. 199. Nietzsche was never so right as when he talked in terms of laughter. This is the most affirmative and benign version of the order of rank, in no small part because he was talking about "my" suffering, not the other's. The fault lies only in Nietzsche's intractable inclination to rank-order

people, as if he had either the right or the means to do so, instead of letting people be. To translate Nietzsche's point into an empirical example, George Colt records a case of a person who called a suicide prevention center and who upon getting a recorded message instead of a counselor burst into laughter at the absurdity of the situation. That burst of laughter burst the tension and the crisis. The laughter was salvific. See George Howe Colt, *The Enigma of Suicide* (New York: Simon and Schuster, 1991), pp. 304–305. Colt offers a helpful, jargon-free, and comprehensive survey of the question of suicide that includes numerous and quite illuminating case studies of suicides.

23. For texts and an exposition, see Caputo, *The Mystical Element in Heidegger's Thought*, pp. 122–24.

24. Whence the recent controversy concerning "Dr. Death" (Jack Kevorkian), a physician who has devised a technology to assist people in taking their own lives, and the controversy surrounding Derek Humphry's *Final Exit*. Humphry is the founder of the Hemlock Society, a group dedicated to making information available on the means of committing suicide.

25. There is growing evidence of correlation between suicide and an insufficiency of a neurotransmitter called serotonin; see Colt, *Enigma of Suicide*, pp. 203–205.

26. My thanks to Drucilla Cornell for "glamorized masculine anxiety" and "the lone phallus," formulations which I have neither the will nor the wit to improve. I can only add a little supplement, that when I was a child I thought it was "the long Ranger rides again."

27. See Hume's essay "On suicide" in *Essays Moral, Political and Literary* (London: Oxford University Press, 1963).

28. Verena Andematt Conley, "Communal Crisis," in *Community at Loose Ends*, ed. by the Miami Theory Collective (Minneapolis: University of Minnesota Press, 1991), p. 68.

29. In my view, Levinas describes the dynamics of faith as well as anybody. Indeed, I think that what Levinas provides is above all a metaphysics of the religious, of faith, which organizes faith around the trace of the Infinite Other. I myself take the present work to be, among other things, a background for a possible account of faith; and I take the notion of *différance* as a propaedeutic to a theory of faith.

30. I am intentionally offering an alternate gloss to Heidegger's commentary on this poem in *Poetry, Language, Thought*, pp. 189ff.

31. I am at this point running Trakl's poem together with James Joyce's short story "The Dead" in *Dubliners* (New York: Penguin Books, 1967), pp. 175–223. I am intentionally running together Trakl with an Irish novelist much favored by Derrida.

32. *Dubliners*, p. 223. "One by one they were all becoming shades" (p. 222).

John D. Caputo: Selected Bibliography

Books

More Radical Hermeneutics: On Not Knowing Who We Are. Bloomington: Indiana University Press, forthcoming.

Edited, with Michael J. Scanlon, *God, the Gift, and Postmodernism.* Bloomington: Indiana University Press, 1999.

Deconstruction in a Nutshell: A Conversation with Jacques Derrida. New York: Fordham
University Press, 1997.
The Prayers and Tears of Jacques Derrida: Religion without Religion. Bloomington: Indi-
ana University Press, 1997.
*Against Ethics: Contributions to a Poetics of Obligation with Constant Reference to Decon-
struction.* Bloomington: Indiana University Press, 1993.
Demythologizing Heidegger. Bloomington: Indiana University Press, 1993.
With James Marsh and Merold Westphal, *Modernity and Its Discontents.* New York:
Fordham University Press, 1992.
Radical Hermeneutics: Repetition, Deconstruction and the Hermeneutic Project. Blooming-
ton: Indiana University Press, 1987.
Heidegger and Aquinas: An Essay on Overcoming Metaphysics. New York: Fordham Uni-
versity Press, 1982.
The Mystical Element in Heidegger's Thought. Athens: Ohio University Press, 1978.
Revised, paperback edition with a new introduction. New York: Fordham Uni-
versity Press, 1986.

Chapters in Edited Volumes and Journal Articles

"Reason, History and a Little Madness: Towards an Ethics of the Kingdom." In *Ques-
tioning Ethics: Contemporary Debates in Philosophy,* ed. Richard Kearney and Mark
Dooley. New York: Routledge, 1999.
"God Is Wholly Other—Almost." In *The Otherness of God,* ed. Orrin F. Summerell.
Charlottesville: University of Virginia Press, 1998.
"Dreaming of the Innumerable: Derrida, Drucilla Cornell, and the Dance of Gen-
der." In *Derrida and Feminism: Recasting the Question of Woman,* ed. Ellen K. Feder,
Mary C. Rawlinson, Emily Zakin. New York: Routledge, 1997.
"A Community without Truth: Derrida and the Impossible Community." *Research in
Phenomenology* 26 (1996).
"Heidegger, Kierkegaard and the Foundering of Metaphysics." In *International Kier-
kegaard Commentary,* vol. 6: *Fear and Trembling and Repetition,* ed. Robert L. Per-
kins. Macon, Ga.: Mercer University Press, 1993.
"In Search of the Quasi-Transcendental: The Case of Derrida and Rorty." In *Working
through Derrida,* ed. Gary B. Madison. Evanston: Northwestern University Press,
1993.
"On Not Knowing Who We Are: Madness, Hermeneutics and the Night of Truth."
In *Foucault and the Critique of Institutions,* ed. John D. Caputo and Mark Yount.
University Park, Pa.: Pennsylvania State University Press, 1993.
"How to Avoid Speaking of God: The Violence of Natural Theology." In *The Prospects
for Natural Theology,* ed. Eugene Thomas Long. Washington, D.C.: Catholic Uni-
versity of America Press, 1992.
"Spirit and Danger." In *Ethics and Danger,* ed. Arleen B. Dallery and Charles E. Scott.
Albany: State University of New York Press, 1992.
"Mysticism and Transgression: Derrida and Meister Eckhart." *Continental Philosophy*
2.24–39 (1989).
"An Ethics of Dissemination." In *The Ethics of the Other,* ed. Charles E. Scott. Albany:
State University of New York Press, 1989.
"On Mystical and Other Phenomena." In *Phenomenology in America,* ed. Calvin O.
Schrag. Dordrecht: Reidel, 1988.
"Beyond Aestheticism: Derrida's Responsible Anarchy." *Research in Phenomenology*
18 (1988).

"Derrida: A Kind of Philosopher." *Research in Phenomenology* 17 (1987).

"The Economy of Signs in Husserl and Derrida: From Uselessness to Full Employment." In *Deconstruction and Philosophy,* ed. John Sallis. Chicago: University of Chicago Press, 1987.

"Telling Left from Right: Hermeneutics, Deconstruction, and the Work of Art." *Journal of Philosophy* 83 (1986).

"Three Transgressions: Nietzsche, Heidegger, Derrida." *Research in Phenomenology* 15 (1985).

"'Supposing Truth to Be a Woman . . . ': Heidegger, Nietzsche, Derrida." *Tulane Studies in Philosophy* 32 (1984).

"Kant's Ethics in Phenomenological Perspective." In *Kant and Phenomenology,* ed. Thomas M. Seebohm and Joseph J. Kockelmans. Washington, D.C.: University Press of America, 1984.

"The Thought of Being and the Conversation of Mankind: The Case of Heidegger and Rorty." In *Hermeneutics and Praxis,* ed. Robert Hollinger. Notre Dame: Notre Dame University Press, 1985.

"Heidegger's God and the Lord of History." *New Scholasticism* 57 (1983).

"Fundamental Themes in Eckhart's Mysticism." *Thomist* 42 (1978).

"The Question of Being and Transcendental Phenomenology: Husserl and Heidegger." *Research in Phenomenology* 7 (1977).

11

In-the-Name-of-the-Father

The Law?

WILLIAM J. RICHARDSON

William J. Richardson's monumental work on Heidegger, *Through Phenomenology to Thought*, published in 1974, was a landmark in the rapid development of Heidegger studies in America. His work offered a classic overview of the movement of Heidegger's thought from his early lecture courses prior to *Being and Time* up to his later writings on *Ereignis* and *Gelassenheit* and the problem of technology. Richardson's insight that Heidegger's thought from early to late was not a matter of separate stages but a movement of thinking was embraced by Heidegger himself, who often spoke of the task of thinking as a pathway. Martin Heidegger wrote a preface to Richardson's work that encouraged a generation of continental philosophers in America to focus on the question of their experience as Americans in the age of technology. Among its many contributions, Richardson's work presented an insightful commentary on Heidegger's courses and still to be translated works, setting the stage for the enormous interest in Heidegger's *Collected Works*, which are now being published and translated into English.

Richardson has again been at the forefront more recently, responsible in part for the reception of Lacanian psychoanalysis into the discourse of American continental philosophy. His philosophical orientation has led to the attempt to articulate the relevance of Heidegger to those once popular efforts to delineate an "existential" method of psychoanalytical treatment. After psychoanalytical training with the William Alanson White Institute in New York, Richardson became interested in Lacan's interpretation of Freud, particularly in his claim that Freud's insight was, above all else, an ethical one. This led Richardson to a careful study of Lacan's Seminar VII, *The Ethics of Psychoanalysis*. Along with John P. Muller, Richardson has published *Lacan and Language: A Reader's Guide to the Écrits* and edited *The Purloined Poe: Lacan, Derrida, and Psychoanalytic Reading*. Richardson's principal concern is with questions about the human subject as an ethical subject in the context of the postmodern challenge to its validity. Since the discovery of the unconscious by psychoanalysis opened up a new dimension of the human subject, the focus of Richardson's interest has shifted specifically to the ethics of psychoanalysis itself.

In the essay included here, Richardson argues that any formal ethics must address the issue of the nature of the moral law. For Lacan the primordial law is the law of the symbolic order, i.e., what he calls "the law of the Father." To query the relationship between the law of the Father and the moral law as they relate to the ethical subject, Richardson probes the heart of both Freud's and Lacan's experience.

⋅⊷═◉═◒⊷⋅

The Court wants nothing from you. It receives you when you come and it dismisses you when you go.

— *Franz Kafka,* The Trial

The scene is the darkened, otherwise empty cathedral in Prague. Rain is falling outside. For a moment, there is no other sound:

> The priest had already taken a step or two away from him, but [Joseph K.] cried out in a loud voice. "Please wait a moment." "I am waiting," said the priest. "Don't you want anything from me?" asked K. "No," said the priest. . . . "[But] you are the prison chaplain," said K, groping his way nearer to the priest again. . . . "That means I belong to the Court," said the priest. "So why should I want anything from you? The Court wants nothing from you, it receives you when you come and dismisses you when you go."[1]

The words are familiar: they come from the penultimate chapter of Franz Kafka's landmark novel, *The Trial*. When the conversation began, it was clear that the chaplain was aware of the accusation against K. but unaware of the state of the process. By the end, the chaplain had heard well enough K.'s protestation of innocence but was equally convinced of the hopelessness of his cause. Condemnation, he knew, was inevitable. Execution of the verdict would follow immediately.

Precisely on his thirty-first birthday, one year to the day after the process began, it happened. Toward nine o'clock in the evening, two men in frock coats showed up at his dwelling, and K., already dressed in black, appeared to be waiting for them. Through the city streets and out to the quarry they led him, where they looked for an appropriate place to lay him on the ground to perform the deed, propping his head against a rock. Then one drew out of a sheath concealed under his cloak a long, double-edged butcher's knife that in a grotesque ritual they passed ceremoniously between them over K.'s supine body, as if somehow he were supposed to interrupt them and perform the deed himself. But he "could not completely rise to the occasion." Finally, one of the two grabbed K.'s throat while the other "thrust the knife deep into his heart and turned it there twice." Dying "like a dog," he whispered, as if the shame of it would outlive him. The pity of it was that he was innocent, or so he claimed to the very end.[2]

This strange tale of guilt, innocence, and the Law (concretized here in the Court) that Kafka himself left unfinished, intending that it be destroyed, was nonetheless published posthumously (1925) by his friend, Max Brod, and has challenged interpreters ever since. Some, like George Steiner, find in it an echo of Kafka's Judaic heritage:

> Self evidently Franz Kafka meditates on the Law. It is the original mystery and subsequent application of the Law, of legalism and judgment, which are the essential concern of Talmudic questioning. If, in the Judaic perception, the language of the Adamic [myth] was that of love, the grammars of fallen man are those of the legal code. It is the modulation from one to the other, as commentary and commentary on commentary seek to hammer it out, which is one of the centers of *The Trial*.[3]

Others find in it a more Christian cast, where "the grammars of fallen man" include a faint hope of redemption. As he was about to die:

> [K.'s] gaze fell on the top story of the house adjoining the quarry. With a flicker as of a light going up, the casements of a window there suddenly flew open; a human figure, faint and insubstantial at that distance and that height, leaned abruptly forward and stretched both arms still farther. Who was it? A friend? A good man? Someone who sympathized? Someone who wanted to help? Was it one person only? Or was it mankind? Was there help at hand? Were there arguments in his favor that had been overlooked? . . . He raised his hands and spread out all his fingers.[4]

Others, like Eric Heller, find in it a thorough-going Gnosticism, while still others find nothing religious in it at all: no more than a remarkably prophetic anticipation of the anonymous brutality of the legal system of the Third Reich.[5] These are matters of literary criticism, however, and are best left to literary critics. Yet Kafka's work belongs to us all, and if one chooses to reflect on "The Paradox of the Law," K.'s insights into Law and its paradoxes (he was, after all, a trained lawyer) are so evocative and provocative that it seems legitimate to let him supply a congenial heuristic context within which to interrogate the relation between Law and psychoanalysis as this functions in the desiring (i.e., ethical) subject in the work of Freud and Lacan.

To begin, again the essential story: on the morning of his thirtieth birthday, two strangers come to the apartment of Joseph K., a junior bank officer, to notify him that he is under arrest. They refuse to explain the reason for his arrest, saying only that he would be interrogated. They lead him to another room to be confronted by an inspector, but he, likewise, gives no reason—only that the arrest has been ordered by a higher authority. A few days later K. receives a note telling him to report before the Court for interrogation at a certain address the following Sunday, but without saying when. Arriving at the address, he finds only an apparently empty warehouse. Eventually he finds his way to the fifth floor and meets a washerwoman, who seems to expect him and who directs him to the meeting room, filled with old men wearing badges, where the judge tells him he is one hour and ten minutes *late*. He soon harangues the Court on the injustice of its methods and stomps out after refusing to have anything more to do with the process. After waiting a whole week expecting another summons, K. returns to the meeting hall on his own initiative to find only the washerwoman there. She regrets that the Court is not in session but assures him that it was only a lower body anyway; if one were acquitted by this Court it meant little, because a higher Court might very well rearrest the prisoner on the same charge. Eventually, K.'s uncle recommends hiring an advocate who, in fact, stays in bed most of the time and, after several months, does nothing but think about writing a petition in his name. Finally, in desperation, K. consults the portrait painter to the Court, Titorelli by name. Titorelli tells K. he can hope for little: no one is ever really acquitted and sometimes cases can be prolonged indefinitely.

It is at that point that the bank asks K. to give a tour of the cathedral to a visiting client from Italy, who, in fact, never shows up—perhaps because of the rainstorm that rages outside. It is then, in the darkened, empty cathedral, that K. notices the solemn figure, robed in black, ascend a pulpit as if to deliver a sermon. "Joseph K.," calls the priest:

> "You are Joseph K.?" said the priest. . . . "You are an accused man. . . . I am the prison chaplain. . . . I had you summoned here. . . . You are held to be guilty. Your case will perhaps never get beyond a lower Court. Your guilt is supposed, for the present, at least, to have been proved." "But I am not guilty," said K.; "it's a mistake. And, if it comes to that, how can any man be called guilty? We are all simply men here, one as much as the other." "That's true," said the priest, "but that's how all guilty men talk."[6]

Guilt, guilt! But guilt for what? Notice that neither the priest nor K. seems to know. More important, K. does not ask—he simply protests his innocence. Soon the priest descends from the pulpit, and the two engage in a conversation that, if not warm, is at least professionally courteous. Finally, the priest, in order to acquaint K. with the nature of the Law, narrates to him, from the writings that serve as preface to the Law, one of Kafka's most famous parables:

> Before the Law stands a door-keeper. To this door-keeper there comes a man from the country who begs for admittance to the Law. But the door-keeper says that he cannot admit the man at the moment. The man, on reflection, asks if he will be allowed, then, to enter later. "It is possible," answers the door-keeper, "but not at this moment." Since the door leading into the Law stands open as usual and the door-keeper steps to one side, the man bends down to peer through the entrance. When the door-keeper sees that, he laughs and says: "If you are so strongly tempted, try to get in without my permission. But note that I am powerful. And I am only the lowest door-keeper. From hall to hall, keepers stand at every door, one more powerful than the other. And the sight of the third man is already more than I can stand." These are difficulties which the man from the country has not ex-

pected to meet [think of the tortuous process of a long analysis]; the Law, he thinks, should be accessible to every man and at all times, but when he looks more closely at the door-keeper in his furred robe, with his huge pointed nose and long thin, Tartar beard, he decides that he had better wait until he gets permission to enter. The door-keeper gives him a stool and lets him sit down at the side of the door. There he sits waiting for days and years. . . . In the first years he curses his evil fate aloud; later, as he grows old, he only mutters to himself. He grows childish, and since in his prolonged study of the door-keeper he has learned to know even the fleas in his fur collar, he begs the very fleas to help him and to persuade the door-keeper to change his mind. Finally his eyes grow dim and he does not know whether the world is really darkening around him or whether his eyes are deceiving him. But in the darkness he can now perceive a radiance that streams inextinguishably from the door of the Law. Now his life is drawing to a close. Before he dies, all that he has experienced during the whole time of his sojourn condenses in his mind into one question, which he has never yet put to the door-keeper. He beckons the door-keeper, since he can no longer raise his stiffening body. The door-keeper has to bend far down to hear him, for the difference in size between them has increased very much to the man's disadvantage. "What do you want to know now?" asks the door-keeper, "you are insatiable." "Every-one strives to attain the Law," answers the man, "how does it come about, then, that in all these years no one has come seeking admittance but me?" The door-keeper perceives that the man is nearing his end and his hearing is failing, so he bellows in his ear: "No one but you can gain admittance through this door, since this door was intended only for you. I am now going to shut it."[7]

Notice that the Law here remains *the* Law, with an absolute, quasi-transcendent character. Yet it is not, strictly speaking, something "universal," i.e., equally accessible to all. Access to it is unique to every individual. K. and the chaplain discuss the parable at length, K. maintaining that the door-keeper deceived the man from the country by failing to tell him the truth from the beginning. The chaplain denies deception but adds: "[I]t is not necessary to accept everything as true, one must only accept it as necessary."[8] The Law, then, is not necessarily "true," but it *is* truly necessary. It is at this point that the chaplain turns in frustration to leave, and K. asks: "Don't you want anything more from me?" "No . . . I belong to the Court," comes the answer. "So why should I want anything from you. . . . The [Law]/Court receives you when you come and it dismisses you when you go."[9] There is nothing else to say!

What may be inferred from all this that might clarify the role of the Law from the perspective of psychoanalysis? Without going any further into an easily expandable interpretation of Kafka, I take him to be suggesting that the Law condemning Joseph K., despite his denial of culpability, is neither a civil-socio-political one that could serve as a paradigm for Nazi totalitarianism, nor a religious one (whether Judaic, Christian, or Gnostic) that could hold him guilty of some unspecified moral transgression. It is a Law that functions on a level deeper than consciousness can disclose, inscribed in Joseph K.'s being human as such, and it is from this fundamental

Law that other laws in one way or other derive their meaning. In psychoanalysis, it is with this Law that the desiring subject must fundamentally deal, it is here that the ethical question is most radically raised. I propose to consider the nature of this Law first as Freud understands it, then as Lacan understands it, and to conclude with two remarks of my own.

⋯⊨◉⊫⋯

To be sure, the term "law" is used loosely in Freud and has been taken to refer to such generalized phenomena as the "pleasure principle" or his basic theory of sexual development. More fundamentally, however, and more precisely, we may take the most basic Law for Freud to be that of the oedipal structure of every human being, whose principal moral injunction is the prohibition of incest. Forced to account for a phenomenon that he had discovered very early in his own self-analysis and confirmed over and over in clinical experience with patients, Freud finally, in good Platonic fashion, fabricated his own myth to explain it. It is the myth of the Father of the primal horde that, without any scientifically anthropological evidence to justify the hypothesis, has nonetheless become part of the phylogenetic strain. No need to repeat the myth here, certainly, except, perhaps, to underline the consequences for the sons who murder the Father and for the sons upon sons that come after them: incestuous desire remains in the progeny and is only scotched, not killed, by the prohibiting taboo; more important for us, the sons' love/hate/resentment toward the Father abides with remorse for killing him, thus compounding the unconscious burden of guilt, the unpayable debt *(Schuld)* that, in a sort of parody of the religious conception of original sin, passes from generation to generation. How the incest taboo combined with the taboo against killing the totem animal (representing the Father) expanded into a conception of God and into a taboo against fratricide (eventually into the interdiction of murder)—all this belongs to the lore by which Freud, on the basis of the myth, accounts for the origins of both civilization and culture.[10] What historians consider to be the origins of Law, whether these be mythical (e.g., Aeschylus's sixth century B.C. account in the *Oresteia*),[11] cultural (e.g., the Code of Hammurabi, dating [we are told] from the eighteenth century B.C.)[12] or religious (e.g., the Decalogue and the Law of Moses in the Bible's book of Exodus, dating probably from the twelfth century B.C.)[13] derive from subsequent (and much different kinds of) sources. Whatever is to be said for traditional myths, Freud's construction is a characteristically modern one. "In truth," Lacan remarks later, "this myth is nothing other than something that is inscribed in the clearest of terms in the spiritual reality of our time, namely, the death of God."[14]

An oedipal interpretation of Kafka's work in general and of *The Trial* in particular, given the notoriety of his relationship to the man who begot him, Hermann Kafka, revealed in the famous *Letter to His Father* (1919), is not difficult to make.[15] There the unequal struggle between father and son is manifest from the beginning:

I was, after all, weighed down by your mere physical presence. I remember, for instance, how we often undressed in the same bathing hut. There was I, skinny, weakly, slight; you strong, tall, broad. Even inside the hut I felt a miserable specimen, and what's more, not only in your eyes but in the eyes of the whole world, for you were for me the measure of all things. But then when we stepped out of the bathing hut before all the people, you holding me by my hand, a little skeleton, unsteady, barefoot on the boards, frightened of the water, incapable of copying your swimming strokes, which you, with the best of intentions, but actually to my profound humiliation, always kept showing me, then I was frantic with desperation and at such moments all my bad experiences in all spheres fitted magnificently together.[16]

In *The Trial*, to be sure, we do not find the cruelty of *The Judgment*, where a father condemns his son to die,[17] or of *Metamorphosis*,[18] where he mortally wounds the son with an apple, or of *Amerika*,[19] where he brutally exiles the son to an uncertain fate. Nor do we sense the bitterness of the son's desire to kill in return, as *In the Penal Colony*, where there is question of an exquisitely designed torture instrument that inflicts a slow and agonizing death by stitching the name of the crime in the victim's flesh through a mechanism using needles of steel.[20] In *The Trial*, the father has been abstracted, generalized, and depersonalized into a heartless, anonymous Court of Law that "wants nothing from you. It receives you when you come and it dismisses you when you go." But the import is clear: "My writing was all about you; all I did there, after all, was to bemoan what I could not bemoan upon your breast."[21] Thus, by the time Kafka turned to writing, he says, "I had lost my self-confidence where you were concerned, and in its place had developed a boundless sense of guilt. (In recollection of this boundlessness I once wrote of someone, accurately [e.g., at the end of *The Trial*]: '[It was] as if the shame of it must outlive him')."[22]

For Kafka, then, the Law that permeated his very being may be thought in Freudian terms as the Law of the oedipal father. The purely sexual aspects of the interpretation (from his relation with his mother through the failed attempts at marriage to the chaplain's reproach in *The Trial* ("you cast about too much for outside help, especially from women")[23] are perfectly coherent with this hypothesis but cannot be elaborated here. I should add, however, that some critics see in this scenario not only the theme of an oedipal destiny but a certain "existential" quality, according to which the story unfolds as a sequence of choices that K. makes that reveal who he is. This suggests that if K. dies "like a dog," that is because he "chose" to not ask the right question in the first place: instead of proclaiming his innocence, he might have faced up to the allegation of his guilt by asking about the reason for it.[24] I shall return to this.

But is the Freudian Law of the oedipal father as exemplified in Franz Kafka *the* Law of *the* Father as Lacan uses that expression in his much celebrated "return to Freud"? Not exactly—there is a difference. After seventeen years of preoccupation with what he came to call the "imaginary" (i.e., image-bound) dimension of the analytic experience, Lacan begins to talk about "Law" only after discovering in the early fifties how Lévi-Strauss had gone about discovering the "laws" of Cultural Anthropology by adopting the methods for discovering the "laws" of General Linguistics as first proposed in the work of Ferdinand de Saussure and developed by his followers. Thus, in the famous "Rome Discourse" of 1953 (some call it the *magna charta* of his thought), entitled "The Function and Field of Speech and Language in Psychoanalyis,"[25] Lacan observes:

> No one is supposed to be ignorant of the Law; this somewhat humorous formula taken direct from our Code of Justice nevertheless expresses the truth in which our experience is grounded, and which our experience confirms. No man is actually ignorant of it, since the Law of man has been the Law of language since the first words of recognition presided over the first gifts. . . . [T]hese gifts, their act and their objects, their erection into signs, and even their fabrication, were so much a part of speech that they were designated by its name.[26]

The gifts, Lacan claims, involved above all the exchange of women and were governed by the laws of marriage ties that, to subsequent social anthropologists, were discernible in terms of a logic of numerical combinations of which the participants would be totally unconscious.[27] "The primordial Law is therefore that which in regulating marriage ties superimposes the kingdom of culture on that of a nature abandoned to the Law of mating. The prohibition of incest is merely its subjective pivot. . . . This Law, then, is revealed clearly enough as identical with an order of language."[28] This is why Lacan can ask (rhetorically): "Isn't it striking that Lévi-Strauss, in suggesting the implication of the structures of language with that part of the social laws that regulate marriage ties and kinship, is already conquering the very terrain in which Freud situates the unconscious?"[29] There in a nutshell is the reason for Lacan's fundamental claim that "the unconscious [discovered by Freud] is structured in the most radical way like a language."[30] Be that as it may, the whole conception is unified under the figure of fatherhood:

> It is *in the name of the father* that we must recognize the support of the symbolic function which, from the dawn of history, has identified his person with the figure of the Law. This conception enables us to distinguish clearly, in the analysis of a case, the unconscious effects of this function from the narcissistic [i.e., imaginary] relations, or even from the real [i.e., actual but non-representable] relations that the subject sustains with the image and action of the [concrete] person who embodies it.[31]

Note that the identification of the symbolic function with the notion of "father" is a purely contingent one that *de facto,* as a matter of (at least Western) history "has identified his person with the figure of the Law."

The Law that is the symbolic function of language, then, is conceived (as early as 1953) in terms of the name "father"—clearly to be distinguished, however, from some imaginary father that one might merely fantasize, or, in Kafka's case, from the actual father, Hermann Kafka, of lived historical experience. This conception of a symbolic order (the term comes from Lévi-Strauss) as identifiable with the name "father" is formalized two years later in Lacan's seminar, *The Psychoses* (1955–56),[32] and summarized in a briefer essay, "On a Question Preliminary to Any Possible Treatment of Psychosis" (1958).[33] Lacan is examining here the nature of psychosis apropos of Freud's analysis of the Schreber case[34] and proposes to think of the essence of psychosis as a failure to gain access to, or as exclusion from (Lacan uses the Freudian word "foreclosure" [*Verwerfung*] of) the symbolic order. To do this, he explains the normal manner of gaining access to it through the achieving of what he calls the "paternal metaphor."

The word metaphor here is obviously a trope of language: he is using it to articulate in purely linguistic terms the initiation of the subject into the symbolic order as an active participant in that Order, in which it has participated passively, of course, since the first moment of its conception. As a trope of language, metaphor signifies the substitution of a signifier for another signifier. In the "paternal metaphor," the substituting signifier is the name "Father," which, as we have seen, designates for Lacan the signifying function as such—the entire symbolic order, understood now as *the* Law of *the* Father, designating *the* Law of all laws. This much is clear enough. But what signifier does this primordial signifier substitute *for* so that it may be called a "metaphor" in the first place? It substitutes for what is understood to be the signifier of what precedes it in the evolution of the infant (*infans:* non-speaking child) up to the moment when it is sufficiently developed to be able to become a speaking subject, i.e., an active participant in the symbolic order, as subject to the Law of the Father.

The matter is difficult for the uninitiated but, reduced to the simplest terms, it comes to this: the infant's initiation into the active use of language takes place at the moment typified by the discovery of the o-o-o and the a-a-a of the *fort/da* experience of Freud's grandson as described in *Beyond the Pleasure Principle*.[35] This signifies as well the beginning of separation from the mother, which means the loss of her as a counterpart with which up to that point the infant has been, at least in some imaginary way, fused. This loss of the mother as imaginary counterpart induces a lack in the infant, a "want" of the mother as an object that has been lost, and this want[ing] of the mother, now lost, becomes the inchoative subject's radical—indeed insatiable (because that object is lost forever)—want[ing], i.e., its desire. What the signifying system (now named "Father," i.e., the Name-of-the-Father) substitutes for, then, is the desire of the mother, the signifier for which, in Lacan's terminology, is the phallus. This means that henceforth the subject's access to the mother, whether as actually another human subject or as lost object, will be possible only through the mediation of language and its signifying chains (Lacan will speak of this in linguistic fashion [to complement his use of "metaphor" here] as the "metonymy" of desire).[36] This moment of induction of the subject into the symbolic order Lacan speaks of as the "splitting" of the subject, i.e., the division in the subject between a conscious dimension of experience as imaginary "ego" and an unconscious dimension where the Other of language, the "subject of the unconscious" (i.e., the unconscious *as* subject) has its say.

Now Lacan also speaks of this entire process of submission by the subject to the symbolic order as the generation of a "debt" with regard to it. Thus in 1953 he tells us: "it is the virtue of the Word [i.e., the whole signifying system] that perpetuates the movement of the Great Debt whose economy Rabelais, in a famous metaphor, extended to the stars themselves."[37] I take this to mean that the Law of the symbolic order for Lacan governs not only the language that speaks humans but the entire physical cosmos as well. It is as if submission to the symbolic order implied an indebtedness: something owed, some kind of lack that the subject is responsible for paying off, if only by obedience to the Law. The terminology returns in an odd way in 1958 when Lacan is focusing on Freud's tendency to conjoin the themes of the father and death:

> How, indeed, could Freud fail to recognize such an affinity, when the necessity of his reflection led him to link the appearance of the signifier of the Father, as author of the Law, with death, even to the murder of the Father—thus showing that if this murder is the fruitful moment of debt through which the subject binds himself for life to the Law, the symbolic Father is, in so far as he signifies this Law, the dead Father.[38]

I take this to mean that Lacan clearly wants to identify the symbolic order, under the name Father, with the dead (murdered) Father of the Freudian myth and somehow make equivalent the debt of the sons toward their dead Father with the debt of the subject toward the symbolic order. But how is this possible? The debt of murdering sons toward a murdered Father (e.g., the Menendez brothers) is essentially a moral debt. The debt of the subject toward the symbolic order can only be a symbolic (i.e., structural) one, born of the subject's dependence upon this order as a consequence of its ineluctable finitude. It is paid off, I presume, simply by compliance with this Order. Recalling that "debt" in German would be *Schuld*, i.e., "guilt," we are facing here the question of how to evaluate Joseph K.'s debt, i.e., indebtedness to a Law before a Court that accuses him of a guilt of which he is unaware and which he steadfastly denies. What kind of debt is at stake here?

The whole problem of Law is lifted to another level of refinement in Lacan's Seminar VII, *The Ethics of Psychoanalysis* (1959–60),[39] four years after the seminar *Psychoses*. Here the issue is not a general ethics that is applied to psychoanalytic problems, as a business or medical ethics might do for each respective discipline, but the ethics of the process as such: what *ought* it be/ do in order to be true to itself. For Lacan, the task of psychoanalysis is to help the analysand to discern "the relationship between action and the desire that inhabits it":[40]

> If analysis has a meaning, desire is nothing other than that which supports an unconscious theme, the very articulation of that which roots us in a particular destiny, and that destiny demands insistently that the debt be paid,

and desire keeps coming back, keeps returning, and situates us once again in a given track, the track of something that is specifically our business.[41]

And it is because we know better than those who went before how to recognize the nature of desire, which is at the heart of this experience, that a reconsideration of ethics is possible, that a form of ethical judgment is possible, of a kind that gives this question the force of a Last Judgment: Have you acted in conformity with the desire that is in you?[42]

[That is why], from an analytic point of view, the only thing of which one can be guilty is of having given ground relative to (céder sur) one's desire.[43]

So far, so good. But where is the Law in all this? What Law governs desire? The answer is loud and clear: the Law of the symbolic order; for it is to this Law that the subject, through its splitting, submits when initiated into active participation in the functioning of language; it is this Law that through the metonymy of signifying chains mediates the subject's want of the lost object. But the lost object (the imaginary fusion with the mOther) is gone—gone forever; it can never be regained through symbolic structures. The *dictio* of language *inter*-venes between desire and its object (the irretrievably lost "fusion" with the mOther), making access to the lost object impossible; and it is *this* impossibility that constitutes the Law's inter-*diction* of incest. It is in this sense that, according to a famous homophony, the "Name" of the Father (*Nom du Père*) and the "No" of the Father (*Non du Père*) are but one.

Whereas for Freud, then, the fundamental human desire is for incest, and the primordial Law constituting both morality and culture is the prohibition of it,[44] for Lacan the fundamental desire is for the lost object, and the Law that inter-dicts incest is not a moral injunction but the simple fact of structural impossibility: "It is to the extent that the function of the pleasure principle is to make man always search for what he has to find again, but which he never will attain, that one reaches the essence, namely, that sphere or relationship which is known as the Law of the prohibition of incest."[45] As for the specification of this inter-diction in terms of the moral demands of social life, this is the function of what Western culture has come to know as the "ten commandments." Though "in the beginning, at a period that is not so remote in the past, [the ten commandments] were collected by a people that sets itself apart as a chosen people,"[46] they regulate for humanity at large the distance between desire and its lost object, the full "range of what are properly speaking our [characteristically] human actions."[47]

Now, there is an important subtext in the *Ethics of Psychoanalysis* seminar that involves a confrontation between Kant and the Marquis de Sade. I shall return to it in a moment. For now let it suffice to say that the same confrontation is orchestrated again in an essay entitled "Kant with Sade" (1963),[48] where the essentials of the foregoing analysis are rearticulated: desire, as mediated by the Law, is the "other side of the Law,"[49] for "Law and repressed desire are one and the same thing."[50] And the Law? Still the

symbolic order to which the subject is submitted through the initial splitting of the subject: "[T]he bipolarity by which the moral Law institutes itself is nothing other than this splitting of the subject which occurs in any
intervention of the signifier. . . . The moral Law has no other principle."[51]
Are the Law of the symbolic order and the Law of morality one and the
same? Is *that* the paradox of the Law?

⤙≡◉≡⤚

All this suggests there is much to say, but I shall restrict my remarks
to two:

A. To identify the symbolic order as such with the Law/Name-of-the-
Father presents an obvious difficulty, for it suggests that the Law for Lacan
is patriarchal in structure and thereby identifies it with the odious name of
"patriarchy." The impression is understandable but misleading, for the Law
of symbolic functioning as a structural (i.e., synchronic) phenomenon is
clearly to be distinguished from the diachronic concretization of that Law
in any given historical culture. If Lacan associates it with the name "Father," it is because, in his view, "from the dawn of history" the Father's
person has been identified "with the figure of the Law."[52] But the Law of
symbolic functioning prescinds from sexual differentiation; it would be as
essential to matriarchal as to patriarchal societies and inevitably instantiated in either. It specifies us all, simply as human beings (Lévi-Strauss);
it makes human communication possible. It should be thought of, I suggest, as *neither* patriarchal *nor* matriarchal but rather as "ambiarchal" or
"biarchal" or simply "archal" (understand: *arche*) if we must name it in
these terms at all.

B. The second point is more delicate and deals with the relation between
the symbolic order as archal Law on one hand and as moral Law on the
other, for "the moral Law," we are told in "Kant with Sade," "has no other
principle" than the "splitting of the subject which occurs in any intervention of the signifier." This is a hard saying. The essay elaborates a thesis
already suggested in the *Ethics of Psychoanalysis* to the effect that the Marquis de Sade, in his novel *Philosophy in the Boudoir* (1795),[53] which appeared
seven years after Kant's *Critique of Practical Reason* (1788),[54] actually "completes" the former and yields up its "truth."[55] What is meant is that Kant has
achieved the great advance of developing an ethics that is not grounded in
some metaphysics of the "good" (e.g., à la Aristotle) that Kant himself had
discredited in the first *Critique,* but in the interiority of a transcendental
subject. This means that the moral Law is determined by pure reason alone,
where the universality and necessity of the Law are discerned after the
manner of a categorical imperative (e.g., "so act that the maxim of your will
could always hold at the same time as a principle of universal Law giving").[56] Truly moral action must proceed out of respect for the Law and not
be contaminated by any lesser motivation, such as desire for secondary gain
or some affect, no matter how noble (e.g., compassion, love, remorse). This
makes Kantian morality a rather austere business, as we all know, and even

Kant admits: "we can see *a priori* that the moral Law as ground of determination of the will, by thwarting our inclinations, cannot help but produce a feeling which can be called pain."[57] Besides the feeling of respect for the Law, pain, too, would be an *a priori* sign of one's compliance with it.

This is the Kantian conception that Sade, for Lacan, "completes" and reveals in its "truth." For Sade, too, has a moral Law that Lacan, in Sade's name, formulates as follows: "I have the right of enjoyment over your body, anyone can say to me, and I will exercise this right, without any limit stopping me in the capriciousness of the exactions that I might have the taste to gratify."[58] It has the generality of Law, after all, for, in Kantian language, "the will is only obligated to dismiss from its practice any reason which is not that of its maxim itself."[59] Moreover, the Law is exemplified by the liturgy of pain that Sade dramatizes with his usual delicacy in *Philosophy in the Boudoir.* The analogy with Kant is evident—but for Lacan, Sade improves on Kant and "completes" him. How? By making it clear that the "voice" that articulates the Law is not simply some voice from "within" but the voice of the Other, i.e., the symbolic order as archal Law: "The Sadian maxim, by pronouncing itself from the mouth of the Other, is more honest than appealing to the voice within, since it unmasks the splitting, usually conjured away [in a purely Kantian reading] of the subject."[60] In such a position, Sade yields up "the truth" of Kant's *Critique.*

How one may react to this intriguing sleight of hand is worth a much longer pause than is possible here. I wish merely to reflect momentarily on what it implies about the "moral Law," if this "has no other principle" than the "splitting" by which the subject is submitted to the symbolic order.[61] For it suggests that the Name-of-the-Father, the Law that mediates desire, acknowledges no difference, from a structural point of view, between the rituals of Sadian cruelty and the prescriptions of the ten commandments. And how could it? The Law of language, foundation of both, shines like the sun upon all indifferently.

What price "ethics of psychoanalysis," then? Is it enough to say that "from an analytic point of view, the only thing of which one can be guilty is of having given ground relative to one's desire," when one's desire is simply the "other side" of the Law, since "the Law and repressed desire are one and the same thing"?[62] For "Law" here is the archal Law of the symbolic order, as valid and validating for the Marquis de Sade as for Moses in the desert of Sinai. The symbolic order, I submit, is not simply morally neutral, it is morally empty, and simple insertion into it cannot be the "principle" of any moral Law—i.e., Law that determines what a human being "ought" to be/ do in order to be specifically human—at all. As primordial Law of the symbolic order, the Name-of-the-Father "wants nothing from you. It receives you when you come and it dismisses you when you go." That is all.

Where, then, does that leave us with regard to the nature of Law, once Lacan contextualizes it this way in terms of an eventual ethics of psychoanalysis? How might Joseph K. have dealt with the accusations of the Court if he had sought and found help from a Lacanian analyst? Assuming that

Joseph K. represents one version, in fantasy form, of Kafka himself, I shall consider them here as one. My expectation is that the task of trying to help K. become aware of a debt *(Schuld)* of which he is unconscious and whose existence he firmly denies would begin by trying to help him appreciate the difference between the symbolic Father as primordial Law upon which every human being is dependent (and to which, in that sense, every human is indebted) and his actual (real, historical) father, by whom Kafka, at least, was tyrannized and toward whom one might feel (like Kafka) a crushing burden of guilt *(Schuld)*. There is a trace of this distinction in *The Trial,* where the tyrannical father of experience has been sanitized into the detached, depersonalized form of the Law as instantiated in the Court—Law/Court that wants nothing from the subject—that receives the subject when it comes and dismisses it when it goes. Such a conception of the Law of the Father gives some sense to the ambiguity of the opening conversation in the cathedral:

> "Your guilt is supposed, for the present, at least, to have been proved," [says the priest.] "But I am not guilty," said K.; "it's a mistake. And, if it comes to that, how can any man be called guilty? We are all simply [human beings] here, one as much as the other." "That is true," said the priest, "but that's how all guilty men talk."[63]

The ambiguity turns on the meaning of "guilt" *(Schuld):* a structural indebtedness to the symbolic order grounded ultimately in the finitude of the subject (Lacan's conception) vs. a quasi-moral guilt for patricide transmitted by phylogenetic inheritance (Freud's conception)—both of them distinct from any personal guilt of which K. would be consciously aware. In the situation of fact, K. is unconscious of these differences, but it would be the task of analysis to help him appreciate them and understand what his symbolic (as opposed to imaginary) indebtedness might consist in and how he might deal with it.

I say that the subject's debt to the symbolic order is grounded in finitude. By that I mean that the subject K.-as-Kafka is inducted into a symbolic order that is determined (therefore negated) in all sorts of ways beyond the constrictions imposed by a domineering father in the flesh. The order is determined for Kafka by such things as the Judaism of his heritage, the political turbulence of his time, the accident of the language available to him to write in (born a Czech, he chose to write in German)—all added to the contingencies of his personal idiosyncratic circumstances (e.g., the frailty of health in an already fragile body). All such determinations would add up to constrictions, i.e., a set of negations that cut the subject off from what it might otherwise have been and for that reason constitute what Lacan calls "castration"—symbolic, of course. At a given moment he even makes his own Heidegger's language of "ontological guilt," so that Lacan's "symbolic castration" and Heidegger's "Being-unto-death" are thought of as one. The Law of the symbolic order, then, despite its absolute, quasi-transcendent character, is tailor-made to each individual. That would account for the poignancy of the door-keeper's final shout to the dying man from the country: "No one but you could gain admittance through this door, since this door was intended only for you. I am now going to shut it."[64]

How could he have gained admittance? Staying with a Lacanian reading (though this would have been a bit much for a poor man from the country), I submit that it would be through an appropriate awareness of his desire, for "the Law and repressed desire are one and the same thing." I understand this to mean that desire, as the wanting of the lost object, is, through the splitting of the subject, submitted to a symbolic order that is trammeled by such limitations as we have just seen. Mediated by *this* Law, desire is inevitably a castrated desire. This does not mean, of course, that desire cannot transgress the Law in its pursuit of the lost object, as if there were an "erotics" by which it stretches beyond the Law,[65] but this simply emphasizes the irretrievability of the object as lost. Desire may indeed strive to transgress the Law, but it cannot transcend its own castration. How does all this pertain to Joseph K.? Obviously the question of his desire was never raised, still less the fact of its castration. He never passed muster before that Last Judgment: "have you acted in conformity with the desire that is in you?"—but then he was never analyzed. To be sure, desire remained alive in him—how else explain that last flicker of hope on the edge of death when "the casements of a window there suddenly flew open and . . . a human figure . . . leaned abruptly forward and stretched both arms still farther. . . . [And] he [in turn] raised his hands and spread out all his fingers."[66] But it was too late. "The hands of one of the partners were already at K.'s throat." If he felt that he died "like a dog" and that the "shame of it must outlive him," my sense is that the humiliation lay in the dumb passivity of it all—never to have understood and embraced his desire, made it is own— even in, especially in—its very castration as Being-unto-death.

To conclude:

1) What has been offered here is an attempt to spell out what I think can be said for an "ethics of psychoanalysis" that addresses the relation between an act and the desire that dwells in it, where this desire is the inverse of the Law of the symbolic order under the guise of Name-of-the-Father. I have in effect said nothing about the symbolic order as a Law of morality. To do so in such fashion as Lacan seems to do, i.e., by making the symbolic order found a moral Law that permits it to smile equally on the Moses at Sinai and the Marquis de Sade, strikes me as gratuitous, hyperbolic non-sense. This is all the more grievous, it seems to me, since psychoanalysis does have serious moral issues raised for it that an ethics of psychoanalysis worth its name ought to address. I am thinking, for example, of the Argentinian analyst who reported having once refused to take into analysis a professional torturer, lest the analysis make him a better torturer. Here the problem of desire, both of analyst and of analysand, is posed in all its urgency. Again, when Lacan tells us that from the viewpoint of psychoanalysis, "the only thing one can be guilty of is to give ground relative to one's desire,"[67] are we

to take this to mean that there are no constraints whatsoever, constituted, say, by the social fabric of the analysand's life (e.g., by certain indissoluble relations with others), that are to be respected? If such constraints appear to exist, how are they to be assayed? Finally, how does the analyst reconcile his/her own desire with constraints extrinsic to desire, say, of the civil law, where, in cases of potential violence, civil society may command that the analyst make exception to the demands of professional confidentiality in the interest of the common good? Questions like these cannot be answered by the *ipse dixit* of Lacan about some abstract refusal to compromise desire. Answers will be forthcoming only when we will have thought through more carefully than has been done up to now the full implications of the absolute primacy of the efficacious word in psychoanalysis in conjunction with the liberation of desire.

2) Finally, if "a reconsideration of ethics is possible, [if a] form of ethical judgment is possible, of a kind that gives this question the force of a Last Judgment: have you acted in conformity with the desire that is in you?" then the subject must be capable of choosing to conform or not conform to, i.e., to give up or not give up on (*céder sur*), its desire. But such a choice implies a con-sistency in the psychoanalytic subject that makes possible the coherence of the hermeneutic narrative by reason of which it is capable of assuming "responsibility" for such a choice, i.e., "answering for" it over time. For my part I do not yet see how Lacan's manner of conceiving of the split subject—split, that is, between an imaginary ego (which is no more than a distorting reflection of a disorganized subject-to-be that functions on the level of consciousness) and the unconscious subject (i.e., subject of the unconscious/unconscious as subject), which is essentially the symbolic or-der itself, however individualized in a dynamic, idiosyncratic identity—leaves room for an *ethical* subject, i.e., a desire capable of choosing to be true to itself. Only such a subject is the properly human subject. Unless we can account for this specifically human dimension of a responsible subject, every subject must in the end die in an inhuman passivity, the way Joseph K. felt he did, "like a dog."

Notes

1. Franz Kafka, *The Trial*, trans. Willa and Edwin Muir (New York: Schocken Books, 1992), p. 222.

2. See ibid., pp. 223–29.

3. George Steiner, "Introduction," ibid., p. ix.

4. Ibid., p. 228.

5. See J. P. Stern, "The Law of *The Trial*," in *On Kafka. Semi-Centenary Perspectives*, ed. Franz Kuna (London: Paul Elek, 1976), pp. 22–41.

6. Kafka, *The Trial*, pp. 209–10.

7. Ibid., pp. 213–15.

8. Ibid., p. 220.

9. Ibid., p. 222.

10. See Sigmund Freud, *Totem and Taboo* (1913), in *The Standard Edition of the Complete Psychological Works of Sigmund Freud*, trans. James Strachey (London: Hogarth Press, 1968), vol. 13, pp. vii–xv, 1–162, 140–46 (hereafter *SE*). Cf. *Civilization and Its Discontents* (1930), *SE*, vol. 21, pp. 57–145.

11. Aeschylus, *The Oresteia*, trans. Robert Fagles (New York: Penguin, 1977).

12. See Rollin Chambliss, *Social Thought from Hammurabi to Comte* (New York: Dryden, 1954), pp. 13–41.

13. *The New Jerome Biblical Commentary*, ed. Raymond E. Brown, Joseph A. Fitzmyer, and Roland E. Murphy (Englewood Cliffs, N.J.: Prentice Hall, 1990), p. 1037.

14. Jacques Lacan, *The Seminar of Jacques Lacan. Book VII. The Ethics of Psychoanalysis*, ed. Jacques-Alain Miller, trans. Dennis Porter (New York: W.W. Norton, 1992), p. 143.

15. Franz Kafka, *Letter to His Father*, trans. Ernst Kaiser and Eithne Wilkins (New York: Schocken Books, 1966).

16. Ibid., pp. 19–21.

17. Franz Kafka, *The Judgment*, trans. Willa and Edwin Muir (New York: Modern Library, 1952). See also Walter H. Sokel, "The Programme of K.'s Court: Oedipal and Existential Meanings of *The Trial*," in *On Kafka*, pp. 1–21.

18. Franz Kafka, *The Metamorphosis*, trans. Stanley Corngold (New York: Bantam, 1972).

19. Franz Kafka, *Amerika*, trans. Edwin Muir (New York: New Directions, 1962).

20. See Franz Kafka, *In the Penal Colony*, in *The Metamorphosis in the Penal Colony and Other Stories*, trans. Willa and Edwin Muir (New York: Schocken Books, 1995).

21. Kafka, *Letter to His Father*, p. 87.

22. Ibid., p. 73. Cf. Kafka, *The Trial*, p. 229.

23. Kafka, *The Trial*, p. 211.

24. See Sokel, "The Programme of K.'s Court," pp. 1–21.

25. Jacques Lacan, "The Function and Field of Speech and Language in Psychoanalysis," *Écrits*, trans. Alan Sheridan (New York: W.W. Norton, 1977), pp. 30–113. Cf. *The Language of the Self: The Function of Language in Psychoanalysis*, trans. Anthony Wilden (Baltimore: Johns Hopkins University Press, 1968), pp. 9–87. Wilden's translation is always provocative, his notes and commentary still (1996) invaluable.

26. Ibid., p. 61.

27. See ibid., pp. 65–66.

28. Ibid., p. 66.

29. Ibid., p. 73.

30. Ibid., p. 234.

31. Ibid., p. 67.

32. Jacques Lacan, *The Seminar of Jacques Lacan. Book III. The Psychoses. 1955–1956*, ed. Jacques-Alain Miller, trans. Russell Grigg (New York: W.W. Norton, 1993).

33. Lacan, "On a Question Preliminary to Any Possible Treatment of Psychosis," *Écrits*, pp. 179–225.

34. Sigmund Freud, *Psycho-Analytic Notes on an Autobiographical Account of a Case of Paranoia (Dementia Paranoides)* (1911), *SE*, vol. 12, pp. 1–82.

35. Freud, *Beyond the Pleasure Principle* (1920), *SE*, vol. 18, pp. 14–17.

36. Lacan, *Écrits*, p. 167.

37. Ibid., p. 67.

38. Ibid., p. 199.

39. Jacques Lacan, *The Seminar of Jacques Lacan. Book VII. The Ethics of Psycho-*

analysis, ed. Jacques-Alain Miller, trans. Dennis Porter (New York: W.W. Norton, 1992).

40. Ibid., p. 313.
41. Ibid., p. 319.
42. Ibid., p. 314.
43. Ibid., p. 319.
44. Ibid., pp. 66–67.
45. Ibid., p. 68.
46. Ibid., p. 80.
47. See ibid., pp. 68–69. Cf. "We are then brought back again to the moral law insofar as it is incarnated in a certain number of commandments. I mean the ten commandments, which in the beginning, at a period that is not so remote in the past, were collected by a people that sets itself apart as a chosen people" (ibid., p. 80).
48. Jacques Lacan, "Kant with Sade," trans. James B. Swenson Jr., *October* 51 (1989): 55–104.
49. Ibid., p. 73.
50. Ibid., p. 68.
51. Ibid., p. 59.
52. Lacan, *Écrits,* p. 67.
53. See Marquis de Sade, *The Complete Justine, Philosophy in the Bedroom and Other Writings,* trans. Richard Seaver and Austryn Wainhouse (New York: Grove, 1965), pp. 177–367. Lacan builds his case on the interlude essay, "Yet another effort, Frenchmen, if you would become Republicans," pp. 296–339.
54. Immanuel Kant, *Critique of Practical Reason,* trans. Lewis White Beck (New York: Macmillan, 1993 [1956]).
55. Lacan, "Kant with Sade," p. 55.
56. Kant, *Critique of Practical Reason,* p. 30.
57. Ibid., p. 76.
58. Ibid., p. 58.
59. Ibid., pp. 58, 59.
60. Ibid., p. 59.
61. See ibid..
62. Cf. ibid., pp. 73, 68.
63. Kafka, *The Trial,* p. 231.
64. Ibid., p. 236.
65. See Lacan, *Ethics of Psychoanalysis,* p. 84.
66. Kafka, *The Trial,* pp. 250–51.
67. Lacan, *Ethics of Psychoanalysis,* p. 321.

William J. Richardson: Selected Bibliography

Books

With J. P. Muller, *The Purloined Poe: Lacan, Derrida, and Psychoanalytic Reading.* Baltimore: Johns Hopkins University Press, 1988.
With J. P. Muller, *Lacan and Language. A Reader's Guide to the Écrits.* New York: International Universities Press, 1982.
Heidegger: Through Phenomenology to Thought. Preface by Martin Heidegger. The Hague: Martinus Nijhoff, 1963.

Chapters in Edited Volumes and Journal Articles

"In-the-Name-of-the-Father: The Law?" In *Questioning Ethics,* ed. R. Kearney and M. Dooley. London: Routledge, 1998.

"From Phenomenology through Thought to a Festschrift." *Heidegger Studies* 13 (1997).

"Long Day's Journey into Sublimation." *Journal of British Society for Phenomenology* 28 (1997).

"Heidegger's Fall." *American Catholic Philosophical Quarterly* 44 (1995).

"The Irresponsible Subject." In *Ethics as First Philosophy: The Significance of Emmanuel Levinas for Philosophy, Literature and Religion,* ed. Adriaan Peperzak. New York: Routledge, 1995.

"Lacan and the Enlightenment: Antigone's Choice." *Research in Phenomenology* 24 (1994).

"Dasein and the Ground of Negativity: A Note on the Fourth Movement of the Beiträge Symphony." *Heidegger Studies* 9 (1993).

"The Word of Silence." In *Speculations after Freud. Psychoanalysis, Philosophy and Culture,* ed. S. Shamdasani and M. Münchow. London: Routledge, 1994.

"The Third Generation of Desire." *The Letter* 1 (1994).

"Heidegger's Truth and Politics." In *Ethics and Danger: Essays on Heidegger and Continental Thought,* ed. A. Dallery and C. Scott with H. Roberts. Albany: State University of New York Press, 1992.

"Desire and Its Vicissitudes." In *Phenomenology and Lacanian Psychoanalysis.* Proceedings of the Eighth Annual Symposium of the Simon Silverman Phenomenology Center. Pittsburgh: Duquesne University, 1992.

"'Like Straw': Psychoanalysis and the Question of God." In *Eros and Eris. Liber Amicorum en hommage à Adriaan Peperzak.* The Hague: Kluwer Academic Publishers, 1992.

"Love and the Beginning." *Contemporary Psychoanalysis* 28 (1992).

"Heidegger among the Doctors." In *Reading Heidegger: Commemorations,* ed. John Sallis. Bloomington: Indiana University Press, 1990.

"Heidegger's Concept of 'World.'" In *Reconsidering Psychology: Perspectives from Continental Philosophy,* ed. P. Williams and J. Falconer. Pittsburgh: Duquesne University Press, 1990.

"Lacan and Non-Philosophy." In *Philosophy and Non-Philosophy since Merleau-Ponty: Continental Philosophy,* ed. H. Silverman. New York: Routledge, Chapman and Hall, 1988.

"Lacan and the Problem of Psychosis." In *Psychosis and Sexual Identity: Towards a Post-Modern View of the Schreber Case,* ed. D. Allison, P. de Oliveira, M. Roberts, and A. Weiss. Albany: State University of New York Press, 1988.

"Ethics and Psychoanalysis." *Journal of the American Academy of Psychoanalysis* 40 (1987).

"Psychoanalysis and Anti-Humanism: Lacan's Legacy." *Krisis* 5–6 (1986–87).

"Psychoanalysis and the God-Question." *Thought* 56 (1986).

"Psychoanalysis and the Being-Question." In *Interpreting Lacan,* ed. J. H. Smith and W. Kerrigan. New Haven: Yale University Press, 1983.

"Lacan and the Subject of Psychoanalysis." In *Interpreting Lacan,* ed. J. H. Smith and W. Kerrigan. New Haven: Yale University Press, 1983.

"The Mirror Inside: Problem of the Self." *Review of Existential Psychology and Psychiatry* 26 (1978–79).

"Martin Heidegger: In Memoriam." *Commonweal* 104 (1977).

"Heidegger's Critique of Science." *New Scholasticism* 62 (1968).

"Kant and the Late Heidegger." In *Phenomenology in America,* ed. J. M. Edie. Chicago: Quadrangle, 1967.

"The Place of the Unconscious in Heidegger." *Review of Existential Psychology and Psychiatry* 5 (1965).

12

Toward an Ethics of *Auseinandersetzung*

RODOLPHE GASCHÉ

Rodolphe Gasché represents better than perhaps any other leading American continental philosopher the interdisciplinary character of continental philosophy. Gasché is as well known in the field of literary theory as he is in philosophy. In his early work, Gasché was mainly concerned with the scientific character of the human sciences, especially sociology, anthropology, and psychoanalysis. Two issues interested him in this context: the specific character of the science that the human sciences could muster by importing hard science models into their discourses (Gasché's early book *Die hybride Wissenschaft* fits this category), as well as how certain human sciences sought to push the hard science models to their limits by exhibiting their underlying phantasmatic structures (his book on Bataille exemplifies this kind of work). Shortly after arriving in the United States, Gasché began his attempt to elaborate on the philosophical dimensions of Derridian deconstruction and to situate it in the history of philosophy and in respect to its antecedents in phenomenology. This work led to the publication of *The Tain of the Mirror* and *Inventions of Difference*. Part of this work also entailed demarcating Derridian deconstruction from deconstruction in literary criticism, in particular the Yale School of deconstruction. His book *The Wild Card of Reading: On Paul de Man* aimed to clarify de Man's thinking and to distinguish it from that of Derrida. Since completing this work, Gasché has embarked on a variety of other endeavors. He is currently finishing a book on Kant's *Aesthetics*, which will reinterpret the Kantian notion of form. His projects concern the status of thinking in post-phenomenological thought, as well as a project on the philosophical notion of "Europe."

 The overall concern that has guided his thinking through its different phases is the difference that philosophical thinking makes with respect to other discourses and the sense that the difference is never a given but constantly needs to be reactualized, reasserted, rethought, and defended. In this context, the question of how it is still possible to philosophize in the aftermath of the rise of the natural sciences, the Holocaust, and postmodernism, and what philosophical thinking can and must mean under these circumstances, is a central part of Gasché's work.

The essay included here is part of a project that seeks to show that the task of philosophical thinking today can no longer "uncritically" endorse the critical gesture. Without altogether abandoning critique, the gesture must become aware of the metaphysics of criticism, especially criticism's aim of drawing impenetrable borders and separating off what is heterogeneous or other—understood here as including not only the human other but everything that is singular. The way in which one's own philosophical thought becomes tied to the thought of another thinker, as in Heidegger's notion of *Auseinandersetzung*, is a first step in the direction of a mode of philosophizing that thinks from the other, a philosophizing whose modalities, gestures, and ways are determined by this relation to the other.

⊶❍⊷

In a process now all too predictable, critical and theoretical concepts such as "critical theory" or "deconstruction" are abandoned, long before their full potential has even begun to be tapped, in favor of seemingly new and more promising terms. *Auseinandersetzung* is one such notion now beginning to make its appearance in texts of literary and cultural criticism. As opposed to the alleged abstraction of critical theory and the obscurantism of deconstruction, *Auseinandersetzung* promises a more intimate and more engaged, if not more visceral, relation to texts, works, or thoughts. In *Auseinandersetzung*, the critic comes face to face in a direct confrontation with the thought of an Other. Out of the ensuing clash of ideas, real and concrete issues come to word, while the debate itself mobilizes energies that themselves testify to the urgency and seriousness of the problems in question. Moreover, *Auseinandersetzung*, by virtue of its greater intimacy and engagement with texts or ideas, takes shape as a relation in which critical vigilance, paired with truly concrete concerns, guards against dogmatic positions and conclusions. In confrontation as *Auseinandersetzung*, opponents meet stripped of ideological masquerade. It is a debate that suggests honesty, responsibility, and a shared commitment to things that truly matter.

It is no secret that the term *Auseinandersetzung* is lifted from Heidegger. Returning to what this term implies and seeks to achieve in its original context, the following discussion of *Auseinandersetzung* intends not only to confront its current use with its strict definition but to set conditions for fruitfully putting this term to work. Indeed, recourse to *Auseinandersetzung*, as a refuge either from concepts that have come under attack or from unresolved difficulties adhering to these concepts, may serve to recontextualize and clarify the very nature of criticism and deconstruction. There is at least a chance that a sustained and informed confrontation with the Heideggerian concept in question could lead to a productive re-evaluation of the critical and deconstructive "relation." This debate, however, may show *Auseinandersetzung* to be more than a simple alternative to the relations in question. Located in an array of positions from which to choose, *Auseinandersetzung* may be a privileged vantage point from which insight into the limits, promises, and achievements of critique and deconstruction may be gained. It is in view of such critical re-evaluation that the subsequent developments have been undertaken.

Auseinandersetzung is a term that, in the mid-thirties, abruptly appears in Heidegger's work, in particular in his lectures on Nietzsche and in *An Introduction to Metaphysics*. From the outset, this word, devoid of any anterior philosophical meaning, indicating, in addition to its juridical meaning of partition, only the explication of something, a debate or dispute, functions as a *terminus technicus*. The Nietzsche lectures advance the term in question as *the* philosophical and hermeneutic mode of relating to the subject matter of a philosopher's thought. The term serves to conceptualize the relation to that which, in a thinker's thought, resists access, by its very nature, to any extraneous approach, namely, that which cannot "be determined anywhere else than from within itself." *Auseinandersetzung* is the exclusive relation to that which, in a thinker's thought, is "true philosophy,"[1] that is, to what in his thought obeys the law of thinking, thinking's own law. As such, it dictates a bracketing of anything that in thinking is of heteronomous origin, anything that would reveal concerns extrinsic to those of thinking itself.

In the "Author's Foreword to all Volumes," Heidegger notes that the object of *Auseinandersetzung*, for which these lectures are to pave the way, is to be "the matter" *(die Sache)* of Nietzsche's thought. *Die Sache* is *der Streitfall*, Heidegger continues, showing that he has in mind the original Germanic meaning of *die Sache* as legal matter, legal case, a case taken to court. *Auseinandersetzung* thus understands that which, in the thinking of a philosopher, is determined only from within itself, as a point in question, a case or conflict under dispute. More precisely, "the matter, the point in question, is in itself a confrontation (*Auseinandersetzung*)."[2] The philosophically autonomous core of a thinker's thought is *Auseinandersetzung* not only because it must be construed or established through the proceedings of the debate but also because having in itself the structure of debate, "the matter" itself invites the confrontational relation in which "the matter" is to be determined as what it is. Being responsive to such a "matter" of thinking is neither talking "about" it, nor judging it "from outside," but rather entering into a relation of *Auseinandersetzung* with it. Thinking, insofar as it is determined only from within itself, invites only one mode of responsible response, namely, one of *Auseinandersetzung* with the case in dispute.

In the first pages of *The Will to Power as Art*, the reason Heidegger proposes for the fact that such an *Auseinandersetzung* with Nietzsche's thought has not yet begun, that even its prerequisites are still to be established, reveals a decisive structural feature without which any debate with that which has the law in itself cannot take place. He writes: "Nietzsche's thought and speech are still too contemporary for us. He and we have not yet been sufficiently separated (*auseinandergesetzt*) in history; we lack the distance (*Abstand*) necessary for a sound appreciation of the thinker's strength."[3] From this we see that any debate of the kind in question requires a setting-apart, a distance, across which the thinker's strength may come into view and justice may be done to his specific achievements. As long as Nietzsche remains caught up in present-day concerns, no glimpse of him as a true philosopher can be had. But the distance implicit to all *Auseinandersetzung* must also be seen as a function of the definition of "the matter" of thinking itself, that is, as that which is determined solely from within itself. If what matters in thinking is thinking free from all heteronomy, then thinking itself is constitutive of the distance which allows any appreciating *Auseinandersetzung* to get off the ground. While confrontation assures that a thinker's thought be recognized in its true strength, such strong thought itself engenders the distance required to appreciate it. *Auseinandersetzung* debates that which in thinking is determined by itself alone, but it does so from a respectful distance, allowing such thought to unfold from itself and in itself.

Before further discussion of the complex structural features of the notion of *Auseinandersetzung* now beginning to emerge, let me first open the dictionaries. *Auseinander,* Grimm's *Deutsches Wörterbuch* tells us, is the result of drawing together in one word what remains separate in living speech while at the same time inverting the natural order of the words, that is, putting the preposition *aus* in *ein aus dem anderen* ahead of the other words. This operation engenders what Grimm calls a hardened and motionless linguistic mass. If moreover, *auseinander* is connected to verbs implying an idea of separation or dissection, "a variety of the most ponderous compounds arise."[4] *Auseinandersetzung* is one of them. This linguistic monster solidifies in one ponderous compound that which is, by nature, discrete, distinct, and separate, and which can only be drawn together by neutralizing the sense of separation inherent to both *ein aus dem anderen* and *setzen.* In *Trübner's Deutsches Wörterbuch,* Goetze prefaces his presentation of the historical evolution of the meaning of the term by noting that it is a very weak verb in New High German and has no basis *(nirgends Boden hat)* in any of the dialects. According to Goetze's dictionary, the legal meaning of *auseinandersetzen,* referring to the partition of the common property of parties who have shared ownership, is historically primary. The verb later acquired the more general meaning of a "clarification of a legal matter, of awarding to each litigant what is properly his or her own," but was subsequently transposed by representatives of the Enlightenment—Johann Christian Gottsched, for instance—to the realm of literary representation, where it acquired the meaning of "presenting in such a manner that all viewpoints are given due attention (*zu ihrem Rechte kommen*)." The contemporary use of the word in the sense of explaining, examining, presenting, or laying out, Goetze adds, derives from this meaning of *auseinandersetzen.*[5] Finally, in *Handwörterbuch der deutschen Sprache,* from a purely semantic account of the term, Heyse determines that *auseinander* signifies "a development *(Entstehen),* a succession or consequence *(Folge),* of one thing from another, or a distancing *(Entfernung)* of one thing from another. Consequently, *auseinandersetzen properly* means, to set apart from one another; *improperly,* to elucidate or explain a representation to someone by dissolving it into its components; *sich über etwas auseinandersetzen* is to annul or dissolve the community with others regarding a matter, to reach a settlement about such a matter (an inheritance, for instance)." He concludes by saying that *die Auseinandersetzung* can be taken in *all* the meanings of the verb.[6]

· Yet, how are we to understand Heidegger's use of the term? Speaking of the necessity of an *Auseinandersetzung* with Nietzsche in the appendices to his 1941–42 lectures on "Nietzsche's Metaphysics," Heidegger writes: "We take the word *Auseinandersetzung* literally. We seek to posit his and our thought apart from and into a relation of opposition to one another *(außer einander und in das Gegeneinander über zu setzen)*; but in a thinking, and not in a comparative mode."[7] Heidegger's literal understanding of the term stresses the *separation* of the two kinds of thoughts, the *distance* thus created between them, as well as the relation of *adverseness* into which they come to stand, or rather, into which they are *set,* or posited. Consequently, the common meaning of *Auseinandersetzung* as debate and confrontation, explanation and exposition, ought not to incur in its philosophical meaning. Still, the literal *(wörtlich)* meaning of the term is not exhausted by the traits of separation, distance, or adverseness; and furthermore, Heidegger makes it such a compound of traits that it literally ceases to be a word.

As shall become increasingly clear, Heidegger's valorization of the word derives from both the history *and* semantics of *Auseinandersetzung*. As a philosophical term, *Auseinandersetzung* is a term not to be found in the dictionaries, for it combines the semantically primary meaning of setting apart, or distancing, with the historically primary meaning of awarding each party what is properly its own. In other words, *Auseinandersetzung* is a formation that draws together in one intimate linguistic whole meanings thoroughly alien to one another. The word, if it still is one, allows semantically and historically irreducible senses of *auseinandersetzen* to dwell together. Moreover, the different ways Heidegger writes the word—*Auseinandersetzung, Aus-einandersetzung, Aus-einander-setzung*—suggest a complex synthesis in which multiple and different modes of separation and belonging-together cohabit. Finally, it also means struggle, conflict, and is thus, as we shall see, a translation of *polemos.*

Yet, linguistic condensation is not the sole means by which Heidegger forges this new philosophical concept. He further differentiates *Auseinandersetzung* from critique by determining it as genuine or authentic critique. He writes: "Confrontation *(Auseinandersetzung)* is genuine criticism. It is the supreme way, the only way, to a true estimation of a thinker. In confrontation we undertake to reflect on his thinking *(seinem Denken nachzudenken)* and to trace it in its effective force, not in its weaknesses. To what purpose? In order that through the confrontation we ourselves may become free for the supreme exertion of thinking."[8]

As genuine critique, confrontation is not negative. In *Die Frage nach dem Ding*, he remarks that the common meaning of critique is "to find fault with, to check mistakes, to bring out deficiencies, and subsequently to reject something."[9] In the appendices to the original lectures that make up *The Will to Power as Art* (written between 1936 and 1937 and published in volume 43 of the Gesamtausgabe), Heidegger is clear about this. We read: *"Auseinandersetzung ≠ Bemängelung."* Nor does it manifest itself as a polemic. But confrontation as genuine critique must also be distinguished from the meaning of critique that emerges in the second half of the eighteenth century, particularly in the context of reflections on art and aesthetics, where it signifies "fixing standards, rules, where it means legislation, that is, an emphasis of the universal over the particular."[10] Finally, Heidegger's genuine critique has nothing in common with critique in the Kantian sense. From Heidegger's developments with respect to Kant's use of the term in *Die Frage nach dem Ding*, we can conclude that *Auseinandersetzung* is not identical with a systematic mapping, based on the model of intelligibility particular to modern mathematics, of the powers of pure reason. It is not the method by which reason comes to know itself and through which it achieves its most intimate rationality.

What, then, is genuine critique? It is critique in the originary sense, Heidegger holds in *Die Frage nach dem Ding*. The established root of critique is *krinein*, commonly translated as "to separate," "put asunder," "distinguish," "decide," etc. In conformity with this originary meaning of the word *krinein*, concepts of criticism ranging from the common notion of criticism as estimation to its dialectical form based on determined negation have consistently articulated a faith in the possibility of pure, if not absolute, distinction. The critical operation thrives on the dream of a pure difference guaranteeing that the separated suffers no contamination by that from which it is cut off, and allowing the determination of essence to proceed in a realm free of all intrusions and within which decision is clear and without ambiguity. This is the philosophical meaning and thrust of critique established by the tradition out of the original meaning of *krinein*. But is it in this sense that we are to understand *Auseinandersetzung?* In *Die Frage nach dem Ding*, Heidegger, too, takes recourse to the original Greek word *krinein*. Yet he translates it as follows: "'sondern', 'absondern,' und so 'das Besondere herausheben'"; in English: to separate, to isolate, and *to thus bring out the particular*. From the beginning, Heidegger's translation subordinates separation to the end of bringing out the particular. However, before drawing out the consequences entailed by this translation for an understanding of "confrontation," we need to read in full the passage in which Heidegger establishes the originary meaning of critique:

> "Critique" comes from the Greek *krinein;* this means: "to separate," "to isolate," and thus to "bring out the particular." Such contrasting (*Abheben*) against other (*gegen anderes*) arises from a lifting (*Hinaufheben*) to a new standing. The meaning of the word "critique" is not negative at all; on the contrary

it means the most positive of the positive, namely the positing of that which in all positing (*Setzung*) must be presupposed (*im voraus angesetzt*) as what determines and decides. Critique is decision in such a positing sense. Only afterwards—since critique is separating and emphasis of the particular, the uncommon and at the same time of what gives the measure (*des Maßgeben-den*)—critique also becomes rejection of the common and the inappropriate.[11]

Critique in a genuine sense is thus neither negative nor determined by the goal of establishing an invulnerable limit. Rather than a severing of one thing from another in pure difference and free of all contamination, critique, in the authentic sense, serves to raise what is separated into its proper rank precisely by contrasting it to what it is separated from. Critique secures propriety and property as it locates its possibility in the other. Critique allows particularity to arise on both sides of the divide, indeed, it is the very condition through which something can come into its most proper own. In this sense critique is the same as *Auseinandersetzung*. In the operation of setting apart by setting against, the particular is posited as such for the first time. Genuine critique is thus what is most positive, since the very possibility of innermost propriety—which, however, is only what it is against what is on the other side of the divide, and vice versa—rests on the decision that it brings about. *Auseinandersetzung* understood this way is thus as much characterized by the setting apart as by the intimate interrelation of what occupies the respective sides of the division.

Before I analyze this complex economy of *Auseinandersetzung* occurring in one thinker's dialogue (*Zwiegespräch*) with the subject matter of another thinker's true philosophy—Nietzsche, in this case—it may be appropriate to recall that for Heidegger, in *An Introduction to Metaphysics, Auseinandersetzung* translates *polemos*. In the following, it will indeed be necessary to demarcate *Auseinandersetzung* as *polemos* from the confrontation that characterizes the genuine dialogue of philosophies. *Polemos* is, of course, not just any war, struggle, or conflict; nor is it war, struggle, or conflict in general. It is also distinct from "mere polemics . . . the machinations and intrigues of man within the realm of the given."[12] Rather, *polemos*—the reference, obviously, is to fragment 53 of Heraclitus—names "the original struggle, for it gives rise to the contenders as such; it is not a mere assault on something already there."[13] The *polemos* of fragment 53, Heidegger writes, "is a conflict that prevailed prior to everything divine and human, not a war in the human sense. This conflict, as Heraclitus thought it, first caused the realm of being to separate into opposites (*läßt im Gegeneinander das Wesende allererst ausein-andertreten*); it first gave rise to position, order, and rank. In such separation (*Auseinandertreten*), cleavages, intervals, distances, and joints opened. In the conflict (*Auseinandersetzung*) a world comes into being."[14] In other words, *polemos*, in which is seen not "mere quarreling and wrangling but the conflict of the conflicting (*der Streit des Streitbaren*), that sets the essential and the nonessential, the high and the low, in their limits and that makes them manifest,"[15] shows *Auseinandersetzung* to be not only a separation that enables the particular to be what it is, in contrast to what it is set against, but a unification as well. Heidegger remarks: "Conflict (*Auseinandersetzung*) does not split, much less destroy unity. It constitutes unity, it is a binding-together, *logos*. *Polemos* and *logos* are the same."[16] *Polemos* binds together in that it gathers in an intimate bond what stands in a relation of the highest antagonism. In this sense, *polemos* is the same as *Geist*, spirit, of which Heidegger writes in *Erläuterungen zu Hölderlins Dichtung*: "Spirit reigns as the sober but audacious *Aus-einandersetzung* which institutes everything present into the clearly distinct boundaries and arrangements of the present's presencing. Such *Aus-einandersetzen* is essential thinking. The 'Spirit's' ownmost proper are the thoughts. Through them everything, because it is separated (*auseinandergesetzt*), belongs together. Spirit is unifying unity. This unity lets the being-together of everything real appear in its gathering."[17] Heidegger's comments, in the appendices to volume 4 of the Gesamtausgabe, as to what he identifies as Hölderlinian guiding words—*Alles ist innig*—reveal intimacy (*Innigkeit*) as indeed the very criterion for what is in a mode of *Auseinandersetzung*. Heidegger remarks: "*Alles ist innig*. This means: One is appropriated into the Other (*Eines ist in das Andere vereignet*), yet in such a way that in this appropriation it remains in its own (*in seinem Eigenen bleibt*). More precisely, through this appropriation into the Other it acquires its ownness to begin with: gods and men, earth and sky. Intimacy does not signify a fusion and dissolution of differences. Intimacy names the belonging-together of what is alien to one another, the happening of *Befremdung* [of being taken (aback) by the Other, or alien]. . . ."[18] Setting apart is thus the condition under which *Befremdung* can occur, that is, a being-affected by the Other through which selfhood is granted to self. The being-appropriated into Other, by which One, or self, is always already disappropriated, is at the same time the very relation in which One, or self, acquires, through the Other, selfhood and Oneness. The proper and the Other stand here in a relation of mutual implication and disimplication. In *Auseinandersetzung* as *polemos*—and as *logos*, which is the same thing—a harmonious ringing takes place in which there is no priority, neither of the One nor of the Other. Indeed, One and the Other both presuppose *das Walten der Befremdung*.

Everything we shall still see shows *Auseinandersetzung* as genuine critique—as the "method" of the dialogue between philosophies—to exhibit the same basic attitude as in the originary struggle, *polemos*. Still, differences obtain between *polemos* and genuine critique that prove significant for any evaluation of the ethics of *Auseinandersetzung*. If in the following I thus try to underline not only the parallels but also the differences between the play of the proper and the Other in *polemos* and genuine critique, it is in order to circumscribe, with as much precision as possible, certain limits that haunt the dialogue between thinkers. Undoubtedly, *Auseinandersetzung* has a clear advantage over critique, for rather than putting separation to work as a means to exclude the Other, or non-proper, in *Auseinandersetzung*, separation, as the space from which *Befremdung* occurs, is the very condition by which not only justice is done to the Other but in which the constitution of propriety shows itself to be a function of the Other's (dis)appropriating address. Yet it seems that *Auseinandersetzung* is not identical to the harmonious interplay between the One and the Other, the harmony of differences in play characteristic to *polemos*. *Auseinandersetzung* is oriented. It follows a path and has a purpose. As the introductory pages to Heidegger's *Nietzsche* demonstrate, *Auseinandersetzung* with Nietzsche's thought seeks to determine to what extent the few thoughts that determine the whole of Nietzsche's thinking remain thought-worthy. Such evaluation, moreover, is not disinterested. If it is true that one must get on the way (*unterwegs*) to *die Sache* of Nietzsche's thinking, it is true, too, that the debate with him—the *Auseinandersetzung* with the matter of Nietzsche the philosopher—*comes from* somewhere and *goes* somewhere. Indeed, through confrontation with the Other, Heidegger's thought seeks to achieve an essential historicality for itself.[19]

Before addressing this question of *Auseinandersetzung's* orientation, let us first see how, as a struggle, a debate, or a confrontation, it adheres to the basic features of the original struggle of *polemos*. In the addenda to volume 43, Heidegger describes the *Zwiegespräch* between thinkers in the following way: "Only in *Auseinandersetzung* does creative interpretation become possible, an interpretation in which Nietzsche comes to stand with respect to himself in his strongest position (*auf sich selbst in seiner stärksten Stellung zum stehen kommt*)."[20] Only through *Auseinandersetzung* does Nietzsche, or the thought of any other great thinker, acquire a relation to itself that is, moreover, of the strongest kind. In *Beiträge*, Heidegger notes that "*Aus-einandersetzung* with the great philosophies—as fundamental metaphysical positions within the history of the guiding question—must be structured in such a manner that each philosophy comes to stand essentially as a mountain among mountains, and thus brings to a stand what is most essential about it."[21] The confrontation in question allows the opponent to stand in what is greatest about him, to acquire his strongest properties. In addition, by reflecting on the opponent's thinking, on its effective force rather than on its weaknesses, he who confronts a thinker becomes free as well "for the supreme exertion of thinking."[22] *Auseinandersetzung* is consequently a relation "in which the opponent is chosen, and in which we and he are brought into a position of confrontation, more precisely, into a struggle for the essential."[23] By being intended in a manner such that the opponent comes to stand in a relation of strength with respect to himself, and such that he who confronts the opponent becomes thus capable of the supreme task of thinking, *Auseinandersetzung* virtually guarantees that rather than leading to antagonism, the struggle, free from extraneous concerns, will be solely for what is essential and determined from within itself. Heidegger continues: "Such 'bringing-the-opponent-into-position' requires the development of the most essential questions; the opponent must be unfolded from the innermost depth of his work to what is most extreme about him."[24] In short, an *Auseinandersetzung* begins only when the most essential questions are being raised, that is, when a confrontation with Nietzsche, for instance, "is at the same time conjoined to a confrontation in the realm of the grounding question of philosophy."[25] In other words, a confrontation requires not only that a thinker and his opponent come to stand in their strongest position with respect to themselves, but also that the struggle be over the most essential, that is, the most binding concern and thereby entail an essential intimacy between the opponents. In the addenda to volume 43, Heidegger remarks that "the rigor of *Auseinandersetzung* is possible only when it is based on the most intimate affinity or relationship. It is possible only where there is a Yes to the essential."[26] Genuine critique binds together as much as it sets apart. In *Auseinandersetzung, logos* or *Geist* dominates as much as *polemos* or *Streit.* In confrontation, the essential is fought for and gained *(erstritten)* in opposition, and hence mutually. This essential, causing the opponents to coil into what they are in strength and most properly as they struggle over something that they share, is constitutive of confrontation in the strict sense; and it suggests that ultimately it is not the opponents that truly matter in this conflict but rather that for which the struggle is waged, since it is the struggle that assigns the places of the opponents. And yet, without the opponents' strife, nothing essential could occur. Is thus the *Auseinandersetzung* between dialoguing thinkers, or rather between one and the matter of the true philosophical thought of the Other, identical with the appropriating and disappropriating play of the proper and the Other that we have encountered with the originary struggle? Is it comparable to the harmonious constitution of One and Other in mutual *Befremdung* that we had seen to characterize *polemos?*

At this point, and before attempting an answer to the preceding question, we do not escape the issue of the range, or sweep, of *Auseinandersetzung.* As a relation in which thinkers, or rather the matter of their thought, comes to stand in what most powerfully characterizes them, and in which justice is done to the Other as Other, a question arises as to the specificity of *Auseinandersetzung.* Is it a relation valid for all dialogue, or a model with only one application, restricted to the dialogue with Nietzsche's thought alone? Is the very nature of Nietzsche's philosophical achievement such that any appropriate relation to it must have the form of *Auseinandersetzung,* and is this relation to Nietzsche unique? Although evidence points to a certain generalizability of *Auseinandersetzung* as the structure for all thinking dialogue, there seems to be a certain tension in Heidegger's writings, especially in those from the mid-thirties, concerning this question. Admittedly, in *Beiträge,* he speaks at one point of Nietzsche's *Auseinandersetzung* with Schopenhauer;[27] in the lectures on thinking and poetry from 1944–45, he even seems to suggest an *Auseinandersetzung* with Hölderlin's poetry;[28] and more important, in the seminar of 1968 at Le Thor he is said to have spoken of the necessity "to embark on an *Auseinandersetzung* with Hegel, in order for Hegel *to speak* to us."[29] But is it not significant that, in *Beiträge,* after having reviewed the different stages in the history of metaphysics in need of historical treatment—Leibniz, Kant, Schelling, Nietzsche—only in the case of Nietzsche is such treatment called an *Auseinandersetzung*? He writes: "to venture the *Auseinandersetzung* with Nietzsche as him who is closest, and yet, to recognize that he is most remote from the question of Being."[30] Finally, what is the significance of the fact that Heidegger elaborates the concept of *Auseinandersetzung* itself exclusively in the Nietzsche lectures, and only with respect to his debate with the latter? In response to these questions, I would argue that *Auseinandersetzung* is primarily cut to fit the debate with Nietzsche, a thinker still too close to be engaged in a just dialogue and with respect to whom the distance across which his true philosophical contribution, his strongest self, can come into view, has yet to be attained. But, as we shall now see, another reason may certainly hold the key to why confrontation is cut to fit Nietzsche more than anyone else.

In the addenda to *The Will to Power as Art*, Heidegger notes that the battle positions in a genuine *Auseinandersetzung* "must be historical—Nietzsche's and ours, and this again in the perspective of the mountain range (*in der Richtung der Höhenzüge*) of the essential history of philosophy."[31] Indeed, *Auseinandersetzung* is a kind of debate that *comes from*, and is *waged from* and *for*, what Heidegger calls in *Nietzsche*, but in particular in *Beiträge*, "*der andere Anfang*," the other beginning. Once that has been established, a definite limitation of *Auseinandersetzung* to the case of Nietzsche's thought will not fail to come into view. Nietzsche, we are told at the beginning of *The Will to Power as Art*, proceeds within the vast orbit of the ancient guiding question (*Leitfrage*) of philosophy.[32] This guiding question, which has been *the* question of the history of metaphysics, is the question constitutive of "the first beginning" *(der erste Anfang)*, and consists of the question: "What is Being?" It is a question that inquires into the essence of beings in terms of existence, in terms of an *existing* essence. In what is to follow, it is essential to distinguish this guiding question from what Heidegger calls the grounding question *(Grundfrage)*, the question "What is the truth of Being?" This question does not itself unfold in the history of philosophy as such, yet it inaugurates "the other beginning." Now, as Heidegger remarks, his lectures on Nietzsche intend "to elucidate the fundamental position within which Nietzsche unfolds the guiding question of Western thought and responds to it. Such elucidation is needed in order to prepare a confrontation (*Auseinandersetzung*) with Nietzsche. If in Nietzsche's thinking the prior tradition of Western thought is gathered and completed in a decisive respect, then the confrontation with Nietzsche becomes one with all Western thought hitherto."[33] As is well known, Heidegger's point in *Nietzsche* is that Nietzsche completed the guiding question that he persisted in thinking, and he thus brought the whole of Western thought into a view that, presupposing a distance to this whole, implicitly harbors another beginning. Showing that Nietzsche has brought the first and, as Heidegger stresses, greatest beginning, to an end—and has thus become "a transition"—Heidegger has also brought his opponent into the position in which he stands to himself in his strongest relation. In the addenda mentioned above, he notes that to be a transition is "the highest that can be said of a thinker. A transition, that prepares transitions to the second beginning."[34] Moreover, in *Beiträge* Heidegger writes, "the transitional is the authentic struggle."[35] From this it follows that the true opponent, Nietzsche at his strongest, as transition and authentic struggle, is in himself *Auseinandersetzung*. In him, and for the first time, the first and the second beginning are at war. Thus, it would seem that the mode of dialogue called *Auseinandersetzung* must be restricted to Nietzsche, that is, to the only thinker who, by having completed the first beginning, is in virtual transition to the other beginning. *Auseinandersetzung* seems to be limited to a debate in the name of the other beginning. As Heidegger emphasizes, such a debate with Nietzsche has not yet begun because we are still too close to him. Any *Auseinandersetzung* requires that we be sufficiently set apart from Nietzsche. Indeed, what must come into view is that Nietzsche, bringing the first beginning to an end, has achieved a position of exteriority of some sort to it. As Heidegger remarks in *Beiträge*, in order to experience what began in and as that beginning, it is necessary "to occupy a distancing position (*Fernstellung*). For *without* this position of distance—and only the position in the *other* beginning is a sufficient one—we always remain too close to the beginning, and this in an incriminating (*verfänglich*) fashion. . . . The position of distance with respect to the first beginning makes it possible to experience that there the question of truth (*aletheia*) remained necessarily unquestioned and that this nonoccurring has from the start made Western thinking 'metaphysical' thinking."[36] In short, then, *Auseinandersetzung* is strictly speaking a debate with a position characterized by distance (*Fernstellung*), namely, distance to the first beginning, and which as such is at least virtually in transition to the other beginning. *Auseinandersetzung* presupposes that the subject matter to be confronted has set itself *apart* from the first beginning and that this distance is what unites the thinkers in opposition. *Auseinandersetzung* requires a distance to one's opponent that permits a sight of the extent to which the thinker has already taken a position of distance from the first beginning. However, since, according to Heidegger, Nietzsche occupies the privileged position in the history of Western thought of having brought himself into opposition to the whole of Western thought while at the same time being furthest away from the grounding question, from the *Seinsfrage*, Nietzsche must be the opponent par excellence, the exemplary thinker whose matter, unlike that of any other thinker in the history of metaphysics, demands a confrontation in the mode of *Auseinandersetzung*.

The role of the other beginning constitutive to any appreciation of what Heidegger calls *Auseinandersetzung* clearly shows it as an oriented debate. Heidegger's contention that bringing the opponent into a position of strength is the condition by which he becomes free "for the supreme exertion of thinking" rings with ambiguity. *Auseinandersetzung* has the look of an unequal struggle in which justice is done to the Other for the mere benefit of the *explicit* development of the question that, while remote to

Nietzsche, is Heidegger's opening question. But let us not come to a hasty conclusion. Indeed, as Heidegger would have it, what counts in this debate is not the person "Nietzsche," or even "Heidegger" for that matter, but the essential Yes that both share, the Yes to the essential question. Moreover, the unfolding of that question in an *Auseinandersetzung* with a properly posited Nietzsche could well be the unfolding of a kind of thought that, according to its very nature, while potentially harboring in itself the promise of another beginning for all the voices that have made up the whole of the Western metaphysical tradition, the whole of the first beginning, is only to be gained in a biased struggle. To sustain such a point, I return to the question of the first and the other beginning.

The necessity of the other beginning, Heidegger reminds us in *Beiträge*, arises from the originary positing of the first beginning itself. More precisely, the first beginning not only explains the necessity of the other beginning, it necessarily sets the other beginning apart from and opposite to itself (*Die Auseinandersetzung der Notwendigkeit des anderen Anfangs aus der ursprünglichen Setzung des ersten Anfangs*).[37] The first beginning is characterized by the experience and positing of the truth of beings (*die Wahrheit des Seienden*), yet since "what thus became disclosed in the first beginning, being as being, necessarily overpowers everything else, the question concerning truth as such is not asked here."[38] Indeed, the more extreme the forgetting of the question of truth becomes, the more imperiously metaphysics sets the space for another beginning apart from and opposite to itself. However, with the other beginning, only that which could not be questioned in the first beginning—as a result of the sheer overpowering disclosure of being as being—is questioned: truth itself. By explicitly asking the question of the truth of being, the other beginning conceptualizes what in the first necessarily receded into oblivion in order for there to be a first beginning in the first place, but from which alone the first beginning draws its true meaning. In the confrontation with the first beginning, this first beginning—metaphysics in other words—is not denounced as error. No demarcation of the other beginning from the first can possibly be a turning down or belittling.[39] On the contrary, to cite Heidegger, "the leap into the other beginning is a return into the first and vice versa. Yet return into the first beginning (the "*Wieder-holung*") is not a taking back into something past as if the latter could be made "real" in the common sense. The return into the first beginning is precisely a distancing (*Entfernung*) from it."[40] In the *Auseinandersetzung*, the other beginning is only the repetition of the first beginning, yet in such manner that the explicit questioning of the forgotten question constitutive of the first beginning leads to a deepening of it and hence to its complete recasting. Heidegger writes: "The other beginning helps from a renewed originarity the first beginning to achieve the truth of its history and, consequently, its own most inalienable Otherness (*zu seiner unveräußerlichen eigensten Andersheit*), which becomes only fruitful in the historical dialogue of the thinkers."[41] In short, in the *Auseinandersetzung* between the first beginning and the other beginning and necessarily set forth by the first, the first beginning, by coming into its own, by achieving what it is most properly, and hence what is most inalienably other about it, becomes the greatest of the beginnings. In addition, only by having come to an end, by having in its most extreme position reached its own limits, is it possible, in the confrontational dialogue, for the first beginning to fulfill that greatness.

What, then, does this imply for the dialogue, the confrontation between Nietzsche and Heidegger? If the other beginning, from which the *Auseinandersetzung* takes place, is the condition under which Nietzsche's thought can be established in its greatest strength, in what is most proper to it, then an *Auseinandersetzung* is not only what does justice to Nietzsche's thought, it also takes place in a place necessarily called upon by that thought itself. Hence, the unequal struggle at which we pointed, as well as the orientation of the confrontation toward enabling Heidegger to exert the supreme task of thinking, is demanded by *the matter* of Nietzsche's thought itself. For without it, the thought of the thinker cannot achieve what is most inalienably other about it and hence also most inalienably proper to it. *The matter* of Nietzsche's thinking—in itself *Auseinandersetzung*—itself entails a certain injustice, or delay in justice, such that justice can be done to *the matter* in the first place.

Although Nietzsche's thought necessitates from within a certain injustice on Heidegger's part in order that it be recognized in its greatest strength, this necessary injustice, this limitation of justice to do justice, is at the same time the condition by which Heidegger will be able to exert the supreme task of thinking. The very specificity of Heidegger's philosophical achievement is a function of that interpretation called upon by Nietzsche's thought "itself." Consequently, what looked at first like an unequal relation by virtue of the historical nature of the battle positions now appears to have all the characteristics of the rather harmonious play of contestants in the originary struggle of the *polemos*. Undoubtedly, interpreting Nietzsche's thought from the perspective of the other beginning restricts it to representing "only"—"an 'only' that is not a limitation, but the demand for something more originary"[42]—a completion of the first beginning. In that, however, Nietzsche's thought achieves a greatness it could not have had by itself in itself. For there is no such thing as a thought, even a thought exclusively determined from within itself, which is solely of itself, is only thought. The thought of the other beginning, by contrast, is a thought whose necessity has always been required by the first beginning. It is what it is "only" in so far as without it, the first beginning could never have been the greatest beginning. In the *Auseinandersetzung* between Nietzsche's thought and Heidegger's thinking, the necessity of the latter's thought is staged in view of the needs of the first. On the other hand, the thought of the other beginning requires that it be demarcated from what it must construe as the first beginning, and this demarcation reflects the thought of the other beginning into its own. In *Auseinandersetzung* the bias is shared. One and the Other, the first beginning and the other beginning, Nietzsche and Heidegger, without priority, reflect each other into their own by calling upon the respective Other's biased approach.[43] In such *Auseinandersetzung*, one thinker's thought and that of another play into by playing against one another. This movement shares the allure of dialectics but differs from it in the important respect that in it the One and the Other, far from being poles destined for eventual supersession, constitute themselves as themselves to begin with. Their irreducible, inalienable difference from one another hinges upon the mutual call for disappropriation. More importantly, however, *Auseinandersetzung* differs from dialectics in what might be called the *generalized biasing*, or *systematic slant* that characterizes its movements. As we have seen, only in view of the thought of the other beginning does Nietzsche achieve what is most inalienably proper to him, and conversely, does Heidegger's own thought come into its own only through its demarcation from a Nietzsche "reductively" interpreted as having completed the first beginning. Unlike critique, *Auseinandersetzung* accords a necessary, a constitutive function to the Other. Yet, it is also clear from what we have developed so far that the possibility of recognition itself of the Other and *Befremdung* of the One by the Other hinge on a presentation of the One and the Other from a special angle. *Auseinandersetzung,* and thus the existence of a One and an Other in the first place, is only possible on the condition of a slanted, slightly unjust understanding that does not see the One and the Other as being what it is solely in and out of itself. This injustice not only causes Nietzsche to appear in his greatest strength and hence as Other to begin with but also makes Heidegger's "supreme exertion of thinking" *merely* the humble recasting of the first beginning. Consequently, one slant counterbalances the other. No dissymmetry prevails here, and hence, in *Auseinandersetzung,* the One and the Other merely secure their respective places by unseating one another in a movement of reciprocal reference or *Befremdung.* Yet, although this symmetric play between the One and the Other seems to reveal a definite limitation on the ability of *Auseinandersetzung* to take in the Other as Other, it also brings into view a clear limit on the extent to which propriety—the ownmost in its inalienable Otherness—may be attributed to an opponent in dialogue. It is in light of this essential limit, without which there would not be any *Auseinandersetzung,* that the following remarks by Heidegger on the limits of greatness must be read. In the addenda to *The Will to Power as Art*, Heidegger remarks that to valuate a thinker does not mean to overlook what he has not overcome. The fateful belongs to greatness, he notes.[44] While *Auseinandersetzung* is not a finding fault or scoring of mistakes, it is nonetheless "a fixing of limits." "Limits belong to greatness. They do not exist in order to be regarded as something faulty, for they are the border—of the other and the created," Heidegger writes.[45] Confrontation as genuine critique thus points out the *necessary* limits to greatness, limits that belong intimately, inalienably, to thinking. If these limits become thematic, in *Auseinandersetzung,* "it is in order to take up the task once again and to know the necessity of the limits. The limits of all greatness—the moment of its birth."[46] The very Otherness of greatness calls for the repetition of a thinker's thought, demanding that *the matter* be taken up again, and in thinking its limits, be developed, or rather, be thought further.

Notes

1. Martin Heidegger, *Nietzsche* (volume 1: *The Will to Power as Art*; volume 2: *The Eternal Recurrence of the Same*), trans. David Farrell Krell (San Francisco: HarperCollins, 1991).

2. Ibid., p. xxxix.

3. Ibid., p. 4.

4. Jacob and Wilhelm Grimm, *Deutsches Wörterbuch* (Leipzig: Hirzel, 1854).

5. *Trübner's Deutsches Wörterbuch*, ed. Alfred Goetze (Berlin: Walter de Gruyter, 1939).

6. J. C. A. Heyse, *Handwörterbuch der deutschen Sprache* (1833) (Hildesheim: Olms, 1968).

7. Martin Heidegger, *1. Nietzsches Metaphysik. 2. Einleitung in die Philosophie. Denken und Dichten*, Gesamtausgabe, volume 50 (Frankfurt a.M.: Vittorio Klostermann, 1990), p. 84.

8. Heidegger, *Nietzsche*, trans. Krell, pp. 4–5.

9. Martin Heidegger, *Die Frage nach dem Ding. Zu Kants Lehre von den transzendentalen Grundsätzen* (Tübingen: Niemeyer, 1975), p. 93.

10. Martin Heidegger, *Nietzsche: Der Wille zur Macht als Kunst*, Gesamtausgabe, volume 43 (Frankfurt a.M.: Vittorio Klostermann, 1985), pp. 277, 279.

11. Heidegger, *Die Frage nach dem Ding*, p. 93.

12. Martin Heidegger, *An Introduction to Metaphysics*, trans. Ralph Manheim (New Haven: Yale University Press, 1959), p. 63.

13. Ibid., p. 62.

14. Ibid.

15. Ibid., pp. 113–14.

16. Ibid., p. 62.

17. Martin Heidegger, *Erläuterungen zu Hölderlins Dichtung*, Gesamtausgabe, volume 4 (Frankfurt a.M.: Vittorio Klostermann, 1981), p. 60.

18. Ibid., p. 196. In Heidegger's analysis in "Language" of Georg Trakl's "A Winter Evening," intimacy becomes determined as the very middle from which the intimate "divides itself cleanly and remains separated." Intimacy here names the middle from which the extremes are held apart *(auseinander)* so that they are at one with each other *(zueinander einig)*. See Martin Heidegger, *Poetry, Language, Thought*. trans. Albert Hofstadter (New York: Harper & Row, 1971), pp. 202–204.

19. Heidegger, *Nietzsche*, trans. Krell, pp. xxix–xl.

20. Heidegger, *Nietzsche*, Gesamtausgabe, vol. 43, pp. 275–76.

21. Martin Heidegger, *Beiträge zur Philosophie*, Gesamtausgabe, volume 65 (Frankfurt a.M.: Vittorio Klostermann, 1989), p. 187.

22. Heidegger, *Nietzsche*, trans. Krell, pp. 4–5. In the addenda to the lecture on "Nietzsche's Metaphysics" from 1941–42, as well as in the lecture "Introduction into Philosophy: Thinking and Poetry" from 1944–45, Heidegger conceives of *Auseinandersetzung* not only primarily as a confrontation with Nietzsche but as a debate that secures "our thinking: that which is thought-worthy for us" as well (p. 84). He writes: "'*Auseinandersetzen.*' Thinking confronts thinking (*Denken setzt sich mit dem*

Denken auseinander). Only thus can one thinking encounter another. Only in this manner is there response (*Entgegnung*). In this manner alone, thinking frees itself from standing against one another in opposition (*aus dem Gegen der Gegnerschaft*)— into the belonging into the same" (p. 87). "In an *Auseinandersetzung* the thoughts that address us and our own thinking bring themselves into a relation of opposition. With this separation *(Auseinandertreten)* the distance occurs from which perhaps an appreciation matures of what constitutes one's own essentiality and the unattainable strength of the encountered thought. Genuine *Auseinandersetzung* does not track down weaknesses and mistakes, does not criticize; rather, it brings the historically encountered thinking before our thinking, and in the open of a decision which the encounter renders inevitable. Therefore we can meditate on the thought of Nietzsche, as well as on all other thinking, only through *Auseinandersetzung*, through which alone we are included into the fundamental feature *(Grundzug)* of historically encountered thought, in order to respond to it in a historical manner" (Heidegger, *1. Nietzsches Metaphysik. 2. Einleitung in die Philosophie. Denken und Dichten*).

23. Heidegger, *Nietzsche,* Gesamtausgabe, vol. 43, p. 276.

24. Ibid.

25. *Nietzsche,* trans. Krell, p. 5.

26. Heidegger, *Nietzsche,* Gesamtausgabe, vol. 43, p. 277.

27. Heidegger, *Beiträge,* p. 181.

28. Heidegger, *1. Nietzsches Metaphysik. 2. Einleitung in die Philosophie. Denken und Dichten,* p. 100.

29. Martin Heidegger, *Vier Seminare* (Frankfurt a.M.: Vittorio Klostermann, 1977), p. 24.

30. Heidegger, *Beiträge,* p. 176.

31. Heidegger, *Nietzsche,* Gesamtausgabe, vol. 43, p. 276.

32. Heidegger, *Nietzsche,* trans. Krell, p. 4.

33. Ibid.

34. Heidegger, *Nietzsche,* Gesamtausgabe, vol. 43, p. 278.

35. Heidegger, *Beiträge,* p. 179.

36. Ibid., pp. 185–86.

37. Ibid., p. 169.

38. Ibid., p. 179.

39. Ibid., p. 178.

40. Ibid., p. 185.

41. Ibid., p. 187.

42. Ibid., p. 175.

43. This is perhaps the point to anticipate a possible objection to the preceding developments. It might be argued that the confrontation between Heidegger and Nietzsche, as we have outlined it, would correspond, at best, to Heidegger's treatment of Nietzsche in the lectures on *The Will to Power as Art,* whereas in the later lectures, Nietzsche will become restricted to such a degree that it would be truly misleading to still characterize the discussion in terms of an *Auseinandersetzung.* Yet, let us recall that the "Author's Foreword" of 1961 prefaces "all volumes." Indeed, is not the radically constricted Nietzsche of the later lectures—in which the completion of metaphysics becomes "reduced" to, or "substituted" by technology as the fulfillment of metaphysics—precisely the opponent at its strongest, "unfolded from the innermost depth of his work to what is most extreme about him," as required by all genuine *Auseinandersetzung?*

44. Heidegger, *Nietzsche,* Gesamtausgabe, vol. 43, p. 278.
45. Ibid., p. 277.
46. Ibid.

Rodolphe Gasché: Selected Bibliography

Books

On Minimal Things: Essays on the Notion of Relation. Stanford: Stanford University Press, 1999.

The Wild Card of Reading: On Paul de Man. Cambridge, Mass.: Harvard University Press, 1998.

Inventions of Difference: On Jacques Derrida. Cambridge, Mass.: Harvard University Press, 1994.

The Tain of the Mirror: Derrida and the Philosophy of Reflection. Cambridge, Mass.: Harvard University Press, 1986.

System und Metaphorik in der Philosophie von Georges Bataille. Bern: Peter Lang, 1978.

Chapters in Edited Volumes and Journal Articles

"Transcendentality, in Play." In *Kants Ästhetik/Kant's Aesthetics/L'esthétique de Kant,* ed. Herman Parret. Berlin and New York: Walter de Gruyter, 1998.

"The Witch Metapsychology," trans. J. Patrick. In *Return of the "French Freud": Freud, Lacan and Beyond,* ed. T. Dufresne. New York: Routledge, 1997.

"Heliocentric Exchange," trans. M. Parslow. In *The Logic of the Gift: Toward an Ethic of Generosity,* ed. Alan Schrift. London: Routledge, 1997.

"Alongside the Horizon." In *The Sense of Philosophy: On Jean-Luc Nancy,* ed. S. Sheppard et al. London: Routledge, 1997.

"Under the Heading of Theory." In *Institution in Cultures: Theory and Practice,* ed. R. Lumsden and R. Patke. Amsterdam: Rodopi, 1996.

"The Sober Absolute: On Benjamin and the Early Romantics." In *Walter Benjamin: Theoretical Questions,* ed. David S. Ferris. Stanford: Stanford University Press, 1996.

"The Felicities of Paradox: Blanchot on the Null-Space of Literature." In *Maurice Blanchot: Literature, Philosophy, and Ethics,* ed. C. B. Gill. London: Routledge, 1996.

"Comparatively Theoretical." In *Germanistik und Komparatistik: DEF-Symposium 1993,* ed. Hendrik Birus. Stuttgart: Metzler, 1995.

"The Heterological Almanac," trans. Leslie Anne Boldt-Irons. In *On Bataille: Critical Essays,* ed. Leslie Anne Boldt-Irons. Albany: State University of New York Press, 1995.

"Deconstructive Criticism." In *Contemporary Literary Criticism.* New York: Gale Research, 1995.

"On Re-Presentation, or Zigzagging with Husserl and Derrida." *Southern Journal of Philosophy* 32 (1993).

"Perhaps—a Modality? On the Way with Heidegger to Language." *Graduate Faculty Philosophy Journal* 16.2 (1993).

"Floundering in Determination." In *Commemorations: Reading Heidegger,* ed. John Sallis. Bloomington: Indiana University Press, 1993.

"On Critique, Hypercriticism, and Deconstruction: The Case of Benjamin." *Cardozo Law Review* (1991).

"God, for Example." In *Phenomenology and the Numinous.* Pittsburgh: Simon Silverman Phenomenology Center Press, Duquesne University, 1988.

"Postmodernism and Rationality." *Journal of Philosophy* 85.10 (1988).

"Nontotalization without Spuriousness: Hegel and Derrida on the Infinite." *Journal of the British Society for Phenomenology* 17.3 (1986).

"On Aesthetic and Historical Determination." In *Poststructuralism and the Question of History,* ed. R. Young et al. Cambridge: Cambridge University Press, 1986.

"The Internal Border," and "The Operator of Difference." In *The Ear of the Other: Otobiography, Transference, Translation. Texts and Discussions with Jacques Derrida,* trans. P. Kamuf. New York: Schocken Books, 1985.

"Quasi-Metaphoricity and the Question of Being." In *Hermeneutics and Deconstruction,* ed. Hugh J. Silverman and Don Ihde. Albany: State University of New York Press, 1985.

"Joining the Text: From Heidegger to Derrida." In *The Yale Critics: Deconstruction in America,* ed. Jonathan Arac, Wlad Godzich, and Wallace Martin. Minneapolis: University of Minnesota Press, 1983.

"Autobiography as *Gestalt:* F. Nietzsche's *Ecce Homo.*" *Boundary 2* (1981).

"Deconstruction as Criticism." *Glyph* 6 (1979).

Part 5

Voices of the Other

13

Subjection, Resistance, Resignification

Between Freud and Foucault

JUDITH BUTLER

Judith Butler is one of the most well-known feminist philosophers in America. She is widely recognized for her original voice in bringing an awareness of the importance of such issues as embodiment, gender, and sexuality to philosophy. She studied with Hans-Georg Gadamer in Heidelberg, where she became immersed in his theory of language and its implications for thinking about subjective experience in culture. This interest led her to the Frankfurt School and eventually to a dissertation on Hegel's *Phenomenology of Spirit*. Simone de Beauvoir's concept of the body and of the agency of gender became the basis for her subsequent and enormously influential work in feminist theory. Foucault has been a primary interlocutor for Butler, and her work has explored the convergence of Foucauldian and psychoanalytic perspectives. *Bodies that Matter* sets forth her influential feminist philosophy of embodiment, and *Excitable Speech: A Politics of the Performative* discusses this issue further and takes up its relationship to language and textuality. Her most recent work focuses on Antigone and the problem of defiance as it becomes defined in terms of the power relations it opposes and the psychic mechanisms that undermine its aim.

Butler has been concerned primarily with the relation between desire and recognition. This issue has framed much of her work in continental philosophy, continental feminist philosophy, and queer theory. Much of her philosophical work has involved the question of the subject, its emergence in language, and the meaning of its agency in a post-humanist light. In her treatment of the subject, she brings together social views of the subject (from Hegel on) with those that are more psychological in orientation, especially as they are defined by Nietzsche and Freud. Her work has been enormously important in the current philosophical discussion of the social constitution of the subject, its relation to power, and the possibilities for innovation that emerge within that framework. This concern about the subject and power comes together in the treatment of subjection she offers in *The Psychic Life of Power*.

Butler's contribution to this volume, "Subjection, Resistance, Resignification: Between Freud and Foucault," attempts to orchestrate a dialogue between social theory and psychoanalysis. On the one hand, she
expresses concern about those psychological accounts of the subject
that deride or derogate the social dimension of the subject's constitution; but, on the other hand, she also shows the difficulties one encounters in social accounts, even at times in those of Foucault, which
repudiate the mechanism and hold of the psyche. She employs a notion of the unconscious of power itself as a way of understanding the
possibility of resignification that makes subject formation and re-formation possible.

-->=◎☞<-

*My problem is essentially the definition of the implicit systems in which we find ourselves
prisoners; what I would like to grasp is the system of limits and exclusion which we practice without knowing it; I would like to make the cultural unconscious apparent.*
　　　　　　　　　　—Michel Foucault, "Rituals of Exclusion"

Consider, in *Discipline and Punish,* the paradoxical character of what Foucault describes as the subjectivation of the prisoner. The term "subjectivation" carries the paradox in itself: *assujetissement* denotes both the becoming of the subject and the process of subjection—one inhabits the figure of
autonomy only by becoming subjected to a power, a subjection that implies a radical dependency. For Foucault, this process of subjectivation takes
place centrally through the body. In *Discipline and Punish* the prisoner's body
not only appears as a *sign* of guilt and transgression, as the embodiment of
prohibition and the sanction for rituals of normalization, but is framed and
formed through the discursive matrix of a juridical subject. The claim that a
discourse "forms" the body is no simple one, and from the start we must
distinguish how such "forming" is not the same as a "causing" or "determining"; still less is it a notion that bodies are somehow made of discourse
pure and simple.[1]

Foucault suggests that the prisoner is not regulated by an *exterior* relation
of power, whereby an institution takes a pregiven individual as the target of
its subordinating aims. On the contrary, the individual is formed or, rather,
formulated through his or her discursively constituted "identity" as prisoner. Subjection is, literally, the *making* of a subject, the principle of regulation according to which a subject is formulated or produced. Such subjection is a kind of power that not only unilaterally *acts on* a given individual as
a form of domination but also *activates* or forms the subject. Hence, subjection is neither simply the domination of a subject nor its production, but
designates a certain kind of restriction *in* production, a restriction without
which the production of the subject cannot take place, a restriction through

which that production takes place. Although Foucault occasionally tries to argue that historically *juridical* power—power acting on, subordinating, pregiven subjects—precedes productive power—the capacity of power to *form* subjects—with the prisoner it is clear that the subject produced and the subject regulated or subordinated are one and that compulsory production is its own form of regulation.

Foucault warns against those within the liberal tradition who would liberate the prisoner from the prison's oppressive confines, for the subjection signified by the exterior institution of the prison does not act apart from the invasion and management of the prisoner's body. What Foucault describes as the full siege and invasion of that body by the signifying practices of the prison—namely, inspection, confession, the regularization and normalization of bodily movement and gesture, the disciplinary regimes of the body—have led feminists to consult Foucault in order to elaborate the disciplinary production of gender.[2] The prison thus acts on the prisoner's body, but it does so by forcing the prisoner to approximate an ideal, a norm of behavior, a model of obedience. This is how the prisoner's individuality is rendered coherent, totalized, made into the discursive and conceptual possession of the prison; it is, as Foucault insists, the way in which "he becomes the principle of his own subjection."[3] This normative ideal inculcated, as it were, into the prisoner is a kind of psychic identity, or what Foucault will call a "soul." Because the soul is an imprisoning effect, Foucault claims that the prisoner is subjected "in a more fundamental way" than by the spatial captivity of the prison. Indeed, in the following passage, the soul is figured itself as a kind of spatial captivity, indeed, as a kind of prison, which provides the exterior form or regulatory principle of the prisoner's body. This becomes clear in the formulation that "the man described for us, whom we are invited to free, is already in himself the effect of a subjection [*assujetissement*] much more profound than himself. . . . the soul is the prison of the body."[4]

Although Foucault is specifying the subjectivation of the prisoner here, he appears also to be privileging the metaphor of the prison to theorize the subjectivation of the body. What are we to make of imprisonment and invasion as the privileged figures through which Foucault articulates the process of subjectivation, the discursive production of identities? If discourse produces identity by supplying and enforcing a regulatory principle which thoroughly invades, totalizes, and renders coherent the individual, then it seems that every "identity," insofar as it is totalizing, acts as precisely such a "soul that imprisons the body." In what sense is this soul "much more profound" than the prisoner himself? Does this mean that the soul preexists the body that animates it? How are we to understand such a claim in the context of Foucault's theory of power?

Rather than answer that question directly, one might for the purposes of clarification counterpose the "soul," which Foucault articulates as an imprisoning frame, to the psyche in the psychoanalytic sense.[5] In the psyche, the subject's ideal corresponds to the ego-ideal, which the super-ego is said to consult, as it were, in order to measure the ego. Jacques Lacan redescribes this ideal as the "position" of the subject within the symbolic, the norm that installs the subject within language and hence within available schemes of cultural intelligibility. This viable and intelligible being, this subject, is always produced at a cost, and whatever resists the normative demand by which subjects are instituted remains unconscious. Thus the psyche, which includes the unconscious, is very different from the subject: the psyche is precisely what exceeds the imprisoning effects of the discursive demand to inhabit a coherent identity, to become a coherent subject. The psyche is what resists the regularization that Foucault ascribes to normalizing discourses. Those discourses are said to imprison the body *in the soul,* to animate and contain the body within that ideal frame, and to that extent reduce the notion of the psyche to the operations of an externally framing and normalizing ideal.[6] This Foucauldian move appears to treat the psyche as if it received unilaterally the effect of the Lacanian symbolic. The transposition of the soul into an exterior and imprisoning frame for the body vacates, as it were, the interiority of the body, leaving that interiority as a malleable surface for the unilateral effects of disciplinary power.

I am in part moving toward a psychoanalytic criticism of Foucault, for I think that one cannot account for subjectivation and, in particular, for becoming the principle of one's own subjection without recourse to a psychoanalytic account of the formative or generative effects of restriction or prohibition. Moreover, the formation of the subject cannot fully be thought—if it ever can be—without recourse to a paradoxically enabling set of grounding constraints. Yet as I elaborate this critique, some romanticized notions of the unconscious defined as necessary resistance will come under critical scrutiny, and that criticism will entail the reemergence of a Foucauldian perspective *within* psychoanalysis. The question of a suppressed psychoanalysis in Foucault—raised by Foucault himself in the reference to a "cultural unconscious" quoted in the epigraph to this essay—might be raised more precisely as the problem of locating or accounting for resistance. Where does resistance to or in disciplinary subject formation take place? Does the reduction of the psychoanalytically rich notion of the psyche to that of the imprisoning soul eliminate the possibility of resistance to normalization and to subject formation, a resistance that emerges precisely from the incommensurability between psyche and subject? How would we understand such resistance, and would such an understanding entail a critical rethinking of psychoanalysis along the way?

In what follows, I will ask two different kinds of questions, one of Foucault, and another of psychoanalysis (applying this term variously to Freud and to Lacan).[7] First, if Foucault understands the psyche to be an imprisoning effect in the service of normalization, then how might he account for psychic resistance to normalization? Second, when some proponents of psychoanalysis insist that resistance to normalization is a function of the unconscious, is this guarantee of psychic resistance merely sleight of hand? More precisely, is the resistance upon which psychoanalysis insists socially and discursively produced, or is it a kind of resistance to, an undermining of, social and discursive production *as such*? Consider the claim that the unconscious only and always resists normalization, that every ritual of conformity to the injunctions of civilization comes at a cost, and that a certain unharnessed and unsocialized remainder is thereby produced which contests the appearance of the law-abiding subject. This psychic remainder signifies the limits of normalization. That position does not imply that such resistance wields the power to rework or rearticulate the terms of discursive demand, the disciplinary injunctions by which normalization occurs. To thwart the injunction to produce a docile body is not the same as dismantling the injunction or changing the terms of subject constitution. If the unconscious, or the psyche more generally, is defined as resistance, what do we then make of unconscious attachments to subjection, which imply that the unconscious is no more free of normalizing discourse than the subject? If the unconscious escapes from a given normative injunction, to what other injunction does it form an attachment? What makes us think that the unconscious is any less structured by the power relations that pervade cultural signifiers than is the language of the subject? If we find an attachment to subjection at the level of the unconscious, what kind of resistance is to be wrought from that?

Even if we grant that unconscious resistance to a normalizing injunction guarantees the failure of that injunction fully to constitute its subject, does such resistance do anything to alter or expand the dominant injunctions or interpellations of subject formation? What do we make of a resistance that can only undermine, but that appears to have no power to rearticulate the terms, the symbolic terms—to use Lacanian parlance—by which subjects are constituted, by which subjection is installed in the very formation of the subject? This resistance establishes the incomplete character of any effort to produce a subject by disciplinary means, but it remains unable to rearticulate the dominant terms of productive power.

Before continuing this interrogation of psychoanalysis, however, let us return to the problem of bodies in Foucault. How and why is resistance denied to bodies produced through disciplinary regimes? What is this notion of disciplinary production, and does it work as efficaciously as Foucault appears to imply? In the final chapter of the first volume of *The History of Sexuality*, Foucault calls for a "history of bodies" that would inquire into "the manner in which what is most material and vital in them has been invested."[8] In this formulation, he suggests that power acts not only *on* the body but also *in* the body, that power not only produces the boundaries of a subject but pervades the interiority of that subject. In the last formulation, it appears that there is an "inside" to the body which exists before power's invasion. But given the radical exteriority of the soul, how are we to understand "interiority" in Foucault?[9] That interiority will not be a soul, and it will not be a psyche, but what will it be? Is this a space of pure malleability, one that is, as it were, ready to conform to the demands of socialization? Or is this interiority to be called, simply, the body? Has it come to the paradoxical point where Foucault wants to claim that the soul is the exterior form and the body the interior space?

Although Foucault wants on occasion to refute the possibility of a body which is not produced through power relations, sometimes his explanations require a body to maintain a materiality ontologically distinct from the power relations that take it as a site of investment.[10] Indeed, the term "site" seemingly appears in this phrase without warrant, for what is the relation between the body as *site* and the investments which that site is said to receive or bear? Does the term "site" stabilize the body in relation to those investments while deflecting the question of how investments establish, contour, and disrupt what the phrase takes for granted as the body's "site" (that is, does the term "site" deflect the project of Lacan's "mirror stage")? What constitutes an "investment," and what is its constituting power? Does it have a visualizing function, and can we understand the production of the bodily ego in Freud as the projected or spatialized modality of such investments?[11] Indeed, to what extent is the body's site stabilized through a certain projective instability, one that Foucault cannot quite describe and which would perhaps engage him in the problematic of the ego as an imaginary function?

Discipline and Punish offers a different configuration of the relation between materiality and investment. There the soul is taken to be an instrument of power through which the body is cultivated and formed. In a sense, it acts as a power-laden schema that produces and actualizes the body. We can understand Foucault's references to the soul as an implicit reworking of the Aristotelian formulation in which the soul is understood to be the form and principle of the body's matter.[12] Foucault argues in *Discipline and Punish* that the soul becomes a normative and normalizing ideal according to which the body is trained, shaped, cultivated, and invested; it is a historically specific imaginary ideal *(idéal speculatif)* under which the body is materialized.

This "subjection" or *assujetissement* is not only a subordination but a securing and maintaining, a putting into place of a subject, a subjectivation. The "soul brings [the prisoner] to existence"; not unlike in Aristotle, the soul, as an instrument of power, forms and frames the body, stamps it, and in stamping it, brings it into being. In this formulation, there is no body outside of power, for the materiality of the body—indeed, materiality itself—is produced by and in direct relation to the investment of power. The materiality of the prison, Foucault writes, is established to the extent that *(dans la mésure)* it is a vector and instrument of power.[13] Hence, the prison is *materialized* to the extent that it is *invested with power*. To be grammatically accurate, there is no prison prior to its materialization; its materialization is coextensive with its investiture with power relations; and materiality is the effect and gauge of this investment. The prison comes to be only within the field of power relations, more specifically, only to the extent that it is saturated with such relations and that such a saturation is formative of its very being. Here the body—of the prisoner and of the prison—is not an independent materiality, a static surface or site, which a subsequent investment comes to mark, signify upon, or pervade; the body is that for which materialization and investiture are coextensive.

Although the soul is understood to frame the body in *Discipline and Punish,* Foucault suggests that the production of the "subject" takes place to some degree through the subordination and even destruction of the body. In "Nietzsche, Genealogy, History," Foucault remarks that only through the destruction of the body does the subject as a "dissociated unity" appear: "the body is the inscribed surface of events (traced by language and dissolved by ideas), the locus of a dissociated self (adopting the illusion of a substantial unity), and a volume in perpetual disintegration."[14] The subject appears at the expense of the body, an appearance conditioned in inverse relation to the disappearance of the body. The subject not only effectively takes the place of the body but acts as the soul which frames and forms the body in captivity. Here the forming and framing function of that exterior soul works against the body; indeed, it might be understood as the sublimation of the body in consequence of displacement and substitution.

In thus redescribing the body in Foucault, I have clearly wandered into a psychoanalytic vocabulary of sublimation. While there, let me pose a question to return to the issue of subjection and resistance. If the body is subordinated and to some extent destroyed as the dissociated self emerges, and if that emergence might be read as the sublimation of the body and the self be read as the body's ghostly form, then is there some part of the body which is not preserved in sublimation, some part of the body which remains unsublimated?

This bodily remainder, I would suggest, survives for such a subject in the mode of already, if not always, having been destroyed, in a kind of constitutive loss. This body is not a site on which a construction takes place; it is a destruction on the occasion of which a subject is formed. The formation of this subject is at once the framing, subordination, and regulation of the body, and the mode in which that destruction is preserved (in the sense of sustained and embalmed) *in* normalization.

If, then, the body is now to be understood as that which not only constitutes the subject in its dissociated and sublimated state, but also exceeds or resists any effort at sublimation, how are we to understand this body that is, as it were, negated or repressed so that the subject might live? One might expect the body to return in a non-normalizable wildness, and there are of course moments in Foucault when something like that happens. But more often than not, in Foucault the possibility of subversion or resistance appears (a) in the course of a subjectivation that exceeds the normalizing aims by which it is mobilized, for example, in "reverse-discourse," or (b) through convergence with other discursive regimes, whereby inadvertently produced discursive complexity undermines the teleological aims of normalization.[15] Thus resistance appears as the effect of power, as a part of power, its self-subversion.

In the theorization of resistance, a certain problem arises which concerns psychoanalysis and, by implication, the limits of subjectivation. For Foucault, the subject who is produced through subjection is not produced at an instant in its totality. Instead, it is in the process of being produced, it is repeatedly produced (which is not the same as being produced anew again and again). It is precisely the possibility of a repetition which does not consolidate that dissociated unity, the subject, but which proliferates effects which undermine the force of normalization. The term which not only names but forms and frames the subject—let us use Foucault's example of homosexuality—mobilizes a reverse discourse against the very regime of normalization by which it is spawned. This is, of course, not a pure opposition, for the same "homosexuality" will be deployed first in the service of normalizing heterosexuality and second in the service of its own depathologization. This term will carry the risk of the former meaning in the latter, but it would be a mistake to think that simply by speaking the term one either transcends heterosexual normalization or becomes its instrument.

The risk of renormalization is persistently there: consider the one who, in defiant "outness," declares his/her homosexuality only to receive the response, "Ah yes, so you are that, and only that." Whatever you say will be read back as an overt or subtle manifestation of your essential homosexuality. (One should not underestimate how exhausting it is to be expected to be an "out" homosexual all the time, whether the expectation comes from gay and lesbian allies or their foes.) Here Foucault cites and reworks the possibility of resignification, of mobilizing politically what Nietzsche, in *On the Genealogy of Morals,* called the "sign chain." There Nietzsche argues that the uses to which a given sign is originally put are "worlds apart" from the uses to which it then becomes available. This temporal gap between usages produces the possibility of a reversal of signification but also opens the way for an inauguration of signifying possibilities that exceed those to which the term has been previously bound.

The Foucauldian subject is never fully constituted in subjection, then; it is repeatedly constituted in subjection, and it is in the possibility of a repetition that repeats against its origin that subjection might be understood to draw its inadvertently enabling power. From a psychoanalytic perspective, however, we might ask whether this possibility of resistance to a constituting or subjectivating power can be derived from what is "in" or "of" discourse. What can we make of the way in which discourses not only constitute the domains of the speakable but are themselves bounded through the production of a constitutive outside: the unspeakable, the unsignifiable?

From a Lacanian perspective, one might well question whether the effects of the psyche can be said to be exhausted in what can be signified or whether there is not, over and against this signifying body, a domain of the psyche which contests legibility. If, according to psychoanalysis, the subject is not the same as the psyche from which it emerges and if, for Foucault, the subject is not the same as the body from which it emerges, then perhaps the body has come to substitute for the psyche in Foucault—that is, as that which exceeds and confounds the injunctions of normalization. Is this a body pure and simple, or does "the body" come to stand for a certain operation of the psyche, one which is distinctly different, if not directly opposed to, the soul figured as an imprisoning effect? Perhaps Foucault himself has invested the body with a psychic meaning that he cannot elaborate within the terms that he uses. How does the process of subjectivation, the disciplinary production of the subject, break down, if it does, in both Foucauldian and psychoanalytic theory? Whence does that failure emerge and what are its consequences?

Consider the Althusserian notion of interpellation, in which a subject is constituted by being hailed, addressed, named.[16] For the most part, it seems, Althusser believed that this social demand—one might call it a symbolic injunction—actually produces the kinds of subjects it names. He gives the example of the policeman on the street yelling, "Hey you there!" and concludes that this call importantly constitutes the one it addresses and sites. The scene is clearly a disciplinary one; the policeman's call is an effort to bring someone back in line. Yet we might also understand it in Lacanian terms as the call of symbolic constitution. As Althusser himself insists, this performative effort of naming can only *attempt* to bring its addressee into being: there is always the risk of a certain *misrecognition*. If one misrecognizes that effort to produce the subject, the production itself falters. The one who is hailed may fail to hear, misread the call, turn the other way, answer to another name, insist on not being addressed in that way. Indeed, the domain of the imaginary is demarcated by Althusser as precisely the domain that makes *misrecognition* possible. The name is called, and I am sure it is my name, but it isn't. The name is called, and I am sure that a name is being called, my name, but it is in someone's incomprehensible speech, or worse, it is someone coughing, or worse, a radiator which for a moment approximates a human voice. Or I am sure that no one has noticed my transgression, and that it is not my name being called but only a coughing passerby, the high pitch of the heating mechanism—but it is my name, and yet I do not recognize myself in the subject that the name, at this moment, installs.[17]

Consider the force of this dynamic of interpellation and misrecognition when the name is not a proper name but a social category,[18] and hence a signifier capable of being interpreted in a number of divergent and conflictual ways. To be hailed as a "woman" or "Jew" or "queer" or "Black" or "Chicana" may be heard or interpreted as an affirmation or an insult, depending on the context in which the hailing occurs (where context is the effective historicity and spatiality of the sign). If that name is called, there is more often than not some hesitation about whether or how to respond; for what is at stake is whether the temporary totalization performed by the name is politically enabling or paralyzing, whether the foreclosure, indeed the violence, of the totalizing reduction of identity performed by that particular hailing is politically strategic or regressive or, if paralyzing and regressive, also enabling in some way.

The Althusserian use of Lacan centers on the function of the imaginary as the permanent possibility of *misrecognition,* that is, the incommensurability between symbolic demand (the name that is interpellated) and the instability and unpredictability of its appropriation. If the interpellated name seeks to accomplish the identity to which it refers, it begins as a performative process which is nevertheless derailed in the imaginary; for the imaginary is surely preoccupied with the law, structured by the law, but does not immediately obey the law. For the Lacanian, then, the imaginary signifies the impossibility of the discursive—that is, symbolic—constitution of identity. Identity can never be fully totalized by the symbolic, for what it fails to order will emerge within the imaginary as a disorder, a site where identity is contested.

Hence, in a Lacanian vein, Jacqueline Rose formulates the unconscious as that which thwarts any effort of the symbolic to constitute sexed identity coherently and fully, an unconscious indicated by the slips and gaps that characterize the workings of the imaginary in language. I quote a passage which has benefited many of us who have sought to find in psychoanalysis a principle of resistance to given forms of social reality:

> The unconscious constantly reveals the "failure" of identity. Because there is no continuity of psychic life, so there is no stability of sexual identity, no position for women (or for men) which is ever simply achieved. Nor does psychoanalysis see such "failure" as a special-case inability or an individual deviancy from the norm. "Failure" is not a moment to be regretted in a process of adaptation, or development into normality, . . . "failure" is something endlessly repeated and relived moment by moment throughout our individual histories. It appears not only in the symptom, but also in dreams, in slips of the tongue and in forms of sexual pleasure which are pushed to the sidelines of the norm . . . there is a resistance to identity at the very heart of psychic life.[19]

In *Discipline and Punish,* Foucault presumes the efficacy of the symbolic demand, its performative capacity to constitute the subject whom it names. In *The History of Sexuality, Volume 1,* however, there is both a rejection of "a single locus of Revolt"—which would presumably include the psyche, the imaginary, or the unconscious within its purview—and an affirmation of multiple possibilities of resistance enabled by power itself. For Foucault, resistance cannot be *outside* the law in another register (the imaginary) or in that which eludes the constitutive power of the law:

> there is no single locus of great Refusal, no soul of revolt, source of all rebellions, or pure law of the revolutionary. Instead there is a plurality of resistances, each of them a special case: resistances that are possible, necessary, improbable; others that are spontaneous, savage, solitary, concerted, rampant, or violent; still others that are quick to compromise, interested, or sac-

rificial; by definition, they can only exist in the strategic field of power relations. But this does not mean that they are only a reaction or rebound, forming with respect to the basic domination an underside that is in the end always passive, doomed to perpetual defeat.[20]

This last caricature of power, although clearly written with Marcuse in mind, recalls the effect of the Lacanian law, which produces its own "failure" at the level of the psyche but which can never be displaced or reformulated by that psychic resistance. The imaginary thwarts the efficacy of the symbolic law but cannot turn back upon the law, demanding or effecting its reformulation. In this sense, psychic resistance thwarts the law in its effects but cannot redirect the law or its effects. Resistance is thus located in a domain that is virtually powerless to alter the law that it opposes. Hence, psychic resistance presumes the continuation of the law in its anterior, symbolic form and, in that sense, contributes to its status quo. In such a view, resistance appears doomed to perpetual defeat.

In contrast, Foucault formulates resistance as an effect of the very power that it is said to oppose. This insistence on the dual possibility of being both *constituted* by the law and *an effect of resistance* to the law marks a departure from the Lacanian framework, for where Lacan restricts the notion of social power to the symbolic domain and delegates resistance to the imaginary, Foucault recasts the symbolic as relations of power and understands resistance as an effect of power. Foucault's conception initiates a shift from a discourse on law, conceived as juridical (and presupposing a subject subordinated by power), to a discourse on power, which is a field of productive, regulatory, and contestatory relations. For Foucault, the symbolic produces the possibility of its own subversions, and these subversions are unanticipated effects of symbolic interpellations.

The notion of "the symbolic" does not address the multiplicity of power vectors upon which Foucault insists, for power in Foucault not only consists in the reiterated elaboration of norms or interpellating demands but is formative or productive, malleable, multiple, proliferative, and conflictual. Moreover, in its resignifications, the law itself is transmuted into that which opposes and exceeds its original purposes. In this sense, disciplinary discourse does not unilaterally constitute a subject in Foucault, or rather, if it does, it *simultaneously* constitutes the condition for the subject's de-constitution. What is brought into being through the performative effect of the "subject" created is not for that reason fixed in place: it becomes the occasion for a further making. Indeed, I would add, a subject only remains a subject through a reiteration or rearticulation of itself as a subject; and this dependency of the subject on repetition for its own coherence may constitute that subject's incoherence, its incomplete character. This repetition or, better, iterability, thus becomes the non-place of subversion, the possibility of a re-embodying of the subjectivating norm that can redirect its normativity.

Consider the inversions of "woman" and "woman," depending on the staging and address of their performance, of "queer" and "queer," depending on pathologizing or contestatory modes. Both examples concern not an opposition between reactionary and progressive usage but rather a progressive usage that requires and repeats the reactionary in order to effect a subversive reterritorialization. For Foucault, then, the disciplinary apparatus produces subjects; but as a consequence of that production, it brings into discourse the conditions for subverting that apparatus itself. In other words, the law turns against itself and spawns versions of itself which oppose and proliferate its animating purposes. The strategic question for Foucault is, then, how can we work the power relations by which we are worked, and in what direction?

In his later interviews, Foucault suggests that identities are formed within contemporary political arrangements in relation to certain requirements of the liberal state, ones which presume that the assertion of rights and claims to entitlement can only be made on the basis of a singular and injured identity. The more specific identities become, the more totalized an identity becomes by that very specificity. Indeed, we might understand this contemporary phenomenon as the movement by which a juridical apparatus produces the field of possible political subjects. Because for Foucault the disciplinary apparatus of the state operates through the totalizing production of individuals, and because this totalization of the individual extends the jurisdiction of the state (that is, by transforming individuals into subjects of the state), Foucault will call for a remaking of subjectivity beyond the shackles of the juridical law. In this sense, what we call identity politics is produced by a state which can only allocate recognition and rights to subjects totalized by the particularity that constitutes their plaintiff status. In calling for an overthrow, as it were, of such an arrangement, Foucault is not calling for the release of a hidden or repressed subjectivity, but rather, for a radical making of subjectivity formed in and against the historical hegemony of the juridical subject:

> Maybe the target nowadays is not to discover what we are, but to refuse what we are. We have to imagine and build up what we could be to get rid of this kind of political "double bind," which is the simultaneous individualization and totalization of modern power structures. . . . The conclusion would be that the political, ethical, social, philosophical problem of our days is not to try to liberate the individual from the state, and from the state's institutions, but to liberate us from the state and the type of individualization which is linked to the state. We have to promote new forms of subjectivity through the refusal of this kind of individuality which has been imposed on us for several centuries.[21]

Two sets of questions emerge from the above analysis. First, why can Foucault formulate resistance in relation to the disciplinary power of sexuality in *The History of Sexuality*, whereas in *Discipline and Punish* disciplinary power appears to determine docile bodies incapable of resistance? Is there something about the relationship of *sexuality* to power that conditions the possibility of resistance in the first text, and a noted absence of a consideration of sexuality from the discussion of power and bodies in the second? Note that in the *History of Sexuality* the repressive function of the law is undermined precisely through becoming itself the object of erotic investment and excitation. Disciplinary apparatus fails to repress sexuality precisely because the apparatus is itself eroticized, becoming the occasion for the *incitement of sexuality* and, therefore, undoing its own repressive aims.

Second, with this transferable property of sexual investments in mind, we might ask what conditions the possibility Foucault invites, that of refusing the type of individuality correlated with the disciplinary apparatus of the modern state? And how do we account for *attachment* to precisely the kind of state-linked individuality that reconsolidates the juridical law? To what extent has the disciplinary apparatus that attempts to produce and totalize identity become an abiding object of passionate attachment? We cannot simply throw off the identities we have become, and Foucault's call to "refuse" those identities will certainly be met with resistance. If we reject theoretically the source of resistance in a psychic domain that is said to precede or exceed the social,[22] as we must, can we reformulate psychic resistance *in terms of the social* without that reformulation becoming a domestication or normalization? (Must the social always be equated with the given and the normalizable?) In particular, how are we to understand not merely the disciplinary production of the subject but the disciplinary cultivation of *an attachment to subjection?*

Such a postulation may raise the question of masochism—indeed, the question of masochism in subject-formation—yet it does not answer the question of the status of "attachment" or "investment." Here emerges the grammatical problem by which an attachment appears to precede the subject who might be said to "have" it. Yet it seems crucial to suspend the usual grammatical requirements and consider an inversion of terms such that certain attachments precede and condition the formation of subjects (the visualization of libido in the mirror stage, the sustaining of that projected image through time as the discursive function of the name). Is this then an ontology of libido or investment that is in some sense prior to and separable from a subject, or is every such investment from the start bound up with a reflexivity that is stabilized (within the imaginary) as the ego? If the ego is composed of identifications, and identification is the resolution of desire, then the ego is the residue of desire, the effect of incorporations which, Freud argues in *The Ego and the Id*, trace a lineage of attachment and loss.

In Freud's view, the formation of conscience enacts an attachment to prohibition which founds the subject in its reflexivity. Under the pressure of the ethical law, a subject emerges who is capable of reflexivity, that is, who takes him/herself as an object and so mistakes him/herself since he/she is, by virtue of that founding prohibition, at an infinite distance from his/her origin. Only on the condition of a separation enforced through prohibition does a subject emerge, formed through the attachment to prohibition (in obedience to it, but also eroticizing it). And this prohibition is all the more savory precisely because it is bound up in the narcissistic circuit that wards off the dissolution of the subject into psychosis.[23]

For Foucault, a subject is formed and then invested with a sexuality by a regime of power. If the very process of subject formation, however, requires a preemption of sexuality, a founding prohibition that prohibits a certain desire but itself becomes a focus of desire, then a subject is formed through the prohibition of a sexuality, a prohibition that at the same time forms this sexuality—and the subject who is said to bear it. This view disputes the Foucauldian notion that psychoanalysis presumes the exteriority of the law to desire, for it maintains that there is no desire without the law that forms and sustains the very desire it prohibits. Indeed, prohibition becomes an odd form of preservation, a way of eroticizing the law that would abolish eroticism but that works only by compelling eroticization. In this sense, a "sexual identity" is a productive contradiction in terms, for identity is formed through a prohibition on some dimension of the very sexuality it is said to bear, and sexuality, when it is tied to identity, is always in some sense undercutting itself.

This is not necessarily a static contradiction, for the signifiers of identity are not structurally determined in advance. If Foucault could argue that a sign could be taken up, used for purposes counter to those for which it was designed, then he understood that even the most noxious terms could be owned, that the most injurious interpellations could also be the site of radical reoccupation and resignification. But what lets us occupy the discursive site of injury? How are we animated and mobilized by that discursive site and its injury such that our very attachment to it becomes the condition for our resignification of it? Called by an injurious name, I come into social being, and because I have a certain inevitable attachment to my existence, because a certain narcissism takes hold of any term that confers existence, I am led to embrace the terms that injure me because they constitute me socially. The self-colonizing trajectory of certain forms of identity politics are symptomatic of this paradoxical embrace of the injurious term. As a further paradox, then, only by occupying—being occupied by—that injurious term can I resist and oppose it, recasting the power that constitutes me as the power I oppose. In this way, a certain place for psychoanalysis is secured in that any mobilization against subjection will take subjection as its resource, and that attachment to an injurious interpellation will, by way of a necessarily alienated narcissism, become the condition under which resignifying that interpellation becomes possible. This will not be an unconscious outside of power but rather something like the unconscious of power itself, in its traumatic and productive iterability.

If, then, we understand certain kinds of interpellations to confer identity, those injurious interpellations will constitute identity through injury. This is not the same as saying that such an identity will remain always and forever rooted in its injury as long as it remains an identity; but it does imply that the possibilities of resignification will rework and unsettle the passionate attachment to subjection without which subject formation—and re-formation—cannot succeed.

Notes

1. The following discussion borrows from and expands upon chapter 1 of my *Bodies That Matter: On the Discursive Limits of "Sex"* (New York: Routledge, 1993), pp. 33–36.

2. See Sandra Bartky, *Femininity and Domination* (New York: Routledge, 1990).

3. Michel Foucault, *Discipline and Punish: The Birth of the Prison*, trans. Alan Sheridan (New York: Random House, 1979), p. 203; *Surveiller et punir: Naissance de la prison* (Paris: Gallimard, 1975), p. 202.

4. Foucault, *Discipline and Punish*, p. 30.

5. It is important to distinguish between the notion of the psyche, which includes the notion of the unconscious, and that of the subject, whose formation is conditioned by the exclusion of the unconscious.

6. For an extended and rich discussion of how norms work to subjectivate and, in particular, how norms are to be understood as transitive actions, see Pierre Macherey, "Towards a Natural History of Norms," in Timothy J. Armstrong, trans. and ed., *Michel Foucault/Philosopher* (New York: Routledge, 1992), pp. 176–91. In the same volume, for a discussion of Foucault as writing indirectly about Lacan, see Jacques-Alain Miller, "Michel Foucault and Psychoanalysis," pp. 58–63. On the problem of the dynamic relation between ethical demands and the subjectivity to which they are addressed, see the very useful comparative discussion of Foucault and Lacan in John Rajchman, *Truth and Eros: Foucault, Lacan, and the Question of Ethics* (New York: Routledge, 1991).

7. This is not to suggest that psychoanalysis is only to be represented by these two figures, although in this analysis it will be.

8. Michel Foucault, *The History of Sexuality, Volume 1: An Introduction*, trans. Robert Hurley (New York: Random House, 1978), p. 152; *La volonté de savoir* (Paris: Gallimard, 1978), p. 200.

9. This question is raised in a different way by Charles Taylor when he asks whether there is a place for Augustinian "inwardness" in Foucault; see his "Foucault on Freedom and Truth," in David Couzens Hoy, ed., *Foucault: A Critical Reader* (New York: Blackwell, 1986), p. 99. It is also taken up in an interesting way by William Connolly in his *The Augustinian Imperative* (Newbury Park, Calif.: Sage Press, 1993).

10. See my "Foucault and the Paradox of Bodily Inscriptions," *Journal of Philosophy* 86.11 (November 1989): 257–79.

11. See discussions of the bodily ego in Freud, "The Ego and the Id," *The Standard Edition of the Complete Psychological Works of Sigmund Freud*, ed. and trans. James Strachey, 24 vols. (London: Hogarth, 1953–74), vol. 19, p. 26, and in Margaret Whitford, *Luce Irigaray: Philosophy in the Feminine* (London: Routledge, 1991), pp. 53–74.

12. For a fuller explanation of Foucault's reworking of Aristotle, see "Bodies That Matter," in my *Bodies That Matter*, pp. 32–36.

13. "What was at issue was not whether the prison environment was too harsh or too aseptic, too primitive or too efficient, but its very materiality as an instrument and vector of power" (*Discipline and Punish*, p. 30 [*Surveiller et punir*, p. 35]).

14. See Foucault, "Nietzsche, Genealogy, History," in *The Foucault Reader*, ed. Paul Rabinow (New York: Pantheon Books, 1984), p. 83.

15. See Zakia Pathak and Rajeswari Sunder Rajan, "Shahbano," in Judith Butler and Joan Scott, eds., *Feminists Theorize the Political* (New York: Routledge, 1992), pp. 257–79.

16. Louis Althusser, "Ideology and Ideological State Apparatuses (Notes Towards an Investigation)," *Lenin and Philosophy and Other Essays*, trans. Ben Brewster (New York: Monthly Review Press, 1971), pp. 170–77.

17. For an excellent book that appropriates this Althusserian problematic for feminism, see Denise Riley, *"Am I That Name?": Feminism and the Category of 'Women' in History* (Minneapolis: University of Minnesota Press, 1988).

18. See Slavoj Žižek on the social interpellation of the proper name in *The Sublime Object of Ideology* (London: Verso, 1989), pp. 87–102.

19. Jacqueline Rose, *Sexuality in the Field of Vision* (London: Verso, 1987), pp. 90–91.

20. Foucault, *The History of Sexuality, Volume 1*, pp. 95–96.

21. Foucault, "The Subject and Power," in *Michel Foucault: Beyond Structuralism and Hermeneutics*, 2nd ed., ed. Hubert L. Dreyfus and Paul Rabinow (Chicago: University of Chicago Press, 1983), p. 216.

22. See the preface to Victor Burgin, James Donald, and Cora Kaplan, eds., *Formations of Fantasy* (London: Methuen, 1986), for a psychoanalytic warning against "collapsing" the psychic and the social.

23. In the preceding paragraph, the terms "attachment" and "investment" might be understood as intentional in the phenomenological sense, that is, as libidinal movements or trajectories that always take an object. There is no free-floating attachment that subsequently takes an object; rather, an attachment is always an attachment to an object, where that to which it is attached alters the attachment itself. The transferability of attachment presupposes that the object to which an attachment is made may change but that the attachment will persist and will always take some object, and that this action of binding to (tied always to a certain warding off) is the constitutive action of attachment. This notion of attachment seems close to certain efforts to account for drives in non-biologistic terms (to be distinguished from efforts that take the biological seriously). Here one might seek recourse to Gilles Deleuze's reading of drives in *Masochism* (New York: Zone, 1989; *Presentation de Sacher-Masoch* [Paris: Minuit, 1967]), in which he suggests that drives may be understood as the pulsionality of positing or valuation. See also Jean Laplanche's recent discussions in which "the drive" becomes indissociable from its cultural articulation: "we think it necessary to conceive of a dual expository stage: on the one hand, the preliminary stage of an organism that is bound to homeostasis and self-preservation, and, on the other hand, the stage of the adult cultural world in which the infant is immediately and completely immersed" (*Jean Laplanche: Seduction, Translation, Drives*, ed. John Fletcher and Martin Stanton [London: Institute of Contemporary Arts, 1992], p. 187).

Judith Butler: Selected Bibliography

Books

Antigone's Claim: Kinship between Life and Death. New York: Columbia University Press, forthcoming.

The Psychic Life of Power: Theories in Subjection. Stanford: Stanford University Press, 1997.

Excitable Speech: A Politics of the Performative. New York: Routledge, 1997.

Bodies That Matter: On the Discursive Limits of "Sex." New York: Routledge, 1993.

Gender Trouble: Feminism and the Subversion of Identity. New York: Routledge, 1990.

Subjects of Desire: Hegelian Reflections in Twentieth-Century France. New York: Columbia University Press, 1987.

Chapters in Edited Volumes and Journal Articles

"Moral Sadism and Doubting One's Own Love." In *Reading Melanie Klein,* ed. Lyndsey Stonebridge and John Phillips. London: Routledge, 1998.

"Bodies and Pleasures Reconsidered." *Theory, Culture, and Society* (1998).

"'Merely Cultural.'" *Social Text* (1997).

"Sovereign Performatives in the Contemporary Scene of Utterance." *Critical Inquiry* (1997).

"Universality in Culture." In Martha Nussbaum, *For Love of Country: Debating the Limits of Patriotism,* ed. Joshua Cohen. Boston: Beacon Press, 1996.

"Burning Acts: Injurious Speech." In *Performativity and Performance,* ed. Eve Kosofsky Sedgwick and Andrew Parker. New York: Routledge, 1995.

"Stubborn Attachment, Bodily Subjection: Rereading Hegel on the Unhappy Consciousness." In *Intersections: Nineteenth-Century Philosophy and Contemporary Theory,* ed. David Clarke and Trillotama Rajan. Albany: State University of New York Press, 1995.

"Collected and Fractured." In *Identities,* ed. K. Anthony Appiah and Henry Louis Gates. Chicago: University of Chicago Press, 1995.

"Poststructuralism and Postmarxism." *Diacritics* 23.4 (1994).

"Kierkegaard's Speculative Despair." In *German Idealism,* ed. Robert Solomon and Kathleen Higgins. London: Routledge, 1993.

"Contingent Foundations: Feminism and the Question of 'Postmodernism.'" *Praxis International* 11.2 (1991).

"Imitation and Gender Insubordination." In *Inside/Out: Gay Theories/Lesbian and Gay Studies Reader,* ed. Diana Fuss. New York: Routledge, 1991.

"The Nothing That Is: Wallace Stevens' Hegelian Affinities." In *Theorizing American Literature: Hegel, the Sign, and History,* ed. Joseph Kronick and Bainard Cowan. Baton Rouge: Louisiana State University Press, 1991.

"The Body Politics of Julia Kristeva." *Hypatia: A Journal of Feminist Philosophy* 3.3, special issue, ed. Nancy Fraser and Sandra Bartky (1989).

"Phenomenological Description and Sexual Ideology in Merleau-Ponty's *Phenomenology of Perception.*" In *The Thinking Muse: Feminist Philosophy and Modern French Philosophy,* ed. Iris Young and Jeffner Allen. Bloomington: Indiana University Press, 1989.

"Variations on Sex and Gender: Beauvoir, Wittig, and Foucault." *Praxis International* (1986).

"Sex and Gender in Beauvoir's *Second Sex.*" *Yale French Studies, Simone de Beauvoir: Witness to a Century* 72 (1986).

14

The Invisibility of Racial Minorities in the Public Realm of Appearances

ROBERT BERNASCONI

Robert Bernasconi can be said to represent the eccentric character of the American continental voice. Although he is British, he lives and teaches in Memphis and has a deep understanding of the uniquely American cultural experience to be had there. He has been among those responsible for the introduction of contemporary French philosophers, especially Emmanuel Levinas, to America. No doubt Bernasconi's work on Levinas, which is beautifully sensitive to the ethical dimension of human experience and to the problem of alterity, which is so often excluded from philosophical consideration, has provided the impetus for his work devoted to the philosophy of race.

Bernasconi was initially drawn to the phenomenology of Heidegger, Sartre, Merleau-Ponty, and Arendt while he was a student in England, despite the domination of analytic philosophy in British universities. The focus of his early work involved the question of how to philosophize with and after Heidegger—as well as Hegel. This led him to Levinas and Derrida and a concern for issues of ethics and politics that needed to be reopened after phenomenology.

Bernasconi is one of those thinkers for whom a radical shift in the direction of his thought can be traced. Perhaps this turn occurred when he moved to the United States in 1988. In any case, the experience of living in a society divided by race began to influence his philosophy. He began to question racism within philosophy, both its institutions and its theories. His research focused on philosophies of racism and also on the ethnocentrism of the philosophy of history of many of the philosophers to whom he had been drawn previously. This concern is reflected in a number of Bernasconi's recent essays and remains a key element in his works in progress.

If indeed Bernasconi has discovered in the very name "continental philosophy" a certain ethnocentrism, he has not abandoned continental philosophy's concerns but has instead subjected them to examination. This has led to a renewal of his early interest in what may be called less sophisticated versions of phenomenology, such as that in

Sartre's work. Bernasconi considers Sartre to be a philosopher who provides the resources to explore the issue of racism within society, especially through his "phenomenology of the oppressor." This possibility is more apparent when one adds a genealogical perspective to Sartrean discourse.

The essay included here reflects Bernasconi's use of phenomenology as a resource, albeit a limited one, for exposing some of the structures of racism within society. The voices of Sartre, Arendt, Levinas, Schutz, and other continental thinkers are intertwined with the distinctively American voices of those who address the experience of racism in America, for instance, W.E.B. Du Bois, Kwame Anthony Appiah, Ralph Ellison, bell hooks, and Lewis R. Gordon.

-→-≡◎≡-←-

During the strike that preceded the assassination of Martin Luther King Jr., the sanitation workers of Memphis and their African American supporters paraded with posters that read, "I AM A MAN." This was not only a labor dispute in which the right of public employees to strike against a city was in question but was also, given the historical context and especially the racial identity of most of the sanitation workers, immediately recognized as an important chapter in the Civil Rights Movement. There were signs that read "JOBS JOBS JOBS," "UNIONIZATION FOR THE SANITATION WORKERS," and "JUSTICE AND EQUALITY FOR ALL MEN." But most signs read simply, "I AM A MAN"; and the photographs of scores of black protesters holding these signs provide the abiding image of the strike. They wanted economic justice and recognition of their union, but contemporary accounts record that more than anything else they wanted to be "recognized" for themselves.[1]

Even when Whites have not gone to the extreme of explicitly denying the humanity of Blacks, they have frequently found numerous ways, institutional and personal, in which to demean Blacks. The need to declare one's humanity arises as a response to this kind of racism. Beyond the appeal to civil rights due to someone as a citizen, there is also, at least since their recognition in the eighteenth century, the appeal to human rights due to a person on the basis of their humanity. Human rights stand as a testimony to the power of the universal. They have given the oppressed of the world a new basis on which to protest discrimination based on the particularities of class, sex, nationality, religion, or race. Human Rights are widely acknowledged as providing a standard that transcends national and cultural boundaries. But does universality offer an adequate defense against racism? Does the appeal to the universal provide a means for overcoming discrimination against groups on the basis of racial differences? Or is racism thereby being addressed by a cosmopolitanism that keeps white privilege intact?

A recent example may serve to clarify what is at stake. During the 1996 election campaign the opponents of affirmative action liked to quote Martin Luther King's "I Have a Dream" speech with its vision of a land where everyone would "not be judged by the color of their skin but by the content of their character."[2] Policies that made explicit use of racial designations were said to be discriminatory. Meanwhile, the opponents of affirmative action chose to ignore King's support for such programs under the heading of "compensatory or preferential treatment." King had written:

> It is impossible to create a formula for the future which does not take into account that our society has been doing something special *against* the Negro for hundreds of years. How then can he be absorbed into the mainstream of American life if we do not do something special *for* him now, in order to balance the equation and equip him to compete on a just and equal basis?[3]

This attempt to enlist Martin Luther King's support against affirmative action is part of a disingenuous attempt to deny minorities a political identity while leaving in place the legacy of the racial oppression they have suffered in the name of that identity. This could not be more different from the call of the Memphis sanitation workers, which was a call for justice, respect, and recognition, but not a call for homogenization.

Within the universal order of humanity there is a question about the political status to be accorded to solidarity based on gender, race, linguistic grouping, class, nationality, and so on. Are these divisions merely divisive? Is their value at best only strategic? Or do these differences have positive value so that appeals to cosmopolitanism or to global identity must be looked upon with suspicion? In this essay I focus on racial difference, with particular attention to anti-Black racism among Whites in contemporary America; but the issues are larger. Frantz Fanon wrote, "I wanted to be a man, nothing but a man."[4] His book, *Black Skin, White Masks*, shows that racism cannot be overcome without addressing the effects of racism. But Fanon's formulation, like the quotation from Martin Luther King in the previous paragraph, now strikes us as insensitive to issues of sexual difference, inviting Sojourner Truth's response: "Ar'n't I a woman?"[5] In the face of overlapping identities and a tendency to experience identities as more tyrannical than liberating, there is a temptation to want to employ singularity and abstract humanism as the main resources in the battle against discrimination. But this is to overlook the need for identities that offer a sense of community, that inspire loyalty, and that promote a common interest, especially among members of an oppressed group.

There is much still to be learned about how and why the classification of people into races took hold at the end of the eighteenth century and was quickly regarded as obvious.[6] At almost exactly the same time that the concept of race was given precision, the American Declaration of Independence proclaimed human equality. Since the Enlightenment one of the great political puzzles has been the combination of cosmopolitan ideals and racist practices. One does not see an initial failure to meet a new higher set of standards so much as a series of appalling blindspots in the application of the noble and profound statements of human dignity that are the hallmark of the period. Declarations of universal rights were authored and pronounced by people who were apparently oblivious of whole classes of people to whom those rights nominally applied but to whom hardly anyone thought to apply them: the poor, women, nonWhites, and, above all, poor, nonWhite, women.[7]

Take slavery, for example. There were few European voices against the slavery of Blacks until the last half of the eighteenth century. That is why one rarely finds justifications or defenses of this form of slavery until that time. The institution did not raise moral problems. It was somehow taken for granted, so long as it was contained within certain parameters that limited slavery to nonWhites and, although this proviso had to be dropped under pressure from the missionaries, to nonChristians. The puzzle is that, when the principle of the equality of all human beings was enunciated by the American colonists, they failed to apply it to the Black slaves in their midst. For a society of slaveowners under the rule of a colonial power to demand liberation from "slavery" for themselves at the same time that they themselves relied for their prosperity on an especially brutal system of slavery was nothing new in the history of morals. What was new was the universal language that they brought to their cause while at the same time apparently being oblivious of its real meaning.

One can say that this contradiction is evidence of brazen hypocrisy, although that would not explain why they insisted on postulating the universal principles that produced the contradiction. One can refer to racism, although that is to name the problem rather than to explain it. One can construct a philosophy of history that would attempt to resolve the contradiction by postulating that, against such deep-seated prejudice, the principle had first to be stated almost unwittingly long before its full application could be envisaged. But this philosophy of history, predicated on progress, would have to explain whether the broadening of the principle's application was the only way for history to resolve the contradiction inherent in the founding documents. The particularly virulent form of racism produced in the United States in the late nineteenth century, in which the very humanity of Blacks was questioned, can also be understood as an attempt at resolving the contradiction.[8] However, the focus of this paper is not the history of the contradiction between the principle and the practice but the underlying phenomenological truth that racial difference, as what is most visible, is within the public realm rendered invisible to the extent that the dominant group succeeds in overlooking a minority, denying its members their place in the sun.[9]

What does it tell us about the nature of the political realm that those who are most visible phenomenally for the dominant group can nevertheless at the same time be rendered invisible within the public realm of appearances? In referring to the public realm of appearances, I am alluding to Hannah Arendt's notion that in the public or political sphere, appearance constitutes reality, albeit without underwriting the precise terms in which she insists on a division between the public and the private.[10] I have addressed elsewhere what I regard to be the systemic failure of Hannah Arendt's phenomenological conception of politics to accommodate an appreciation of the issues raised by race in American society, and I will not rehearse that analysis here.[11] However, I refer to her here to make the point that the political realm is the realm of appearances and that, because appearances can be manipulated, reality can also be manipulated. Furthermore, it is sufficient that race be visible in the sense that racial identities can be marked with sufficient clarity, either physiognomically or by dress code, to give rise to a consistent system of identifications, for its political reality to be secure.

Only philosophers with an impoverished conception of perception could imagine that the category of race, let alone racism itself, could be contested by exposing the distinction between the phenomenal appearance of certain physical characteristics and what is said to lie "behind" that appearance once the appearance has been isolated.[12] The problem is that within a racialized society to see skin color is to see someone as of another race with all that entails. However unjustified the stereotypes may be, they are part of the political reality. To that extent, racism has made race "real" without making it true. As Tshembe explains to the American journalist, Charlie Morris, in Lorraine Hansberry's play *Les Blancs*, race once invented takes on a reality of its own: "it is pointless to pretend it doesn't *exist*—merely because it is a *lie*!"[13] The fact that we now reject the racial science that taught previous generations to treat race as an indicator of character and even of moral worth does not mean that the stereotypes that are deeply embedded in popular culture and that are reinforced by the media can be broken by pointing out that they are unjustified. It is not just with reference to skin color that people are judged by appearances. Sexism often operates in the same way. Nothing is to be gained by pretending that racism and sexism can be eradicated by the introduction of a few skillfully chosen distinctions and the policing of ordinary language to ensure that these distinctions are respected. Rather, we must try to understand better the process by which society sustains, in this case, racism.

Those who are most invisible in the public realm, in the sense of being powerless, mute, and deprived of human rights, are often most visible to those who disempower them, silence them, and exploit them. During segregation in the United States, Whites as a class never lacked the capacity to see the Blacks that waited on their tables, did their yard work, and passed them on the sidewalks. Their invisibility was in some sense deliberate or, at least, programmed. As Ralph Ellison wrote in *Invisible Man*, describing the experience of a black man in a white society, "I am invisible, understand, simply because people refuse to see me."[14] It has not been necessary for Whites to look Blacks in the face because Blacks were taught to divert their gaze. bell hooks has described this process in the following terms:

> One mark of oppression was that black folks were compelled to assume the mantle of invisibility, to erase all traces of their subjectivity during slavery and the long years of racial apartheid, so that they would be better, less threatening servants. An effective strategy of white supremacist terror and dehumanization during slavery centered around white control of the black gaze.[15]

This practice was so striking that Sartre remarked on the phenomenon in a newspaper article published after only his first visit to the United States: "if by chance their eyes meet yours, it seems to you that they do not see you and it is better for them and you that you pretend not to have noticed them."[16] The refusal of Whites to see Blacks was predicated on the fact that they knew who was there to be seen and sought to control them by choosing not to see them. That is to say, Whites saw Blacks without seeing them. How was this possible? In no small measure by controlling the Black gaze so that Whites did not experience themselves as they were seen by Blacks.[17]

Prejudice wants to make those against whom it is directed disappear. It wants to exterminate them but usually has to satisfy itself with hiding them away. It turns them into outcasts. Christians expelled the Jews or forced the Jews to live in ghettos. Whites today produce the same effect by staying in the suburbs and refusing to go downtown for fear that they would have to share the sidewalk with Blacks who might return their gaze. In this context to exaggerate one's difference as Jew or Black is to make a gesture of defiance. But if the prejudiced find this threatening, they are even more threatened by the possibility of being fooled, as when they mistake a foe for a friend. Thus Jews were obliged to wear a yellow badge as a sign of their Jewishness. This was so there would be no mistake, which was to admit that otherwise a Jew could be mistaken for a Gentile. The pressure on Jews to assimilate highlights racism at the point where the demand to assimilate seems to have succeeded. That is why the persecution directed against the Marranos is regarded as one of the original instances of modern racism.[18] Fear of failing to identify those from whom one differentiated oneself led racial scientists in Nazi Germany to instruct people on how to identify the distinctive features of each race.[19] The visibility of blackness in a "white world"—that space carved out by Whites for themselves—gave anti-Black racism a unique self-confidence. And yet one of the historical obsessions of anti-Black racism in the United States has been the fear that there are Blacks who can pass as White. This problem is of racism's own making. Because Whites in the United States have for much of their history been concerned with their own racial purity, they operated by "one-drop" rule that produced a class of people for whom passing was an option. Such people looked White but were counted as Black. To the members of this racialized society their "appearance" belied their "reality," not because skin color did not mean something but because their skin color was a misleading indicator of how society classified them. When, as in Nella Larsen's *Passing,* a white man found that his apparently white wife in fact counted as black, that man did not conclude that the idea of racial essence was false.[20] So far as he was concerned, it was not his idea of race that had deceived him but his wife, because he now saw her as black, something that, in this case, he had already seen—hence his use of "Nig" as a nickname for her—but which at the same time he had refused to see. Racism wants to make its targets disappear, but it does not want them to disappear into anonymity. It wants to see them without seeing them. It wants to identify its targets unambiguously without having to face them.

This is accomplished in part by controlling how Blacks are made to appear. In slavery times, Whites saw Blacks as slaves: freed Blacks had to be able to prove their status. Furthermore, under slavery, Blacks were supposed to appear happy; under segregation, submissive; and today the stereotypes are manipulated in the form of images of the welfare queen, the teenage mother, the gang member, and the drug addict. As a result of the construction of these stereotypes that are disseminated through the media and through hearsay, many Whites are threatened simply by the sight of a young black man. If he is not already known to us, the stereotype intervenes. We Whites have trouble seeing past the stereotype, as if it formed a layer of invisibility. It is a case of seeing without seeing.

It is not that Blacks are invisible to Whites. On one diagnosis that means that their humanity is invisible to those Whites who are nevertheless most aware of them. Given that there can be few racists left, if any, who deny the biological humanity of Blacks, this raises the question of how modern-day racists express a belief in the equality of all human beings and at the same time treat Blacks as inferior. This blatant contradiction is in part sustained by the persistence of stereotypes. How do the stereotypes hold sway even among people who know better? One can begin to address this problem by noting what it is one does and does not see. One does not in the standard case see another human being as simply that, another human being. If one did, it would not have been necessary for the Memphis sanitation workers to line the street with their signs that read: "I AM A MAN." In a racialized society, everyone is seen in terms of the racial categories of the moment. Today they are seen *as* Blacks, Whites, Hispanics, or Asians. This is so prevalent that there are times in such a society when it seems that it is impossible for an audience to follow an anecdote or a news story until the racial identity of the protagonist has been established: "Was he black or white?" Within the context of racism, particularity intervenes between universality and singularity. This analysis is what leads to the widespread claim that if one could only look beyond the particularity of race, class, gender, and so on, then one would encounter a person in his or her singularity and there would be no obstacle against arriving at the universal designation "human" in terms of which all are equal.

Levinas must be counted among those who have claimed that the "as" structure, according to which the individual is given to perception as being of a certain type, lends itself to racism:

> It is evident that it is in the knowledge of the other *(autrui)* as a simple individual—individual of a genus, a class, or a race—that peace with the other *(autrui)* turns into hatred; it is the approach of the other as "such and such a type."[21]

Not surprisingly, given the problems that his treatment of the feminine had already raised for him, Levinas did not say whether the sex of the individual should also be included in those characteristics that need to be overlooked for the encounter with the Other to take place. Nevertheless, although he said in an interview that to encounter the Other it is best not to notice the color of his or her eyes, one should beware jumping to the conclusion that Levinas offered this as a practical proposal, still less as an injunction.[22] Although Levinas is not always read this way, it seems to me that he construes singularity not as a phenomenon that can be unveiled but as an enigma. That is to say, it is "up to me" to retain its exorbitant meaning.[23] Singularity interrupts the system of social identity that inevitably returns or, more precisely, always remains intact. To see someone in his or her singularity would not be unlike addressing them in their singularity in what Levinas calls "saying" *(le dire)*.[24] Just as the "saying without a said" that Levinas sometimes invoked is always in fact accompanied by a said because one addresses the Other in language, so even what might be called "overlooking" someone's race, sex, or class thereby to see them in their singularity does not leave them deprived of all characteristics. The following passage from "The Rights of Man and the Rights of the Other," dating from 1985, shows Levinas attempting to negotiate what is for him a difficult problem:

> These rights of man . . . express the alterity or absolute of every person, the suspension of all *reference:* a violent tearing loose *(arrachement)* from the determining order of nature and the social structure in which each of us is obviously involved; an alterity of the *unique* and the incomparable, due to the belonging of each one to mankind *(au genre humain)*, which, *ipso facto and paradoxically*, is annulled precisely to leave each man *the only one of his kind (unique dans son genre)*.[25]

Levinas found himself forced to acknowledge that to relate to someone in his or her singularity through a certain dissolution of the particularity that would reduce that person to being a representative of a certain type, nevertheless still allows at least a passing reference of this singular person to the human genus. The question is whether this paradoxical structure, once allowed, could not also accommodate a passing reference to class and race.

Somewhat surprisingly given Levinas's personal history as a target of anti-Semitism, his account, at least in his philosophical as opposed to his confessional writings, bypasses the attachment to social identity that is often found on the part of the oppressed.[26] It ignores the fact that many people who have been discriminated against and persecuted want to be accepted, not just as a member of humanity, or for their singularity, but in the same terms under which they had previously been rejected. It is not enough to be "a man," "a woman," "a human being, nothing but a human being." Even if this were possible, it is not regarded as desirable. This is not only true of many Blacks, who choose to appropriate and transform the meaning of the labels assigned to them in the course of their oppression. Arendt also acknowledged this point on the basis of her experience of National Socialism: "If one is attacked as a Jew, one must defend oneself *as a Jew*. Not as a German, not as a world citizen, not as an upholder of the Rights of Man."[27] Similarly, one can recall Benny Lévy's response to Sartre's *Anti-Semite and Jew* many years after first reading it. Sartre had led him to discover what he dreamt of discovering: "I am a man, not a Jew." However, Lévy subsequently recognized the price for doing so: he had embraced a form of self-denial.[28] He had sacrificed his identity in a way that, had it been sustained, would have been a victory for his oppressors, who would themselves still have seen him not in his humanity but as a Jew.

Already in 1797 de Maistre wrote that "In my lifetime I have seen Frenchmen, Italians, Russians, etc.; thanks to Montesquieu, I even know that *one can be Persian*. But as for *man*, I declare that I have never in my life met him."[29] To see another as this or that, as a Black, East Asian, or White, as male or female, young or old, to see someone as a representative of some class or group, is an irreducible aspect of social experience, even though the precise terms under which this takes place are culturally determined and the emphasis that is given to one of the terms in relation to the others can change historically with reference to the general context. Acknowledging that someone is of a certain race, sex, or class does not necessarily reduce that person to being a representative of a type, a *persona*. It can also mean, among other things, recognizing and being sensitive to aspects of their experience that one might not have shared oneself but that one knows have touched them deeply. Only for the kind of people who, for example, preface a racist remark by declaring that some of their best friends are black, could it make sense to say that they must "overlook" race to relate to someone. But they are precisely the kind of people most likely to make that same racist remark in front of their black friends, precisely because they overlook race. The double bind that racism imposes on its targets lies in demanding assimilation while at the same time denying its possibility. Racism says, "Become like us," while always reasserting under its breath, "You can never become like us, because you are not one of us and we will not mistake you for one of us." The current proposal to move without delay to a society without racial designations has all the appearance of being, and perhaps sometimes is, a further example of Whites attempting to determine how, for example, African Americans may present themselves in society. The phenomenological studies of Alfred Schutz are a helpful resource for understanding this kind of racism.[30]

In the course of his 1957 essay "Equality and the Meaning Structure of the World," Alfred Schutz offered an account of the impact of imposed typifications on groups.[31] Each group not only has a view of itself, it also has a view of other correlative groups with which it is in contact. Drawing on distinctions that he had already outlined in his classic 1932 study *The Phenomenology of the Social World,* but which he now reformulated in the terminology of William Sumner, Schutz set out to describe how the meaning of the world as seen by an in-group or We-group relates to that of an Others-group or out-group.[32] Each group takes its own perspective for granted. It regards itself as the center of everything and rates everyone else in terms of their divergences from its own practices. Again borrowing from Sumner, Schutz called this perspective "ethnocentrism."[33] Furthermore, each group is inclined to feel itself misunderstood by the other groups; and the more misunderstood its members feel, the more they pull closer together in order to protect themselves from criticism. They are also liable to regard these misunderstandings as evidence of a hostility on the part of the other group, which vindicates their own initial antipathy and serves to fuel it. This has a serious impact on how the group understands itself, leading it, for example, to insist on ever more stringent forms of loyalty on the part of its members.[34]

The relevance of these considerations to the present inquiry is enhanced by the fact that Schutz went on to consider specifically the example of interaction between different races in the United States. Schutz considered race to be, in Max Scheler's terminology, a material factor or *Realfaktor,*[35] alongside such things as geopolitical structure, political power relationships, the conditions of economic production, and so on. However, it is immediately apparent from the context that Schutz did not thereby mean that race was a determining factor in the sense that it would be in a biologism, but rather that membership of a race, unlike membership of a voluntary group, locates one within "a preconstituted system of typifications, relevances, roles, positions, statues" which are not of one's own making but are handed down "as a social heritage."[36] One's race, like one's sex or the national group into which one is born, is, according to Schutz, an existential element of one's situation in the sense that it is something with which one has to come to terms. In a text contemporary with "Equality and the Social Meaning Structure," Schutz explained that the *Realfaktoren* belong to "the world of everyday life taken for granted in the common-sense thinking of the actors on the social scene with which they have to come to terms."[37] Having already established that the view one group has of another group can, under certain conditions, serve to modify the way that second group comes to regard itself, Schutz introduced the question of the case where a group's world has come to be dominated by a perspective arising from another group that is hostile to it. According to Schutz, even though one cannot choose to which race one belongs, one should be free, among other things, to determine with what force one participates in group membership and what importance one gives to that identity.[38] He then proceeded to show how in the first half of the twentieth century African Americans were denied that freedom.

Schutz took as his example the "separate but equal" doctrine formulated by the Supreme Court in *Plessy v. Ferguson*. Whatever its proponents claimed, the repercussions of the decision rendered were discriminatory:

> Even under the assumption that separation was not meant to involve an inferiority in the colored race, segregation is taken as an insult by the Negro and he becomes sensitive about it. His being treated as a type induces self-typification with an inverted sign. Even if he never intended to travel by sleeping car, the principled denial of its use becomes to him relevant in his own terms. He has a new problem to grapple with.[39]

Schutz argued that the imposition of a typification by one group on another correlative group is inevitable but not necessarily discriminatory.[40] Discrimination takes place only when the typification from outside is imposed in such a way as to become part of the experience of the afflicted individual. This may not coincide with what is ordinarily understood by discrimination, but the account does succeed in drawing attention to the fact that where one group is in a position to impose a typification on an individual as a member of another group, that individual becomes alienated from his or her own self-characterization and becomes a mere representative of the typified characteristics. Schutz added that such a person would be deprived of the right to the pursuit of happiness.[41] Schutz clearly wanted to draw on all the deep resonances that phrase has within the context of the United States, but it also shows the extent to which Schutz's analysis is governed by and to a certain extent limited to a specific context. In any case, in such circumstances the members of a minority group would not be content to seek equality with the dominant group in the form of assimilation but would, Schutz noted, insist on being granted special rights to secure *real* equality, in addition to mere formal equality.[42]

In an attempt to explain what led African Americans to demand "special" rights for themselves, Schutz appealed to Myrdal's account of how "the white man's rank order of discriminations" was the inverse of "the Negro's rank order." Myrdal's study of this difference in priorities between Whites and Blacks showed that Blacks were right to believe that even full realization of the principle of non-discrimination would secure them only formal equality with the dominant group and not real equality. Myrdal had observed that whereas Whites in the United States tended to focus on laws against intermarriage and sexual intercourse involving white women as the most important type of discrimination to correct, followed in importance by the demeaning social etiquette imposed on Blacks in their relation to Whites and by the legal barriers against interracial social intercourse, Blacks were more concerned with discrimination in economic matters such as securing land, credit, jobs, and public relief, with discrimination in the law courts and by the police next in the order of priority.[43] Schutz did not say what special rights Blacks were claiming, but clearly "compensatory or preferential treatment" of the kind Martin Luther King subsequently advocated would meet the description. In other words, Schutz showed how such a demand arises as a consequence of the form of racism to which Blacks are subjected in the United States. Contemporary attempts to cast such demands as another form of racism are thereby exposed as a form of blindness to the concrete context, a form of blindness that serves to perpetuate White blindness to the Black gaze.

Schutz employed the example of life under segregation to highlight the way that European Americans held a view of African Americans that made itself felt in many aspects of the lives of African Americans. The White stereotype of Blacks was, of course, contested by the meaning that African Americans gave and continue to give to being African American; and it led to the inner conflict that W.E.B. Du Bois described as "double consciousness."[44] In *The Autobiography of an Ex-Colored Man*, James Weldon Johnson provided a description of this "sort of dual personality" and drew the inevitable conclusion: "I believe it to be a fact that the colored people of this country know and understand the white people better than the white people know and understand them."[45] European Americans were largely oblivious to the way African Americans saw them and, to a large extent, they still are. Schutz did not explore this asymmetry. Instead, he took his analysis in the direction of Sartre's account of the look.

A few years prior to the "Equality" essay, Schutz had criticized Sartre's description of the look as a site of conflict in which one is either the seer or the seen: it left no place for mutual interaction in freedom.[46] This is not the place to examine Schutz's objections or the resources that Sartre subsequently developed for addressing this problem. Nor do I intend to determine the extent to which Schutz, having clearly shown how discriminatory practices arise, was able to conceive of a society without discrimination. One might think that because Schutz traced discrimination back to the inevitable discrepancy between the way a group looks at itself and the way it is seen by others, it was hard for him to explain the situation where discrimination did not arise, and when it did, how it might diminish instead of grow. The problem was exacerbated in the case of groups organized in terms of race or sex as one's participation in those groups was not voluntary.[47] Schutz was, therefore, consistent when he conceded that "we had better courageously face the fact that prejudices are themselves elements of the interpretation of the social world and even one of the mainsprings that make it tick."[48] However, Schutz did recognize that when a minority group is satisfied with its relationship to the predominant group, that minority group is liable to see assimilation as the way forward.[49] When a group feels that its opportunities have been deliberately restricted by another group, an entirely different situation obtains. For the dominant group to insist upon assimilation as a precondition of economic empowerment, while at the same time excluding the possibility of assimilation from the outset, guarantees conflict. In other words, if the dominant group insists upon assimilation because it perceives a specific minority group as failing to conform to the standards it imposes, in all likelihood this is because it is operating with stereotypes that render it impossible for that group to meet the demand. The conditions that underlie the issuing of the demand make it impossible for the demand to be met: the demand to act white is addressed not to Whites but to those who are seen, for example, *as* black. In the rare case in which Whites fail to act White, as in the case of young suburban Whites imitating the forms of dress associated with rap, they are not under the same pressure to conform: it is believed that they will outgrow it, because it is all an act. It is not real.

The invisibility of African Americans in the public realm of appearances, as I have presented it in this essay, refers to the way European Americans silence African Americans, shield themselves from the gaze of African Americans, so as to remain comfortable and uncontested in a white world that does not acknowledge itself as such. The invisibility of racial minorities arises from a refusal on the part of the majority to see them or, more precisely, to listen to them. My analysis does not deny that at various times and in various arenas European Americans have had access to African American perspectives on the world and on themselves. These have always been available; they have been the focus of attention from time to time, as at the time of the debate over the abolition of slavery and during the Civil Rights Movement, albeit often filtered through white media. What is new is that Blacks, who have always contested the meaning of blackness imposed on them, have forced this contestation into the public realm. Whites cannot avoid hearing it and cannot avoid seeing how it implicates them. They now find their own identity being challenged by the meaning Blacks impose on them. This is the context in which an increasing number of Whites declare that they would prefer to drop all talk of race. That they should make this proposal now is not surprising. It is too easy for academics and politicians to consider all talk of racial difference taboo in their own sphere while at the same time race organizes society, as, for example, with residential apartheid. Racial identity will only cease to be salient when one can say of a newborn baby that its racial identity will have no significant impact on the kind of life he or she is likely to lead. But the conditions that would make it possible to say that cannot be brought about without a radical transformation of society of a kind that most Whites would not even contemplate.

To devote our efforts now to trying to determine how long it will be before we can get beyond the particularity of race seems hardly worthwhile, because even if it is sometimes possible for some people in some contexts to do so in some sense, even the minimal goal of a society in which people are not judged by the color of their skin is a long way off. Once it is recognized that in the present context it makes no sense to ask people suddenly to become literally color blind, as if one could ask them not to notice skin color or other physiognomic differences that have been given a meaning in contemporary society, attention can then pass to the construction and interaction of the various stereotypes. This is where the phenomenological studies of Schutz can be of assistance. The focus of this essay has not been the incoherence of the system of racial classification, nor the institutional segregation of American society that sustains the ignorance that fuels the racial stereotypes, but the imposition of the stereotypes and the conflicts that arise from them. However, if Schutz is correct, as I believe he is, White stereotypes of Blacks have an importance that, for example, White stereotypes of Japanese or Black stereotypes of Whites do not have, not because African Americans are more sensitive than other ethnic groups but because so many African Americans remain economically disempowered. They recognize that these stereotypes seriously impact their lives both personally, for example, in terms of job promotions or loan approvals, and institutionally, for example, in terms of how those stereotypes work to determine where they live and thus what educational or job opportunities are available to them and their children. Consider, for example, the stereotypes of Jews or of the Irish that still operate in the United States. However unjust and unwarranted these typifications are, they tend not to have the impact they once had, because in contemporary North America the Jews and the Irish are not economically disempowered in the way African Americans and some more recent immigrant groups are. When employers insist as a condition of employment that prospective employees have attained a level of assimilation that far exceeds what is necessary to do the work satisfactorily, one has a clear case in which issues of recognition and of economic justice cannot be kept separate.[50] Of course, employers would probably insist that they were acting this way because their customers demanded it. It is the same kind of excuse used by white houseowners who do not want African Americans living next door. They usually insist that they have no personal objection but that they are worried about how the value of their house might suffer once the general perception of the neighborhood changes. These are some of the ways in which racism can permeate a society in which hardly anyone admits being a racist. An individual can proclaim the invisibility of racial minorities by insisting on the invisibility, the non-existence, of race; but this does not change anything, so long as one assumes that "everyone (all other Whites) except me" is operating with the stereotypes.

It is now possible to offer a provisional answer to my earlier question about what we know about the public realm of appearances given that those who are most visible for the dominant group can at the same time be rendered invisible within it. Treating African Americans as invisible or, more precisely, rendering them invisible was, among other things, a mechanism by which European Americans could protect themselves from encountering a point of view that conflicted with their own self-understanding. One can then better understand why European Americans go to such lengths to avoid experiencing themselves as seen by African Americans. That is a major part of why these two groups do not more often share the same schools, churches, clubs, factories, malls, playgrounds, and, above all, the same housing districts. The invisibility of African Americans, the suppression of their presence and thus of their gaze, has also been one of the ways Whites have secured their own disappearance as white. There are different kinds of racism operating by different logics but, according to, for example, the dominant logic of anti-Black racism within the United States,

Whites do not thematize their identity but disappear into the norm.[51] This is the invisibility of the dominant group within the public realm of appearances. It sustains institutional racism by concealing it. Racial science often does not characterize the white race which, in Kant's formulation, "contains all impulses and talents in itself."[52] In such cases racial science proceeds by characterizing the particularity of the other races. Within such a system of thought, Whites set the standard. They represent the universality to which others are supposed to aspire but from which they are excluded by virtue of the limitations of their race. Such prejudices lend themselves to a universalism that is not so much in opposition to racism as it is an instrument of racism. In this context, what it means to be human is contested and the statement "I AM A MAN" is anything but an underwriting of abstract humanism, because a certain model of humanity is covert within such a humanism. From this perspective, nothing is less surprising than the apparent contradiction between Enlightenment ideas about universal human equality and Enlightenment racism, so long as there is a dominant group that controls the look and thus the discourse of equality. In such a setting racism remains an irreducible component of the universalistic discourse, not its contrary, which is why we must always be suspicious of fine words and sentiments, as when people celebrate their color blindness by declaring race to be invisible.

On a personal note, I may not have been in the United States long enough to be called a European American, but I have not forgotten that from the moment I arrived I was seen as white. Coming from England, I came from a context where, alongside class and gender, what mattered was being English. This was also, in a sense, a racial designation. In Europe in the nineteenth century, what today might be called national identities, ethnic identities, and racial identities, were understood as interrelated. In spite of my resistance to being designated simply as white, I was forced to recognize that this is how I appear in the United States. I do not ever expect to be comfortable with this label. But, however much I would like to imagine that I could disappear into being a singular human being and nothing more, in a polarized society I cannot deny my social identity.[53] Fortunately, I cannot, and certainly should not, be reduced to this social identity or any of my other social identities: like everyone else my singularity is mediated by several overlapping identities. To inherit a history is to assume the privileges, opportunities, and burdens that it brings, including certain responsibilities, among which is the responsibility to respond to how one is seen. Insofar as we fail to do so, it is we Whites who are trying to maintain our invisibility. But we will not be able to hide much longer.

Notes

1. For an account of the strike, see Joan Turner Beifuss, *At the River I Stand* (Memphis: St. Luke's Press, 1990), esp. pp. 285–86, 453.

2. *A Testament of Hope. The Essential Writings of Martin Luther King, Jr.*, ed. James M. Washington (San Francisco: Harper & Row, 1986), p. 219.

3. Martin Luther King Jr., *Why We Can't Wait* (New York: Signet, 1964), p. 134.

4. Frantz Fanon, *Peau noire, masques blancs* (Paris: Seuil, 1975), p. 91; trans. Charles Lam Markmann, *Black Skin, White Masks* (New York: Grove, 1982), p. 113.

5. Olive Gilbert, *Narrative of Sojourner Truth* (Oxford: Oxford University Press, 1991), p. 134. For a discussion of whether Sojourner Truth actually used the phrase, see Jeffrey Stewart's introduction, pp. xxxiii–xxxiv.

6. I presented a preliminary account of the history of the development of a scientific conception of race in the eighteenth century at a conference on Race and the Academy organized by Kevin Miles at Villanova University in 1996. My paper, "Who Invented the Concept of Race?" gave a central place to Kant's 1775 essay, "Von den verschiedenen Racen der Menschen." See Immanuel Kant, *Gesammelte Schriften*, vol. 2 (Berlin: Walter de Gruyter, 1968), pp. 427–43. See also Emmanuel Eze's "The Color of Reason: The Idea of 'Race' in Kant's Anthropology," in *Postcolonial African Philosophy*, ed. Emmanuel Chukwudi Eze (Oxford: Blackwell, 1997), pp. 103–40.

7. The best example is, of course, Thomas Jefferson. See his "Notes on the State of Virginia," in *Writings*, ed. Merrill Peterson (New York: Library of America, 1984), pp. 264–67. See also Paul Finkelman, "Jefferson and Slavery: 'Treason against the Hopes of the World,'" in *Jeffersonian Legacies*, ed. Peter S. Onuf (Charlottesville: University Press of Virginia, 1993), pp. 181–221.

8. See, for example, Charles Carroll, *"The Negro a Beast"* (1900), reprint edition (Salem, N.H.: Ayer, 1991).

9. I must emphasize at the outset that this essay is self-consciously one-sided insofar as it is a contribution to what Sartre called a "phenomenology of the oppressor." See Jean-Paul Sartre, *Notebooks for an Ethics*, trans. David Pellauer (Chicago: University of Chicago Press, 1992), p. 561 *(Cahiers pour une morale* [Paris: Gallimard, 1983], p. 579). Even though I have attempted to balance my observations by including testimony from those who have experienced discrimination, it is still inevitably one-sided with the identity—and the location—of the author clearly marked.

10. Hannah Arendt, *The Human Condition* (Chicago: University of Chicago Press, 1958), p. 50. It is perhaps hard to see how Hannah Arendt's concept of the public realm of appearances can function as a definition of politics within the contemporary world, especially as a major part of Arendt's analysis in *The Human Condition* is an attempt to show that the distinctions that sustain the integrity of the public realm have become confused in the modern world. However, by borrowing her conception, it is still possible to clarify the relation of the ethical and the political, which is what is at issue here.

11. See Robert Bernasconi, "The Double Face of the Political and the Social: Hannah Arendt and America's Racial Divisions," *Research in Phenomenology* 16 (1996): 3–24.

12. This tendency is operative within contemporary attempts first to reduce racial difference to ethnic difference and then to deny that what used to be called races can successfully sustain an ethnic identity. See the writings of Kwame Anthony Appiah, including "'But Would That Still Be Me?' Notes on Gender, 'Race,' Ethnicity, as Sources of 'Identity,'" *Journal of Philosophy* 87.10 (October 1990): 493–99. For an account of some of the unspoken assumptions underlying the historical development of this position, see Kamala Visweswaran "Race and the Culture of Anthropology," *American Anthropologist* 100.1 (1998): 1–14.

13. Lorraine Hansberry, *Les Blancs: The Collected Last Plays*, ed. Robert Nemiroff (New York: Random House, 1972), p. 122.

14. Ralph Ellison, *Invisible Man* (New York: Vintage Books, 1989), p. 3.

15. bell hooks, *Killing Rage: Ending Racism* (New York: Henry Holt, 1995), p. 35.

16. Jean-Paul Sartre, "Return from the United States," trans. T. Denean Sharpley-Whiting, in *Existence in Black*, ed. Lewis R. Gordon (New York: Routledge, 1997), p. 84 ("Retour des Etats-Unis. Ce que j'ai appris du problème noir," *Le Figaro*, June 16, 1945, p. 2).

17. See Lewis R. Gordon, *Bad Faith and Antiblack Racism* (New Jersey: Humanities Press, 1995), p. 102: "The white body is expected not to be looked at by black bodies. This is because the black body's situation of being-without-a-perspective cannot be maintained if blacks are able to unleash the Look." For an account of Sartre's application of his analysis of the look from *Being and Nothingness* to the struggle between the races, see Robert Bernasconi, "Sartre's Gaze Returned: The Transformation of the Phenomenology of Racism," *Graduate Faculty Philosophy Journal* 18.2 (1995): 201–21.

18. See Richard H. Popkin, "The Philosophical Bases of Modern Racism," in *The High Road to Pyrrhonism* (San Diego: Austin Hill Press, 1980), pp. 79–80.

19. See, for example, Ludwig Ferdinand Claus, *Rasse und Seele. Eine Einführung in den Sinn der leiblichen Gestalt* (Berlin: Büchergilde Gutenberg, 1939).

20. Nella Larsen, *Passing* (New York: Alfred A. Knopf, 1929).

21. Emmanuel Levinas, "Peace and Proximity," trans. Peter Atterton and Simon Critchley, in *Emmanuel Levinas: Basic Philosophical Writings*, ed. Adriaan Peperzak et al. (Bloomington: Indiana University Press, 1996), p. 166 ("Paix et Proximité," in *Emmanuel Levinas. Les cahiers de la nuit surveillée*, ed. Jacques Rolland [Lagrasse: Verdier, 1984], p. 343).

22. Emmanuel Levinas, *Ethics and Infinity*, trans. Richard A. Cohen (Pittsburgh: Duquesne University Press, 1985), p. 85 (*Éthique et infini* [Paris: Fayard, 1982], p. 89).

23. Emmanuel Levinas, "Enigma and Phenomenon," trans. Alphonso Lingis, in *Basic Philosophical Writings*, p. 70 ("Enigme et phénomène," in *En découvrant l'existence avec Husserl et Heidegger* [Paris: Vrin, 1967], pp. 208–209).

24. Emmanuel Levinas, *Otherwise than Being or Beyond Essence*, trans. Alphonso Lingis (The Hague: Martinus Nijhoff, 1981), pp. 37–38, 45–51 (*Autrement qu'être ou au-delà de l'essence* (The Hague: Martinus Nijhoff, 1974), pp. 47–49, 58–65).

25. Emmanuel Levinas, *Outside the Subject*, trans. Michael B. Smith (Stanford: Stanford University Press, 1994), p. 117 ("Les droits de l'homme et les droits d'autrui," *Hors sujet* [Saint Clement: Fata Morgana, 1987], p. 176).

26. For a more sustained treatment of this aspect of Levinas's thought, see Robert Bernasconi, "Who Is My Neighbor? Who Is the Other?" in *Ethics and Responsibility in the Phenomenological Tradition* (Pittsburgh: Simon Silverman Phenomenology Center, Duquesne University, 1992), pp. 1–31. I now regard as inadequate the attempt I made there to find further resources in Levinas to address racism. For a more detailed examination of the issues, see Robert Bernasconi, "Wer ist der Dritte? Überkreuzung von Ethik und Politik bei Levinas," trans. Antje Kapust, in *Der Anspruch des Anderen. Perspektiven phänomenologischer Ethik*, ed. Bernhard Waldenfels and Iris Därmann (Munich: Fink, 1998), pp. 87–110.

27. Hannah Arendt, "What Remains? The Language Remains," trans. Joan Stambaugh, in *Essays in Understanding 1930–1954*, ed. Jerome Kohn (New York: Harcourt Brace, 1994), p. 12. See also Hannah Arendt, "On Humanity in Dark Times: Thoughts about Lessing," in *Men in Dark Times* (New York: Harcourt, Brace and World, 1968), pp. 17–18.

28. Benny Lévy, *L'espoir maintenant* (Paris: Verdier, 1991), p. 72.

29. Joseph de Maistre, *Considerations on France*, trans. Richard A. Lebrun (Montreal: McGill–Queens University Press, 1974), p. 97 (*Considérations sur la France*, ed. R. Johannet and F. Vermale [Paris: Vrin, 1936], p. 81.,

30. The continuing relevance of Schutz's analyses of anonymity for the understanding of contemporary racism has already been demonstrated by Lewis Gordon. See his *Fanon and the Crisis of European Man* (New York: Routledge, 1995), pp. 37–66, and "Existential Dynamics of Theorizing Black Invisibility," in *Existence in Black*, ed. Lewis R. Gordon (New York: Routledge, 1997), pp. 69–79.

31. Alfred Schutz, "Equality and the Meaning Structure of the Social World," in *Collected Papers*, vol. 2 (The Hague: Martinus Nijhoff, 1964), pp. 226–73.

32. Ibid., p. 244. The distinction between the in-group or We-group and the Others-group or they-group was borrowed by Schutz from William Graham Sumner, *Folkways* (Boston: Ginn, 1906), pp. 12–13. However, Schutz related it to a distinction, which he had already borrowed from Max Weber in 1932, between subjective meaning, which involves reference to a particular person, such as the producer of a product, and objective meaning, which is abstracted from and independent of particular persons. See Alfred Schutz, *The Phenomenology of the Social World* (London: Heinemann, 1972), pp. 132–36. In "Equality and the Meaning Structure of the Social World," Schutz modified his presentation of the distinction by acknowledging that "objective meaning" is relative to the observer or scientist who produced it. See *Collected Papers*, vol. 2, p. 227.

33. Schutz, *Collected Papers*, vol. 2, p. 244. Cf. Sumner, *Folkways*, p. 13.

34. Schutz, *Collected Papers*, vol. 2, pp. 244–247.

35. Ibid., p. 249. Schutz adopted this term from Max Scheler. See the latter's *Probleme einer Soziologie des Wissens*, in *Die Wissensformen und die Gesellschaft*, Gesammelte Werke 8, (Bern and Munich: Francke, 1960), pp. 20–23, 44–51.

36. Schutz, *Collected Papers*, vol. 2, p. 252.

37. Alfred Schutz, "In Search of the Middle Ground," in *Collected Papers*, vol. 4 (Dordrecht: Kluwer Academic Publishers, 1996), p. 149.

38. Schutz, *Collected Papers*, vol. 2, p. 254.

39. Ibid., p. 261.

40. Ibid., pp. 258–62.

41. Ibid., pp. 256–57. There is a further limitation that arises from the fact that Schutz had in effect defined discrimination not only in terms of an act or a motive but also in terms of the power to impose a typification. This would seem to render the structures of discrimination ultimately inaccessible to phenomenological description, at least as Schutz practiced it, and call for the addition of other kinds of analysis. I am grateful to Kevin Thompson for pointing this out.

42. Ibid., pp. 265, 267–68. Schutz presented "formal equality" as full equality before the law and full political equality but suggested that where assimilation has not taken place "real equality" would be liable to entail special rights, such as the protection of one's national language in schools and before the courts.

43. Gunnar Myrdal, *An American Dilemma* (New York: Harper, 1944), pp. 60–61.

44. W.E.B. Du Bois, *The Soul of Black Folk*, in *Writings*, ed. Nathan Huggins (New York: Library of America, 1986), pp. 363–65.

45. James Weldon Johnson, *The Autobiography of an Ex-Colored Man* (New York: Penguin, 1990), pp. 14–15.

46. Alfred Schutz, "Sartre's Theory of the Alter Ego," *Collected Papers*, vol. 1 (The Hague: Martinus Nijhoff, 1967), p. 203.

47. Schutz, in his commentary on certain documents issued by the United Nations, appears to underwrite the suggestion that "each individual should be able

to decide voluntarily whether or not he [*sic*] belongs to a specific minority." See Schutz, *Collected Papers*, vol. 2, p. 266.

48. Ibid., p. 262.

49. Ibid., p. 265.

50. For the contemporary debate between the supporters of redistribution versus the upholders of recognition, see the essays by Nancy Fraser and Iris Young in Cynthia Willett, ed., *Theorizing Multiculturalism* (Oxford: Blackwell, 1998).

51. The problem with norms and with normalcy, against which one must always be on guard, is unwittingly exposed by Edmund Husserl in *Die Krisis der europäischen Wissenschaften und die transzendentale Phänomenologie*, Husserliana 6 (The Hague: Martinus Nijhoff, 1962), pp. 141–42; trans. by David Carr as *The Crisis of the European Sciences and Transcendental Phenomenology* (Evanston, Ill.: Northwestern University Press, 1970), p. 139. See further Jacques Derrida's comments in Edmund Husserl, *L'origine de la géométrie* (Paris: Presses Universitaires de France, 1962), pp. 74–75; trans. by John P. Leavey as *Edmund Husserl's Origin of Geometry* (New York: Nicholas Hays, 1978), pp. 79–80.

52. Immanuel Kant, *Vorlesungen über Anthropologie*, Gesammelte Schriften, vol. 25, pt. 2 (Berlin: Walter de Gruyter, 1997), p. 1187.

53. For an explanation of this point, see Albert Memmi, *Portrait du colonisé* (Paris: Gallimard, 1985); trans. by H. Greenfield as *The Colonizer and the Colonized* (Boston: Beacon Press, 1967).

Robert Bernasconi: Selected Bibliography

Books

Heidegger in Question: The Art of Existing. Atlantic Highlands: Humanities Press, 1993.

Edited with Simon Critchley, *Re-Reading Levinas*. Bloomington: Indiana University Press, 1991.

Edited with David Wood, *Derrida and Différance*. 2nd rev. ed. Evanston, Ill.: Northwestern University Press, 1988.

The Question of Language in Heidegger's History of Being. Atlantic Highlands: Humanities Press, and London: Macmillan, 1985.

Chapters in Edited Volumes and Journal Articles

"The Third Party." *Journal of the British Society for Phenomenology* 30.1 (1999).

"Different Styles of Eschatology: Derrida's Take on Levinas's Political Messianism." *Research in Phenomenology* 28 (1998).

"Can Development Theory Break with Its Past? Endogenous Development in Africa and the Old Imperialism." *African Philosophy* 11.1 (1998).

"Hegel at the Court of the Ashanti." In *Hegel after Derrida*, ed. Stuart Barnett. London: Routledge, 1998.

"'Stuck Inside of Mobile with the Memphis Blues Again.'" In *Theorizing Multiculturalism*, ed. Cynthia Willett. London: Blackwell, 1998.

"'An Ethics of Violence Justifying Itself: 'Sartre's Explorations of Violence and Oppression." *Bulletin de la Société Américaine de Philosophie* 10.2 (1998).

"African Philosophy's Challenge to Continental Philosophy." In *Postcolonial African Philosophy*, ed. Emmanuel Eze. Oxford: Blackwell, 1997.

"What Goes Around Comes Around: Derrida and Levinas on the Economy of the

Gift and the Gift of Genealogy." In *The Logic of the Gift: Toward an Ethic of Generosity,* ed. Alan Schrift. New York: Routledge, 1997.

"Eckhart's Anachorism." *Graduate Faculty Philosophy Journal* 19.2, 20.1 (1997).

"The Violence of the Face: Peace and Language in the Thought of Levinas." *Philosophy and Social Criticism* 23.6 (1997).

"The Double Face of the Political and the Social: Hannah Arendt and America's Racial Divisions." *Research in Phenomenology* 26 (1996).

"'You Don't Know What I'm Talking About': Alterity and the Hermeneutic Ideal." In *The Specter of Relativism,* ed. Lawrence K. Schmidt. Evanston, Ill.: Northwestern University Press, 1995.

"'Only the Persecuted . . .': Language of the Oppressor, Language of the Persecuted." In *Ethics as First Philosophy,* ed. Adriaan Peperzak. New York: Routledge, 1995.

"'I Will Tell You Who You Are': Heidegger on Greco-German Destiny and *Amerikanismus.*" In *From Phenomenology to Thought, Errancy, and Desire,* ed. Babette E. Babich. Dordrecht: Kluwer Academic Publishers, 1995.

"Sartre's Gaze Returned: The Transformation of the Phenomenology of Racism." *Graduate Faculty Philosophy Journal* 18.2 (1995).

"Heidegger and the Invention of the Western Philosophical Tradition." *Journal of the British Society for Phenomenology* 26.3 (1995).

"Heidegger's Other Sins of Omission." *American Catholic Philosophical Quarterly* 69.2 (1995).

"Repetition and Tradition: Heidegger's Destruction of the Distinction between Essence and Existence in *Basic Problems of Phenomenology.*" In *Reading Heidegger from the Start: Essays in His Earliest Thought,* ed. T. Kisiel and J. van Buren. Albany: State University of New York Press, 1994.

"Politics beyond Humanism: Mandela and the Struggle against Apartheid." In *Working through Derrida,* ed. Gary Madison. Evanston, Ill.: Northwestern University Press, 1993.

"On Deconstructing Nostalgia for Community within the West: The Debate between Nancy and Blanchot." *Research in Phenomenology* 23 (1993).

"Who is My Neighbor? Who is the Other? Questioning 'the Generosity of Western Thought.'" In *Ethics and Responsibility in the Phenomenological Tradition,* ed. Richard Rojcewicz. Pittsburgh: Simon Silverman Phenomenology Center, Duquesne University, 1992.

"One-Way Traffic: The Ontology of Decolonization and Its Ethics." In *Ontology and Alterity in Merleau-Ponty,* ed. Galen A. Johnson and Michael B. Smith. Evanston, Ill.: Northwestern University Press, 1990.

"The Ethics of Suspicion." *Research in Phenomenology* 20 (1990).

"Seeing Double: Destruction and Deconstruction." In *Dialogue and Deconstruction: The Gadamer-Derrida Encounter,* ed. R. Palmer and D. Michelfelder. Albany: State University of New York Press, 1989.

"Heidegger's Destruction of Phronesis." *Southern Journal of Philosophy* 28 (1989).

"Rereading *Totality and Infinity.*" In *The Question of the Other: Essays in Contemporary Continental Philosophy,* ed. A. Dallery and C. Scott. Albany: State University of New York Press, 1989.

"Levinas: Philosophy and Beyond." In *Philosophy and Non-Philosophy since Merleau-Ponty,* ed. H. J. Silverman. New York: Routledge & Kegan Paul, 1988.

"Levinas and Derrida: The Question of the Closure of Metaphysics." In *Face to Face with Levinas,* ed. R. Cohen. Albany: State University of New York Press, 1986.

15

Feminist Theory and Hannah Arendt's Concept of Public Space

SEYLA BENHABIB

Seyla Benhabib has emerged as one the foremost thinkers in the field of social and political philosophy. She is one of those responsible for the infusion of critical theory, especially the work of Jürgen Habermas, into the American debate about principles of justice and the Enlightenment model of rationality. Her work is often at the crossroads between reconstruction and critique, drawing out radical strands from the tradition that serve to move the discussion of political life in a new and original direction. Her insight is recognized across the spectrum of continental and Anglo-American philosophy as one that allows disparate contemporary intellectual voices—feminism, postmodernism, communitarianism, and universalism—to come into dialogue with one another. As Professor of Government at Harvard, her philosophical work has increasingly become involved with liberal moral and political theory and its link to Kantian practical philosophy.

In her work, Benhabib seeks to reconstruct, without wholly dismantling, certain ideals of political universalism, such as respect for the individual human being; individual autonomy and liberty; equality as the foundation for principles of social and economic justice; and democratic community. She maintains that a post-Enlightenment defense of what she calls interactive universalism, without the trappings of metaphysics, is still possible and politically beneficial. Such a new form of universalism that recognizes gender difference and contextual relevance sheds the hidden privileging of the legislative, indifferent, and patriarchal ego that lies behind the traditional claim to being gender blind. In her book *The Reluctant Modernism of Hannah Arendt* and elsewhere, Benhabib has developed a theory of public space that is sensitive to the individual stories and the need for particular moral judgments and actions that is at the heart of our experience of community.

The essay included in this volume discusses the possibility of a critical exchange between Hannah Arendt's political philosophy and contemporary feminist theory that can be illuminating for both sides. In this essay, she pursues a strategy of questioning which she describes as "thinking with Arendt against Arendt." This method of philosophizing is present throughout Seyla Benhabib's work.

⋅►▅◉▅◄⋅

For contemporary feminist theory, Hannah Arendt's thought remains puzzling, challenging, and, at times, infuriating. The sense of disappointment and anger one experiences as a feminist theorist when confronted with some of Arendt's characteristic distinctions, such as those between freedom and necessity, the public and the private, the male and the female, has best been expressed in the following sharp words by Hanna Pitkin:

> Can it be that Arendt held so contemptible a doctrine—one that denies the possibility of freedom, a truly human life, and even reality, to all but a handful of males who dominate all others and exclude them by violence from privilege? And when the excluded and miserable do enter history, can it be that Arendt condemns them for their rage, their failure to respect the "impartiality of justice and laws"? Impartiality! Justice! Where were these principles when that immense majority was relegated to shame and misery?[1]

Following this devastating commentary, Pitkin herself voices the second most common reaction experienced in the face of Arendt's works by contemporary feminist theorists, namely, puzzlement: "But there is more wrong here than injustice. On this account, I suggest, one cannot even make sense of politics itself."[2] Noting that something is wrong with this vision imputed to Arendt, Pitkin in the rest of her essay moves to a subtler account of Arendt's concept of the political and of the relation between the public and the private: "Yet, can this really be what Arendt means?" she writes. "Why should she so undermine her own efforts to save public, political life?"[3]

There is no simple answer to this question. Consider some of the opening passages of *The Human Condition:*

> The fact that the modern age emancipated the working classes and women at nearly the same historical moment must certainly be counted among the characteristics of an age which no longer believes that bodily functions and material concerns should be hidden. It is all the more symptomatic of the nature of these phenomena that the few remnants of strict privacy even in our own civilization relate to the "necessities" in the original sense of being necessitated by having a body.[4]

It is as if for Arendt the modern age is based on a category mistake, rather upon a series of mistakes, one of which is to assume that "bodily functions" and "material concerns" can become "public matters." What implications does this have for women? Does it mean that the emancipation of women is even more problematic than that of laborers because they seem to be "representatives of the realm of the body"—although we are not told how or why? In entering the public realm women seem to be bringing with them a principle of reality into this sphere, namely, the necessities which originate with having a body and which, from Arendt's point of view, strictly have no place in the public. Expressed more pointedly, the emancipation of women subverts the architectonic of Hannah Arendt's political philosophy and her claim that "each human activity points to its proper location in the world."[5] It is thus hard to avoid the impression that in these early passages of *The Human Condition*, Arendt ontologizes the division of labor between the sexes and those biological presuppositions which have historically confined women to the household and to the sphere of reproduction alone.[6]

If this is all that can be said on the significance of Hannah Arendt's political philosophy for contemporary feminist theory, then perhaps we should simply relegate Arendt to the category of those few women who, being exceptionally gifted and brilliant, were, to use a phrase of Arendt's, "pariahs," outsiders. Although as pariahs these women did not belong in the predominantly male community of scholarship and thought, neither did they convert their pariah status into a collective challenge and questioning of the "intellectual property which they were asked to administer."[7] Why not simply admit that Hannah Arendt was a prefeminist, or maybe even an antifeminist who, according to her biographer Elisabeth Young-Bruehl, "was suspicious of women 'who gave orders,' skeptical about whether women should be political leaders, and steadfastly opposed to the social dimensions of Women's Liberation."[8]

Yet a critical exchange between Hannah Arendt's political philosophy and contemporary feminist theory can be illuminating for both sides. Since the second wave of the women's movement has made the motto "the personal is political" one of its few and continuing rallying points, there is a challenging conceptual and political problem which feminists must face when reading Arendt. Maybe not Arendt's thought but feminism itself rests on a category mistake, and the attempt to "politicize" the private leads not to the emancipation of women but to the elimination of the last vestiges of human freedom in the modern world? From Theodor Adorno and Christopher Lasch on the left, to Gertrud Himmelfarb and Irving Kristol on the right, with liberals like Ronald Dworkin, John Rawls, and Bruce Ackerman straddling the middle, there is an important argument in Western political thought that maintaining some boundaries between the public and the private spheres is essential to preserving human freedom. Have feminist theorists told us where this line needs to be drawn, or is the phrase "the personal is political" an invitation to another version of authoritarian politics?

For contemporary feminist theory, Hannah Arendt's thought is also challenging in that there are a number of fascinating portraits of women in her work. From her early book on *Rahel Varnhagen* (1957) to her essay on Rosa Luxemburg (1955), and her portrait of Isak Dinesen (1955), women figures and masterful reflections on their lives are present as a theme, even if not a major one, in the Arendtian corpus.[9] Fitting these women, their lives and aspirations, and Arendt's views of them into the categorial structure of her political thought is a hermeneutic task still to be undertaken. Finally, there are also contemporary feminists who argue not only that, despite the apparent hostility and antagonism between feminist goals and Arendt's political thought, a deeper reading of her work will yield categories which bear a genuine affinity to the radical claims of contemporary feminism, but also that in the experience of the women's movement one has rediscovered those phenomenological aspects of revolutionary politics which Arendt had so brilliantly analyzed. The first argument has been put forward by Nancy C. M. Hartsock and the second by Ann M. Lane.

In her book *Money, Sex and Power: Toward a Feminist Historical Materialism,* Nancy Hartsock writes:

> Arendt's argument about the close relation of power, community and action could be regarded as idiosyncratic. The modifications she makes tend, overall, to reduce tension and opposition and to provide a vision of the political community as a shared and common world in which the individual both merges with others and distinguishes himself. Issues of exercising power over others are defined in terms of "empowerment," and the exercise of power becomes instead potentiality and capacity. But these modifications of the agonal model of politics and power share some important features with the ideas of several other theorists of power.[10]

Hartsock then analyzes the views of Dorothy Emmet, Hanna Pitkin, and Berenice Carroll, discovering in their work the shift already initiated by Arendt in thinking about power in political philosophy.[11] Common to these thinkers is a shift in vision from the instrumental conception of power, so characteristic of the tradition from Thomas Hobbes to Max Weber, toward a collaborative one; instead of viewing power as divisive these thinkers view power as integrative; instead of considering it as domination, they think of power as "empowerment," as liberatory activity.

It is precisely these aspects of Arendt's political thought that Ann M. Lane also emphasizes in her attempt to show that Arendt's "phenomenology of oppression and liberation" (my words) continues to illuminate women's struggles. Urging us to refocus our attention on Arendt's earlier works, and particularly upon her encounter with Zionism in the 1930s,[12] Ann Lane writes:

> Even if she is not a feminist, Arendt's political theory shares much with those who are. . . . Even as she turns away from Arendt, Rich [Lane is referring to Adrienne Rich] identifies the same issues for feminism that Arendt highlighted for Zionism: the quality of life as an outsider; the implicit tradition of identity for the pariah that provides resources for re-creating collectivity; the social experiments that are models for the whole community.[13]

In this essay, I pursue a strategy of questioning which I describe as "thinking with Arendt against Arendt." I am most sympathetic to those theorists like Pitkin, Hartsock, Lane, and, most recently, Mary Dietz,[14] who attempt to retrieve from Arendt's political thought those gems of insight which can still illuminate our struggles as contemporaries. Much as Arendt herself appropriated the political tradition of the West, not in the spirit of a scholastic exercise but in the spirit of questioning and dialogue such as to orient the mind in the present, we too can engage with her work today to illuminate some of the deepest political perplexities of our times. One of these perplexities is the changing boundaries of the political in our societies,[15] and with it the shifting line between the public and private realms. I argue that to engage in a "dialectical conversation" with Hannah Arendt about the concepts of the public and the private is crucial at this historical juncture. This is the case not only because these concepts are so essential to our political life that any apparently simplistic subversion of them will at the best lead us as feminists to lose political allies and at the worst land us in authoritarian utopias, but also because this task is important theoretically. Contemporary feminist theory needs a concept of public space if it is to articulate a liberatory vision of human relations. In this dialectical conversation, the partners do not remain unchanged: while I modify Arendt's concept of public space in the direction of a dialogic and procedural model, I suggest that contemporary feminist theory, in its refusal to articulate a positive conception of privacy, has undermined some of its own emancipatory thrust.

Throughout this essay I write of "feminist theory" in the singular. This usage does not reflect my assumption that there is only one authoritative or defining tradition in feminist theory. At present, feminist theory reflects all the fractures and fractions of current disputes in the humanities, ranging from postmodernism to neo-pragmatism, from liberalism to psychoanalytical feminism. In the present context though, I think it is safe to assume that there is one common assumption which unites feminist theorizing and which distinguishes this body of work from gender-blind theories like Arendt's. The category of "gender," that is, the study of the social and cultural construction, interpretation, internalization, and reproduction of sexual difference, is the *differentia specifica* of feminist theory, although feminists will differ in explaining and interpreting these processes.

Two Models of the Public Space

Without a doubt Hannah Arendt is the central political thinker of this century whose work has reminded us with great poignancy of the "lost treasures" of our tradition of political thought, and specifically of the "loss" of public space, of *der öffentliche Raum*, under conditions of modernity.[16] Hannah Arendt's major theoretical work, *The Human Condition*, is usually, and not altogether unjustifiably, treated as an anti-modernist political work. By "the rise of the social" Arendt means the institutional differentiation of modern societies into the narrowly political realm on the one hand and the economic market and the family on the other. As a result of these transformations, economic processes which had hitherto been confined to the "shadowy realm of the household" emancipate themselves and become public matters. The same historical process which brought forth the modern constitutional state also brings forth "society," that realm of social inter-action which interposes itself between the "household" on the one hand and the political state on the other.[17] Arendt sees in this process the occlud-ing of the political by the "social" and the transformation of the public space of politics into a pseudo-space of interaction in which individuals no longer "act" but "merely behave" as economic producers, consumers, and urban city-dwellers.

This relentlessly negative account of the "rise of the social" and the de-cline of the public realm has been identified as the core of Arendt's nostal-gic "anti-modernism."[18] Yet it would be grossly misleading to read Hannah Arendt only or even primarily as a nostalgic thinker. She devoted as much space in her work to analyzing the dilemmas and prospects of politics under conditions of modernity as she did to the decline of public space in moder-nity. If we are not to read her account of the disappearance of the public realm as a *Verfallsgeschichte* (a history of decline), then how are we to inter-pret it?[19] If one locates Arendt's concept of "public space" in the context of her theory of totalitarianism, the term acquires a range of meanings rather different from the ones dominant in *The Human Condition*. This topographi-cal figure is suggested early on in her work, at the end of *The Origins of Totalitarianism* (1950), to compare various forms of political rule. Constitu-tional government is likened to moving within a space where the law is like the hedges erected between the buildings and one orients oneself upon known territory. Tyranny is like a desert; under conditions of tyranny: one moves in an unknown, vast open space where the will of the tyrant occa-sionally befalls one like the sandstorm overtaking the desert traveler. To-talitarianism has no spatial topology; it is like an iron band, compressing people increasingly together until they are formed into one.[20]

The concepts "agonistic" vs. "associational" public space can capture this contrast. According to the "agonistic" view, the public realm represents that space of appearances in which moral and political greatness, heroism, and preeminence are revealed, displayed, shared with others. This is a competi-tive space in which one competes for recognition, precedence, and acclaim. The agonal space is based on competition rather than collaboration; it indi-viduates those who participate in it and sets them apart from others; it is exclusive in that it presupposes strong criteria of belonging and loyalty from its participants.

By contrast, according to the "associational" view such a public space emerges whenever and wherever, in Arendt's words, "men act together in concert." On this model, public space is the space "where freedom can ap-pear."[21] It is not a space in any topographical or institutional sense: a town hall or a city square where people do not "act in concert" is not a public space in this Arendtian sense. A private dining room in which people gather to hear a *Samizdat* or in which dissidents meet with foreigners can become a public space; just as a field or a forest can also become a public space if they are the object and the location of an "action in concert," of a demon-stration to stop the construction of a highway or a military air base, for example. These diverse topographical locations become public spaces in that they become the "sites" of power, of common action coordinated through speech and persuasion. For Arendt herself, examples of the recovery of such public spaces under conditions of modernity were present not only in the American but also in the French Resistance during the Second World War, in the Hungarian uprising in 1956, and in the civil rights and anti-war movements of the late 1960s in the United States.

All these historically disparate instances repeated one experience.[22] Violence can occur in private and in public, but its language is essentially private because it is the language of pain. Force, like violence, can be located in both realms. In a way, it has no language, and nature remains its quintessential source. It moves without having to persuade or to hurt. Power, however, is the only force that emanates from action, and it comes from the mutual action of a group of human beings: once in action, one can make things happen, thus becoming the source of a different kind of "force."

The Feminist Critique of Hannah Arendt's Concept of Public Space

While all genuine politics and power relations involve an agonistic dimension, in the sense of a vying for distinction and excellence, agonal politics also entails an associative dimension based on the power of persuasion and consensus. In this sense the sharp differentiation between these models needs to be softened. But there is a less benign aspect to the agonal space, one which makes many feminists denounce it as articulating the predominantly male experiences of death through war and domination. In her perceptive analysis, Nancy Hartsock points out:

> In the case of the warrior-hero, then, each aspect of *eros* takes negative form. Relations with others take the form of the struggle for victory in battle, a struggle for dominance that requires the other's submission or even his death. . . . The body and its needs, even for life itself, are held to be irrelevant. . . . Finally, creativity and generation, issues centering on life, are replaced for the warrior-hero by a fascination with death.[23]

One of the curious aspects of Arendt's account of the agonal space of the *polis* is that she subdues and, yes, "domesticates" the Homeric *warrior-hero* to yield the Aristotelian *deliberative citizen*. She writes:

> Thought was secondary to speech, but speech and action were considered to be coeval and coequal, of the same rank and the same kind: and this originally meant not only that most political action, in so far as it remains outside the sphere of violence, is indeed transacted in words, but more fundamentally that finding the right words at the right moment, quite apart from the information or communication they may convey, is action. Only sheer violence is mute.[24]

In her rejection of violence as a form of political activity, and in substituting *phronesis* in speech for valor in war, which after all was the existential experience of the Homeric warrior-hero (think here of Achilles and his "mute" rage), Arendt appears to have undertaken a quiet feminist transformation of the Homeric warrior ideal into the "tamer" and "more reasonable" Aristotelian deliberative citizen.

The agonal model of the public sphere needs also to be criticized from a further perspective, which is neither exclusively nor uniquely feminist. One can criticize this model from a perspective that is more attuned to the political experience of modernity. Since many of Arendt's negative observations on modernity have implications for the transformations of women's lives in the modern world as well, the defense of the more modernist conception of politics, found in her associative model, and the defense of the entrance of women into the public sphere are closely related. The agonal space of the *polis* was made possible by a morally homogeneous and politically egalitarian, but exclusive, community, in which action could also be a revelation of the self to others. Under conditions of moral and political homogeneity and lack of anonymity, the "agonal" dimension, the vying for excellence among peers, could take place. For the moderns, public space is essentially porous; neither access to it nor its agenda of debate can be predefined by criteria of moral and political homogeneity. With the entry of every new group into the public space of politics after the French and American Revolutions, the scope of the public gets extended. The emancipation of workers made property relations into a public-political issue; the emancipation of women has meant that the family and the so-called private sphere become political issues; the attainment of rights by non-white and non-Christian peoples has put cultural questions of collective self- and other-representations on the "public" agenda. Not only is it the "lost treasure" of revolutions that eventually all can partake in them, but equally, when freedom emerges from action in concert, there can be no agenda to predefine the topic of public conversation. The struggle over what gets included in the public agenda is itself a struggle for justice and freedom.

The episode which best illustrates this blind spot in Hannah Arendt's thought is that of school desegregation in Little Rock, Arkansas. Arendt likened the demands of the black parents to have their children admitted into previously all-white schools, demands upheld by the U.S. Supreme Court, to the desire of the social parvenu to gain recognition in a society that did not care to admit her. This time around Arendt failed to make the "fine distinction" in political matters which she otherwise so cultivated; and she confused an issue of public justice—equality of educational access—with an issue of social preference—who my friends are or whom I invite to dinner. It is to her credit, however, that after the intervention of the black novelist Ralph Ellison she had the grace to reverse her position.[25]

At the root of Arendt's vacillations as to what is and what is not an appropriate matter to be discussed in the public realm lies another more important problem, namely, her "phenomenological essentialism." By this I mean her belief that each type of human activity has its proper "place" in the world, and that this place is the only authentic space in which this kind of activity can truly unfold.[26] In accordance with essentialist assumptions, "public space" is frequently either defined as that space in which only a certain *type of activity*, namely, action as opposed to work or labor, takes place; or it is delimited from other "social" spheres with reference to the *substantive content* of the public dialogue. Both strategies, in my opinion, are indefensible and lead Arendt to limit her concept of public space in ways which are not compatible with her own associative model.[27] Different action-types, like work and labor, can become the locus of "public space" if they are reflexively challenged and called into question from the standpoint of the asymmetrical power relations governing them. To give a few examples: obviously productivity quotas in the factory workshop, how many chips per hour a worker should produce, can become a matter of "public concern" if the legitimacy of those setting the quotas, their right to do so, their reasons for doing so are challenged. Likewise, as experiences in the 1980s have shown us, even the most intricate questions of nuclear strategy, the number of nuclear warheads on a missile, the time required to defuse them—all these dauntingly technical issues—can be reclaimed by a public under conditions of democratic legitimacy and become part of what our res publica is about. Arendt, by contrast, relegated certain types of activity like work and labor, and by extension issues of economics and technology, to the "social" realm, ignoring that these activities and relations, insofar as they are based on power hierarchies, could become matters of public-political dispute as well.

Equally, I regard as futile Arendt's attempt to define "public space" by setting the agenda of the public conversation. Even on her terms, the effect of collective action in concert will be to put ever new and unexpected items on the agenda of public debate. Thus the "associational" model develops not a substantive but *a procedural* concept of public space which is in fact compatible with this view. What is important here is not so much *what* public discourse is about as the *way* in which this discourse takes place: force and violence destroy the specificity of public discourse by introducing the "dumb" language of physical superiority and constraint and by silencing the voice of persuasion and conviction. Only power is generated by public discourse and is sustained by it. From the standpoint of this procedural model, neither the distinction between the social and the political nor the distinction between work, labor, or action are that relevant. At stake is the reflexive questioning of issues by all those affected by their foreseeable consequences and the recognition of their right to do so.

If, however, neither matters of economics nor of technology belong in the "social" realm alone, by virtue of the kinds of human activities which sustain them, but can become public-political matters to the degree to which the power relations which structure them are challenged, why can we not say the same about typically female activities like housework, care for the emotional and sexual needs of the body, the bearing and rearing of children? If Arendt's essentialism is implausible in these other areas, then is it not likewise implausible when applied to the activities specific to the household, unless, of course, there is a sense in which these activities are more fundamentally "private"? The following passage supports this reading:

> Although the distinction between private and public coincides with the opposition of necessity and freedom, of futility and permanence, and, finally, of shame and honor, it is by no means true that only the necessary, the futile, and the shameful have their proper place in the private realm. The most elementary meaning of the two realms indicates that there are things that need to be hidden and others that need to be displayed publicly if they are to exist at all.[28]

In these and other passages, Arendt appears to me to be proposing some conception of human balance and psychic integrity, which could only be maintained if the private and the public realms stood in a certain relation to one another. In this context, Arendt does not mean by "privacy" the freedom of religion and conscience which historically has been understood as the fundamental privacy right in the liberal polity; nor does Arendt think that there is a privacy right to economic wealth.[29] By privacy in the above quote—"there are things that need to be hidden and others that need to be displayed publicly"—Arendt means primarily the necessity that some aspect of the "domestic-intimate" sphere be hidden from the glare of the public eye. What aspect, then, of this "domestic-intimate" sphere must remain hidden from the public eye and sheltered from political action? An answer to this question can be interpolated by considering the distinction in her thought between "privacy" and "intimacy." And here a surprising meeting between certain feminist concerns and Arendt's political theory becomes visible.

Intimacy vs. Privacy in Hannah Arendt's Work

Hannah Arendt distinguishes between "intimacy" and "privacy," and between "the social" and "the political" as modes of public life.[30] In the emergence of modernity in the West in the course of the sixteenth and seventeenth centuries, Arendt sees not only the transformation of the political-public into the social-public but also the transformation of the private into the "intimate." For her, the preoccupation with intimacy and with individual subjectivity are aspects of the same process. Isolating individuals and forcing them into the confines of anonymous public activities like the exchange and commodity market, the modern age also brings forth the cult of individuality, the preoccupation and concern with the uniqueness, authenticity, and psychic harmony of the self. Rousseau's *Confessions* are the pinnacle of this preoccupation with the self and its inner space. For Arendt, the mark of the turn to individuality and to intimacy is the accompanying "worldlessness" of these human relations. With the rise of the social, modern writers cease to locate the identity essential to the self in the public realm: the public realm in the form of the "social," and I am referring here primarily to the market of the free exchange of commodities, ceases to be the sphere in which individuality is most authentically displayed. From Rousseau to Marx, modern theorists thematize the "alienation" of the self from others in the social world. In Hegel's memorable phrase, "virtue" and "the course of the world" part company.[31]

Arendt here is privileging a sense of privacy distinct from intimacy and its worldlessness. She writes:

> The second outstanding non-privative characteristic of privacy is that the four walls of one's private property offer the only reliable hiding place from the common public world, not only from everything that goes on in it but also from its very publicity, from being seen and being heard. A life spent entirely in public, in the presence of others, becomes, as we would say, shallow. While it retains its visibility, it loses the quality of rising into sight from some darker ground which must remain hidden if it is not to lose its depth in a very real non-subjective sense. The only efficient way to guarantee the darkness of what needs to be hidden against the light of publicity is private property, a privately owned place to hide in.[32]

Certainly, Arendt's call in this passage for "a privately owned place to hide in" is not a call to own a condominium or a private house—as far as I know she rented an apartment in New York City and never owned anything. To approach Arendt's meaning, recall here Virginia Woolf's *A Room of One's Own*. The commonalities in this search for a space that provides the self with a center, with a shelter, with a place in which to unfold capacities, dreams and memories, to nurture the wounds of the ego, and to lend to it that depth of feeling which, as Arendt puts it, allows it to rise into sight "from some darker ground," are striking. This passage is an affirmation of "the home." Viewed against the background of massive homelessness today, the perspicacity of Arendt's insight is clear: the home not only lends the self the depth without which it is nothing but a shadow in the streets, the home also provides that space that protects, nurtures, and makes the individual fit to appear in the public realm. The homeless self is the individual ready to be ravaged by the forces of the social against which it must daily fight to protect itself.

With Arendt's concept of the home—not her terminology but mine—we reach the most significant sense of "privacy" in her theory, one that feminist theorists must not only share but also cultivate. Let me distinguish, though, between a specific domestic structure, the monogamous nuclear male-headed family, and the "home." This is a distinction which Hannah Arendt herself did not make and which is the central reason why her affirmation of the private realm so often reads like an ahistorical justification of a specific gender division of labor which historically confined modern bourgeois women to the home. While feminists have shown that the patriarchal family was no "home" for most women, the gay liberation movements in the last two decades have also made public that there are many ways to be a family and to share a home. New legislation passed in various U.S. cities, most notably in New York City and Cambridge, Massachusetts, names these types of human associations "domestic partnerships," thus distinguishing between the "home" structure and a certain type of psychosexual and intimate relationship. Contained in the concept of "privacy," particularly as it has applied to the "domestic-familial realm," have been several moral and political principles. They may be named intimacy, domesticity, and the space of individuality. What form of sexual relations best expresses intimacy can no longer be dictated in terms of categories of biologically grounded gender identity; homosexual as well as heterosexual human relations may succeed or fail in creating intimacy for the individuals involved. Domestic arrangements geared toward the sustenance of the human body and of its daily needs, the running of a home in which embodied selves need to be sheltered, the raising, nurture, and education of children, can be carried out, and historically have been carried out, by many different forms of kinship and family-like arrangements. Intimacy and domesticity together contribute to the nourishment and unfolding of individuality. In this sense, the primary moral and cultural purpose of the household under conditions of modernity is the development and flourishing of autonomous individualities. Although this explication expands Hannah Arendt's categories considerably and takes them in directions which she herself could not have anticipated, they are compatible with her deep reflections on the meaning of the private sphere. One very important consequence of this reformulated concept of privacy is not only the redefinition of the family unit but also the encouragement of legislation protecting children and their care providers on the basis of the right to a home, understood as the moral and political entitlement of the individual to the physical, material, and spiritual preconditions for the development of the personality.

Hannah Arendt's concept of privacy and some concerns of contemporary feminist theory about "a room of one's own" can be made compatible with each other along the lines suggested above. What about her highly problematic distinction between "the social" and "the political" as modalities of public life? Is it useful in thinking about contemporary women's struggles?

"The Social" vs. "The Political": Toward a Reconsideration of Arendt's Distinctions

At present there are three different strands of research among feminist theorists which, in different ways, throw new and hitherto undetected light on the concept of the public sphere and the related concepts of the social and the political. First, there is a growing body of *alternative feminist historiographies of the genesis of the public sphere.* Joan Landes's *Women and the Public Sphere in the Age of the French Revolution* (1988) and Linda Kerber's *Women of the Republic: Intellect and Ideology in Revolutionary America* (1986) are among the most notable works of scholarship in this area. Despite some differences in their assessment of specific authors, for example, Montesquieu and Rousseau, both works tackle a common problem: namely, the gender contradictions of early bourgeois republics that advocate universal equality and freedom on the one hand, but confine the citizen's wife and her claims to freedom to the domestic sphere alone. These works suggest but do not answer the conceptually more challenging question: Is it a historically contingent fact, eventually corrected, so to speak, in the course of subsequent democratic and revolutionary struggles, that the ideology of the emergent bourgeois public sphere confined women to the private realm alone?

Or is it the case that this historical constellation of events shows that there is a deep incompatibility between the very model of the bourgeois public sphere and the inclusion of women? Theorists who answer this second question in the affirmative can be named *advocates of the alternative model of public sphere*. Their work constitutes the second most significant strand of research among feminist theorists working on this topic. Iris Young has put forth the most challenging arguments on this issue: criticizing the liberal-Kantian model of the values of impartiality, objectivity, and detachment in practical reason, Young develops the model of a "civic public," which would be partial to the hitherto excluded and repressed interests of certain groups, which would be perspectival, engaged, embedded, and embodied. Altering the normative bases of this model of impartiality would yield a pluralistic, heterogeneous, to some extent anonymous, but more erotic and more carnivalesque public space than the more republican and sedate versions imagined by either the French or the American revolutionaries. Young sees the civic space of the city and its neighborhoods as exemplifying this ideal.[33]

Finally, there is a strand of feminist theorizing which is inspired by the critical social theory of late capitalism developed by Jürgen Habermas and Claus Offe and for which the concept of public space is important from the standpoint of articulating a *feminist and radical democratic critique of the late welfare-state capitalist democracies*. Nancy Fraser's work has been one of the most significant contributions in this area.[34]

Although these three areas of research are closely related and naturally lead into each other, in the present context I can only suggest how Arendt's distinction between the "social" and the "political" would be significant from the standpoint of the third enterprise, that is, for developing a feminist critique of welfare-state-type, late-capitalist societies within which I would situate my own attempt to reread Hannah Arendt. Undoubtedly, our societies are undergoing tremendous transformations at present. In really existing Western democracies, under the impact of corporatization, the mass media, and the growth of business-style political associations such as political action committees and other lobbying groups, the public sphere of democratic legitimacy has shrunk. The autonomous citizen, whose reasoned judgment and participation were the sine qua non of the public sphere, has been transformed into the "citizen consumer" of packaged images and messages, or the "electronic mail target" of large lobbying groups and organizations. This impoverishment of public life has been accompanied by the growth of the society of surveillance and voyeurism on the one hand (Foucault), and the "colonization of the lifeworld" on the other (Habermas). Not only has public life been transformed, private life as well has undergone tremendous changes, only some of which can be welcome for furthering the values of democratic legitimacy and discursive will formation. Hannah Arendt's prediction that modern societies would be increasingly dominated by the "social," with the concomitant rule of the bureaucracy on the one hand, and an obsessive preoccupation with intimacy on the other, has proved remarkably prescient.

As the sociologist Helga Maria Hernes has remarked, in some ways welfare-state societies are ones in which "reproduction" has gone public.[35] When, however, issues like child-rearing; care for the sick, the young and the elderly; reproductive freedoms; domestic violence; child abuse and the constitution of sexual identities go "public," more often than not a "patriarchal-capitalist-disciplinary bureaucracy" has resulted.[36] These bureaucracies have frequently disempowered women and other affected groups and have set the agenda for public debate and participation. In reflecting about these issues feminist theory has lacked a *critical model of public space and public discourse.* A critical model of public space is necessary to enable us to draw the line between "juridification," *Verrechtlichung* in Jürgen Habermas's term, or between making "social" and "administering to," in Arendtian terms, on the one hand, and between making "public," in the sense of making accessible to debate, reflection, action, and moral-political transformation on the other. To make issues of common concern "public" in this second sense means making them increasingly accessible to associative models of political interaction; it means to democratize them. As feminists, we have lacked a critical model which could distinguish between the bureaucratic administration of needs and collective democratic empowerment over them. More often than not, debates among feminists have been blocked by the alternatives of a legalistic liberal reformism (the National Organization of Women [NOW] agenda; American Civil Liberties Union [ACLU] positions) and a radical feminism which can hardly conceal its own political and moral authoritarian undertones.[37]

While Hannah Arendt's agonistic model is at odds with the sociological reality of modernity, as well as with modern political struggles for justice, her associative model of the public sphere may be an essential beginning point in the feminist critique of the transformation of public life under late capitalism. Feminist politics, particularly in the United States, has been an accomplice to the process by which the sphere of the public has extended itself while its influence and legitimacy have shrunk. The public has been all too glibly and thoughtlessly identified with the legal system and the media. As a nation of voyeurs sat watching courtroom testimonies of abusive parents, domestic violence, marital rape, child molestation, I for one have at times cringed in shame at what, in Arendt's words, was the making public of what needed to be kept private. I do not want to be misunderstood: insofar as the rights of these women, children, spouses were destroyed and abused, the law must protect them. Yet the law is too blunt an instrument at times to redress the wounds of individuals whose "home" has been their "hell." As feminists, we have seen the transformation of the public into the social, into the rule by nobody, by an anonymous army of experts, judges, attorneys, social workers, psychiatrists, and welfare officials. Certainly we must accept here the inevitable dialectic of social movements which, if successful at all, will create institutions and even bureaucracies to advocate and fulfill their claims in the public sphere; in other words, there is a certain interdependence between bureaucratization and democratization. Yet there is also a sphere of politics which exhausts itself neither in the bureaucratic administration of needs nor in the clientalistic pressing forward of claims within established institutional mechanisms. This is the dimension of the political which involves transforming private shame into a public claim, private darkness and blindness into public light and visibility. This kind of politics involves giving "each other the world." In this task of recovering the political, we can do worse than to think with Hannah Arendt against Hannah Arendt.

Notes

1. Hanna Pitkin, "Justice: On Relating Private and Public," *Political Theory* 9.3 (1981): 336.

2. Ibid.

3. Ibid., p. 338.

4. Hannah Arendt, *The Human Condition* (Chicago: University of Chicago Press, 1973 [1958], p. 73.

5. Ibid.

6. In a recent article Mary Dietz has given a feminist reading of the "gender subtext" of Arendt's ostensibly gender-neutral analysis of the "human" activities of work, labor, and action. Dietz shows quite persuasively that although these activities are not associated by Arendt herself with any specific gender organization, it is of course the women who perform those activities most essential to Arendt's understanding of labor: cooking, cleaning, sewing, mending, tidying up—those activities necessary for the daily continuation of life and the regeneration of the body; and of course those reproductive and nurturing activities, like the bearing and care of children, but also of the elderly, the sick, and the needy (see Arendt, *Human Condition,* pp. 96ff.; and Mary Dietz, "Hannah Arendt and Feminist Politics," in *Feminist Interpretations and Political Theory*, ed. Mary Shanley and Carole Pateman [London: Polity Press, 1990], pp. 232–53).

7. This is the phrase that Arendt herself cites from Morris Goldstein in the context of discussing the difficulty that the German Jews faced in administering a "property," that is, the German intellectual tradition that was not their own and that excluded them. See Moritz Goldstein, "Deutsch-Jüdischer Parnass," as quoted in Hannah Arendt, "Walter Benjamin," in *Men in Dark Times* (New York: Harcourt, Brace, Jovanovich, 1968 [1955]), pp. 18–34. The exact quote from Goldstein reads: "We Jews administer the intellectual property of a people which denies us the right and the ability to do so."

8. Elisabeth Young-Bruehl, *For Love of the World* (New Haven, Conn.: Yale University Press, 1982), p. 238.

9. See Hannah Arendt, *Rahel Varnhagen: The Life of a Jewish Woman* (New York: Harcourt, Brace, Jovanovich, 1974 [1957]). For the essay on Rosa Luxemburg, see Arendt, *Men in Dark Times*, pp. 33–57; and for the portrait of Isak Dinesen, see ibid., pp. 95–111.

10. Nancy C. M. Hartsock, *Money, Sex and Power: Toward a Feminist Historical Materialism* (Boston: Northeastern University Press, 1985), p. 222.

11. Ibid., pp. 222–30.

12. Some of the less known aspects of Arendt's lifelong occupation with Jewish identity and Jewish politics have been documented by Dagmar Barnouw in *Visible Spaces: Hannah Arendt and the German-Jewish Experience* (Baltimore: Johns Hopkins University Press, 1990).

13. Ann M. Lane, "The Feminism of Hannah Arendt," *Democracy* 3.3 (1983): 111.

14. Dietz, "Hannah Arendt and Feminist Politics," pp. 232–53.

15. See Charles S. Maier, ed., *Changing Boundaries of the Political* (Cambridge: Cambridge University Press, 1987), pp. 12ff., on the welfare state, women's issues, and changing boundaries of the political; see also Lauro Balbo, "Family, Women and the State: Notes toward a Typology of Family Roles and Public Intervention," in ibid., pp. 201–21.

16. See further Seyla Benhabib, "Hannah Arendt and the Redemptive Power of Narrative," *Social Research* 57.1 (1990): 167–96.

17. Arendt, *Human Condition*, pp. 38–49.

18. See Christopher Lasch, "Introduction," *Salmagundi* 60 (1983); and Jürgen Habermas, "Hannah Arendt's Communications Concept of Power," *Social Research* 44, Hannah Arendt Memorial Issue (1977).

19. I have argued elsewhere that the key here is Arendt's odd methodology, which conceives of political thought as "story-telling." Viewed in this light, her "story" of the transformation of public space is an "exercise" of thought. Such thought exercises dig under the rubble of history in order to recover those "pearls" of past experience, with their sedimented and hidden layers of meaning, so as to cull from them a story that can orient the mind in the future. The vocation of the theorist as "story-teller" is the unifying thread of Arendt's political and philosophical analyses from the origins of totalitarianism to her reflections on the French and American Revolutions to her theory of public space and to her final words to the first volume of *The Life of the Mind* on "Thinking" (1971). Read in this light, Arendt's account of the "rise of the social" and the decline of public space under conditions of modernity cannot be viewed as a nostalgic *Verfallsgeschichte* but must be understood as the attempt to think through the human history sedimented in layers of language. We must learn to identify those moments of rupture, displacement, and dislocation in history. At such moments language is the witness to the more profound transformations taking place in human life. Nonetheless, Arendt is not free of assumptions deriving from an *Ursprungsphilosophie*, which posits an original state or temporal point as the privileged source to which one must trace back the phenomena so as to capture their "true" meaning. As opposed to rupture, displacement, and dislocation, this view emphasizes the continuity between the past origin and the present condition and seeks to uncover at the origin the lost and concealed essence of the phenomena. There are really two strains in Hannah Arendt's thought, one corresponding to the method of fragmentary historiography, and inspired by Walter Benjamin; the other, inspired by the phenomenology of Husserl and Heidegger, and according to which memory is the mimetic recollection of the lost origins of phenomena as contained in some fundamental human experience.

In accordance with this latter approach, reminders abound in *The Human Condition* of "the original meaning of politics" or of the "lost" distinction between the "private" and the "public." See Benhabib, "Hannah Arendt and the Redemptive Power of Narrative," for a fuller discussion of the methodological puzzles of Arendt's analysis of totalitarianism.

20. Hannah Arendt, *The Origins of Totalitarianism* (New York: Harcourt, Brace, Jovanovich, 1967), p. 466.

21. Arendt, *Men in Dark Times*, p. 4.

22. Arendt, *Human Condition*, p. 26.

23. Hartsock, *Money, Sex and Power*, p. 189.

24. Arendt, *Human Condition*, p. 26.

25. See Hannah Arendt, "Reflections on Little Rock," *Dissent* 6.1 (1959): 45–56; Ralph Ellison, in *Who Speaks for the Negro?* ed. Robert Penn Warren (New York: Random House, 1965), pp. 342–44; and Arendt to Ralph Ellison in a letter of July 29, 1965, as cited by Young-Bruehl, *For the Love of the World*, p. 316.

26. Arendt, *Human Condition*, pp. 73ff.

27. See note 30 below for a discussion of some of the puzzles surrounding Arendt's use of this term.

28. Arendt, *Human Condition*, p. 73.

29. For Arendt property and wealth are distinct. While property, in the sense of a place of my own and that part of the world which sustains my daily well-being, is private, wealth is public, and its appropriation always subject to political action and public policy (Arendt, ibid., pp. 109ff.).

30. Although it often seems as if Arendt equates the "rise of the social" with "the decline of the public sphere" as such, upon close scrutiny it would be more appropriate to emphasize the "transformation" of the public sphere under conditions of modernity from the political to the social public. Social life, in Arendt's sense of the term, is also enacted in public; but this is a different kind of "publicness," one bound together by the forces of the life-process itself and not by political action: "Society is the form in which the fact of mutual dependence for the sake of life and nothing else assumes public significance and where the activities connected with sheer survival are permitted to appear in public" (Arendt, ibid., p. 46). In this essay I am not addressing the fact that Arendt nowhere in *The Human Condition* thematizes that aspect of the rise of modernity that has been considered such a crucial feature of this epoch for thinkers as diverse as G. W. F. Hegel, Alexis de Tocqueville, Jürgen Habermas, and Talcott Parsons. This is the formation of an independent sphere of "civic and political associations," and secondary institutions within the social, which have the function, among others, of mediating between the narrowly political state on the one hand and society, in the broad sense of differing and competing social groups, on the other. Hannah Arendt's sociology of modernity is curiously truncated, but as a political and cultural historian she operates with a much richer conception of the modern social sphere. In my book *The Reluctant Modernism of Hannah Arendt* (Newbury Park, Calif.: Sage, 1996), I argue that Arendt did not neglect this dimension of modernity in her historical writings but that she did not thematize its philosophical import until much later in her life.

31. G. W. F. Hegel, *The Phenomenology of Spirit*, trans. A. V. Miller (Oxford: Clarendon Press, 1977 [1807]), p. 71.

32. Arendt, *Human Condition*, p. 71.

33. See Iris Young, "Impartiality and the Civic Public," in *Feminism as Critique*, in Seyla Benhabib and Drucilla Cornell, eds. (London: Polity Press, 1987), pp. 56–77; and Iris Young, "The Ideal of Community and the Politics of Difference," in

Feminism and Postmodernism, ed. Linda Nicholson (New York: Routledge, 1990), pp. 300–24.

34. Nancy Fraser, *Unruly Practices: Power, Discourse and Gender in Contemporary Social Theory* (London: Polity Press, 1990).

35. See Helga Maria Hernes, *Welfare State and Woman Power: Essays in State Feminism* (London: Norwegian University Press, 1987).

36. Fraser, *Unruly Practices;* and Nancy Fraser, "Women, Welfare and the Politics of Need Interpretation," *Hypatia: A Journal of Feminist Philosophy* 2 (1987): 103–21.

37. For a good example of the first trend, see Rosemarie Tong, *Women, Sex and the Law* (Totowa, N.J.: Rowman & Littlefield, 1984). For the second trend, consult Catharine MacKinnon's work and the amazing "return of the repressed" Marxist orthodoxy of the state and the law in her writings in, for example, her early article, "Feminism, Marxism, Method and the State: An Agenda for Theory," in *Feminist Theory: A Critique of Ideology*, ed. N. O. Koehane, M. Z. Rosaldo, and B. C. Gelpi (Chicago: University of Chicago Press, 1982), pp. 1–30; and her more recent *Feminism Unmodified: Discourses on Life and Law* (Cambridge, Mass.: Harvard University Press, 1987).

Seyla Benhabib: Selected Bibliography

Books

Democracy and Identity: Problems of Political Incorporation in the Global Era. Princeton: Princeton University Press, forthcoming.

Democracy and Difference: Contesting Boundaries of the Political. Princeton: Princeton University Press, 1996.

The Reluctant Modernism of Hannah Arendt. Thousand Oaks, Calif.: Sage, 1996.

With Judith Butler, Drucilla Cornell, and Nancy Fraser. *Feminist Contentions: A Philosophical Exchange*. New York: Routledge, 1994.

Situating the Self: Gender, Community and Postmodernism in Contemporary Ethics. New York: Routledge, 1992.

Feminism as Critique: On the Politics of Gender. Minneapolis: University of Minnesota Press, 1987.

Critique, Norm and Utopia: A Study of the Foundations of Critical Theory. New York: Columbia University Press, 1986.

Chapters in Edited Volumes and Journal Articles

"Democracy and Identity: In Search of the Civic Polity." *Philosophy and Social Criticism* 24.2–3 (1998).

"The Embattled Public Sphere: Hannah Arendt, Jürgen Habermas and Beyond." *Theoria: A Journal of Social and Political Theory* 90 (December 1997).

"On Reconciliation and Respect, Justice and the Good Life: Response to Herta Nagl-Docekal and Rainer Forst." *Philosophy and Social Criticism* 23.5 (1997).

"The Local, the Contextual and/or Critical." *Constellations* 3.1 (1996).

"Identity, Perspective and Narrative in Hannah Arendt's *Eichmann in Jerusalem.*" *History and Memory* 8.2 (1996).

"Judith Shklar's Dystopic Liberalism." *Social Research* 61 (1994).

"Deliberative Rationality and Models of Democratic Legitimacy." *Constellations* 1.1 (1994).

"Feminist Theory and Hannah Arendt's Concept of Public Space." *History of the Human Sciences* 6.2 (1993).

"Feminism and Postmodernism: An Uneasy Alliance." *Praxis International* 11.2
   (1991).
"Hannah Arendt and the Redemptive Power of Narrative." *Social Research* 57.1
   (1990).
"Critical Theory and Postmodernism: On the Interplay of Ethics, Aesthetics and
   Utopia in Critical Theory." *Cardozo Law Review* 11.5–6 (1990).
"On Contemporary Feminist Theory." *Dissent* 36.3 (1989).
"The Shadow of Aristotle and Hegel: Communicative Ethics and Current Contro-
   versies in Practical Philosophy." *Philosophical Forum* 21.1–2 (1989).
"Judgment and the Moral Foundations of Politics in Arendt's Thought." *Political
   Theory* 16 (1988).

CONTRIBUTORS

Seyla Benhabib is Professor of Government at Harvard University and Senior Research Associate at the Center for European Studies.

Robert Bernasconi is Moss Professor of Philosophy at the University of Memphis.

Walter Brogan is Professor of Philosophy at Villanova University.

Judith Butler is Maxine Elliot Professor of Rhetoric and Comparative Literature at the University of California, Berkeley.

John D. Caputo is the David R. Cook Chair of Philosophy at Villanova University.

Edward S. Casey is Professor and Chair of Philosophy at the State University of New York, Stony Brook.

Drucilla Cornell is Professor of Law at Rutgers University–Newark.

Rodolphe Gasché is Eugenio Donato Professor of Comparative Literature at the State University of New York, Buffalo.

David Farrell Krell is Professor of Philosophy at DePaul University.

Alphonso Lingis is Professor of Philosophy at Pennsylvania State University.

William J. Richardson is Professor of Philosophy at Boston College.

James Risser is Professor of Philosophy at Seattle University.

Richard Rorty is Professor of Comparative Literature at Stanford University.

John Sallis is Liberal Arts Professor of Philosophy at Pennsylvania State University.

Dennis J. Schmidt is Professor of Philosophy at Villanova University.

Calvin O. Schrag is the George Ade Distinguished Professor of Philosophy at Purdue University.

Charles E. Scott is the Edwin Erle Sparks Professor of Philosophy at Pennsylvania State University.

INDEX